In an effort to **go green**, Oxford University Press is providing a **Sampler Edition** of *Of the People: A History of the United States*, Fourth Edition. This **Sampler includes** chapters 15–20, the full table of contents and front matter, and the index. By using less paper in this Sampler, we're saving more trees. By providing the full text in a digital format, we lessen carbon emissions with reduced shipping. The cost savings from these green initiatives will help fund our mission to support Oxford University's objective of excellence in research, scholarship, and education.

If you are considering the text for adoption and would like to see more, you can view the complete text via eBook or receive a full printed copy of the text. Simply contact your Oxford University representative or call 800.280.0280 to request a copy.

Less paper = more trees saved

eBook = no carbon emission from shipping

Cost savings = more money to fund OUP's mission

D1598991

# What's New to the

- **NEW FEATURES THROUGHOUT:**
FOURTEEN new **AMERICAN PORTRAIT**,
FIVE new **AMERICAN LANDSCAPE**,
TEN new **AMERICA AND THE WORLD**, and
THREE new **STRUGGLES FOR DEMOCRACY** features

## AMERICAN PORTRAIT

### John Turchinetz

In January 1946, John Turchinetz finally headed home to Boston, Massachusetts, from World War II. Just out of high school, this son of a Romanian-born father and Ukrainian-born mother had joined the Navy three years earlier at the age of 18. Serving as a seaman aboard the cruiser named for his home city, John had manned an antiaircraft gun, suffered a disabling injury, and won medals in the Pacific. After the Japanese surrender, he and some of his shipmates from the *Boston* toured the city of Hiroshima, devastated by the first atomic bomb. "It was unbelievable," the seaman recalled. Like other Americans, John and his shipmates had had enough of war. "We were glad that it was over," he said. "We wanted peace."

At first, they found it. Back in Boston, John had a joyful reunion with his family. The mayor threw a big party for the crew of the *Boston*. Living with his parents again, John went to work at the federal Navy Yard in the harbor. The government needed the veteran, but not his beloved ship, in the new era of peace: the *Boston* was taken out of service—"mothballed," they called it. Although John, like many veterans, "felt a little different," his neighborhood and his country seemed the same. After the experience of war, people were friendly and united. "We were trying to help each other," John remembered. "We were trying to be normal."

The sense of normality—the feeling of friendliness, and peace—did not last long at all. Before the end of 1946, the cold war, a tense confrontation with the Soviet Union, began to disrupt American life. Soviet influence quickly spread in Eastern Europe. The USSR absorbed Ukraine, the homeland of John Turchinetz's father, and took territory from Romania, his mother's homeland, which then became a Soviet ally. Convinced the Soviets would keep trying to expand their power and spread communism across Europe, US leaders challenged their former allies. While the cold war developed, Americans also faced the task of maintaining prosperity in peacetime. Laborers, women, and African Americans struggled to preserve and extend their rights and opportunities. President Harry Truman and the Democratic Party struggled as well to preserve their power and implement a liberal agenda.

The cold war quickly became the dominant fact of national life in the late 1940s. To contain Soviet and communist expansion, the US government took unprecedented peacetime actions. But massive foreign aid, new alliances, and a military buildup did not prevent the cold

## AMERICAN LANDSCAPE

### "Gitmo"

From the camera eye of a satellite miles above, Guantánamo Bay stood out from the rest of eastern Cuba. The inlet was a horseshoe of brown and gray amid the lush green of the island and the bright blue of the Atlantic. To the administration of George W. Bush, Guantánamo Bay was a gray area, too: one of the few places on earth that was American and yet not American, a drab anomaly perfect for one of the most controversial phases of the war on terror.

Guantánamo Bay, 520 miles from Miami, Florida, had been an anomaly for more than a century. After the Spanish-American War of 1898, the US government had taken the spot for a well-protected naval base. The Cuban-American Treaty of 1903 effectively gave America perpetual control over the base. For less than $4,000 a year, the United States could keep the facility and both Washington and Cuba agreed to end

base and the only one in a Communist country.

Gitmo became less and less valuable over the years. As the cold war ended and the United States closed down military bases, there was no real need for a naval installation so close to the US mainland. Then the war on terror began. The Bush administration needed to put captured Taliban fighters and other "enemy combatants" somewhere safe. It was too risky to leave detainees in unstable Afghanistan or Iraq, but it was also too risky to bring them to the United States, where courts, Congress, and public opinion could interfere in their imprisonment. So the Bush administration looked, in the words of Secretary of Defense Donald Rumsfeld, for "the least worst place" to hold those captured in the war on terror.

They found it at Guantánamo Bay. The US military controlled the base, but US

## AMERICA AND THE WORLD

### American Tourists in Cold War Europe

"THIS IS YOUR YEAR FOR EUROPE," an American Airlines magazine ad proclaimed in 1948. "Anyone with only a week or two—or even a few days—can enjoy a fascinating trip to the 'Old World,' traveling by time-saving American Flagship. Don't put off that dreamed-of-journey abroad. Make this your year—your family's year—for Europe!"

Hundreds of thousands of Americans were eager to follow the airline's advice. The Great Depression and then World War II had reduced overseas tourism to almost nothing. But now, Americans were prosperous again and war-torn Europe was at peace and eager for dollars. Technological advances made steam-powered ships and propeller-driven airplanes, such as American Airlines' Flagship, faster and more affordable than ever. In 1949, over half a million Americans traveled overseas; in 1955, that number soared past a million. With the advent of jet-powered air travel, that figure would reach over 2 million by 1961.

Various impulses spurred American tourists. Americans wanted to relax, enjoy themselves, and explore exotic places. A nation of immigrants, Americans wanted

For the US government, American tourism represented something else altogether: a weapon in the cold war. In a letter to recipients of new passports, President Eisenhower explained that "you represent us all in bringing assurance to the people you meet that the United States is a friendly nation and one dedicated to the promotion of the well-being and security of the community of nations." Echoing that sentiment, Americans and foreigners alike spoke of US tourists as "unofficial ambassadors" abroad.

Those ambassadors did a mixed job. In Europe, an unflattering stereotype of the American tourist emerged. "He is a mobile human armed with cameras and broad-rimmed sunglasses, dressed-up in many-colored shirts and multi-colored neckties, who chewing-gums his way across an old and alien continent," wrote a European tour guide. American travelers were stereotyped as too loud, too critical, too unsophisticated, and too demanding: they actually wanted cold beer and private bathrooms!

Americans pushed back. Some of the criticism, they suggested, was the product of envy and insecurity: Europeans, their nations' wealth and power dimin-

on such a trip becomes magnified and is finally blamed on the United States as a whole."

American travelers developed another image, one rooted in the 1950s ideal of a democratic United States without social classes. "What the Italians like most about Americans is their free and easy manner," a journalist reported in 1957. "They consider Americans truly democratic, since they show not the slightest trace of class consciousness, and deal considerately and politely with one and all." Despite the reputation of some, the mass of travelers seemed to promote a positive understanding of their country, as US officials hoped. "Americans who are traveling abroad this Summer," said a Swiss teen in 1948, "are good ambassadors."

Travel also helped Americans get past some of their own stereotypes and prejudices. For instance, Americans who traveled to Moscow were in for a surprise. "Many American tourists here profess astonishment . . . that the Russians are people, that they smile and laugh and talk like people, that there are automobiles here. . . ," a writer noted in 1959. "Almost invariably, the Russians leave a tourist bumps into and talks with are friendly, helpful, deeply curious about the United States."

The encounters appeared to ease some of the cold war tensions and fears of the Soviets, too. "Some Russians who have

# Fourth Edition?

STRUGGLES FOR DEMOCRACY

## The Russian Attack on Democracy

It was a strange, almost paradoxical aspect of democracy: the simple, even boring act of standing in line and then checking a box or pulling a lever could have a dramatic impact on the future of the richest, most powerful country in the world. For all the attention given to who had the right to vote, Americans seldom devoted much thought to the mechanism of casting a ballot. After states and localities took firm control of the voting process from political parties around the turn of the twentieth century, fears of fraud decreased. With increased federal oversight of elections during and after the civil rights movement, those fears largely vanished.

Then, during the 2016 presidential election, strange, unsettling events occurred. In June, some voters turned up at the polls for California's primary only to find that they were mysteriously no longer registered. Hackers had gotten into the official computer system and altered their voting records. Similar break-ins happened in at least 20 more places around the country before the end of voting in November.

Meanwhile, US intelligence agencies revealed that the Russian government was behind the hacking and release of the emails of Hillary Clinton's campaign manager and the Democratic National Committee. The agencies also disclosed that Russia had used social media to spread false stories in another effort to affect the election. Despite these revelations, President Obama avoided public retaliation against Russia: he did not want to seem to be helping Clinton, who looked likely to win anyway. Instead, the president privately warned Russia's president, Vladimir Putin, not to interfere further.

After Donald Trump's surprising victory, Obama finally took public action. Late in 2016, the United States sanctioned Russian individuals and groups, seized two Russian compounds in the United States, and ordered 35 Russian diplomatic personnel to leave the country. "Russia's cyber activities were intended to influence the election, erode faith in US democratic institutions, sow doubt about the integrity of our electoral process, and undermine confidence in the institutions of the US government," the White House explained. "These actions are unacceptable and will not be tolerated."

Even so, it was unclear how the United States could stop further Russian activity. It was unclear, too, how to protect the sprawling machinery of elections, much of it computer based, controlled by so many states and communities.

Moreover, Americans were divided about Russian hacking, as they were about so many things in the 2010s. Putin had not only wanted to make Americans lose faith that elections were genuine. The Russian president, who loathed Hillary Clinton for her strong opposition to his country's foreign policy, had also wanted to elect Donald Trump. For Trump and his supporters, stories of Russian hacking and manipulation of social media seemed like an attempt by Democratic sore losers to undermine his legitimacy. But other Americans believed the government should aggressively pursue the Russian campaign. Suspicious of Trump's refusal to criticize Putin or fully acknowledge the Russian hacking, some people believed that the Trump campaign had colluded with Russians to get him elected.

As the nation awaited reports by Congress and the special counsel, information about Russian activity continued to emerge. Facebook admitted that starting the month Trump announced his candidacy in 2015, the company had unknowingly let Russian "troll farms" run fake, divisive advertisements, sometimes pro-Trump, on the social media site. Another Russian source bought ads on Google's Gmail and YouTube platforms.

Americans were left wondering about a distinctively twenty-first century problem: whether a foreign government could use technology to influence voters, keep some from casting ballots, elect a president, and undermine confidence in democracy itself.

## ■ More than thirty new primary sources

### 30.6 DONALD TRUMP, EXTRACT OF REMARKS AT A "MAKE AMERICA GREAT AGAIN" RALLY IN HARRISBURG, PENNSYLVANIA (2017)

After his election as president, Donald Trump continued holding campaign-style rallies for his supporters around the country. Feeding off the energy of the crowd, Trump articulated his right-wing populist message in the Rustbelt community of Harrisburg, Pennsylvania. Whom does he blame for the condition of the country?

As you may know, there's another big gathering taking place tonight in Washington, D.C. Did you hear about it?

AUDIENCE: Booo—

THE PRESIDENT: A large group of Hollywood actors and Washington media are consoling each other in a hotel ballroom in our nation's capital right now. (Applause.) They are gathered together for the White House Correspondents Dinner—without the President. (Applause.) And I could not possibly be more thrilled than to be more than 100 miles away from Washington Swamp—(applause)—spending my evening with all of you, and with a much, much larger crowd and much better people. Right? (Applause.) Right?

AUDIENCE: U-S-A! U-S-A!

THE PRESIDENT: And look at the media back there. . . .

AUDIENCE: Booo—

THE PRESIDENT: That's right.

AUDIENCE: CNN Sucks! CNN Sucks!

THE PRESIDENT: Media outlets like CNN and MSNBC are fake news. Fake news . . .

The truth is, there is no place I'd rather be than right here in Pennsylvania to celebrate our 100-day milestone to reflect on an incredible journey together, and to get ready for the great, great battles to come, and that we will win in every case, okay? We will win. (Applause.) Because make no mistake, we are just beginning in our fight to make America great again. (Applause.)

Now, before we talk about my first 100 days, which has been very exciting and very productive, let's rate the media's 100 days. Should we do that? Should we do it? Because, as you know, they are a disgrace. . . .

So just as an example of media, take the totally failing New York Times.

AUDIENCE: Booo—

THE PRESIDENT: But that's what we have. They're incompetent, dishonest people. . .

So here's the story. If the media's job is to be honest and tell the truth, then I think we would all agree the media deserves a very, very, big fat failing grade.

AUDIENCE: Booo—

- To improve narrative flow and to better align with syllabi, the number of Gilded Age chapters has been reduced from three to two

- New and revised coverage throughout  (see pp. xxxii-xxxv in the Preface for details)

### Economic Change and a Divided Nation

As so often in American history, anxieties about religion, race, and gender partly reflected anxieties about economic change. In the twenty-first century, the implications of deindustrialization, digitization, and globalization became increasingly clear. Despite the recovery from the Great Recession, the economy seemed to divide Americans into unequal groups: the rich and everyone else; men and women; old and young; urban and rural.

#### Jobs and Growth

By the 2010s, some optimistic forecasts about the information revolution and globalization were not coming true. New technologies and freer trade turned out to be more disruptive than expected. While observers anticipated that globalization would threaten some American manufacturing, they were unprepared for the sharp decline in the twenty-first century. Instead of increasing, jobs in manufacturing dropped 20 percent

- A revised and significantly expanded Chapter 30: "A Nation Transformed," The Twenty-First Century (formerly the Epilogue), that covers the span of years since 2001

**"Make America Great Again"** Donald Trump rallies his supporters during the 2016 presidential campaign.

- Numerous new photos

# Praise for *Of the People*

"This is an excellent book. It covers topics and ideas well, branches into subjects that other books gloss over, appeals to many different groups of students, and can be used not only to teach, but to spur discussion."

—Michael Frawley, *University of Texas of the Permian Basin*

"This is a great book that will bring students into deep discussion about the American story. It is accessible to students and comprehensible enough to make instructors happy."

—Matthew Campbell, *Lone Star College–Cypress Fairbanks*

"*Of the People* is the complete package. Its engaging narrative captures the grand sweep of U.S. history and animates the diverse lives that populate the past. The book is interesting and accessible, and the price is right. The volume also comes with many add-ons that can be useful in the classroom or online."

—Matthew Oyos, *Radford University*

"*Of the People* has some strong themes. In addition, the special features are intriguing and can be effectively woven into classroom discussions, and the selection of primary documents is good."

—Brenden Rensink, *Brigham Young University*

# Learning Resources

- **INSTRUCTOR'S RESOURCE MANUAL**
  Includes, for each chapter, a detailed chapter outline, suggested lecture topics, learning objectives, and approximately forty multiple-choice, short-answer, true-or-false, fill-in-the-blank, and essay questions for each chapter

- **POWERPOINTS AND COMPUTERIZED TEST BANK**
  Includes PowerPoint slides and JPEG files for all the maps and photos in the text. The Computerized Test Bank includes all of the test items from the Instructor's Resource Manual.

- **THE US HISTORY VIDEO LIBRARY**
  Produced by Oxford University Press, each 3–5 minute video covers a key topic in U.S. history, from Squanto to John Brown and from Mother Jones to the "disco wars" of the late 1970s/early 1980s. Combining motion pictures, stills, audio clips, and narration, these videos are ideal for both classroom discussion or as online assignments.

- **THE US HISTORY IMAGE LIBRARY**
  Includes more than 2,000 images organized by period, topic, and region.

To view a demo video from the **US History Video Library** or sample images from the **US History Image Library**, go to: **https://oup-arc.com/access/us-history.**

- **OXFORD FIRST SOURCE**
  This database includes hundreds of primary source documents in world history. The documents cover a broad variety of political, economic, social, and cultural topics and represent a cross section of American voices. Special effort was made to include as many previously disenfranchised voices as possible. The documents are indexed by date, author, title, and subject. Short documents (one or two pages) are presented in their entirety while longer documents have been carefully edited to highlight significant content. Each document is introduced with a short explanatory paragraph and accompanied by study questions.

A complete **Course Management cartridge** is also available to qualified adopters.

**Student Companion Website at www.oup.com/us/oakes-mcgerr:** The open-access Online Study Center helps students to review what they have learned from the textbook and explore other resources online. Practice quizzes allow them to assess their knowledge of a topic before a test.

# Enhanced Study Resources

Students who purchase a new copy of *Of the People*, Fourth Edition, can redeem an access code to access these additional study resources, at no extra charge:

- Twenty-five quizzes per chapter that offer an explanation and page reference for each question

- A study guide that provides note-taking worksheets and chapter summaries for each chapter

- Animated maps that deepen understanding of key developments in American history. Each animation is accompanied by quiz questions.

- Video quizzes that assess comprehension of key topics in American history

- Students can also purchase access to these enhanced study resources at the Ancillary Resource Center: **www.oup.com/us/oakes-mcgerr**.

Please visit **www.oup.com/us/oakes-mcgerr** for a demo of the enhanced study resources.

- **PRIMARY SOURCE COMPANION AND RESEARCH GUIDE**, a brief online Research Primer with a library of annotated links to primary and secondary sources in U.S. history

- **INTERACTIVE FLASHCARDS**, using key terms and people listed at the end of each chapter; these multimedia cards help students remember who's who and what's what

## Of the People: A History of the United States, Fourth Edition, is available in these volumes:

**VOL. I: TO 1877 (CHAPTERS 1–15)**
**EBOOK:** 978-0-19-093211-4
**LOOSE-LEAF:** 978-0-19-091062-4
**STUDENT EDITION:** 978-0-19-091020-4

**VOL. II: SINCE 1865 (CHAPTERS 15–30)**
**EBOOK:** 978-0-19-093212-1
**LOOSE-LEAF:** 978-0-19-091063-1
**STUDENT EDITION:** 978-0-19-091021-1

### *WITH SOURCES*

**VOL. I: TO 1877** *WITH SOURCES*
**EBOOK:** 978-0-19-093209-1
**LOOSE-LEAF:** 978-0-19-091012-9
**STUDENT EDITION:** 978-0-19-090996-3

**VOL. II: SINCE 1865** *WITH SOURCES*
**EBOOK:** 978-0-19-093210-7
**LOOSE-LEAF:** 978-0-19-091013-6
**STUDENT EDITION:** 978-0-19-090997-0

# Package and Save!

*Sources for Of the People* (978-0-19-091015-0): Edited by Maxwell Johnson, this two-volume companion sourcebook includes approximately eighty primary sources, both textual and visual. Chapter introductions, document headnotes, and study questions provide learning support. The sourcebook is only **$5.00 per volume** when bundled with *Of the People*.

*Of the People* V1 + Sourcebook V1 = Pkg ISBN 978-0-19-094139-0
*Of the People* V2 + Sourcebook V2 = Pkg ISBN 978-0-19-094141-3
*Of the People* V1 w/ Sources + Sourcebook V1 = Pkg ISBN 978-0-19-094140-6
*Of the People* V2 w/ Sources + Sourcebook V2 = Pkg ISBN 978-0-19-094142-0

 **Mapping United States History: A Coloring and Exercise Book** (978-0-19-092166-8): Providing both full-color reference maps and eighty outline maps, this two-volume coloring and exercise book offers students opportunities to strengthen their geographical and spatial-learning skills. *Mapping United States History* is **FREE** when bundled with *Of the People*.

*Of the People* V1 + Mapping V1 = Pkg ISBN 978-0-19-094184-0
*Of the People* V2 + Mapping V2 = Pkg ISBN 978-0-19-094183-3
*Of the People* V1 w/ Sources + Mapping V1 =
Pkg ISBN 978-0-19-094185-7
*Of the People* V2 w/ Sources + Mapping V2 =
Pkg 978-0-19-094186-4

Save your students **20%** when you package *Of the People* with any other Oxford book!

**Suggested titles:**

*Writing History: A Guide for Students*, Fifth Edition, by William Kelleher Storey

*The Information-Literate Historian: A Guide to Research for History Students*, Third Edition, by Jenny Presnell

# Of the People

# Of the People

A HISTORY OF THE UNITED STATES  *Fourth Edition*
WITH SOURCES

**VOLUME II** Since 1865

Michael McGerr

Jan Ellen Lewis

James Oakes

Nick Cullather

Mark Summers

Camilla Townsend

Karen M. Dunak

New York   Oxford
Oxford University Press

Oxford University Press is a department of the University of Oxford.
It furthers the University's objective of excellence in research, scholarship,
and education by publishing worldwide. Oxford is a registered trademark of
Oxford University Press in the UK and certain other countries.

Published in the United States of America by Oxford University Press
198 Madison Avenue, New York, NY 10016, United States of America.

© 2019, 2017, 2013, and 2011 by Oxford University Press

For titles covered by Section 112 of the US Higher Education
Opportunity Act, please visit www.oup.com/us/he for the latest
information about pricing and alternate formats.

All rights reserved. No part of this publication may be reproduced, stored in
a retrieval system, or transmitted, in any form or by any means, without the
prior permission in writing of Oxford University Press, or as expressly permitted
by law, by license, or under terms agreed with the appropriate reproduction
rights organization. Inquiries concerning reproduction outside the scope of the
above should be sent to the Rights Department, Oxford University Press,
at the address above.

You must not circulate this work in any other form
and you must impose this same condition on any acquirer.

ISBN: 978-0-19-090997-0

9 8 7 6 5 4 3 2 1
Printed by LSC Communications, United States of America

Jeanne Boydston
1944–2008
Historian, Teacher, Friend

# Brief Contents

**Maps** xxvi
**Features** xxviii
**Preface** xxx
**About the Authors** xliii

Chapter 15    Reconstructing a Nation, 1865–1877    458
Chapter 16    The Triumph of Industrial Capitalism, 1850–1890    496
Chapter 17    The Culture and Politics of Industrial America, 1870–1892    524
Chapter 18    Industry and Empire, 1890–1900    556
Chapter 19    A United Body of Action, 1900–1916    588
Chapter 20    A Global Power, 1914–1919    618
Chapter 21    The Modern Nation, 1919–1928    648
Chapter 22    A Great Depression and a New Deal, 1929–1940    678
Chapter 23    The Second World War, 1941–1945    708
Chapter 24    The Cold War, 1945–1954    742
Chapter 25    The Consumer Society, 1945–1961    772
Chapter 26    "The Table of Democracy," 1960–1968    804
Chapter 27    Living with Less, 1968–1980    836
Chapter 28    The Triumph of Conservatism, 1980–1991    868
Chapter 29    The Globalized Nation, 1989–2001    902
Chapter 30    "A Nation Transformed," The Twenty-First Century    934

**Appendix A**    **Historical Documents**    A-1
**Appendix B**    **Historical Facts and Data**    B-1
**Glossary**    G-1
**Photo Credits**    C-1
**Index**    I-1

# Contents

**Maps**   xxvi
**Features**   xxviii
**Preface**   xxx
      New to the Fourth Edition   xxxii
      Hallmark Features   xxxv
      Learning Resources for *Of the People*   xxxv
      Acknowledgments   xxxvii
**About the Authors**   xliii

## CHAPTER 15 Reconstructing a Nation, 1865–1877   458

AMERICAN PORTRAIT: John Dennett Visits a Freedmen's Bureau Court   460

Wartime Reconstruction   461
    Lincoln's Ten Percent Plan Versus the Wade-Davis Bill   462
    The Meaning of Freedom   463
    Experiments with Free Labor   464

Presidential Reconstruction, 1865–1867   465
    The Political Economy of Contract Labor   466
    Resistance to Presidential Reconstruction   467
    Congress Clashes with the President   467
    Origins of the Fourteenth Amendment   467

Congressional Reconstruction   470
    The South Remade   470
    The Impeachment and Trial of Andrew Johnson   470
    Radical Reconstruction in the South   472
    Achievements and Failures of Radical Government   472
    The Political Economy of Sharecropping   474
    The Gospel of Prosperity   475
    A Counterrevolution of Terrorism and Economic Pressure   477

AMERICA AND THE WORLD: Reconstructing America's Foreign Policy   478

A Reconstructed West   478
    The Overland Trail   479
    The Origins of Indian Reservations   480
    The Destruction of Indian Subsistence   482

The Retreat from Republican Radicalism   483
    Republicans Become the Party of Moderation   483

Reconstructing the North    484

    The Fifteenth Amendment and Nationwide African American Suffrage    484
    Women and Suffrage    485

The End of Reconstruction    485

    Corruption Is the Fashion    486
    Liberal Republicans Revolt    487
    "Redeeming" the South    487

STRUGGLES FOR DEMOCRACY: An Incident at Coushatta, August 1874    488

    The Twice-Stolen Election of 1876    490
    Sharecropping Becomes Wage Labor    491

Conclusion    494

Chapter 15 Primary Sources

    15.1  Petroleum V. Nasby [David Ross Locke], *A Platform for Northern Democrats* (1865)    S15-0
    15.2  Mississippi Black Code (1865)    S15-1
    15.3  Sharecropping Contract Between Alonzo T. Mial and Fenner Powell (1886)    S15-4
    15.4  Joseph Farley, An Account of Reconstruction    S15-5
    15.5  A Southern Unionist Judge's Daughter Writes the President for Help (1874)    S15-6
    15.6  Red Cloud Pleads the Plains Indians' Point of View at Cooper Union (1870)    S15-7

## CHAPTER 16 The Triumph of Industrial Capitalism, 1850–1890    496

AMERICAN PORTRAIT: Rosa Cassettari    498

The Political Economy of Global Capitalism    499

    The "Great Depression" of the Late Nineteenth Century    499

AMERICA AND THE WORLD: The Global Migration of Labor    501

The Economic Transformation of the West    502

    Cattlemen: From Drovers to Ranchers    502
    Commercial Farmers Remake the Plains    503
    Changes in the Land    503

AMERICAN LANDSCAPE: Mining Camps in the West    504

    America Moves to the City    506

The Rise of Big Business    508

    The Rise of Andrew Carnegie    508
    Carnegie Dominates the Steel Industry    509
    Big Business Consolidates    510

A New Social Order   512
   Lifestyles of the Very Rich   512
   The Consolidation of the New Middle Class   513
   The Industrial Working Class Comes of Age   514
   Social Darwinism and the Growth of Scientific Racism   516

STRUGGLES FOR DEMOCRACY: "The Chinese Must Go"   518
   The Knights of Labor and the Haymarket Disaster   520

Conclusion   522

Chapter 16 Primary Sources
   16.1  Russell H. Conwell, "Acres of Diamonds" (1860s–1920s)   S16-0
   16.2  Visual Document: Alfred R. Waud, "Bessemer Steel Manufacture"
         (1876)   S16-1
   16.3  George Steevens, Excerpt from *The Land of the Dollar* (1897)   S16-2
   16.4  Emma Lazarus, "The New Colossus" (1883)   S16-4
   16.5  Josiah Strong, Excerpts from "The Superiority of the Anglo-Saxon Race"
         (1885)   S16-4
   16.6  James Baird Weaver, *A Call to Action* (1892)   S16-6

## CHAPTER 17  The Culture and Politics of Industrial America, 1870–1892   524

AMERICAN PORTRAIT: Luna Kellie and the Farmers' Alliance   526

The Elusive Boundaries of Male and Female   527
   The Victorian Construction of Male and Female   527
   The Victorian Crusade for Morality   528
   Urban Culture   529

A New Cultural Order: New Americans Stir Old Fears   531
   Josiah Strong Attacks Immigration   531
   From Immigrants to Ethnic Americans   532
   The Catholic Church and Its Limits in Immigrant Culture   533
   Immigrant Cultures   534
   The Enemy at the Gates   535

Two Political Styles   536
   The Triumph of Party Politics   536
   Masculine Partisanship and Feminine Voluntarism   538
   The Women's Christian Temperance Union   538
   The Critics of Popular Politics   539

STRUGGLES FOR DEMOCRACY: The "Crusade" Against Alcohol   540

Economic Issues Dominate National Politics    540
Greenbacks and Greenbackers    541
Weak Presidents Oversee a Stronger Federal Government    542

AMERICA AND THE WORLD: Foreign Policy: The Limited Significance of Commercial
Expansion    546

Government Activism and Its Limits    547
States Discover Activism    548
Cities: Boss Rule and New Responsibilities    548

Challenging the New Industrial Order    549
Henry George and the Limits of Producers' Ideology    549
Edward Bellamy and the Nationalist Clubs    551
Agrarian Revolt    551
The Rise of the Populists    552

Conclusion    554

Chapter 17 Primary Sources
17.1 *New York World*, "How Tim Got the Votes" (1892)    S17-0
17.2 *Tammany Times*, "And Reform Moves On" (1895)    S17-1
17.3 Henry George, Excerpts from "That We Might All Be Rich" (1883)    S17-2
17.4 Jacob Riis, Excerpt from *How the Other Half Lives* (1890) and Visual
Document: Jacob Riis, "Bandits' Roost" (1887)    S17-4
17.5 Visual Documents: "Gift for the Grangers" (1873) and the Jorns Family of Dry
Valley, Custer County, Nebraska (1886)    S17-6

## CHAPTER 18 Industry and Empire, 1890–1900    556

AMERICAN PORTRAIT: J. P. Morgan    558

The Crisis of the 1890s    559
Hard Times and Demands for Help    560
The Overseas Frontier    560
The Drive for Efficiency    562
The Struggle Between Management and Labor    562
Corporate Consolidation    564

A Modern Economy    564
Currency: Gold Versus Silver    565
The Cross of Gold    565
The Battle of the Standards    565

The Retreat from Politics    567
The Lure of the Cities    567

AMERICAN LANDSCAPE: Galveston, Texas, 1900   568

Inventing Jim Crow   570
The Atlanta Compromise   571
Disfranchisement and the Decline of Popular Politics   571

STRUGGLES FOR DEMOCRACY: The Wilmington Race Riot   572

Organized Labor Retreats from Politics   574

American Diplomacy Enters the Modern World   575

Sea Power and the Imperial Urge   575
The Scramble for Empire   577
War with Spain   577
The Anti-Imperialists   581
The Philippine-American War   581
The Open Door   582

Conclusion   586

Chapter 18 Primary Sources

18.1  Frederick Winslow Taylor, Excerpts from *The Principles of Scientific Management* (1911)   S18-0
18.2  Booker T. Washington, "The Atlanta Compromise" (1895)   S18-2
18.3  Theodore Roosevelt, Excerpts from "The Strenuous Life" (1899)   S18-4
18.4  Visual Document: Louis Dalrymple, "School Begins" (1899)   S18-6

CHAPTER 19   A United Body of Action, 1900–1916   588

AMERICAN PORTRAIT: Helen Keller   590

Toward a New Politics   591

The Insecurity of Modern Life   591
The Decline of Partisan Politics   593
Social Housekeeping   593
Evolution or Revolution?   595

The Progressives   596

Social Workers and Muckrakers   596

STRUGGLES FOR DEMOCRACY: Public Response to *The Jungle*   598

Dictatorship of the Experts   600
Progressives on the Color Line   600

Progressives in State and Local Politics   602

Redesigning the City   602
Reform Mayors and City Services   603
Progressives and the States   603

A Push for "Genuine Democracy" and a "Moral Awakening"   605

The Executive Branch Against the Trusts   605
The Square Deal   606

Conserving Water, Land, and Forests    607
TR and Big Stick Diplomacy    608
Taft and Dollar Diplomacy    609

AMERICAN LANDSCAPE: The Hetch Hetchy Valley    610

Rival Visions of the Industrial Future    612
The New Nationalism    612
The 1912 Election    613
The New Freedom    615

Conclusion    616

Chapter 19 Primary Sources
19.1  Jane Addams, Excerpts from *Twenty-Years at Hull House with
      Autobiographical Notes* (1910)    S19-0
19.2  Upton Sinclair, Excerpts from *The Jungle* (1906)    S19-2
19.3  Visual Documents: Lewis Wickes Hine, National Child Labor Committee
      Photographs (Early 1900s)    S19-5
19.4  Helen Keller, Excerpts from "Blind Leaders" (1913)    S19-7

CHAPTER **20**  A Global Power, **1914–1919**    788

AMERICAN PORTRAIT: Walter Lippmann    620

The Challenge of Revolution    621
The Mexican Revolution    622
Bringing Order to the Caribbean    622
A One-Sided Neutrality    623
The *Lusitania*'s Last Voyage    624

The Drift to War    624
The Election of 1916    625
The Last Attempts at Peace    625
War Aims    626
The Fight in Congress    626

Mobilizing the Nation and the Economy    627
Enforcing Patriotism    627

STRUGGLES FOR DEMOCRACY: Eugene V. Debs Speaks Out Against the War    628
Regimenting the Economy    630
The Great Migration    632
Reforms Become "War Measures"    633

Over There    634
Citizens into Soldiers    635
The Fourteen Points    635
The Final Offensive    636

Revolutionary Anxieties   639
   Wilson in Paris   639
   The Senate Rejects the League   640
   Red Scare   641

AMERICA AND THE WORLD: The American Red Cross and Wartime Civilian Aid   642

Conclusion   645

Chapter 20 Primary Sources
   20.1  World War I–Era Music: "I Didn't Raise My Boy to Be a Soldier" (1915) and
         "Over There" (1917)   S20-0
   20.2  Eugene V. Debs, Excerpts from Canton, Ohio, Speech (1918)   S20-1
   20.3  George Creel, Excerpts from How We Advertised America (1920)   S20-4
   20.4  Woodrow Wilson, "Fourteen Points" Speech (1918)   S20-6

## CHAPTER 21   The Modern Nation, 1919–1928   648

AMERICAN PORTRAIT: "America's Sweetheart"   650

A Dynamic Economy   651
   The Development of Industry   651
   The Trend Toward Large-Scale Organization   652
   The Transformation of Work and the Workforce   653
   The Defeat of Organized Labor   654
   The Decline of Agriculture   654
   The Urban Nation   655

A Modern Culture   655
   The Spread of Consumerism   656
   New Pleasures for a Mass Audience   657
   A Sexual Revolution   659
   Changing Gender Ideals   659

STRUGGLES FOR DEMOCRACY: Flappers and Feminists   660

AMERICAN LANDSCAPE: "Flaming Youth" on Campus   662
   The Family and Youth   662
   The Celebration of the Individual   663

The Limits of the Modern Culture   664
   The Limits of Prosperity   664
   The "Lost Generation" of Intellectuals   664
   Fundamentalist Christians and "Old-Time Religion"   665
   Nativists and Immigration Restriction   666
   The Rebirth of the Ku Klux Klan   666

Mexican Americans    667
African Americans and the "New Negro"    668

## A "New Era" in Politics and Government    670

The Modern Political System    670
The Republican Ascendancy    671
The Politics of Individualism    672
Republican Foreign Policy    673
Extending the "New Era"    673

**AMERICA AND THE WORLD:** J. Walter Thompson and International Markets    674

## Conclusion    676

## Chapter 21 Primary Sources

21.1   Hiram Wesley Evans, Excerpts from "The Klan: Defender of Americanism"
(1925)    S21-0
21.2   Bruce Barton, Excerpts from *The Man Nobody Knows: A Discovery of the Real
Jesus* (1925)    S21-1
21.3   Visual Document: Colgate & Co. Advertisement (1925)    S21-4
21.4   Robert Lynd and Helen Lynd, Excerpt from "Remaking Leisure in Middletown"
(1929)    S21-5

## CHAPTER 22   A Great Depression and a New Deal, 1929–1940    678

**AMERICAN PORTRAIT:** Dorothea Lange    680

## The Great Depression    681

Causes    681
Descending into Depression    682
Hoover Responds    685

## The First New Deal    687

The Election of 1932    687
FDR Takes Command    689
Federal Relief    690
The Farm Crisis    691

**STRUGGLES FOR DEMOCRACY:** The Civilian Conservation Corps and a New Brand of
Environmentalism    692

The Blue Eagle    694

## The Second New Deal    695

Critics Attack from All Sides    695
The Second Hundred Days    696

Social Security for Some    697
Labor and the New Deal    698
The New Deal Coalition    699

## Crisis of the New Deal    701

Conservatives Counterattack    701

**AMERICA AND THE WORLD: The 1936 Olympics    702**

The Liberal Crisis of Confidence    704

## Conclusion    705

## Chapter 22 Primary Sources

22.1  Franklin D. Roosevelt, First Inaugural Address (1933)    S22-0
22.2  Visual Documents: Dorothea Lange, Farm Security Administration
      Photographs (1930s)    S22-3
22.3  Letters to Eleanor Roosevelt (1936)    S22-4
22.4  Remembering the Great Depression, Excerpts from Studs Terkel's *Hard Times*
      (1970)    S22-5

## CHAPTER 23  The Second World War, 1941–1945    708

**AMERICAN PORTRAIT: A. Philip Randolph    710**

## Island in a Totalitarian Sea    711

A World of Hostile Blocs    711
The Good Neighbor    712
America First?    713
Means Short of War    714

## Turning the Tide    716

Midway and Coral Sea    716

**AMERICA AND THE WORLD: The Carrier    718**

Gone with the Draft    719
The Winning Weapons    721
The Second Front    723

## Organizing for Production    724

A Mixed Economy    725
Industry Moves South and West    725
New Jobs in New Places    726
Women in Industry    727

## Between Idealism and Fear    728

Japanese Internment    730
No Shelter from the Holocaust    731

**STRUGGLES FOR DEMOCRACY: The Zoot Suit Riots    732**

Closing with the Enemy    732
   Taking the War to Europe    734
   Island Hopping in the Pacific    735
   Building a New World    736
   The Fruits of Victory    737

Conclusion    739

Chapter 23 Primary Sources
   23.1  Franklin D. Roosevelt, "Four Freedoms" Speech (1941)    S23-0
   23.2  Charles Lindbergh, America First Committee Address (1941)    S23-4
   23.3  Letter from James G. Thompson to the Editor of the *Pittsburgh Courier*
          (1942)    S23-6
   23.4  Letters from Polly Crow to Her Husband During World War II (1944)    S23-7

## CHAPTER 24  The Cold War, 1945–1954    742

AMERICAN PORTRAIT: John Turchinetz    744

Origins of the Cold War    745
   Ideological Competition    745
   Uneasy Allies    746
   From Allies to Enemies    747

National Security    747
   The Truman Doctrine    748
   Containment    749
   Taking Risks    750
   Global Revolutions    751

AMERICAN LANDSCAPE: The Nevada Test Site    752
   Korea    754
   NSC-68    756

The Reconversion of American Society    756
   The Postwar Economy    756
   The Challenge of Organized Labor    757
   Opportunities for Women    758
   Civil Rights for African Americans    759

The Frustrations of Liberalism    761
   The Democrats' Troubles    761
   Truman's Comeback    762

Fighting the Cold War at Home    763
   Doubts and Fears in the Atomic Age    764
   The Anti-Communist Crusade    764

STRUGGLES FOR DEMOCRACY: The Hollywood Ten    766

   The Hunt for Spies    767
   The Rise of McCarthyism    769

Conclusion    770

Chapter 24 Primary Sources
   24.1  X (George F. Kennan), Excerpts from "The Sources of Soviet Conduct"
       (1947)    S24-0
   24.2  High School and College Graduates in the Cold War (1948–1950)    S24-1
   24.3  Statements by the United Auto Workers and General Motors (1945)    S24-3
   24.4  Harry S. Truman, Excerpts from Special Message to the Congress
       Recommending a Comprehensive Health Program (1945)    S24-4
   24.5  Joseph McCarthy, Excerpts from Wheeling, West Virginia Speech (1950)    S24-6

CHAPTER 25  The Consumer Society, 1945–1961    772

AMERICAN PORTRAIT: The Ricardos    774

Living the Good Life    775
   Economic Prosperity    775

AMERICAN LANDSCAPE: Eisenhower's Interstate Highway System    776
   The Suburban Dream    776
   The Pursuit of Pleasure    778

A Homogeneous Society?    780
   The Discovery of Conformity    780
   The Decline of Class and Ethnicity    781
   The Resurgence of Religion and Family    781
   Maintaining Gender Roles    782
   Persisting Racial Differences    783
   The Survival of Diversity    785

The Eisenhower Era at Home and Abroad    786
   "Ike" and 1950s America    787
   Modern Republicanism    787

STRUGGLES FOR DEMOCRACY: "The Fantastic, Real-Life, Dream-Come-True Adventure of
                the Barstow Family of Wethersfield, Connecticut"    788
   An Aggressive Cold War Strategy    788
   Avoiding War with the Communist Powers    791
   Crises in the Third World    792

AMERICA AND THE WORLD: American Tourists in Cold War Europe    794

Challenges to the Consumer Society    796
   Rebellious Youth    796
   The Beat Movement    797

The Rebirth of Environmentalism    797
The Struggle for Civil Rights    798
The Crisis of "Misplaced Power"    801

Conclusion    802

Chapter 25 Primary Sources
25.1  Gael Greene, "The Battle of Levittown" (1957)    S25-0
25.2  H. H. Remmers and D. H. Radler, Excerpts from "Teenage Attitudes" (1958)    S25-2
25.3  Visual Documents: Automobile Advertisements (1953–1955)    S25-4
25.4  United States Office of Civil and Defense Mobilization, Excerpts from "Survive Nuclear Attack" (1960)    S25-6

## CHAPTER 26 "The Table of Democracy," 1960-1968    804

AMERICAN PORTRAIT: The A&T Four    806

New Approaches to Power    807
Grassroots Activism for Civil Rights    807
The New Liberalism    807
The New Conservatism    808
The New Left    808
The Presidential Election of 1960    809

The New Frontier    809
Style and Substance    809
Civil Rights    811

AMERICAN LANDSCAPE: "Spaceport USA"    812
Flexible Response and the Third World    814
Two Confrontations with the Soviets    815
Kennedy and Vietnam    816

The Great Society    817
Lyndon Johnson's Mandate    817
"Success Without Squalor"    817
Preserving Personal Freedom    819
The Death of Jim Crow    820

The American War in Vietnam    821
Johnson's Decision for War    821
Fighting a Limited War    822
The War at Home    824

The Great Society Comes Apart    825
The Emergence of Black Power    825
The Youth Rebellion    827

STRUGGLES FOR DEMOCRACY: Protest in the Schools    828

The Rebirth of the Women's Movement    830
Conservative Backlash    831
1968: A Tumultuous Year    832

Conclusion    834

Chapter 26 Primary Sources

26.1 Martin Luther King Jr., "Statement to the Press at the Beginning of the Youth Leadership Conference" (1960) and Student Nonviolent Coordinating Committee, Statement of Purpose (1960)    S26-0
26.2 John F. Kennedy, Excerpts from Inaugural Address (1961)    S26-1
26.3 Testimony of Marian Wright, Examination of the War on Poverty; Hearings Before the Subcommittee on Employment, Manpower, and Poverty of the Committee on Labor and Public Welfare (1967)    S26-2
26.4 Lyndon B. Johnson, Excerpts from Address at Johns Hopkins University, "Peace Without Conquest" (1965)    S26-5
26.5 John Wilcock, "The Human Be-In" and "San Francisco" (1967)    S26-7

## CHAPTER 27  Living with Less, 1968–1980    836

AMERICAN PORTRAIT: "Fighting Shirley Chisholm"    838

A New Crisis: Economic Decline    839
Weakness at Home    839
The Energy Crisis    840
Competition Abroad    841
The Multinationals    841
The Impact of Decline    841

AMERICAN LANDSCAPE: The South Bronx    842

Confronting Decline: Nixon's Strategy    844
A New Foreign Policy    844
Ending the Vietnam War    846
Chile and the Middle East    847
Taming Big Government    848
An Uncertain Economic Policy    849

Refusing to Settle for Less: Struggles for Rights    849
African Americans' Struggle for Racial Justice    849

STRUGGLES FOR DEMOCRACY: "ROAR"!    850

Women's Liberation    852
Mexican Americans and "Brown Power"    853
Asian American Activism    854
The Struggle for Native American Rights    855
Gay Power    856

Backlash: From Radical Action to Conservative Reaction     857
"The Movement" and the "Me Decade"     857
The Plight of the White Ethnics     858
The Republican Counterattack     858

Political Crisis: Three Troubled Presidencies     859
Watergate: The Fall of Richard Nixon     859
Gerald Ford and a Skeptical Nation     860
"Why Not the Best?": Jimmy Carter     862

Conclusion     866

Chapter 27 Primary Sources
27.1  Testimony of Gerald Dickey, Mergers and Industrial Concentration; Hearings
        Before the Subcommittee on Antitrust and Monopoly of the Committee on the
        Judiciary (1978)     S27-0
27.2  Nixon Decides on the Christmas Bombing (1972)     S27-2
27.3  New York Radical Women, *Principles* (1968) and Pat Maxwell, "Homosexuals
        in the Movement" (1970)     S27-4
27.4  Statements by Roman Pucinski, Ethnic Heritage Studies Centers; Hearings
        Before the General Subcommittee on Education of the Committee on
        Education and Labor (1970)     S27-6
27.5  Jimmy Carter, Address to the Nation on Energy and National Goals: "The
        Malaise Speech" (1979)     S27-7

## CHAPTER 28  The Triumph of Conservatism, 1980–1991     868

AMERICAN PORTRAIT: Linda Chavez     870

Creating a Conservative Majority     871
The New Economy     871
The Rehabilitation of Business     872

AMERICAN LANDSCAPE: Silicon Valley     873
The Rise of the Religious Right     874
The 1980 Presidential Election     874

The Reagan Revolution at Home     876
The Reagan Style     876
Shrinking Government     877
Reaganomics     877
The 1984 Presidential Election     879

The Reagan Revolution Abroad     879
Restoring American Power     880
Confronting the "Evil Empire"     881

The Reagan Doctrine in the Third World    881
The Middle East and Terrorism    883

AMERICA AND THE WORLD: The Ethiopian Famine    884
The United States and the World Economy    886

The Battle over Conservative Social Values    886
Attacking the Legacy of the 1960s    887
Women's Rights and Abortion    887
Gays and the AIDS Crisis    889
African Americans and Racial Inequality    890
"The Decade of the Hispanic"    892

From Scandal to Triumph    893
Business and Religious Scandals    893
Political Scandals    893
Setbacks for the Conservative Agenda    894
A Vulnerable Economy    894
Reagan's Comeback    896

STRUGGLES FOR DEMOCRACY: Reagan at the Berlin Wall    898

Conclusion    900

Chapter 28 Primary Sources
28.1 Visual Document: US Centers for Disease Control, AIDs Awareness Poster
    (1980s)    S28-0
28.2 Jerry Falwell, Excerpts from *Listen, America!* (1980)    S28-1
28.3 Ronald Reagan, Excerpts from "Address to the Nation on the Economy"
    (1981)    S28-2
28.4 National Conference of Catholic Bishops, Excerpts from "The Challenge of
    Peace: God's Promise and Our Response" (1983)    S28-4
28.5 Excerpts from the Republican and Democratic Party Platforms on the State of
    the American Family (1984)    S28-6

CHAPTER 29  The Globalized Nation, 1989–2001    902

AMERICAN PORTRAIT: James Sharlow    904

The Age of Globalization    905
The Cold War and Globalization    905
New Communications Technologies    905
Multinationals and NGOs    906
Expanding Trade    906
Moving People    907
Contesting Globalization    907

AMERICA AND THE WORLD: *Titanic* and the Globalization of Hollywood    908

A New Economy    910
  From Industry to Information    910
  A Second Economic Revolution?    910
  Downsizing America    911
  Boom and Insecurity    912

Democratic Deadlock    912
  George H. W. Bush and the End of the Reagan Revolution    913
  The Rebellion Against Politics as Usual    914
  Clinton's Compromise with Conservatism    916
  Domestic Dissent and Terrorism    917

STRUGGLES FOR DEMOCRACY: "Temporarily Closed," 1995–1996    918
  Scandal    920
  The Presidential Election of 2000    920

Culture Wars    921
  African Americans in the Post–Civil Rights Era    921
  "Family Values"    923
  Multiculturalism    924
  Women in the Postfeminist Era    925
  Contesting Gay and Lesbian Rights    925

Redefining Foreign Policy in the Global Age    927
  The New World Order    927
  The Persian Gulf War    928
  Retreating from the New World Order    929
  A New Threat    931

Conclusion    932

Chapter 29 Primary Sources
  29.1  Kenichi Ohmae, "Declaration of Interdependence Toward the World—
        2005" (1990) and Helena Norberg-Hodge, "Break Up the Monoculture"
        (1996)    S29-0
  29.2  Solomon D. Trujillo, "Opportunity in the New Information
        Economy" (1998)    S29-2
  29.3  Visual Document: Aziz + Cucher, "Man with Computer"
        (1992)    S29-3
  29.4  Excerpts from National Defense Authorization Act of 1994
        (1993) and Defense of Marriage Act (1996)    S29-4
  29.5  George H. W. Bush, Excerpts from "Address Before a Joint Session
        of the Congress on the Cessation of Hostilities in the Persian Gulf
        Conflict" (1991)    S29-6

# CHAPTER 30 "A Nation Transformed," The Twenty-First Century 934

AMERICAN PORTRAIT: Lt. Craig Mullaney    936

Twin Crises    937
Bush 43    937
9/11    937
The Global War on Terror    938
The Iraq War    939
Iraq and Afghanistan in Turmoil    939
Financial Crisis    940

Obama and the Promise of Change    941

AMERICAN LANDSCAPE: "Gitmo"    942
The Presidential Election of 2008    942
Confronting Economic Crisis    944
Ending the Wars in Afghanistan and Iraq    945
The Politics of Frustration    946
A Second Term    946
Climate Change    947
Unending War?    947

Diversity and Division    950
A Diverse Society of Color    950
Tolerance and Intolerance    951
LGBTQ Rights    952
Shifting Religious Beliefs and Practices    953

Economic Change and a Divided Nation    953
Jobs and Growth    953
The Rich, the Poor, and the Middle Class    954
Women and Men    956
Baby Boomers and Millennials    956
Urban and Rural    957

Democracy Under Stress    957
Money and Politics    957
Polarized Politics    958
Four Political Approaches    959
The Presidential Election of 2016    959
"Make America Great Again"    961

STRUGGLES FOR DEMOCRACY: The Russian Attack on Democracy    962

Conclusion    964

## Chapter 30 Primary Sources

30.1  George W. Bush, Excerpts from "Address Before a Joint Session of the Congress on the United States Response to the Terrorist Attacks of September 11" (2001)    S30-0

30.2  Barack Obama, Keynote Address, Democratic Party Convention (2004)    S30-2

30.3  Debate in the House of Representatives on a Resolution "That Symbols and Traditions of Christmas Should Be Protected" (2005)    S30-3

30.4  Harry M. Reid, "The Koch Brothers" (2015)    S30-5

30.5  Steve A. King, "Illegal Immigration," House of Representatives (2007)    S30-6

30.6  Donald Trump, Extract of Remarks at a "Make America Great Again" Rally in Harrisburg, Pennsylvania (2017)    S30-7

# Appendices

## Appendix A Historical Documents    A-1

The Declaration of Independence    A-1

The Constitution of the United States of America    A-3

Articles    A-13

Lincoln's Gettysburg Address    A-22

## Appendix B Historical Facts and Data    B-1

US Presidents and Vice Presidents    B-1

Admission of States into the Union    B-3

**Glossary**    G-1

**Photo Credits**    C-1

**Index**    I-1

# Maps

15–1    Reconstruction and Redemption    *471*
15–2    Sharecropping    *475*
15–3    The Effect of Sharecropping in the South: The Barrow Plantation in Oglethorpe County, Georgia    *476*
15–4    The Overland Trail    *479*
15–5    The Presidential Election, 1876    *491*
16–1    Patterns of Global Migration, 1840–1900    *500*
16–2    The Growth of Railroads, 1850–1890    *508*
16–3    Major American Industries, ca. 1890    *511*
17–1    Houses of Prostitution, 1850–1859 and 1900–1909    *530*
17–2    Population of Foreign Birth by Region, 1880    *532*
17–3    The Election of 1888    *545*
18–1    The Election of 1896    *566*
18–2    The Spanish-American War: (a) Caribbean Theater; (b) Pacific Theater    *580*
18–3a   The Imperial World: Asia, Africa, and the Middle East    *584*
18–3b   The Imperial World: the Pacific and the Americas    *585*
19–1    Growth of Public Lands    *608*
19–2    United States in the Caribbean    *612*
19–3    The Election of 1912    *614*
20–1    The US Invasions of Mexico, 1914, 1917    *623*
20–2    Western Front, 1918    *637*
21–1    The Election of 1928    *676*
22–1    Extent of the Dust Bowl    *684*
22–2    The Presidential Election of 1932    *688*
22–3    TVA Projects    *694*
23–1    World War II in the Pacific, 1942–1945    *717*
23–2    World War II in Europe, 1942–1945    *724*
23–3    The Manhattan Project    *726*
24–1    Cold War in Europe, 1950    *751*
24–2    The Korean War, 1950–1953    *755*
24–3    The 1948 Presidential Election    *763*
25–1    America's Cold War Alliances in Asia    *793*
25–2    America's Cold War Alliances in the Middle East    *796*
25–3    African Americans Attending Schools with White Students in Southern and Border States, 1954    *798*
26–1    The Presidential Election, 1960    *810*
26–2    America's War in Vietnam, 1965–1968    *823*
26–3    Race Riots, 1965–1968    *825*
26–4    The Presidential Election, 1968    *834*
27–1    Movement from Rustbelt to Sunbelt    *844*

27–2    The Equal Rights Amendment (ERA)    *853*
27–3    Native American Population, 1980    *855*
27–4    The Presidential Election, 1976    *862*
28–1    The Growth of Evangelical Christianity    *875*
28–2    The Presidential Election, 1980    *876*
28–3    The Reagan Doctrine in Central America and the Caribbean    *882*
28–4    Abortion in the 1980s    *889*
29–1    Aging in America    *913*
29–2    The Persian Gulf War    *928*
30–1    US Military Deployments in the Age of Terror    *949*
30–2    Percentage Change in Minority Population by County: 2000 to 2010    *950*

# Features

## AMERICAN PORTRAIT

John Dennett Visits a Freedmen's Bureau Court (Chapter 15)

Rosa Cassettari (Chapter 16)

Luna Kellie and the Farmers' Alliance (Chapter 17)

J. P. Morgan (Chapter 18)

Helen Keller (Chapter 19)

Walter Lippmann (Chapter 20)

"America's Sweetheart" (Chapter 21)

Dorothea Lange (Chapter 22)

A. Philip Randolph (Chapter 23)

John Turchinetz (Chapter 24)

The Ricardos (Chapter 25)

The A&T Four (Chapter 26)

"Fighting Shirley Chisholm" (Chapter 27)

Linda Chavez (Chapter 28)

James Sharlow (Chapter 29)

Lt. Craig Mullaney (Chapter 30)

## AMERICAN LANDSCAPE

Mining Camps in the West (Chapter 16)

Galveston, Texas, 1900 (Chapter 18)

The Hetch Hetchy Valley (Chapter 19)

"Flaming Youth" on Campus (Chapter 21)

The Nevada Test Site (Chapter 24)

Eisenhower's Interstate Highway System (Chapter 25)

"Spaceport USA" (Chapter 26)

The South Bronx (Chapter 27)

Silicon Valley (Chapter 28)

"Gitmo" (Chapter 30)

## AMERICA AND THE WORLD

Reconstructing America's Foreign Policy (Chapter 15)

The Global Migration of Labor (Chapter 16)

Foreign Policy: The Limited Significance of Commercial Expansion (Chapter 17)

The American Red Cross and Wartime Civilian Aid (Chapter 20)

J. Walter Thompson and International Markets (Chapter 21)

The 1936 Olympics (Chapter 22)

The Carrier (Chapter 23)

American Tourists in Cold War Europe (Chapter 25)

The Ethiopian Famine (Chapter 28)

*Titanic* and the Globalization of Hollywood (Chapter 29)

## STRUGGLES FOR DEMOCRACY

An Incident at Coushatta, August 1874 (Chapter 15)

"The Chinese Must Go" (Chapter 16)

The "Crusade" Against Alcohol (Chapter 17)

The Wilmington Race Riot (Chapter 18)

Public Response to *The Jungle* (Chapter 19)

Eugene Debs Speaks Out Against the War (Chapter 20)

Flappers and Feminists (Chapter 21)

The Civilian Conservation Corps and a New Brand of Environmentalism (Chapter 22)

The Zoot Suit Riots (Chapter 23)

The Hollywood Ten (Chapter 24)

"The Fantastic, Real-Life, Dream-Come-True Adventure of the Barstow Family of Wethersfield, Connecticut" (Chapter 25)

Protest in the Schools (Chapter 26)

"ROAR"! (Chapter 27)

Reagan at the Berlin Wall (Chapter 28)

"Temporarily Closed," 1995–1996 (Chapter 29)

The Russian Attack on Democracy (Chapter 30)

# Preface

At Gettysburg, Pennsylvania, on November 19, 1863, President Abraham Lincoln dedicated a memorial to the more than 3,000 Union soldiers who had died turning back a Confederate invasion in the first days of July. There were at least a few ways that the president could have justified the sad loss of life in the third year of a brutal war dividing North and South. He could have said it was necessary to destroy the Confederacy's cherished institution of slavery, to punish southerners for seceding from the United States, or to preserve the nation intact. Instead, at this crucial moment in American history, Lincoln gave a short, stunning speech about democracy. The president did not use the word, but he offered its essence. The term *democracy* came from the ancient Greek word *demos*—for "the people." To honor the dead of Gettysburg, Lincoln called on northerners to ensure "that government of the people, by the people, for the people, shall not perish from the earth."

With these words, Lincoln put democracy at the center of the Civil War and at the center of American history. The authors of this book share his belief in the centrality of democracy; his words, "of the people," give our book its title and its main theme. We see American history as a story "of the people," of their struggles to shape their lives and their land.

Our choice of theme does not mean we believe that America has always been a democracy. Clearly, it has not. As Lincoln gave the Gettysburg Address, most African Americans still lived in slavery. American women, North and South, lacked rights that many men enjoyed; for all their disagreements, white southerners and northerners viewed Native Americans as enemies. Neither do we believe that there is only a single definition of democracy, either in the narrow sense of a particular form of government or in the larger one of a society whose members participate equally in its creation. Although Lincoln defined the northern cause as a struggle for democracy, southerners believed it was anything but democratic to force them to remain in the Union at gunpoint. As bloody draft riots in New York City in July 1863 made clear, many northern men thought it was anything but democratic to force them to fight in Lincoln's armies. Such disagreements have been typical of American history. For more than 500 years, people have struggled over whose vision of life in the New World would prevail.

It is precisely such struggles that offer the best angle of vision for seeing and understanding the most important developments in the nation's history. In particular, the democratic theme concentrates attention on the most fundamental concerns of history: people and power.

Lincoln's words serve as a reminder of the basic truth that history is about people. Across the 30 chapters of this book, we write extensively about complex events. But we also write in the awareness that these developments are only abstractions unless they are grounded in the lives of people. The test of a historical narrative, we believe, is whether its characters are fully rounded, believable human beings.

The choice of Lincoln's words also reflects our belief that history is about power. To ask whether America was democratic at some point in the past is to ask how much power various groups of people had to make their lives and their nation. Such questions of power necessarily take us to political processes, to the ways in which people work separately and collectively to enforce their will. We define politics quite broadly in this book. With the feminists of the 1960s, we believe that "the personal is the political," that power relations shape people's lives in private as well as in public. *Of the People* looks for democracy in the living room as well as the legislature, and in the bedroom as well as the business office.

Focusing on democracy, people, and power, we have necessarily written as wide-ranging a history as possible. In the features and in the main text, *Of the People* conveys both the unity and the great diversity of the American people across time and place. We chronicle the racial and ethnic groups who have shaped America, differences of religious and regional identity, the changing nature of social classes, and the different ways that gender identities have been constructed over the centuries.

While treating different groups in their distinctiveness, we have integrated them into the broader narrative as much as possible. A true history "of the people" means not only acknowledging their individuality and diversity but also showing their interrelationships and their roles in the larger narrative. More integrated coverage of Native Americans, African Americans, Latinos, and other minority groups appears throughout the fourth edition.

*Of the People* also offers comprehensive coverage of the different spheres of human life—cultural as well as governmental, social as well as economic, environmental as well as military. This commitment to comprehensiveness is a reflection of our belief that all aspects of human existence are the stuff of history. It is also an expression of the fundamental theme of the book: the focus on democracy leads naturally to the study of people's struggles for power in every dimension of their lives. Moreover, the democratic approach emphasizes the interconnections between the different aspects of Americans' lives; we cannot understand politics and government without tracing their connection to economics, religion, culture, art, sexuality, and so on.

The economic connection is especially important. *Of the People* devotes much attention to economic life, to the ways in which Americans have worked and saved and spent. Economic power, the authors believe, is basic to democracy. Americans' power to shape their lives and their country has been greatly affected by whether they were farmers or hunters, plantation owners or slaves, wage workers or capitalists, domestic servants or bureaucrats. The authors do not see economics as an impersonal, all-conquering force; instead, we try to show how the values and actions of ordinary people, as well as the laws and regulations of government, have made economic life.

We have also tried especially to place America in a global context. The history of America, or any nation, cannot be adequately explained without understanding its relationship to transnational events and global developments. That is true for the first chapter of the book, which shows how America began to emerge from the collision of Native Americans, West Africans, and Europeans in the fifteenth and sixteenth centuries. It is just as true for the last chapters of the book, which demonstrate how globalization and the war on terror transformed the United States at the turn of the twenty-first century. In the chapters in between, we detail how the world has changed America and how America has changed the world. Reflecting the concerns of the rest of the book, we focus particularly on the movement of people, the evolution of power, and the attempt to spread democracy abroad.

Abraham Lincoln wanted to sell a war, of course. But he also truly believed that his audience would see democracy as quintessentially American. Whether he was right is the burden of this book.

# New to the Fourth Edition

We are grateful that the first, second, and third editions of *Of the People* have been welcomed by instructors and students as a useful instructional aid. In preparing the fourth edition, our primary goal has been to maintain the text's overarching focus on the evolution of American democracy, people, and power; its strong portrayal of political and social history; and its clear, compelling narrative voice. To that end, the broad representation of Native Americans, African Americans, and other minority groups in this text shows the full diversity of the American people. One of the text's strengths is its critical-thinking pedagogy because the study of history entails careful analysis, not mere memorization of names and dates.

History continues, and the writing of history is never finished. For the fourth edition, we have updated the following elements based on the most recent scholarship:

## Number of Chapters

The book has been condensed from 30 chapters and an epilogue to 30 chapters: the number of Gilded Age chapters has been reduced from three (formerly Chapters 16, 17, and 18 in the third edition) to two (Chapters 16 and 17 in the fourth edition) to streamline the narrative flow and more evenly balance the distribution of chapters to allow for more coverage of recent history. The chapter content has been redistributed as follows to accommodate this restructuring.

### Chapter 15: Reconstructing a Nation, 1865–1877
- Includes a new section titled "A Reconstructed West," which is comprised of the following sections from the third edition's Chapter 16:
  - The Overland Trail
  - The Origins of Indian Reservations
  - The Destruction of Indian Subsistence
- The chapter-ending section "The End of Reconstruction" now concludes with "Sharecropping Becomes Wage Labor" from the third edition's Chapter 16.

### Chapter 16: The Triumph of Industrial Capitalism, 1850–1890
- Includes the section "Social Darwinism and the Growth of Scientific Racism" from the third edition's Chapter 17
- Includes "Struggles for Democracy: 'The Chinese Must Go'" from the third edition's Chapter 17
- Includes the section "The Knights of Labor and the Haymarket Disaster" from the third edition's Chapter 18

### Chapter 17: The Culture and Politics of Industrial America, 1870–1892
- Formerly Chapter 18 in the third edition
- Includes the section "The Elusive Boundaries of Male and Female," which is comprised of the following sections from the third edition's Chapter 17:
  - The Victorian Construction of Male and Female
  - Victorians Who Questioned Traditional Sexual Boundaries

- Content from the third edition's Chapter 17 "American Portrait: Anthony Comstock's Crusade Against Vice" is incorporated into the discussion "The Victorian Crusade for Morality."
- Includes the section "The Varieties of Urban Culture" from the third edition's Chapter 17, now simply titled "Urban Culture."
- Includes the section "A New Cultural Order: New Americans Stir Old Fears," which is comprised of the following sections from the third edition's Chapter 17:
  - Josiah Strong Attacks Immigration
  - From Immigrants to Ethnic Americans
  - The Catholic Church and Its Limits in Immigrant Culture
  - Immigrant Cultures
- Includes the section "The Rise and Fall of the National Labor Union" from the third edition's Chapter 15

**Chapter 30: "A Nation Transformed," The Twenty-First Century**

Formerly the Epilogue, this chapter has been revised and significantly expanded to cover the span of years since 2001.

- Revised discussion of Obama's second term in office
- New discussions on:
  - Climate change
  - The rise of the Islamic State
  - Diversity, division, and discrimination in the United States, with emphasis on the justice system's treatment of African Americans and Deferred Action for Childhood Arrivals (DACA)
  - Expanded discussion of LGBTQ rights
  - Shifting religious beliefs and practices in the United States
  - The implications of deindustrialization, digitization, and globalization on jobs and growth
  - The growing income inequality gap
  - How economic change has impacted the status of women, men, baby boomers, and millennials, as well as increased the divide between urban and rural areas
  - How growing wealth inequality has intensified the problem of money in politics
  - The emergence of four contending political approaches
  - The Presidential Election of 2016

## New Additions to American Portrait, American Landscape, America and the World, and Struggles for Democracy Features

These popular features from the third edition have been updated with eight new American Portraits, four new American Landscapes, eight new America and the World features, and three new Struggles for Democracy.

## Photos

Approximately one-third of the photos have been revised throughout the chapters and sources.

## Primary Sources

A version of the text is available with end-of-chapter primary source documents, both textual and visual, designed to reinforce students' understanding of the material by drawing connections among topics and thinking critically. Nearly all chapters include at least one new source document:

- Source 2.3 Father Pierre Cholonec, Life of Kateri (1715)
- Source 3.1 Edward Waterhouse's Report on the Uprising of 1622
- Source 5.4 George Whitefield, Account of a Visit to Georgia (1738)
- Source 6.5 The Stamp Act Riots: The Destruction of Thomas Hutchinson's House (1765)
- Source 7.2 Alexander Hamilton Recommends Arming Slaves and George Washington Rejects the Idea (1779)
- Source 8.2 Thomas Jefferson's Letter to Philip Mazzei (1796)
- Source 9.5 Elder David Purviance's Description of the Cane Ridge Revival (1801)
- Source 10.5 Frances Kemble's Journal (1838–1839)
- Source 11.2 Angelina Grimké, Excerpt from *An Appeal to the Women of the Nominally Free States* (1838)
- Source 12.5 María Amparo Ruiz, *The Squatter and the Don* (1885)
- Source 13.4 Abraham Lincoln, Speech at Springfield, Illinois (1857)
- Source 14.1 John Sherman, A Letter on the Crisis to Philadelphians (1860)
- Source 14.3 Cornelia Hancock, Letter to Her Sister (1863)
- Source 14.4 John Beauchamp Jones Observes the Deterioration on the Confederate Home Front (1863–1864)
- Source 15.5 A Southern Unionist Judge's Daughter Writes the President for Help (1874)
- Source 15.6 Red Cloud Pleads the Plains Indians' Point of View at Cooper Union (1870)
- Source 16.6 James Baird Weaver, *A Call to Action* (1892)
- Source 17.5 Visual Documents: "Gift for the Grangers" (1873) and the Jorns Family of Dry Valley, Custer County, Nebraska (1886)
- Source 18.1 Frederick Winslow Taylor, Excerpts from *The Principles of Scientific Management* (1911)
- Source 20.1 World War I–Era Music: "I Didn't Raise My Boy to Be a Solider" (1915) and "Over There" (1917)
- Source 21.1 Hiram Wesley Evans, Excerpts from "The Klan: Defender of Americanism" (1925)
- Source 22.4 Remembering the Great Depression, Excerpts from Studs Terkel's *Hard Times* (1970)
- Source 23.2 Charles Lindbergh, America First Committee Address (1941)
- Source 24.2 High School and College Graduates in the Cold War (1948–1950)
- Source 25.1 Gael Greene, "The Battle of Levittown" (1957)
- Source 25.3 Visual Documents: Automobile Advertisements (1953–1955)
- Source 26.5 John Wilcock, "The Human Be-In" and "San Francisco" (1967)
- Source 27.2 Nixon Decides on the Christmas Bombing (1972)
- Source 28.1 Visual Document: US Centers for Disease Control, AIDS Awareness Poster (1980s)

- Source 29.3 Visual Document: Aziz + Cucher, "Man with Computer" (1992)
- Source 30.2 Barack Obama, Keynote Address, Democratic Party Convention (2004)
- Source 30.3 Debate in the House of Representatives on a Resolution "That Symbols and Traditions of Christmas Should Be Protected" (2005)
- Source 30.4 Harry M. Reid, "The Koch Brothers" (2015)
- Source 30.5 Steve A. King, "Illegal Immigration," House of Representatives (2007)
- Source 30.6 Donald Trump, Extract of Remarks at a "Make America Great Again" Rally in Harrisburg, Pennsylvania (2017)

## Hallmark Features

- Each chapter opens with an **American Portrait** feature, a story of someone whose life in one way or another embodies the basic theme of the pages to follow.
- Select chapters include an **American Landscape** feature, a particular place in time where issues of power appeared in especially sharp relief.
- To underscore the fundamental importance of global relationships, select chapters include a feature on **America and the World**.
- Each chapter includes a **Struggles for Democracy** feature, focusing on moments of debate and public conversation surrounding events that have contributed to the changing ideas of democracy, as well as the sometimes constricting but overall gradually widening opportunities that evolved for the American people as a result.
- **Common Threads** focus questions at chapter openings.
- **Time Lines** in every chapter.
- A list of chapter-ending key terms, **Who, What, Where**, helps students recall the important people, events, and places of that chapter.
- All chapters end with both **Review Questions**, which test students' memory and understanding of chapter content, and **Critical-Thinking Questions**, which ask students to analyze and interpret chapter content.

## Learning Resources for *Of the People*

Oxford University Press offers instructors and students a comprehensive ancillary package for qualified adopters.

### Ancillary Resource Center (ARC)

This online resource center, available to adopters of *Of the People*, includes the following:

- Instructor's Resource Manual: Includes, for each chapter, a detailed chapter outline, suggested lecture topics, and learning objectives, as well as approximately 40 multiple-choice, short-answer, true-or-false, fill-in-the-blank, and 10 essay questions for each chapter
- A Computerized Test Bank that includes all of the test items from the Instructor's Resource Manual
- PowerPoints and Computerized Test Bank: Includes PowerPoint slides and JPEG and PDF files for all the maps and photos in the text, and approximately 1,000 additional PowerPoint-based slides from OUP's US History Image Library, organized by themes and periods in American history.

- The US History Video Library, Produced by Oxford University Press: Each 3- to 5-minute video covers a key topic in US history, from Squanto to John Brown, from Mother Jones to the "disco wars" of the late 1970s/early 1980s. Combining motion pictures, stills, audio clips, and narration, these videos are ideal for both classroom discussion or as online assignments.

## Oxford First Source

This database includes hundreds of primary source documents in US history. The documents cover a broad variety of political, economic, social, and cultural topics and represent a cross section of American voices. Special effort was made to include as many previously disenfranchised voices as possible. The documents are indexed by date, author, title, and subject. Short documents (one or two pages) are presented in their entirety while longer documents have been carefully edited to highlight significant content. Each document is introduced with a short explanatory paragraph and accompanied with study questions.

A complete **Course Management cartridge** is also available to qualified adopters. Instructor's resources are also available for download directly to your computer through a secure connection via the instructor's side of the companion website. Contact your Oxford University Press sales representative for more information.

## Student Companion Website at www.oup.com/us/oakes-mcgerr

The open-access Online Study Center designed for *Of the People: A History of the United States*, Fourth Edition helps students to review what they have learned from the textbook as well as explore other resources online.

## Sources for *Of the People: A History of the United States, Volume I to 1877* (ISBN 978019091014) and *Of the People: A History of the United States, Volume II Since 1865* (ISBN 9780190910150)

Edited by Maxwell Johnson, and organized to match the table of contents of *Of the People*, this two-volume sourcebook includes five to six primary sources per chapter, both textual and visual. Chapter introductions, document headnotes, and study questions provide learning support. Each volume of the sourcebook is only $5.00 when bundled with *Of the People*.

## Mapping and Coloring Book of US History

This two-volume workbook includes approximately 80 outline maps that provide opportunities for students to deepen their understanding of geography through quizzes, coloring exercises, and other activities. *The Mapping and Coloring Book of US History* is free when bundled with *Of the People*.

## E-Books

Digital versions of *Of the People* are available at many popular distributors, including Chegg, RedShelf, and VitalSource.

## Other Oxford Titles of Interest for the US History Classroom

Oxford University Press publishes a vast array of titles in American history. The following list is just a small selection of books that pair particularly well with *Of the People: A History of the United States*, Fourth Edition. Any of these books can be packaged with *Of the People* at a significant discount to students. Please contact your Oxford University Press sales representative for specific pricing information or for additional packaging suggestions. Please visit www.oup.com/us for a full listing of Oxford titles.

### *Writing History: A Guide for Students*, Fifth Edition, by William Kelleher Storey, Professor of History at Millsaps College

Bringing together practical methods from both history and composition, *Writing History* provides a wealth of tips and advice to help students research and write essays for history classes. The book covers all aspects of writing about history, including **finding topics and researching** them, **interpreting source materials, drawing inferences from sources, and constructing arguments.** It concludes with three chapters that discuss writing effective sentences, using precise wording, and revising. Using numerous examples from the works of cultural, political, and social historians, *Writing History* serves as an ideal supplement to history courses that require students to conduct research. The fifth edition includes expanded sections on peer editing and topic selection, as well as new sections on searching and using the Internet. *Writing History* can be packaged with *Of the People: A History of the United States*, Fourth Edition. Contact your Oxford University Press sales representative for more information.

### *The Information-Literate Historian: A Guide to Research for History Students*, Third Edition, by Jenny Presnell, Information Services Library and History, American Studies, and Women's Studies Bibliographer, Miami University of Ohio

This is the only book specifically designed to teach today's history student how to most successfully select and use sources—primary, secondary, and electronic—to carry out and present their research. Written by a college librarian, *The Information-Literate Historian* is an indispensable reference for historians, students, and other readers doing history research. *The Information-Literate Historian* can be packaged with *Of the People: A History of the United States*, Fourth Edition. Contact your Oxford University Press sales representative for more information.

# Acknowledgments

We are grateful to our families, friends, and colleagues who encouraged us during the planning and writing of this book. We would like once again to thank Bruce Nichols for helping launch this book years ago. We are grateful to the editors and staff at Oxford University Press, especially our acquisitions editor, Charles Cavaliere, and our development editor, Maegan Sherlock. Charles's commitment made this text possible and Maegan deftly guided the development of the fourth edition. Thanks also to our talented production team, Barbara Mathieu, senior production editor, and Michele Laseau, art director, who helped to fulfill the book's vision. And special thanks go to Leslie Anglin, our copyeditor; to Rowan Wixted, assistant editor; and to the many other people behind the scenes at Oxford for helping this complex project happen.

The authors and editors would also like to thank the following people, whose time and insights have contributed to the first, second, third, and fourth editions.

## Expert Reviewers of the Fourth Edition

Daniel Anderson
*Cincinnati State University*

Tramaine Anderson
*Tarrant County College*

Matthew Campbell
*Lone Star College–Cypress Fairbanks*

Gregg S. Clemmer
*Carroll Community College*

John Patrick Daly
*College at Brockport, State University of New York*

Maureen Elgersman Lee
*Hampton University*

Michael Frawley
*University of Texas of the Permian Basin*

Robert Genter
*Nassau Community College*

Sakina M. Hughes
*University of Southern Indiana*

Katrina Lacher
*University of Central Oklahoma*

Robert Lee
*St. Louis Community College–Meramec*

Matthew Oyos
*Radford University*

Stephen Todd Pfeffer
*Columbus State Community College*

Brenden Rensink
*Brigham Young University*

Marie Stango
*California State University, Bakersfield*


## Expert Reviewers of the Third Edition

Greg Hall
*Western Illinois University*

Ross A. Kennedy
*Illinois State University*

Randall M. Miller
*Saint Joseph's University*

David W. Morris
*Santa Barbara City College*

Adam Pratt
*University of Scranton*

Judith Ridner
*Mississippi State University*

Robert A. Smith
*Pittsburg State University*

Timothy B. Smith
*University of Tennessee at Martin*

Linda D. Tomlinson
*Fayetteville State University*

Gerald Wilson
*Eastern Washington University*


## Expert Reviewers of the Second Edition

Marjorie Berman
*Red Rocks Community College–Lakewood*

Will Carter
*South Texas Community College*

Jonathan Chu
*University of Massachusetts, Boston*

Sara Combs
*Virginia Highlands Community College*

Mark Elliott
*University of North Carolina–Greensboro*

David Hamilton
*University of Kentucky*

James Harvey
*Houston Community College*

Courtney Joiner
*East Georgia College*

Timothy Mahoney
*University of Nebraska–Lincoln*

Abigail Markwyn
*Carroll University*

Brian Maxson
*Eastern Tennessee State University*

Matthew Oyos
*Radford University*

John Pinheiro
*Aquinas College*

James Pula
*Purdue University–North Central*

John Rosinbum
*Arizona State University*

Christopher Thrasher
*Texas Tech University*

Jeffrey Trask
*University of Massachusetts–Amherst*

Michael Ward
*California State University–Northridge*

Bridgette Williams-Searle
*The College of Saint Rose*

## Expert Reviewers of the First Edition

Thomas L. Altherr
*Metropolitan State College of Denver*

Luis Alvarez
*University of California–San Diego*

Adam Arenson
*University of Texas–El Paso*

Melissa Estes Blair
*University of Georgia*

Lawrence Bowdish
*Ohio State University*

Susan Roth Breitzer
*Fayetteville State University*

Margaret Lynn Brown
*Brevard College*

W. Fitzhugh Brundage
*University of North Carolina–Chapel Hill*

Gregory Bush
*University of Miami*

Brian Casserly
*University of Washington*

Ann Chirhart
*Indiana State University*

Bradley R. Clampitt
*East Central University*

William W. Cobb Jr.
*Utah Valley University*

Cheryll Ann Cody
*Houston Community College*

Sondra Cosgrove
*College of Southern Nevada*

Thomas H. Cox
*Sam Houston State University*

Carl Creasman
*Valencia Community College*

Christine Daniels
*Michigan State University*

Brian J. Daugherity
*Virginia Commonwealth University*

Mark Elliott
*University of North Carolina–Greensboro*

Katherine Carté Enge
*Texas A&M University*

Michael Faubion
*University of Texas–Pan American*

John Fea
*Messiah College*

Anne L. Foster
*Indiana State University*

Matthew Garrett
*Arizona State University*

Tim Garvin
*California State University–Long Beach*

Suzanne Cooper Guasco
*Queens University of Charlotte*

Lloyd Ray Gunn
*University of Utah*

Richard Hall
*Columbus State University*

Marsha Hamilton
*University of South Alabama*

Mark Hanna
*University of California–San Diego*

Joseph M. Hawes
*University of Memphis*

Melissa Hovsepian
*University of Houston–Downtown*

Jorge Iber
*Texas Tech University*

David K. Johnson
*University of South Florida*

Lloyd Johnson
*Campbell University*

Catherine O'Donnell Kaplan
*Arizona State University*

Rebecca M. Kluchin
*California State University–Sacramento*

Michael Kramer
*Northwestern University*

Louis M. Kyriakoudes
*University of Southern Mississippi*

Jason S. Lantzer
*Butler University*

Shelly Lemons
*St. Louis Community College*

Charlie Levine
*Mesa Community College*

Denise Lynn
*University of Southern Indiana*

Lillian Marrujo-Duck
*City College of San Francisco*

Michael McCoy
*Orange County Community College*

Noeleen McIlvenna
*Wright State University*

Elizabeth Brand Monroe
*Indiana University–Purdue
University Indianapolis*

Kevin C. Motl
*Ouachita Baptist University*

Todd Moye
*University of North Texas*

Charlotte Negrete
*Mt. San Antonio College*

Julie Nicoletta
*University of Washington–Tacoma*

David M. Parker
*California State University–Northridge*

Jason Parker
*Texas A&M University*

Burton W. Peretti
*Western Connecticut State University*

Jim Piecuch
*Kennesaw State University*

John Putman
*San Diego State University*

R. J. Rockefeller
*Loyola College of Maryland*

Herbert Sloan
*Barnard College, Columbia University*

Vincent L. Toscano
*Nova Southeastern University*

William E. Weeks
*San Diego State University*

Timothy L. Wood
*Southwest Baptist University*

Jason Young
*SUNY–Buffalo*

## Expert Reviewers of the Concise Second Edition

Hedrick Alixopulos
*Santa Rosa Junior College*

Guy Alain Aronoff
*Humboldt State University*

Melissa Estes Blair
*Warren Wilson College*

Amanda Bruce
*Nassau Community College*

Jonathan Chu
*University of Massachusetts–Boston*

Paul G. E. Clemens
*Rutgers University*

Martha Anne Fielder
*Cedar Valley College*

Tim Hacsi
*University of Massachusetts–Boston*

Matthew Isham
*Pennsylvania State University*

Ross A. Kennedy
*Illinois State University*

Eve Kornfeld
*San Diego State University*

Peggy Lambert
*Lone Star College–Kingwood*

Shelly L. Lemons
*St. Louis Community College*

Carolyn Herbst Lewis
*Louisiana State University*

Catherine M. Lewis
*Kennesaw State University*

Daniel K. Lewis
*California State Polytechnic University*

Scott P. Marler
*University of Memphis*

Laura McCall
*Metropolitan State College of Denver*

Stephen P. McGrath
*Central Connecticut State University*

Vincent P. Mikkelsen
*Florida State University*

Julie Nicoletta
*University of Washington Tacoma*

Caitlin Stewart
*Eastern Connecticut State University*

Thomas Summerhill
*Michigan State University*

David Tegeder
*Santa Fe College*

Eric H. Walther
*University of Houston*

William E. Weeks
*University of San Diego*

Kenneth B. White
*Modesto Junior College*

Julie Winch
*University of Massachusetts–Boston*

Mary Montgomery Wolf
*University of Georgia*

Kyle F. Zelner
*University of Southern Mississippi*

**Expert Reviewers of the Concise First Edition**

Hedrick Alixopulos
*Santa Rosa Junior College*

Guy Alain Aronoff
*Humboldt State University*

Melissa Estes Blair
*Warren Wilson College*

Amanda Bruce
*Nassau Community College*

Jonathan Chu
*University of Massachusetts–Boston*

Paul G. E. Clemens
*Rutgers University*

Martha Anne Fielder
*Cedar Valley College*

Tim Hacsi
*University of Massachusetts–Boston*

Matthew Isham
*Pennsylvania State University*

Ross A. Kennedy
*Illinois State University*

Eve Kornfeld
*San Diego State University*

Peggy Lambert
*Lone Star College–Kingwood*

Shelly L. Lemons
*St. Louis Community College*

Carolyn Herbst Lewis
*Louisiana State University*

Catherine M. Lewis
*Kennesaw State University*

Daniel K. Lewis
*California State Polytechnic University*

Scott P. Marler
*University of Memphis*

Laura McCall
*Metropolitan State College of Denver*

Stephen P. McGrath
*Central Connecticut State University*

Vincent P. Mikkelsen
*Florida State University*

Julie Nicoletta
*University of Washington Tacoma*

Caitlin Stewart
*Eastern Connecticut State University*

Thomas Summerhill
*Michigan State University*

David Tegeder
*Santa Fe College*

Eric H. Walther
*University of Houston*

William E. Weeks
*University of San Diego*

Kenneth B. White
*Modesto Junior College*

Julie Winch
*University of Massachusetts–Boston*

Mary Montgomery Wolf
*University of Georgia*

Kyle F. Zelner
*University of Southern Mississippi*

# About the Authors

**Michael McGerr** is the Paul V. McNutt Professor of History at Indiana University–Bloomington. He is the author of *The Decline of Popular Politics: The American North, 1865–1928* (1986) and *A Fierce Discontent: The Rise and Fall of the Progressive Movement, 1870–1920* (2003), both from Oxford University Press. He is writing *"The Public Be Damned": The Kingdom and the Dream of the Vanderbilts*. The recipient of a fellowship from the National Endowment for the Humanities, Professor McGerr has won numerous teaching awards at Indiana, where his courses include the US Survey; War in Modern American History; Rock, Hip Hop, and Revolution; Big Business; The Sixties; and American Pleasure. He has previously taught at Yale University and the Massachusetts Institute of Technology. He received his BA, MA, and PhD from Yale.

**Jan Ellen Lewis** is Professor of History and Dean of the Faculty of Arts and Sciences, Rutgers University–Newark. She also teaches in the history PhD program at Rutgers, New Brunswick, and was a visiting professor of history at Princeton. A specialist in colonial and early national history, she is the author of *The Pursuit of Happiness: Family and Values in Jefferson's Virginia* (1983) as well as numerous articles and reviews. She has coedited *An Emotional History of the United States* (1998), *Sally Hemings and Thomas Jefferson: History, Memory, and Civic Culture* (1999), and *The Revolution of 1800: Democracy, Race, and the New Republic* (2002). She has served as president of the Society of Historians of the Early American Republic, as chair of the New Jersey Historical Commission, and on the editorial board of the *American Historical Review*. She is an elected member of the Society of American Historians and the American Antiquarian Society. She received her AB from Bryn Mawr College and MAs and PhD from the University of Michigan.

**James Oakes** has published several books and numerous articles on slavery and antislavery in the nineteenth century, including *The Radical and the Republican: Frederick Douglass, Abraham Lincoln, and the Triumph of Antislavery Politics* (2007), winner of the Lincoln Prize in 2008. Professor Oakes is Distinguished Professor of History and Graduate School Humanities Professor at the City University of New York Graduate Center. In 2008, he was a fellow at the Cullman Center at the New York Public Library. His new book is *Freedom National: The Destruction of Slavery in the United States* (February 2013).

**Nick Cullather** is a historian of US foreign relations at Indiana University–Bloomington. He is author of three books on nation building: *The Hungry World* (2010), a story of foreign aid, development, and science; *Illusions of Influence* (1994), on US–Philippines relations; and *Secret History* (1999 and 2006), a history of the CIA's overthrow of the Guatemalan government in 1954. He received his PhD from the University of Virginia.

**Mark Summers** is the Thomas D. Clark Professor of History at the University of Kentucky–Lexington. In addition to various articles, he has written *Railroads, Reconstruction, and the Gospel of Prosperity* (1984), *The Plundering Generation* (1988), *The Era of Good Stealings*

(1993), *The Press Gang* (1994), *The Gilded Age; or, The Hazard of New Functions* (1997), *Rum, Romanism and Rebellion* (2000), *Party Games* (2004), and *A Dangerous Stir* (2009). At present, he has just completed a book about a Tammany politician, *Big Tim and the Tiger*. He is now writing a survey of Reconstruction and a book about 1868. He teaches the American history survey (both halves), the Gilded Age, the Progressive Era, the Age of Jackson, Civil War and Reconstruction, the British Empire (both halves), the Old West (both halves), a history of political cartooning, and various graduate courses. He earned his BA from Yale and his PhD from the University of California–Berkeley.

**Camilla Townsend** is Professor of History at Rutgers University–New Brunswick. She is the author of five books, among them *Annals of Native America* (2016), *Malintzin's Choices: An Indian Woman in the Conquest of Mexico* (2006), and *Pocahontas and the Powhatan Dilemma* (2004), and she is the editor of *American Indian History: A Documentary Reader* (2010). The recipient of fellowships from the National Endowment for the Humanities and the John Simon Guggenheim Memorial Foundation, she has also won awards at Rutgers and at Colgate, where she used to teach. Her courses at the graduate and undergraduate level cover the colonial history of the Americas, as well as Native American history, early and modern. She received her BA from Bryn Mawr and her PhD from Rutgers.

**Karen M. Dunak** is Associate Professor of History at Muskingum University in New Concord, Ohio. She is the author of *As Long as We Both Shall Love: The White Wedding in Postwar America* (2013), published by New York University Press. She currently is working on a book about media representations of and responses to Jacqueline Kennedy Onassis. Her courses include the US Survey, Women in US History, Gender and Sexuality in US History, and various topics related to modern US history. She earned her BA from American University and her PhD from Indiana University.

**Jeanne Boydston** was Robinson-Edwards Professor of American History at the University of Wisconsin–Madison. A specialist in the histories of gender and labor, she was the author of *Home and Work: Housework, Wages, and the Ideology of Labor in the Early American Republic* (1990); coauthor of *The Limits of Sisterhood: The Beecher Sisters on Women's Rights and Woman's Sphere* (1988); and coeditor of *Root of Bitterness: Documents in the Social History of American Women*, second edition (1996). The recipient of numerous teaching awards, she gave courses in women's and gender history, the United States before the Civil War, and global and comparative history. Her BA and MA were from the University of Tennessee, and her PhD was from Yale University.

# Of the People

# Reconstructing a Nation

## 1865–1877

## COMMON THREADS

In what ways did emancipation and wartime Reconstruction overlap?

When did Reconstruction begin?

Did Reconstruction change the South? If so, how? If not, why not?

How did Reconstruction affect the West?

What brought Reconstruction to an end?

## OUTLINE

**AMERICAN PORTRAIT: John Dennett Visits a Freedmen's Bureau Court**

Wartime Reconstruction
  Lincoln's Ten Percent Plan Versus the Wade-Davis Bill
  The Meaning of Freedom
  Experiments with Free Labor

Presidential Reconstruction, 1865–1867
  The Political Economy of Contract Labor
  Resistance to Presidential Reconstruction
  Congress Clashes with the President
  Origins of the Fourteenth Amendment

Congressional Reconstruction
  The South Remade
  The Impeachment and Trial of Andrew Johnson
  Radical Reconstruction in the South
  Achievements and Failures of Radical Government
  The Political Economy of Sharecropping
  The Gospel of Prosperity
  A Counterrevolution of Terrorism and Economic Pressure

**AMERICA AND THE WORLD: Reconstructing America's Foreign Policy**

A Reconstructed West
  The Overland Trail
  The Origins of Indian Reservations
  The Destruction of Indian Subsistence

The Retreat from Republican Radicalism
  Republicans Become the Party of Moderation

Reconstructing the North
  The Fifteenth Amendment and Nationwide African American Suffrage
  Women and Suffrage

The End of Reconstruction
  Corruption Is the Fashion
  Liberal Republicans Revolt
  "Redeeming" the South

**STRUGGLES FOR DEMOCRACY: An Incident at Coushatta, August 1874**

  The Twice-Stolen Election of 1876
  Sharecropping Becomes Wage Labor

Conclusion

< Terror in the South

459

## AMERICAN PORTRAIT

# John Dennett Visits a Freedmen's Bureau Court

John Richard Dennett arrived in Liberty, Virginia, on August 17, 1865, on a tour of the South reporting for the magazine *The Nation*. The editors wanted accurate weekly accounts of conditions in the recently defeated Confederate states, and Dennett was the kind of man they could trust: a Harvard graduate, a firm believer in the sanctity of the Union, and a member of the class of elite Yankees who thought of themselves as the "best men" the country had to offer.

At Liberty, Dennett was accompanied by a Freedmen's Bureau agent. The Freedmen's Bureau was a branch of the US Army established by Congress to assist the freed people. Dennett and the agent went to the courthouse because one of the Freedmen's Bureau's functions was to adjudicate disputes between the freed people and southern whites.

The first case was that of an old white farmer who complained that two blacks who worked on his farm were "roamin' about and refusin' to work." He wanted the agent to help find the men and bring them back. Both men had wives and children living on his farm and eating his corn, the old man complained. "Have you been paying any wages?" the Freedmen's Bureau agent asked. "Well, they get what the other niggers get," the farmer answered. "I a'n't payin' great wages this year." There was not much the agent could do, but one of his soldiers volunteered to go and tell the blacks that "they ought to be at home supporting their wives and children."

A well-to-do planter came in to see if he could fire the blacks who had been working on his plantation since the beginning of the year. Warned not to beat his workers the way he would slaves, the planter complained that they were unmanageable without what he considered proper punishment. Under the circumstances, the planter wondered, "Will the Government take them off our hands?" The agent suspected that the planter was looking for a way to dismiss his workforce unpaid at the end of the growing season. "If they've worked on your crops all the year so far," the agent told the planter, "I guess they've got a claim on you to keep them a while longer."

Next came a "good-looking mulatto man" representing a number of African Americans worried that they would be forced into five-year contracts with their employers. "No, it a'n't true," the agent said. Could they rent or buy land to work themselves? "Yes, rent or buy," the agent said. But with no horses, mules, or plows, the former slaves wanted to see "if the Government would help us out after we get the land." All that the agent could offer was a note from the bureau authorizing them to acquire farms of their own.

The last case involved a field hand whose master had beaten him with a stick. The agent sent the field hand back to work. "Don't be sassy, don't be lazy when you've got work to do; and I guess he won't trouble you." A minute later, the worker returned to procure a letter to his master "enjoining him to keep the peace, as he feared the man would shoot him, he having on two or three occasions threatened to do so."

Most of the cases Dennett witnessed centered on labor relations, which often spilled over into other matters, including the family lives of former slaves, their civil rights, and their ability to buy land. The freed people preferred to work their own land but lacked the resources to rent or buy farms. Black workers and white owners who negotiated wage contracts had trouble figuring out each other's rights and responsibilities. The former masters clung to all their old authority that they could. Freed people wanted as free a hand as possible.

The Freedmen's Bureau was in the middle of these conflicts. Generally, agents tried to see to it that freed people had written contracts guaranteeing their essential right to work as free laborers, uncoerced by whip, club, or gun. Southern whites resented any intrusion with people they still saw as essentially property, and they let civil authorities know it. The Freedmen's Bureau became a lightning rod for the political conflicts of the Reconstruction period.

Conditions in the South elicited sharply different responses from lawmakers in Washington. At one extreme was President Andrew Johnson, who believed in small government and a speedy readmission of the southern states and looked on the Freedmen's Bureau with suspicion. At the other extreme were radical Republicans calling on the federal government to redistribute confiscated land to former slaves, give African American men the vote, and take it away from whites who were not loyal to the United States during the war. In between, there were moderate Republicans who at first tried to work with the president and were content simply to guarantee African Americans' basic civil rights. But as reports of violence and the abusive treatment of the freed people reached Washington, Republicans shifted in more radical directions.

Back and forth it went: events in the South triggered policy decisions in Washington, which in turn shaped events in the South. What John Dennett saw in Liberty, Virginia, was a good example of this. Policies set in Washington shaped what the Freedmen's Bureau agent could do for former masters and slaves. However, those policies shifted when the Bureau's reports and those of journalists, like Dennett, exposed just how troubled southern conditions were. From this interaction the politics of Reconstruction, and with it a "New South," slowly emerged.

# Wartime Reconstruction

Even as emancipation began, the US government began experimenting with reconstructing the Union. The two goals merged: by creating new, loyal southern states and making their abolition of slavery a condition for reunion, Lincoln could enact emancipation there without court challenge. Through a generous policy of pardons, he could encourage Confederates to make their peace with the Union, speeding the war's end.

Despite the chorus of cries for hanging Jefferson Davis from a sour-apple tree, few northerners wanted to pursue bloody punishments for the million Confederate soldiers who were technically guilty of treason. In the end, Confederate generals went home unharmed to become lawyers, businessmen, and planters; General Robert E. Lee became a college president. No civil leader was hanged for treason, not even Jefferson Davis. Two years after his arrest, he walked out of prison, thanks to bail put up by northerners like editor Horace Greeley. In later years, former Confederates became senators, governors, and federal judges. Months before the war ended, northerners were raising money to rebuild the southern economy and feed its destitute people. What the North wanted was not vengeance, but guarantees of lasting loyalty and a meaningful freedom. Questions arose with no easy answers: What did it take to reunite America? Should it be restored, or reconstructed, and if the latter, how drastically? How far could yesterday's enemies be trusted? What did freedom mean, and what rights should the "freed people" enjoy? In reconstructing society, how far did the government's power go?

## Lincoln's Ten Percent Plan Versus the Wade-Davis Bill

Lincoln moved to shape a postwar South based on free labor and to replace military control, Banks's included, with new civil governments. However, wartime Reconstruction had to take Confederate resistance into account. Any terms the president set would need to attract as much white southern support as it could and hold out an inducement to those at war with the United States to return to their old loyalties. In December 1863, Lincoln issued a Proclamation of Amnesty and Reconstruction, offering a full pardon and the restoration of civil rights to all those who swore loyalty to the Union, excluding only a few high-ranking Confederate military and political leaders. When the number of loyal whites in a former Confederate state reached 10 percent of the 1860 voting population, they could organize a new state constitution and government. But Lincoln's "Ten Per Cent Plan" also required that the state abolish slavery, just as Congress had demanded before admitting West Virginia to the Union earlier in the year. Attempts to establish a loyal government foundered, but circumstances in Louisiana proved more promising. Under General Banks's guidance, Free State whites met in New Orleans in 1864 and produced a new state constitution abolishing slavery.

By that time, however, radical Unionists were expecting more. Propertied and well educated, the free black community in New Orleans pleaded that without equal rights to education and the vote, mere freedom would not be enough. Impressed by their argument, Lincoln hinted to Louisiana authorities that he would welcome steps opening the vote for at least some blacks. The hints were ignored.

Black spokesmen found a friendlier audience among radical Republicans in Congress, among them Thaddeus Stevens of Pennsylvania and Charles Sumner of Massachusetts. Believing that justice required giving at least some blacks the vote and setting a more rigorous standard of loyalty for white southerners than Lincoln's plan offered, they shared a much wider concern that any new government must rest on statutory law, not presidential proclamations and military commanders' decrees. They were not at all prepared to treat Lincoln's "loyal" states as fit to return to Congress—not when so much of Louisiana and Arkansas remained in Confederate hands and was excluded from the new constitution-making—not when a speckling of enclaves pretended to speak for the state of Virginia.

As doubts grew about Louisiana's Reconstruction, Congress edged away from Lincoln's program. In mid-1864, Senator Benjamin F. Wade of Ohio and Congressman Henry Winter Davis of Maryland proposed a different plan, requiring a majority of a state's white voters to swear allegiance to the Union before Reconstruction could begin. Slavery must also be abolished and full equality before the law must be granted to African Americans. Lincoln pocket-vetoed the Wade-Davis bill to protect the governments that were already under way toward reform. However, he could not make Congress admit a single one of his newly reconstructed states.

## The Meaning of Freedom

"We was glad to be set free," a former slave remembered years afterward. "I didn't know what it would be like. It was just like opening the door and lettin' the bird fly out. He might starve, or freeze, or be killed pretty soon but he just felt good because he was free." Blacks' departure came as a terrible shock to masters lulled into believing that their "servants" appreciated their treatment. Some former slave owners persuaded themselves that they were the real gainers of slavery's abolition. "I was glad and thankful—on my own account—when slavery ended and I ceased to belong, body and soul, to my negroes," a Virginia woman later insisted. Forced to do their own cooking or washing, other mistresses fumed at blacks' ingratitude. In fact, many African Americans left, not out of unkindness, but simply to prove that they could get along on their own. White fears that blacks, once free, would murder their masters proved groundless.

Leaving the plantation was the first step in a long journey for African Americans. Many took to the roads, some of them returning to their old homes near the coasts, from which masters had evacuated as Union armies approached. Others went searching for family members, separated from them during slavery. For 20 years, black newspapers carried advertisements, appealing for news of a husband or wife long since lost. Those who had not been separated went out of their way to have their marriages secured by law. That way, their children could be made legitimate and their vows made permanent. Once married, men sought sharecropping contracts that allowed their families to live with them on plantations. Because black women across the South had become what the law called "domestic dependents," husbands could refuse employers their wives' services and keep them home. In fact, freedwomen were likelier to work outside the home than white women. They tended the family garden, raised children, hired out as domestics, and, as cotton prices fell, shared the work of hoeing and picking in the fields just so the family could make ends meet.

The end of slavery meant many things to freed people. It meant that they could move about their neighborhoods without passes, and that they did not have to step aside to let whites pass them on the street. They could own dogs or carry canes, which had always been the master's exclusive privilege. They could dress as they pleased or choose their own names, including, for the first time, a surname.

Freedom liberated African Americans from the white minister's take on Christianity. No longer were large portions of the Bible closed off to them. Most southern blacks withdrew from white churches and established their own congregations, particularly in the Methodist and Baptist faith. In time, the church emerged as a central institution in the southern black community, the meeting place, social center, and source of comfort that larger society denied them. A dozen years after the war, South Carolina had a thousand ministers of the African Methodist Episcopal Church alone.

To read the Gospel, however, freed people needed schooling. One former slave remembered his master's parting words on this matter: "Charles, you is a free man they say, but Ah tells you now, you is still a slave and if you lives to be a hundred you'll STILL be a slave, 'cause you got no education, and education is what makes a man free!" Even before the war ended, northern teachers poured into the South to set up schools. When the fighting stopped, the US Army helped recruit and organize thousands of northern women as teachers, but they could never send enough. Old and young spared what time they had from work, paying teachers in eggs or produce when coin was scarce. Black classes met wherever they could: in mule stables and cotton houses, even the slave pen in New Orleans, where the old auction block became a globe stand. Due to a lack of school-books, they read dictionaries and almanacs. On meager resources, hundreds of thousands of southern blacks learned to read and write over the course of the next generation. The first black colleges would be founded in the postwar years, including Hampton Institute in Virginia and Howard University in Washington, DC. The American Missionary Associa-tion established seven, among them Atlanta and Fisk Universities.

Finally, freedom allowed freed people to congregate, to celebrate the Fourth of July or Emancipation Day, or to petition for equal rights before the law. Memorial Day may have begun with blacks gathering to honor the Union dead whose sacrifices had helped make them free.

## Experiments with Free Labor

Many whites insisted that blacks would never work in freedom and foresaw a South ruined forever. Freed people proved just the opposite though. When Union troops landed on the Sea Islands off South Carolina in November 1861, the slaveholders fled, leaving behind between 5,000 and 10,000 slaves. Within months the abandoned plantations of the Sea Islands were being reorganized. Eventually black families were given small plots of their own land to cultivate, and in return for their labor they received a "share" of the year's crop. When the masters returned after the war to reclaim their lands, the labor system had already proven itself. Much modified, it would form the basis for the arrange-ment known as "sharecropping."

The sugar and cotton plantations around New Orleans provided another opportunity to shape the future of free labor. When the Union army came to occupy New Orleans in 1862, the tens of thousands of field hands on these plantations were no longer slaves, but the landowners still held possession of the land. Unlike the Sea Islands, these plantations could not be broken up. And sugar plantations could not be effectively organized into small sharecropping units.

Hoping to stem the flow of black refugees to Union lines and cut the loss of black lives in the contraband camps, Union general Nathaniel Banks issued stringent regulations to put the freed people back to work quickly in Louisiana. At the time, Banks was the com-mander of the Department of the Gulf during the occupation of New Orleans and his policy, known as the Banks Plan, required freed people to sign yearlong contracts to work on their former plantations. Workers would be paid either 5 percent of the proceeds of the crop or three dollars per month. The former masters would provide food and shelter, and African American workers were forbidden to leave the plantations without permission. Established planters welcomed the plan, but many critics protested that Banks had simply replaced one form of slavery with another; however, most freed people knew the differ-ence and accepted the work conditions. The Banks Plan became the model for plantations throughout the lower Mississippi Valley.

Understandably, freed people wanted land of their own. Only then could they avoid working for their old masters on any terms. "The labor of these people had for two hun-dred years cleared away the forests and produced crops that brought millions of dollars annually," H. C. Bruce explained. "It does seem to me that a Christian Nation would, at least, have given them one year's support, 40 acres of land and a mule each." As the war ended, many African Americans expected the government's help in becoming landowners. Union general William Tecumseh Sherman heard an appeal from freed people on the Sea Islands. "The way we can best take care of ourselves is to have land," they argued, "and turn it out and till it by our own labor." Convinced, Sherman issued Special Field Order No. 15 granting captured land to the freed people. By June, 400,000 acres had been distributed to 40,000 former slaves.

Congress did not leave matters there. In March 1865, the Republicans established the Bureau of Refugees, Freedmen, and Abandoned Lands, commonly known as the Freedmen's Bureau. In the area of labor relations, the Bureau sometimes sided with landowners against the interests of the freed people. But it also provided immediate relief for thousands of people of both races. Indeed, of more than 18 million rations distributed over three years, more than 5 million went to whites in need. The Bureau joined with northern religious groups in creating some 4,000 black schools. It ran charity hospitals and provided medical services. Freed people came to Bureau agents for justice when white-dominated courts denied it and took counsel when labor contracts were to be negotiated. Some agents sided instinctively with the former masters. Most courted white hostility by protecting freed people from violence, settling their complaints, advising them on labor contracts, and seeing that employers paid as promised.

The Freedmen's Bureau also became involved in the politics of land redistribution and controlled the disposition of 850,000 acres of confiscated and abandoned Confederate lands. In July 1865, General Oliver Otis Howard, the head of the Bureau, directed his agents to rent the land to the freed people in 40-acre plots that they could eventually purchase. Many agents believed that to reeducate them in the values of thrift and hard work, the freed people should be encouraged to save money and buy land for themselves. A Freedman's Savings Bank helped many do just that.

Moderate and radical Republicans alike were determined to press for more than a nominal freedom for blacks. Equally important, Congress made it clear that it would insist on being consulted in any Reconstruction policy.

# Presidential Reconstruction, 1865–1867

Andrew Johnson took office in April 1865 as a great unknown. Born in a log cabin and too poor to attend school, he began his career on a tailor's bench where he had shown grit and enterprise. In time he had risen to moderate wealth in the eastern Tennessee hill country, enough to own slaves, but he never forgot his humble beginnings. Before the war, he had defended slavery and the common man, called for taxpayer-supported public schools, and free homesteads. A courageous Union Democrat in wartime, he had run roughshod over Tennessee Confederates as military governor. He hated treason and the rich planters that he blamed for the war. Johnson deserved much of the credit for Tennessee abolishing slavery; however, he alarmed some radicals along the way who found more pardons than penalties in his policies. Convinced that a lasting reunion of the states could only come by earning white southerners' good will and determined to see the Thirteenth Amendment ratified quickly, the president started Reconstruction six months before Congress convened and left it entirely in white hands. In doing so, he offended not only the radicals favoring a color-blind suffrage but also the moderates who believed that Reconstruction must be done by law and not executive order.

## The Political Economy of Contract Labor

Presidential Reconstruction began in late May 1865, when President Johnson offered amnesty and the restoration of property to white southerners who swore loyalty to the Union, excluding only high-ranking Confederate military and political leaders and very rich planters. He named provisional governors in seven seceded states and told them to organize constitutional conventions. For readmission to the Union and restoration of their full privileges, conventions must adopt the Thirteenth Amendment, void their secession ordinances, and repudiate their Confederate war debt. Most of the constitutional conventions met the president's conditions, though with grumbling and legal quibbling. Many made clear that they still thought the South had been right all along. They only bowed to military force. "We have for breakfast salt-fish, fried potatoes, and treason," a lodger at a Virginia boarding house wrote. "Fried potatoes, treason, and salt-fish for dinner. At supper the fare is slightly varied, and we have treason, salt-fish, fried potatoes, and a little more treason."

Elections under these new constitutions would then choose civil governments to replace provisional authority. Only white men covered by the amnesty proclamation or subsequent pardons could vote, but by September Johnson was signing pardons wholesale. Secessionists flocked to the elections that followed the conventions. Freshly pardoned Confederates won some of the most prominent offices, former Confederate vice president Alexander Stephens among them.

White southerners welcomed Johnson's leniency. Once pardoned, they petitioned for restoration of their confiscated or abandoned properties. In September 1865, Johnson ordered the Freedmen's Bureau to return the lands to their former owners. By late 1865, former slaves were being forced off the 40-acre plots that the government agency had given them.

No sooner did conservative legislatures meet than they fashioned "Black Codes" defining, or rather confining, blacks' new freedom. Some states ordered different punishments: fines for whites and whipping or sale for black offenders. Elsewhere, lawmakers forbade freed people from renting land, owning guns, or buying liquor. Vagrancy laws gave police wide discretion to collar any black and subject him or her to forced labor, sometimes for an old master. Apprenticeship statutes let the courts take away black children without parents' consent and bind them out to years of unpaid labor. Blacks were allowed to testify only in certain cases. They were taxed to pay for white schools, but the Johnsonian state governments provided them with none of their own.

Landowners gave their black employees as little as they could. With the legal machinery backing them up, they forced them into labor contracts that stipulated what they could do with their private time. One planter required his black workers to "go by his direction the same as in slavery time." Other landowners denied them the right to leave the plantation without their "master's" consent. Some arrangements allotted as little as a tenth of the crop in wages, and many employers found an excuse to turn their field hands off unpaid as soon as the crop was in. It was no wonder that many freedmen saw contract labor as slavery under a new name, or that thousands refused to sign any terms at the year's end.

## Resistance to Presidential Reconstruction

An undercurrent of violence underlay conservative control. In North Carolina, a resident wrote, the Negro was "sneered at by all and informed daily yes hourly that he is incompetent to care for himself—that his race is now doomed to perish from off the face of the Earth—that he will not work—that he is a thief by nature[,] that he lies more easily and naturally than an honest man breathes." Blacks were assaulted for not showing proper deference to whites, for disputing the terms of labor contracts, or for failing to meet the standards that white employers demanded. Black churches were burned, rebuilt, and burned again. A Freedmen's Bureau agent in Kentucky classified the incidents in just a few counties: twenty-three "cases of severe and inhuman beating and whipping of men; four of beating and shooting; two of robbing and shooting; three of robbing; five men shot and killed; two shot and wounded; four beaten to death; one beaten and roasted; three women assaulted and ravished; four women beaten, two women tied up and whipped until insensible; two men and their families beaten and driven from their homes, and their property destroyed; two instances of burning of dwellings and one of the inmates shot." White witnesses refused to acknowledge what they knew to be true, white judges dismissed cases involving black defendants, and white juries invariably acquitted the offenders. If Johnson expressed content with the speedy restoration of loyalty in the South, a growing chorus of complaints from freed people and Unionists down South told a different story.

## Congress Clashes with the President

Troubled by presidential Reconstruction's failings, a Republican Congress refused to readmit former Confederate states without investigation. A Joint Committee on Reconstruction was formed to examine their loyalty and the safety of white and black Unionists' rights. At the same time, moderate Republicans also wanted to establish a program for readmission that Johnson would support. By expanding the power of the Freedmen's Bureau and proposing a Civil Rights bill, they thought they had the makings of a compromise.

The first extended the Bureau's life, strengthened its powers, and permitted it to set up courts that allowed black testimony. The second overturned the Dred Scott decision by granting United States citizenship to American men regardless of race. This marked the first time that the federal government intervened in states' rights to guarantee due process and basic civil rights.

To Republicans' amazement, Johnson vetoed both bills and in terms that made no compromise possible. Hinting that Congress had no right to reconstruct until the southern states were readmitted and doubting blacks' fitness to enjoy the same civil rights as whites, the president declared Reconstruction completed. Unable to override the Freedmen's Bureau bill veto, Congress did pass the Civil Rights bill, which served as the foundation for section one of the Fourteenth Amendment, and later that summer a new Freedmen's Bureau bill.

## Origins of the Fourteenth Amendment

During the spring of 1866, the Joint Committee on Reconstruction proposed a Fourteenth Amendment to the Constitution, outlining the conditions that Republicans thought were essential for a just and lasting peace. Provisions guaranteed payment of the national debt and prevented payment of the Confederate one. Confederates who had held public office before the war were barred from office until Congress removed

**Anti-Freedmen's Bureau Poster** Led by President Andrew Johnson, attacks on the Freedmen's Bureau became more and more openly racist in late 1865 and 1866. This Democratic Party broadside was circulated during the 1866 election.

their disabilities. Replacing the Constitution's three-fifths clause, which allowed slaves to be counted as three-fifths of a human being for the purpose of taxation and representation, representation in Congress would now be based on a state's voting population. If freed blacks entitled southern states to additional House seats, that representation entitled blacks to the right to vote (see Table 15–1). "Happy will our disappointment be if this dry stalk shall bud and blossom into Impartial Suffrage," one radical wrote, doubtfully. Even if it did not, the South would return to Congress weaker in strength than it had left. But the crucial provision wrote civil rights guarantees into fundamental law, guaranteeing citizenship to all males born in the United States. Few of its authors could foresee how, over the century to come, its promise would expand the national commitment to furthering equality, not just for men but for women and other disadvantaged groups; nor could they see how far it could be used to expand the government's authority to set things right.

Deserted by the party that had elected him, Johnson fought on. He launched the National Union movement, a bipartisan coalition of conservatives whose goal was to defeat Republicans at the midterm elections. A railroad tour from Chicago and back to Washington allowed him to make his case to the American people. However, the National Union movement fizzled; hardly any Republican thought the proposed Amendment presented

**Table 15-1** Reconstruction Amendments, 1865–1870

| Amendment | Main Provisions | Congressional Passage (two-thirds majority in each house required) | Ratification Process (three-quarters of all states including ex-Confederate states required) |
|---|---|---|---|
| 13 | Slavery prohibited in the United States | January 1865 | December 1865 (27 states, including 8 southern states) |
| 14 | 1. National citizenship for all men and women born in the United States | June 1866 | Rejected by 12 southern and border states, February 1867 |
| | 2. State representation in Congress reduced proportionally to number of voters disenfranchised | | Radicals make readmission of southern states hinge on ratification |
| | 3. Former high-ranking Confederates denied right to hold office until Congress removes disabilities | | Ratified July 1868 |
| | 4. Confederate debt repudiated | | |
| 15 | Denial of franchise because of race, color, or past servitude explicitly prohibited | February 1869 | Ratification required for readmission of Virginia, Texas, Mississippi, and Georgia; ratified March 1870 |

unfair terms for a defeated South. Johnson's "Swing Around the Circle" tour ended in crowds trading insults with the president.

Two incidents confirmed northern fears that presidential Reconstruction had left southern Unionists defenseless. On May 1, 1866, after two drivers—one black, one white—had a traffic accident, Memphis police arrested the black one. A group of black veterans tried to prevent the arrest and, as a result, a white crowd gathered. A riot broke out. Over the next three days, white mobs burned hundreds of homes, destroyed churches, and attacked black schools. Five black women were raped; nearly fifty people, all but two of them black, were killed.

Three months later, violence of an explicitly political dimension broke out in New Orleans. Alarmed at former Confederates' return to power in Louisiana, "Free Staters" sought to recall the state's 1864 constitutional convention. They may have meant to open voting rights to some blacks or cut "rebels" out, but they never got the chance. On July 30, 1866, when a few dozen delegates assembled at Mechanics Institute, white mobs set on the convention's supporters, who were mostly black. Led by police and firemen, many of them Confederate veterans, rioters opened fire on a black parade and broke into the convention hall. "The floor was covered with blood," one victim remembered, "and in walking downstairs the blood splashed under the soles of my boots." Blacks trying to surrender were gunned down. By the time the attackers dispersed, 34 blacks and 3 white supporters had been killed, and another 100 had been injured.

# Congressional Reconstruction

The elections of 1866 became a referendum on whether Johnson's policies had gone far enough to assure the permanent safety of the Union. But they also posed competing visions of what American democracy should mean. For President Johnson, "democracy" meant government by local majorities, which often meant white supremacy. For African Americans and a growing number of Republicans in Congress, genuine democracy demanded a firm foundation of equal civil and political rights. The sweep that followed brought in an even more solidly Republican Congress than before and doomed presidential Reconstruction. Congressional Reconstruction would be far different. It was an extraordinary series of events, second only to emancipation in its impact on the history of the United States.

## The South Remade

Republicans had agreed on the Fourteenth Amendment's provisions as a final settlement of the war's issues. Southern states that ratified it would be readmitted, whether they enfranchised blacks or not. Tennessee ratified the amendment and was readmitted to Congress immediately. But in the remaining southern states, conservatives rejected the amendment by wide margins, and with the president's encouragement. As unpunished assaults on Unionists and freed people continued, Congress lost patience. In the short run, the army could keep order, but a long-term solution was needed. Moderate Republicans came to agree with radicals: only by putting loyal men, regardless of race, in charge could a loyal, just South come into being. The only other alternative would be an open-ended national commitment to rule the South by force.

Although they were far from what radical Republicans had hoped for, in March 1867, Congress passed two Reconstruction Acts. Leaving the Johnsonian state governments in office, the acts declared them provisional and their officeholders subject to removal if they hamstrung the Reconstruction process. Ten ex-Confederate states were divided into five military districts and placed under army supervision (see Map 15–1). The army would register voters, both white and black, except for the comparatively small number disqualified by the not-yet-ratified Fourteenth Amendment. To regain congressional representation, each state must call a constitutional convention and draw up a new constitution providing for equal civil and political rights. Voters then must ratify it, and the newly elected governments must adopt the Fourteenth Amendment. Military oversight would end as civil authority replaced it. Thus, most white southern men had a say in constructing the new political order, and when those states were readmitted, they were granted the same rights as others. For all the laws' limits, remaking state governments and requiring a broader male suffrage promised a Radical Reconstruction indeed.

## The Impeachment and Trial of Andrew Johnson

Johnson could not stop congressional Reconstruction. But he could temper it. Battling now to protect the executive's powers, Johnson shared Democrats' fears that Congress had veered far from the Constitution, placing military authority above civil authority and overturning what he saw as the natural order of society, where blacks were kept in subordination.

In vain, radical Republicans called for Johnson's impeachment. Instead, Congress tried to restrain him by law. The Tenure of Office Act kept the president from removing

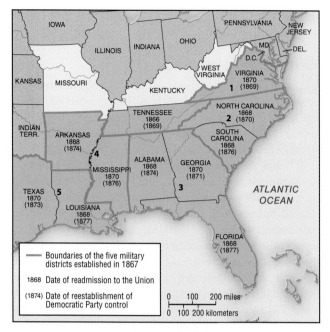

**Map 15-1    Reconstruction and Redemption** By 1870, Congress had readmitted every southern state to the Union. In most cases the Republican Party retained control of the "reconstructed" state governments for only a few years.

officials who had been appointed in his administration with Senate confirmation. Another law required that every presidential order to the military pass through General Ulysses S. Grant. Johnson could still dismiss district commanders (and did when they interpreted their powers differently than he did), but as long as Grant headed the army and Edwin M. Stanton the War Department, Republicans felt that they had safeguarded the Reconstruction Acts against a potential coup.

Provoked by these challenges to his authority, Johnson issued interpretations of the Reconstruction Acts to permit wider conservative registration, forcing Congress into special session to revise the law with a Third Reconstruction Act. He issued broader amnesty proclamations for former Confederates, forced the dismissal of Republican officers, and, abiding by the Tenure of Office Act, suspended Stanton in August 1867. When the Senate reinstated him the following winter, Johnson ordered him ejected. "What good did your moderation do you?" radical Republican Thaddeus Stevens taunted moderates. "If you don't kill the beast, he will kill you." With the law seemingly broken, the House impeached Johnson.

The expected removal never happened. Rejecting Stevens's argument that presidential obstruction was enough for conviction, senators required an intentional violation of law. The Tenure of Office Act's wording was so unclear that it may not have applied to Stanton. When the president promised to restrain himself and selected a successor to Stanton that moderates trusted, the impeachment process lost momentum. In May, the Senate fell one vote short of the two-thirds needed to convict. Within a month, Congress had readmitted seven southern states, thus limiting Johnson's power to thwart Reconstruction in those states; with Grant's election to the presidency that fall, the new governments had whatever support the army could afford them.

## Radical Reconstruction in the South

With the help of Union Leagues, auxiliaries of the Republican Party whose goal was to mobilize and educate black voters, and with military protection against conservative violence in place, Radical Reconstruction transformed the Cotton South dramatically. Within six months, 735,000 blacks and 635,000 whites had registered to vote. Blacks formed electoral majorities in South Carolina, Florida, Mississippi, Alabama, and Louisiana and in most states they found white support in the so-called scalawags, white Southerners who supported Reconstruction and Republican policies. Wartime Unionists, hill farmers neglected by planter-dominated governments, debtors seeking relief, development-minded businessmen seeking a new, more diversified South, and even some Confederate leaders and planters all welcomed Radical Reconstruction. Carpetbaggers, northerners who had come south to farm, invest, preach, or teach, were few in numbers, but they took a front rank among the leaders in black-majority states.

Starting in the fall of 1867, ten states called constitutional conventions, heavily Republican and predominantly, but not exclusively, white. The results of these conventions, so-called Black and Tan constitutions, guaranteed a color-blind right to suffrage, mandated public school systems, and overhauled the tax structure. They also included a right to bear arms in their bills of rights. Only a few states shut any Confederates out of the vote, and most of those that did removed the electoral disabilities before a year was out.

## Achievements and Failures of Radical Government

Later caricatured as a dire era of "bayonet" and "negro rule," Radical Reconstruction was neither. The Republican governments won in fairer elections and with greater turnouts than any that the South had known up until that time. Republican leadership remained overwhelmingly white and, for the most part, southern born. While some 700 blacks served in state legislatures, only in South Carolina and possibly Louisiana did they ever outnumber whites. No state elected a black governor, while only 16 blacks served in Congress, 2 of whom were senators. Still, the contrast between what had been and what would follow as a result of Reconstruction was revolutionary. These Reconstruction legislatures were more representative of their constituents than most legislatures in nineteenth-century America (see Figure 15–1). While some African American officeholders were indeed

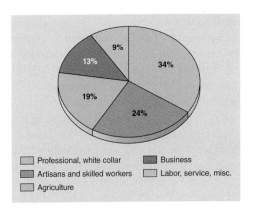

Professional, white collar
Artisans and skilled workers
Agriculture
Business
Labor, service, misc.

**Figure 15–1  Occupations of African American Officeholders During Reconstruction** Although former slaves were underrepresented among black officeholders, the Reconstruction governments were among the most broadly representative legislatures in US history.

illiterate, former slaves who did not own land, a disproportionate number came from the tiny prewar free African American elite of ministers, teachers, and small business owners. Freed people also filled hundreds of county offices. They served as sheriffs, bailiffs, judges, and jurors, offering the promise, at least, of a fair hearing in court for black defendants and litigants. Sharing power locally meant a greater chance for black communities to share in the benefits of public expenditures.

Republican rule delivered on its promises. The whipping post and debtor's prison vanished. The new governments funded insane asylums, roads, and prisons. Homestead exemptions protected debtors' real estate, and lien laws gave tenant farmers more control over the crops they grew and awarded artisans a first right to their employer's assets. The right of married women to hold property in their own name was expanded. Across the Deep South, laws took on racial discrimination on streetcars and railroad lines, mandating equal treatment. Most important, most Reconstruction governments built or extended access to the free public school system to African Americans. Underfunded and segregated, those schools nonetheless boosted literacy rates, especially among freed people.

**Radical Members** One of the greatest achievements of congressional Reconstruction was the election of a significant number of African Americans to public office.

## The Political Economy of Sharecropping

Radical Reconstruction made it easier for the former slaves to negotiate the terms of their labor contracts. Workers with grievances had a better chance of securing justice, as southern Republicans became sheriffs, justices of the peace, and county clerks, and as southern courts allowed blacks to serve as witnesses and sit on juries.

The strongest card in the hands of the freed people was a shortage of agricultural workers in the South. After emancipation, thousands of blacks sought opportunities in towns and cities or in the North. Though most blacks remained in the South as farmers, they reduced their working hours in several ways. Black women still worked the fields but spent more time nursing their infants and caring for their children. And the children went to school when they were able. The resulting labor shortage forced white landlords to renegotiate their labor arrangements with the freed people.

The contract labor system that had developed during the war and under presidential Reconstruction was replaced with a variety of regional arrangements. On the Louisiana sugar plantations, the freed people became wage laborers. But in tobacco and cotton regions, where most freed people lived, a new system of labor, sharecropping, developed. Under this system, an agricultural worker and his family typically agreed to work for one year on a particular plot of land, with the landowner providing the tools, seed, and work animals. At the end of the year, the crop was split, perhaps one-third going to the share-cropper and two-thirds to the owner.

Sharecropping shaped the economy of the postwar South by transforming the production and marketing of cash crops. Landowners broke up their plantations into family-sized plots, worked by sharecroppers in family units with no direct supervision. Each sharecropping family established its own relationship with local merchants to sell crops and buy supplies. Merchants became crucial to the southern credit system, because most southern banks could not meet the banking standards established by Congress during the Civil War. Storekeepers, usually the only people who could extend credit to sharecroppers, provided sharecroppers with food, fertilizer, animal feed, and other provisions during the year until the crop was harvested.

These developments had important consequences for white small farmers. More merchants fanned out into up-country areas inhabited mostly by ordinary whites, areas now served by railroads sponsored by the Reconstruction legislatures. With merchants offering credit and railroads offering transportation, small farmers started to produce cash crops. Thus, Reconstruction sped the process by which southern yeomen abandoned self-sufficient farming for cash crops.

Sharecropping spread quickly among black farmers in the Cotton South. By 1880, 80 percent of cotton farms had fewer than 50 acres, and the majority of those farms were operated by sharecroppers (see Maps 15–2 and 15–3). Sharecropping had several advantages for landlords. It reduced their risk when cotton prices were low and encouraged workers to increase production without costly supervision. Further, if sharecroppers changed jobs before the crop was harvested, they lost a whole year's pay. But there were also advantages for the workers. For freed people with no hope of owning their own farms, sharecropping at least rewarded their hard work. The bigger the crop, the more they earned. It gave them more independence than contract labor.

Sharecropping also allowed the freed people to work in families rather than in gangs. Freedom alone had rearranged the powers of men, women, and children within the families

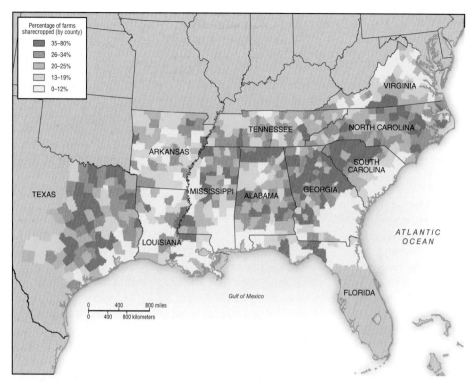

**Map 15-2  Sharecropping** By 1880, the sharecropping system had spread across the South. It was most common in the inland areas, where primarily cotton and tobacco plantations existed before the Civil War.

of former slaves. Parents gained new control over their children. They could send sons and daughters to school or put them to work. Successful parents could give their children an important head start in life. Similarly, African American husbands gained new powers.

The marriage laws of the mid-nineteenth century that defined the husband as the head of the household were irrelevant to slaves, because their marriages had no legal standing. With emancipation, these patriarchal assumptions of American family law shaped the lives of freed men and women. Once married, women often found that their property belonged to their husbands. The sharecropping system further assumed that as head of the household the husband made the economic decisions for the entire family. Men signed most labor contracts, and most contracts assumed that the husband would take his family to work with him.

Sharecropping shaped the social system of the postwar South. It influenced the balance of power between men and women. It established the balance of power between landowners and sharecroppers. It tied the southern economy to agriculture, in particular to cotton production, impeding the region's overall economic development.

## The Gospel of Prosperity

Only a diversified economy could break the planters' hold over a black labor force; railroads could lower farmers' shipping costs and tap the South's coal and iron resources.

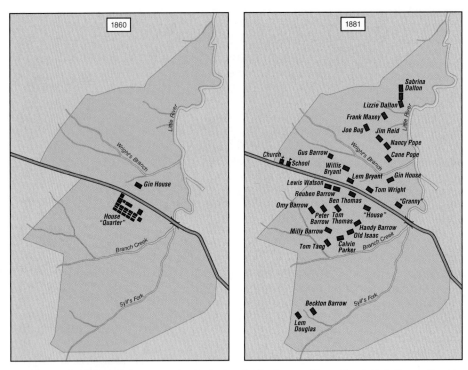

**Map 15-3    The Effect of Sharecropping in the South: The Barrow Plantation in Oglethorpe County, Georgia** Sharecropping cut large estates into small landholdings worked by sharecroppers and tenants, changing the landscape of the South.

Economic development might even give the South an independence worth having: it was no longer required to look north for its investment capital or finished goods. A program that made all classes prosper seemed ready-made to recruit more whites for a party and push racial issues into the background. Republicans preached a "gospel of prosperity" that would use government aid to build a richer South and benefit ordinary white southerners. Reconstruction governments committed the states' credit and funds to building its industrial base.

The strategy had big drawbacks. Diverting scarce resources to railroads and corporations left less for black constituencies' needs, especially school systems. Investors hesitated to invest in bonds issued by governments at risk of violent overthrow. Hungry corporations hounded the legislature for favors and made bribery their clinching argument. State-owned railroads were sold to private firms for a song—and a payoff. States already spending heavily to repair the damage of the war and to build new state services on a much-reduced tax base obligated themselves for millions more. As taxes soared, white farmers became increasingly receptive to Democratic claims that they were being robbed, their money wasted by swag-grabbing outsiders and ignorant black upstarts in office. The passage of civil rights bills, ending discrimination in public transportation, only alienated former scalawags further and stirred conservatives to bring the stay-at-homes to the polls. Everywhere, Republicans were split over how far to trust former Confederates. That division lost Virginia and Tennessee to the "Redeemers," conservative white Democrats, in 1869. In Arkansas, two Republicans claimed the governorship in 1872, and two years later they raised armies to fight it out. The "Brooks-Baxter war" ended with the Democrat-backed contestant winning and a new constitution that put both Republicans out for good.

## A Counterrevolution of Terrorism and Economic Pressure

Republicans' policy failures alone did not destroy them. Terrorism and economic pressure did. Everywhere planters used their power to keep black tenants from voting. White radicals found themselves shunned by society. They were denied credit or employment unless they left politics. As early as 1867, secret organizations were arising, bent on Reconstruction's overthrow and the restoration of white dominance, which, effectively, meant bringing Democrats into power by threats, beatings, and killings. From the Carolinas to Texas, the Ku-Klux Klan and similar organizations shot Republican lawmakers and burned black schools and churches, often in broad daylight. Black landowners and renters were targeted. African American employees or tenants who complained about being cheated faced flogging or assassination for "insolence." Teachers, party organizers, and white wartime Unionists all fell victim. Politically active blacks were threatened, driven from their homes, whipped, or shot. Their wives were raped and their homes plundered while Democratic newspapers defamed the victims. In a single year, authorities counted well over 500 killings in Georgia alone—and just about no arrests, much less indictments. Witnesses refused to testify, intimidated juries dared not convict, and sheriffs dared not arrest. In Arkansas, Texas, and Tennessee, Republican governors mustered a white militia and broke the terrorist movement. Elsewhere they found themselves powerless or outgunned. Terrorism carried North Carolina, Alabama, and Georgia for the Democrats in 1870, crippling Reconstruction in the first state and effectively ending it in the other two. By 1872, Redeemers had regained control of the whole upper and border South. After that, they rigged the election laws to curb the black vote and put any Republican comeback out of reach.

Reconstruction had not been meant to work that way. Instead of being able to defend themselves, Reconstruction governments found themselves desperately dependent on national support. But that support had been dissipating ever since the passage of the Reconstruction Acts.

As terrorism mounted, Congress legislated to protect a free, fair vote. The most important, the 1871 "Ku Klux" Act, gave the US government the power to suppress the Klan, even suspending the writ of habeas corpus. President Grant moved cautiously, however, because the newly created Justice Department lacked both funds and personnel. When the time limit on the law's most effective provisions expired, Congress did not renew them and did nothing to expand the government's ability to cope with violence when it broke out again, a few years later. Still, thousands of arrests and hundreds of convictions ended the Klan, restoring peace in time for the 1872 presidential elections.

## AMERICA AND THE WORLD

# Reconstructing America's Foreign Policy

As the Civil War approached, slavery's expansionists tainted manifest destiny for everyone but Democrats. Republicans had no intention of spreading an empire of the unfree—nor of letting any European power do so. In Mexico, the French emperor had installed a puppet state headed by Maximilian, the Austrian archduke. The Johnson administration helped force France to withdraw its troops. Unbacked, Maximilian's regime collapsed. Spreading the republic's bounds would only spread liberty. It might even give black southerners a place free of race prejudice where they could fulfill their potential. Secretary of State William Seward dreamed of all North America, perhaps even most of the Caribbean, as one vast federation; Senator Charles Sumner suggested that the United States ease Canada into the Union.

Nothing of the kind happened. Seward's biggest success came in 1867, in purchasing Alaska from Russia. A few months later, however, the Senate rejected a treaty buying the Virgin Islands from Denmark and held off on leasing a naval base in Santo Domingo. A treaty with Colombia giving the United States exclusive rights to build a canal across the Isthmus of Panama came to nothing. Canadians showed no interest in joining the Union and instead forged a union of their own separate provinces.

Not all the wealth of the West Indies could carry the United States beyond trade to the taking of territory. Slavery's end killed most of the zest for annexing Cuba; the fact that its people were Catholics and racially diverse alarmed even some Republicans. When a rebellion broke out there in 1868, Congress did nothing about it. Similar inhibitions thwarted Grant's plan to annex Santo Domingo in 1870. As head of the Senate Foreign Relations Committee, Sumner's opposition doomed the treaty and, ironically, himself; as a result, Grant and Fish forced the Senate to depose him from his chairmanship.

# A Reconstructed West

Events out west may have contributed to the nation's declining interest in southern affairs. The lands beyond the Missouri River were being reconstructed just as dramatically, and, when it came to their original inhabitants, far more brutally. In the West, most troops occupied states and territories and kept the peace. Here, too, the Gospel of Prosperity promised a new civilization, based on outsiders settling and bringing their eastern values and eastern capital with them. Passed during the Civil War, the Homestead Act was meant to populate the West with independent small farmers. Millions came in the 40 years that followed and continued to take out titles until 1934; millions more bought land at nominal prices under supplementary laws. Their movement has become the stuff of legend. But these hardy individuals did not settle an empty prairie. Native people held it already.

## The Overland Trail

In popular images, the West was a haven for rugged men who struck out on their own, but most migrants went in family groups, and the families were mostly middle class. Few poor people could afford the journey and still hope to buy land and set up a farm.

The journey across the Overland Trail (see Map 15-4) had become safer over the years. The US government built forts to supply migrants and protect the trail from (rare) Indian attacks. Mormon settlers in Utah had built Salt Lake City into a major stopping point and the heart of a thriving economy. On May 10, 1869, two railroads, the Central Pacific, building from California, and the Union Pacific, building from the Missouri River, joined at Promontory Point, Utah. This first transcontinental railroad line effectively replaced the five-month journey of covered wagons with a trip of a little less than a week. Four more transcontinentals would reach the Pacific over the next generation. Out from them radiated branch lines and side spurs, to tie the West into eastern markets. Where the companies set down depots, towns sprang up, unlike in the East, where the towns came first and the railroads afterward. Irresponsibly and sometimes crookedly financed, subsidized by all levels of government, their construction almost guaranteeing an eventual wreck (actual and financial), railroads became the symbol for the age. They represented to many Americans the enterprising spirit, the intrepid nature, and the arrogance of industrial capitalism. They turned Minnesota's Red River valley into a sea of wheat and dominated California's government. They also gave the army an unprecedented mobility that it would very much need. By the time the railroad presidents drove the golden spike at Promontory Point, the government had become occupied by the growing problem of Native American–white relations in the West.

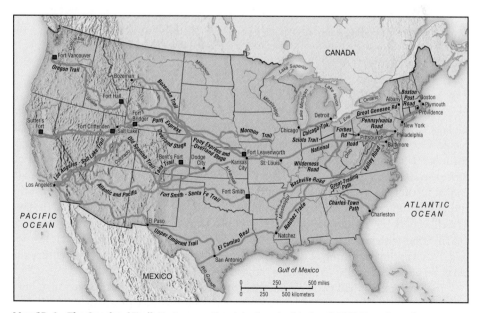

**Map 15-4    The Overland Trail**  No transcontinental railroad existed until 1869. Even thereafter, most settlers moved west on a series of well-developed overland trails.

**Chinese Laborers Building Railroad** This 1877 picture of a Southern Pacific Railroad trestle shows the crude construction methods used to build the first line across the Sierra Nevada.

## The Origins of Indian Reservations

In 1851, more than 10,000 Native Americans from across the Great Plains converged on Fort Laramie in Wyoming Territory. All the major Indian peoples were represented: Sioux, Cheyenne, Arapaho, Crow, and many others. They came to meet with government officials who hoped to develop a lasting means of avoiding Indian–white conflict. Since the discovery of gold a few years earlier, white migrants had been crossing through Indian territory on their way to California, most of them already prejudiced against the Indians. US officials wanted to prevent outbreaks of violence between whites and Indians as well as between Indian nations. They proposed creating a separate territory for each Indian tribe, with government subsidies to entice the Indians to stay within their territories. This was the beginning of the reservation system, and for the rest of the century the US government struggled to force the Indians to accept it.

The government had good reason to advocate for reservations. At their worst, both whites and Indians behaved ferociously. Civilians in one territory raised $5,000 for Indian scalps, promising $25 for any "with ears on." At Sand Creek, Colorado, militia slaughtered and scalped over 100 friendly Indians, two-thirds of them women and children. Fingers were cut off for the rings, body parts for souvenirs. In the northern Rockies, warriors led by the Northern Plains Indian leader Red Cloud lured forces from Fort Phil Kearny, killed them all, and stripped and mutilated the bodies. But Red Cloud could also say truthfully, "When the white man comes in my country, he leaves a trail of blood behind him." The reservation system was corrupt and badly handled. Agents for the Bureau of Indian Affairs cheated Indians and the government alike, sometimes reaping huge profits. But the reservations failed mostly because not all Indians agreed to stay within their designated territories, leading to armed confrontations and reprisals. "The more we can kill this year, the less will have to be killed the next war," General William Tecumseh Sherman declared.

Instead of extermination, the government opted for a more comprehensive reservation policy. Two treaties divided the Great Plains into two vast Indian territories. The Medicine Lodge Treaty, signed in Kansas in 1867, organized thousands of Indians across the southern plains. In return for government supplies, most of the southern plains peoples agreed to restrict themselves to the reservation. The Northern Plains Indians did not agree so readily. Inspired by Red Cloud, some insisted that the United States abandon forts along the Bozeman Trail. When the government agreed, Red Cloud signed the Fort Laramie Treaty in 1868. (It was one of the last. Starting in 1871, the government stopped treating the tribes as separate nations. They were subject peoples, nothing more.)

Red Cloud abided by the treaties for the rest of his life. They failed all the same. Not all the tribes approved of the treaties, and on the southern plains, raiding parties gave the army all the excuse it needed for payback. On Thanksgiving Day, 1868, the Seventh Cavalry, led by Lieutenant-Colonel George Armstrong Custer, massacred Cheyennes at Washita Creek, Oklahoma. Among the fallen was Black Kettle, who had survived the Sand Creek massacre in Colorado and whose influence had brought other tribes to make peace at Medicine Lodge. President Grant's "Peace Policy" had replaced selfish politicians with high-minded ministers as its go-betweens to the tribes and emphasized negotiation and assimilation over war and expulsion. However, there was no peace out West; not for the Comanches, Navajos, Modocs, or Lakota Sioux. And those last, in one general's opinion, were the greatest light cavalry in history.

The Lakota had a chance to prove their skill in battle. In Dakota Territory the discovery of gold in the Black Hills in 1874 brought thousands of whites onto Indian territory. When the Lakota refused to cede their lands to the miners, the government sent in the army, led by the charismatic, headstrong Lieutenant-Colonel Custer. In June 1876, Custer made two critical mistakes: he split his forces, and he failed to keep them in communication with each other. He and hundreds of his men were slaughtered at Little Bighorn, Montana, by 2,000 Indian warriors led by Crazy Horse.

"Custer's Last Stand" was the stuff of legends, but the real story came afterward. The Lakota could win battles, but not the war. Significantly, Crow warriors died with Custer. As in most other struggles, Native Americans served as US scouts, adjuncts, and allies. There was never a united Indian resistance, because, as far as Native Americans were concerned, there were no such things as Indians. There were Blackfoots, Nez Percés, Arapahoes, and Comanches. They could be broken and beaten one by one, or turned against one another—and they were. The longer a war went on, the more tribes gave up or switched sides. The army had learned to adapt to a different kind of fighting. It hit the enemy in winter, when its forces were pinned down as they had been at Washita Creek. It destroyed not only Indian soldiers but also villages and crops to starve them into submission. In the Southwest, it used Apaches to hunt down other Apaches and adopted mule trains in place of slow, cumbersome supply wagons.

## The Destruction of Indian Subsistence

At the same time as the discovery of gold in the Black Hills, the demand for hides brought a different kind of gold rush to the plains: the mass slaughter of buffalo herds. Profit and sport drove the hunt, but cattlemen had no objection to opening up the range for their own stock. The army saw a bonus in anything wiping out subsistence for Indians off the reservation. "Kill every buffalo you can," a colonel urged one hunter. "Every buffalo dead is an Indian gone." Railroads joined in, sponsoring mass kills from slow-moving trains on the prairies. Some 13 million bison in 1850 dwindled by 1880 to a few hundred. The only buffalo a westerner was likely to see by 1920 was the one on the back of the nickel.

In the Northwest in 1877, the Nez Percés, fleeing from Union troops, began a dramatic trek across the mountains in an attempt to reach Canada. The Nez Percés eluded the troops and nearly made it over the Canadian border. However, hunger and the elements forced Chief Joseph and his exhausted people to agree to go to their reservations.

Pursued and deprived of allies one by one, Chief Sitting Bull and his last few warriors gave up in 1881. By then, most Indian wars were like jail breakouts: small, sporadic, and ugly. The ugliest came at Wounded Knee, South Dakota, in 1890. Fearing that the Ghost Dance religious revival movement would stir up rebellion, soldiers gunned down over 200 Native American men, women, and children. Sitting Bull did not live to see it. He had been shot resisting arrest days before.

**Indian Village Routed, Geronimo Fleeing from Camp** Oil on canvas by Frederic Remington, 1896.

Sharing none of the settlers' fear of and less of their contempt for Indians, reformers hoped that reservations would function not just as holding pens, but as schools and civilizers. Lincoln's commissioner of Indian Affairs, William P. Dole, believed that "Indians are capable of attaining a high degree of civilization." Like other reformers, Dole equated civilization with a belief in individual property rather than communal holdings, Christian values rather than native religions, and the discipline of the regular hours that farmers and workers, rather than hunters, observed. Accordingly, reformers set out, as one of them put it, to destroy the Indian and save the person. They introduced government schools on reservations to teach the virtues of private property, individual achievement, and social mobility.

The reformers' influence peaked in 1887 when Congress passed the Dawes Severalty Act, the most important Indian legislation of the century, and the very kind of confiscation never done on freed peoples' behalf. Reservation land was broken up into separate plots and distributed among individual families. The goal was to force Indians to live like white farmers. But the lands allotted were generally so poor, and the plots so small, that their owners quickly sold them. Large tracts were kept in trust by the government and gradually sold off, purportedly to pay for uplifting and assimilating the Indians. By the early twentieth century only a few, sharply diminished reservations remained outside the desert Southwest. Native American cultures endured, but many Native Americans did not. Poverty, overcrowding, and epidemic disease brought their population to its lowest point. For many eastern onlookers, those conditions only proved how unworthy the race was to compete in the struggle for life—a conclusion all too many had drawn about African Americans from Reconstruction's downfall.

# The Retreat from Republican Radicalism

A series of makeshift laws and improvisations, congressional Reconstruction had stirred misgivings among moderate Republicans who were fearful of stretching the Constitution too far and uneasy with using the expanded authority that war had given them in peacetime. New steps, such as confiscating planters' property, say, or a nationally funded school system, were out of the question. Even the Freedmen's Bureau was cut back and, except for education, closed down completely when reconstructed states were readmitted to Congress. Public backlash against radicalism gave Democrats heavy gains in the 1867 elections. In order to survive, Reconstruction had to consolidate its gains and leave the new state governments to fulfill its promises.

### Republicans Become the Party of Moderation

By then, the 1868 presidential campaign was under way. Running the war hero General Ulysses S. Grant for president, Republicans could offer a candidate who was above politics. His slogan, "Let us have peace," emphasized that the party meant to restore the Union, rather than advance radicalism. The platform endorsed congressional Reconstruction and defended black voting in the South, but it insisted that states not covered by Reconstruction should decide the issue of suffrage for themselves. Positioning themselves as protectors of the war's accomplishments came all the more easily after Democrats nominated former New York governor Horatio Seymour on a platform declaring the Reconstruction Acts as illegal, null and void. Their fiercest spokesmen swore that if Democrats won, they would overturn the newly elected southern governments and install white conservative ones. Voiding those governments would invalidate the Fourteenth Amendment, ratified by southern legislatures; some partisans even argued that every measure passed since southern congressmen walked out in 1861 had no legal force. Bondholders, fearful that Democrats would turn their national securities into waste paper or pay them in depreciated "greenbacks," thought Grant the safer choice, even without Republicans' shouting that Seymour's election would reward traitors and bring on civil war again.

Northern voters got a taste of what Democratic rule would mean in an epidemic of violence across the South. Riots and massacres in Louisiana and Georgia kept Republicans from voting and carried both states for Seymour. In the North, the outrages may have been decisive in electing Grant. Carrying the electoral college by a huge margin, he won the popular vote more narrowly with just 53 percent, and then only because of a heavy black turnout in his favor.

# Reconstructing the North

Although Reconstruction was aimed primarily at the South, the North was affected as well, especially by the struggle over the black vote. The transformation of the North was an important chapter in the history of Reconstruction.

### The Fifteenth Amendment and Nationwide African American Suffrage

Segregated into separate facilities or excluded entirely, denied the right to vote in nearly every state outside of New England, blacks in wartime fought to end discrimination in the North. Biracial efforts chipped away at many states' discriminatory "Black Laws" and the Fourteenth Amendment eliminated the rest nationwide. Streetcar lines in some cities stopped running separate cars, black testimony was admitted on the same terms as white, and in a few northern communities, black children began attending white schools. Ending the color bar on voting and jury service proved to be more difficult: when impartial suffrage went on the ballot, most northern states voted against it (though most Republicans favored it and Congress mandated it in the territories and the District of Columbia).

The shocking electoral violence of 1868 persuaded Republicans that equal suffrage in the South needed permanent protection. In 1869, Congress added a Fifteenth Amendment to the Constitution forbidding the use of "race, color, or previous condition of servitude" as a bar to suffrage in the North as well as the South. For those states not yet readmitted to the Union (Virginia, Mississippi, and Texas), it made ratification of the amendment an additional condition. On March 30, 1870, the Fifteenth Amendment became part of the Constitution.

Revolutionary as it was, the Fifteenth Amendment had serious limitations that would weaken its impact later. As the Supreme Court would note, it did not confer a right to vote on anybody. It simply limited the grounds on which it could be denied. States could impose property or taxpaying qualifications or a literacy test if they pleased, as long as the restrictions made no distinction on the basis of race. They could set up residency requirements or limit the vote to naturalized citizens, or to men.

## Women and Suffrage

The issue of black voting added to tensions among northern radicals. Feminists and abolitionists had worked together in the struggle for emancipation, but signs of trouble appeared as early as May 1863 at the convention of the Woman's National Loyal League in New York City. The League had been organized to assist in defeating the slave South. One of the convention's resolutions declared that "there never can be a true peace in this Republic until the civil and political rights of all citizens of African descent and all women are practically established." For some delegates, this went too far. They argued that it was inappropriate to inject the issue of women's rights into the struggle to restore the Union.

With the war's end, the radical crusade for black suffrage intensified debate among reformers. Elizabeth Cady Stanton and others pointed out the injustice of letting "Patrick and Sambo and Hans and Yung Tung" vote while propertied, educated women were denied suffrage. The Fourteenth Amendment, by privileging male inhabitants' right to vote explicitly, appalled Stanton, and the Fifteenth Amendment's failure to address gender discrimination at the polls only confirmed her suspicion that what one abolitionist called "the Negro's hour" would never give way to one for women. Friendly to women's suffrage though they were, abolitionists like Frederick Douglass and suffragists like Lucy Stone argued that the critical issue was the protection of the freed people. "When women, because they are women, are dragged from their homes and hung upon lamp-posts," Douglass reminded an audience, "when their children are torn from their arms and their brains dashed to the pavement; when they are the objects of insult and outrage at every turn; when they are in danger of having their homes burnt down over their heads; when their children are not allowed to enter schools; then they will have an urgency to obtain the ballot." In 1869, radical and abolitionist allies parted ways. The women's suffrage movement divided into rival organizations, Stanton's National Woman Suffrage Association and Stone's American Woman Suffrage Association.

Some radicals, Charles Sumner among them, favored women's suffrage, but most Republicans did not. The territories of Wyoming and Utah enfranchised women. Elsewhere, lawmakers let women participate in school-board elections, but voting reform went no further. Most states refused even to put the issue on the ballot. When they did so, it was voted down. Denying women's appeal that as citizens they were entitled to vote, the Supreme Court declared that the Fourteenth Amendment's right of citizenship did not carry that right with it.

# The End of Reconstruction

Events outside the South helped speed Reconstruction's collapse. Reform-oriented Republicans felt alarm at the spread of political corruption after the war. Convinced, too, that full reconciliation must come, now that the war's goals had been met, they broke with the party and abandoned their support for federal intervention in southern affairs. Additionally, a depression took voters' minds off Reconstruction issues. By 1876, "Redemption" had carried white Democrats to power in all but a few southern states. Yet a hotly disputed presidential election and divided power would doom even those.

## Corruption Is the Fashion

Never before had corruption loomed so large in the United States. With more money to spend, more favors to give, and more functions to perform, both state and federal governments found themselves besieged by supplicants, and officeholders found opportunities to turn a dishonest penny where none had existed before. In New York City, infamous state senator William M. Tweed used the Tammany Hall political machine to steal tens of millions of dollars. Senators bought their seats in Kansas and South Carolina, while Tennessee congressmen sold appointments to West Point. The Standard Oil Company allegedly controlled Pennsylvania's legislature. As Henry Clay Warmoth, the governor of Louisiana put it, corruption was "the fashion." He, incidentally, was very fashionable himself.

With an honest but credulous chief executive, Grant's administration became notoriously corrupt. Customs collectors shook down merchants and used their employees to manage party conventions. With help from administration insiders, the notorious speculators Jay Gould and Jim Fisk tried to corner the nation's gold supply and brought on a brief, ruinous panic on Wall Street. Grant's private secretary was even exposed as a member of the "Whiskey Ring," a group of distillers and revenue agents who cheated the government out of millions of dollars in taxes. Charges of making money by swindling the Indians forced the Secretary of Interior out of office. Months later, the Secretary of War quit when investigators traced kickbacks to his wife. Having overcharged the government for supplies while building the Union Pacific Railroad, the fraudulent Credit Mobilier contracting firm shared mammoth profits with nearly a dozen top congressmen. The Republican platform, one critic snarled, was just a conjugation of the verb "to steal."

Southern corruption reflected national patterns. In the worst states, both parties stole, bribed, and profited. But in the South, Democrats blamed such action on ignorant black voters and nonlandowning white Republicans. Shifting the issue from equal rights to honest government, they insisted that clean, cheap government, run by society's natural leaders (white and well-heeled), would benefit all races. Every scandal discredited Republican rule further, including the many

**President Grant as a Strong Man** Despite solid accomplishments and his own honesty, Ulysses S. Grant would be remembered for scandals in just about every department. Here he upholds various corrupt "rings" and the thieves and hacks that mulcted the War and Navy Departments, the government of the District of Columbia, and the custom-house service.

upright and talented leaders, both black and white, that fought against corruption. This helped galvanize the opposition, destroying Republican hopes of attracting white voters and weakening support for Reconstruction. By 1875, northerners assumed the worst of any carpetbagger, even one fighting to cut taxes and block cheats.

## Liberal Republicans Revolt

Voicing widely held concerns, a small, influential group of northern Republican intellectuals, editors, and activists challenged a political system that, in their view, rested on greed, selfishness, partisanship, and politicians' keeping war hatreds alive. Known as "liberal Republicans," they viewed bosses and political machines, which were out to loot the Treasury, and special interests as detrimental to good government. They were weary of railroads receiving land grants, of steamship lines receiving subsidies, and government clerkships that were given to cronies. Decrying corruption and disenchanted with Reconstruction, they called for reform: a lower tariff, a stable currency system based on gold, a merit-based civil service system for appointments to office, and full, universal amnesty for former Confederates.

When Democrats announced a "New Departure," accepting the three constitutional amendments, liberal Republicans took them at their word. Despairing of preventing Grant's renomination, they nominated the eccentric, reform-minded editor Horace Greeley for president in 1872. The platform promised to end all political disabilities and reconcile North and South, in essence by ending all federal intervention on black southerners' behalf. Desperate to win, Democrats endorsed the editor, their lifelong enemy, but thousands stayed home on election day rather than vote for him. Having cut the tariff and restored the office-holding rights of all but a handful of ex-Confederates, Republicans won many reformers back. Greeley lost in a landslide and died in a sanitarium less than a month later.

Grant's reelection bought Reconstruction time, but it could not do more than that. Northerners, even Republican ones, became increasingly alarmed every time the national government used its power to act on behalf of Reconstruction governments and deal with issues that should be handled by local authorities. As a result, the president found it increasingly hard to justify intervening on the behalf of black voters.

## "Redeeming" the South

In September 1873, America's premier financial institution, Jay Cooke & Company, went bankrupt after overextending itself on investments in the Northern Pacific Railroad. Within weeks, hundreds of banks and thousands of businesses failed. The country sank into a depression that lasted five years. Unemployment rose to 14 percent as corporations slashed wages. Bitter strikes in textile plants, coal fields, and on the railroad lines ended in failure and violence. As America turned its attention to issues of corruption, labor unrest, and economic depression, Reconstruction took a backseat.

Between the corruption scandals buffeting the Grant administration and the economic crisis, northern voters' interest in Reconstruction plummeted. Those who had favored government intervention to keep "Rebels" from coming to power no longer saw the need. Former Confederates stood by the flag as earnestly as Unionists. In the 1874 elections, Democrats made a dramatic comeback. For the first time since 1859, they carried the House, guaranteeing a deadlocked Congress. Outgoing Republicans

## STRUGGLES FOR DEMOCRACY

# An Incident at Coushatta, August 1874

If biracial democracy had a chance anywhere in Reconstruction Louisiana, it was upstate in Red River parish. With African Americans outnumbering whites more than two to one, majority rule meant Republican government. As in so many other black counties, whites held the choicest offices: sheriff, tax collector, and mayor of the parish seat in Coushatta. A Vermont-born Union veteran, Marshall Harvey Twitchell, represented Red River in the state senate. Most of the wealth and nearly all the property stayed in native white hands, just as it had before the war. Blacks continued to raise and harvest the cotton on other people's land.

Nevertheless, Reconstruction made a difference for African Americans. They elected members of their own race to the police jury that did most of the parish's day-to-day governing. Several justices of the peace who handled minor civil cases were black. Farmers, field hands, and day laborers performed jury duty. What freed people wanted most, however, was what white conservatives had long denied

them, a functioning public school system. Twitchell saw that they got one, with separate schools for whites and blacks. So prosperous was Red River under "Negro rule," Twitchell bragged, that it was evident to "the most perfect stranger."

Having the most votes was not enough, however. All the influential newspapers and nearly all the property and firepower in Red River parish remained with the Democrats. When hard times hit, Republicans' enemies organized rifle clubs and a White League, which acted as the military arm of the Democratic Party. Unlike the Ku Klux Klan, it operated in the open and without disguises. By mid-1874, death threats against Republican officials were being posted on the streets of Coushatta. "Your fate is sealed," one letter warned judges. "Nothing but your blood will appease us." Alarmed, the police jury resigned and white Republicans left the parish.

That August, White Leaguers pretended to have uncovered a black plot to slaughter white residents. On that excuse, they arrested several dozen black Republican

made one last advance, passing Charles Sumner's civil rights bill, which outlawed discrimination in public places. The law left segregated schools and cemeteries alone, and most southern establishments ignored even those provisions that did pass. But with Congress's adjournment in March 1875, Republicans no longer had any chance of bolstering Reconstruction with legislation, or even funding an army big enough to protect a fair vote at the polls.

Supreme Court rulings made implementing Reconstruction legislation harder still. In the 1873 *Slaughterhouse* cases, a majority decided that the Fourteenth Amendment's protection of equal rights under the law covered only those rights associated with national citizenship. Rights affiliated with state citizenship—for example, the right to butcher cattle

**Terror in the South** Thomas Nast's 1874 cartoon depicts a White League member and a Klan member joining hands over a terrorized black family. Nast's point was not that emancipation had been a mistake, but that without national protection, freed people's fate was worse than slavery.

leaders and all the white parish officers. To save their lives, the officials resigned. The vigilantes promised them an armed escort out of the parish, but instead, it led them into an ambush. Mounted gunmen from the neighboring parish killed six prisoners. Later they rode into Coushatta and hanged two of the captured blacks as well. Absent on political business, Twitchell alone survived. When he returned in 1876, an unknown gunman shot him, costing him both arms. From then on, Republican majorities counted for nothing. Democrats did the voting and governing and thus radical Reconstruction's gains melted away.

Coushatta's fate was Louisiana's. White Leaguers overthrew the governor in September 1874. Federal intervention restored him, but it could not save local Republican governments like Red River's. "The State government has no power outside of the United States Army . . . no power at all," an officer confessed. "The White League is the only power in the State."

when a Louisiana state law gave a monopoly to one particular firm—could only be upheld by the state. In 1876, the justices whittled down the national government's power to protect black voters from intimidation and violence or even their right to bear arms and hold public meetings. In *United States v. Cruikshank*, the Court took up a horrific massacre of some 150 black state militiamen at Colfax, Louisiana, on Easter Sunday, 1873; it decided that the equal protection clause applied only to state governments' actions, not that of the paramilitaries responsible. In *Hall v. DeCuir* (1878), the Supreme Court invalidated a Louisiana law prohibiting racial segregation on public transportation. In the Civil Rights Cases of 1883, the Supreme Court declared that the Fourteenth Amendment did not cover discriminatory practices by private persons.

Even before the 1874 elections, southern Reconstruction was collapsing. As the number of white Republicans fell, the number of black Republicans holding office in the South increased. But the persistence of black officeholders only reinforced the Democrats' determination to "redeem" their states from Republican rule. Blaming hard times on "carpetbagger" corruption and high taxes, conservatives formed taxpayers' leagues and armed themselves in White Leagues, paramilitary groups whose goal was to remove Republicans from office and prevent freedmen from voting. Crude appeals to white supremacy and harsh economic pressure forced most scalawags to drop out of politics, making it easier to draw a sharp color line. Paramilitaries then applied violence and intimidation to keep blacks from the polls. By the fall of 1874, they were overthrowing local governments in Mississippi and Louisiana. White Leagues took over the streets in New Orleans and briefly ousted the governor. Terrorism helped "redeem" Alabama that November, among other places.

That left two securely Republican states, both with considerable black majorities: South Carolina and Mississippi. In 1875, Democrats in the latter mounted the most blatant show of force yet. Governor Adelbert Ames begged for federal help and was told to look to his own resources first. The election that followed was as quiet as White League shotguns could make it. In the end, enough blacks were disfranchised and enough scalawags voted their racial prejudices to hand power to the Democrats. Within months they forced Ames's resignation. In 1876, South Carolina whites adopted the "Mississippi Plan" with an even more open commitment to violent overthrow of the Republican majority. Mounted, armed men broke up Republican rallies. In Hamburg, white paramilitaries besieged the local black militia and, after their surrender, killed seven of them. "We write to tell you that our people are being shot down like dogs, and no matter what democrats may say," one South Carolinian wrote the president, "unless you help us our folks will not dare go to the polls." In Louisiana, Redeemer violence may have been worse still.

## The Twice-Stolen Election of 1876

Amid a serious economic depression, and with an electorate tired of Reconstruction, the Democrats stood a good chance of winning the presidency in 1876. The Democratic candidate, New York governor Samuel J. Tilden, had won a reputation for fighting thieves in his own party. On election night, Tilden won 250,000 more votes than his Republican opponent, Ohio governor Rutherford B. Hayes (see Map 15–5). But Republican "returning boards" in three southern states—Florida, South Carolina, and Louisiana—counted Hayes in and gave him a one-electoral vote victory.

Democrats swore that they had been cheated out of the presidency, though even without white violence and manipulation, Hayes probably would have won not just in the three disputed states but elsewhere in the South. Both houses of Congress deadlocked on counting the electoral votes. Cries of "Tilden or Blood" rang through the air. In the end, both sides compromised by choosing a special electoral commission to settle the matter. In an eight-to-seven vote, it awarded Hayes every disputed state. House Democrats could not stop "His Fraudulency" from being sworn in, but their southern members, cutting the best deal they could, agreed to drop their obstruction in return for assurances that Hayes would not aid in the survival of the last two Reconstruction governments. A month after taking office, Hayes withdrew the regiments guarding Republican statehouses in South Carolina and Louisiana; by that time Redeemer Democrats had full control of the states

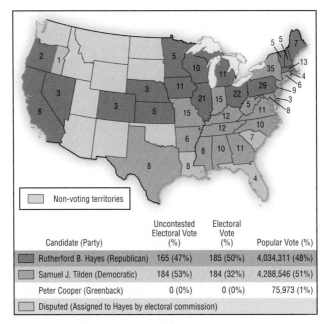

**Map 15-5   The Presidential Election, 1876** In 1876, the Democratic presidential candidate, Samuel Tilden, won what popular vote white southern Democrats permitted to be cast, but he was denied the presidency because Republicans claimed that a fair count gave Louisiana, South Carolina, Oregon, and Florida to their candidate, Rutherford B. Hayes.

anyway. This order marked Reconstruction's symbolic end. Hereafter, the president would emphasize goodwill between the North and South and trust Redeemers' promises to protect black rights—a trust that was speedily betrayed, and nowhere more so than on the farms where most freed people worked for a white landowner.

## Sharecropping Becomes Wage Labor

As the southern economy recovered from the devastation of the Civil War, many observers predicted a bright future for the region. Optimists saw a wealth of opportunities from untapped natural and human resources, a South freed from the inefficient slave labor system and ripe for investment.

Americans were building railroads at an exuberant clip, but southerners built them faster—with northern money. By 1890, steel mills lit the night skies of Birmingham, Alabama. Textile mills dotted the Piedmont Plateau (along the eastern foothills of the Appalachian Mountains from Virginia to Georgia). Southerners were migrating from the countryside to the towns, expanding cotton production into new areas, like the rich Mississippi delta soil. Yet ordinary southerners, especially African Americans, did not share in the New South's prosperity.

Redemption shifted the terms of the new labor relationship between landlords and sharecroppers in landowners' direction. The most important question was who owned the cotton crop at the end of the year: the sharecropper who raised it, the landlord who owned the farm, or the merchant who lent the supplies to bring the crop in.

Legal resolution in favor of the landlord came by the middle of the 1880s. The courts defined a sharecropper as a wage laborer. The landlord owned the crop and paid his workers a share of it as a wage. Landlords also won a stronger claim on the crop than the merchant creditors. Under the circumstances, merchants were reluctant to advance money to sharecroppers. Many left plantation districts and moved up-country, doing business with white yeomen farmers. Trapped in a cycle of debt, white farmers in the 1880s began losing their land and falling into tenancy. Meanwhile, in the "black belt" (where most African Americans lived and most of the cotton was produced), successful landlords became merchants while successful merchants purchased land and hired sharecroppers of their own. By the mid-1880s, black sharecroppers worked as wage laborers for the landlord-merchant class across much of the South.

Sharecropping differed in two critical ways from the wage work of industrial America. First, sharecropping was family labor, depending on a husband and father who signed the contract and delivered the labor of his wife and children to the landlord. Second, because sharecropping contracts were yearlong, the labor market was restricted to a few weeks at the end of each year. If croppers left before the end of the year, they risked losing everything.

The political economy of sharecropping impoverished the South by binding the region to cotton, a crop that steadily depleted the soil even as prices fell. Yet most southern blacks found few alternatives. In time a few black farmers purchased their own land, but their farms were generally tiny and the soil poor. The skilled black artisans who had worked on plantations before the Civil War moved to southern cities, where they took unskilled, low-paying jobs. Northern factories were segregated, as were the steel mills of Birmingham, Alabama, and the Piedmont textile mills. Black women worked as domestic

## Time Line

▼**1851**
Fort Laramie Treaty establishes Indian reservations

▼**1862**
Passage of Homestead Act

▼**1863**
Lincoln's Proclamation of Amnesty and Reconstruction

▼**1864**
Wade-Davis Bill

▼**1865**
Thirteenth Amendment adopted and ratified

Freedmen's Bureau established
Confederate armies surrender
Lincoln assassinated; Andrew Johnson becomes president
Johnson creates provisional governments in the South; new civil governments begin
Joint Committee on Reconstruction established by Congress

▼**1866**
Congress renews Freedmen's Bureau; Johnson vetoes it
Civil Rights Act vetoed by Johnson; Congress overrides veto

Congress passes Fourteenth Amendment
New Orleans and Memphis massacres
Republicans sweep midterm elections

▼**1867**
First, Second, and Third Reconstruction Acts passed
Tenure of Office Act
Medicine Lodge Treaty

▼**1868**
Second Fort Laramie Treaty
Washita Massacre

servants to supplement their husbands' meager incomes. Wage labor transformed southern blacks' lives, but it brought no prosperity.

The "New South" of industry and diversified agriculture opened southern forests to northern timber companies and dotted southern rivers with textile mills, but it did not break the stranglehold that cash crops and plantations had over the economy. It made the region more dependent on northern capital and finished goods than ever. Most of all, for the freed people outside a few large cities, it did not prove new at all. They found themselves excluded from juries and unprotected from white harassment and attack. White judges, white police, and white sheriffs guaranteed a white justice that treated every black witness's testimony as suspect and turned petty larceny into an excuse for jail time and permanent disfranchisement. Black convicts stood more chance of serving on the chain gang, often hired out as cheap labor to employers who paid the state pennies a day for the work done. In the Deep South, lynchings became almost an everyday occurrence, and, to judge from the souvenir sellers and excursion trains bringing in viewers, a kind of obscene spectator sport. Prejudice closed the door to blacks seeking to become professionals or craftsmen and guaranteed the skimpiest of funding for their schools. In a few states, the whipping post made a comeback. With the laws and the lawless working together to keep most blacks from voting, freedom meant much less than it had in Reconstruction days. But now, there were few northerners willing to listen when black southerners appealed for help.

Hoping to escape poverty and discrimination, some former slaves moved west. One group, the Exodusters, moved to the Kansas prairie during the mid-1870s. By 1880, more than 6,000 blacks had joined them, searching for cheap land for independent farms. Like white farmers, the Exodusters fought with cattlemen. Blacks who settled in cow towns such as Dodge City and Topeka found the same discrimination they had known in the South. Still, some of the Exodusters did buy land and build farms.

Johnson fires Secretary of War Stanton

House of Representatives impeaches Johnson

Senate trial of Johnson ends in acquittal

Fourteenth Amendment ratified

Waves of Klan violence sweep Cotton South

Ulysses S. Grant elected president

▼1869
Congress passes Fifteenth Amendment

▼1870
Fifteenth Amendment ratified

▼1872
"Liberal Republican" revolt
Grant reelected

▼1873
Financial "panic" sets off depression

▼1875
"Mississippi Plan" succeeds
Civil Rights Act enacted

▼1876
Disputed presidential election of Rutherford B. Hayes and Samuel J. Tilden
Custer's Last Stand at Little Bighorn

▼1877
Electoral commission names Rutherford B. Hayes president
Last Reconstruction governments collapse

▼1887
Dawes Severalty Act

# Conclusion

Inspired by a vision of society based on equal rights and free labor, Republicans expected emancipation to transform the South. Freed from the shackles of the slave power, the region might yet become a shining example of democracy and prosperity. Twenty years later, events seemed to mock that promise. The South was scarcely more industrial than before the war and, as far as former slaves were concerned, far from completely free. Cotton, sugar, rice, and tobacco still defined the South's economy far more than the hoped-for mines and mills. Only a small fraction of freed people had become landowners, and most of them would never escape poverty and dependence on propertied whites. After the Panic of 1873, sharecropping eliminated most blacks' hope of real economic independence. As fears of a new rebellion dimmed, Republicans lost their zeal for federal intervention in the South. Republican state authorities could not save themselves, much less their black constituents. Chastened by Reconstruction's defects, Americans began to turn their attention to the new problems of urban, industrial America and to the epic success story, as they saw it, of the "winning of the West."

Even so, the achievements of Reconstruction were monumental. In the West, it settled vast multitudes of people—and unsettled multitudes more. Over two generations, it created as many states as had gone into rebellion in 1861. Across the South, African Americans carved out a space in which their families could live more freely than before. Black and white men elected to office some of the most democratic state legislatures of the nineteenth century. Thousands of black workers had escaped a stifling contract-labor system for the comparatively wider autonomy of sharecropping. Hundreds of thousands of former slaves learned to read and write and were able to worship in churches of their own making. Most important, Reconstruction added three important amendments to the Constitution that transformed civil rights and electoral laws throughout the nation. For the first time, the protections in the Bill of Rights would apply not just against national encroachment but that of the states as well. As a result of those changes in fundamental law, Reconstruction, then, was not so much a promise broken as one waiting to be fulfilled.

# Who, What, Where

Banks, Nathaniel  464

Black Codes  466

Dennett, John  460

Fifteenth Amendment  484

Fort Laramie  480

Fourteenth Amendment  467

Freedmen's Bureau  460

Grant, Ulysses S.  471

Greeley, Horace  462

Homestead Act  478

Howard, Oliver Otis  465

Johnson, Andrew  461

"Liberal Republicans"  487

Massacre at Wounded Knee, South Dakota  482

Overland Trail  479

Red Cloud  481

Redemption  471

Reservations  480

Sharecropping  463

Sitting Bull  482

Stanton, Elizabeth Cady  485

Ten Percent Plan  462

Tenure of Office Act  470

# Review Questions

1. What made congressional Reconstruction "radical"?
2. How did conditions for the readmission of states into the Union change over time?
3. How did Reconstruction change the South?
4. How did western Indians respond to westward expansion?
5. How did Reconstruction change the North?
6. What were the major factors that brought Reconstruction to an end?

# Critical-Thinking Questions

1. Compare and contrast wartime Reconstruction, presidential Reconstruction, and congressional (radical) Reconstruction. What were the key differences between the three phases?
2. How critical was the failure of land redistribution for blacks? Was sharecropping an acceptable substitute for achieving economic freedom? Why or why not?
3. How did terrorism and economic pressure both hinder and help the Reconstruction of the South?

# Suggested Readings

Foner, Eric. *Reconstruction: America's Unfinished Revolution, 1863–1877.* New York: HarperCollins, 2014.

Hahn, Steven. *A Nation Under Our Feet: Black Political Struggles in the Rural South from Slavery to the Great Migration.* Cambridge, MA: Harvard University Press, 2003.

Litwack, Leon. *Been in the Storm So Long: The Aftermath of Slavery.* New York: Oxford University Press, 1979.

Summers, Mark Wahlgren. *The Ordeal of the Reunion: A New History of Reconstruction.* Chapel Hill: University of North Carolina Press, 2014.

**For further review materials and resource information, please visit www.oup.com/us/oakes-mcgerr**

# CHAPTER 15: RECONSTRUCTING A NATION, 1865–1877

Primary Sources

## 15.1 PETROLEUM V. NASBY [DAVID ROSS LOCKE], *A PLATFORM FOR NORTHERN DEMOCRATS* (1865)

David Ross Locke, the editor of the *Toledo Blade*, made his fortune under another name: Petroleum V. Nasby, a fictional postmaster and sometimes pastor, whose letters gave a Republican spoof of what Copperhead Democrats believed. Bad spelling was a common way of signaling to readers that a piece was meant to be humorous, though Locke also meant to show that Nasby's ideas were not only vicious and absurd but founded on a virtually illiterate ignorance.

Saint's Rest (wich is in the Stait uv Noo Jersey), June the 23d, 1865

These is the dark days uv the dimokrasy. The misforchoons that befell our armies in front uv Richmond, the fall uv our capital, follered by the surrender uv our armies to Grant and Sherman, hez hurt us. Our leaders are either pinin in loathsome dunguns, incarseratid by the hevin-defyin, man-destroyin, tyrannical edix uv our late lamented President, or are baskin in the free air uv Italy and Canady. We hev no way uv keepin our voters together. Opposin the war won't do no good, for before the next elecshun the heft uv our voters will hev diskiverd that the war is over. The fear uv drafts may do suthin in some parts uv Pennsylvany and suthern Illinoy, for sum time yuit, but that can't be depended on.

But we hev wun resource for a ishoo—ther will alluz be a dimokrasy so long as ther's a nigger.

Ther is a uncompromising dislike to the nigger in the mind uv a ginooine dimekrat. The Spanish bullfighter, when he wants to inflame the bull to extra cavortin, waves a red flag afore him. When yoo desire a dimekrat to froth at the mouth, yoo will find a black face will anser the purpose. Therefore, the nigger is, today, our best and only holt. Let us use him.

For the guidance uv the faithful, I shel lay down a few plain rools to be observed, in order to make the most uv the capital we hev:

(1) Alluz assert that the nigger will never be able to take care uv hisself, but will alluz be a public burden. He may, possibly, give us the lie by goin to work. In sich a emergency, the dooty uv every dimekrat is plane. He must not be allowed to work. Associashens must be organized, pledged to neither give him employment, to work with him, to work for anyone who will give him work, or patronize any wun who duz. (I wood sejest that sich uv us ez hev bin forchoonit enuff to git credit, pay a trifle on account, so ez to make our patronage worth suthin.) This course, rigidly and persistently follered, will drive the best uv em to stealin, and the balance to the poorhouses, provin wat we hev alluz claimed, that they are a idle and vishus race. Think, my brethren, wat a inspirin effeck our poorhouses and jails full uv niggers wood hev on the people! My sole expands ez I contemplate the deliteful vision.

(2)  Likewise assert that the nigger will come North, and take all the good places, throwin all
our skilled mechanics out uv work by underbiddin uv em. This mite be open to two objec-
shuns, to-wit: It crosses slitely rool the 1, and white men mite say, ef there's jist enuff labor
for wat's here, why not perhibit furriners from comin? I anser: It's the biznis uv the voter to
reconcile the contraicshun—he may believe either or both. Ez to the second objeckshun,
wher is the Dimekrat who coodent be underbid, and stand it even to starvashen, ef the
underbiddin wux dun by a man uv the proud Caukashen race? And wher is the Dimekrat
so lost to manhjood ez not to drink blood, ef the same underbiddin is dun by a nigger?
The starving for work ain't the question—it's the color uv the cause uv the starvashen that
makes the difference.

Nigger equality may be worked agin to advantage. All men, without distincshun uv sex,
are fond uv flatrin theirselves that somebody's lower down in the scale uv humanity than they
is. Ef 'twan't for niggers, what wood the dimokrasy do for sumbody to look down upon? It's also
shoor to enlist wun style uv wimmen on our sides. In times gone by, I've notist gushin virgins
uv forty-five, full sixteen hands high and tough ez wire, holdin aloft banners onto which wuz
inscribd—"Save us from Nigger Equality." Yoo see it soothed em to hev a chase uv advertising,
1st, That they wuz frail, helplis critters; and, 2d, That, anshent and tough ez they wuz, some wun
wuz still goin for em.

Ef ther ain't no niggers, central commities must furnish em. A half dozen will do for a
ordinary county, ef they're hustled along with energy. Ef they won't steal, the central commities
must do it theirselves. Show yer niggers in a township in the morning, an the same nite rob the
clothes-lines and hen-roosts. Ever willin to sacrifice myself for the cause, I volunteer to do this
latter dooty in six populous counties.

These ijees, ef follered, will, no doubt, keep us together until our enemies split, when we will
reap the reward uv our constancy and fidelity. May the Lord hasten the day.

Petroleum V. Nasby
Lait Paster uv the Church uv the Noo Dispensashun

*Source:*  David Ross Locke/Petroleum V. Nasby, *A Platform for Northern Democrats*, from Locke, *The Struggles, Social,
Financial and Political of Petroleum V. Nasby* (Boston, 1888), quoted in William Benton, publ., *The Annals
of America. Volume 9, 1858–1865: The Crisis of the Union* (Chicago: Encyclopedia Britannica, Inc., 1968),
pp. 597–598.

# 15.2 MISSISSIPPI BLACK CODE (1865)

Faced with the speedy emancipation of nearly half of Mississippi's population, the
first all-white postwar legislature set out to define what rights blacks should enjoy in
freedom. Some of the most basic were guaranteed, including the right to marry and
hold property, and to testify under certain limited circumstances. Others were denied,
among them the right to vote, sit on juries, hold office, or intermarry with whites.
Most controversially, the Apprentice and Vagrancy Laws created a structure, color-
blind in its outward workings, that effectively allowed white authorities to comman-
deer blacks and force them into involuntary labor or even to sell their labor to white
bidders at auction.

## Apprentice Law

Section 1. *Be it enacted by the legislature of the state of Mississippi,* that it shall be the duty of all sheriffs, justices of the peace, and other civil officers of the several counties in this state to report to the Probate courts of their respective counties semiannually, at the January and July terms of said courts, all freedmen, free Negroes, and mulattoes under the age of eighteen within their respective counties, beats, or districts who are orphans, or whose parent or parents have not the means, or who refuse to provide for and support said minors; and thereupon it shall be the duty of said Probate Court to order the clerk of said court to apprentice said minors to some competent and suitable person, on such terms as the court my direct, having a particular care to the interest of said minors:

Provided, that the former owner of said minors shall have the preference when, in the opinion of the court, he or she shall be a suitable person for that purpose.

Section 2. *Be it further enacted,* that the said court shall be fully satisfied that the person or persons to whom said minor shall be apprenticed shall be a suitable person to have the charge and care of said minor and fully to protect the interest of said minor. The said court shall require the said master or mistress to execute bond and security, payable to the state of Mississippi, conditioned that he or she shall furnish said minor with sufficient food and clothing; to treat said minor humanely; furnish medical attention in case of sickness; teach or cause to be taught him or her to read and write, if under fifteen years old; and will conform to any law that may be hereafter passed for the regulation of the duties and relation of master and apprentice:

Provided, that said apprentice shall be bound by indenture, in case of males until they are twenty-one years old, and in case of females until they are eighteen years old.

Section 3. *Be it further enacted,* that in the management and control of said apprentices, said master or mistress shall have power to inflict such moderate corporeal chastisement as a father or guardian is allowed to inflict on his or her child or ward in common law:

Provided, that in no case shall cruel or inhuman punishment be inflicted.

Section 4. *Be it further enacted,* that if any apprentice shall leave the employment of his or her master or mistress without his or her consent, said master or mistress may pursue and recapture said apprentice and bring him or her before any justice of the peace of the county, whose duty it shall be to remand said apprentice to the service of his or her master or mistress; and in the event of a refusal on the part of said apprentice so to return, then said justice shall commit said apprentice to the jail of said county, on failure to give bond, until the next term of the country court; and it shall be the duty of said court, at the first term thereafter, to investigate said case; and if the court shall be of opinion that said apprentice left the employment of his or her master or mistress without good cause, to order him or her to be punished, as provided for the punishment of hired freedmen, as may be from time to time provided for by law, for desertion, until he or she shall agree to return to his or her master or mistress:

Provided, that the court may grant continuances, as in other cases; and provided, further, that if the court shall believe that said apprentice had good cause to quit his said master or mistress, the court shall discharge said apprentice from said indenture and also enter a judgment against the master or mistress for not more than $100, for the use and benefit of said apprentice, to be collected on execution, as in other cases.

Section 5. *Be it further enacted,* that if any person entice away any apprentice from his or her master or mistress, or shall knowingly employ an apprentice, or furnish him or her food or clothing, without the written consent of his or her master or mistress, or shall sell or give said apprentice ardent spirits, without such consent, said person so offending shall be deemed guilty of a high misdemeanor, and shall, on conviction thereof before the county court, be punished as provided for the punishment of persons enticing from their employer hired freedmen, free Negroes, or mulattoes.

. . . Section 10. *Be it further enacted*, that in all cases where the age of the freedman, free Negro, or mulatto cannot be ascertained by record testimony, the judge of the county court shall fix the age.

## Vagrancy Law

Section 2. *Be it further enacted,* that all freedmen, free Negroes, and mulattoes in this state over the age of eighteen years found on the second Monday in January 1966, or thereafter, with no lawful employment or business, or found unlawfully assembling themselves together either in the day or nighttime, and all white persons so assembling with freedmen, free Negroes, or mulattoes, or usually associating with freedmen, free Negroes, or mulattoes on terms of equality, or living in adultery or fornication with a freedwoman, free Negro, or mulatto, shall be deemed vagrants; and, on conviction thereof, shall be fined in the sum of not exceeding, in the case of a freedman, free Negro, or mulatto, $50, and a white man, $200, and imprisoned at the discretion of the court, the free Negro not exceeding ten days, and the white man not exceeding six months.

Section 3. *Be it further enacted,* that all justices of the peace, mayors, and aldermen of incorporated towns and cities of the several counties in this state shall have jurisdiction to try all questions of vagrancy in their respective towns, counties, and cities; and it is hereby made their duty, whenever they shall ascertain that any person or persons in their respective towns, counties, and cities are violating any of the provisions of this act, to have said party or parties arrested and brought before them and immediately investigate said charge; and, on conviction, punish said party or parties as provided for herein. . . .

Section 5. *Be it further enacted,* that all fines and forfeitures collected under the provisions of this act shall be paid into the county treasury for general county purposes; and in case any freedman, free Negro, or mulatto shall fail for five days after the imposition of any fine or forfeiture upon him or her for violation of any of the provisions of this act to pay the same, that it shall be, and is hereby made, the duty of the sheriff of the proper county to hire out said freedman, free Negro, or mulatto to any person who will, for the shortest period of service, pay said fine or forfeiture and all costs:

*Provided,* a preference shall be given to the employer, if there be one, in which case the employer shall be entitled to deduct and retain the amount so paid from the wages of such freedman, free Negro, or mulatto then due or to become due; and in case such freedman, free Negro, or mulatto cannot be hired out he or she may be dealt with as a pauper.

Section 6. *Be it further enacted,* that the same duties and liabilities existing among white persons of this state shall attach to freedmen, free Negroes, and mulattoes to support their indigent families and all colored paupers; and that, in order to secure a support for such indigent freedmen, free Negroes, and mulattoes, it shall be lawful, and it is hereby made the duty of the boards of county police of each county in this state, to levy a poll or capitation tax on each and every freedman, free Negro, or mulatto, between the ages of eighteen and sixty years, not to exceed the sum of $1 annually, to each person so taxed, which tax, when collected, shall be paid into the county treasurer's hands and constitute a fund to be called the Freedman's Pauper Fund, which shall be applied by the commissioners of the poor for the maintenance of the poor of the freedmen, free Negroes and mulattoes of this state, under such regulations as may be established by the boards of county police, in the respective counties of this state.

Section 7. *Be it further enacted,* that if any freedman, free Negro, or mulatto shall fail or refuse to pay any tax levied according to the provisions of the 6th Section of this act, it shall be prima facie evidence of vagrancy, and it shall be the duty of the sheriff to arrest such freedman, free Negro, or mulatto, or such person refusing or neglecting to pay such tax, and proceed at once to hire, for the shortest time, such delinquent taxpayer to anyone who will pay the said tax, with accruing costs, giving preference to the employer, if there be one.

Section 8. *Be it further enacted,* that any person feeling himself or herself aggrieved by the judgment of any justice of the peace, mayor, or alderman in cases arising under this act may, within five days, appeal to the next term of the county court of the proper county, upon giving bond and security in a sum not less than $25 nor more than $150, conditioned to appear and prosecute said appeal, and abide by the judgment of the county court, and said appeal shall be tried *de novo* in the county court, and the decision of said court shall be final.

Source:  Mississippi Black Code, 1865, from *Laws of the State of Mississippi, Passed at a Regular Session of the Mississippi Legislature* (Jackson, 1866), pp. 82–93, 165–167, quoted in William Benton, publ., *The Annals of America. Volume 9, 1858-1865: The Crisis of the Union* (Chicago: Encyclopedia Britannica, Inc., 1968), pp. 628–634.

# 15.3 SHARECROPPING CONTRACT BETWEEN ALONZO T. MIAL AND FENNER POWELL (1886)

For Republicans, the essence of "free labor" was the *contract*, the notion that either a governing figure and his people, or a wealthy man and those who labored for him, both had to subscribe voluntarily to an explicit agreement outlining their mutual responsibilities in order for their relationship to be binding. Unfortunately, after the war, southern blacks freed from slavery but without land sometimes had little choice but to sign stringent labor contracts with landlords, who were often former slave owners. A system emerged known as sharecropping. The tenant, or "cropper," would sign an annual contract to work a plot of land in return for a share of the crop. The following is a sharecropping contract from 1886, between a landlord named A. T. Mial and a sharecropper named Fenner Powell.

This contract made and entered into between A. T. Mial of one part and Fenner Powell of the other part both of the County of Wake and state of North Carolina—

Witnesseth—That the Said Fenner Powell hath bargaaned and agreed with the Said Mial to work as a cropper for the year 1886 on Said Mial's land on the land now occupied by Said Powell on the west Side of Poplar Creek and a point on the east Side of Said Creek and both South and North of the Mial road, leading to Raleigh, That the said Fenner Powell agrees to work faithfully and diligently without any unnecessary loss of time, to do all manner of work on Said farm as may be directed by Said Mial, And to be respectful in manners and deportment to Said Mial.

And the Said Mial agrees on his part to furnish mule and feed for the same and all plantation tools and Seed to plant the crop free of charge, and to give the said Powell One half of all crops raised and housed by Said Powell on Said land except the cotton seed. The Said Mial agrees to advance as provisions to Said Powell fifty pound of bacon and two sacks of meal per month and occasionally some flour to be paid out of his the Said Powell's part of the crop or from any other advance that may be made to Said Powell by Said Mial. As witness our hands and seals this the 16th day of January A.D. 1886.

Source:  Contract between Alonzo T. Mial and Fenner Powell, January 1886, in Roger Ransom and Richard Sutch, *One  Kind of Freedom: The Economic Consequences of Emancipation* (New York: Cambridge University Press, 1977), p. 91.

# 15.4 JOSEPH FARLEY, AN ACCOUNT OF RECONSTRUCTION

Joseph Farley, born in 1843 in Virginia, ran away and joined the Union army. Later he was given a pension. "At that time I never thought about dying," he remembers. "I never thought about anybody shooting me; I just thought about shooting them." Interviewed in 1930 by a black student from Fisk University, he gave a rambling account, from which the postwar material has been excerpted. As with all distant recollections, Farley's may have been affected by the lapse of time and the person conducting the interview.

It was a long, long time before everything got quiet after the war. On Franklin Street here I saw once 100 Ku Klux Klans, with long robes and faces covered. You don't know anything of them. They were going down here a piece to hang a man. There were about 600 of us soldiers, so we followed them to protect the man. The Klan knew this, and passed on by the house and went on back to town and never did bother the man.

One time a colored soldier married a white woman over here at Fort Bruce. The man belonged to my company. His name was Sergeant Cook. About twenty of the soldiers went to the wedding, and they had about five or six white men who said he couldn't marry this woman. Old Dr. Taylor . . . came over to marry them. He stood near me and I told him to go on and marry this couple or else someone here would die. He looked around and saw all these soldiers and he knew about us and that we meant for him to do as he had been told. He married them and we guarded our hack over to the war boat on the Cumberland. They went over to Nashville and lived there. They had a daughter whose name was Mrs. Gnatt. When they married was in 1866. Mrs. Gnatt could tell you her father was named Cyrus Cook. Guess you know you can't do that now, no sir; you just can't do that now. At one time a colored man could ride anywhere he wanted to, but now he can't do it. I am one of the first voters of Montgomery County. They told me at one time that I was not to come to the polls or I would be met by 600 men on horses. So about six or eight hundred of us armed and went to the polls with our bayonets. That man that had told me that did not show up. So we voted, and voted for whom we wanted. At that time the Rebels who rebelled against this country could not vote and they said that these Negroes shouldn't vote but we showed them. Of course, they came down and stood and looked at us but they didn't bother us. We went there armed and prepared for fighting so that if they started anything, there would be trouble. When they mustered me out from the army, I brought my gun from Nashville right here to Clarksville and kept it twenty-five years. Finally I let an old soldier have it.

When I first came here we had no teachers here but white teachers. They would call the roll same as calling the roll for soldiers. They taught school in the churches before they had school houses. They used to go to school at night and work all day. Clarence C. White's father, Will White, was the first teacher or principal of the school here in Clarksville.

. . . .

When the War was over some of the colored returned to their white folks, but I didn't want to be under the white folks again. I was glad to get out. Once, for fifteen years here, I run a saloon and livery stable. One time I worked on a boat. When I was on my first boat, one time I went to vote. A white man told me that if I voted Republican he would fire me, so I told him to fire me then. I just told him he could fire me right now for I didn't want to work anyway. I went on and voted the Republican ticket, and they told me they liked my principle and I could go on and go to work.

I still got my discharge from way back in 1866. I keeps it and I mean to keep it as long as I live. I am proud of it.

Source:   George P. Rawick, ed. *The American Slave: A Composite Autobiography. Volume 18. Unwritten History of Slavery* (Fisk University) (Westport, CT: Greenwood, 1972), pp. 121–128.

# 15.5 A SOUTHERN UNIONIST JUDGE'S DAUGHTER WRITES THE PRESIDENT FOR HELP (1874)

Mrs. S. A. Wayne was the daughter of an Alabama Unionist, Judge James A. Abrahams. As the 1874 political campaign grew more violent, she wrote begging President Grant to send protection to Republicans like herself. Soon after the letter was sent, Abrahams was shot by persons unknown. Shortly after that, Grant sent troops to Livingston County. It was not enough to give black and white voters the security they needed; Democratic "Redeemers" swept the election.

I feel more like addressing you as my dear Father & Friend for such you have proven to me & mine—but—Oh, my God! you have no conception of the trouble we are in—War is declared in our midst and though the U. S. troops are here the Ku Klux are worse than before they came—And who are they fighting? The poor defenseless negroes—Why? For voting or rather expressing their determination to vote the Republican ticket—This evening the lives of my husband—father & brother were threatened—with the intention of making them renounce their principles—God only knows what the end will be—I have seen the Capt & Lt stationed at this place—& they say the only hope is Martial law—& that is the only remedy—Since I last wrote you some four or five negroes have been killed in this County—& the Ku Klux are now at Belmont 16 miles from this place in force & will probably murder as many more—They are exasperated against the three white Republicans in this place because they refused to go with them on one of their raids last weeks—hence the threats against their lives—My Father left this evening & I pray God he may not return until Martial law is declared—Oh my dear Sir *you can save* the country—oh protect the Union loving men against those who despise it & are doing all to overthrow it—I write you this not thinking my enlisting in the cause will help it, but because I feel it my duty to let you know how great our trouble is—No excuse can be given by these murderers—for since the assassination of Mr Billings not one single

Republican meeting has been held in this county—And this is what the Democrats are fighting for—Unless Martial law is declared hundreds of the poor negroes will be killed—even now they do not sleep in their houses & are hunted down like wild beasts by the Democracy because they will not vote their ticket—Oh! My dear Sir act & be our friends. God knows the innocent only suffer—& the blush of shame mantles my cheek when I read the pitiable excuses in the Democratic papers—apologizing for their cowardly deeds—No brave man is afraid of a few of them in open daylight but a hundred or two banded together; making night hideous with their demoniac yells is enough to make the stoutest heart quail—I have written you hurriedly—There is no security in the mails & I send this by a U.S. Paymaster who arrived here this afternoon & leaves to night—Again I beg you to help us in this dreadful emergency—No U.S. Marshall has been here & if they were to come they could not punish these murderers immediately—& they ought to be dealt with severely & immediately—This is private & I write as to my own dear Father & confide to you our troubles—We have lived in the midst of it since the war & it is more terrible now than ever—Every Union man will be killed if active steps are not taken by the Government to stop it—I am ever your true & loving Union woman.

*Source:*   S. A. Wayne to Ulysses S. Grant, September 18, 1874, quoted in John Y. Simon, ed., *The Papers of Ulysses S. Grant: Volume 25: 1874* (Carbondale: Southern Illinois University Press, 2003), pp. 195–196.

# 15.6 RED CLOUD PLEADS THE PLAINS INDIANS' POINT OF VIEW AT COOPER UNION (1870)

As one of the foremost leaders of the Teton Sioux, Red Cloud had kept the US Army at bay for several years. The war, as his speech pointed out, had never been his own doing. He, like many other Indians, sought a fair peace; like them, he found that all the power to define what peace meant and how it would be enforced lay in the hands of the indifferent, the ill-informed, and the insatiable.

My brethren and my friends who are here before me this day, God Almighty has made us all, and He is here to bless what I have to say to you today. The Good Spirit made us both. He gave you lands and He gave us lands; He gave us these lands; you came in here, and we respected you as brothers. God Almighty made you but made you all white and clothed you; when He made us He made us with red skins and poor; now you have come.

When you first came we were very many, and you were few; now you are many, and we are getting very few, and we are poor. You do not know who appears before you today to speak. I am a representative of the original American race, the first people of this continent. We are good and not bad. The reports that you hear concerning us are all on one side. We are always well-disposed to them. You are here told that we are traders and thieves, and it is not so. We have given you nearly all our lands, and if we had any more land to give we would be very glad to give it. We have nothing more. We are driven into a very little land, and we want you now, as our dear friends, to help us with the government of the United States.

The Great Father made us poor and ignorant—made you rich and wise and more skillful in these things that we know nothing about. The Great Father, the Good Father in Heaven, made you all to eat tame food—made us to eat wild food—gives us the wild food. You ask anybody who has gone through our country to California; ask those who have settled there and in Utah, and you will find that we have treated them always well. You have children; we have children. You want to raise your children and make them happy and prosperous; we want to raise and make them happy and prosperous. We ask you to help us to do it.

At the mouth of the Horse Creek, in 1852, the Great Father made a treaty with us by which we agreed to let all that country open for fifty-five years for the transit of those who were going through. We kept this treaty; we never treated any man wrong; we never committed any murder or depredation until afterward the troops were sent into that country, and the troops killed our people and ill-treated them, and thus war and trouble arose; but before the troops were sent there we were quiet and peaceable, and there was no disturbance. Since that time there have been various goods sent from time to time to us, the only ones that ever reached us, and then after they reached us (very soon after) the government took them away. You, as good men, ought to help us to these goods.

Colonel Fitzpatrick of the government said we must all go to farm, and some of the people went to Fort Laramie and were badly treated. I only want to do that which is peaceful, and the Great Fathers know it, and also the Great Father who made us both. I came to Washington to see the Great Father in order to have peace and in order to have peace continue. That is all we want, and that is the reason why we are here now.

In 1868 men came out and brought papers. We are ignorant and do not read papers, and they did not tell us right what was in these papers. We wanted them to take away their forts, leave our country, would not make war, and give our traders something. They said we had bound ourselves to trade on the Missouri, and we said, no, we did not want that. The interpreters deceived us. When I went to Washington I saw the Great Father. The Great Father showed me what the treaties were; he showed me all these points and showed me that the interpreters had deceived me and did not let me know what the right side of the treaty was. All I want is right and justice. . . . I represent the Sioux Nation; they will be governed by what I say and what I represent. . . .

Look at me. I am poor and naked, but I am the Chief of the Nation. We do not want riches, we do not ask for riches, but we want our children properly trained and brought up. We look to you for your sympathy. Our riches will . . . do us no good; we cannot take away into the other world anything we have—we want to have love and peace. . . . We would like to know why commissioners are sent out there to do nothing but rob [us] and get the riches of this world away from us?

I was brought up among the traders and those who came out there in those early times. I had a good time for they treated us nicely and well. They taught me how to wear clothes and use tobacco, and to use firearms and ammunition, and all went on very well until the Great Father sent out another kind of men—men who drank whisky. He sent out whisky-men, men who drank and quarreled, men who were so bad that he could not keep them at home, and so he sent them out there. I have sent a great many words to the Great Father, but I don't know that they ever reach the Great Father. They were drowned on the way, therefore I was a little offended with it. The words I told the Great Father lately would never come to him, so I thought I would come and tell you myself.

And I am going to leave you today, and I am going back to my home. I want to tell the people that we cannot trust his agents and superintendents. I don't want strange people that we know nothing about. I am very glad that you belong to us. I am very glad that we have come here and found you and that we can understand one another. I don't want any more such men sent out there, who are so poor that when they come out there their first thoughts are how they can fill their own pockets.

We want preserves in our reserves. We want honest men, and we want you to help to keep us in the lands that belong to us so that we may not be a prey to those who are viciously disposed. I am going back home. I am very glad that you have listened to me, and I wish you good-bye and give you an affectionate farewell.

Source:  *New York Times*, July 17, 1870, cited in William Benton, publ., *Annals of America, Volume 10: Reconstruction and Industrialization* (Chicago: Encyclopedia Britannica, Inc., 1968), 242–244.

# The Triumph of Industrial Capitalism

## 1850-1890

## COMMON THREADS

In what ways were the problems of Reconstruction and the problems of industrialization similar?

What made "big business" different from earlier enterprises?

How did the new social order of the late nineteenth century resemble what came before it, and how was it different later?

## OUTLINE

**AMERICAN PORTRAIT: Rosa Cassettari**

The Political Economy of Global Capitalism
  The "Great Depression" of the Late Nineteenth Century

**AMERICA AND THE WORLD: The Global Migration of Labor**

The Economic Transformation of the West
  Cattlemen: From Drovers to Ranchers
  Commercial Farmers Remake the Plains
  Changes in the Land

**AMERICAN LANDSCAPE: Mining Camps in the West**

  America Moves to the City

The Rise of Big Business
  The Rise of Andrew Carnegie
  Carnegie Dominates the Steel Industry
  Big Business Consolidates

A New Social Order
  Lifestyles of the Very Rich
  The Consolidation of the New Middle Class
  The Industrial Working Class Comes of Age
  Social Darwinism and the Growth of Scientific Racism

**STRUGGLES FOR DEMOCRACY: "The Chinese Must Go"**

  The Knights of Labor and the Haymarket Disaster

Conclusion

< **The Eads Bridge**

## AMERICAN PORTRAIT

# Rosa Cassettari

**I**n 1884, Rosa Cassettari left an Italian village near Milan and joined the stream of migrants from all across Europe bound for America. Others went full of dreams. "The country where everyone would find work! Where wages were so high that no one had to go hungry! Where all men were free and equal and where even the poor could own land!"

But Rosa left behind her son to rejoin her brutal, abusive husband, Santino, an iron miner in Missouri. Unable to read or write, she expected the worst, and rightly. "All us poor people had to go down through a hole to the bottom of the ship," she remembered. Crowded in darkness, sleeping on wooden shelves, feeding from tin plates, Rosa felt no relief to see land. Cheated in New York and forced to make her way to Missouri with nothing to eat, she arrived in a shabby cluster of tents and shanties, where she added to Santino's wages by cooking for a dozen miners. With no doctors or midwives available, Rosa gave birth to a premature child alone on the floor of her cabin. The last straw came when Santino used his savings to open a house of prostitution. Rosa fled for her life, and friends helped her move to Chicago. Was this the Promised Land?

Rosa thought so. She worked hard all her life, knew hunger in bad times, and just got by in good ones. But she always found friends to help her and religious faith to comfort her. In time she found work at Chicago Commons, a settlement house founded to help immigrants get by in a strange, often bewildering city. She discovered a strength and courage she had never known at home. When she went back to Italy to bring over her son, villagers gaped. She was wearing a hat and new shoes and "they thought I was something wonderful." When she told them that poor people in America ate meat every day, they could not believe it. And she lived to see her children doing better than she had—not rich, but not in want.

Rosa was one of millions of people uprooting themselves worldwide in the late nineteenth century. They moved from the countryside to the city or from town to town. They shifted from less developed regions to places where industrialization was well under way. The magnet for most of the movement was a core of industrial capitalist societies, and the United States was just one destination among many.

Common laborers moved from place to place because jobs were unsteady, or they moved when work was finished. Hired hands plodded the roads in autumn following the harvest, spent winters working in Washington's lumber camps, and toiled by summer along the Erie Canal. African American sharecroppers in the South moved at year's end, eventually into cotton-growing districts, into towns and cities, or out of the South. White tenant farmers found new homes and better living conditions in company-owned coal- and textile-mill towns. Native Americans, their domains already in flux for centuries, now lost most of their lands to white settlement and were herded onto reservations. And all across America, the children of farmers traded the charm and endless labor of rural life for the bright-lit, squalid metropolises of the East.

They went seeking work, and that meant working for somebody else, on terms that the employer set. It meant working with new, complicated machines, with foul air, dirty rivers, or ravaged land. Working people had been freed from the things that once tied them to the land, such as feudal dues and slavery. But wage labor often compelled men and women to shift from country to country, and finally from continent to continent. To watch Rosa Cassettari as she traveled from Italy to Chicago is to witness one small part of a process set in motion by global needs and once-unimaginable aspirations.

# The Political Economy of Global Capitalism

The economic history of the late nineteenth century was sandwiched between two great financial panics in 1873 and 1893. Both were followed by prolonged periods of high joblessness and labor strife. Between the two panics, prices dropped. Farmers with crops selling for less felt the crushing weight of money borrowed when prices were high. Manufacturers cut costs by increasing production, by replacing skilled labor with technology, and by drawing on the international labor market for a cheaper workforce. Still, amid bouts of hard times, the American economy transformed dramatically and, for consumers and many workers, for the better.

### The "Great Depression" of the Late Nineteenth Century

On July 16, 1877, workers for the Baltimore and Ohio Railroad struck at Martinsburg, West Virginia, over one wage cut too many. Within days, the strike spread to the Pennsylvania Railroad, the New York Central, the Great Western, and the Texas Pacific. Governors ordered the strikers to disperse. They asked for federal troops and got them. Soldiers fired on protestors in Pittsburgh, and for a while, confrontations between workers and armed forces fanned the flames of insurrection. "Other workingmen followed the example of the railroad employees," explained Henry Demarest Lloyd, a prominent social critic. "At Zanesville, Ohio, fifty manufactories stopped work. Baltimore ceased to export petroleum. The rolling mills, foundries, and refineries of Cleveland were closed. . . . Merchants could not sell, manufacturers could not work, banks could not lend. The country went to the verge of a panic." The strike was broken, though a hundred lives were lost by that time. Alarmed state authorities went on an armory-building binge and recruited a National Guard to keep order or break strikes in the future. Between 1875 and 1910, state troops were called out nearly 500 times.

The "Great Railroad Strike" of 1877 was fueled by an economic depression that began with the Panic of 1873 (see Chapter 15) and spread throughout the developed world. Immigrant arrivals in New York—200,000 every year between 1865 and 1873—fell to less than 65,000 in 1877. Although employment (and immigration) recovered in the 1880s, prices and wages continued to fall. Then, in 1893, another panic struck. Major railroads went bankrupt, including four of the five transcontinentals. Over 500 banks and 15,000 businesses shut down.

The world was shrinking. In 1866, Cyrus Field's telegraph cable was laid under the Atlantic Ocean. Now Americans could read Europe's latest news the next morning. They could cluster at the depot to hear the latest box score, sent by telegraph even as the game went on. Railroads carried Pillsbury's flour from Minneapolis mills to Massachusetts; refrigerated cars carried Chicago's "dressed beef" carcasses to California; and the catalog brought the goods of a nation to every farm on the high plains so efficiently that consumers swore "by God, the Ten Commandments, and Sears, Roebuck." Thanks to the steamship, midwestern wheat fed customers in Russia, and boards cut from the forests of the Cascades turned into flooring for plantations in Malaya. In Pittsburgh's steel mills, Slavic languages and Hungarian were as common as German and Russian in Lower East Side New York's needle trades. Capitalism, not just transportation, had mingled peoples together.

An industrializing and liberalizing Europe had cut families free from their traditional ties to the land. Many migrated to better themselves: some within Europe, some to South America or Canada, and many to America (see Map 16–1). In many Irish families,

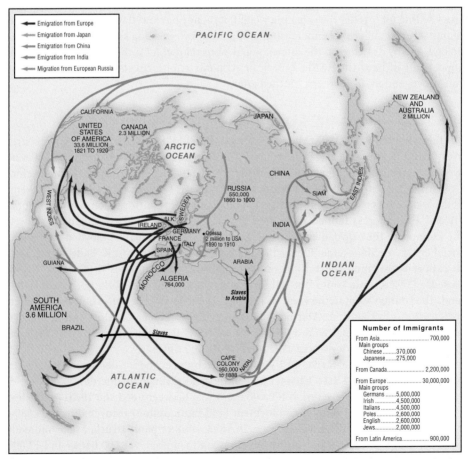

**Map 16-1  Patterns of Global Migration, 1840-1900** Emigration was a global process by the late nineteenth century. But more immigrants went to the United States than to all other nations combined. *Source*: London Times Atlas.

## AMERICA AND THE WORLD

# The Global Migration of Labor

Nineteenth-century migrants tended to leave areas already in the grip of social and economic change. Rosa Cassettari, for example, had worked in a silk-weaving factory in Italy. At first, the largest numbers emigrated from the most developed nations, such as Great Britain and Germany. Later in the century, as industrial or agricultural revolution spread, growing numbers of immigrants came from Scandinavia, Russia, Italy, and Hungary (see Map 16–1). As capitalism developed in these areas, small farmers were forced to produce for a highly competitive international market. The resulting upheaval sent millions of rural folk into the worldwide migratory stream.

Improvements in transportation and communication made migration easier. In 1856, more than 95 percent of immigrants came to America aboard sailing vessels. By the end of the century, more than 95 percent came in steamships. The Atlantic crossing took one to three months under sail, but only 10 days by steam. Beginning in the 1880s, fierce competition among steamship lines lowered the cost of a transatlantic ticket. But the great migrations were also related to economic and political turmoil. After 1890, immigration from northern and western Europe fell off sharply, as industrial growth soaked up surplus labor. At the same time, agrarian crises drove out peasants from eastern and southern Europe. Southern Italy could barely compete with Florida and California's lemons and oranges and found the American protective tariff closing off its biggest overseas wine market. Straitened Italian farmers started coming to the United States.

Jewish immigration was propelled by different impulses. In the Russian empire, pogroms, anti-Jewish riots, erupted in 1881–1882, 1891, and 1905–1906. Many Jews were killed. Anti-Semitic laws confined Russian Jews to the so-called Pale of Settlement along the empire's western and southern borders. The May Laws of 1882 severely restricted their religious and economic life. Starting in the 1880s, anti-Semitic riots brought fire and murder into the Jewish ghettoes. Sometimes the police looked on; sometimes they joined the rioters. The government not only encouraged the persecution; at times, it provoked it. By 1890, Russian Jews were making new homes for themselves in America. Swanky hotels snubbed them, clubs blackballed them, but here they could publish newspapers in Yiddish or Hebrew, worship freely, hope for schooling, even a college education, for their children, and make a living. A few went to Congress. One later became the prime minister of Israel.

Most immigrants, though, just came to America looking for work. Many planned to make money and then return home, as thousands of Italians and Slovaks did. (Some, discovering to their surprise that they had become more American than they expected, came back to stay.) Some came with education and skills, most with little more than their ability to work. They usually found their jobs through families, friends, and fellow immigrants. Letters from America told of high wages and steady employment. Communities of immigrant workers provided the support that newcomers like Rosa Cassettari needed. Some immigrants settled directly on farms, but the overwhelming mass lived in cities.

sending sons and daughters abroad meant money packets sent home to allow the rest to stay behind. Italians and eastern Europeans, known as "birds of passage," often came west only to earn money and return. But their cheap labor and that of millions who came to stay built the railroads and forged the steel. They slaughtered sheep and cattle in Chicago's stockyard district, "Packingtown," for Philip Armour and Gustavus Swift. Others worked as domestic servants, served behind store sales counters, or ran the sewing machines that met a national demand for ready-made clothing.

# The Economic Transformation of the West

For novelists, the West seemed like a separate world from the industrial transformation of the East: a land where the old-fashioned manly virtues of the cowboy, the trapper, the prospector, and the homesteader carved a destiny out of the wilderness. In fact, the economic revolution may have changed the West more than anywhere else. Lawless violence and wild speculation were part of the western experience, but so were the struggling families, start-up companies, and hard-working immigrants that remade Cleveland and Chicago. By 1900, thanks to the revolution that eastern-run railroads made, the West provided Americans with the meat and bread for their dinner tables, the wood that built their homes, and the gold and silver that backed up their currency. The West was being drawn into the political economy of global capitalism. As much as any eastern city, it had become diverse and ethnically and economically complex well before the director of the US Census declared the frontier "closed" in 1890. And when it came to savage labor strife, there was nothing Pittsburgh's victims could have told the miners in Cripple Creek or Leadville, Colorado.

## Cattlemen: From Drovers to Ranchers

The cowboy is the mythic figure of the American West: a rugged loner who scorned society for the freedom of the trail. In fact, cowboys were usually single men. They worked hard and played harder, spending their earnings on a shave, a new suit of clothes, and a few good nights in town. Civil War veterans, former slaves, displaced Indians, and Mexicans all became cowboys. Their pay was low, their work dangerous and unsteady, and their chances of reaching real independence were slim.

Longhorn cattle were as much a part of western legend as the cowboys who drove them. With the westward spread of the railroads, Texas ranchers began driving huge herds of Texas longhorns up the Chisholm Trail north onto the Great Plains. They brought the herds to railroad towns from which the cattle could be shipped, such as Abilene, Wichita, or Dodge City, Kansas. Cattlemen sold half of their stock to eastern markets and the other half in the West, some to the government for feeding soldiers and reservation Indians.

But the Texas longhorn had several drawbacks: it was tough and rangy, it produced more bone and sinew than meat, it carried a tick that devastated many of the other grazing animals, and it took a long time to fatten up. Investors began to breed hybrid cattle that were less hardy but beefier and of higher quality. By the early 1880s, investors were pouring capital into mammoth cattle-herding companies. The Great Plains became seriously overstocked. The depleted grazing lands left the cattle weak from malnutrition, and in the late 1880s several devastating winters wiped out whole herds. It was said that a person could walk across Kansas and never touch ground, just stepping from carcass to carcass.

Open-range herding became so environmentally destructive that it was no longer economically feasible. Long drives became increasingly difficult as farmers fenced in the plains, but they also became less necessary because railroads could pick up cattle just about everywhere. By the 1890s, huge cattle companies were giving way to smaller ranches that raised hybrid cattle. Cowboys became ranch hands with regular wages, like miners and factory workers.

In the mid-1880s, more than 7 million head of cattle roamed the Great Plains, but as their numbers declined, sheep replaced them. Although sheep proved even more ecologically destructive than cattle, by 1900 sheepherding had largely taken the place of the cattle industry in Wyoming and Montana and was spreading to Nevada. Sheepherding had the advantage of not interfering with small farmers as much as cattle driving did.

## Commercial Farmers Remake the Plains

Between 1860 and 1900, the number of farms in America nearly tripled, thanks largely to the economic development of the West. On the Great Plains and in the desert Southwest, farmers took up former Indian lands. In California, white settlers poached on the estates of Spanish-speaking landlords, stripping them of their natural resources and undermining their profitability. Over time, Hispanic ranchers gave way to European American farmers. The Hispanic population of Los Angeles fell from 82 percent in 1850 to 19 percent in 1880. A similar pattern occurred in New Mexico and Texas.

This ethnic shift signaled profound changes in the ecology and political economy of the West, driven by the exploding global demand for western products. Cattle ranchers were feeding eastern cities. Lumber from the Pacific Northwest found its way to Asia and South America. By 1890, western farmers produced half of the wheat grown in the United States, and they shipped it across the globe.

But farming in the arid West was unlike eastern farming. The 160-acre homesteads that lawmakers proposed in the original Homestead Act proved too small for guaranteeing a viable living on the parched prairies, though hundreds of thousands staked claims—and kept on doing so until 1934. Farmers needed costly equipment and extensive irrigation to produce wheat and corn for international markets. To make these capital investments, they mortgaged their lands. For mechanized, commercial agriculture to succeed on mortgaged land, western farms had to be much bigger than 160 acres.

Government homesteads made up only a fraction of all the lands sold. Speculators may have bought up as much as 350 million acres from state or federal governments or from Indian reservations. Railroads were granted another 200 million acres by the federal government. They sold much of it at bargain rates. The more farmers the railroads could settle on their lands, the more customers they would have, and the more farm produce there would be to ship. Railroads set up immigration bureaus and offered settlers cheap transportation, credit, and agricultural aid. The Great Plains filled with settlers from the East Coast and from Ireland, Germany, and Scandinavia.

## Changes in the Land

No Garden of Eden welcomed prairie farmers. "All Montana needs is rain," a promoter was said to have told one settler—who agreed: but that was also all that Hell needed. Rain fell rarely and in sparse amounts on the Great Plains and the desert Southwest.

## AMERICAN LANDSCAPE

# Mining Camps in the West

Rosa Cassettari's mining camp experience had none of the glamour that mythology lends those farther West. The greatest strike came in 1848 when James Marshall found gold at John Sutter's mill site in the California foothills. Prospectors poured in by the thousands, creating boomtowns like Ophir and You-Be-Damned overnight—and ghost towns just as quickly, when the lode gave out. Findings actually peaked years after the Forty-Niners' gold rush. New discoveries pulled prospectors eastward, into Colorado in 1859, Idaho in 1862, and Montana in 1864. In Nevada, prospectors hit the largest vein of all, the Comstock Lode. It would yield $350 million worth of gold and silver over 20 years.

Western mining camps were raw, violent, male-dominated, and diverse. New England Yankees mingled with Australians, Mexicans, Chinese, and African Americans. Alone or in small groups, they panned for gold, squatting in icy stream beds. Once the surface gold had been captured, miners shoveled dirt into boxes or sluices to capture ore by running water over it. A few miners struck it rich. The biggest winners may have been the storekeepers who sold blasting powder, shovels, and groceries. Four became partners and built the western half of America's first transcontinental railroad. They had such a stranglehold on California's transit system that locals called their company "the Octopus." Levi Strauss, a German immigrant, came to sell canvas tents and made a fortune turning them into pants—and Levis, as they came to be called, sell worldwide today.

Penniless Irish-born Marcus Daly did even better. Pooling resources, he and some San Francisco investors dug for silver in Montana and hit one of the world's largest veins of copper. The Anaconda mine made Daly millions. Its high-grade copper entered worldwide markets, wherever cities and industries needed copper wire to harness electricity's power. Partly due to

Howling blizzards, blistering summers that warped railroad track out of alignment, sky-blackening clouds of locusts, and loneliness meant ruin for some, despair for others. Yet settlers came, worked, endured, and improvised. With little wood or stone available, many farmers built sod houses—even sod schoolhouses. Joseph Glidden's invention, barbed wire, provided them fencing. Strong steel plows cut a sod so knotted with grass roots that hoes bounced off it like paving. Windmills rose from the prairie to pump water from hundreds of feet below ground and over time drain much of it dry. Mennonite settlers from Russia brought durum wheat, ideal for the harsh climate. Everywhere, families built schools, churches, and communities alongside the now-ubiquitous railroad stations.

The western environment was newly made. Wolves, elk, and bears were exterminated as farmers brought in pigs, cattle, and sheep. Tulare Lake, covering hundreds of square miles of California's Central Valley, was sucked dry by 1900. Mines sent tons of earth and

**Chinese and Anglo Miners near Sacramento, California, 1852** Digging for gold paid off mostly in aches, misery, and loneliness. The so-called Forty-Niners included immigrants from across the Pacific and from Latin America, but just about no women.

Anaconda, by 1883 the United States led the world in producing copper.

Daly's venture represented the future. By the 1870s, gold veins ran too deep for lone prospectors to reach; heavy, costly machines were needed. Minerals like zinc and copper required a heavier initial investment that would take much longer to be repaid. Mine shafts needed timber supports in a treeless land, as well as blowers to cool the 130-degree temperatures deep underground. Deep mines needed constant pumping: 2 million gallons of water seeped into the Comstock every day. Copper or silver took smelting. Thus, corporations alone could tap most of the West's mineral wealth. Engineers and wage laborers, managed from boardrooms miles away, extracted, smelted, and shipped the ore. Even Comstock's 750 miles of tunnels 3,000 feet underground were corporation run. Companies built the railroads to carry ore to market and to the towns where miners lived. These were shabby, utilitarian places without libraries, parks, schools—or the chance to strike it rich on one's own. The Comstocks had given way to the Cassettaris.

rock down the rivers of the Sierra Nevada, threatening entire cities with flooding. The skies above Butte, Montana, turned gray from pollutants released by copper-smelting plants. Sheepherding destroyed the vegetation on the eastern slopes of the Rocky Mountains and the Sierra Nevada. But the West was also dotted with communities and railroad depots. California oranges found a market in New England, and Washington apple orchards filled the stalls in eastern markets.

By the turn of the century, states and reservations stood where the Cheyenne, Dakota, and Comanche nations had commanded vast domains. Settlers of many ethnicities—Swedish, Finnish, Hispanic, and others—experienced the bounty and hardship of what had once been Indian land. Corporate enterprises and mechanized farms now shared the West with the homesteaders and storekeepers. Farmers had connected to world markets. They were clothed and supplied by cities' industries. They owed eastern railroad corporations their access to the world, and they owed nearly everything else to eastern mortgage holders. Mining and lumber corporations employed tens of thousands of wage laborers. Thanks to the gold rush, San Francisco rose from 5,000 inhabitants midcentury to 150,000 twenty years later. Denver was incorporated in 1861 with a population just below 5,000. By 1870, it had grown twentyfold.

## America Moves to the City

Between 1850 and 1900, the map of the United States was redrawn, thanks to the appearance of dozens of new cities (see Figure 16–1). In 1850, the largest city in the United States was New York, with a population of just over half a million. By 1900, New York, Philadelphia, and Chicago each had more than a million residents.

The industrial city was different from its predecessors. By the middle of the nineteenth century the modern "downtown" was born, a place where people shopped and worked but did not necessarily live. Residential neighborhoods separated city dwellers from the downtown districts and separated the classes from one another. Streetcars and commuter railroads brought middle-class clerks and professionals from their homes to their jobs and back, but the fares were beyond the means of the working class. The rich built their mansions uptown, but workers had to stay within walking distance of their jobs.

Cities became more crowded, unsanitary, and unsafe. Yellow fever and cholera epidemics were frequent. Fires periodically wiped out entire neighborhoods. In October 1871, much of Chicago went up in flames. Immigrant slums sprang up in most major cities of America, as well as in mill towns and mining camps. In 1890, Jacob Riis published *How the Other Half Lives*, exposing conditions in downtown New York, the breeding grounds of vice, crime, and despair. He described a dark three-room apartment that six people shared. The two bedrooms were tiny, the beds nothing more than boxes filled with "foul straw." Such conditions were a common feature of urban poverty in the late nineteenth century.

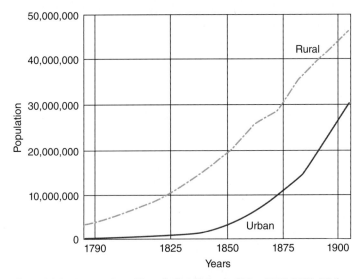

**Figure 16-1   Proportion of Population Living in Cities, 1790–1900**  While a growing proportion of Americans lived in cities, city dwellers would outnumber rural Americans only in the twentieth century.

Yet during these same years urban reformers and technology made city life less dangerous and more comfortable. Professional fire and police departments protected cities from fire outbreaks and violence. Boards of health and quarantine laws brought epidemics under control. By the century's end, city dwellers could count on clean drinking water, efficient transportation, great museums, public libraries, parks, and a variety of entertainment unimaginable in the countryside.

By 1900, travelers walking down New York City's Bowery at midnight could feel safer, basking in the blaze of electric lights. Thomas Alva Edison's invention of the commercially viable incandescent light bulb in 1879 was only one invention among many to dispel that darkness. He and other inventors created the dynamo to generate electricity, as well as alternating current to transmit power more efficiently. City dwellers would be the first to light their homes with electricity, the first to install telephones, and those most likely to receive mail every day, Sundays included. They would also be the ones most likely to eat fruits and vegetables out of season. Thanks to mass production, Gilded Age manufacturers would introduce canned foods into American diets. For those with money to spare, nothing could compare with the new, gigantic department stores, able to sell an endless variety of goods at the lowest prices because they dealt in such tremendous volume. Where else but Philadelphia would have Wanamaker's, with three acres of selling area and 129 counters, stretching two-thirds of a mile? Where else but New York would have a Heinz food sign six stories high, requiring 1,200 light bulbs? Cities showed off industrial capitalism's riches at their best, as well as its victims at their worst.

Nobody represented both sides of capitalism as well as a young Scots immigrant who came with his parents to

**Wanamaker's Grand Depot Department Store, 1876** "Big business" in the late nineteenth century not only mass-produced goods but also sold them in large quantities at low prices. John Wanamaker's Philadelphia department store was among the most famous of these large, new retailers and funded Wanamaker's political activity against corrupt city officials.

Pittsburgh and started out in a textile mill for $1.20 a week. Fifty years later, Andrew Carnegie sold his steel mills to J. Pierpont Morgan for $480 million.

# The Rise of Big Business

Before the Civil War the only enterprises in the United States that could be called "big businesses" were the railroads (see Map 16–2). Indeed, railroads became the model for a new kind of business—big business—that emerged during the 1880s. Big businesses had massive bureaucracies managed by professionals rather than owners and were financed through a national banking system centered on Wall Street. They marketed their goods and services across the world and generated wealth in staggering concentrations, giving rise to a class of men whose names—Carnegie, Rockefeller, Morgan, and Vanderbilt— became synonymous with American capitalism.

### The Rise of Andrew Carnegie

Andrew Carnegie was an immigrant, whereas most businessmen were native born. His childhood in Scotland was marked by poverty, whereas most of America's leading men of business were raised in comfort. Nevertheless, Andrew Carnegie was the perfect reflection of the rise of big business. In the course of his career, Carnegie mastered the telegraph, railroad, petroleum, iron, and steel industries and set the example for modern management techniques and strict accounting procedures in manufacturing. Other great industrialists and financiers made their mark in the last half of the nineteenth century. Canadian-born James J. Hill's railroad empire filled the grain elevators with wheat

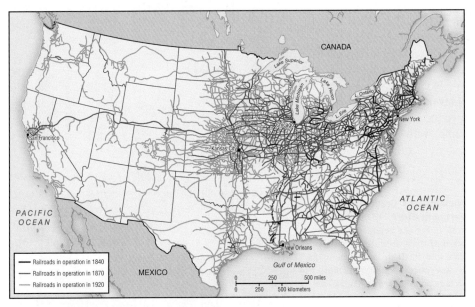

**Map 16–2   The Growth of Railroads, 1850–1890** Railroads were more than a means of transportation; they were also America's first "big business." They set the model for running huge industrial corporations, and the growth of railroads fostered the iron and steel industries.

that made Minneapolis the country's great flour-making center; his money built copper smelters in Montana and an apple-growing industry in Washington. German-born Friederich Weyerhäuser's timber company logged the West and furnished the boards that homesteaders on the treeless prairie needed so desperately. However, none had lives that took on the mythic proportions of that of the Scottish lad who came to America at the age of 12 and ended up the world's richest man.

Not content with his job at a textile mill, Carnegie enrolled in a night course to study accounting, and a year later he got a job as a messenger boy in a telegraph office. So astute and hard-working was Andrew that by 1851 he was promoted to telegraph operator. There he displayed a rare talent for leadership. He recruited bright, hard-working men and organized them with such stunning efficiency that the Pennsylvania Railroad offered Carnegie a job, first as a private secretary and later in management.

Carnegie came to the firm at a time when rail construction was soaring. Petroleum refiners shipped their kerosene by rail. Mining corporations needed railroads to ship their coal and iron. By the mid-1850s, the largest factory in the country, the Pepperell Mills in Biddeford, Maine, employed 800 workers, whereas the Pennsylvania Railroad then had more than 4,000 employees. If an engineer arrived late, or if a fireman came to work drunk, trains were wrecked, lives were lost, and business failed. The railroads thus borrowed the disciplinary methods and bureaucratic structure of the military to ensure that the trains ran safely and on time. J. Edgar Thomson, the Pennsylvania's president, established an elaborate bookkeeping system providing detailed knowledge of every aspect of the Pennsylvania's operations. Based on that data, the company could reward managers who improved the company's profits and eliminate those who failed.

Carnegie succeeded. As superintendent of the western division, he helped make the Pennsylvania a model of efficiency. By 1865, with 30,000 employees and lines stretching east to New York City and west to Chicago, it was the largest private company in the world. It was also necessarily one of the most financially intricate. Railroads dwarfed all previous business enterprises in the amount of investment capital they required and in the complexity of their financial arrangements. A major line might require over a hundred separate kinds of account books. Railroads were the first corporations to issue stocks through sophisticated trading mechanisms that attracted investors from around the world. To organize the market in such vast numbers of securities, the modern investment house was developed.

## Carnegie Dominates the Steel Industry

By 1872, Carnegie had taken on other interests as well. His Keystone Bridge Company built the first steel arch bridge over the Mississippi. Acquiring a controlling interest in the Union Iron Company, Carnegie had overhauled it, adapting the Pennsylvania's managerial techniques and accounting practices. He also integrated operations: unlike other firms, his would not just melt iron ore into pig iron, but make bars of it, and turn those bars into beams and plates. Eliminating middlemen meant savings, and savings let him sell for less. As Carnegie put it, "Watch the costs and the profits will take care of themselves."

More important, his railroad experience taught him that steel, not iron, was the future. Under the loads of larger, heavier trains, iron rails simply could not hold up for long. Though prohibitively expensive at first, steel rails lasted 20 years, whereas iron ones

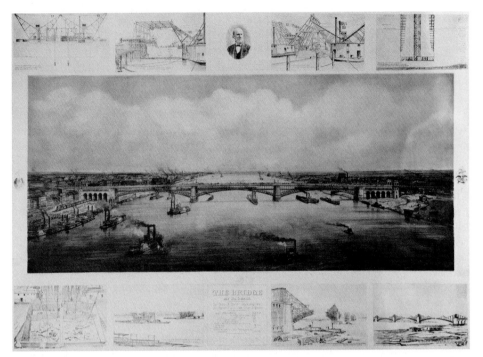

**The Eads Bridge** The steel arches of the Eads Bridge across the Mississippi River at St. Louis were both an engineering marvel and a triumph of Andrew Carnegie's managerial skills.

needed replacement at 5. Steel also proved better for making locomotives, boilers, and railroad cars. In the 1860s, two developments cleared the path for the transition from iron to steel. First, Henry Bessemer's patented process for turning iron into steel became available to American manufacturers. Second, iron ore began flowing from deposits in northern Michigan. With access to investment capital and Thomson for his partner, Carnegie opened a steel plant in 1873. Despite a worldwide depression, it turned a profit immediately.

## Big Business Consolidates

In the late nineteenth century, every great industry conjured up the name of a magnate: Carnegie in steel, Gustavus Swift or Philip Armour in meatpacking, John D. Rockefeller in oil refining, James J. Hill or Collis P. Huntington in railroads, and J. P. Morgan in financing (see Map 16–3). Actually, no single individual or family could own most big businesses because they required too much capital (financial resources). They were run by professionally trained managers. The highest profits went to companies with the most efficient bureaucracies. Because the businesses were so big and their equipment so expensive, they had to operate continuously. In an economic slowdown, an average factory could close its doors for a while, but big businesses could not.

With railroads and telegraph lines opening up national markets and new technology allowing mass production at lower costs, industries faced unprecedented competition. They met this challenge of competition and the need for a regular source of supply by adopting *vertical integration*. This was the attempt to control as many aspects of a business

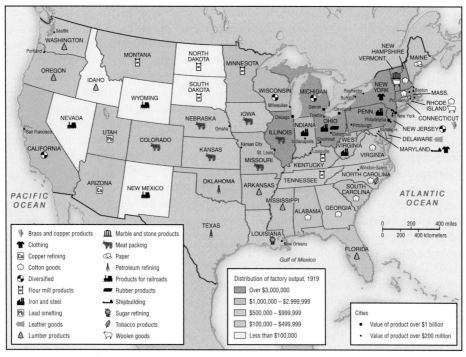

**Map 16-3    Major American Industries, ca. 1890**  An industrial map of late nineteenth-century America shows regions increasingly defined not by what they grew but by what they made.

as possible, from the production of raw materials to the sale of the finished product. Carnegie did not just manufacture steel; he owned the iron mines and handled the marketing of finished steel. He also grasped two profit-making strategies that other firms, from breweries to makers of canned goods, had learned: economies of scale and *continuous flow*. Bigger furnaces could produce steel more cheaply. Running them 24 hours a day, seven days a week, made every minute count. And with the help of the Jones Mixer, a container keeping pig iron molten, the biggest component in steel would be ready for immediate use. Rails poured into molds did not even wait in the plant to cool. Flatcars carried them outside, while others lined up to be filled. By such means over 15 years, Carnegie cut steel prices in half. Without these innovations, the gridwork of steel railroad lines would never have been—nor that new, lighter superstructure of girders that allowed the first skyscrapers to tower above Chicago and New York.

The same commitment to continuous flow made Philip D. Armour and Gustavus Swift into the nation's premier meatpackers. Instead of the local slaughterhouse, firms in Chicago's "Packingtown" had assembly lines carrying a steady stream of carcasses, with each employee assigned one task in the disassembling of pigs and cattle. To save on freight rates for live cattle, the packers built refrigerator cars to carry the "dressed beef" alone to distant markets. Armour also realized that by making money off the rest of the animal, he could lower the price for which he sold his meat. By 1900, the fat, bones, blood, and bristles were turned into hairbrushes, fertilizer, soap, and even the stuffing for automobile cushions—and Armour could sell his beef at four cents a pound.

John D. Rockefeller tried the other solution to cutthroat competition, *horizontal consolidation*: control of one step in the industrial process. Rockefeller had founded Standard Oil in 1867 in Cleveland, Ohio. Like Carnegie, Rockefeller hired the best managers and financiers to build and run the most efficient modern refineries and cut his dependence on railroad transport by investing in pipelines to carry the oil. However, he was also more willing than Carnegie to wipe out his competitors by any means available. Rockefeller squeezed from the railroads preferential shipping rates and rebates, the return of part of the standard price charged to other refiners—a critical advantage in a savagely competitive business. As president of the National Refiners' Association, he formed cartels, alliances with the major operators in other states. But the cartels were too weak to eliminate independent refiners.

Rockefeller found his solution in merging all the major companies under Standard Oil leadership. In 1882, the Standard Oil combine was formalized as a "trust," an elaborate legal device by which different producers came together under the umbrella of a single company that could police competition internally. In 1889, the New Jersey legislature passed a law allowing corporations based in that state to form "holding companies" that controlled companies in other states. Thus, the trust gave way to the holding company, with Standard Oil of New Jersey its most prominent example. Within a decade, holding companies dominated some of America's largest industries.

Standard Oil became a notorious example of how big business had changed the American economy—and, some thought, for the worse. Rockefeller's many charities never buried his reputation as a "robber baron," a term thrown at the titans of industry, transport, and finance. Exceptional in an age when most firms remained small and most industries stayed competitive (railroads mercilessly so), these "captains of industry" were admired and feared in equal measure.

# A New Social Order

Americans took pride in having no such rigid class system as in Europe. Anyone could rise, and, as Rosa Cassettari noticed, the poor need not doff their caps before the rich. But class divisions ran deep all the same. One could see that clearly, just by comparing Carnegie's Scottish castle with Painters' Row, where his unskilled workers lived in unventilated wooden houses without running water and with privies for all perched up the hill.

### Lifestyles of the Very Rich

Between 1850 and 1890, the proportion of the nation's wealth owned by the 4,000 richest families nearly tripled. At the top of the social pyramid clustered some 200 families worth more than $20 million each. Concentrated in the Northeast, New York especially, these families flaunted their opulence. Spread more evenly across America were the several thousand millionaires made rich by cattle ranching, agricultural equipment, mining, commerce, and real estate. Most of America's millionaires traced their ancestry to Great Britain. Usually they were Protestant, mostly Episcopalians, Presbyterians, or Congregationalists. By the standards of their day they were unusually well educated and, more often than not, voted Republican. (Southerners remained firmly Democratic.)

The upper classes lived in mammoth houses. Some addresses became celebrated for their wealth: Fifth Avenue in Manhattan, Nob Hill in San Francisco, and Boston's Back Bay. Wealthy suburbs (Brooklyn Heights, Philadelphia's Main Line, and Brookline, Massachusetts) became privileged retreats. The richest families also built country estates that rivaled the stately homes of England and the chateaus of France, such as the palace-sized "cottages" along the Newport, Rhode Island, shoreline. The leading figures in New York's high society competed to stage the most lavish balls and dinner parties, in one case with hundred-dollar bills as party favors. It was left to the new middle class to display the traditional virtues of thrift and self-denial.

## The Consolidation of the New Middle Class

In 1889, the *Century Dictionary* introduced the phrase "middle class" in the United States. The new term reflected a fresh awareness that American society had distinct gradations. Professionals were the backbone of the new middle class of the nineteenth century. All professions organized themselves into associations—some 200 between 1870 and 1890 alone—that set educational and ethical standards for admission and practice. Corporations needed professional managers, not swashbuckling gamblers. Business schools arose, teaching the science of accounting and the art of management. By 1920, 1,700 schools trained nurses, nearly all of them women. (At the same time, doctors' associations used their power over licensing to get rid of midwives; Rosa Cassettari was not the only one to do without.) Educators even gave a professional veneer to housekeeping by inventing "home economics" courses. States had a vested interest in professionalism, too. By 1900, most required association-drafted bar exams for lawyers and medical exams for doctors.

Behind the new professional managers marched an expanding white-collar army of cashiers, clerks, and government employees, mostly men. Their annual incomes far outpaced independent craftsmen and factory workers. They also had a better chance to rise. A beginning clerk might make only $100 a year, but within five years his salary could approach $1,000. At a time when a skilled Philadelphia factory hand made under $600, over 80 percent of the male clerks in the Treasury Department earned twice that.

Improved roads and mass-transit systems allowed middle-class families to escape the city's clamor and crowdedness, though suburbs, like city neighborhoods, were made for every income. The invention of oil-based house paints in the 1870s allowed owners to give the outside any color they pleased. Thanks to the mass-produced "Excelsior" mower and romantic associations with the Old South, the normal middle-class residence had a front porch and a lawn; but the crabgrass got blamed on eastern European immigrants, who supposedly brought it with them.

Only the most successful craftsmen matched the incomes and suburban lifestyles of white-collar clerks. Butchers might earn more than $1,600 annually, for example, but shoemakers averaged little more than $500. But while a shoemaker earned little more than a skilled factory worker, if he owned his own shop, he enjoyed an independence that middle-class Americans cherished. A cigar maker working on high-priced "seed and Havanas" had skills that gave him far more say in his work than the unskilled employees making two-cent "stogies" with a cigar mold. Pride and power, not just pay, defined job satisfaction. In carpentry and in the coal mines, specialized skills made workers hard to replace. But around them, labor-saving machinery was increasing a far more dependent industrial working class made up of people like Rosa Cassettari.

## The Industrial Working Class Comes of Age

"When I first went to learn the trade," John Morrison told a congressional committee in 1883, "a machinist considered himself more than the average workingman; in fact, he did not like to be called a workingman. He liked to be called a mechanic." Morrison identified one of the great changes in nineteenth-century America. "Today," Morrison lamented, the mechanic "is simply a laborer." Technological innovations replaced artisans with semiskilled or unskilled factory laborers. For traditional mechanics, this felt like downward mobility.

Because most factory workers and common laborers were migrants (or children of migrants) from small towns, farms, or abroad, few experienced factory work as a degradation of their traditional skills, as Morrison did. They had a chance to move upward from unskilled to skilled positions. Shop foremen might become storekeepers. Working-class families took comfort that their children had a still better chance of moving into the middle class. But industrial labor was a harsh existence for all factory operatives, who toiled long hours in difficult conditions performing repetitive tasks with little job security. Most luckless and hardest pressed were the common laborers, earning their keep by physical exertion. Their numbers grew throughout the century until by 1900 unskilled labor made up a third of the industrial workforce.

In 1900, women accounted for nearly one of every five Americans gainfully employed, mostly in unskilled or semiskilled labor. In northern middle-class homes, young Irish women worked as domestics, jobs held in the South by African American women. Jewish women sewed garments for as little as three dollars for a six-day week, and Italians worked on lace and paper flowers in their tenements. A smaller proportion of women held white-collar jobs, as teachers, nurses, or low-paid clerical workers and salesclerks behind department store counters.

The same hierarchy that favored men in the white-collar and professional labor force existed in the factories and sweatshops. In the clothing industry, for example, units dominated by male workers were higher up the chain of command than those dominated by women. Indeed, as the textile industry became a big business, the proportion of women working in textile mills steadily declined. The reverse trend affected white-collar workers. As department stores expanded in the 1870s and 1880s, they hired women, often Irish immigrants, for jobs with low wages and none of the prospects for promotion men still had. White-collar work did not confer middle-class status upon women as it did upon men in the late nineteenth century.

Few working-class wives and mothers took jobs outside the home, but many took in boarders or did laundry. The poorer working-class families survived by sending their children to work. The rich sent their daughters to finishing schools and their sons to boarding schools; middle-class parents sent their children to public schools; anything beyond grade school ranked as a luxury among those less well off than that. Ten-year-olds could be found tending the cotton spindles or picking shale off the conveyor belts coming up from the coal mines. They ran barefoot through New York's streets hawking newspapers and lugged red-hot, newly cast bottles from the furnaces in glass factories. Only in Horatio Alger novels did "Mark the Match-Boy" strike it rich.

Division of labor allowed more goods to be made for much lower per-unit labor costs. The introduction of the sewing machine in the 1850s, for example, gave rise to sweatshops where work was subdivided into simple, repetitive tasks. One group produced collars for men's shirts, another produced sleeves, and another stitched the parts together. Division of labor saved employers on training, and in industries where turnover was high, it kept the machinery running. Factory work was at best insecure, subject to swings in the business cycle. But unskilled workers also lacked the leverage to improve their own conditions. If Carnegie's workers, blinded or crippled on the job, got nothing more than the privilege of begging at the mill gates—if lung diseases were as common in textile factories as the "mill child's cough" and gangrene of the jaw among boys making matches—workers had no options beyond leaving and being fired.

Workmen's compensation was rare, and retirement pensions were unknown. Helplessness and the pool of surplus labor made organizing unions a challenge among the unskilled. Men laying railroad track or digging subway tunnels were always moving on, with common labor often seasonal and factory turnover high. In some meatpacking houses, turnover came close to 100 percent annually. A strike depleted workers' savings

**Cannery in Sunnyvale, California** The mass production of food involved a large female labor force, as this picture shows. Quite possibly, employers hired so readily not just because they could pay women less, but because anything involving the preparation of food fit in with the stereotype of "woman's work."

quickly. Exceptionally mobile and easily replaceable, immigrants increasingly came from places unfamiliar with the idea of organized labor and from cultures where religion defined identity more than class. Employers knew that by using them or, better still, black Americans as strikebreakers, they could turn race against race, native against foreigner. "Scabs," as those taking strikers' places were called, faced insult and threat. Some were beaten, others killed. Some firms built private armies to enforce control, but they could usually count on the police and state militia to help them win a strike.

## Social Darwinism and the Growth of Scientific Racism

As ethnicity identification developed in the late nineteenth century, class divisions were increasingly difficult to isolate from cultural distinctions. The middle class, for example, was overwhelmingly native born, white, Anglo-Saxon, and Protestant. By contrast, the working class came largely from racial and religious minorities, many of them foreign born (see Figure 16–2). By 1900, 75 percent of manufacturing workers were immigrants or their children, and in large cities, nearer 85 percent. The South's laborers were overwhelmingly black sharecroppers. As educated elites defined high culture, they drew on

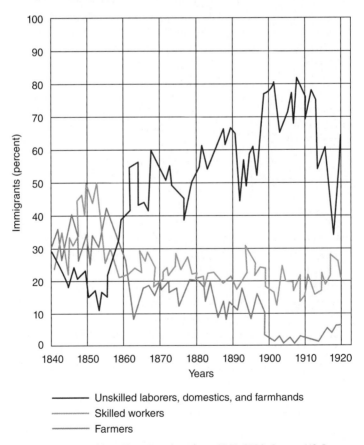

──── Unskilled laborers, domestics, and farmhands
──── Skilled workers
──── Farmers

**Figure 16-2  Working-Class Immigration, 1840-1920** *Source*: US Bureau of Census.

traditions and tastes formed by the propertied classes of a less culturally diverse America, one increasingly under challenge.

Pundits and professors argued that this form of society, stratified by class, race, ethnicity, and gender, was not only how things had to be, but how natural law required them to be. In 1859, Charles Darwin published his masterpiece of evolutionary theory, *On the Origin of Species*. Several scientists had already suggested that life had evolved over a long period of time, but Darwin offered the first persuasive explanation of how this had taken place. He argued that a process of "natural selection" favored those biological changes that were most suited to the surrounding environment. American scientists took readily to Darwinism. Asa Gray at Harvard and Joseph LeConte at the University of California spread the evolutionary word in their influential textbooks on botany and geology. By 1900, virtually all American high school science textbooks embraced evolution.

Darwin's influence did not stop with the natural sciences. Social scientists applied the theory of natural selection to social evolution. This combination of social theory with evolutionary science was known as Social Darwinism. Social Darwinists argued that human inequality was the outcome of a struggle for survival in which the fittest rose to the top. This theory made the rich seem more fit than the poor and blacks seem less fit than whites. To Social Darwinists, inequality was the natural order of things. In this way, Darwin's theory was hijacked to defend the new social order of industrial capitalism.

Natural selection was also invoked to show an inherent African racial inferiority (and that of Indians as well). Racists had argued that without slavery, freed blacks could not compete—or even survive. After the war, newspapers predicted the disappearance of African Americans by century's end and of Indians within a generation or two more. The 1890 census seemed to show a declining African American population, and racial theorists published influential studies "proving" that competition with whites was killing blacks off. Their only salvation, biologist Joseph LeConte argued, would come through permanent subordination. Only white overlordship could save blacks from their natural fate.

Far more influential than LeConte was statistician Frederick L. Hoffman's full-length treatise *Race Traits and Tendencies of the American Negro*, published in 1896. The book's many tables and figures gave the authoritative air of social science to Hoffman's conclusion: ever since leaving the shelter of slavery, blacks had been degenerating morally. Evolutionary theory doomed them to poverty and social inferiority.

Social Darwinism had plenty of defenders, notably Professor William Graham Sumner of Yale University. "Before the tribunal of nature," he asserted, "a man has no more right to life than a rattlesnake." Any government intervention to help the unfortunate interfered with natural selection. It would be useless in the long run and a harmful interference with the rigid economic laws of supply and demand in the short run. But the Sumners of the world found themselves under increasing challenge well before the century ended. Ministers, who saw man as a moral, rather than an economic, animal, rejected the concept of a natural selection process based on selfishness and scramble. Economist Richard T. Ely argued that even in economic decisions, self-interest did not play the all-controlling role that Social Darwinism presumed. Success, a younger generation of economists and social scientists argued, depended not just on a person's natural gifts but also on the surrounding conditions. Change the conditions—replace a slum with clean and healthy apartments, an alley with a playground or a park, a pittance with a living wage—and the man or woman with abilities might have the chance to use them to rise.

## STRUGGLES FOR DEMOCRACY

# "The Chinese Must Go"

For the Chinese, immigrating to America proved a disastrous success. With no other group did the promise of a new beginning suffer so badly in the translation.

In the mid-nineteenth century, the Chinese fled the convulsions of the Taiping Rebellion, a massive civil war that left 20 million dead. Some immigrants found work in the California gold fields; others dug the mines or laid track on the transcontinental railroad. Contractors swore by them: they did the hardest work at the lowest wage and never complained. Mines in Idaho and Montana imported Chinese labor. In California's inland valley, they earned a dollar a day digging the irrigation ditches for the great farms. As tourist hotels opened in southern California, they welcomed the Chinese as cooks and help. Along the Pacific coast, their vessels hauled in shoals of fish, ready to be dried, salted, and barreled for sale in China. Others dove for abalone; well-polished, the shells sold by the hundreds of thousands in Europe. They planted the vineyards north of San Francisco Bay and harvested the orchards south of it. The Bing cherry was developed by a Chinese horticulturist in Oregon, the frost-resistant orange by a Chinese immigrant in Florida. Saving their money, the thriftier Chinese opened up laundries and retail shops. Every major city had its "Chinatown," colorful, congested, and overwhelmingly male: the first generations of Chinese were sojourners, meaning to prosper and return home. They rented rather than bought homes and left their families behind. Those who died in America, if they could afford it, had their remains shipped back to their native soil for burial.

Hard-working, resourceful, sober, willing, and almost obsessive about paying what they owed, the Chinese were the very personification of the Horatio Alger

In that sense, the modern university reflected the inequalities of the age—and the promise. Leading scholars in the new "social sciences" of sociology, anthropology, and political science gave authority to Social Darwinism's conjectures, by dividing the world into great and inferior nations. At the top were the so-called Teutonic nations of Western Europe and North America. This hierarchy, far from reflecting the biases of its creators, was grounded in the objective methods of pure science—or so anthropologists, sociologists, and professional economists claimed. However, a vocal minority, just as well trained abroad, came back to apply objective standards to Social Darwinism and expose its fallacies.

Colleges thus helped reinforce elite power while opening the door a crack to those wanting to enter that elite realm. Only a tiny fraction of Americans attended college, mostly native-born and well-to-do males. Nevertheless, it was a larger fraction than ever before. One reason was that the first Morrill Land Grant Act of 1862 had endowed the states with great tracts to fund institutions teaching "agriculture and the mechanic ideal for success. That, however, was just the problem. White workers resented their cheap labor and the corporations that used them as strikebreakers. Keeping apart and failing to assimilate, Chinese immigrants remained alien, closed off by differences in language and religion from their neighbors. It was widely believed that the Chinese ate birds' nests, rats, squirrels, and, worst of all, abalone. Ignorance only kindled fantasies among whites, of a Chinatown crowded with opium dens, racketeers, and prostitution rings—all of which did exist—and not much else. Alarmist writers forecast a race war, where the "Celestials" conquered the world for their emperor.

Even as other immigrants became voters, the Chinese found themselves isolated and imperiled. Courts refused Chinese testimony because of the race's supposed habit of lying. Trade unions refused to admit them. Rioters in Los Angeles tore through the Asian community, beating up and killing whomever they could find and looting every store; a city councilman led the mob, and the chief of police sealed Chinatown off so that the victims could not escape.

Vigilantes burned down Chinatowns across the West. Farmers employing Chinese laborers had their barns and fields torched. By 1877, anger against the Chinese and railroad barons had become a political uprising, with the cry, "The Chinese must go!" California's new constitution barred them from public schools and taxed them out of the mining and fishing industries. National laws over the next 20 years would close the doors to new immigration and make it harder for residents to visit home and return to the United States.

Closing the doors to their home country had an unexpected effect. Cut off from their Old World communities, forced to make a lifetime commitment to their new homeland, the survivors learned English, brought their families over, and remade themselves as Chinese Americans. They adopted Western clothing; their sons and daughters went to Sunday school, joined the Boy Scouts, and organized chapters of the YMCA and YWCA. All the same, full assimilation would not come in their lifetimes, nor their grandchildren's. In more than a mere physical sense, the Statue of Liberty faced away from the newcomers of the Pacific Rim.

arts." Seventy "land grant" institutions were founded, including the major state university systems of New York, Illinois, Michigan, and California. Those in the Midwest admitted women as well as men. Women's colleges also opened their doors: six of the "Seven Sisters" began after the Civil War. By 1910, two in five college students were women. If blacks found themselves largely shut out of the elite schools (which also set quotas limiting Jewish admissions), they, too, had new opportunities in land grant institutions as well as in black colleges like Fisk University in Tennessee or Booker T. Washington's Tuskegee Institute in Alabama.

Social scientists such as Ely and Hoffman prided themselves on their commitment to the truth as facts and statistics revealed it. Like advocates of high culture, sociologists and anthropologists claimed to have isolated the definitive truths of human society. But not all "realists" sought solace in statistics. Some of America's best artists responded to the realities of a diverse, urban, industrial America. They could see what it took no advanced degree to grasp: that a many-cultured society was being enriched and reshaped by those very people that Social Darwinists had dismissed as the losers in humankind's struggle to advance.

## The Knights of Labor and the Haymarket Disaster

Workers had known that all along, their share fell far behind what their labor deserved. Between 1860 and 1890, wages overall grew by 50 percent, but elite skilled and semi-skilled workers in a handful of industries, such as printing and metalworking, got the lion's share of the gains. The vast majority of workers suffered directly from deflation and economic instability. By 1880, 40 percent of industrial workers lived at or below the poverty line, and the average worker was unemployed for 15 to 20 percent of the year. To relieve their plight, American workers sought political solutions to economic problems.

Inspired by the radicalism of the Civil War and Reconstruction, industrial workers across the North organized dozens of craft unions, Eight-Hour Leagues, and working-men's associations, all designed to protect northern workers who were overworked and underpaid. They called strikes, initiated consumer boycotts, and formed consumer cooperatives. In 1867 and 1868, workers in New York and Massachusetts campaigned for laws restricting the workday to eight hours. Soon, workers began electing their own candidates to state legislatures.

Before the Gilded Age, labor organizations had never drawn many workers. The tradition of individuals lifting themselves up bred a distrust of collective solutions. Founded in 1866, the National Labor Union (NLU) was the first significant postwar effort to organize all "working people" into a national union. William Sylvis, an iron molder, founded the NLU and became its president in 1868. He denied any "harmony of interests" between workers and capitalists. On the contrary, every wage earner was at war with every capitalist, whose "profits" robbed working people of the fruits of their labor.

Under Sylvis's direction, the NLU advocated a wide range of political reforms, not just bread-and-butter issues. Sylvis believed that through organization American workers could take the "first step toward competence and independence." He argued for a doubling of the average worker's wages. He supported voting rights for blacks and women. Nevertheless, after a miserable showing in the elections of 1872, the NLU fell apart.

Despite the collapse of the NLU, a more successful alternative had already begun. In 1869, some Philadelphia garment makers formed the Noble and Holy Order of the

## Time Line

▼**1848**
Andrew Carnegie emigrates to the United States

▼**1857**
Henry Bessemer develops process for making steel

▼**1859**
Oil discovered in western Pennsylvania and the petroleum boom begins

▼**1862**
Homestead Act

▼**1866**
First successful transatlantic telegraph cable begins operation

▼**1869**
Opening of the first transcontinental railroad

Knights of Labor. The Knights were inspired by the producers' ideology and admitted everyone from self-employed farmers to unskilled factory workers. Stressing the need for uplift and temperance, the Knights advocated a host of reforms, including the eight-hour day, equal pay for men and women, the abolition of child and prison labor, inflation of the currency to counteract the deflationary spiral, and a national income tax.

Only a strong national organization able to hold various locals together and provide necessary funds would give the Knights credibility among potential recruits. In the late 1870s, a new constitution required all members to pay dues and let the national organization support local boycotts. Open to women as well as men, skilled and unskilled, black and white (but not Chinese), the Knights grew rapidly, from 19,000 members in 1881 to 111,000 in 1885. Terence Powderly, leader of this largely working-class movement, believed in neither socialism nor the notion that there was any necessary conflict between labor and capital. Wage earners were "producers," and he meant to overthrow "wage slavery," not capitalism itself. Powderly favored arbitration and conciliation over confrontation, and the consumer boycott over the strike. Local assemblies struck anyhow. They even forced a settlement out of the railroads of the Southwest, including those of the notorious Jay Gould, who had bragged that he "could hire one half of the working class to kill the other half." The Knights' lobbying helped put through the Chinese Exclusion Act in 1882 and a federal law against imported contract labor three years later. By 1886, membership swelled to nearly a quarter of a million. Labor parties elected mayors and city councilmen; only vote fraud kept them from making Henry George mayor of New York. They even talked of fielding a presidential ticket.

But the more the Knights of Labor grew, the more the strains among its members showed. Shopkeepers and small-factory owners had very different interests from wage laborers, especially when it came to strikes. By 1886, work stoppages were twice what they had been the year before. The "Great Upheaval" had begun. The more Knights there were, the more militant they sounded. The culmination came when trade unions called for a nationwide strike for the eight-hour day. On May 1, 1886, workers across the country walked off their jobs in one of the largest labor walkouts in American history. In Chicago 80,000 workers went out on strike. The Chicago strike was largely peaceful until May 4, when, at an anarchist rally at Haymarket Square, someone from the crowd tossed a bomb into a line of police. Eight policemen were killed. Police shot into the crowd. Four people died. Many more were wounded. The bomb thrower was never identified.

▼**1871**
Great Chicago Fire

▼**1872**
Andrew Carnegie's steel works open near Pittsburgh

▼**1873**
Financial panic, followed by depression

▼**1877**
The "Great Railroad Strike"

▼**1882**
John D. Rockefeller forms Standard Oil trust
Thomas Edison develops the first commercially viable incandescent electric light

▼**1890**
Jacob Riis publishes *How the Other Half Lives*
Director of US Census declares frontier "closed"

▼**1893**
Financial panic, followed by depression

**Haymarket Riot** The Haymarket "riot," as it was misnamed, set off a wave of middle-class hysteria against foreigners, radicals, and labor unions. This image correctly shows police firing into the crowd. Inaccurately, it shows members of the crowd firing back, the orator apparently urging them on. It also leaves out the women and children who attended.

Anarchists—who questioned the legitimacy of all government power—had little influence on the labor movement, but their fiery rhetoric invoking the use of violence made them conspicuous. In a blatantly unfair trial with perjured testimony, eight of them were found guilty of inciting the "Haymarket riot." Four were hanged, one committed suicide, and the others went to prison. (In 1893, Governor John Peter Altgeld pardoned the survivors. He knew it would doom him politically; it did.) Haymarket was a turning point in American labor politics. A wave of revulsion against labor agitation swept the country, and state anti-labor laws sprinkled the statute books. The Knights never recovered from the Haymarket disaster. Instead, the labor movement found its new leadership in Samuel Gompers's American Federation of Labor, which concentrated on organizing skilled workers and making demands that could be met immediately, without waiting for political reforms: "bread-and-butter unionism," as some called it.

## Conclusion

Rosa Cassettari and Andrew Carnegie—two immigrants whom the new global economy of industrial capitalism helped draw overseas—met wholly different destinies. Not just their origins, but gender roles, opportunity, and good luck explained how they ended up. Yet both shared the same striving spirit that held out at least the chance for them to better themselves (as Cassettari did, however modestly) and their adopted country. Cassettari's experience with failure impelled her to search for something better. Carnegie's success made him yearn for more than money. By 1900, having thrown his energies into getting, Carnegie threw them all into giving. He set up endowments, funded universities, and founded an institute for peace. He had helped create an industrial nation. Now he set out to re-create American culture. Ironically, the Rosa Cassettaris of the world had beaten him to it.

## Who, What, Where

Bessemer process  510

Carnegie, Andrew  508

Cassettari, Rosa  498

Chisholm Trail  502

Haymarket Square  521

Jones Mixer  511

Knights of Labor  520

Longhorn cattle  502

Lower East Side  500

National Labor Union  520

Pittsburgh  499

Powderly, Terence  521

Riis, Jacob  506

Scabs  516

Sharecropping  498

Social Darwinism  516

Sylvis, William  520

Tenement  514

Trust  512

## Review Questions

1. Define "industrial capitalism." How was industrial capitalism a global phenomenon in the late nineteenth century?

2. What were the differences in lifestyle and in opportunities for those in America's upper, middle, and lower classes, and how did those differences widen or narrow during the late nineteenth century?

3. How was the West absorbed into the national and international markets?

## Critical-Thinking Questions

1. How and why did the effects of industrial capitalism differ in the South, West, and North?

2. Historians often refer to this period as the "Gilded Age." "Gilded" refers to something of base or common substance coated with a thin layer of gold, so that it seems far brighter and more valuable than it is. In view of America's industrial development at this time, do you think the term "Gilded Age" is appropriate? Why or why not?

3. Aside from the expansion of industrial capitalism, what factors affected American development during this period? How important are those factors in comparison to capitalism's growth?

## Suggested Readings

Chandler, Alfred D. *The Visible Hand: The Managerial Revolution in American Business.* Cambridge, MA: Harvard University Press, 1977.

Cronon, William. *Nature's Metropolis: Chicago and the Great West.* New York: W. W. Norton, 1991.

White, Richard. *The Republic for Which It Stands: The United States During Reconstruction and the Gilded Age, 1865–1896.* New York: Oxford University Press, 2016.

**For further review materials and resource information, please visit www. oup.com/us/oakes-mcgerr**

# CHAPTER 16: THE TRIUMPH OF INDUSTRIAL CAPITALISM, 1850–1890
## Primary Sources

---

## 16.1 RUSSELL H. CONWELL, "ACRES OF DIAMONDS" (1860s–1920s)

A Baptist pastor from Philadelphia, Russell H. Conwell's most widely known work was his sermon "Acres of Diamonds," first prepared in 1861 when he was 18, and added to and improved upon years later. Over a half century, he would deliver it more than 6,000 times, earning some $8 million from lecture fees. It expressed the faith of the age that any enterprising person could succeed and that individual effort was sure to be rewarded.

---

You and I know there are some things more valuable than money; of course, we do. Ah, yes! By a heart made unspeakably sad by a grave on which the autumn leaves now fall, I know there are some things higher and grander and sublimer than money. Well does the man know, who has suffered, that there are some things sweeter and holier and more sacred than gold. Nevertheless, the man of common sense also knows that there is not any one of those things that is not greatly enhanced by the use of money. Money is power.

Love is the grandest thing on God's earth, but fortunate the lover who has plenty of money. Money is power: money has powers; and for a man to say, "I do not want money," is to say, "I do not wish to do any good to my fellowmen." It is absurd thus to talk. It is absurd to disconnect them. This is a wonderfully great life, and you ought to spend your time getting money, because of the power there is in money. And yet this religious prejudice is so great that some people think it is a great honor to be one of God's poor. I am looking in the faces of people who think just that way.

I heard a man once say in a prayer-meeting that he was thankful that he was one of God's poor, and then I silently wondered what his wife would say to that speech, as she took in washing to support the man while he sat and smoked on the veranda. I don't want to see any more of that kind of God's poor. Now, when a man could have been rich just as well, and he is now weak because he is poor, he has done some great wrong; he has been untruthful to himself; he has been unkind to his fellowmen. We ought to get rich if we can by honorable and Christian methods, and these are the only methods that sweep us quickly toward the goal of riches.

. . . A young man came to me the other day and said, "If Mr. Rockefeller, as you think, is a good man, why is it that everybody says so much against him?" It is because he has gotten ahead of us; that is the whole of it—just gotten ahead of us. Why is it Mr. Carnegie is criticized so sharply by an envious world! Because he has gotten more than we have. If a man knows more than I know, don't I incline to criticize somewhat his learning? Let a man stand in a pulpit and preach to thousands, and if I have fifteen people in my church, and they're all asleep, don't I criticize him? We always do that to the man who gets ahead of us. Why, the man you are criticizing has one hundred millions, and you have fifty cents, and both of you have just what you are worth.

. . . If you have no capital, I am glad of it. You don't need capital; you need common sense, not copper cents.

A. T. Stewart, the great princely merchant of New York, the richest man in America in his time, was a poor boy; he had a dollar and a half and went into the mercantile business. But he lost eighty-seven and a half cents of his first dollar and a half because he bought some needles and thread and buttons to sell, which people didn't want.

Are you poor? It is because you are not wanted and are left on your own hands. There was the great lesson. Apply it whichever way you will it comes to every single person's life, young or old. He did not know what people needed, and consequently bought something they didn't want, and had the goods left on his hands a dead loss. A. T. Stewart learned there the great lesson of his mercantile life and said "I will never buy anything more until I first learn what the people want; then I'll make the purchase." He went around to the doors and asked them what they did want, and when he found out what they wanted, he invested his sixty-two and a half cents and began to supply a "known demand." I care not what your profession or occupation in life may be; I care not whether you are a lawyer, a doctor, a housekeeper, teacher or whatever else, the principle is precisely the same. We must know what the world needs first and then invest ourselves to supply that need, and success is almost certain.

. . . In our city especially, there are great opportunities for manufacturing, and the time has come when the line is drawn very sharply between the stockholders of the factory and their employees. Now, friends, there has also come a discouraging gloom upon this country and the laboring men are beginning to feel that they are being held down by a crust over their heads through which they find it impossible to break, and the aristocratic money-owner himself is so far above that he will never descend to their assistance. That is the thought that is in the minds of our people. But, friends, never in the history of our country was there an opportunity so great for the poor man to get rich as there is now and in the city of Philadelphia. The very fact that they get discouraged is what prevents them from getting rich. That is all there is to it. The road is open, and let us keep it open between the poor and the rich.

*Source:*  Russell H. Conwell, *Acres of Diamonds*, foreword by Russell F. Weigley (Philadelphia: Temple University Press, 2002), pp. 23–42.

# 16.2 VISUAL DOCUMENT: ALFRED R. WAUD, "BESSEMER STEEL MANUFACTURE" (1876)

The manufacture of steel began in the Middle Ages in Europe and Asia, but industrialization enabled the manufacture of high-quality steel in massive quantities. The transformation of iron ore into steel was an intensive process. The arrival of huge converters in enormous steel mills caused some observers to consider both the wondrousness of the new technology and the hell-like conditions that employed it. While the United States benefited from large quantities of steel for railroads, construction, and equipment, steel workers labored under harsh conditions. The forges poured liquid hot metal; workers were exposed to air pollution; and wages provided little to no income for long hours and an extensive workweek with no substantial breaks.

*Source:*  Alfred R. Waud, 1828–1891, artist. "Bessemer Steel Manufacture" (1876). Library of Congress Prints and Photographs Division, Washington, DC.

## 16.3 GEORGE STEEVENS, EXCERPT FROM *THE LAND OF THE DOLLAR* (1897)

George Steevens, a British journalist, came across the Atlantic in 1896 to collect material for *The Land of the Dollar*. While visiting Philadelphia, he went to one of the most celebrated department stores in the country, Wanamaker's. His guess that the owner had been a "rattling good" Cabinet officer was half right. In terms of efficiency, Wanamaker proved excellent; as a partisan Republican, he willingly saw to the discharge of as many Democratic postmasters as he could manage, and his readiness to forbid mailing materials that he considered indecent stirred outrage among authors.

In Philadelphia everybody goes to Wanamaker's. Mr. [John] Wanamaker was once Postmaster-General of the Republic, and I should think he was a rattling good one. His store was already the largest retail drapery and hosiery and haberdashery, and all that sort of business, in the world, when by the recent purchase of a giant establishment in New York he made it more largest still. Now the working of Wanamaker's, as I am informed, is this. It is no use going there to get what you want. You must go to get what Mr. Wanamaker wants to sell. He tells you each morning in the newspapers what he has got today, and if you want it you had better go and get it; the chances are it will be gone tomorrow. The head of each department is entrusted with a certain amount of capital, and buys his goods at his own discretion. But woe unto him if he does not turn over his capital quickly. There is a rule that no stock may be in the house more than, I think, three months; after that off it must go at any sacrifice.

"You can always tell when Mr. Wanamaker's in town," said a shopwalker, "because there's always some change being made." And then he added, in a half-voice of awestricken worship, "I believe Mr. Wanamaker loves change for its own sake." For the sake of custom, I should say; for this formula of change for change's sake is one of the master-keys of American character. Mr. Wanamaker keeps a picture-gallery, with some really fine modern paintings, to beguile his patrons. To-day he will have an orchestrion playing, tomorrow a costume exhibition of spinning—girls from all the lands of the earth,—every day something new. One day, by moving a table six feet, so that people had to walk round it instead of past it, he increased the sales of an article from three shillings to hundreds of pounds. If that is not genius, tell me what is.

But the really Napoleonic—I was going to say daemonic—feature of the Wanamaker system is the unerring skill with which it reaps its profits out of the necessities of others. Fixing his price according to the economic doctrine of final utility—taking no account, that is, of the cost of production, but only of the price at which most people will find it worth their while to buy—Mr. Wanamaker realizes 10 per cent for himself, and an enormous saving for the consumers. A cargo of rose-trees had been consigned from Holland to a firm of florists, which failed while the plants were in mid-ocean. They went a-begging till Mr. Wanamaker bought them up and put them on the market at about half the rate current in Philadelphia. In ten days not one of the twenty thousand was left. A firm which manufactured hundred-dollar bicycles found itself without cash to meet its liabilities. Mr. Wanamaker bought up the stock and altered the maker's label as well as one peculiarity of the gear. Then he broke the price to sixty-six dollars, and subsequently to thirty-three. They all went off in a week or so. He bought the plates of a huge edition of the hundred-dollar Century Dictionary, altered the title-page, bound them for himself, and put the article on the market at fifty-one dollars and a half. In six weeks he had sold two thousand. A firm in California, which manufactures an excellent kind of blanket, was in difficulties. Mr. Wanamaker bought up the stock, and sold it at a third of the normal price in three days.

All this is magnificent for the customer, and apparently not unprofitable to Mr. Wanamaker. But plainly somebody has to pay, and who? The small trader. After the rose-tree deal nobody wanted to buy roses of the florists of Philadelphia. The city is stocked with bicycles and Century Dictionaries, and nobody within a radius of miles will want to buy a pair of blankets for a generation. Mr. Wanamaker sends out three hundred and sixty-five thousand parcels to his customers in the slackest month of the year, and turns over thirteen million dollars annually. The small people, it is presumed, are ground to powder against the wall.

*Source:* George Steevens, *The Land of the Dollar* (New York, 1897), quoted in David Colbert, ed., *Eyewitness to America: 500 Years of America in the Words of Those Who Saw It Happen* (New York: Pantheon Books, 1997), pp. 305–306.

# 16.4 EMMA LAZARUS, "THE NEW COLOSSUS" (1883)

Emma Lazarus became a prominent writer against anti-Semitism, particularly the Russian empire's pogroms against Jewish people. As an organizer of relief agencies, she was deeply involved in the struggle to keep America's doors open to immigration. Her sonnet, titled "The New Colossus," was inscribed on the pedestal of the Statue of Liberty, which was dedicated in late 1886.

Not like the brazen giant of Greek fame,
With conquering limbs astride from land to land;
Here at our sea-washed, sunset gates shall stand
A mighty woman with a torch, whose flame
Is the imprisoned lightning, and her name
Mother of Exiles. From her beacon-hand
Glows world-wide welcome; her mild eyes command
The air-bridged harbor that twin cities frame.
"Keep, ancient lands, your storied pomp!" cries she
With silent lips. "Give me your tired, your poor,
Your huddled masses yearning to breathe free,
The wretched refuse of your teeming shore.
Send these, the homeless, tempest-tost to me,
I lift my lamp beside the golden door!"

*Source:*  Emma Lazarus, "The New Colossus," quoted in William Benton, publ., *The Annals of America. Volume 11, 1884–1894: Agrarianism and Urbanization* (Chicago: Encyclopedia Britannica, Inc., 1968), p. 107.

# 16.5 JOSIAH STRONG, EXCERPTS FROM "THE SUPERIORITY OF THE ANGLO-SAXON RACE" (1885)

As the new secretary to the Congregational Home Missionary Society, Josiah Strong began with a revision of the society's manual and ended up publishing a book, combining his notions of social Darwinism and his fears that a white America stood imperiled by what he felt were inferior races: not just African Americans and Chinese immigrants, but the Irish, the Italians, the Slavs, and those of the Jewish faith. Strong's *Our Country* was first published in 1885.

It is not necessary to argue to those for whom I write that the two great needs of mankind, that all men may be lifted up into the light of the highest Christian civilization, are, first, a pure, spiritual Christianity, and second, civil liberty. Without controversy, these are the forces which, in the past, have contributed most to the elevation of the human race, and they must continue to be, in the future, the most efficient ministers to its progress. It follows, then, that the Anglo-Saxon, as the great representative of these two ideas, the despositary of these two greatest blessings, sustains peculiar relations to the world's future, is divinely commissioned to be, in a peculiar sense, his brother's keeper. Add to this the fact of his rapidly increasing strength in modern times, and we have well-nigh a demonstration of his destiny. . . . In one century the United States has increased its territory ten-fold, while the enormous acquisition of foreign territory by Great Britain—and chiefly within the last hundred years—is wholly unparalleled in history. This mighty Anglo-Saxon race, though comprising only one-thirteenth part of mankind, now rules more than one-third of the earth's surface, and more than one-fourth of its people. And if this race, while growing from 6,000,000 to 120,000,000, thus gained possession of a third portion of the earth, is it to be supposed that when it numbers 1,000,000,000, it will lose the disposition, or lack the power to extend its sway? . . .

America is to have the great preponderance of numbers and of wealth, and by the logic of events will follow the scepter of controlling influence. This will be but the consummation of a movement as old as civilization—a result to which men have looked forward for centuries. John Adams records that nothing was "more ancient in his memory than the observation that arts, sciences and empire had traveled westward; and in conversation it was always added that their next leap would be over the Atlantic into America." He recalled a couplet that had been inscribed or rather drilled, into a rock on the shore of Monument Bay in our old colony of Plymouth:

The Eastern nations sink, their glory ends,
And empire rises where the sun descends . . .

. . . Looking at the distant future, I do not think that the Rev. Mr. Zincke takes an exaggerated view when he says: 'All other series of events—as that which resulted in the culture of mind in Greece, and that which resulted in the Empire of Rome—only appear to have purpose and value when viewed in connection with, or rather as subsidiary to, the great stream of Anglo-Saxon emigration to the West.'"

There is abundant reason to believe that the Anglo-Saxon race is to be, is, indeed, already becoming, more effective here than in the mother country. The marked superiority of this race is due, in large measure, to its highly mixed origin. Says Rawlinson: "It is a general rule, now almost universally admitted by ethnologists, that the mixed races of mankind are superior to the pure ones"; and adds: "Even the Jews, who are so often cited as an example of a race at once pure and strong, may, with more reason, be adduced on the opposite side of the argument." The ancient Egyptians, the Greeks, and the Romans, were all mixed races. Among modern races, the most conspicuous example is afforded by the Anglo Saxons. . . . There is here a new commingling of races; and, while the largest injections of foreign blood are substantially the same elements that constituted the original Anglo-Saxon admixture, so that we may infer the general type will be preserved, there are strains of other bloods being added, which, if Mr. Emerson's remark is true, that "the best nations are those most widely related," may be expected to improve the stock, and aid it to a higher destiny. If the dangers of immigration, which have been pointed out, can be successfully met for the next few years, until it has passed its climax, it may be expected to add value to the amalgam which will constitute the new Anglo-Saxon race of the New World. . . .

It may be easily shown, and is of no small significance, that the two great ideas of which the Anglo-Saxon is the exponent are having a fuller development in the United States than in Great Britain. There the union of Church and State tends strongly to paralyze some of the members of the body of Christ. Here there is no such influence to destroy spiritual life and power. Here, also, has been evolved the form of government consistent with the largest possible civil liberty. Furthermore, it is significant that the marked characteristics of this race are being here emphasized most. Among the most striking features of the Anglo-Saxon is his moneymaking power—a power of increasing importance in the widening commerce of the world's future. We have seen . . . that, although England is by far the richest nation of Europe, we have already outstripped her in the race after wealth, and we have only begun the development of our vast resources.

Again, another marked characteristic of the Anglo-Saxon is what may be called an instinct or genius for colonizing. His unequaled energy, his indomitable perseverance, and his personal independence, made him a pioneer. He excels all others in pushing his way into new countries. It was those in whom this tendency was strongest that came to America, and this inherited tendency has been further developed by the westward sweep of successive generations across the continent. So noticeable has this characteristic become that English visitors remark it. Charles Dickens once said that the typical American would hesitate to enter heaven unless assured that he could go farther west.

What is the significance of such facts? These tendencies infold the future; they are the mighty alphabet with which God writes his prophecies. May we not, by a careful laying together of the letters, spell out something of his meaning? It seems to me that God, with infinite wisdom and skill, is training the Anglo-Saxon race for an hour sure to come in the world's future. Heretofore there has always been in the history of the world a comparatively unoccupied land westward, into which the crowded countries of the East have poured their surplus populations. But the widening waves of migration, which millenniums ago rolled east and west from the valley of the Euphrates, meet today on our Pacific coast. There are no more new worlds. The unoccupied arable lands of the earth are limited, and will soon be taken. The time is coming when the pressure of population on the means of subsistence will be felt here as it is now felt in Europe and Asia. Then will the world enter upon a new stage of its history—the *final competition of races, for which the Anglo-Saxon is being schooled.* Long before the thousand millions are here, the mighty *centrifugal* tendency, inherent in this stock and strengthened in the United States, will assert itself. Then this race of unequaled energy, with all the majesty of numbers and the might of wealth behind it—the representative, let us hope, of the largest liberty, the purest Christianity, the highest civilization—having developed peculiarly aggressive traits calculated to impress its institutions upon mankind, will spread itself over the earth. If I read not amiss, this powerful race will move down upon Mexico, down upon Central and South America, out upon the islands of the sea, over upon Africa and beyond. And can any one doubt that the results of this competition of races will be the "survival of the fittest?" "Any people," says Dr. Bushnell, "that is physiologically advanced in culture, though it be only in a degree beyond another which is mingled with it on strictly equal terms, is sure to live down and finally live out its inferior. Nothing can save the inferior race but a ready and pliant assimilation. Whether the feebler and more abject races are going to be regenerated and raised up, is already, very much of a question. What if it should be God's plan to people the world with better and finer material?"

*Source:* Josiah Strong, "The Superiority of the Anglo-Saxon Race," quoted in William Benton, publ., *The Annals of America. Volume 11, 1884–1894: Agrarianism and Urbanization* (Chicago: Encyclopedia Britannica, Inc., 1968), pp. 72–76.

# 16.6 JAMES BAIRD WEAVER, *A CALL TO ACTION* (1892)

A Union officer and later an insurgent Iowa Republican, James B. Weaver moved first into the Greenback Party and then joined the Populists. As their presidential candidate in

1892, he issued *A Call to Action*, exposing the gap between the lifestyles of the rich and the conditions of the underprivileged.

---

If the master builders of our civilization one hundred years ago had been told that at the end of a single century, American society would present such melancholy contrasts of wealth and poverty, of individual happiness and widespread infelicity as are to be found to-day throughout the Republic, the person making the unwelcome prediction would have been looked upon as a misanthropist, and his loyalty to Democratic institutions would have been seriously called in question. Our federal machine, with its delicate inter-lace work of National, State and municipal supervision, each intended to secure perfect individual equality, was expected to captivate the world by its operation and insure domestic contentment and personal security to a degree never before realized by mankind.

But there is a vast difference between the generation which made the heroic struggle for Self-government in colonial days, and the third generation which is now engaged in a mad rush for wealth. The first took its stand upon the inalienable rights of man and made a fight which shook the world. But the leading spirits of the latter are entrenched behind class laws and revel in special privileges. It will require another revolution to overthrow them. That revolution is upon us even now.

Two representative characters—Dives and Lazarus—always make their appearance side by side in disturbing contrast just before the tragic stage of revolution is reached. They were present at the overthrow of ancient civilizations; the hungry multitude stood outside the gates when Belshazzar's impious feast was spread; they were both at the cave of Adullam when the scepter was about to depart from the tyrant Saul to the hands of the youthful David; they stood side by side when Alaric thundered at the gates of Rome; they confronted one another in the fiery tempest of the French revolution and they are sullenly face to face in our own country to-day. . . .

## The Banker's Banquet

The following editorial appeared in the *Kansas City Times*, August 30, 1889:

"The contract for serving the banquet for the convention of the American Bankers' Association was yesterday awarded to C.M. Hill, of the Midland Hotel. There were sixty competitors. The price is such as to insure one of the finest banquets ever served in this country. No expense will be spared to make the affair a grand success, even aside from the menu. The banquet will be given in the Priests of Pallas' Temple, at Seventh and Lydia. It will be necessary to build and furnish an annex, where the cooking can be done for 1,500 covers. The preparations seem to take into contemplation a great flow of wine, as there will be six thousand wine glasses and about forty wine servers. There will be in all nearly three hundred waiters. It is estimated that the entire cost of the banquet will be from $15,000 to $20,000. Mr. Hill anticipates some difficulty in securing efficient waiters, and with this particular object in view, will make a trip to New York and Chicago."

This impious feast which took place in the very heart of the mortgage-ridden and debt-cursed West, was the most shocking and brazen exhibition of wanton extravagance and bad morals combined, which the laboring millions of America were ever called upon to behold. What a travesty upon common sense and the ordinary instinct of self-preservation to intrust the finances of a great Nation and the welfare of labor to the hands of such men.

This carousal was but history repeating itself. It is not necessary in our day that an armless hand shall come out of the darkness and write the decree of Heaven upon the wall of the palace while the drunken carousal is being held, as in the time of Belshazzar; nor does it now require an expert Hebrew prophet, like Daniel, to disclose to the King that the sword is about to enter, and that a greater than Darius is thundering at the gates of Babylon, commissioned from on high to restore the stolen treasures of the temple, and to transfer the kingdom to another." . . .

## At the Rich Man's Gate

About the time these princely entertainments were given, and in the same year with some of them, one of the metropolitan journals caused a careful canvass to be made of the unemployed of that city. The number was found to be one hundred and fifty thousand persons who were daily unsuccessfully seeking work within the city limits of New York. Another one hundred and fifty thousand earn less than sixty cents per day. Thousands of these are poor girls who work from eleven to sixteen hours per day.

In the year 1890, over twenty-three thousand families, numbering about one hundred thousand people, were forcibly evicted in New York City owing to their inability to pay rent, and one-tenth, of all who died in that city during the year were buried in the Potters Field.

In the *Arena* for June, 1891, will be found a description of tenement house horrors, by Mr. B.O. Flower. He has done a valuable service to humanity by laying before the world the result of his investigations. After describing a family whose head was unable to find work, Mr. Flower says:

"This poor woman supports her husband, her two children and herself, by making pants at twelve cents a pair. No rest, no surcease, a perpetual grind from early dawn, often till far into the night; and what is more appalling, outraged nature has rebelled; the long months of semi-starvation and lack of sleep have brought on rheumatism, which has settled in the joints of her fingers, so that every stitch means a throb of pain. The afternoon we called she was completing an enormous pair of custom-made pants of very fine blue cloth, for one of the largest clothing houses in the city. The suit would probably bring sixty or sixty-five dollars, yet her employer graciously informed his poor white slave that as the garment was so large he would give her an extra cent. Thirteen cents for fine custom-made pants, manufactured for a wealthy firm, which repeatedly asserts that its clothing is not made in tenement houses! Thus with one of the most painful diseases enthroned in that part of the body which must move incessantly from dawn till midnight, with two small dependent children and a husband powerless to help her, this poor woman struggles bravely, confronted ever by a nameless dread of impending misfortune. Eviction, sickness, starvation—such are the ever present spectres, while every year marks the steady encroachment of disease and the lowering of the register of vitality. Moreover, from the window of her soul falls the light of no star athwart the pathway of life.

"In another tenement Mr. Flower found a poor widow with three children, making pants at twelve cents a pair. One of the children had been engaged, since she was two and one-half years old in overcasting the long seams of the garments, made by her mother! In the attic of another tenement a widow was found weeping and working by the side of a cradle where lay a sick child, whose large luminous eyes shone with almost phosphorescent brilliancy from great cavernous sockets, as they wandered from one to another, with a wistful, soul-querying gaze. Its forehead was large and prominent, so much so that looking at the upper part of the head one would little imagine the terrible emaciation of the body, which was little more than skin and hones, and the sight of which spoke more eloquently than words of the ravages of slow starvation and wasting disease. The woman was weeping because she had been notified that if one week's rent was not paid on Saturday she would be evicted, which meant death to her child who was suffering from a rupture, and for whom she was unable to purchase a truss.

"The making at home of clothing, cigars, etc., in New York and Brooklyn is paid at prices on which no women could live were there not other workers in the family. Some of their occupations involved great risks to girls, such as the loss of joints, of fingers, of the hand, or sometimes of the whole arm." . . .

*Source:*  James Baird Weaver, *A Call to Action: An Interpretation of the Great Uprising, Its Sources and Causes* (Des Moines: Iowa Printing Company, 1892), 362–363, 367–370.

# The Culture and Politics of Industrial America

## 1870–1892

## COMMON THREADS

How did the social construction of gender impact men's and women's lives in the late nineteenth century?

How did both culture and politics reflect sharp distinctions between men and women?

How did culture and politics break those distinctions down?

What was the overriding issue of American politics in the late nineteenth century?

Was American politics headed for a crisis in the 1890s?

## OUTLINE

**AMERICAN PORTRAIT: Luna Kellie and the Farmers' Alliance**

The Elusive Boundaries of Male and Female
  The Victorian Construction of Male and Female
  The Victorian Crusade for Morality
  Urban Culture

A New Cultural Order: New Americans Stir Old Fears
  Josiah Strong Attacks Immigration
  From Immigrants to Ethnic Americans
  The Catholic Church and Its Limits in Immigrant Culture
  Immigrant Cultures
  The Enemy at the Gates

Two Political Styles
  The Triumph of Party Politics
  Masculine Partisanship and Feminine Voluntarism
  The Women's Christian Temperance Union
  The Critics of Popular Politics

**STRUGGLES FOR DEMOCRACY: The "Crusade" Against Alcohol**

Economic Issues Dominate National Politics
  Greenbacks and Greenbackers
  Weak Presidents Oversee a Stronger Federal Government

**AMERICA AND THE WORLD: Foreign Policy: The Limited Significance of Commercial Expansion**

Government Activism and Its Limits
  States Discover Activism
  Cities: Boss Rule and New Responsibilities

Challenging the New Industrial Order
  Henry George and the Limits of Producers' Ideology
  Edward Bellamy and the Nationalist Clubs
  Agrarian Revolt
  The Rise of the Populists

Conclusion

< **Protestors Outside an Ohio Saloon**

# Luna Kellie and the Farmers' Alliance

As a girl, Luna Kellie dreamed of raising a family on her own farm. Her father, a railroad worker on the Northern Pacific line, did try to make a go of farming in Minnesota but when the farm failed, he moved the family to St. Louis, Missouri. There Luna met and married James T. Kellie. At the age of 18, Luna moved with her husband and their infant to a homestead near Hastings, Nebraska.

Life on the prairie fell far short of her dreams. The Kellies lived in an 8-by-12-foot sod house dug into a hillside. She gave birth to 12 children. Two died. Weakened by the strain of childbirth and constant toil, Luna dreamed of a brighter future, a holiday to Yellowstone's geysers. "Our trip never materialized," she recalled years later, "but we put in some happiest hours of life planning it."

The life of sturdy independence that farmers supposedly enjoyed turned out to be a pinched, isolated existence. Luna tried to connect with friends and neighbors, but there was not much choice. Her family attended a Methodist church until James quarreled with the pastor. Schools were even scarcer than churches, but Luna went out of her way to become active in the school district, where she took part in discussions over whether women should have the right to vote.

Like many rural women, Luna shared the responsibility for managing the farm. She kept a garden, which helped feed the family and brought in extra income from the sale of chickens and eggs. Luna also learned how to tend livestock and grow fruit trees. Her husband tried to grow spring wheat, but between falling prices and high interest rates, their work never freed them from debt. After seven years, the Kellies lost the farm. They struggled to survive by raising chickens, sheep, and livestock.

Like so many prairie farmers just barely scraping by, Luna Kellie turned to the Farmers' Alliance, the largest and most powerful association that coped with agricultural woes. She was not alone: 250,000 women joined the Alliance, making it the largest women's organization in the United States.

For Kellie, the Alliance held out the hope of realizing the dreams of her youth. Its program could break down the isolation of rural life, bringing farmers together in cooperative enterprises while giving them the advantages that the "money power" had taken away. In 1892, when the Nebraska Farmers' Alliance affiliated with the National Farmers' Alliance and Industrial Union, Kellie was elected state secretary. She worked as tirelessly on Alliance business as she had on her own farm, writing countless letters. She edited and set the type for articles for the Alliance newspaper.

Without setting foot outside her home, Luna Kellie found herself at the center of a vast network of farmers who learned from each other by discussing key issues. Starting in efforts to improve rural Americans' lives, the movement quickly advanced into broader questions of political reform. By 1892, the Farmers' Alliance had fostered the most important political insurgency of the late nineteenth century, the Populist Party.

# The Elusive Boundaries of Male and Female

Luna Kellie's involvement in politics was a sign that the old assumptions about a "woman's place" in society were shifting, along with notions of how to preserve the independence, opportunity, and equal voice that the republic once had promised to ordinary people. In fact, the political economy of industrial capitalism and the triumph of wage labor helped men and women rethink traditional concepts of masculinity and femininity. As they did so, new cities and newfound leisure time offered unprecedented opportunities to test the conventional boundaries of sexual identity.

## The Victorian Construction of Male and Female

Until the mid-1700s, most European doctors believed that there was only one sex: females were simply inferior, insufficiently developed males. Sometime after 1750, however, scientists and intellectuals began to argue that males and females were fundamentally different, that they were "opposite" sexes. For the first time it was possible to argue that women were naturally less interested in sex than men or that men were "active" whereas women were "passive." Nature itself seemed to justify the infamous double standard that condoned sexual activity by men but punished it in women.

Nineteenth-century society drew even more extreme differences between men and women. Taking its name from the long reign of Britain's Queen Victoria, the Victorian era is often stereotyped as an age of sexual repression and cultural conservatism, and it was, up to a point. Boys reading moralistic stories of heroes who overcame their fears prepared for the competitive worlds of business and politics, both largely male preserves. To be a "man" in industrial America was to work in the rough-and-tumble world of the capitalist market. Men proved themselves by their success at making a living and thereby at taking care of a wife and children.

Victorian men defined themselves as rational creatures threatened by insistent sexual drives. Physical exertion was an important device for controlling a man's powerful sexual urges, just as masturbation was deemed an unacceptable outlet for these drives. Men were urged to channel their sexual energies into strenuous activities such as sports and, conveniently enough, wage labor.

Where masculinity became a more rigid concept, femininity became less certain. Women's schools established their own sports programs. Affluent women took up bicycling, tennis, swimming, and croquet. Yet the stereotype persisted that women were too frail for the hurly-burly of business and enterprise. Lacking the competitive instinct of the male, the female was best fitted to become a wife and mother within the protective confines of the home. Just as men joined social clubs and sports teams, a "female world of love and ritual" developed. Middle-class women often displayed among themselves a passionate affection that was often expressed in nearly erotic terms. But genuinely passionate female sexuality disturbed the Victorians. Evidence of sexual passion among women was increasingly diagnosed, mostly by male doctors, as a symptom of a new disorder called "neurasthenia."

Over time, the differences between men and women were defined in increasingly medical terms. Victorian doctors redefined homosexuality as a medical abnormality, a perversion, and urged the passage of laws outlawing homosexual relations. The new science of gynecology powerfully reinforced popular assumptions about gender differences.

Leading male physicians argued that the energy women expended in reproduction left them unable to withstand the rigors of higher education. In extreme cases, physicians would excise a woman's clitoris to thwart masturbation or remove her ovaries to cure neurasthenia.

On the assumption that motherhood was a female's natural destiny, doctors pressed to restrict women's access to contraception and to prohibit abortion. Before the Civil War, many Americans tolerated abortion in the first three months of pregnancy, though they did not necessarily approve of it. This began to change as the medical profession laid claim to the regulation of female reproduction. The American Medical Association (AMA, founded in 1847) campaigned to suppress abortionists and criminalize abortion. The AMA also supported passage of the Comstock Law, which in addition to being the first federal law to ban the production, distribution, and public display of obscenity, outlawed the sale of contraceptive devices. "Our Heavenly Father never sends more mouths than He can feed," one doctor explained. To hear an advocate of the law tell it, the only naysayers were "long-haired men and short-haired women"—the unmanly and unfeminine.

To bolster traditional marriage, states passed laws raising the age of consent, forbidding common-law and interracial marriage, punishing polygamists, and tightening restrictions on divorce. Only in the West did authorities allow incompatibility grounds for ending a marriage. Many places set up family courts to handle desertion and juvenile delinquency. Congress passed several antipolygamy laws to protect Mormon wives and, as a fringe benefit, to take the vote away from a religious group known to lean Democratic.

## The Victorian Crusade for Morality

In the Victorian era, reformers saw the city as a place where traditional morality broke down, particularly standards of sexual propriety. With corrupt police lackadaisical about enforcing morality, reformers established private organizations to smite smut with prosecutions and citizens' arrests. Moral crusader Anthony Comstock's New York Society for the Suppression of Vice (SSV) inspired many others. It deputized itself to enforce laws "for the suppression of the trade in, and circulation of, obscene literature and illustrations, advertisements, and articles of indecent or immoral use." Comstock's chief concern was the protection of children. In his book *Traps for the Young* (1883), he warned that obscenity was luring American youngsters into deviant ways by stoking youthful wants and passions until they had "a well-nigh irresistible mastery over their victim." As head of the society, Comstock acted as a special post office agent. "You must hunt these men as you hunt rats," Comstock declared, "without mercy." In many cases, that meant without respecting the rights of due process. Reformers entrapped perpetrators by enticing and then arresting them. Comstock caught America's most notorious abortionist that way. He felt no remorse when she cut her throat rather than go to trial.

Such efforts, however, could not reverse the underlying trends. Illegal contraceptive devices were widely known and used. In major cities, abortionists charged $10 for their services. As for the divorce rate, it increased 15 times over. By 1915, the United States had the highest divorce rate in the world, affecting one marriage in seven. In a new economy based on wage labor, single young men found the city ideal for cutting

**Anthony Comstock** Crediting himself with 4,000 arrests and destroying 400,000 pictures, New York's most notorious vice crusader showed how governments could take action, in the so-called era of laissez-faire, against views that middle-class moralists found objectionable. This 1906 illustration shows Comstock as a monk thwarting shameless displays of flesh, whether that of women, horses, or dogs.

loose at comparatively little risk. Workers had more leisure and white-collar employees more still. Those looking for prostitutes found them readily available (see Map 17–1). In many towns, they had their own neighborhood, the "red-light district," and sometimes the "sporting trade" published guidebooks detailing different houses' specialties. The relative anonymity of urban life and the cash value set on everything made sin pay better than ever before and perpetrators less fearful of being shamed for it. With prostitutes renting their bodies for as little as 50 cents a trick and with saloon keepers doubling as brothel keepers (or tripling as aldermen), the SSV might win battles, but never the war.

## Urban Culture

Cities reflected the diversity and vitality of a changing America, far from the rhythms of Luna Kellie's world and the cherished ideal of the self-sufficient farmer. Urban centers crystallized Americans' larger ambivalence about the social changes of the era. Boasting of how up-to-date their country was, Americans longed for a reassuring past. Tenement kids cheered Buffalo Bill Cody's romanticized re-creations of the plains wars and loved the chance to see Sitting Bull himself. (Sitting Bull liked "Buffalo Bill" more than he liked white civilization. He puzzled at how a society so rich could leave homeless children begging in the streets.) Yankees paid good money for tickets to minstrel shows about happy plantation life down South, and everybody read Joel Chandler Harris's "Uncle Remus" stories, recasting African folk tales with a kindly old slave as their narrator.

At the same time, city culture took on a life all its own. From the 1880s on, it meant bright lights: electricity, in place of dimmer gaslight, and a vigorous "night life." Electric trolleys and

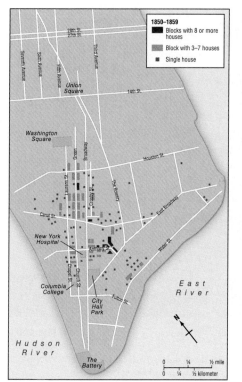
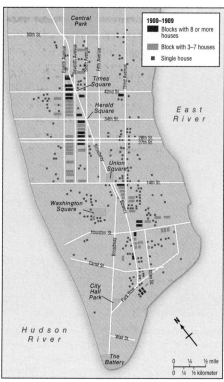

**Map 17-1  Houses of Prostitution, 1850–1859 and 1900–1909** One measure of the sexual freedom characteristic of city life was the explosive increase in prostitution. As the demand for prostitution rose, so did attempts to suppress it.
*Source:* Timothy J. *Gilfoyle, City of Eros* (New York: W. W. Norton, 1992), p. 33.

suburban rail networks drew tens of thousands downtown (see Figure 17–1), to department stores, firms, and factories by day and to theaters, music halls, and concert saloons by night.

One did not have to venture far in the biggest cities to find shows flouting Victorian standards of propriety by using sexual titillation to entertain audiences. Can-can girls, off-color jokes, and comedy skits focusing on the war of the sexes played well in working-class districts. Even among the "respectable classes," both men's and women's clothing became simpler, looser, and more comfortable. Within limits, popular culture idealized the sensuous human body, while for the first time male sports heroes were openly admired for their physiques. Police cracked down on homosexual conduct more severely than before, but the old rules still applied: private and consensual behavior involved relatively little risk.

While reformers like Comstock saw the cities' vice and corruption, linking both to immigrant slums, some of America's best artists created art that reflected the gritty truths of everyday life and celebrated the cities' vitality. If Comstock's admirers defined "culture" as limited to only the great works in the Western European tradition (even suppressing some, such as those by Voltaire, Walt Whitman, Aristophanes, and Ovid), city dwellers embraced a wider array of influences. Out of "Storyville," the red-light district in New Orleans, came the beginnings of jazz; out of the honky-tonks came the first great composers

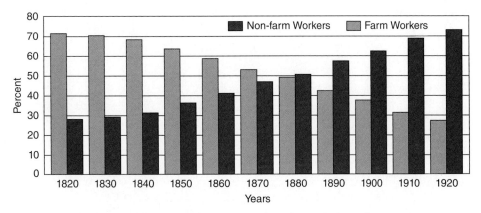

**Figure 17-1    Growth of the Nonfarm Sector** Underpinning the rise of urban culture was the emergence of a wage-earning labor force. Concentrated in cities, wage earners had cash at their disposal to spend on the amusements cities had to offer.

of ragtime. And a canny publicity agent knew how to sell a faintly risqué painting, *September Morn*: he got Comstock to arrest the gallery owner for indecency. Firms running off copies of it could not keep up with the demand.

# A New Cultural Order: New Americans Stir Old Fears

When novelist Henry James returned to the United States in 1907 after a quarter of a century in Europe, he was appalled by the pervasive presence of immigrants in New York City. On the streetcars, he confronted "a row of faces, up and down, testifying, without exception, to alienism unmistakable, alienism undisguised and unashamed." James was one of the many native-born Americans who assumed that their culture was Protestant, democratic, and English speaking. They saw a threat in vast numbers of immigrants who were none of those things and in the roots that ethnic subcultures were setting down in the cities. Yet among immigrants and their children, an ethnic identity was often traded for a broader assimilation into American culture.

### Josiah Strong Attacks Immigration

"Every race which has deeply impressed itself on the human family has been the representative of some great idea," clergyman Josiah Strong wrote in *Our Country*. Greek civilization was famed for its beauty, he explained; the Romans for their law; and the Hebrews for their purity. The Anglo-Saxons claimed two great ideas: the love of liberty and "pure spiritual Christianity." Strong was optimistic that as representatives of "the largest liberty, the purest Christianity, the highest civilization," the Anglo-Saxon race would "spread itself over the earth." Published in 1885, Strong's best-selling book went through many editions and was serialized in newspapers across America. Like him, many native-born Americans saw themselves as the defenders of Anglo-Saxon culture.

But there was a problem. Strong and his followers saw the arrival of millions of immigrants as a challenge to Anglo-Saxon America. By 1900, more than 10 million Americans

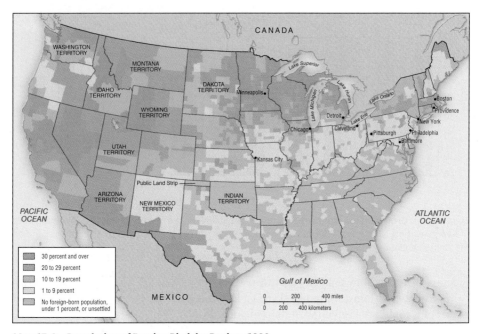

**Map 17-2   Population of Foreign Birth by Region, 1880**
*Source:* Clifford L. Lord and Elizabeth H. Lord, *Historical Atlas of the United States* (New York: Holt, 1953).

were foreign born. The typical immigrant, he warned, was not a freedom-loving Anglo-Saxon Protestant but a narrow-minded "European peasant" whose "moral and religious training has been meager or false." Immigrants brought crime to America's cities and, voting in blocs, undermined the nation's politics. "[T]here is no more serious menace to our civilization," Strong warned, "than our rabble-ruled cities."

For Strong, the problem was that immigrants were coming in such huge numbers that assimilation was becoming impossible (see Map 17–2). Worst of all—in Strong's view—the Catholic Church held millions of immigrants in its grip, filling their heads with superstition rather than "pure Christianity." Through its parochial schools, the Catholic Church was training new generations to love tyranny rather than liberty.

Strong and his readers need not have worried (and to be fair, Strong himself saw the real solution in what came to be called the Social Gospel, the active involvement of Protestants in helping those less well off than themselves). Indeed, they misread their own evidence. By cultivating the German vote or the Irish vote, for example, politicians brought immigrants into American culture. Nor were immigrants as slavishly subservient to the Catholic Church as Strong thought.

## From Immigrants to Ethnic Americans

In the middle of the nineteenth century, most immigrants came with loyalties to their regions and villages, not to a nationality. German-speaking immigrants thought of themselves primarily as Bavarian or Prussian rather than German, just as Rosa Cassettari thought of herself as Tuscanese and did not count Sicilians as Italians at all. For many Slavs, identification went no further than the parish whose church bells they heard on Sunday morning.

Regional differences faded, an ocean away from home, but they would have done so anyhow. Nationalism as a self-identifying concept was spreading throughout the Western world. It was reflected in a unifying Italy, a consolidated German Reich, the czar's "Russification" program that laid the whip on Jewish backs and made Russian, not French, the language of the St. Petersburg elite. The patriotic fervor that the Civil War unleashed in the United States, liberal revolutions did in Paris and Berlin. Immigrants brought an increasingly robust sense of their ethnic identities with them. At the same time, in the United States secular fraternal organizations and mutual aid societies, designed to help newcomers find jobs and housing, forged wider ethnic identities. In 1893, mine workers formed the Pennsylvania Slovak Catholic Union to help cover burial expenses for those killed in the mines. Most often, however, middle-class immigrants or local priests took the lead in forming fraternal organizations, which eventually counted about half of all immigrants as members.

Some immigrant businessmen led the drive toward larger ethnic definitions. Because regional loyalties among his workers hindered efficiency, Marco Fontana, who ran the Del Monte Company in California, encouraged the growth of an "Italian" identity.

## The Catholic Church and Its Limits in Immigrant Culture

The Roman Catholic Church played a complicated role in the development of ethnic immigrant cultures. Many ethnic communities collected donations to build churches to preserve their Old World traditions. But the church also eased the transition into American life. Polish churches in Chicago and German parishes in Milwaukee used their women's groups and youth clubs as mutual aid societies for newcomers.

The church sometimes unintentionally sped the development of ethnic identities. The Irish became more devout in America as they came to rely on the church for help resisting an overwhelmingly Protestant culture. Through the church, Germans also overcame their regional differences. But the more they came to equate their German identity with Catholicism, the more they resented Irish domination of the church hierarchy. German Catholics worked to establish their own churches, with sermons preached in German. By contrast, the Italians distrusted and distanced themselves from the official church. Ethnic diversity made it all the more important for Catholic leaders to find some middle ground. Bishops across North America worked on standardizing Catholic rituals and ceremonies into a uniquely American blend. They published uniform catechisms, established powerful bureaucracies, and discouraged the folk rituals that Italians, Irish, and Slavs had carried with them.

Unlike in Europe, the church had to struggle just to share in the education of immigrant children; controlling it lay wholly beyond their power. Public schools were heavily Protestant. Shifting the focus away from the classics and toward "practical" education and language training, reformers hoped to shape reliable workers and patriotic citizens. But immigrants balked at "Americanization" efforts beyond providing them with skills they could use to get ahead, and the bulwark of their resistance was the church.

During the second half of the nineteenth century, both the Catholic and Lutheran Churches established parochial school systems to give immigrant children an alternative to the biases of public education. In most states and cities, tax revenues went for public schools only, and Germans set up their own parish schools. Even so, parochial education did its part toward eventual assimilation to the New World. Schools in Irish Catholic or German Lutheran parishes fostered distinctly American ethnic identities, as well as a Catholicism and Lutheranism that diverged from Old World norms.

## Immigrant Cultures

Newcomers adjusted to American culture on their own terms. Some changed their names to English equivalents: Piccolo became Little, Wahlgren became Green, and Schmidt became Smith. Even those who did not set out to assimilate found that the longer they stayed, the more their customs diverged from those of the Old World. Irish Americans fused together songs from various parts of Ireland and added piano accompaniment. Polish immigrant bands expanded beyond the traditional violin by adding accordions, clarinets, and trumpets. Hundreds of immigrant theaters offered productions that adjusted traditional plot lines to the New World. Jewish plays told of humble peddlers who outwitted their prosperous patrons. Italian folktales celebrated the importance of the family. In these ways, distinctive ethnic identities adapted to urban and industrial America.

At a time when middle-class families had only two or three children, immigrant families remained large. At the turn of the century, Italian mothers in Buffalo, New York, had an average of 11 children. Among Polish wives, the average was closer to 8. In Pennsylvania's coal-mining district, working-class immigrant women had 45 percent more children than native-born women. They had sound economic reasons: families often needed

**Immigrants** Immigrants often crowded into "tenements," a new form of apartment building that actually improved living conditions for many of America's poor city dwellers.

children's income to get by. However, the death rate among immigrant children was also high. In 1900, one out of three Polish and Italian mothers had seen one of their children die before his or her first birthday.

## The Enemy at the Gates

Culture was contested ground, as much a part of urbanization as class conflict and political upheaval. Rural Americans were drawn by urban culture's freedom but troubled by its licentiousness. Native-born Protestants, often truly concerned with helping immigrants, were also suspicious of immigrant folkways. Victorian moralists assailed the collapse of traditional gender distinctions. All these struggles reflected the efforts of Americans to cope with dramatic social transformations. There were no clear winners—unless diversity and a wide array of choices made everyone a winner.

Big-city life stirred images of an alarming diversity: "Chinatowns" in San Francisco and Los Angeles, Polish athletics clubs and German *schutzenvereine* (shooting clubs), pushcart peddlers haggling in Yiddish, Irish Americans demanding that New York's City Hall fly the Irish flag on St. Patrick's Day, Catholics expecting a day off from school on Good Friday. Native-born Protestants fretted that "E Pluribus Unum" might no longer apply: How could we become one, out of so many?

Political opposition to immigration, known as nativism, had enjoyed a brief success in the 1850s. Even foreign-born workers resented low-paid Chinese labor, and in 1882, Congress passed the first Chinese exclusion act. Not the least of the Tammany Hall political machine's sins, in New York reformers' eyes, was how Irish it was, and how public funds endowed Catholic schools there. Especially in the Midwest, anti-Catholicism drew on Protestant nightmares of the Inquisition and beliefs that the church's leaders combined

**As the Number of Immigrants to America Swelled, So Did Opposition to Them** This 1891 cartoon blames immigration for causing a host of social and political evils.

religious intolerance with a hatred of free government. In the 1890s, the American Protective Association (APA) threw its weight behind candidates favoring Protestant interests.

As immigration increased, nativist rhetoric grew more racist and drew on the dubious sociology of Social Darwinism (see Chapter 16). The threat was no longer merely from radicals and Catholics but also from darker-skinned peoples from Italy, Russia, and eastern Europe. Experts proclaimed the inherent intellectual inferiority of such peoples, giving the imprimatur of science to the most vicious stereotypes. Italians were said to be genetically predisposed to organized violence, Jews to thievery and manipulation. Anti-immigrant societies appeared across America. Mob violence sacked Chinese neighborhoods in Los Angeles in 1871, and 11 Italians were lynched by a New Orleans mob, on charges of having murdered the police chief.

But Protestant cultural politics failed to shut out immigration from southern and eastern Europe; the United States would not even require immigrants to pass a literacy test until 1917. The APA died quickly when politicians recognized that they did better by appealing to immigrant voters. They passed resolutions favoring Irish "home rule" (rather than English occupation), denounced the Russian czar's persecution of Jews, and made Columbus Day a holiday. The real cultural fights came at the state level over issues like outlawing boxing, charging prohibitively high licenses on working-class saloons, making Jewish stores close on the Protestant Sabbath, requiring Protestant Bible reading in public schools, and forcing parochial schools to use Protestant state-mandated textbooks.

# Two Political Styles

In a multicultural America, politics did more to assimilate newcomers than to make them feel unwelcome. With only two major parties vying for power, neither could afford to alienate all immigrant groups; however, some Republicans scapegoated the Catholic and Irish ones. Each organization welcomed the foreign-born into its ranks and adjusted its policies at the state and local level to keep their loyalty.

Politics came in two flavors in the Gilded Age: the male-dominated partisanship of voters, political operatives, and officeholders; and the voluntarism of those who put cause above party, from reform societies and women's organizations to labor unions and farmers' groups. The politicians had every advantage on their side. Because the "spoils system" let them appoint every official down to janitor when they took power, they could extort a share of government employees' wages to fund a campaign. They chose the candidates and counted the returns. In close elections, they had "soap" (payoffs to voters) to buy a winning margin. Most of the newspapers framed the news in one party's way. Political organizations became more sophisticated and much more centralized. In this age, people began to speak of "bosses" and "political machines" in which, supposedly, the leader rallied his party followers like an army to carry every election and fill every office: the Democratic hordes in New York City that the Tammany Hall machine mobilized, for example. But time and again, politicians—even Tammany's—found themselves forced to accommodate outside pressures, and by the 1890s, those pressures had remade the very basis of the political game.

## The Triumph of Party Politics

Ever since Lincoln's day, most Americans had voted the straight party line every time. Political parties printed and passed out their own ballots for loyalists to drop in the right box. Nobody needed to be literate to make his choice (no state gave women the vote until Wyoming's admission in 1890). Partisans could remove candidates' names from these ballots, and organizers often bribed voters. Intimidation also played a role. In much of the South, passing out Republican ballots was nearly as fatal as yellow fever. "Resurrectionists" voted in dead men's names, "colonizers" crossed state lines to vote in crucial elections, and political agents might even march their purchased public to vote in "blocks of five," as one Indiana Republican advised in 1888. But most voters cast honest ballots and cared so strongly that if they could have voted a dozen times they would have—as, in big cities, some did!

From the 1840s through the 1860s, an average of 69 percent of those eligible voted in presidential elections. During the final quarter of the century, the average rose to 77 percent (see Figure 17–2). Southern figures lagged slightly: between 1876 and 1892, nearly two out of three southern men voted in presidential elections, compared with 82 percent of northern ones. The gap would widen as Democrats perfected the tools for keeping African Americans from casting a ballot or southern Republicans from having the least hope of a free vote and a fair count.

Newspapers played a critical role in maintaining this level of political participation. Much of the press acted as cheerleaders and opinion makers. Most papers survived with the help of party and government advertisements as well as contracts to print ballots and campaign documents. Papers slanted stories their party's way, and proudly. "Republican in everything, independent in nothing," the *Chicago Inter Ocean* boasted.

Campaign hoopla offered voters unrivaled spectacle. Political clubs and military companies paraded. Marchers rang bells, flew banners, and escorted floats with pretty girls representing Liberty, Columbia, or the various states. A good mass meeting combined barbecue, rousing oratory, band music, and fireworks. Together, they made politics America's most popular participatory sport.

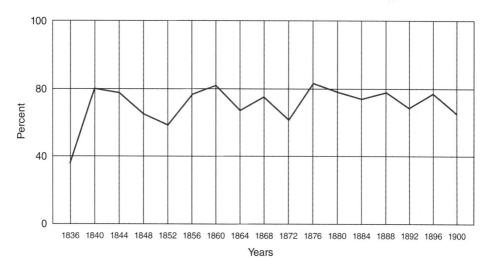

**Figure 17-2    Percent of Eligible Voters Casting Ballots** Between 1840 and 1896, a huge proportion—often 80 percent—of those eligible to vote did so in presidential elections. In the twentieth century, turnout dropped substantially.

However, politics was more than sport. Civil War veterans were reminded, "Vote as you shot!" Roused by the Union veterans' organization, the Grand Army of the Republic, and speeches that used the memory of the war to inflame sectional grievances, Union veterans typically backed the Republican Party. Black Americans also usually supported the party that had ended slavery. Confederates mostly voted Democratic. Democrats spoke for states' rights, small government, and white supremacy. In their eyes, Republicanism meant state and local laws telling people what to drink and how to use their Sundays. As Democrats saw it, "the party of moral ideas" protected the national banker, the railroad tycoon, and the upstart Negro. To Republicans, Democrats were the party of "rum, Romanism, and rebellion," of Catholics, saloon keepers, violence, and vice. They themselves spoke for the northern middle class, especially the better-educated ones. Government, local and national, had a duty to make Americans better off. As the Republicans told it, their party's symbol was the schoolhouse while the Democrats' was the whipping post of slavery. And each side knew that the republic's fate depended on its winning.

## Masculine Partisanship and Feminine Voluntarism

The public sphere of campaigns and voting was a man's world; the private sphere of home and family was widely celebrated as a woman's. In practice, though, women shared in popular politics. They decorated the meeting halls, prepared the food, watched and sometimes joined the parades. By the end of the 1880s, both parties pitched part of their appeals to wives and families. Nevertheless, politically active women opted for a different style of politics.

A stereotype that had previously limited female political activity now gave women their chance to enter public debate. Seen as the special protectors of the family's values, women found that their views on marriage, morality, and the need to protect America's children would get a respectful hearing from lawmakers. Women's supposed superior virtue gave them a privileged position in moral reform movements. These included anti-alcohol temperance societies and campaigns for laws to keep the Christian Sabbath holy—by keeping barbershops, museums, and baseball parks closed on Sunday. To protect the private sphere, many women claimed the right to enter the public one.

Women could pursue politics only as representatives of voluntary associations dedicated to specific reforms. Voluntarism mostly recruited members from the educated middle class, who brought their class biases with them.

Sometimes women's associations copied the style of partisan politics, staging mass marches and rallies. But the marching, chanting, military flavor of mass politics did not sit well with society's image of women's traditional role. So activists were likely to concentrate less on rousing voters than on educating them and lobbying elected officials. Men also joined voluntary associations, but they were dismissed by mainstream politicians as "namby-pamby, goody-goody gentlemen." In the late nineteenth century, voluntarism was associated with feminine politics, and party politics was associated with masculinity.

## The Women's Christian Temperance Union

Still, voluntarism could do wonders, and over time, the boundaries of the women's sphere became increasingly unclear. One of the most prominent female-backed political movements, the Women's Christian Temperance Union (WCTU), emerged in 1874 to battle the ravages of alcohol. Led by Frances Willard from 1879 until her death in 1898, the WCTU built itself on women's calling as protectors of the home. A decentralized structure allowed groups to tailor their activities to local needs. Women found in the WCTU a source of camaraderie as well as political activism. They made it among the largest women's political organizations in the late nineteenth century, with 150,000 adult members. (The National American Woman Suffrage Association had only 13,000.) The WCTU convened huge rallies with none of the masculine rowdiness of party conventions. Willard and her associates gave speeches, wrote articles, published books and newspaper columns on the evils of drink, organized petition campaigns, and lobbied officeholders.

Under Willard, the crusade against alcohol broadened to tackle the problems of a new industrial society. The WCTU endorsed women's suffrage and formed an alliance with the country's largest labor union. Willard supported laws restricting the workday to eight hours and prohibiting child labor. By the 1890s Willard was treating drunkenness as a public health issue rather than a personal sin, a social problem rather than an individual failure. Temperance advocates supported reforms designed to relieve poverty, improve public health, raise literacy, alleviate the conditions of workers, reform prisons, suppress public immorality, and preserve peace.

In the cities, especially up north, temperance remained a middle-class reform movement, with little appeal in immigrant neighborhoods. The WCTU's strongly evangelical Protestant identity and its association of saloons with aliens and Catholics spoke louder than its official policy of religious toleration. Irish Catholics and German Lutherans resented a campaign aimed to replace altar wine with grape juice in Christian services.

## The Critics of Popular Politics

The mix of partisanship and voluntarism made American politics more "popular" than ever before, attracting women and men, blacks and whites, immigrants and the native born, working class and middle class. But some Americans saw behind the spectacle to the games professional politicians played. After the Civil War, a small but influential group known as Liberals (and later as Mugwumps) challenged the party-run state. Alarmed at its selfishness, corruption, and incompetence, they called for government by professionals and independent agencies. Though some agreed with Charles Francis Adams that "[u]niversal suffrage can only mean in plain English the government of ignorance and vice," most believed that with a cleaner politics and "campaigns of education," the people would see where their true interests lay. A merit system must reward ability in the public service; a government-issued official (Australian) ballot distributed only at polling places must give every voter the chance to choose, in privacy, among all the possibilities. Tasks like setting a fair railroad rate or tariff duty, running a park system, or policing a great city should no longer be left to vote-getters. Education and expertise, not political pull, must drive policy.

Thanks to Liberals, the nonpartisan secret ballot was adopted everywhere. In 1881, supporters of good government organized the National Civil Service Reform League to prevent political parties from filling government positions. Victory came two years later with the establishment of a Civil Service Commission that would assign federal jobs on the basis of merit rather than patronage. Some states followed suit. But regarding the problems of rapid industrialization, Liberals' solutions fell short.

Most Americans approached their politics looking backward to the issues of the Civil War and Reconstruction. Every president but one between 1869 and 1901 had

# The "Crusade" Against Alcohol

Just before Christmas in 1873, Dr. Diocletian Lewis arrived in Hillsboro, Ohio, to speak on the evils of alcohol. He had given the speech many times before, but this time the women who came proved unusually responsive. The next morning a group of Hillsboro women met for prayer and then marched through the town urging local merchants to stop selling liquor. Inspired by their success, the women kept up the pressure through the winter of 1873–1874. Neither jail nor a rain of curses, eggs, and sour beer could dampen their spirits.

The Crusade, as it came to be called, spread quickly into 31 states and territories. Druggists and hotel keepers promised to quit selling alcohol. Nearly 70 breweries closed. The women's fervor inspired crusaders to establish a permanent organization, the WCTU. In years to come, like-minded reformers set up "temperance saloons" that served ice cream or coffee. They opened YMCA chapters with reading rooms and employment agencies to co-opt services that bars had provided. Sunday schools recruited children to break from their parents' habits and to parade, chanting, "Tremble, King Alcohol! We shall grow up!"

But Americans' drinking habits hardly changed at all. Saloons throve. People went there not just to drink but to find companionship and release. Italians went there to read newspapers in their own language. Workers went there to find jobs listings, and foremen to do hiring. Bartenders knew everybody, which was one reason that saloons were tied closely to party machines. The fastest way to empty a Chicago council meeting, residents joked, was to shout, "Your saloon's on fire!"

In the end, lasting change took political action, first by creating local or statewide majorities for prohibiting alcohol, and then by forcing the minority to give way. So across the West, states and territories

served in the Civil War (and the one exception, Grover Cleveland, sent a substitute). But many Americans also came to feel deep concerns about a society becoming more diverse, urban, and industrial. Such issues would dominate public life by the close of the century.

# Economic Issues Dominate National Politics

By the late nineteenth century, Americans were used to the idea that government should oversee the distribution of the nation's natural resources. After the Civil War, federal officials distributed public lands to homesteaders and railroads and granted rights to mining, ranching, and timber companies. During those same decades, the rise of big business led many Americans to believe that the government should regulate the outlawed the sale of alcohol, with the "dry" countryside imposing its will on the "wet" cities. Because women took leading roles in the cause, prohibitionists became the foremost advocates of woman suffrage.

For good reason, Frances Willard was the first woman honored with a statue in the US Capitol; for good reason, saloon keepers fought for a males-only suffrage to the last.

**Protestors Outside an Ohio Saloon** The WCTU's fight against alcohol could never have succeeded without the active support of many men. They felt as deep a concern at the moral and social consequences of too much tippling.

currency. Many others saw salvation in trade barriers to protect American commerce and workers from ruinous foreign competition. Because the two major parties commanded nearly even support at the national level, the outcome was that no issue could be finally settled. Shaped by clusters of special interests until they covered over 4,000 items, tariffs rose, fell, and rose again. Congresses tinkered with the currency, even while gold continued to hold a privileged place as backing for paper money. The bolder a policy initiative, the likelier it was to founder.

## Greenbacks and Greenbackers

The money question demonstrated the inability of Gilded Age politicians to act decisively on major issues. To support the Union effort during the Civil War, the US government printed $450 million worth of "greenbacks," paper bills backed by the government's word but not by the traditional reserves of specie, meaning gold or silver. When the war ended, most Americans agreed that the greenbacks should be withdrawn from circulation until any paper dollar could be exchanged for a dollar in specie at the bank. But with the onset of the 1870s, wage cuts and tight money led to a debate. Resumptionists, those who wanted to return to the gold standard, found themselves battling debtors and industrialists who thought that a shrinking money supply would worsen the economy. Greenbackers went further. They called for issuing even more greenbacks, without any requirement that precious metals back the notes up. In the middle were many Republicans and Democrats who favored inflation, but by backing dollars in silver as well as gold. The currency had been backed in this way before Congress legislated silver out of its privileged place with the "Crime of 1873," as the Coinage Act of 1873 came to be called. Later reformers blamed a bankers' plot for the change: gold, in shorter supply, meant a smaller money supply, big enough for eastern needs and small enough to make every dollar more valuable. A dollar that could buy three times as much forced a farmer to work three times as hard to pay off debts contracted before the "Crime of '73." Holders of mortgages and bonds, agrarians shouted, had legislated themselves a bonanza.

To gold's defenders, any shift to silver or paper meant national dishonor. "Honest money," they cried, was morality itself. A flood of silver into Treasury vaults meant a flood of paper, with wild speculation, inflation out of control, and debts paid off in such depreciated currency that creditors would face ruinous losses. The Greenback-Labor Party peaked in 1878, when it garnered over a million votes and elected 14 congressmen. However, as economic skies brightened, its appeal dwindled. In 1879, resumption took place, with the $300 million in circulating greenbacks made convertible into gold. Support for silver did not die away, and every time the economy contracted, calls for limited silver coinage rose across the West and South. Farmers there found loans hardest to get, except at interest rates that (to their thinking) verged on extortion. Until times improved all over, neither side could win a final victory. They could take only half steps in one direction or the other.

## Weak Presidents Oversee a Stronger Federal Government

Starting in the mid-1870s, the Democrats and Republicans had nearly equal electoral strength (see Table 17–1). From 1876 through 1896, no president took office with an overwhelming electoral mandate. The results of the 1880 election were typical of the era. Republican James A. Garfield won by a tiny margin. He received 48.5 percent of the votes, and Democrat Winfield Scott Hancock received 48.1 percent. Grover Cleveland won a plurality in 1888, but he lost the Electoral College. In both cases, the losers accused vote-buying Republicans of making the difference. But Republicans could reply that in the South, Republican votes never received a fair count. No president enjoyed a full term during which his own party controlled both houses of Congress. Reelected in 1872, Grant was the last president in the century to serve two consecutive terms.

In some cases, a president took office already discredited by the electoral process, as did Rutherford B. Hayes in 1877 (see Chapter 15). Furious that their presidential candidate, Samuel J. Tilden, had been "counted out" by three southern states juggling the returns to make Hayes the winner, Democrats threatened "His Fraudulency" with impeachment. Hayes's fellow Republicans protested his overtures to win over southern conservatives at the expense of protection for black voters, and guests resented his ban on liquor at state

**Table 17-1** Razor-Thin Electoral Margins in the Gilded Age

| Year | Popular Vote | % of Popular Vote | Electoral Vote |
| --- | --- | --- | --- |
| 1876 | 4,036,572 | 48.0 | 185 |
|      | 4,284,020 | 51.0 | 184 |
| 1880 | 4,453,295 | 48.5 | 214 |
|      | 4,414,082 | 48.1 | 155 |
|      | 308,578   | 3.4  | —   |
| 1884 | 4,879,507 | 48.5 | 219 |
|      | 4,850,293 | 48.2 | 182 |
| 1888 | 5,477,129 | 47.9 | 233 |
|      | 5,537,857 | 48.6 | 168 |

dinners. The party bosses raged at his steps toward a professional civil service. Hayes forbade his party to exact tribute from Republican officeholders. He fought Roscoe Conkling, New York's ruthless Republican boss, for control of the New York Customs House—the most lucrative source of patronage in America. When the English writer Samuel Johnson defined patriotism as the last refuge of a scoundrel, Conkling snarled, he little anticipated the possibilities of the word "reform." With cabinet officers controlling civil service appointments, improvements were patchier than Hayes would have liked, and civil service reformers were crestfallen.

By sending federal troops to suppress the 1877 railroad strike (see Chapter 16), Hayes set an important precedent for federal intervention in industrial disputes. He vetoed the Chinese immigration exclusion legislation passed by Congress in 1879. Troubled as he was by widespread suffering, Hayes had no cure for the economic slump of the 1870s. To protect the public credit, he opposed any steps to end the deflation of currency that had forced wages and prices down so sharply and brought ruin to farmers and industrial workers. In 1878, he vetoed the Bland-Allison Act, hailed as a way to modestly inflate the currency by coining silver in amounts tied to the amount of gold being minted. (It passed anyway, with little effect on the money supply.) Though prosperity returned soon after, Republicans felt as much relief to see his term end as he did. They did not protest his decision not to stand for reelection.

Economic, rather than racial, issues dominated the 1880 campaign, although Democratic state governments were rolling back the gains blacks had made during Reconstruction. Both parties relied on the patronage system too much to press civil service reform. Democrats favored lower tariffs than the Republicans, though both parties had strong protectionist blocs (supporting high tariffs to protect American producers) as well as members who favored lower tariff rates. Neither party wanted free trade; the government needed the revenue from tariff duties. So Garfield's victory in 1880 did not foreshadow any major shifts in government policy. It took a national tragedy to bring that about.

On July 2, 1881, a neglected office seeker shot the president. Garfield died two months later, and Chester A. Arthur, the product of Conkling's patronage machine, became president. The assassination made it dangerous for the new president to resist the swell of popular support for civil service reform. The Republicans in control of Congress did resist, however, and Democrats swept into office on a tide of resentment against Republican corruption and patronage. The following year Congress passed, and President Arthur signed, the landmark Pendleton Civil Service Act. The Pendleton Act prohibited patronage officeholders from contributing to the party machine that gave them their jobs. More important, the law authorized the president to establish a Civil Service Commission to administer competitive examinations for federal jobs. Before the century ended, the majority of federal jobs were removed from the reach of the patronage machines. The Pendleton Act was a major turning point in the creation of a stable and professional civil service.

Dying of a kidney disease, Arthur could not win renomination. The corrupt Republican candidate, James G. Blaine, offended Liberals and gave Democrats a chance. They nominated Governor Grover Cleveland, who was elected after a mud-spattered campaign, complete with anti-Catholic slurs and a scandal about Cleveland's illegitimate child. His slogan, "Public office is a public trust," expressed the Liberals' ideal. However, Blaine would have won had he not alienated irate prohibitionists and had the black vote not been suppressed in the South.

Cleveland was upright, downright, and forthright. He carried out the Pendleton Act to the letter, though not much beyond it, and harried railroad interests that exploited public land, including some of his campaign contributors. Special veterans' pension bills met ringing vetoes. So did a bill to relieve drought victims on the plains. Union veterans shouted when he tried to return captured Confederate flags to the southern states, and for once Cleveland backed down. Believing in a cheap, limited national government, he offered no great programs, but neither did he thwart congressional moves to broaden government's scope. He signed legislation raising the Agriculture Department to cabinet status and the Dawes Severalty Act, parceling out a fraction of the Indians' land to them as private property (see Chapter 16). Equally important, he approved the Interstate Commerce Act, creating an Interstate Commerce Commission (ICC) with power to regulate the railroads. Ever since the 1860s, states had been creating similar commissions, some of them setting railroad rates and all of them able to investigate and publicize abuses. Although weak and sometimes captive to the interests they regulated, they represented a growing state role overseeing many activities. Like the state agencies, the ICC promised more in the way of controlling rates and unfair practices than it could deliver, especially with court decisions hobbling the regulators.

With few accomplishments beyond a White House wedding to Frances Folsom and ominous political rumblings at the midterm elections, Cleveland needed a stirring issue. He found it in the high protective tariff. The tariff had done its work too well. Government surpluses had been growing, tightening credit as Treasury vaults locked away more and more of the nation's money, and tempting politicians to spend the revenue for pensions and subsidies. Critics saw the tariff as taking money from consumers' pockets to fill those of the monopolists, who, safe from foreign competition, could keep their prices high. Cautious presidents like Arthur had left the tariff alone, but Cleveland devoted his annual message to Congress in December 1887 to tariff reform. Favoring free trade would be political suicide, but adjustments downward, especially for raw materials, might make American exports more competitive and drive prices down.

It might drive wages down, too; so Republicans warned. Shouting that rate reductions would shutter factories and flood America in cheaper British goods, they had the Senate votes to block any bill that the House passed. Even one less skewed to serve southern

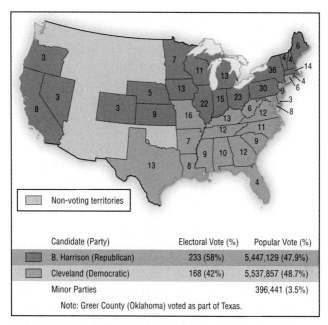

| Candidate (Party) | Electoral Vote (%) | Popular Vote (%) |
|---|---|---|
| B. Harrison (Republican) | 233 (58%) | 5,447,129 (47.9%) |
| Cleveland (Democratic) | 168 (42%) | 5,537,857 (48.7%) |
| Minor Parties | | 396,441 (3.5%) |

Note: Greer County (Oklahoma) voted as part of Texas.

**Map 17–3 The Election of 1888** With the Solid South locked up, Democrats only needed two of the biggest northern states to win. They failed this year—just barely. But for Republicans, it was a wake-up call: either they must admit enough new states to pack the Electoral College their way or they must pass a law protecting a free, fair vote down South.

interests than the House-begotten Mills bill would have had no chance. Better in pointing the way than in working out the details of an actual measure, Cleveland did not push for the Mills bill or even for a strong endorsement of tariff reform in the 1888 Democratic platform. All the same, the issue dominated the campaign, with Republicans charging that free-trading England wanted a Cleveland victory. He won a majority of the popular vote but lost the Electoral College to Benjamin Harrison (see Map 17–3).

Having won House, Senate, and presidency on a protectionist platform, Republicans had two years to deliver. Under the forceful leadership of "Czar" Thomas Brackett Reed and with influence from President Harrison, the "Billion Dollar Congress" put through the new, higher McKinley Tariff, named for Congressman William McKinley of Ohio. At the same time, Congress gave the president the authority to lower tariffs with nations opening their markets to American goods, granting him important new power in the conduct of foreign affairs. Congress also passed a lavish Dependents' Pension Law, subsidies to encourage shipping, and a silver-purchase act that westerners hoped would inject more coinage into the money supply. The Sherman Anti-Trust Act of 1890 outlawed "combinations" in "restraint of trade," though what precisely that covered was uncertain. Five years later the Supreme Court even ruled out most manufacturing. Republicans also introduced—but failed to pass—both a federal enforcement bill that might have protected black southern voters and the Blair Education Bill, which might have provided federal money to guarantee black southerners an adequate education.

## AMERICA AND THE WORLD

# Foreign Policy: The Limited Significance of Commercial Expansion

**M**oney was not everything—neither in domestic politics nor in foreign policy. In the 1860s, Secretary of State William Henry Seward shifted the emphasis of American foreign policy from the acquisition of territory to the expansion of American commerce. Working to open markets in the Americas and across the Pacific, Seward saw the nation's influence following its trade. He still dreamed of a nation extending beyond the water's edge. What he discovered was that, however adventurous American empire builders had been, the war had made them stingy in paying for new domains, either in money or in lives.

Expansionism in the Gilded Age, then, meant expanding markets, and even then not always through government action. Between 1860 and 1897, American exports tripled, surpassing $1 billion per year. In 1874, for the first time, Americans sold more than they bought. Nearly 85 percent of those exports were farm goods, but the share of industrial exports grew prodigiously as the century closed. Between 1889 and 1898, iron and steel exports jumped by 230 percent.

Mexico provided a different example of commercial expansion: investment abroad. Political instability had hindered investment, but Porfirio Díaz's seizure of power in 1876 brought decades of reassuring autocracy—at least for investors. They rushed south to build railroads, dig oil wells, sell life insurance, and invest in commercial farming. By 1910, Americans owned 43 percent of all the property in Mexico; Mexicans owned rather less.

Secretaries of state reaffirmed Seward's commitment to commercial expansion. Treaties with Japan and Korea opened new Asian markets. A treaty with King Kalakaua of Hawaii gave the islands' sugar favored treatment on the American market, prompting a huge influx into the United States (along with a backlash by sugar producers on the mainland). Worried that European nations would divert Latin American commerce from the United States, Secretary of State James G. Blaine became the champion of "reciprocity,"

Nothing offends like success. Derided as a "human iceberg," Harrison lacked the common touch. But he was not the problem. Democrats blamed higher prices on the tariff. White southerners rose in alarm at the threat of a full and fair black vote. Reformers considered the pensions a steal, and in the Midwest, Republicans ran into trouble when they tried to regulate parochial and German-language schools—the first step, immigrants cried, to foisting their own values on Catholic children. In 1890 voters put the Democrats back in control of the House of Representatives. Two years later, Cleveland won the presidency, this time with an outright majority.

breaking down American trade barriers in return for special access to foreign markets. In 1889, he convened the first Pan-American conference. Concern for access to foreign markets pushed successive administrations to assert America's exclusive right to build a canal across Central America. But that motive never stood alone—not in a world that every year Americans could see being devoured by European empires, and where Britain's and Germany's flags (and artillery) so often followed where their loans and exporters had ventured first.

Beyond that, America steered clear of foreign entanglements. In the 1880s, the United States, Germany, and England rattled sabers over disputed claims in Samoa; a riot in Valparaiso led to threats of naval force against Chile; and "jingoes," as friends of an aggressive foreign policy were called, complained about English mistreatment of Irish patriots and British claims in Latin America. If they had gotten their way, America would have gone to war to punish Spanish "insolence" in stopping American gunrunners to Cuba and to punish Canadian claims to sovereignty over the offshore fisheries and seal islands. They got no war.

Still, by the 1890s there were inklings of a new American assertiveness, mixing economic interest and a sense of America's mission to spread democracy. That showed itself most clearly in Hawaii. By 1886, two-thirds of the islands' sugar was produced on American-owned plantations. American power in Hawaii grew so great that it provoked a backlash among native Hawaiians. Queen Liliuokalani's ascension to the throne in 1891 meant trouble for sugar growers. Two years later, they helped Hawaiians dethrone the queen and appealed for the United States to annex the islands. Undeceived by white planters pretending to speak for a Polynesian people, the Cleveland administration refused, but McKinley's carried annexation through. Nobody dreamed of statehood for so dark-skinned and foreign an electorate.

Only in the late 1880s did America's hemispheric interests begin to shape military policy. In 1890, Congress approved the construction of the first modern warships, and the Supreme Court extended the president's control over "our international relations." The growing links between commercial and diplomatic interests were reviving the powers of the American presidency. But as the story of domestic politics has made clear, those links were never the whole story—nor did the scramble for markets make America forge a steel navy in a world grown different and more dangerous.

# Government Activism and Its Limits

Two themes dominate the traditional impression of late nineteenth-century political history: first, brazen corruption, and second, limited government that left the new industrial economy to develop as it pleased. The real heroes, according to this view, were those outside the party system, the Liberals and Populists, the moral crusaders and insurgents. While corruption was a problem, the foregoing view falls short as a true picture of the age.

Only by later standards was the national government limited. When peace came, Congress cut taxes, trimmed the army to a mere 25,000 men, and virtually abandoned any oceangoing navy. Yet it never returned to its proportions or role in 1861. Civilian federal employees rose from 53,000 in 1871 to 256,000 30 years later. Congress created a Department of Justice in 1870 and a Department of Agriculture in 1889. The postal service tripled in size over a quarter of a century, delivering 7 billion pieces of mail in 1900. More than a quarter of the national budget in 1900 went for veterans' pensions, awarded to over a million veterans and their dependents.

By the turn of the century, the rudiments of a modern federal government were in place. The Interstate Commerce Commission was able to compel safety machinery like automatic brakes and coupling devices on trains, but it lacked the power to enforce its own rulings, especially where unfair rates were concerned. It had to rely on courts friendly to government action protecting health, safety, and morals, but distrustful of any interference in the marketplace. Crippled by a damaging Supreme Court ruling in 1895, the weak Sherman Anti-Trust Act threatened few monopolies. In both cases, government action had not yet lived up to its potential. By comparison, state and municipal governments responded more aggressively to the problems of a transforming society.

## States Discover Activism

Americans continued to clamor for state constitutions restricting government powers. They resented tax hikes and objected to bureaucrats. They had good reasons to distrust their officials. Lobbyists swarmed the capitols. Standard Oil did everything to the Pennsylvania legislators except refine them, a critic complained. Railroad tycoons, silver-mine owners, and copper kings bought themselves Senate seats, and the insurance lobby in New York spent tens of thousands of dollars making friends in Albany every year.

But lawmakers kept doing more every year—and that, contradictory as it might seem, was what Americans also seem to have wanted. In spite of lobbyists, corporation taxes went up. So did spending. Public school systems expanded. School years lengthened. In 20 years, spending per pupil doubled, and in almost every state outside the South, attendance became compulsory. "Tramp laws" jailed jobless workers for bad reputations or "criminal idleness." Upset that customers might buy "butterine," made from animal or vegetable fats, dairy farmers got legislatures to require the new name "oleomargarine" and, in some places, unappetizing colors like pink. Unions put through laws establishing Labor Day and setting up fact-finding bureaus of labor statistics. Hundreds of laws went through to protect women workers or keep children out of the coal mines, to forbid employers from paying their workers in company-issued paper money, "scrip," and even to set up arbitration machinery, so that industrial disputes could be settled by negotiation rather than confrontation. The laws promised more than they performed: enforcement was sometimes spotty or nonexistent—much less stringent than for laws forbidding boycotting of shop owners and picketing by strikers. The courts weakened or killed many statutes, especially the ones that regulated workers' hours.

## Cities: Boss Rule and New Responsibilities

States also intervened to help govern the swelling municipalities. One reason for that was the cities' reputation for boss rule and control by party machines such as New York City's Tammany Hall. With urban services expanding so fast, the city government had more than enough jobs to do, and every job bought the machine a friend. Trading services for votes, the ward and precinct captains working for the "boss" made government matter in the most personal way. But as reformers pointed out, the money to do that had to come from somewhere: shakedowns and graft, perhaps; protection money from gamblers and saloon keepers; and forced donations from storekeepers afraid to have an enemy in city hall. Government by two-bit politicians out to line their own pockets meant rotten government, and in many ways poorer neighborhoods suffered most. Boss rule meant garbage-choked streets, tenements that were firetraps, and police and fire chiefs turning their services into party armies.

Scandals and abuses gave legislatures the excuse to shift authority away from partisan elected officials to experts and specialists on unelected boards. Mayors, city council members, and aldermen lost much of their authority over budgets, schools, health, transportation, police, and parks to commissions generally staffed by middle-class professionals. The commissioners found help among city reformers, and in many cases, the bosses did not put up much of a fight. With competing private fire companies no longer rushing to a fire and beating each other up, and with patrolmen no longer paying a kickback for their appointment and expected to take it out of saloons, prostitutes, and shopkeepers, the quality of the fire and police departments could only improve.

Bosses were never the uncrowned emperors reformers made them out to be. Nowhere, not even in Tammany's New York, did they have total power. They had to accommodate interest groups, including labor and reform organizations. That was one reason why, in the late nineteenth century, city governments provided broader social services than anywhere else and produced some of the century's great urban achievements: New York's Central Park, San Francisco's Golden Gate Park, and the Brooklyn Bridge. Chicagoans literally reversed the flow of the Chicago River.

# Challenging the New Industrial Order

In the late nineteenth century, disparate voices rose, arguing that something had gone wrong in a new, industrialized America where technology had made a few millionaires, living off the toil of unpropertied millions. Middle-class radicals argued that economic development had undermined individual liberty and equality. Yet although their attacks on capitalism were severe, their assumptions were traditional. They often worried that without substantial reforms, a discontented working class would threaten private property and social order. On the other hand, radicalized workers questioned one of the premises of producers' ideology—that American democracy was secured by a unique harmony between capital and labor. The Knights of Labor had called for a workers' party and carried their tickets in many local elections. In the mills and mines, labor agitation often became violent and was replied to with violence, as happened most notoriously in Haymarket Square in 1886. But even if the harmony of capital and labor had been destroyed, advocates of the producers' ideology continued to hold faith in political solutions to the labor problem.

## Henry George and the Limits of Producers' Ideology

Henry George was born in Philadelphia in 1839 to middle-class parents. Although his formal education was limited, George traveled and read widely. Shocked that as the nation grew richer its number of poor people grew as well, he published his conclusions in 1879 in a best-selling book called *Progress and Poverty*.

George's explanation rested on what historians have called producers' ideology. He assumed that only human labor could create legitimate wealth and that anything of value, such as food, clothing, or steel rails, came from the world's producing classes. By contrast,

**John F. Weir's 1877 Painting Forging the Shaft: A Welding Heat** This painting graphically depicts the forms of industrial wage labor that Henry George feared. He advocated tax policies that would restore a Jeffersonian economy of small, independent producers.

stockbrokers, bankers, and speculators made money from money rather than from the goods they produced. Their wealth was therefore illegitimate. From these premises, George divided the world into two classes: producers and predators.

The harmony of capital and labor was a central theme of producers' ideology. Henry George dreamed of a world in which working people owned their own farms and shops, making them both capitalists and laborers, a vision that recalled Thomas Jefferson's ideal society of small farmers and independent shopkeepers. America used to be that way, George believed, but as society "progressed," the land was monopolized by a wealthy few. Producers were forced to work for wealthy landholders. Employers invested in technology that increased the productivity of their workers but kept the added wealth for themselves. George's solution was a so-called single tax on rents. Because all wealth derived from labor applied to land, he reasoned, rents were an unnatural transfer of wealth from the producers to the landlords. To discourage the landowning class from accumulating land, George suggested prohibitively high taxes on rents and improvements on land. All other taxes would be abolished, including the tariffs protecting big business.

George was no socialist. He presented his single tax as an alternative to the dangerous radical doctrines he thought were spreading among the working class. But his work challenged the Social Darwinists' idea that those who were poor owed it to their own inadequacies, and that the rich owed their place to their superiority. George depicted a world in which the system itself had made a cluster of winners and a host of losers, and in which government policy could right the balance.

## Edward Bellamy and the Nationalist Clubs

In 1888, Edward Bellamy, a Massachusetts editor, published a best-selling critique of capitalism even more powerful than Henry George's. Bellamy's *Looking Backward* was a utopian novel set in the future, where technology had raised the standard of living for all. Industrial civilization's problems had been solved by overcoming the "excessive individualism" of Bellamy's day. Progress came, not through Social Darwinism's competition, but through its opposite: cooperation. Whereas *Progress and Poverty* proposed the restoration of the simple virtues of Jeffersonian society, *Looking Backward* imagined a high-tech future filled with consumer goods. In Bellamy's ideal world, production and consumption would no longer be subject to the whims of the market; instead, they would be harmonized by "nationalism," an obscure process of centralized planning. *Looking Backward* catered to a middle-class craving for order amid the chaos of industrial society. Decisions about what to produce were made collectively, and society as a whole owned the means of production. Whereas Henry George reasserted the values of hard work and self-restraint, Edward Bellamy embraced the modern cult of leisure and looked to the day when there would be little need for government. This vision inspired thousands of middle-class Americans to form "Bellamy Clubs" or "Nationalist Clubs," particularly in New England.

## Agrarian Revolt

The late nineteenth century was a desperate time for American farmers in the grain and cotton belts of the West and South. To compete, they had to buy costly agricultural equipment, often from manufacturers who benefited from tariff protection. Then they had to ship their goods on railroads that charged higher rates to small farmers than to big industrialists. At the market, they faced steadily declining prices.

A global economy put southern cotton in competition with cotton from India and Egypt. Western wheat competed with Russian and eastern European wheat. To keep up, farmers increasingly went into debt, and in a deflationary spiral the money they borrowed to plant their crops was worth more when it came time to pay it back, whereas their crops were worth less. The proportion of owner-occupied farms declined, and the number of tenants rose. A few years of drought meant ruin on the plains. "In God we trusted, in Kansas we busted," one departing farmer wrote on his wagon.

Scattered over large sections of the country, farmers were committed to an ideology of economic independence and cool to government intervention. The industrial transformation of the late nineteenth century taught many of them that they could no longer stand alone. One of the first attempts to organize farmers was the Patrons of Husbandry, generally called the Grange. The Grange claimed 1.5 million members by 1874. Consistent with producers' ideology, the Grange organized cooperatives to eliminate the role of merchants and creditors. By storing grain collectively, farmers held their products back from the market in the hope of gaining control over commodity prices. But inexperience made the Grange cooperatives difficult to organize and sustain. After 1875, their membership dwindled.

The National Farmers' Alliance and Industrial Union, known simply as the Farmers' Alliance, was much more effective than the Grange. Founded in Texas in 1877, the Alliance spread rapidly across the South and West. Its goal was not to restore rural Jeffersonian simplicity but to bring American farmers into the modern world of industry and prosperity. The Alliance focused above all on education, broadly conceived. That meant public schools and the spread of scientific agriculture and sound business practices. The Alliance also built its own network of newspapers and lecturers to free farmers from their isolation. For rural men and women alike, the Farmers' Alliance offered the chance to share in the progress and prosperity of American life.

At its core the Alliance was a reform organization calling for a specific set of economic policies. Above all, the farmers wanted to inflate the currency, whether by the circulation of more silver currency or of more paper currency ("greenbacks") or a combination of the two. Inspired by the successes of highly organized corporations, especially railroads, the Alliance also supported a system of cooperative "subtreasuries" that would provide low-interest loans, backed by farmers' crops, held until the best prices were available.

By the late 1880s, the Farmers' Alliance had drawn millions of members, concentrated in the southern, western, and plains states. Created at a huge meeting at Ocala, Florida, in 1890, the Ocala Platform supported a host of new policies that joined economic progress to democratic reform. The platform called for the free coinage of silver, lower tariffs, government subtreasuries, and a constitutional amendment providing for direct election of senators. Finally, the Alliance called for strict government regulation, and if necessary direct government ownership, of the railroad and telegraph industries.

The Farmers' Alliance steered clear of politics and instead judged political candidates by their support of the Ocala Platform reforms. They elected shoals of congressmen and even a few senators by cooperating with Democrats in the West and, where neither party gave satisfaction, by running independent candidates. Out of these efforts came the most significant third party of the late nineteenth century, the People's Party, otherwise known as the Populists.

### The Rise of the Populists

On February 22, 1892, a coalition of reform organizations met in St. Louis, including representatives of the Knights of Labor and the Farmers' Alliance. Together they founded the People's Party. At Omaha on July 4, they nominated General James B. Weaver of Iowa for president and drew up the Omaha Platform, demanding an inflationary currency policy and a subtreasury system. The Populists also called for a graduated income tax, direct government ownership of railroads and telegraph lines, and the confiscation of railroad land grants. But they also spoke for a government restored to the people by a

## Time Line

▼**1867**
Patrons of Husbandry (the Grange) founded

▼**1869**
Noble and Holy Order of the Knights of Labor founded

▼**1870**
Department of Justice created

▼**1872**
Grant reelected

▼**1873**
"Crusade" against alcohol begins in Hillsboro, Ohio

▼**1874**
Women's Christian Temperance Union (WCTU) is formed

▼**1876**
Rutherford B. Hayes elected president
Porfirio Díaz seizes power in Mexico

▼**1877**
Farmers' Alliance founded

▼**1878**
Bland-Allison Act

▼**1879**
Frances Willard becomes president of the WCTU
Henry George publishes *Progress and Poverty*

▼**1880**
James Garfield elected president

▼**1881**
Garfield assassinated; Chester Arthur becomes president
WCTU endorses women's suffrage

▼**1883**
Pendleton Civil Service Act

**Kansas Farm Families on the Road to a People's Party Gathering** In a state usually locked up for the GOP, the farmer's revolt revived political competition and an evangelical passion about issues absent since the Civil War.

secret ballot, popularly elected senators, and the power of voters to make laws for themselves by initiative and referendum.

Populism took in more than wheat and cotton farmers. Small ranchers joined to fight the politically privileged cattle kings. Townspeople joined to oppose the railroads. Prohibitionists,

▼**1884**
Grover Cleveland elected
    president

▼**1886**
Nationwide strike for eight-hour
    day
Riot at Haymarket Square in
    Chicago

▼**1887**
Interstate Commerce Act
Four Haymarket anarchists
    executed
Dawes Severalty Act

▼**1888**
Benjamin Harrison elected
    president
Edward Bellamy publishes
    *Looking Backward*

▼**1889**
United States convenes first Pan-
    American Conference
Department of Agriculture
    created

▼**1890**
McKinley Tariff
Sherman Anti-Trust Act

Ocala Platform

▼**1891**
Queen Liliuokalani assumes the
    Hawaiian throne

▼**1892**
Omaha Platform of the People's
    Party
Grover Cleveland reelected

▼**1893**
Queen Liliuokalani overthrown

▼**1898**
Frances Willard dies

woman suffragists, and the dwindling membership of the Knights of Labor found friends aplenty in the People's Party. Rallies took on the spirit of a revival, with speakers promising a return to the lost promise of the Revolution. In the 1892 elections, Weaver won about 1 million votes, and the Populists elected several senators, representatives, governors, and state legislators. But wage earners in the industrial North and East still held back. The Populist platform, for all its talk of the unity of the toiling masses, offered industrial workers little. They depended on the protective tariff to shield them from cheap foreign labor. Higher prices for the farmer meant price hikes in the stores, when most workers had no hope of raising their wages to keep up. They knew how paper money worked: many were paid in company-issued "scrip," redeemable only at the company store at a steep discount. Conversely, farmers who hired workers had no zeal for an eight-hour day or laws restricting child labor. Wherever the Populists were strong, mainstream parties adopted their most popular causes.

Southern Populists faced a particularly difficult challenge. To win, they needed help from the largest class of impoverished farmers, black sharecroppers. Only by downplaying racial differences could they make such a coalition work. Not all whites could overcome their prejudices. The Farmers' Alliance had always been strictly segregated, with a separate Colored Farmers' Alliance. And in fact the economic interests of the two groups were not always compatible. Black leaders appreciated the limits of any alliance with white reformers, and most black southerners kept voting Republican. Coalitions between Republicans and Populists sometimes came about. But any multiracial alliance inspired the ugliest race-baiting that Democrats could devise, to break the partners apart and restore the color line. It gave them all the excuse they needed to stuff ballot boxes, count votes creatively, and remake the laws to cut as many Populists, white and black, out of the suffrage as possible—always in the name of reform.

## Conclusion

Luna Kellie was not alone in seeing a nation on the edge of catastrophe by the early 1890s. Americans still went to the polls in record numbers, but the political system was showing serious strains. Strident voices rose, against Catholics, foreigners, Negroes, and Jews. Farmers cried out against the "money power." Bloody strikes convulsed the coalfields and Carnegie's mills. Culture wars disrupted politics in the Midwest, while southern Democrats fended off political challengers by invoking white supremacy in its rawest form. In big cities, reformers cried that boss rule had replaced government by the people. But Gilded Age politics offered more hope than it appeared. In its tumultuous variety, it showed a country bursting with reform impulses, and with the energy to regenerate a nation in crisis.

## Who, What, Where

Comstock, Anthony  528

Farmers' Alliance  526

George, Henry  549

Greenbackers  542

Hawaii  546

Kellie, Luna  526

Mugwumps  539

Nationalist Clubs  551

Omaha Platform  552

Patronage  539

Pendleton Civil Service Act  544

Political machine  535

Populism  553

Sherman Anti-Trust Act  545

Spoils system  536

Subtreasury  552

Tammany Hall  535

Temperance  538

Weaver, James B.  552

Willard, Frances  538

Women's Christian Temperance Union
(WCTU)  538

# Review Questions

1. Discuss how constructions of gender defined what men and women could do and be.

2. How did urbanization and immigration challenge cultural norms in the late nineteenth century?

3. Describe the two major "styles" of politics in the late nineteenth century.

4. Describe the changes in the roles of national, state, and local government during this period.

5. What did Henry George, Edward Bellamy, and Frances Willard have in common? What did the Farmers' Alliance stand for?

# Critical-Thinking Questions

1. Why did Victorian attitudes on gender and morality break down in this period?

2. What was the case that guardians of traditional culture made against a multicultural society?

3. Why did so many people participate in politics in the late nineteenth century? What did they expect to get out of it?

4. To what extent did the industrial revolution described in Chapter 16 affect politics and the issues politicians discussed in this period?

5. What were the major challenges to "politics as usual" in this age, and where did those challenges come from? Why did they arise, and how successful were they in remaking American society?

# Suggested Readings

Burrows, Edwin G., and Mike Wallace. *Gotham: A History of New York to 1898*. New York: Oxford University Press, 1999.

Goodwyn, Lawrence. *The Populist Moment: A Short History of the Agrarian Revolt in America*. New York: Oxford University Press, 1978.

Morgan, H. Wayne. *From Hayes to McKinley: National Party Politics, 1877–1896*. Syracuse, NY: Syracuse University Press, 1969.

**For further review materials and resource information, please visit www.oup.com/us/oakes-mcgerr**

# CHAPTER 17: THE CULTURE AND POLITICS OF INDUSTRIAL AMERICA, 1870–1892

## Primary Sources

## 17.1 *NEW YORK WORLD*, "HOW TIM GOT THE VOTES" (1892)

New York City's Tammany Hall machine was nationally infamous, but no critic could deny that the Democratic organization knew how to bring every supporter to the polls. Local election-district leaders took pride in getting a full turnout, and those with political ambitions spared no effort on Election Day. One of the hardest working politicians was "Big Tim" Sullivan, a state assemblyman and rising star in downtown Manhattan. Helped by his cousins "Big Florry" and "Boston Tim" Sullivan, he demonstrated his skills during the 1892 Cleveland-Harrison presidential election, when he set the goal of carrying every man on the voter rolls.

"Now here comes a duck," whispered Tim, to his cousin Florry, "who's been gettin' drunk on Denny Shea. Watch me fix him."

"Say, young feller," demanded Tim with a frown, surrounded by eight fierce-looking Sullivans, "how are y' goin' to vote?"

"I'm fer Cleevelan' an' th' hull ticket," replied the fellow, with apparent enthusiasm.

"You're lyin' an' y' know it," said Tim, with painful frankness. "Do y' see this paster?"

He did.

"Well, jes' take it, an' slap it on a ballot. An' I want y' to slap it on so I can hear it, too. See?"

"All right," was the reply, "but you've gotto do dis fer me. You gotta promise to look out fer me if de cops take me in fer hittin' de bowl."

The agreement was made on the spot.

This was followed by sixty Tammany ballots which were above suspicion. Then the Republican district captain cast his vote.

"That's one fer Harrison," commented Tim, sadly.

Just then a woman came up to Tim and called him aside, confidentially.

"My husband's so drunk, begorra, he can't walk," she said. "Pfhat are yez goin' to do?"

"How many times have I told that duck," said Tim indignantly, "not to getta jag until after he voted. Here, Florry, get ten cents' worth o' ammonia and straighten 'im out."

Five minutes later the fellow came, supported by two Sullivans.

"You don't needa think I've been drinkin', Mr. Sullivan," he apologized. "I was workin' all night, an' I felt so tired I fell asleep. Hooray for Tim Sullivan an' Cleveland!"

Then there was a lull of five minutes. It was broken by the Republican Supervisor.

"That's two," said Tim, mournfully, "but I'll see that duck don't sling ink around here next year. The bloke who was here last year was a square feller."

There were twenty-eight votes still out by three o'clock, and among them were several who were under suspicion.

"Go hunt up Lake," he instructed his nephew, Tim, Jr: "He's another one o' Denny Shea's gang."

When Lake came he admitted frankly that he was going to vote for Harrison, but he promised to vote for the Tammany ticket.

"Do you wantta ruin my chances to get to th' Senate?" demanded Tim. "Are you goin' to be the only man in the district who's goin' back on me? What do you think Grover Cleveland'll say to me when he sees I let Gilroy have an extra vote? You'll be wantin' a favor, but when I got to Cleveland he'll fire me out."

Much as he loved Harrison, Jake would not have Tim put on the black list if he could help it. So he voted for Cleveland.

"But don't tell Denny," he enjoined Tim.

Next the Republican poll clerk voted. How aggravating it was to see him, with his cynical smile hand over a Republican ballot!

"That duck thinks he's smart," growled Tim, "but I know how to get even with 'im."

There were still half a dozen Baxter street clothiers who had not voted. Tim, Jr., reported they were busy selling clothing. Tim concluded to go around himself.

"Now here, Jake," he said to Jacob Harris, who keeps a store near Walker Street, "you gotta go out an' vote now."

"How can I, Mr. Sullivan," was protested. "I'm waitin' on a customer."

"Yes," responded Dry Dollar, "an' you've been waitin' on him fer two hours. How much are yer dickering over?"

"The gentleman wants it for two dollars less," was explained.

"Well, hully gee!" ejaculated Tim, "is that all? I'll pay the difference."

The Republican inspector had not yet voted. Tim looked in at him wistfully. Then he whistled to him and made a frantic endeavor to coax him out into the street, but the inspector was not in the market. A few minutes later he cast his ballot for Harrison and the agony was over.

"Now look here, Tim," consoled Florry, "wot's the use o' gettin' huffy over four votes? Those ducks couldn't get out of it. They had to vote for Harrison."

"I know," admitted Tim; "but it's pretty tough to come so near carryin' th' distric' unanimous, an' have four stubborn ducks hold out like that."

Judge Patrick Divver, when seen by a *World* reporter, said:

"Yes, Tim did first rate. He did all that could be expected of him. That boy's a good politician, and when he gets older he'll be a wonder."

*Source:* "How Tim Got the Votes," *New York World*, November 10, 1892.

# 17.2 *TAMMANY TIMES*, "AND REFORM MOVES ON" (1895)

In 1894, New York City reformers drove Tammany Hall from power and installed a Republican coalition. It only lasted a single term. When the new police commissioner, Theodore Roosevelt, began enforcing the state law forbidding the sale of alcohol on Sunday, his actions split working-class and immigrant voters from middle-class and native-born ones. The man with the "growler"—the bucket in which workers collected beer to consume on the job—narrowed all reform down to the narrow-mindedness of the prohibitionists. Tammany Hall had a winning issue and knew it, as these lyrics show, set to the tune of a popular favorite, "And the Band Played On."

New York on Sunday is awfully dry,
And Reform moves on,
Can't open the side-door, police standing by,
And Reform moves on.
The growler gets rusty, our throats are so dusty—
Oh dear, when will this end?—
When Roosevelt's dead or tucked snugly in bed,
As Reform moves on.
One Sunday our Roosevelt rode all over town,
When Reform moved on,

For side doors wide open he looked up and down,
As Reform moved on.
They say he was looking to have them closed up, but I'll give you a tip,
He simply was dry and he'd drink on the sly,
As Reform moves on.

Source: *Tammany Times*, November 18, 1895.

---

# 17.3 HENRY GEORGE, EXCERPTS FROM "THAT WE MIGHT ALL BE RICH" (1883)

As the author of *Progress and Poverty*, Henry George became a celebrated authority on class conflict and social injustice in industrializing America. Socialists agreed with his diagnosis of society, though not with his solutions, among which were a single tax falling on landed property and an end to protective tariffs. Nearly winning the New York City mayoral race in 1886 and at the forefront of efforts to create a workers' party, George campaigned on distrust of government and detestation of privilege. Many of his essays were gathered together in the book *Social Problems*, published in 1883.

---

The terms rich and poor are of course frequently used in a relative sense. Among Irish peasants, kept on the verge of starvation by the tribute wrung from them to maintain the luxury of absentee landlords in London or Paris, "the woman of three cows" will be looked on as rich, while in the society of millionaires a man with only $500,000 will be regarded as poor. Now, we cannot, of course, all be rich in the sense of having more than others; but when people say, as they so often do, that we cannot all be rich, or when they say that we must always have the poor with us, they do not use the words in this comparative sense. They mean by the rich those who have enough, or more than enough, wealth to gratify all reasonable wants, and by the poor those who have not.

Now, using the words in this sense, I join issue with those who say that we cannot all be rich; with those who declare that in human society the poor must always exist. I do not, of course, mean that we all might have an array of servants; that we all might outshine each other in dress, in equipage, in the lavishness of our balls or dinners, in the magnificence of our houses. That would be a contradiction in terms. What I mean is, that we all might have leisure, comfort and abundance, not merely of the necessaries, but even of what are now esteemed the elegancies and luxuries of life. I do not mean to say that absolute equality could be had, or would be desirable. I do not mean to say that we could all have, or would want, the same quantity of all the different forms of wealth. But I do mean to say that we might all have enough wealth to satisfy reasonable desires; that we might all have so much of the material things we now struggle for, that no one would want to rob or swindle his neighbor; that no one would worry all day, or lie awake at nights, fearing he might be brought to poverty, or thinking how he might acquire wealth.

Does this seem an utopian dream? What would people of fifty years ago have thought of one who would have told them that it was possible to sew by steam-power; to cross the Atlantic in six days, or the continent in three; to have a message sent from London at noon delivered in Boston three hours before noon; to hear in New York the voice of a man talking in Chicago?

Did you ever see a pail of swill given to a pen of hungry hogs? That is human society as it is.

Did you ever see a company of well-bred men and women sitting down to a good dinner, without scrambling, or jostling, or gluttony, each, knowing that his own appetite will be satisfied, deferring to and helping the others? That is human society as it might be.

"Devil catch the hindmost" is the motto of our so-called civilized society today. We learn early to "take care of No. 1," lest No.1 should suffer; we learn early to grasp from others that we may not want ourselves. The fear of poverty makes us admire great wealth; and so habits of greed are formed, and we behold the pitiable spectacle of men who have already more than they can by any possibility use, toiling, striving, grasping to add to their store up to the very verge of the grave—that grave which, whatever else it may mean, does certainly mean the parting with all earthly possessions however great they be.

In vain, in gorgeous churches, on the appointed Sunday, is the parable of Dives and Lazarus read. What can it mean in churches where Dives would be welcomed and Lazarus shown the door? In vain may the preacher preach of the vanity of riches, while poverty engulfs the hindmost. But the mad struggle would cease when the fear of poverty had vanished. Then, and not till then, will a truly Christian civilization become possible.

And may not this be?

. . .

The passenger who leaves New York on a trans-Atlantic steamer does not fear that the provisions will give out. The men who run these steamers do not send them to sea without provisions enough for all they carry. Did He who made this whirling planet for our sojourn lack the forethought of man? Not so. In soil and sunshine, in vegetable and animal life, in veins of minerals, and in pulsing forces which we are only beginning to use, are capabilities which we cannot exhaust—materials and powers from which human effort, guided by intelligence, may gratify every material want of every human creature. There is in nature no reason for poverty—not even for the poverty of the crippled or the decrepit. For man is by nature a social animal, and the family affections and the social sympathies would, where chronic poverty did not distort and embrute, amply provide for those who could not provide for themselves.

But if we will not use the intelligence with which we have been gifted to adapt social organization to natural laws—if we allow dogs in the manger to monopolize what they cannot use; if we allow strength and cunning to rob honest labor, we must have chronic poverty, and all the social evils it inevitably brings. Under such conditions there would be poverty in paradise.

"The poor ye have always with you." If ever a scripture has been wrested to the devil's service, this is that scripture. How often have these words been distorted from their obvious meaning to soothe conscience into acquiescence in human misery and degradation—to bolster that blasphemy, the very negation and denial of Christ's teachings, that the All-Wise and Most Merciful, the Infinite Father, has decreed that so many of his creatures must be poor in order that others of his creatures to whom he wills the good things of life should enjoy the pleasure and virtue of doling out alms! "The poor ye have always with you," said Christ; but all his teachings supply the limitation, "until the coming of the Kingdom." In that kingdom of God on earth, that kingdom of justice and love for which he taught his followers to strive and pray, there will be no poor. But though the faith and the hope and the striving for this kingdom are of the very essence of Christ's teaching, the staunchest disbelievers and revilers of its possibility are found among those who call themselves Christians. Queer ideas of the Divinity have some of these Christians who hold themselves orthodox and contribute to the conversion of the heathen. A very rich orthodox Christian said to a newspaper reporter, a while ago, on the completion of a large work out of which he is said to have made millions: "We have been peculiarly favored by Divine Providence; iron never was so cheap before, and labor has been a drug in the market."

. . .

The wealth-producing powers that would be evoked in a social state based on justice, where wealth went to the producers of wealth, and the banishment of poverty had banished the fear and greed and lusts that spring from it, we now can only faintly imagine. Wonderful as have been the discoveries and inventions of this century, it is evident that we have only begun to grasp that dominion which it is given to mind to obtain over matter. Discovery and invention are born of leisure, of material comfort, of freedom. These secured to all, and who shall say to what command over nature man may not attain?

It is not necessary that any one should be condemned to monotonous toil; it is not necessary that any one should lack the wealth and the leisure which permit the development of the faculties that raise man above the animal. Mind, not muscle, is the motor of progress, the force which compels nature and produces wealth. In turning men into machines we are wasting the highest powers. Already in our society there is a favored class who need take no thought for the morrow—what they shall eat, or what they shall drink, or wherewithal they shall be clothed. And may it not be that Christ was more than a dreamer when he told his disciples that in that kingdom of justice for which he taught them to work and pray this might be the condition of all?

*Source:*   Henry George, "That We All Might Be Rich," from *Social Problems* (Chicago: 1883) quoted in William Benton, publ., *The Annals of America. Volume 10, 1866–1883: Reconstruction and Industrialization* (Chicago: Encyclopedia Britannica, Inc., 1968), pp. 601–606.

## 17.4 JACOB RIIS, EXCERPT FROM *HOW THE OTHER HALF LIVES* (1890) AND VISUAL DOCUMENT: JACOB RIIS, "BANDITS' ROOST" (1887)

In 1890, the Danish American police reporter Jacob Riis published a book about the slums of New York City entitled *How the Other Half Lives*. Its stark text, excerpted in the following, was accompanied by Riis's haunting photographs. In addition to being a pioneer in photojournalism, Riis contributed to the record that reformers used to advocate for public health programs, government policing of housing, and other public measures to relieve poverty and its accompanying ills.

The "Rock of Ages" is the name over the door of a low saloon that blocks the entrance to another alley, if possible more forlorn and dreary than the rest, as we pass out of the Alderman's court. It sounds like a jeer from the days, happily past, when the "wickedest man in New York" lived around the corner a little way and boasted of his title. One cannot take many steps in Cherry Street without encountering some relic of past or present prominence in the ways of crime, scarce one that does not turn up specimen bricks of the coming thief. The Cherry Street tough is all-pervading. Ask Superintendent Murray, who, as captain of the Oak Street squad, in seven months secured convictions for theft, robbery, and murder aggregating no less than five hundred and thirty years of penal servitude, and he will tell you his opinion that the Fourth Ward, even in the last twenty years, has turned out more criminals than all the rest of the city together.

But though the "Swamp Angels" have gone to their reward, their successors carry on business at the old stand as successfully, if not as boldly. There goes one who was once a shining light in thiefdom. He has reformed since, they say. The policeman on the corner, who is addicted to a professional unbelief in reform of any kind, will tell you that while on the Island once he sailed away on a shutter, paddling along until he was picked up in Hell Gate by a schooner's crew, whom he persuaded that he was a fanatic performing some sort of religious penance by his singular expedition.

. . . .

We have crossed the boundary of the Seventh Ward. Penitentiary Row, suggestive name for a block of Cherry Street tenements, is behind us. Within recent days it has become peopled wholly with Hebrews, the overflow from Jewtown adjoining, pedlars and tailors, all of them. It is odd to read this legend from other days over the door: "No pedlars allowed in this house." These thrifty people are not only crowding into the tenements of this once exclusive district—they are buying them. The Jew runs to real estate as soon as he can save up enough for a deposit to clinch the bargain. As fast as the old houses are torn down, towering structures go up in their place, and

Jacob Riis's powerful exposures of the links between poverty, grime, crime, and exploitation were strengthened by the pictures he took in the slums of downtown New York. Danish-born, the reformer was one of the pioneers in what came to be called photojournalism. *Source:* Photograph by Jacob Riis.

Hebrews are found to be the builders. Here is a whole alley nicknamed after the intruder, Jews' Alley. But abuse and ridicule are not weapons to fight the Israelite with. He pockets them quietly with the rent and bides his time. He knows from experience, both sweet and bitter, that all things come to those who wait, including the houses and lands of their persecutors.

Here comes a pleasure party, as gay as any on the avenue, though the carry-all is an ash-cart. The father is the driver and he has taken his brown-legged boy for a ride. How proud and happy they both look up there on their perch! The queer old building they have halted in front of is "The Ship," famous for fifty years as a ramshackle tenement filled with the oddest crowd. No one knows why it is called "The Ship," though there is a tradition that once the river came clear up here to Hamilton Street, and boats were moored along-side it. More likely it is because it is as bewildering inside as a crazy old ship, with its ups and downs of ladders parading as stairs, and its unexpected pitfalls. But Hamilton Street, like Water Street, is not what it was. The missions drove from the latter the worst of its dives. A sailors' mission has lately made its appearance in Hamilton Street, but there are no dives there, nothing worse than the ubiquitous saloon and tough tenements.

Enough of them everywhere. Suppose we look into one? No. — Cherry Street. Be a little careful, please! The hall is dark and you might stumble over the children pitching pennies back there. Not that it would hurt them; kicks and cuffs are their daily diet. They have little else. Here where the hall turns and dives into utter darkness is a step, and another, another. A flight of stairs. You can feel your way, if you cannot see it. Close? Yes! What would you have? All the fresh air that ever enters these stairs comes from the hall-door that is forever slamming, and from the windows of dark bedrooms that in turn receive from the stairs their sole supply of the elements God meant to be free, but man deals out with such niggardly hand. That was a woman filling her pail by the hydrant you just bumped against. The sinks are in the hallway, that all the tenants may have access—and all be poisoned alike by their summer stenches. Hear the pump squeak! It is the lullaby of tenement-house babes. In summer, when a thousand thirsty throats pant for a cooling drink in this block, it is worked in vain. But the saloon, whose open door you passed in the hall, is always there. The smell of it has followed you up. Here is a door. Listen! That short hacking cough, that tiny, helpless wail—what do they mean? They mean that the soiled bow of white you saw on the door downstairs will have another story to tell—Oh! a sadly familiar story—before the day is at an end. The child is dying with measles. With half a chance it might have lived; but it had none. That dark bedroom killed it.

It was took all of a suddint," says the mother, smoothing the throbbing little body with trembling hands. There is no unkindness in the rough voice of the man in the jumper, who sits by the window grimly smoking a clay pipe, with the little life ebbing out in his sight, bitter as his words sound: "Hush, Mary! If we cannot keep the baby, need we complain—such as we?"

Such as we! What if the words ring in your ears as we grope our way up the stairs and down from floor to floor, listening to the sounds behind the closed doors—some of quarrelling, some of coarse songs, more of profanity. They are true. When the summer heats come with their suffering they have meaning more terrible than words can tell. Come over here. Step carefully over this baby—it is a baby, spite of its rags and dirt—under these iron bridges called fire-escapes, but loaded down, despite the incessant watchfulness of the firemen, with broken household goods, with wash-tubs and barrels, over which no man could climb from a fire. This gap between dingy brick-walls is the yard. That strip of smoke-colored sky up there is the heaven of these people. Do you wonder the name does not attract them to the churches? That baby's parents live in the rear tenement here. She is at least as clean as the steps we are now climbing. There are plenty of houses with half a hundred such in. The tenement is much like the one in front we just left, only fouler, closer, darker—we will not say more cheerless. The word is a mockery. A hundred thousand people lived in rear tenements in New York last year. Here is a room neater than the rest. The woman, a stout matron with hard lines of care in her face, is at the wash-tub. "I try to keep the childer clean," she says, apologetically, but with a hopeless glance around. The spice of hot soap-suds is added to the air already tainted with the smell of boiling cabbage, of rags and uncleanliness all about. It makes an overpowering compound. It is Thursday, but patched linen is hung upon the pulley-line from the window. There is no Monday cleaning in the tenements. It is washday all the week round, for a change of clothing is scarce among the poor. They are poverty's honest badge, these perennial lines of rags hung out to dry, those that are not the washerwoman's professional shingle. The true line to be drawn between pauperism and honest poverty is the clothes-line. With it begins the effort to be clean that is the first and the best evidence of a desire to be honest.

What sort of an answer, think you, would come from these tenements to the question "Is life worth living?" were they heard at all in the discussion?

Source:  Jacob A. Riis, *How the Other Half Lives: Studies Among the Tenements of New York* (New York: Charles Scribner's Sons, 1890), pp. 39–47.

# 17.5 VISUAL DOCUMENTS: "GIFT FOR THE GRANGERS" (1873) AND THE JORNS FAMILY OF DRY VALLEY, CUSTER COUNTY, NEBRASKA (1886)

The image of the self-sufficient "yeoman farmer" in close communion with nature always had been more fantasy than real; but on the bare prairies, where it took a family working full time just to keep body and soul together, the harsh reality made the old myths feel like bitter mockery. These contrasting documents depict two versions of farm life: the ideal and the real.

Source:   "Gift for the Grangers," J. Hale Powers & Co. Fraternity & Fine Art Publishers, Cincinnati; Strobridge & Co. Lith.

Source:   Photograph by Solomon D. Butcher, Library of Congress American Memory Historical Collections.

# Industry and Empire

## 1890–1900

## COMMON THREADS

How did industrial ideals of efficiency and organization change the practice of democracy in America during the early 1900s?

Did the choices Americans made about how to run their economy set the United States on a course for overseas conflict?

What did it mean to be modern? How did the pace of technological change affect Americans' outlook?

## OUTLINE

**AMERICAN PORTRAIT: J. P. Morgan**

The Crisis of the 1890s
  Hard Times and Demands for Help
  The Overseas Frontier
  The Drive for Efficiency
  The Struggle Between Management and Labor
  Corporate Consolidation

A Modern Economy
  Currency: Gold Versus Silver
  The Cross of Gold
  The Battle of the Standards

The Retreat from Politics
  The Lure of the Cities

**AMERICAN LANDSCAPE: Galveston, Texas, 1900**

  Inventing Jim Crow
  The Atlanta Compromise
  Disfranchisement and the Decline of Popular Politics

**STRUGGLES FOR DEMOCRACY: The Wilmington Race Riot**

  Organized Labor Retreats from Politics

American Diplomacy Enters the Modern World
  Sea Power and the Imperial Urge
  The Scramble for Empire
  War with Spain
  The Anti-Imperialists
  The Philippine-American War
  The Open Door

Conclusion

< **The Rough Riders**

## AMERICAN PORTRAIT

# J. P. Morgan

**I**t was a short distance from the Arlington Hotel to the White House, and although it was icy and dark, J. Pierpont Morgan chose to walk. He pulled his scarf up around a scowling face known to millions of newspaper readers. He had not wanted to come to Washington. There were "large interests" that depended on keeping the currency of the United States sound, he told a Treasury official, and those interests were now in jeopardy. The commander in chief of the nation's bankers was going to meet the president to keep the United States from going bankrupt.

The events leading up to this meeting stretched back five years to 1890, when business failures toppled London's Baring Brothers investment house and triggered a collapse in European stock prices. Depression spread through Britain, Germany, and France. Anxious European investors began selling off their large American holdings. In early 1893, the panic reached the United States. The Philadelphia and Reading Railroad folded in February. Fourteen thousand businesses soon followed, along with more than 600 banks.

Summer brought more bad news from abroad. The government of India stopped minting silver, causing US silver dollars to lose one-sixth of their value. Wall Street went into another tailspin. In New York, 55,000 men, women, and girls in the clothing industry were thrown out of work. Banks refused to cash checks, and coins vanished from circulation. Tens of thousands of homeless poor people filled the roads. Breadlines formed. "The world surely cannot remain as mad as it is," the historian Henry Adams observed.

For Grover Cleveland the madness was only starting. The anger of workers and farmers, simmering for decades, was boiling over. The president pledged to keep the dollar on the gold standard, but it was not enough. A wave of strikes swept the country. Unemployed workers battled police on the Capitol grounds. By January 1895 so many panicky investors were cashing government bonds that the Treasury's gold reserve was half gone, and it looked as if the remainder might last only two weeks. Reluctantly, Cleveland agreed to open negotiations with Morgan.

Admired and reviled, Morgan was known as the leading financial manipulator of the late nineteenth century. Born to wealth in Hartford, Connecticut, he had been a Wall Street fixture since before the Civil War. Like two of his contemporaries, steelmaker Andrew Carnegie and oil magnate John D. Rockefeller, Morgan's skill lay in organization. He restructured railroads, rooting out corruption, waste, and competition and driving down wages. Instead of taking risks, he eliminated them. He convinced leaders of warring firms to strike bargains and share the profits. Cleveland was about to place the Treasury in this man's hands.

The president opened the meeting by suggesting that things might not be so bad; a new bond issue might stabilize the dollar. No, Morgan replied flatly, the run on gold would continue until European investors regained confidence. If the president agreed, Morgan would arrange a private loan and personally guarantee the solvency of the US Treasury. After a stunned silence, the two men shook hands. News of the deal instantly calmed the bond markets. The crisis was over. The *New York Sun* reported that the deal "revived a confidence in the wealth and resources of this country," but Populist newspapers denounced it as a conspiracy and a "great bunco game."

Culminating two decades of turbulence, the Panic of 1893 permanently transformed the American political economy. Businessmen such as Morgan created even larger corporate combinations and placed them under professional managers. They used technology and "scientific management" to control the workplace and push laborers to work faster and harder. Workers resisted, and the 1890s saw brutal clashes between capital and labor. Looking for jobs and schools, country people moved to the city and found both promise and danger. Social mobility among African Americans aroused fears in whites, and southerners created a system of formal segregation, enforced by law and terror. Amid growing violence, industrial workers, Native Americans, and African Americans debated how best to deal with the overwhelming forces ranged against them.

The 1890s were also a turning point in American political history. After the 1896 election, many Americans walked away from the electoral process. Others were removed from the voter rolls through a process known as "disfranchisement." African American leaders and union organizers urged their followers to turn away from politics in favor of "bread-and-butter" economic issues. The masculine, public spectacle of nineteenth-century politics with its parades and flag raisings died out. Patriotism, once synonymous with partisanship, now stood for America's global military and economic ambitions. Civic events featured army bands and cannon salutes. Newspapers conjured up foreign threats. As Americans became more conscious of their military power, they watched the horizon for threats to their well-being.

Americans began to feel that their economy's links to the world—and the changes wrought by manufacturing and rapid communications—separated their times from all that had happened before. Morgan's rescue required transactions on two continents, instantaneously coordinated by telegraph. The speed of industry, trade, and information and the way carbon technologies spanned distance and time created a sense that the environment and the future could be controlled. Many felt that those who possessed this newfound control—citizens of modern countries—stood apart from those in other lands whose lives were not guided by science and information.

Between 1890 and 1900 Americans made their country recognizably modern. Those with the means to do so enlarged and refashioned many aspects of work and daily life. Financiers and giant corporations assumed control of the economy. Huge cities grew. The significance of voting declined, and a decade that opened with a global economic catastrophe ended with a dramatic display of the global reach of US power.

# The Crisis of the 1890s

Financial convulsions, strikes, and the powerlessness of government against wealth rudely reminded Americans of how much their country had changed since the Civil War. When Illinois sent Abraham Lincoln to Congress, Chicago's population was less than 5,000; in 1890, it exceeded 1 million. Gone was the America of myth and memory, in which class tensions were slight and upward (or at least westward) and mobility seemed easy. Many Americans foresaw the collapse of civilization. Others, however, felt that the United States was passing into a new phase of history that would lead to still greater trials and achievements.

## Hard Times and Demands for Help

Chicago in 1893 captured the hopes and fears of the new age. To celebrate the 400th anniversary of Columbus's discovery of America, the city staged the World's Columbian Exposition, transforming a lakefront bog into a gleaming vision of the past and the future. Just outside the exposition's gates was the city of the present. In December 1893, Chicago had 75,000 unemployed, and the head of a local relief committee declared that "famine is in our midst." In the nation's second-largest city, thousands lived in shacks or high-rise tenements with only a single bathroom on each densely packed floor. Jobs were scarce, and when men gathered at the exposition's gates to beg for work, the police drove them away.

As the depression deepened, the Cleveland administration ordered troops to guard Treasury branches in New York and Chicago. Jobless people banded together into "industrial armies," many with decidedly revolutionary aims. Hundreds heeded the call of Jacob Coxey, an Ohio landowner and Populist. In 1894, Coxey urged the unemployed to march on Washington and demand free silver and a public road-building program that would hire a half-million workers. When Coxey set out with 100 followers, reporters predicted the ragged band would disintegrate as soon as food ran out, but well-wishers turned out by the thousands to greet the Coxeyites with supplies for the trip.

Industrial armies set out from Boston, St. Louis, Chicago, Portland, Seattle, and Los Angeles. When Coxey arrived in Washington on May 1 with 500 marchers, Cleveland put the US Army on alert. The march ended ignominiously. In front of the Capitol, police arrested Coxey, and his disillusioned army dispersed. Still, no one could deny that something was seriously wrong and that, as Ray Stannard Baker, a reporter for the *Chicago Record*, noted, "the conditions in the country warranted some such explosion."

## The Overseas Frontier

At noon on September 16, 1893, thousands of settlers massed along the borders of the Cherokee Strip, a 6-million-acre tract in northwestern Oklahoma. In the next six hours the last great land rush came to an end, and the line of settlement long marked on census maps ceased to exist.

Frederick Jackson Turner, a historian at the University of Wisconsin, described the implications of this event. Steady westward movement had placed Americans in "touch with the simplicity of primitive life," he explained, and helped renew the process of social development. The frontier furnished "the forces dominating the American character," and without its rejuvenating influence, democracy itself might be in danger. Turner's thesis resonated with Americans' fears that modernity had robbed their country of its unique strengths and that the end of free lands would put free institutions at risk. "There is no unexplored part of the world left suitable for men to inhabit," Populist writer William "Coin" Harvey claimed.

That assertion turned out to be premature. More homesteaders claimed more western lands after 1890 than before, and well into the next century new "resource frontiers"— oil fields, timber ranges, Alaskan ore strikes—were explored. Irrigation technology and markets for new crops created a boom for dry-land farmers. Nonetheless, the upheavals of the 1890s seemed to confirm Turner's contention that new frontiers lay overseas.

Whereas farmers had always needed to sell a large portion of their output abroad, until the 1890s the market for manufactured goods was almost exclusively domestic. As the volume of manufactured goods increased, the composition of exports changed. Oil, steel, textiles, typewriters, and sewing machines made up a larger portion of overseas trade. Americans still bought nine-tenths of domestic manufactures, but by 1898 the extra tenth was worth more than $1 billion (see Figure 18–1).

As American firms entered foreign markets, they discovered that other nations and empires also used restrictive tariffs to guard their markets and promote domestic manufacturing. Government and business leaders saw that the United States might have to use political or military leverage to open foreign markets to gain a larger share of world trade. Their social Darwinist view of the world—as a jungle in which only the fittest nations would survive—justified the global competition for trade and economic survival.

Recognizing that a strong navy could extend America's economic reach, Congress authorized the construction of three large battleships in 1890. Four years later, an official commission investigated the feasibility of a canal across Central America. A newly organized National Association of Manufacturers urged the government to open foreign markets. The administration created a Bureau of Foreign Commerce and urged US consuls to seize opportunities to extend sales of American industrial products abroad.

Congress also knew that tariff rates could influence the expansion of trade. Before 1890, taxes on imports had been set high to raise revenue and to help domestic manufacturers by making foreign goods unaffordable. The Harrison-McKinley Tariff of 1890 did something different. It allowed the president to use the tariff to punish countries that closed their markets to US goods or to reward them for lifting customs barriers. This "bargaining tariff" used the weight of the US economy to open markets around the world.

The United States began reorganizing to compete in a global marketplace. The struggle required the executive branch to enlarge the military and take on additional authority. It also meant that domestic industries had to produce higher quality goods at reduced cost to match those from Germany or Japan. Employers and workers had to gear up for the global contest for profits.

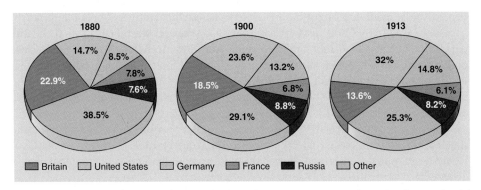

**Figure 18-1   Relative Shares of World Manufacturing** The United States was a significant industrial power by 1880, and by the turn of the century it moved into a position of dominance.

## The Drive for Efficiency

In mines, factories, and mills, production relied on the knowledge of skilled workers. Laborers used their knowledge to set work routines, assure their own safety, and bargain with managers who wanted to change the nature of work. As profits stagnated and competition intensified, employers tried to prevent labor from sharing control over production. Employers relied on three allies: technology, scientific management, and federal power. Workers resisted, organizing themselves and enlisting the support of their communities.

Advances in management techniques enabled employers to dictate new methods. Frederick Winslow Taylor, the first "efficiency expert," reduced each occupation to a series of simple, precise movements that could be easily taught and endlessly repeated. To manage time and motion scientifically, Taylor explained, employers should convert traditional workplace skills and knowledge into "rules, laws, and formulae."

Taylor's stopwatch studies determined everything from how much pig iron a man should load into a boxcar in a day (75 tons) to how he should be paid (3.75 cents per ton). Even office work could be separated into simple, unvaried tasks. "Taylorism" created a new layer of college-educated "middle managers" who supervised production in offices and factories.

Although Taylorism accelerated production, it also increased absenteeism and worker dissatisfaction. Another new technique, "personnel management," promised to solve this problem with tests to select suitable employees, team sports to ward off boredom, and social workers to regulate the activities of workers at home.

As the nineteenth century ended, management was establishing a monopoly on expertise and using it to set the rhythms of work and play, but workers did not easily relinquish control. In the 1890s, the labor struggle entered a new phase. New unions confronted corporations in bloody struggles that forced the federal government to decide whether communities or property had more rights. Skilled workers rallied the labor movement to the cause of retaining control of the conditions of work.

## The Struggle Between Management and Labor

To accelerate production, employers aimed to seize full control over the workplace. They had private detective agencies, the courts, and federal troops on their side and were ready to act. In Pennsylvania and Chicago, this antagonism led to bloody confrontations.

The most modern steelworks in the world, Andrew Carnegie's mill at Homestead, Pennsylvania, made armor plating for American warships and steel rails for shipment abroad. In June 1892, Carnegie's partner, Henry Clay Frick, broke off talks with the plant's American Federation of Labor–affiliated union and announced that the plant would close on July 2 and reopen a week later with a nonunion workforce. The union contended that Frick's actions were an assault on the community, and the town agreed. On the morning of July 6, townspeople equipped with a cannon confronted 300 armed company guards and forced them to surrender.

The victory was short-lived. A week later the governor of Pennsylvania sent in the state militia, and under martial law strikebreakers reignited the furnaces. The battle at Homestead broke the union and showed that corporations, backed by government, would defend their prerogatives at any cost.

The Pullman strike, centered in Chicago, paralyzed the railroads for two weeks in the summer of 1894. It pitted the American Railway Union (ARU) against 24 railroads and

**Homestead Strike** When Carnegie Steel locked out all 3,800 employees of the Homestead Steel Works, local citizens and police battled with Carnegie guards for control of the plant. They believed that as producers they had a right to work and profit from their labor. Carnegie believed that he had a right to hire and fire whom he pleased.

the powerful Pullman Company over the company's decision to cut pay by 30 percent, an action taken in response to the economic crisis of 1893. Eugene V. Debs, the charismatic president of the ARU, urged strikers to obey the law, avoid violence, and respect strike-breakers. When Cleveland sent in the army over the governor's protests, enraged crowds blocked tracks and burned railroad cars. Police arrested hundreds of strikers. Debs went to jail for six months and came out a socialist. Pullman and Homestead showed that the law was now on the side of the proprietors.

Newspapers, magazines, and novels portrayed Pullman and Homestead as two more battles in an unending war against the savage opponents of progress, with the forces of government rescuing civilization from the unions.

The business elite's cultural influence allowed it to define the terms of this contest, to label its enemies as enemies of progress. Workers did not object to efficiency or modernization, but they wanted a share of its benefits and some control over the process of change. With state and corporate power stacked against them, their goals appeared beyond reach.

Just as the massacre at Wounded Knee in 1890 had ended the armed resistance of Native Americans, the violence at Homestead and Chicago marked a new phase in the struggle of industrial workers.

## Corporate Consolidation

In a wave of mergers between 1897 and 1904, investment bankers consolidated leading industries under the control of a few corporate giants, and J. P. Morgan led the movement. His goal was to take industry away from the industrialists and give it to the bankers. Bankers, he felt, had better information about the true worth of an industry and so could make better decisions about its future. They could create the larger, leaner firms needed to take on foreign competitors.

Morgan's greatest triumph was the merger of eight huge steel companies, their ore ranges, rolling mills, railroads, and shipping lines into the colossal U.S. Steel. The 1901 merger created the world's largest corporation. Its capital amounted to 7 percent of the total wealth of the United States (by comparison, the largest US firm in 2008, Exxon Mobil, had assets valued at only six-tenths of 1 percent of gross domestic product). U.S. Steel's investors (Morgan especially) earned profits "greatly in excess of reasonable compensation," according to one government report.

Bankers outnumbered steelmakers on U.S. Steel's board, and they controlled the company. *McClure's* magazine reported that the new company was "planning the first really systematic effort ever made by Americans to capture the foreign steel trade."

# A Modern Economy

Grover Cleveland's bargain with Morgan revived the industrial economy, but farm prices, wages, and the president's popularity remained flat. Cash-strapped farmers in the West and South disliked the president's hard-money policies and cozy relationships with plutocrats such as Morgan. Calling out troops to crush the Pullman strike cost Cleveland the support of northern workers. The escalating cycle of economic and political crises, farmer and labor insurgencies, middle-class radicalism, and upper-class conservatism fractured political parties. Democrats, Republicans, and Populists all called for stronger government action, but each party split over what action to take. In 1896, the "currency question" dominated a watershed election that transformed the two major parties and destroyed the third.

The year 1896 was the last time presidential candidates openly debated great economic questions in terms that had been familiar to voters since Thomas Jefferson ran for president in 1800; 1896 was also the first recognizably modern presidential election, the first time a successful candidate used the advertising and fund-raising techniques of twentieth-century campaigns.

## Currency: Gold Versus Silver

The soundness of the dollar, which Morgan and Cleveland worked so hard to preserve, was a mixed blessing for Americans. Based on gold, the dollar helped sell American goods in foreign markets, especially in Europe, where currencies were also based on gold. The United States traded on a much smaller scale with countries—such as Mexico and China—that used silver. Gold, however, was valuable because it was scarce, and many Americans suffered from that scarcity. The low prices and high interest rates Populists complained of were a result of the gold standard.

Increasing the money supply would reduce interest rates and make credit more available. There were two ways to put more money in circulation: the government could print paper greenbacks, or it could coin silver. "Free silver" advocates generally favored coining a ratio of 16 ounces of silver for each ounce of gold. Both Populists and western mining interests pushed silver. The Republican and Democratic Parties officially endorsed the gold standard, but by 1896 each party had a renegade faction of silverites. In the 1890s, the crucial political issues—jobs, foreign trade, the survival of small farms, and the prosperity of big corporations—boiled down to one question: Would the dollar be backed by gold or silver? The election of 1896 was "the battle of the standards."

## The Cross of Gold

A dark mood hung over Chicago as delegates arrived at the Democratic convention in July 1896. They had come to bury Cleveland and the party's commitment to the gold standard along with him. The draft platform denounced Cleveland for imposing "government by injunction" during the Pullman strike. When the platform came before the full convention, delegates had to decide whether the party would stand for silver or gold and who would replace Cleveland as the candidate for president.

Both questions were decided when a former congressman from Nebraska, William Jennings Bryan, mounted the stage. He was an electrifying speaker. "You come and tell us that the great cities are in favor of the gold standard," he said. "Destroy our farms, and the grass will grow in the streets of every city in the country!" Bryan spoke in the rhythmic cadence of a camp preacher. "We will answer their demand for a gold standard by saying to them"—he paused, stretching out his arms in an attitude of crucifixion—"You shall not press down upon the brow of labor this crown of thorns. You shall not crucify mankind upon a cross of gold!" The hall exploded with cheers. Bryan won the nomination handily.

Two weeks later the Populists, meeting in St. Louis, also nominated Bryan. The Ocala and Omaha platforms, which imagined comprehensive changes in the money system and American institutions, had been reduced to a single panacea: silver. Republicans overwhelmingly adopted a progold plank, drafted with the approval of J. P. Morgan, and nominated William McKinley, the governor of Ohio and a supporter of industry. The parties could hardly have offered two more different candidates or two more different visions of the future.

## The Battle of the Standards

In one of the most exciting electoral contests since the Civil War, the candidates employed new techniques in radically different ways. McKinley ran like an incumbent: he never left his home. Instead, delegations came to him. Some 750,000 people from 30 states trampled McKinley's grass and listened to speeches affirming his commitment to high tariffs and sound money. The speeches were distributed as newspaper columns, fliers, and pamphlets across the country. The campaign used public relations techniques to educate the electorate on the virtues of the gold standard. Posters reduced the campaign's themes to pithy slogans like "Prosperity or Poverty" and "Vote for Free Silver and Be Prosperous Like Guatemala."

The genius behind the campaign was a Cleveland coal-and-oil millionaire named Marcus Hanna who bankrolled his publicity blitz with between $3 million and $7 million raised from industrialists. The combination of big money and advertising revolutionized presidential politics.

With only $300,000 to spend, Bryan ran like a challenger, even though his party occupied the White House. He logged 29,000 miles by rail and buggy and made more than 500 speeches in 29 states. Oratorical ability had won Bryan the nomination, but audiences were unaccustomed to hearing a candidate speak for himself, and many considered it undignified. "The Boy Orator has one speech," wrote an unsympathetic Republican, John Hay. "He simply reiterates the unquestioned truths that . . . gold is vile, that silver is lovely and holy."

Despite the scorn of eastern newspapers, industrialists feared the prospect of a Bryan presidency. Factory owners threatened to close shop if Bryan won. Just before Election Day, the global markets that McKinley praised returned the favor. Crop failures abroad doubled the price of wheat in the Midwest, raising farm incomes and alleviating the anxieties that drove farmers to Bryan. Bryan won the South and West decisively, but McKinley won the populous industrial Northeast and several farm states in the upper Midwest, capturing the Electoral College by 271 to 176 (see Map 18–1).

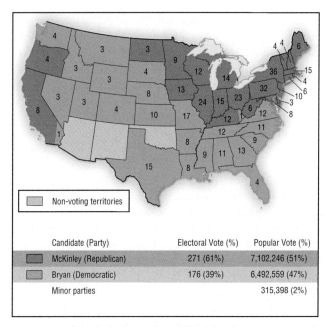

| Candidate (Party) | Electoral Vote (%) | Popular Vote (%) |
|---|---|---|
| McKinley (Republican) | 271 (61%) | 7,102,246 (51%) |
| Bryan (Democratic) | 176 (39%) | 6,492,559 (47%) |
| Minor parties | | 315,398 (2%) |

**Map 18–1 The Election of 1896** William McKinley's "front-porch campaign" carried the northern industrial states, along with the key farm states of Iowa and Minnesota, securing a narrow victory over Bryan.

The election of 1896 changed the style of campaigns and shifted the political positions of both major parties. By pushing currency policies to improve the lives of workers and farmers, Bryan's Democrats abandoned their traditional Jacksonian commitment to minimal government. The Republicans recognized that voters would judge the president on his ability to bring them prosperity. Electoral democracy now had a distinctly economic cast. As president, McKinley asserted his leadership over economic policy, calling Congress into special session to pass the Dingley Tariff Act, which levied the highest taxes on imports in American history. He extended presidential power even more dramatically through an expansionist foreign and military policy.

In the election of 1896, basic economic questions—Who is the economy supposed to serve? What is the nature of money?—were at stake in a closely matched campaign. No wonder voter turnout hit an all-time high. Administrative agencies took over those issues after the turn of the century, but Americans long remembered that raucous campaign when the nation's economic future was up for grabs. As late as the 1960s, schoolchildren still recited the Cross of Gold speech.

# The Retreat from Politics

The economy improved steadily after 1895, but this latest business panic left lasting marks on corporate and political culture. Industrial workers made a tactical retreat in the face of a new political and legal climate. In the South, depression, urbanization, and the modernizing influence of railroads accelerated the spread of legalized racial segregation and disfranchisement. What was happening in the South and the nation was part of a nationwide decline of participatory politics. With the slackening of both agrarian unrest and resistance to corporate capitalism, politics lost some of its value. Voter participation declined, and Americans felt less of a personal stake in elections. Disaffected groups—such as labor and African Americans—had to devise new ways to build community and express resistance.

### The Lure of the Cities

In the South as in the North, people left the countryside and moved to towns and cities. By 1900, one out of six southerners lived in town. Except for Birmingham, Alabama, southern cities were not devoted to manufacturing but to commerce and services. Doctors' offices, clothing and dry goods stores, and groceries could be found near warehouses in which cotton was stored, ginned, and pressed and near the railway station, from which it was shipped to textile mills.

The growth of villages and towns in the South was the product of rural decay. Crop liens, which gave bankers ownership of a crop before it was planted, and debt drove people from farms. The young and the ambitious left first, while older and poorer residents stayed behind.

While white newcomers settled on the outskirts, African Americans moved into industrial districts along the railroad tracks. Still, towns offered things that were missing in the country, such as schools. A Little Rock, Arkansas, resident noted that newly arrived African American parents were "very anxious to send their children to school." Jobs were often available, too, although more frequently for women than for men. Men looked for seasonal labor at farms or lumber camps outside towns. This meant families faced a tough choice between poverty and separation.

AMERICAN LANDSCAPE

# Galveston, Texas, 1900

Looking back, many survivors would remember warning signs: an unusual stillness in the Gulf of Mexico, lightning flashes in a clear sky. But when the winds began to pick up early in the morning on September 8, 1900, the residents of Galveston believed their solid slate-roofed homes would protect them from what turned out to be the deadliest storm in American history.

Galveston was a Gilded Age boomtown, the "New York of the Gulf." Sited like Manhattan on an island at the mouth of a deep-water bay, it was Texas's principal port. Railroads brought cotton and cattle from San Antonio, Dallas, and Fort Worth to the wharves, where they met steamships from Hamburg, Cartagena, and Marseille. Galveston was a major arrival point for immigrants, who had their papers and throats checked at Pelican Island before setting foot in a land advertised as exuberantly fertile. Alongside hotels, offices, boutiques, and the Grand Opera House on the Strand were the consulates of 16 countries, including Russia and Japan.

Like many American cities, Galveston was ostensibly governed by a mayor and a council, comprised of aldermen elected by each of the 12 wards, but an elite of wealthy brokers and merchants maintained the city's dominance through private monopolies. The Galveston Wharf Company charged outrageous port fees and steered trade into the hands of favored clients. The Cotton Exchange set prices for the region's principal crop. Economics and politics were a kind of competition; for boosters it was not enough for Galveston to be prosperous; it also had to trounce its rival, Houston. Traders on the powerful (and unelected) Deepwater Port Commission used their connections to get federal money to dredge the shipping canals, removing protective sandbars and sealing Galveston's lead. Even the weather bureau joined in, playing up the tornado threat to inland cities while dismissing the danger from hurricanes as "an absurd delusion."

Galveston shared the confidence of the country at the dawn of a new century. Leaving the doldrums of the early 1890s, the national economy forged ahead. American armies were victorious in Cuba and Asia, and scientific advances—telecommunications, medicine, steam propulsion, and weather prediction—strengthened a sense that distance, disease, and nature itself could be tamed. Galveston was at the forefront of these changes, the first city in Texas with electric lights and telephones. Its streetcar line defied geography, traveling on elevated trestles over the Gulf itself. The city grew by 30 percent in the previous decade, the Galveston News reported on September 7, and "the prospects are bright even to surpass it."

The 1900 storm was not unprecedented. In 1886, the coastal town of Indianola was

Despite setbacks, newcomers gained a place for themselves in urban life. By 1890, every southern city had an African American business district with churches, insurance companies, lawyers, doctors, undertakers, and usually a weekly newspaper. Benevolent and reform organizations, sewing circles, and book clubs enriched community life.

wiped out by a hurricane. Still, when the red and black storm flags went up, Galvestonians and the thousands of tourists in town for a weekend at the beach sought shelter in the city rather than escaping to the mainland. It was a fatal choice. The storm surge pulverized the commercial district. The streetcar trestle, lifted by the flood, bulldozed through neighborhoods, smashing houses in its path. Thousands were swept out to sea, while thousands more drowned in the wreckage. The clouds cleared over a ruined city. From one end to the other along the high-water mark stretched a ridge of broken timbers, masonry, furniture, and human and animal corpses.

With hospitals, churches, and city hall destroyed, the victims organized their own relief. Middle- and upper-class women distributed thousands of pounds of supplies from the Red Cross. An ad hoc Women's Health Protective Committee rallied survivors to care for the injured, clear debris, and set up tent cities. Meanwhile, the Deep Water Commission struggled to clear wrecked ships and reopen the port. Together, WHPC and port officials petitioned the legislature to replace the city's elected government with a board of appointed commissioners who would head departments of finance, fire, police, water, sewage, and streets. Democratic institutions were not up to the challenge, they agreed; this emergency required experts.

The commissioner system unmasked the control that brokers and merchants had always had over Galveston's politics, but it also revealed the new power of educated women (who still lacked the vote) and reform groups. The commissioners launched an ambitious reconstruction scheme, beginning with data collection. They carefully mapped currents, wave patterns, and the debris wall, using it to mark the outer limits of new construction. Instead of relocating to the mainland, they laid plans for raising the city 17 feet and placing it behind a three-mile-long concrete seawall to hold back any future storm surge. The Women's Committee laid out lots for new houses separated by wide, well-drained streets and barriers of vegetation to disrupt flood currents.

Galveston lost the competition to become the state's largest city. The discovery of oil at Spindletop Dome a year later made Houston the next boomtown. But the commissioner system became a model of progressive reform imitated by over 500 cities, mostly in the Midwest. The "Galveston Plan" offered a cure for the corruption of urban machines. Commissioners agreed that "economy and business methods, not politics" should be the ruling principle. While efficient, it was also undemocratic. Only two members of the board were elected; the rest were appointed by the legislature. None were African American, despite black majorities in two of the wards. Residents were grateful for the speedy action, but uneasy about the new order. "Commission government is far from a perfect plan," wrote a journalist who survived the disaster; "it only marks a transition toward better things."

African American professionals such as lawyers, doctors, and nurses were limited to working within their community. Jobs on the bottom rung of the corporate ladder—clerk, salesman, telephone operator, stenographer, railroad conductor—were reserved for whites.

## Inventing Jim Crow

In June 1892, Homer Plessy boarded the East Louisiana Railway in New Orleans for a trip to Covington, Louisiana. Having purchased a first-class ticket, he attempted to board the whites-only car and was arrested under a Louisiana law that required African Americans and whites to ride in "equal but separate accommodations." Before Judge John H. Ferguson could try the case, Plessy's lawyer appealed on the grounds that the separate-car law violated the Constitution's Fourteenth Amendment.

When *Plessy v. Ferguson* came before the Supreme Court in April 1896, the State of Louisiana argued that the law was necessary to avoid the "danger of friction from too intimate contact" between the races. In separate cars, all citizens enjoyed equal privileges. Plessy's lawyer, Albion Tourgée, replied that the question was not "the equality of the privileges enjoyed, but the right of the state to label one citizen as white and another as colored." In doing so, the government gave unearned advantages to some citizens and not to others. The issue for Tourgée was not racial conflict or even prejudice, but whether the government should be allowed to divide people arbitrarily. The court upheld the "separate but equal" doctrine, and the decision provided legal justification for the system of official inequality that expanded in the twentieth century. Informal segregation had existed since the Civil War, and unwritten local customs usually governed the public interaction of whites and African Americans—at work, in business, or when traveling. By the 1890s those informal customs were being codified in law. Railroads, as symbols of progress, were a chief point of contention.

The political and economic tensions created by the depression helped turn racist customs into a rigid caste division. Competition for jobs fed racial antagonisms, as did the migration into cities and towns of a new generation of African Americans, born since the war, who showed less deference to whites. New notions of "scientific" racism led intellectuals and churchmen to regard racial hostility as natural. Angry southern voters deposed the governing coalitions of landowners and New South industrialists and replaced them with Populist "demagogues."

Between 1887 and 1891, nine states in the South passed railroad segregation laws. Trains included separate cars for African Americans, called "Jim Crow" cars after the name of a character in a minstrel show. Soon Jim Crow laws were extended to waiting rooms, drinking fountains, and other places where African Americans and whites might meet.

Segregation was also enforced by terror. The threat of lynching poisoned relations

**Lynchings Were Public Spectacles** When 17-year-old Jesse Washington was killed in Waco, Texas, in 1916, a crowd of several thousand, including the mayor, police chief, and students from Waco High, attended the event on the lawn of city hall. Afterward, the murderers posed for a photograph and sold their victim's teeth for $5 apiece.

between the races, and African Americans learned that they could be tortured and killed for committing a crime, talking back, or simply looking the wrong way at a white woman. Between 1882 and 1903, nearly 2,000 African American southerners were killed by mobs. Victims were routinely tortured, flayed, castrated, gouged, and burned alive, and members of the mob often took home grisly souvenirs such as a piece of bone or a severed thumb.

Many African American southerners fought segregation with boycotts, lawsuits, and disobedience. Ida Wells-Barnett, a Nashville journalist, organized an international antilynching campaign (see Chapter 19). Segregation was constantly negotiated and challenged, but after 1896 it was backed by the US Supreme Court.

## The Atlanta Compromise

When Atlanta invited African American educator Booker T. Washington to address the Cotton States Exposition in 1895, northern newspapers proclaimed a new era of racial progress. The speech made Washington the most recognized African American in the United States. Starting with 40 students and an abandoned shack, Washington had built Tuskegee Institute into the preeminent technical school for African Americans. Washington was a guest in the stately homes of Newport and at Andrew Carnegie's castle in Scotland. When Atlanta staged an exposition to showcase the region's industrial and social progress, the organizers asked Washington to speak.

Washington's address stressed racial accommodation. It had been a mistake, he argued, to try to attain equality by asserting civil and political rights, and he stated that progress "must be the result of severe and constant struggle rather than artificial forcing." He urged white businessmen to employ African American southerners "who have, without strikes and labor wars, tilled your fields, cleared your forests, builded your railroads and cities." Stretching out his fingers and then closing them into a fist, he summarized his approach to race relations: "In all things that are purely social, we can be as separate as the fingers, yet one as the hand in all things essential to mutual progress." The largely white audience erupted into applause.

Washington's "Atlanta Compromise" stressed the mutual obligations of African Americans and whites. African Americans would give up the vote and stop insisting on social equality if white leaders would keep violence in check and allow African Americans to succeed in agriculture and business. White industrialists welcomed this arrangement, and African American leaders felt that for the moment it might be the best that could be achieved.

## Disfranchisement and the Decline of Popular Politics

After the feverish campaign of 1896, elections began to lose some of their appeal. Attendance fell off at the polls, from 79 percent of voters in 1888 down to 65 percent in 1896. The public events surrounding campaigns also drew thinner crowds, and apathy seemed to have become a national epidemic.

In the South, the disappearance of voters was easy to explain. As Jim Crow laws multiplied, southern states disfranchised African Americans (and one out of four whites) by requiring voters to demonstrate literacy, property ownership, or knowledge of the Constitution in order to register. Louisiana added the notorious grandfather clause,

## STRUGGLES FOR DEMOCRACY

# The Wilmington Race Riot

In 1894, the Populist-Republican "Fusion" ticket won both houses of the North Carolina General Assembly, the powerful state legislature. Fusion officials, anxious to overturn the machine style politics the Democratic Party had established since Reconstruction, set to restoring direct power to the people of North Carolina. Eliminating policies that benefited the white elite at the expense of the farming poor, unskilled labor, and black southerners, Fusionists terminated official appointments and made all positions subject to local election. They enacted new electoral laws and registration practices to encourage black voting. By 1896, the Fusionists, with their focus on class rather than racial solidarity, won every statewide race in North Carolina, and Daniel L. Russell, a Republican, was elected governor. A new brand of truly democratic politics seemed to be on the horizon.

Wilmington, the largest city in North Carolina, had a majority black population and had long been known for the political and economic opportunities it afforded African Americans. But in 1897, when city elections resulted in a Fusionist mayor and several Fusionist aldermen, the tide turned. Anxious at the results achieved by the Populist-Republican pairing, Democratic Party leaders were determined to redeem themselves politically. Embracing the language of "Negro rule" to frighten white voters and "white supremacy" to encourage racial solidarity, Democrats drew a sharp color line among voters, a strategy that coincided with the Jim Crow system of segregation that was rapidly spreading throughout the South.

A public exchange over the question of lynching and interracial relations galvanized the Democratic Party. In August 1897, Rebecca Felton, a Georgia feminist and white supremacist, declared the black rapist to be among the greatest threats faced by southern white farm women. She demanded that white men use vigilante justice to protect the virtue of their women. If necessary, men should be prepared to "lynch a thousand times a week." Alexander Manly, a black Wilmingtonian and editor of the only black-owned daily newspaper in the nation, the *Daily Record*, responded with an editorial in August 1898 in which he defended black men and attempted to dismantle the myth of the black sexual aggressor. He argued that rape claims against black men were exaggerated and that the majority of sexual relations between black men and white women were consensual.

This enraged white southerners. In the aftermath of the Manly editorial, a radical white supremacist faction of the Democratic Party, the Red Shirts, began a campaign of fear and coercion. In October

which denied the vote to men whose grandfathers had been prohibited from voting (see Table 18–1).

Whites saw disfranchisement and segregation as modern, managed race relations. Demonizing African Americans enforced solidarity among white voters otherwise divided by local or class interests.

**Wilmington** White citizens stand before the destroyed *Daily Record* office, 1898.

1898, the Red Shirts terrorized interracial political alliances across eastern North Carolina by breaking up political meetings, destroying property, and committing violent acts. Their goal: keep Republican and Populist voters—especially black voters—from going to the polls. The night before the election, Wilmington Democratic Party leader Colonel Alfred Moor Waddell instructed a mass meeting of white citizens "Go to the polls tomorrow, and if you find the negro out voting, tell him to leave the polls, and if he refuses, kill him."

Democrats' tactics (including stuffed ballots and voter fraud) succeeded, and their candidates secured offices throughout the state. But many of those who had reclaimed Democratic seats in Wilmington were unwilling to accept Fusionists as their peers and colleagues. On November 9, the day after Election Day, a mass meeting of white Wilmingtonians adopted a Wilmington Declaration of Independence, which claimed white supremacy as a right, called for an end to black political participation and interracial politics, and demanded the expulsion of Manly from Wilmington (he had already left).

When black Wilmingtonians responded too slowly to the demands of the Declaration, the white citizenry was all too ready to strike. On November 10, armed, anxious white men filled the Wilmington armory; an early procession of about 500 men grew to 2,000. The first target was Manly's *Daily Record*. A mob ransacked the offices and torched the building. As the crowd marched into one of Wilmington's black neighborhoods, they used repeating rifles to outgun the black men who attempted to defend their property. Hundreds of black citizens escaped Wilmington, hoping to wait out the riot. The number of black deaths remains unknown; most estimates range from 7 to 20.

Those leading the insurrection demanded the resignation of Fusionist officials and then took power for themselves. Political opponents of the rioters were run out of the city. Over the course of the next month, 1,400 African Americans fled Wilmington. No one in Wilmington spoke out against the rioters and no outside forces came to the aid of black citizens. The tactics used in Wilmington spread a clear message throughout the Jim Crow South: those challenging a political system based on white supremacy and elite rule would suffer the consequences.

No new legal restrictions hampered voting in the North and West, but participation fell there, too. This withdrawal from politics reflected the declining importance of political pageantry and the disappearance of intense partisanship. A developing economy with new patterns of social and cultural life undermined partisanship, but so did the new style of campaigns. For American men, the cliffhanger contests of the late

**Table 18-1** The Spread of Disfranchisement

| Year | State | Strategies |
| --- | --- | --- |
| 1889 | Florida | Poll tax |
| 1889 | Tennessee | Poll tax |
| 1890 | Mississippi | Poll tax, literacy test, understanding clause |
| 1891 | Arkansas | Poll tax |
| 1893, 1901 | Alabama | Poll tax, literacy test, grandfather clause |
| 1894, 1895 | South Carolina | Poll tax, literacy test, understanding clause |
| 1894, 1902 | Virginia | Poll tax, literacy test, understanding clause |
| 1897, 1898 | Louisiana | Poll tax, literacy test, grandfather clause |
| 1899, 1900 | North Carolina | Poll tax, literacy test, grandfather clause |
| 1902 | Texas | Poll tax |
| 1908 | Georgia | Poll tax, literacy test, understanding clause, grandfather clause |

nineteenth century had provided a sense of identity that strengthened ethnic, religious, and neighborhood identities.

The new emphasis on advertising, education, and fund-raising reduced the personal stakes for voters. Educated middle- and upper-class voters liked the new style, feeling that raucous campaigns were no way to decide important issues. They sought to influence policy more directly, through interest groups rather than parties. Unintentionally, they discarded traditions that unified communities and connected voters to their country and its leaders.

## Organized Labor Retreats from Politics

Workers followed organized labor as it turned away from political activity and redefined objectives in economic terms. As traditional crafts came under attack, skilled workers created new organizations that addressed immediate issues: wages, hours, and the conditions of work. The American Federation of Labor (AFL), founded in 1886, built a base around skilled trades and grew from 150,000 members to more than 2 million by 1904. The AFL focused on immediate goals to improve the working lives of its members. Its founder, Samuel Gompers, was born in London's East End and apprenticed as a cigar maker at the age of 10. After his family moved to New York, Gompers joined the Cigar Makers' International Union.

Although affiliated with the Knights of Labor, the cigar makers were more interested in shortening work hours and increasing wages than in remaking the economy. High dues and centralized control allowed the union to offer insurance and death benefits to members while maintaining a strike fund. Gompers applied the same practices to the AFL. His "pure and simple unionism" made modest demands, but it still encountered fierce resistance from corporations, which were backed by the courts.

In the 1895 case of *In re Debs*, the Supreme Court allowed the use of injunctions to criminalize strikes. The court then disarmed one of labor's last weapons, the boycott. In *Loewe v. Lawlor* (1908), known as the Danbury Hatters case, the court ruled that advertising a consumer boycott was illegal under the Sherman Anti-Trust Act.

Gompers believed that industrial unions, which drew members from all occupations within an industry, lacked the discipline and shared values needed to face down corporations and government, whereas unions organized around a single trade or craft would be stronger. However, because the AFL was organized by skill, it often ignored unskilled workers, such as women or recent immigrants. Because employers used unskilled newcomers to break strikes or to run machinery that replaced expert hands, Gompers excluded a large part of the labor force. Organizers recruited Irish and German workers while ignoring Italian, African American, Jewish, and Slavic workers. The union attacked female workers for "stealing" jobs that once belonged to men.

Other unions were built to represent the immediate interests of their members. Under Eugene V. Debs, railroad workers merged the old railroad brotherhoods into the ARU in 1893. The United Mine Workers (UMW), founded in 1890, unionized coal mines in Pennsylvania, Ohio, Indiana, and Michigan. The ARU and the UMW were industrial unions that tried to organize all of the workers in an industry. Able to disrupt the energy and transport systems on which the whole economy depended, these new unions had immense potential power. They faced determined opposition from business and its allies in government. "Our government cannot stand, nor its free institutions endure," the National Association of Manufacturers declared, "if the Gompers-Debs ideals of liberty and freedom of speech and press are allowed to dominate."

# American Diplomacy Enters the Modern World

The Republican victory in 1896 gave heart to proponents of prosperity through foreign trade. Before the turn of the century, the new president announced, the United States would control the world's markets. "We will establish trading posts throughout the world as distributing points for American products," Senator Albert Beveridge forecast. "Great colonies, governing themselves, flying our flag and trading with us, will grow about our posts of trade." McKinley sought neither war nor colonies, but many in his party wanted both. These "jingoes" included Assistant Secretary of the Navy Theodore Roosevelt; John Hay, the ambassador to London; and Senators Beveridge and Henry Cabot Lodge. Britain, France, and Germany were seizing territory around the world, and jingoes believed the United States needed to do the same for strategic, religious, and economic reasons. Spain was the most likely target, clinging feebly to the remnants of its once-vast empire in Cuba, the Philippines, Guam, and Puerto Rico. Under Cleveland, the United States had moved away from confrontation with Spain, but McKinley pushed for the creation of an American empire that stretched to the far shores of the Pacific.

## Sea Power and the Imperial Urge

Few men better exemplified the jingoes' combination of religiosity, martial spirit, and fascination with the laws of history than Alfred Thayer Mahan. A naval officer and strategist, he argued that since the Roman Empire, world leadership had belonged to the nation that controlled the sea. Published in 1890, his book *The Influence of Sea Power upon History, 1660–1783* became an instant classic.

Mahan connected naval expansion and empire to the problem of overproduction that the United States faced. A great industrial country needed trade; trade required a merchant fleet; and merchant shipping needed naval protection and overseas bases. Colonies could provide markets for goods and congregations for Christian missionaries, but, more important, they allowed naval forces to protect sea lanes and project power in Asia, Latin America, and Africa.

Mahan urged the United States to build a canal across Central America for better access to Asian markets. He urged the building of naval bases along routes to Latin America and the Far East. Congress and the Navy Department began implementing these recommendations even before McKinley took office (see Figure 18–2).

Mahan was not the only prophet who recalled the Roman Empire. Brooks Adams's *The Law of Civilization and Decay* (1895) detailed the effects of the closed frontier: greater concentration of wealth, social inequality, and eventual collapse. To repeal this "law," the United States needed a new frontier in Asia where it could regenerate itself through combat. Sharing the social Darwinist belief that nations and races were locked in a savage struggle for survival, Mahan and Adams expected the United States to win the approaching conflict.

If subduing continents with the cross, Constitution, and Gatling gun appealed to anyone, it was Theodore Roosevelt. Roosevelt paid keen attention to the forces that were magnifying the power of some nations and diminishing others. Imperialism seemed to him the essential characteristic of modernizing countries. A frontiersman, writer, soldier, and politician, Roosevelt was acutely conscious of how modern forces—globalized trade, instant communications, modern navies, and imperialism—had altered the rules of domestic and international politics. He sought to position the United States at the center of these modernizing currents, a place that would have to be earned, he felt, both on foreign battlefields and at home, where the gains of the nineteenth century had not yet been translated into the social and moral advancement that marked a true civilization.

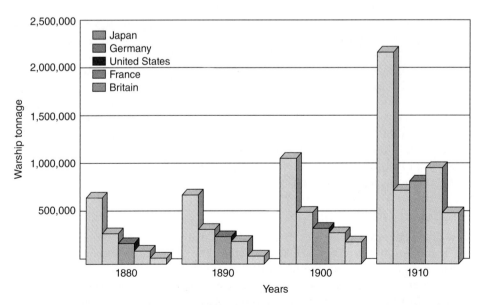

**Figure 18-2   Warship Tonnage of the World's Navies** Naval strength was the primary index of power before World War I. The United States held onto third place in the naval arms race, while Germany and Japan made significant gains.
*Source:* Paul Kennedy, *Rise and Fall of the Great Powers* (New York: Random House, 1987), p. 203.

**Pears' Soap** Advertisements emphasized the celebrated civilizing capacities of imperialism, as shown in this advertisement for Pears' Soap, 1899.

The first step towards lightening

## The White Man's Burden

is through teaching the virtues of cleanliness.

## Pears' Soap

is a potent factor in brightening the dark corners of the earth as civilization advances, while amongst the cultured of all nations it holds the highest place—it is the ideal toilet soap.

## The Scramble for Empire

For jingoes, China was the ultimate prize in the global contest for trade and mastery. It had more people than any other country, hence more customers and more souls for Christ. The number of American missionaries in China doubled in the 1890s, many of them from the Student Volunteer movement, which had chapters on nearly every college campus. Even though no more than 1 or 2 percent of US exports had ever gone to China, manufacturers believed that China could absorb the output of America's overproductive factories. James B. Duke founded the British-American Tobacco Company based on "China's population of 450 million people, and assuming that in the future they might average a cigarette a day." In 1890, Standard Oil began selling kerosene in Shanghai. Fifteen years later, China was the largest overseas market for American oil. Mahan had predicted that China would be the arena for the coming struggle for industrial and military supremacy, and by 1897 he seemed to be right.

In 1894, Japan declared war on China and soon occupied Korea, Manchuria, and China's coastal cities. When the fighting was over, Western powers seized slices of Chinese territory. In 1897, German troops captured the port of Qingdao on the Shandong Peninsula. An industrial area, Shandong was the center of American missionary activity, investment, and trade. To Americans, the invasion of Shandong presaged an imperial grab for territory and influence. In the 1880s, European powers had carved up Africa. Now it appeared that the same thing was about to happen in China. The McKinley administration watched events in China carefully, but in the winter of 1897–1898 it had more pressing concerns closer to home.

## War with Spain

While other European powers were expanding their empires, Spain was barely hanging on to the one it had. Since the 1860s, its two largest colonies, Cuba and the Philippines, had been torn by revolution. Between 1868 and 1878, Cuban nationalists fought for independence. Spain ended the war by promising autonomy but not independence. US officials wanted an end to Spanish rule, but the McKinley Tariff and the Panic of 1893 ruined Cuba's chief export industry, sugar. Under a crushing debt, Spain reneged on its promise, and in 1895 the rebellion resumed. The rebels practiced a scorched-earth policy, dynamiting trains and burning plantations in an attempt to force Spain out.

Spain retaliated with a brutal campaign of pacification, killing nearly 100,000 civilians, but it was no use. The Spanish army was disintegrating. Cuban rebels, in control of the countryside, prepared a final assault on the cities. US officials, many of whom wanted to annex the island, now worried that Cuba would gain full independence. McKinley explored the options of either purchasing it from Spain or intervening on the pretext of ending the strife. William Randolph Hearst's *New York Journal* and other newspapers favored the latter, inciting readers with lurid stories of Spanish atrocities and Cuban rioting. Cuba sold newspapers. McKinley moved quickly toward confrontation. When riots erupted in the Cuban capital, he ordered a warship to Havana. Theodore Roosevelt sent one of the newest battleships, the USS *Maine*. The arrival of the *Maine* reduced tensions for a while, but on February 15 an explosion ripped through the ship, killing 266 of a crew that had numbered 350. Navy investigators later concluded that boilers had exploded accidentally, but the newspapers blamed both Spanish and Cuban treachery. Hearst printed a full-page diagram of the ship being destroyed by a "sunken torpedo."

McKinley hesitated, mindful of the budget and events in China, but Roosevelt ordered Commodore George Dewey's Asiatic Squadron to ready an attack on the Philippines. Congress appropriated $50 million for arms. Spanish emissaries tried to gain support from other European countries, but they were rebuffed.

In March, the economic picture brightened, and McKinley sent Spain an ultimatum demanding independence for Cuba. On April 11, he asked Congress for authorization to use force, and Congress passed a declaration of war. Expansionists such as Roosevelt, Mahan, and Adams would not have succeeded if war had been less popular. Corporate interests favored it, immigrants and southerners saw it as a way to assert their patriotism, and newspapers found it made good copy. "We are all jingoes now," declared the *New York Sun*.

Neither side had many illusions about the outcome. Fighting Spain, novelist Sherwood Anderson wrote, was "like robbing an old gypsy woman in a vacant lot at night after the fair," but the war opened with a cliffhanger that even Hearst could not have invented. On May 1, news arrived that Dewey's forces were fighting the Spanish fleet in Manila Bay in the Philippines. The war had begun, not in Cuba, but instead half a world away. There the information stopped. The telegraph cable from Manila had been cut. Official Spanish reports alleged that the Americans had suffered a "considerable loss of life." Dewey's squadron contained only two modern cruisers, but in contrast to Spain's wooden vessels, all of its ships were steel hulled. For six anxious days Americans awaited word from the far edge of the Pacific.

It arrived early on May 7. The *New York Herald*'s Hong Kong correspondent had been at the battle. Dewey destroyed Spain's entire fleet of 12 warships without a single serious casualty. The country went wild with relief and triumph. New York staged a parade on Fifth Avenue. A Dewey-for-president movement began. In Washington, McKinley consulted a map to see where the Philippines were. Roosevelt quit his job and ordered up a uniform.

The war in Cuba unfolded more modestly. The navy bottled up Spain's ships in the Bay of Santiago de Cuba, and American warships cut the fleet to pieces as it attempted to escape. "Don't cheer, men," an officer ordered the gun crews. "Those poor devils are dying."

In the years before the war, Congress had poured money into the navy but not the army, and it took some time before soldiers could be trained and equipped. Recruits were

**The Rough Riders** Theodore Roosevelt's regiment, with its blend of educated men from the east and rough-and-tumble western frontiersmen, represented his idealized blend of American military manhood.

herded into camps in Florida without tents, proper clothing, or latrines. There were few medical supplies or doctors. In these unsanitary camps, soldiers died of dysentery and malaria. Of the 5,462 US soldiers who died in the war with Spain, 5,083 succumbed to disease, a scandal that forced the government to elevate the status of the surgeon general and to improve sanitation and disease prevention in the military.

The army landed on the Cuban coast and marched inland to engage Spanish defenders. Roosevelt came ashore with the First Volunteer Cavalry, known as the "Rough Riders." He recruited, trained, and publicized the regiment and wrote its history. An assortment of outlaws, cowboys, Ivy League athletes, New York City policemen, a novelist, and a Harvard Medical School graduate, its membership combined frontier heroism with eastern elite leadership. The regiment traveled with its own film crew and a correspondent from the *New York Herald*.

Spanish forces stubbornly resisted around the city of Santiago. At San Juan Hill, 500 defenders forced a regiment of the New York National Guard to retreat. The all–African American 9th and 10th Cavalry fought alongside the Rough Riders. "The negroes saved that fight," a white soldier reported. The capture of Santiago effectively ended Spanish resistance. When fighting ended in August, US troops occupied Cuba, Guam, Puerto Rico, and the city of Manila. The war had lasted only four months.

As American and Spanish diplomats met in Paris to conclude a peace treaty, McKinley had to decide which occupied territories to keep as colonies. Congress, not wanting to inherit the island's $400 million in debt, had already resolved not to annex Cuba. McKinley decided that Guam and Puerto Rico would make ideal naval bases (see Map 18–2).

The president also seized the opportunity to annex the island nation of Hawaii. In 1893, American sugar planters, led by Sanford Dole, overthrew the islands' last queen, Liliuokalani, and petitioned for annexation. They were motivated by the Harrison-McKinley Tariff, which would ruin the planters unless they could reconnect Hawaii's trade to the United States. Annexation was their best chance, and they had a powerful ally in the US Navy. Mahan had identified Pearl Harbor, on Oahu, as a vital base. McKinley decided to take up Dole's annexation offer.

The Philippines were more of a problem. The 7,000 islands were far from the United States and had a population of several million. The United States needed a naval base and supply station close to the China coast, but holding just one island would be impossible if another power controlled the others. Shortly after Dewey's victory, British and German warships anchored in Manila Bay, clearly intending to divide up the territory the United States did not claim. McKinley felt trapped.

Spain recognized Cuban independence and surrendered most of its empire to the United States for free, but it gave up the Philippines only after the United States agreed to

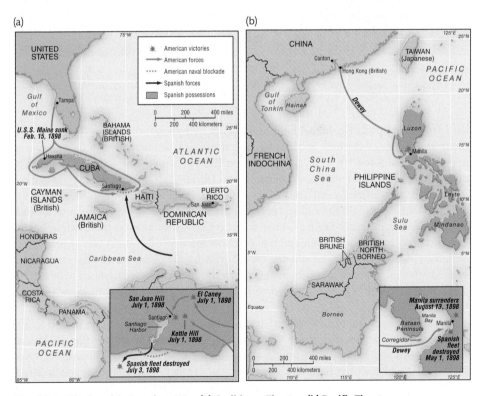

**Map 18–2   The Spanish-American War: (a) Caribbean Theater; (b) Pacific Theater**

pay $20 million, or, as an American satirist calculated, $1.25 for every Filipino. The treaty was signed December 10, 1898.

McKinley did not take into account the fact that the Philippines had already declared independence. With Dewey's encouragement, rebels under the command of Emilio Aguinaldo had liberated the countryside surrounding Manila and laid siege to the city. At Malolos, north of Manila, a national assembly, including lawyers, doctors, professors, and landowners, issued a constitution. By the time the US Army arrived in 1899, Filipinos had overthrown the Spanish and rallied to their new government.

## The Anti-Imperialists

Many prominent Americans opposed both the annexation of new colonies and the approaching war with the Philippines. During the treaty fight in Congress in January 1899, they tried to mobilize opinion against the treaty. The movement included ex-presidents Grover Cleveland and Benjamin Harrison; William Jennings Bryan; labor unionists, including Samuel Gompers and Eugene Debs; writers such as Mark Twain and Ambrose Bierce; and industrialists, including Andrew Carnegie. The anti-imperialists advanced an array of moral, economic, and strategic arguments. Filipinos and Hawaiians, they said, had sought American help in good faith and were capable of governing themselves. The islands could not be defended, and US forces would be exposed to attack at Pearl Harbor or Manila. Carnegie argued that imperialism took tax dollars and attention away from domestic problems. White supremacists asked whether Filipinos would become citizens or be allowed to vote and emigrate to the mainland.

The most moving objections came from those who believed imperialism betrayed America's fundamental principles. To Mark Twain, imperialism was only the newest form of greed: "There is more money in it, more territory, more sovereignty, and other kinds of emolument, than there is in any other game that is played." Opponents of annexation organized an Anti-Imperialist League and lobbied for the rejection of the Paris Treaty.

Congress responded to anti-imperialist objections, banning Philippine immigration, placing the colonies outside the tariff walls, and promising eventual self-government. Jingoes had a military victory on their side. Anti-imperialists could not offer a vision comparable to naval supremacy, the evangelization of the world, or the China market. On February 6, 1899, the US Senate ratified the Paris Treaty and annexed the Philippines. A day earlier, on the other side of the world, the Philippine-American War began.

## The Philippine-American War

McKinley believed he had annexed islands full of near savages "unfit for self-rule," but the Philippines by 1899 had an old civilization with a long tradition of resistance to colonialism. When Magellan discovered the islands in 1521, he found a literate population linked by trade ties to India, Japan, and China. The Spanish converted most Filipinos to Catholicism and established schools and a centralized government. Manila's oldest university was older than Harvard. By 1898, much of the upper class, the *illustrados*, had been educated in Europe.

Dewey gave Aguinaldo his word that America desired no colonies. Aguinaldo continued to trust the Americans despite the arrival of fresh US troops. On February 4, an argument between American and Filipino sentries ended in gunfire. Aguinaldo was despondent: "No one can deplore more than I this rupture. I have a clear conscience that I endeavored to avoid it at all costs."

Kansas volunteers drove the Filipino armies into the mountains. Aguinaldo adopted a guerilla strategy, which proved effective. Some 4,000 Americans were killed during the war and another 3,000 wounded out of a total force of 70,000. Frustrated by guerilla conflict, American soldiers customarily executed prisoners, looted villages, and raped Filipino women. An American general on the island of Samar ordered his soldiers to kill everyone over the age of 10. "No cruelty is too severe for these brainless monkeys," a soldier wrote home. "I am in my glory when I can sight some dark skin and pull the trigger."

The army's preferred mode of torture was "the water cure," in which a soldier forced water down a prisoner's throat until the abdomen swelled, and then kicked the prisoner's stomach to force the water out again. Military officials argued that Filipinos were "half-civilized" and that force was the best language for dealing with them.

Newspaper accounts of torture and massacres fueled American opposition to the war, just as US forces scored some victories. Recognizing that they were fighting a political war, US officers took pains to win over dissidents and ethnic minorities. In 1901, this strategy began to pay off. When American troops intercepted a messenger bound for Aguinaldo's secret headquarters, Brigadier General Frederick Funston devised a bold (and, under the rules of war, illegal) plan. He dressed a group of Filipinos loyal to the American side in the uniforms of captured Filipinos, and, posing as a prisoner, Funston entered Aguinaldo's camp and kidnapped the president.

After three weeks in a Manila prison, Aguinaldo issued a proclamation of surrender. When resistance continued in Batangas Province for another year, the US Army responded by herding people into concentration camps, a practice the United States had condemned in Cuba. It had the same tragic result. Perhaps a third of the province's population died of disease and starvation. On July 4, 1902, President Theodore Roosevelt declared the war over.

The American flag flew over the Philippines until 1942, but the colony never lived up to its imperial promise. Instead of defending American trade interests, US troops were pinned down in garrisons, guarding against uprisings and the threat of Japanese invasion. The costs of occupation far exceeded the profits generated by Philippine trade. The colony chiefly attracted American reformers and missionaries, who built schools, churches, and agricultural colleges. Some colonists sought statehood, but Americans liked their colonial experiment less and less. Labor unions feared a flood of immigration from the islands, and farmers resented competition from Philippine producers; in 1933, Congress voted to phase out American rule.

## The Open Door

As Americans celebrated their victories, European powers continued to divide China into quasi-colonial "concessions." An alarmed imperial court in Beijing began a crash program of modernization, but reactionaries overthrew the emperor and installed the conservative "dowager empress" Cixi. In the countryside, Western missionaries and traders came under attack from local residents led by martial artists known as Boxers. Many Americans feared that the approaching disintegration of China would mean the exclusion of US trade.

Secretary of State John Hay watched events in China carefully. "The inherent weakness of our position is this," he wrote McKinley. "We do not want to rob China ourselves, and our public opinion will not allow us to interfere, with an army, to prevent others from robbing her. Besides, we have no army." Seeking some way to keep China's markets open, McKinley turned to William Rockhill, a legendary foreign service officer who had lived in China and had been the first westerner to visit Tibet. He, in turn, consulted his friend Alfred Hippisley, an Englishman returning from service with the British-run Chinese imperial customs.

Rockhill, Hippisley, and Hay drafted an official letter known as the Open Door Note. Sent to each of the imperial powers, it acknowledged the partitioning of China into spheres and observed that none of the powers had yet closed its areas to the trade of other countries. The note urged the powers to declare publicly their intention to continue this policy. The Open Door was mostly bluff. The United States had no authority to ask for such a pledge and no military power to enforce one. The foreign ministers of Germany, Japan, Russia, Britain, and France replied cautiously at first, but Hay adroitly played one power off another, starting with Britain and Japan. Once the two strongest powers in China had agreed, France and then Russia and Germany followed. The United States had secured access to China without war or partition, but the limits of Hay's success soon became apparent.

In early 1900, the antiforeign Boxer movement swept through Shandong Province. Armed Chinese attacked missions and foreign businesses, destroyed railroads, and massacred Chinese Christians. Empress Cixi recruited 30,000 Boxers into her army and declared war on all foreign countries. The Western powers rushed troops to China, but before they arrived, Chinese armies attacked Western embassies in Beijing. A British, Russian, Japanese, and French force gathered at Tianjin to march to the rescue. European powers appeared all too eager to capture the Chinese capital.

Without consulting Congress, McKinley ordered American troops into battle on the Asian mainland. Five thousand soldiers rushed from Manila to Tianjin. Hay issued a second Open Door Note, asking the allies to pledge to protect China's independence. Again, the imperial powers reluctantly agreed rather than admit their secret plans to carve up China. On August 15, 1900, US cavalry units reached Beijing, along with Russian Cossacks, French Zouaves, British-Indian sepoys, German hussars, and Japanese dragoons. After freeing the captive diplomats, the armies of the civilized world looted the city. The United States was unable to maintain the Open Door in China for long. Russia and Japan established separate military zones in northeast China, but the principle of the Open Door, of encouraging free trade and open markets, guided American foreign policy throughout the twentieth century. It rested on the assumption that, in an equal contest, American firms would prevail, spreading manufactured goods around the world and American influence with them. Under the Open Door, the United States was better off in a world without empires, a world in which consumers in independent nations could buy what they wanted. Just one year after the Spanish-American War, Hay rejected imperial expansion in favor of trade expansion. This new strategy promised greater gains, but it placed the United States on a collision course with the empires of the world (see Map 18–3).

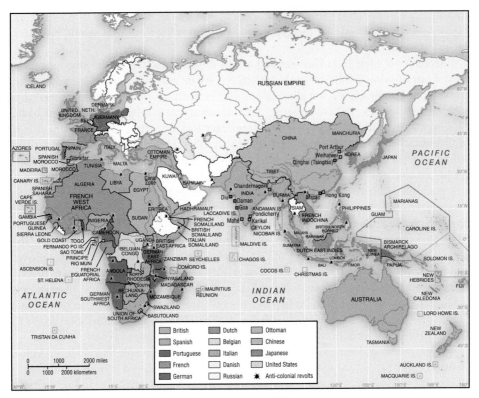

**Map 18-3a   The Imperial World: Asia, Africa, and the Middle East**   Modern imperialism reached its apex between 1880 and 1945. Most of Africa, the Middle East, and Asia, a third of the world's population, was absorbed into global empires linked by telegraph and steamship to centers of government and commerce in London, Paris, Tokyo, and Washington, DC.

## Time Line

### ▼1890

Global depression begins

United Mine Workers founded

Battle of Wounded Knee ends Indian wars

Harrison-McKinley Tariff passed

Alfred T. Mahan publishes *The Influence of Sea Power upon History, 1660-1783*

Standard Oil markets kerosene in China

### ▼1892

Homestead strike

### ▼1893

Financial crisis leads to business failures and mass unemployment

World's Columbian Exposition, Chicago

Cherokee Strip land rush

American sugar planters overthrow Queen Liliuokalani of Hawaii

### ▼1894

Coxey's Army marches on Washington

Pullman strike

US commission charts canal route across Nicaragua

### ▼1895

Morgan agrees to Treasury bailout

National Association of Manufacturers founded

Brooks Adams publishes *The Law of Civilization and Decay*

Booker T. Washington gives "Atlanta Compromise" address

Revolution begins in Cuba

Japan annexes Korea and Taiwan

### ▼1896

*Plessy v. Ferguson* declares "separate but equal" facilities constitutional

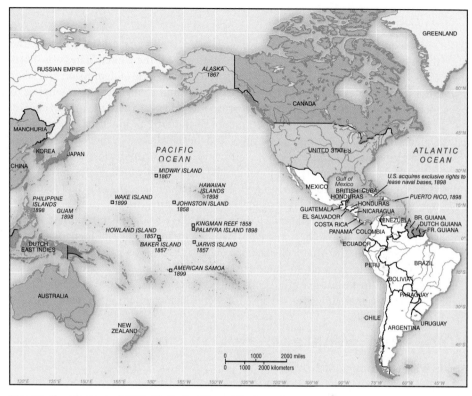

**Map 18–3b    The Imperial World: the Pacific and the Americas**

William McKinley elected president

▼**1897**

Germany captures Qingdao, on China's Shandong Peninsula

McKinley issues formal protest to Spain

▼**1898**

USS *Maine* explodes in Havana's harbor

United States declares war on Spain

Dewey defeats Spanish fleet at Manila Bay

In the Treaty of Paris, Spain grants Cuba independence

and cedes Guam, Puerto Rico, and the Philippines to the United States

Aguinaldo proclaims Philippine independence

▼**1899**

Senate votes to annex Puerto Rico, Hawaii, and the Philippines

Philippine-American War begins

Hay issues first Open Door Note

▼**1900**

Hay issues second Open Door Note

US Army joins British, French, Russian, German, and Japanese forces in capture of Beijing

Great Exposition of Paris showcases American technology

William McKinley reelected

▼**1901**

Aguinaldo captured

McKinley assassinated; Theodore Roosevelt becomes president

▼**1902**

Roosevelt declares Philippine-American War over

# Conclusion

In the turbulent 1890s, the social and economic divisions among Americans widened. The hope that a solution to these divisions could be found outside the United States was short-lived. Imperialism promised new markets and an end to the cycle of depression and labor strife. The United States conquered an overseas empire and challenged other empires to open their ports to free trade, but the goal of prosperity and peace at home proved elusive.

In many ways social Darwinism became a self-fulfilling prophecy, as competition rather than compromise prevailed. Workers and businessmen, farmers and bankers, middle-class radicals and conservatives, whites and African Americans saw each other as enemies. Racial segregation showed that middle ground, on which whites and African Americans could meet on equal terms, had disappeared. Americans now had to decide what was politically possible and devise new bargaining strategies.

Economic recovery and military victory closed the decade on an optimistic note. Prosperity, power, and technology seemed to have rewritten the rules of human affairs to America's advantage. In the American exhibit at the Paris Exposition of 1900, Henry Adams contemplated a 40-foot dynamo—a "huge wheel, revolving within arm's length"—and felt as if he had crossed a "historical chasm." The machine's mysterious silent force, emanating from "a dirty engine house carefully kept out of sight," seemed a metaphor for the modern age.

# Who, What, Where

Bryan, William Jennings  565

Crop liens  567

Cuba  568

Galveston  568

Gold standard  558

Gompers, Samuel  574

Hearst, William Randolph  578

Homestead Steel Works  563

Jim Crow laws  570

Open Door  582

The Philippines  575

Separate but equal  570

Taylorism  562

Washington, Booker T.  571

Wilmington  572

# Review Questions

1. What new techniques and practices made US industries more efficient?
2. What motivated Americans to seek an empire?
3. Why did the weather bureau discount the hurricane threat to Galveston?
4. Which cities were the main centers of industry and culture in the 1890s?

# Critical-Thinking Questions

1. How did the concept of individual rights evolve in reaction to new economic conditions? Name key figures who articulated a concept of democratic rights, and describe their ideas.

2. Contrast the arguments for empire with the rhetoric of the anti-imperialists. Which dangers to the nation and democracy did each side stress?

3. Why was the issue of currency so important to Americans in 1896? What was at stake?

## Suggested Readings

Brewer, Susan A. *Why America Fights: Patriotism and War Propaganda from the Philippines to Iraq.* New York: Oxford University Press, 2009.

Edwards, Rebecca, and DeFeo, Sarah. The Presidential Campaign: Cartoons and Commentary. 2000. http://projects.vassar.edu/1896/1896home.html

Lears, Jackson. *Rebirth of a Nation: The Making of Modern America, 1877–1920.* New York: Harper Perennial, 2010.

Young, Jeremy C. *The Age of Charisma: Leaders, Followers, and Emotions in American Society, 1870–1940.* New York: Cambridge University Press, 2016.

**For further review materials and resource information, please visit www.oup.com/us/oakes-mcgerr**

## 18.1 FREDERICK WINSLOW TAYLOR, EXCERPTS FROM *THE PRINCIPLES OF SCIENTIFIC MANAGEMENT* (1911)

Frederick Winslow Taylor aimed to identify the most basic movements of workplace skills to provide management with the means to train workers to complete tasks with the highest levels of efficiency. With managerial oversight and the cooperation of labor, industry could produce at higher levels, thereby benefiting owners, consumers, and through Taylor's imagined wage increases, workers.

Under the old type of management success depends almost entirely upon getting the "initiative" of the workmen, and it is indeed a rare case in which this initiative is really attained. Under scientific management the "initiative" of the workmen (that is, their hard work, their good-will, and their ingenuity) is obtained with absolute uniformity and to a greater extent than is possible under the old system; and in addition to this improvement on the part of the men, the managers assume new burdens, new duties, and responsibilities never dreamed of in the past. The managers assume, for instance, the burden of gathering together all of the traditional knowledge which in the past has been possessed by the workmen and then of classifying, tabulating, and reducing this knowledge to rules, laws, and formulæ which are immensely helpful to the workmen in doing their daily work. In addition to developing a science in this way, the management take on three other types of duties which involve new and heavy burdens for themselves.

These new duties are grouped under four heads:

First. They develop a science for each element of a man's work, which replaces the old rule-of-thumb method.

Second. They scientifically select and then train, teach, and develop the workman, whereas in the past he chose his own work and trained himself as best he could.

Third. They heartily cooperate with the men so as to insure all of the work being done in accordance with the principles of the science which has been developed.

Fourth. There is an almost equal division of the work and the responsibility between the management and the workmen. The management take over all work for which they are better fitted than the workmen, while in the past almost all of the work and the greater part of the responsibility were thrown upon the men.

It is this combination of the initiative of the workmen, coupled with the new types of work done by the management, that makes scientific management so much more efficient than the old plan. . . .

Perhaps the most prominent single element in modern scientific management is the task idea. The work of every workman is fully planned out by the management at least one day in advance, and each man receives in most cases complete written instructions, describing in detail the task which he is to accomplish, as well as the means to be used in doing the work. And the work planned in advance in this way constitutes a task which is to be solved, as explained above, not by the workman alone, but in almost all cases by the joint effort of the workman and the management. This task specifies not only what is to be done but how it is to be done and the exact time allowed for doing it. And whenever the workman succeeds in doing his task right, and within the time limit specified, he receives an addition of from 30 percent to 100 percent to his ordinary wages. These tasks are carefully planned, so that both good and careful work are called for in their performance, but it should be distinctly understood that in no case is the workman called upon to work at a pace which would be injurious to his health. The task is always so regulated that the man who is well suited to his job will thrive while working at this rate during a long term of years and grow happier and more prosperous, instead of being over-worked. Scientific management consists very largely in preparing for and carrying out these tasks. . . .

Doubtless some of those who are especially interested in working men will complain because under scientific management the workman, when he is shown how to do twice as much work as he formerly did, is not paid twice his former wages, while others who are more interested in the dividends than the workmen will complain that under this system the men receive much higher wages than they did before. . . .

It is not fair, however, to form any final judgment until all of the elements in the case have been considered. At the first glance we see only two parties to the transaction, the workmen and their employers. We overlook the third great party, the whole people—the consumers, who buy the product of the first two and who ultimately pay both the wages of the workmen and the profits of the employers.

[A] glance at industrial history shows that in the end the whole people receive the greater part of the benefit coming from industrial improvements. In the past hundred years, for example, the greatest factor tending toward increasing the output, and thereby the prosperity of the civilized world, has been the introduction of machinery to replace hand labor. And without doubt the greatest gain through this change has come to the whole people—the consumer. . . .

It is no single element, but rather this whole combination, that constitutes scientific management, which may be summarized as:

Science, not rule of thumb.

Harmony, not discord.

Cooperation, not individualism.

Maximum output, in place of restricted output.

The development of each man to his greatest efficiency and prosperity.

The writer wishes to again state that: "The time is fast going by for the great personal or individual achievement of any one man standing alone and without the help of those around him. And the time is coming when all great things will be done by that type of cooperation in which each man performs the function for which he is best suited, each man preserves his own individuality and is supreme in his particular function, and each man at the same time loses none of his originality and proper personal initiative, and yet is controlled by and must work harmoniously with many other men."

Source:  Frederick Winslow Taylor, *The Principles of Scientific Management* (New York: Harper & Brothers, 1911), chapter 2.

# 18.2 BOOKER T. WASHINGTON, "THE ATLANTA COMPROMISE" (1895)

On September 18, 1895, noted black leader Booker T. Washington addressed a predominantly white audience at the Cotton States and International Exposition in Atlanta. The "Atlanta Compromise," as it came to be known, much like the curriculum of Washington's Tuskegee Institute, advocated hard work and morality as the path to upward mobility for the black population. As the South moved increasingly in the direction of Jim Crow segregation, white southerners celebrated the speech, pleased by Washington's emphasis on economic cooperation rather than social integration.

One-third of the population of the South is of the Negro race. No enterprise seeking the material, civil, or moral welfare of this section can disregard this element of our population and reach the highest success. I but convey to you, Mr. President and Directors, the sentiment of the masses of my race when I say that in no way have the value and manhood of the American Negro been more fittingly and generously recognized than by the managers of this magnificent Exposition at every stage of its progress. It is a recognition that will do more to cement the friendship of the two races than any occurrence since the dawn of our freedom.

Not only this, but the opportunity here afforded will awaken among us a new era of industrial progress. Ignorant and inexperienced, it is not strange that in the first years of our new life we began at the top instead of at the bottom; that a seat in Congress or the state legislature was more sought than real estate or industrial skill; that the political convention or stump speaking had more attractions than starting a dairy farm or truck garden.

A ship lost at sea for many days suddenly sighted a friendly vessel. From the mast of the unfortunate vessel was seen a signal, "Water, water; we die of thirst!" The answer from the friendly vessel at once came back, "Cast down your bucket where you are." A second time the signal, "Water, water; send us water!" ran up from the distressed vessel, and was answered, "Cast down your bucket where you are." And a third and fourth signal for water was answered, "Cast down your bucket where you are." The captain of the distressed vessel, at last heeding the injunction, cast down his bucket, and it came up full of fresh, sparkling water from the mouth of the Amazon River. To those of my race who depend on bettering their condition in a foreign land or who underestimate the importance of cultivating friendly relations with the Southern white man, who is their next-door neighbor, I would say: "Cast down your bucket where you are"—cast it down in making friends in every manly way of the people of all races by whom we are surrounded.

Cast it down in agriculture, mechanics, in commerce, in domestic service, and in the professions. And in this connection it is well to bear in mind that whatever other sins the South may be called to bear, when it comes to business, pure and simple, it is in the South that the Negro is given a man's chance in the commercial world, and in nothing is this Exposition more eloquent than in emphasizing this chance. Our greatest danger is that in the great leap from slavery to freedom we may overlook the fact that the masses of us are to live by the productions of our hands, and fail to keep in mind that we shall prosper in proportion as we learn to dignify and glorify common labour, and put brains and skill into the common occupations of life; shall prosper in proportion as we learn to draw the line between the superficial and the substantial, the ornamental gewgaws of life and the useful. No race can prosper till it learns that there is as much dignity in tilling a field as in writing a poem. It is at the bottom of life we must begin, and not at the top. Nor should we permit our grievances to overshadow our opportunities.

To those of the white race who look to the incoming of those of foreign birth and strange tongue and habits for the prosperity of the South, were I permitted I would repeat what I say to my own race, "Cast down your bucket where you are." Cast it down among the eight millions of Negroes whose habits you know, whose fidelity and love you have tested in days when to have proved treacherous meant the ruin of your firesides. Cast down your bucket among these people who have, without strikes and labour wars, tilled your fields, cleared your forests, builded your railroads and cities, and brought forth treasures from the bowels of the earth, and helped make possible this magnificent representation of the progress of the South. Casting down your bucket among my people, helping and encouraging them as you are doing on these grounds, and to education of head, hand, and heart, you will find that they will buy your surplus land, make blossom the waste places in your fields, and run your factories. While doing this, you can be sure in the future, as in the past, that you and your families will be surrounded by the most patient, faithful, law-abiding, and unresentful people that the world has seen. As we have proved our loyalty to you in the past, in nursing your children, watching by the sick-bed of your mothers and fathers, and often following them with tear-dimmed eyes to their graves, so in the future, in our humble way, we shall stand by you with a devotion that no foreigner can approach, ready to lay down our lives, if need be, in defense of yours, interlacing our industrial, commercial, civil, and religious life with yours in a way that shall make the interests of both races one. In all things that are purely social we can be as separate as the fingers, yet one as the hand in all things essential to mutual progress. . . .

Nearly sixteen millions of hands will aid you in pulling the load upward, or they will pull against you the load downward. We shall constitute one-third and more of the ignorance and crime of the South, or one-third [of] its intelligence and progress; we shall contribute one-third to the business and industrial prosperity of the South, or we shall prove a veritable body of death, stagnating, depressing, retarding every effort to advance the body politic.

Gentlemen of the Exposition, as we present to you our humble effort at an exhibition of our progress, you must not expect overmuch. Starting thirty years ago with ownership here and there in a few quilts and pumpkins and chickens (gathered from miscellaneous sources), remember the path that has led from these to the inventions and production of agricultural implements, buggies, steam-engines, newspapers, books, statuary, carving, paintings, the management of drug stores and banks, has not been trodden without contact with thorns and thistles. While we take pride in what we exhibit as a result of our independent efforts, we do not for a moment forget that our part in this exhibition would fall far short of your expectations but for the constant help that has come to our educational life, not only from the Southern states, but especially from Northern philanthropists, who have made their gifts a constant stream of blessing and encouragement.

The wisest among my race understand that the agitation of questions of social equality is the extremest folly, and that progress in the enjoyment of all the privileges that will come to us must be the result of severe and constant struggle rather than of artificial forcing. No race that has anything to contribute to the markets of the world is long in any degree ostracized. It is important and right that all privileges of the law be ours, but it is vastly more important that we be prepared for the exercise of these privileges. The opportunity to earn a dollar in a factory just now is worth infinitely more than the opportunity to spend a dollar in an opera-house.

In conclusion, may I repeat that nothing in thirty years has given us more hope and encouragement, and drawn us so near to you of the white race, as this opportunity offered by the Exposition; and here bending, as it were, over the altar that represents the results of the struggles of your race and mine, both starting practically empty-handed three decades ago, I pledge that in your effort to work out the great and intricate problem which God has laid at the doors of the South, you shall have at all times the patient, sympathetic help of my race; only let this be constantly in mind, that, while from representations in these buildings of the product of field, of forest, of mine, of factory, letters, and art, much good will come, yet far above and beyond material benefits will be that higher good, that, let us pray God, will come, in a blotting out of sectional differences and racial animosities and suspicions, in a determination to administer absolute justice, in a willing obedience among all classes to the mandates of law. This, coupled with our material prosperity, will bring into our beloved South a new heaven and a new earth.

Source:  Louis R. Harlan, ed., *The Booker T. Washington Papers*, vol. 3 (Urbana: University of Illinois Press, 1974), pp. 583–587.

# 18.3 THEODORE ROOSEVELT, EXCERPTS FROM "THE STRENUOUS LIFE" (1899)

Drawing upon a national history that celebrated the rugged individual and the conquest of the frontier, Theodore Roosevelt saw an imperial future for the United States as the nineteenth century concluded. In Chicago in April 1899, he addressed an audience of wealthy businessmen at the Hamilton Club and called for bravery and decisive action from public leaders. Roosevelt believed those who wished to lead had a responsibility to uplift both white civilization and the American nation. Manliness was a fundamental part of national leadership, and Roosevelt believed manly, martial action was the only way for the United States to compete in the modern world.

We of this generation do not have to face a task such as that our fathers faced, but we have our tasks, and woe to us if we fail to perform them! We cannot, if we would, play the part of China, and be content to rot by inches in ignoble ease within our borders, taking no interest in what goes on beyond them, sunk in a scrambling commercialism; heedless of the higher life, the life of aspiration, of toil and risk, busying ourselves only with the wants of our bodies for the day, until suddenly we should find, beyond a shadow of question, what China has already found, that in this world the nation that has trained itself to a career of unwarlike and isolated ease is bound, in the end, to go down before other nations which have not lost the manly and adventurous qualities. If we are to be a really great people, we must strive in good faith to play a great part in the world. We cannot avoid meeting great issues. All that we can determine for ourselves is whether we shall meet them well or ill. Last year we could not help being brought face to face with the problem of war with Spain. All we could decide was whether we should shrink like cowards from the contest, or enter into it as beseemed a brave and high-spirited people; and, once in, whether failure or success should crown our banners. So it is now. We cannot avoid the responsibilities that confront us in Hawaii, Cuba, Porto Rico, and the Philippines. All we can decide is whether we shall meet them in a way that will redound to the national credit, or whether we shall make of our dealings with these new problems a dark and shameful page in our history. To refuse to deal with them at all merely amounts to dealing with them badly. We have a given problem to solve. If we undertake the solution, there is, of course, always danger that we may not solve it aright; but to refuse to undertake the solution simply renders it certain that we cannot possibly solve it aright.

The timid man, the lazy man, the man who distrusts his country, the over-civilized man, who has lost the great fighting, masterful virtues, the ignorant man, and the man of dull mind, whose soul is incapable of feeling the mighty lift that thrills "stern men with empires in their brains"—all these, of course, shrink from seeing the nation undertake its new duties; shrink from seeing us build a navy and an army adequate to our needs; shrink from seeing us do our share of the world's work, by bringing order out of chaos in the great, fair tropic islands from which the valor of our soldiers and sailors has driven the Spanish flag. These are the men who fear the strenuous life, who fear the only national life which is really worth leading. They believe in that cloistered life which saps the hardy virtues in a nation, as it saps them in the individual; or else they are wedded to that base spirit of gain and greed which recognizes in commercialism the be-all and end-all of national life, instead of realizing that, though an indispensable element, it is, after all, but one of the many elements that go to make up true national greatness. No country can long endure if its foundations are not laid deep in the material prosperity which comes from thrift, from business energy and enterprise, from hard, unsparing effort in the fields of industrial activity; but neither was any nation ever yet truly great if it relied upon material prosperity alone. All honor must be paid to the architects of our material prosperity, to the great captains of industry who have built our factories and our railroads, to the strong men who toil for wealth with brain or hand; for great is the debt of the nation to these and their kind. But our debt is yet greater to the men whose highest type is to be found in a statesman like Lincoln, a soldier like Grant. They showed by their lives that they recognized the law of work, the law of strife; they toiled to win a competence for themselves and those dependent upon them; but they recognized that there were yet other and even loftier duties—duties to the nation and duties to the race.

We cannot sit huddled within our own borders and avow ourselves merely an assemblage of well-to-do hucksters who care nothing for what happens beyond. Such a policy would defeat even its own end; for as the nations grow to have ever wider and wider interests, and are brought into closer and closer contact, if we are to hold our own in the struggle for naval and commercial supremacy, we must build up our power without our own borders. We must build the isthmian canal, and we must grasp the points of vantage which will enable us to have our say in deciding the destiny of the oceans of the East and the West.

So much for the commercial side. From the standpoint of international honor the argument is even stronger. The guns that thundered off Manila and Santiago, left us echoes of glory, but they also left us a legacy of duty. If we drove out a medieval tyranny only to make room for savage anarchy, we had better not have begun the task at all. It is worse than idle to say that we have no duty to perform, and can leave to their fates the islands we have conquered. Such a course would be the course of infamy. It would be followed at once by utter chaos in the wretched islands themselves. Some stronger, manlier power would have to step in and do the work, and we would have shown ourselves weaklings, unable to carry to successful completion the labors that great and high-spirited nations are eager to undertake.

The work must be done; we cannot escape our responsibility; and if we are worth our salt, we shall be glad of the chance to do the work—glad of the chance to show ourselves equal to one of the great tasks set modern civilization. But let us not deceive ourselves as to the importance of the task. Let us not be misled by vainglory into underestimating the strain it will put on our powers. Above all, let us, as we value our own self-respect, face the responsibilities with proper seriousness, courage, and high resolve. We must demand the highest order of integrity and ability in our public men who are to grapple with these new problems. We must hold to a rigid accountability those public servants who show unfaithfulness to the interests of the nation or inability to rise to the high level of the new demands upon our strength and our resources. . . .

Our army needs complete reorganization—not merely enlarging—and the reorganization can only come as the result of legislation. A proper general staff should be established, and the positions of ordnance, commissary, and quartermaster officers should be filled by detail from the line. Above all, the army must be given the chance to exercise in large bodies. Never again should we see, as we saw in the Spanish war, major-generals in command of divisions who had never before commanded three companies together in the field. Yet, incredible to relate, the recent Congress has shown a queer inability to learn some of the lessons of the war. There were large bodies, of men in both branches who opposed the declaration of war, who opposed the ratification of peace, who opposed the upbuilding of the army, and who even opposed the pur- chase of: armor at a reasonable price for the battle-ships and cruisers, thereby putting an absolute stop to the building of any new fighting-ships for the navy. If, during the years to come, any disaster should befall our arms, afloat or ashore, and thereby any shame come to the United States, remember that the blame will lie upon the men whose names appear upon the roll-calls of Congress on the wrong side of these great questions. On them will lie the burden of any loss of our soldiers and sailors, of any dishonor to the flag; and upon you and the people of this country will lie the blame if you do not repudiate, in no unmistakable way, what these men have done. The blame will not rest upon the untrained commander of untried troops, upon the civil officers of a department the organization of which has been left utterly inadequate, or upon the admiral with an insufficient number of ships; but upon the public men who have so lamentably failed in forethought as to refuse to remedy these evils long in advance, and upon the nation that stands behind those public men. . . .

When once we have put down armed resistance, when once our rule is acknowledged, then an even more difficult task will begin, for then we must see to it that the islands are administered with absolute honesty and with good judgment. If we let the public service of the islands be turned into the prey of the spoils politician, we shall have begun to tread the path which Spain trod to her own destruction. We must send out there only good and able men, chosen for their fitness, and not because of their partisan service, and these men must not only administer im- partial justice to the natives and serve their own government with honesty and fidelity, but must show the utmost tact and firmness, remembering that, with such people as those with whom we are to deal, weakness is the greatest of crimes, and that next to weakness comes lack of consider- ation for their principles and prejudices.

I preach to you, then, my countrymen, that our country calls not for the life of ease but for the life of strenuous endeavor. The twentieth century looms before us big with the fate of many nations. If we stand idly by, if we seek merely swollen, slothful ease and ignoble peace, if we shrink from the hard contests where men must win at hazard of their lives and at the risk of all they hold dear, then the bolder and stronger peoples will pass us by, and will win for themselves the domination of the world. Let us therefore boldly face the life of strife, resolute to do our duty well and manfully; resolute to uphold righteousness by deed and by word; resolute to be both honest and brave, to serve high ideals, yet to use practical methods. Above all, let us shrink from no strife, moral or physical, within or without the nation, provided we are certain that the strife is justified, for it is only through strife, through hard and dangerous endeavor, that we shall ul- timately win the goal of true national greatness.

*Source:* Theodore Roosevelt, "The Strenuous Life" (April 10, 1899).

# 18.4 VISUAL DOCUMENT: LOUIS DALRYMPLE, "SCHOOL BEGINS" (1899)

Toward the end of the nineteenth century, some Americans expressed concern about the motivation behind American imperial action and empire building. The original caption to Louis Dalyrmple's 1899 cartoon, "School Begins," published in *Puck* magazine read: "School Begins. Uncle Sam (to his new class in Civilization): Now, children, you've got to learn these lessons whether you want to or not! But just take a look at the class ahead of you, and remember that, in a little while, you will feel as glad to be here as they are!" The blackboard in the background reads: "The consent of the governed is a good thing in theory, but very rare in fact. . . . England has governed her colonies whether they consented or not. By not waiting for their consent she has greatly advanced the world's civilization. . . . The U.S. must govern its new territories with or without the consent of the governed until they can govern themselves."

*Source:* *Puck* 44, no. 1142 (January 25, 1899). Copyright 1899 by Keppler & Schwarzmann. Library of Congress Prints and Photographs Division Washington, DC.

19

# A United Body of Action

## 1900–1916

## COMMON THREADS

What political problems arose from the transition to an urban, industrial, and national society?

How did women's activism on social issues change the style and content of politics?

Why did party politics decline at the same time that national interest groups emerged?

How did the new interventionism transform the administration of cities and states?

In what ways did progressivism enlarge the president's powers over foreign policy and the economy?

## OUTLINE

**AMERICAN PORTRAIT: Helen Keller**

Toward a New Politics
   The Insecurity of Modern Life
   The Decline of Partisan Politics
   Social Housekeeping
   Evolution or Revolution?

The Progressives
   Social Workers and Muckrakers

**STRUGGLES FOR DEMOCRACY: Public Response to *The Jungle***

   Dictatorship of the Experts
   Progressives on the Color Line

Progressives in State and Local Politics
   Redesigning the City
   Reform Mayors and City Services
   Progressives and the States

A Push for "Genuine Democracy" and a "Moral Awakening"
   The Executive Branch Against the Trusts
   The Square Deal
   Conserving Water, Land, and Forests
   TR and Big Stick Diplomacy
   Taft and Dollar Diplomacy

**AMERICAN LANDSCAPE: The Hetch Hetchy Valley**

Rival Visions of the Industrial Future
   The New Nationalism
   The 1912 Election
   The New Freedom

Conclusion

< The Hull House Choir in Recital, 1910

## AMERICAN PORTRAIT

# Helen Keller

Like many women of her generation, Helen Keller, born in 1880 to a wealthy family in Tuscumbia, Alabama, attended college. Of her first day, she later wrote, "It was a day full of interest for me. I had looked forward to it for years." In 1904, she graduated cum laude from Radcliffe College, the all-women sister institution to Harvard College. Diploma in hand, Keller joined many turn-of-the-century middle-class Americans as they assessed an America in need of change and dedicated themselves to improving it.

Keller, though, was unlike her peers. Blind and deaf since she had been stricken by "brain fever" when she was 19 months old, Keller had completed her university education with the assistance of her long-time friend and teacher, Anne Sullivan, who signed for Helen all the lectures and readings that were not available in Braille. As the first deaf and blind person to earn a college degree, Helen was an object of public fascination, something of a celebrity. The public celebrated her as an example of the triumph of the individual against the most difficult of circumstances. With hard work and dedication, she had overcome unimaginable hurdles.

But Keller, like so many activists at the turn of the century, rejected this model of individualism. An ongoing commitment to the rights of the disabled, coupled with continued reading on society and philosophy by radical authors such as Karl Marx, H. G. Wells, and Eugene Debs, led Keller, in 1908, to join the American Socialist Party, which assessed modern problems as economic in nature and advocated on behalf of (ideally, non-violent) revolution.

The leading causes of disability in the United States, Keller determined, were related to accidents occurring and diseases acquired in the industrial workplace. These accidents and health issues arose as a result of employer greed and negligence, a refusal to make worker safety a priority. Once disabled, people were dismissed, Keller argued, and constituted a class that, as a rule, were poor. They joined the ranks of the impoverished as they were cut off from educational and employment opportunities, condemned to live in overcrowded slums, and received often limited and insufficient medical care.

While Keller claimed the necessity of a full-scale revolution, she echoed the views of those who believed in the need to reform the existing social structure. In her conception of disability rights, the issue was not that disabled people did not fit into society as it was. The issue was that society was constructed in such a way that it failed to fit all of its existing members. She extended this view to a class analysis, believing that capitalism inevitably subjugated the working class and resulted in tremendous inequality. In a 1913 lecture, she made clear the limits of individualism and the need to change society: "[N]o one of us can do anything alone . . . we are bound together. I do not like this world as it is. I am trying to make it a little more as I would like to have it."

Many of Keller's contemporaries likewise believed in the necessity of cooperation and similarly wished to make the world more as they would like to have it. The majority of

American reformers—known as progressives—did not, however, share her political radicalism. The possibility of a violent conflict between rich and poor seemed a very real threat. As a whole, progressive reformers—social workers, journalists, lawyers—optimistically believed in people's ability to improve society and each other (a radicalism of its own kind). They believed in the need for the establishment of and adherence to a moral, distinctly middle-class model, cultivated and spread by new institutions and enforced by new laws. Progressives employed science and religion to justify their beliefs and, upon that basis, advocated for the supervision of human affairs by qualified experts. Critical of the rich and the poor, progressives believed in the necessity of an activist government to oversee the actions and behaviors of both. The radicalism espoused by socialists like Keller pushed conservatives who had long supported a laissez-faire style of government to respond to progressive calls for reform rather than face the possibility of a full-scale political uprising.

# Toward a New Politics

Progressivism displaced the intensely partisan politics of the late nineteenth century. The political and economic crises of the 1890s left Americans disillusioned with traditional parties. A growing socialist movement threatened more radical action if moderate reform failed. Protestant churches spoke out against capitalism's abuses, and new interpretations of Christian ethics lent a moral urgency to reform. The dangers of urban life gave educated, affluent Americans a sense that civic problems needed to be dealt with immediately. Women took leading roles, using pressure groups to extend their influence while also seeking the vote.

Egged on by the press, progressives organized to solve the problems of the new industrial world. Although they sometimes idealized smaller towns and bygone eras, progressives recognized that large-scale industrial capitalism was here to stay. They worked as troubleshooters to make an erratic and brutal system more predictable, efficient, and humane. In pushing for reform, they were willing to enlarge the power of the state and to use it to tell people what was good for them. As reform gained momentum, mayors, governors, and presidential candidates identified themselves and their agendas as progressive.

## The Insecurity of Modern Life

Most people who lived in cities at the turn of the century had grown up in the country (see Figure 19–1). They remembered living in communities where people knew each other, where much of what they ate and wore was made locally. In the modern city, water, fuel, and transportation were all supplied by large, anonymous corporations. Unknown executives made decisions that affected the livelihoods, savings, and safety of thousands of people. City dwellers felt more sophisticated than their parents but also less secure.

City living carried risks. Inspecting a Chicago market, journalist Upton Sinclair found milk laced with formaldehyde, peas colored green with copper salts, and sausage doctored with toxic chemicals. Dozens of patent medicines—including aspirin, cocaine, and heroin—were sold as remedies for everything from hay fever to cancer.

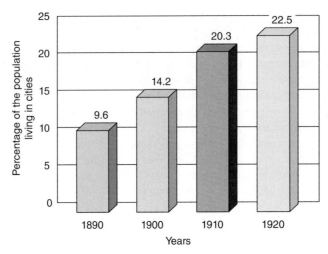

**Figure 19-1 Percentage of the Population Living in Cities, 1890–1920** Cities and towns underwent dramatic growth around the turn of the century. Offices, department stores, and new forms of mass entertainment—from vaudeville to professional sports—drew people to the city center. Railroads and trolleys allowed cities to spread outward, segregating residents by class.
*Source*: Paul Kennedy, *Rise and Fall of the Great Powers* (New York: Random House, 1987), p. 200.

Tenement blocks housing hundreds of people often had no fire escapes or plumbing. Tragedy reminded New Yorkers of these dangers on March 25, 1911, when fire engulfed the Triangle Shirtwaist Company on the top three floors of a 10-story building. Five hundred Jewish and Italian seamstresses were trapped; many jumped from ledges in groups, holding hands. In all, 146 died. Such episodes demonstrated that an unregulated economy could be both productive and deadly.

Government added to the problem. Regulation often created kickbacks and bribery. In 1904 and 1905, journalist Lincoln Steffens uncovered corruption in state after state. In New York, insurance companies paid off elected officials in return for favorable legislation. In San Francisco, boss Abraham Ruef ruled the city with a slush fund from public utilities. The Minneapolis police, along with the mayor's office, protected brothels and gambling dens in return for bribes. Elections made the system less accountable, not more. By creating a demand for campaign funds and jobs, elections became invitations to graft.

The rising middle class found public and corporate irresponsibility infuriating. In stately Victorian "streetcar suburbs," business managers, accountants, engineers, lawyers, and doctors became aware of themselves as a class, but one trapped between two groups, the rich and the masses of wage laborers. Because of education and experience, members of the middle class had their own ideas on how organizations, such as utility companies, cities, and states, should run. Modern corporations needed clear lines of authority, an emphasis on efficiency, and reliable sources of information. Yet these virtues were frustratingly absent from civic life.

**Triangle Shirtwaist Fire**  Disasters often galvanized support for new laws. After the March 25, 1911, fire at the Triangle Shirtwaist Company in Greenwich Village killed 146 young workers, many of whom jumped from the seventh, eighth, and ninth stories of the building to escape flames, New York finally enacted legislation on factory safety.

## The Decline of Partisan Politics

Participation in elections declined by choice and coercion. Nationally, 79 percent of the electorate voted in 1896, but four years later only 73 percent voted, and by 1904 the total fell to 65 percent (see Figure 19–2). Literacy tests accounted for much of the decline in the South, but in all regions the old spectacular style of electioneering, with parades and rallies, gave way to campaigns that were more educational and less participatory. Worse for the parties, the voters split their tickets. The ethnic and sectional loyalties that led to straight party ballots in the late nineteenth century seemed to be weakening.

Increasingly, Americans participated in politics through associations. Voluntary and professional societies took over functions that once belonged to the parties: educating voters and even making policy. These "interest groups" worked outside the system to gather support for a cause or proposal. Many were patterned after corporations, with a board of directors and state and local chapters. Built on the idea that reform was a continuous process, they strove for permanence. Some, such as the National Association for the Advancement of Colored People (NAACP), the Salvation Army, and the Sierra Club, are still prominent.

## Social Housekeeping

The mounting clamor for change aroused political strength in unexpected places. Women's social clubs had been nonpolitical before the turn of the century. Dedicated to developing public talents such as art, speaking, reading, and conversation, they were highly organized, with local, state, and national chapters. A General Federation of Women's Clubs was formed in 1890. Within 10 years, the urgency of social problems led many clubs to campaign for free kindergartens, civil service reform, and public health.

A growing cohort of professional women energized reform. The first generation of graduates from the new women's colleges had reached adulthood, and some, like Helen Keller, had attained advanced degrees at a time when few men went to college. These "new women," as historians have called them, had ambitions and values different from those of their mothers' generation. About half did not marry. With career paths closed to them, educated women found careers by finding problems that needed solving. Florence Kelley, trained as a lawyer, became Illinois's first state factory inspector and later directed the National Consumers League. Margaret Sanger, a New York public health nurse, distributed

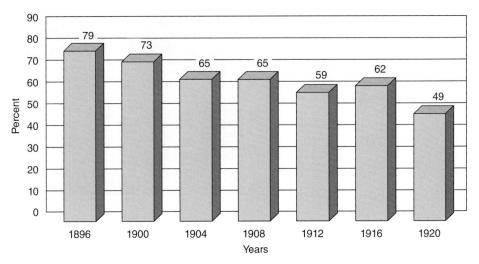

**Figure 19-2   Voter Participation, 1896–1920** After the intense partisanship and high-stakes elections of the 1890s, campaigns became more "educational" and voters lost interest.

literature on birth control and sex education when it was illegal to do so. Sophonisba Breckinridge, with a doctorate from the University of Chicago, led the struggle against child labor. Female activists discovered problems, publicized them, lobbied for new laws, and then staffed the bureaus and agencies administering the solutions.

Women's professional associations, unions, business clubs, ethnic and patriotic societies, and foundations changed the practice of democracy. What was once considered charity or volunteer work became political. Some groups, such as the Young Women's Christian Association (YWCA, 1894) and the International Council of Nurses (1899), had a global reach. The experiences of women's groups taught activists the importance of cooperation, organization, and expertise. When women's clubs built a playground and donated it to the city, they increased their stake in the political system. Likewise, advocating on behalf of women's political role was the National Association of Colored Women's Clubs (NACWC, 1896), which launched campaigns against lynching and Jim Crow laws. All of these organizations gave women new reasons to demand full citizenship.

The women's suffrage movement grew quietly in the early years of the century. Women had gained the vote in four states—Colorado, Wyoming, Utah, and Idaho—but between 1896 and 1910 no other states adopted a women's suffrage amendment. The movement was stubbornly opposed by the Catholic Church, machine politicians, and business interests.

Competing suffrage organizations joined forces under the National American Woman Suffrage Association (NAWSA). Led by Carrie Chapman Catt and Anna Howard Shaw, NAWSA developed a strategy based on professional lobbying and publicity. Suffragists appealed to clubwomen and middle-class reformers by cultivating an image of Victorian respectability and linking suffrage to moderate social causes, such as temperance and education. At first, NAWSA's strategy paid off. After 1910, five states adopted suffrage amendments, but the opposition rallied and defeated referenda in three states.

Frustrated with the glacial pace of progress, Alice Paul's National Woman's Party adopted more radical tactics, picketing the White House and staging hunger strikes. Despite setbacks, women led the transformation of politics through voluntary organizations and interest groups and were on the threshold of even greater gains.

## Evolution or Revolution?

Founded in 1901, the Socialist Party's swelling membership seemed to confirm its claims that the future would be revolutionary rather than progressive. In 1912, Eugene V. Debs, the party's candidate for president, won almost a million votes, or 6 percent of the total. "Gas and water" Socialists, who demanded public ownership of utilities, captured offices in many smaller cities. In the plains states, socialism drew strength from primitive Baptist and Holiness churches and held revival-style tent meetings. In Oklahoma, almost one-quarter of the electorate voted Socialist in 1914.

Although tinged with religion, Socialists' analysis of modern problems was economic. They maintained that the profit motive distorted human behavior, forcing people to compete for survival as individuals instead of joining to promote the common good. Driven by profits, corporations could not be trusted with the welfare of consumers or workers. Socialists demanded the collective ownership of industries, starting with ones that most directly affected people's lives: railroads and city utilities. Socialists had faith that America could make the transition without violence and that socialism was surely "coming like a prairie fire," a Socialist newspaperman told his readers. "Social Gospel" clergymen preached this coming millennium. Washington Gladden, a Congregationalist pastor from Ohio; Walter Rauschenbusch, a Baptist minister from New York; William Dwight Porter Bliss, who founded the Society for Christian Socialists; and George Herron, an Iowa Congregationalist, were among the prominent ministers who interpreted the Bible as a call to social action. Their visions of the Christian commonwealth ranged from reform to revolution, but they all believed that corporate capitalism was organized sin and that the church had an obligation to stand against it.

When the Industrial Workers of the World (IWW) talked about revolution, they meant class war, not elections. Founded in 1905, the IWW (known as the "Wobblies") unionized some of the most rugged individuals in the West: miners, loggers, and even rodeo cowboys (under the Bronco Busters and Range Riders Union). Gathering unskilled workers into "one big union," the Wobblies challenged the AFL's elite unionism and the Socialists' gradualism. With fewer than 100,000 members, the union and its leader, William "Big Bill" Haywood, had a reputation for radicalism. In Lawrence, Massachusetts, and Paterson, New Jersey, IWW strikers clashed with police and paraded under red flags with thousands of marchers. To an anxious middle class, these activities looked like signs of an approaching conflict between rich and poor.

Conservatives and reformers alike felt the hot breath of revolution on their necks, and socialism's greatest influence may have been the push it gave conservatives to support moderate reform. Theodore Roosevelt warned that without reform the United States would divide into two parties, one representing workers, the other capital.

The failure of the two parties to deal with urgent problems created a chance to redefine democracy. As the new century began, Americans were testing their political ideals, scrapping old rules, and getting ready to fashion new institutions and laws to deal with the challenges of modern society.

# The Progressives

Historians have found it difficult to define the progressives. They addressed a wide variety of social problems with many different tactics but appealed to a broad audience. A rally to end child labor, for instance, might draw out young lawyers, teachers, labor unionists, woman suffragists, professors, and politicians. A series of overlapping movements, campaigns, and crusades defined the era from 1890 to 1920.

Progressivism was a political style, a way of approaching problems. Progressives had no illusions that wage labor or industrialism could be eliminated or that it was possible to re-create a rural commonwealth. Big cities and big corporations, they believed, were permanent features of modern life, but progressives were convinced that modern institutions could be made humane, responsive, and moral.

In choosing solutions, progressives relied on scientific expertise as a way to avoid the clash of interests. Those raised during the Civil War knew democracy was no guarantee against mass violence. Rival points of view could be reconciled more easily by impartial authority. Like the salaried managers many of them were, progressives valued efficiency and organization. No problem could be solved in a single stroke, but only by persistent action.

Sure that science and God were on their side, progressives did not balk at imposing their views on other people, even if democracy got in the way. Such measures as naming "born criminals" to be put on probation before committing a crime were called "progressive." To southern progressives, "scientific" principles justified racial segregation. Progressives demanded more democracy when it led to "good government," but if the majority was wrong, in their view, progressives handed power to unelected managers. The basic structure of American society, they felt, should not be open to political debate.

Above all, progressives shared an urgency. "There are two kinds of people," reformer and occupational health expert Alice Hamilton learned from her mother, "the ones who say, 'Someone ought to do something about it but why should it be I?' and the ones who say, 'Somebody must do something about it, then why not I?'" Hamilton and other progressives never doubted which kind they were.

## Social Workers and Muckrakers

Among the first to hear the call to service were the young women and men who volunteered to live among the urban poor in "settlement houses." Stanton Coit established the first on New York's Lower East Side in 1886, but the most famous was Hull House, which opened in Chicago three years later. Its founders, Jane Addams and Ellen Starr, bought a rundown mansion at the center of an inner-city ward thick with sweatshops, factories, and overcrowded tenements. The women of Hull House opened a kindergarten and a clinic, took sweatshop bosses to court, investigated corrupt landlords, criticized the ward's powerful alderman, and built the city's first public playground.

Addams drew together at Hull House a remarkable group of women with similar backgrounds. Florence Kelley organized a movement for occupational safety laws. Julia Lathrop headed the state's Children's Bureau. All three women were raised in affluent Quaker homes during or shortly after the Civil War, and their parents were all abolitionists. Like Helen Keller, all three attended college and traveled or studied in Europe.

As the fame of Hull House spread, women (and some men) organized settlement houses in cities across the country. By the turn of the century there were more than 100, and by 1910 more than 400. Reformers often began by using social science techniques to

**The Hull House Choir in Recital, 1910** Chicago, according to Lincoln Steffens, was "loud, lawless, unlovely, ill-smelling, new; an overgrown gawk of a village." Addams and other settlement workers sought to tame this urban wilderness through culture and activism.

survey the surrounding neighborhoods, gathering information on the national origins, income, housing conditions, and occupations of residents. Addams released *Hull-House Maps and Papers*, a survey of the 19th Ward, in 1895. One of the most ambitious research projects was the Pittsburgh Survey, a massive investigation of city living and working conditions published between 1909 and 1914. Its data confirmed that the causes of poverty were social, not personal, contradicting a common belief that the poor had only themselves to blame. Settlements did "social work" rather than charity.

Surveys also used maps, photographs, and even three-dimensional models. In 1900, housing reformers exhibited a scale cutaway model of a New York tenement block, showing how airless, overcrowded rooms contributed to disease and crime. Shelby Harrison, director of surveys for the Russell Sage Foundation, explained that the survey itself was reform, stimulating popular action with "the correcting power of facts."

This statistical outlook motivated settlement workers to attack urban problems across a broad front. Social workers labored to ensure food safety, repair housing, and sponsor festivals and pageants. Working conditions, especially for women and children, drew special attention, but employers, landlords, and city bosses were not the only targets: those involved in working-class vices—in gambling establishments, saloons, and brothels—were also attacked. The loudest voice of progressivism came from a new type of journalism introduced in 1902. In successive issues, *McClure's* magazine published Lincoln Steffens's investigation of graft in St. Louis and Ida Tarbell's "History of the Standard Oil Company," sensational exposés of the crimes of the nation's political and economic elite. As periodicals competed for readers, the old partisan style of journalism gave way to crusades,

## STRUGGLES FOR DEMOCRACY

# Public Response to *The Jungle*

Like other reform-minded journalists of the Progressive Era, Upton Sinclair believed in the power of the pen to bring attention to various social troubles and inspire demands for social, economic, and political reform. In 1904, Sinclair began an investigation of Chicago's Packingtown during which he learned firsthand of workers' challenges as they attempted to make a living doing the foul work available in Chicago's stockyards. The result of his investigation was the 1906 novel *The Jungle*. The title reflected Sinclair's critique of the United States' capitalist economy—a cutthroat system, he believed, that robbed people of their humanity as they struggled to survive. Chronicling the travails of the working poor and revealing the horrors of the American meatpacking enterprise through the struggles of Lithuanian immigrant Jurgis Rudkus and his family, the book revealed the limits to the rugged individualism so celebrated by Gilded Age leaders and those who touted the virtues of social Darwinism. Sinclair hoped readers would empathize with workers who toiled under atrocious work conditions, lived in squalor,

and suffered from political corruption, all while struggling to achieve the upward mobility they had imagined American life would provide. Socialism, the book concludes, with its focus on equity and cooperation, could lead the American people to a more humane existence.

The novel was an immediate sensation. In the first month and a half after publication, the book sold 25,000 copies. Audiences read Sinclair's fictional account as though it were fact and were outraged by what they read. But the outrage—and calls for reform—differed from what Sinclair had intended. Rather than creating cross-class consciousness or fostering a sense of solidarity with the working-class immigrants described in the text, the novel succeeded in outraging middle-class citizens in their identification as consumers, horrified by descriptions of diseased meat and chemical preservatives in products they might have purchased.

President Theodore Roosevelt, no fan of muckrakers, was persuaded by Sinclair's indictment of the meatpacking industry. A self-identified progressive, Roosevelt was inclined to regulate food and drugs

celebrities, and "sob sister" features. The new 10-cent magazines, such as *Everybody's*, *Cosmopolitan*, and *McClure's*, had audiences and budgets big enough to pay for in-depth investigations. The result was a type of reporting Theodore Roosevelt disdainfully called "muckraking." Readers loved it, and an article exposing some new corporate or public villainy could easily sell half a million copies.

Muckrakers named names. Upton Sinclair described the grisly business of canning beef. Ray Stannard Baker investigated railroads and segregation. Samuel Hopkins Adams catalogued the damage done by narcotics in popular medicines. Tarbell exposed Standard Oil's camouflaged companies, espionage, sweetheart deals, and predatory pricing.

**Meat Inspectors** Hogs receive a final inspection at Swift & Co., Chicago, 1906.

to prevent misbranding and adulteration. Direct response from readers pushed him to act. When angry letters from those who had read *The Jungle* began to arrive at the White House, Roosevelt authorized the Department of Agriculture to investigate meatpacking in Chicago. Their claim that conditions were fine came as no surprise to Sinclair, who told the president that sending those officials was tantamount to sending a criminal to investigate a crime. When the two men met in the aftermath of this first investigation, Roosevelt resolved to send the US labor commissioner Charles P. Neill and Assistant Treasury Secretary James Bronson Reynolds, assisted by Socialist activist and political organizer Ella Reeve Bloor, to conduct an independent investigation. Their June 1906 report matched descriptions from Sinclair's text. They described "a humid atmosphere heavy with the odors of rotten wood, decayed meats, stinking offal, and entrails" and "dirty, blood-soaked, rotting wood floors, fruitful culture beds for the disease germs of men and animals."

In the aftermath of the report—and as a result of the efforts of other muckrakers like Samuel Hopkins Adams, who called attention to the patent medicine industry's false claims and peddling of often dangerous products—President Roosevelt endorsed the Pure Food and Drug Act of 1906 as well as the Federal Meat Inspection Act of the same year. The laws created sanitary standards for the meatpacking industry and federal inspections of animals to be slaughtered, and made criminal the misbranding of food and drugs. Demonstrating the progressive commitment to research, problem solving, and government oversight, the legislation also represented the power of the public voice in effecting real change.

Her series shattered the notion that industrial giants competed in a free market and pushed the Justice Department to sue Standard Oil in 1906 for conspiracy to restrain trade.

The 10-cent magazines projected local problems onto a national canvas. Newspapers had covered municipal corruption before, but Steffens's series in *McClure's* revealed that bribery, influence peddling, and protection rackets operated in nearly every major city. Magazines also reported on progressive victories, allowing solutions adopted in Toledo or Milwaukee to spread quickly. Muckraking declined after 1912, the victim of corporate advertising boycotts and declining readership, but while it lasted, "public opinion" became a force that could shake the powerful.

## Dictatorship of the Experts

For doctors, lawyers, and engineers, reform offered a chance to apply their skills to urgent problems, and the Progressive Era coincided with the rise in influence of the social sciences and the professions. Experts could mediate potentially violent conflicts and eliminate the uncertainties of democracy. Scientific advances seemed to justify this faith. In just a generation, antiseptic techniques, X-rays, and new drugs created a new understanding of disease. Electric light, recorded sound, motion pictures, radio, and flight confirmed science's ability to shape the future.

Social workers copied doctors, diagnosing each case with clinical impartiality. Newly professionalized police forces applied the techniques of fingerprinting, handwriting analysis, and psychology to law enforcement. Dietitians installed bland but nutritionally balanced meals in school cafeterias. Reformers tried (but failed) to simplify spelling and bring "efficiency" to the English language.

Trust in science sometimes led to extreme measures. One was the practice of eugenics, an attempt to rid society of alcoholism, poverty, and crime through selective breeding. "If the knowledge [of eugenics] were applied, the defective classes would disappear within a generation," the president of the University of Wisconsin predicted. Persuaded that genetics could save the state money, the Indiana legislature passed a law in 1907 authorizing the forced sterilization of "criminals, idiots, rapists, and imbeciles." Patients with epilepsy, psychiatric disorders, or mental handicaps who sought help at state hospitals were surgically sterilized. Criminals received the same treatment. Seven other states also adopted the "Indiana Plan."

The emphasis on expertise hid a thinly veiled distrust of democracy. Professional educators, for example, took control of the schools away from local boards and gave it to expert administrators and superintendents. They certified teachers and classified students based on "scientific" intelligence tests. To reformers, education was too important to be left to amateurs, such as teachers, parents, or voters.

Progressivism created new social sciences and made universities centers of advocacy. Sociology was a product of the progressive impulse. The study of government became political science, and "scientific" historians searched the past for answers to modern problems. John R. Commons, Richard Ely, and Thorstein Veblen used economics to study how modern institutions developed and functioned. Legal scholars such as Louis Brandeis and Roscoe Pound called for revising the law to reflect social realities.

This stress on expertise made Progressive Era reforms different from those of earlier periods. Instead of trying to succeed at a single stroke—by passing a law or trouncing a corrupt politician—progressives believed in process and established organizations and procedures that would keep the pressure on and make progress a habit.

## Progressives on the Color Line

In her international crusade against lynching, Ida B. Wells-Barnett pioneered some of the progressive tactics of research, exposure, and organization. A schoolteacher in Memphis, Wells-Barnett documented mob violence against African Americans and mobilized opinion in the United States and Britain. Cities that condoned extralegal executions soon faced a barrage of condemnation from church groups and women's clubs. As her Afro-American Council grew, Wells-Barnett joined forces with white suffragists, social workers, and journalists, but her cause was not fully embraced. Many reform groups sympathized with white southerners or wanted to avoid dividing their membership over race.

**Ida B. Wells-Barnett with Her Children** Ida Wells-Barnett, journalist and activist, made lynching an international issue through her writing and speaking tours.

Reformers debated how much progress non-Anglo-Saxons were capable of, but they were inclined to be pessimistic. Eugenics gave white supremacy the endorsement of science. A new technology, the motion picture, showed its power to rewrite history from a racial viewpoint in D. W. Griffith's classic *Birth of a Nation* (1915), which romanticized the Klan's campaign of terror during Reconstruction. Policy was often based on racial assumptions. Trade schools, not universities, were deemed appropriate for educating Filipinos and Hawaiians. Progressives took Native American children from their families and placed them in boarding schools. Electoral reform in Texas meant disfranchising Spanish-speaking voters.

Wells-Barnett was not alone in finding doors through this wall of racial ideology. William Edward Burghardt DuBois documented the costs of racism in *The Philadelphia Negro* (1898). The survey spoke the progressives' language, insisting that discrimination was not just morally wrong but inefficient, because it took away work and encouraged alcoholism and crime. DuBois transformed the politics of race as profoundly as Addams transformed the politics of cities.

Raised in Massachusetts, DuBois learned Latin and Greek in public schools. At 17, he went to Fisk University in Tennessee, where he "came in contact for the first time with a sort of violence that [he] had never realized in New England." He also had his first encounter with African American religion and gospel music, which was "full of the voices of the past." DuBois later studied at Harvard and Berlin.

DuBois and Booker T. Washington espoused opposing visions of African Americans' place in the United States. Both emphasized the importance of thrift and hard work. DuBois, however, rejected Washington's willingness to accept legal inequality. DuBois came to believe that the Atlanta Compromise (see Chapter 18) led only to disfranchisement and segregation. He disliked the way Washington's influence with white philanthropists silenced other voices. Five years after the Atlanta speech he opened a sustained attack on Washington's "Tuskegee Machine."

In *The Souls of Black Folk* (1903), DuBois argued that the strategy of accommodation contained a "triple paradox": Washington had urged African Americans to seek industrial training, build self-respect, and become successful in business, while asking them to stop striving for higher education, civil rights, or political power. How could a people train themselves without higher education or gain self-respect without having any of the rights other Americans enjoyed—or succeed in business without the power to protect themselves or their property? Economic, political, and educational progress had to move together. Like other progressives, DuBois insisted on the importance of process and organization. African Americans could not stop demanding the vote, equality, or education.

In July 1905, DuBois and 28 African American leaders met on the Canadian side of Niagara Falls (no hotel on the US side would admit them) to organize a campaign against racial violence, segregation, and disfranchisement. The Niagara Movement was one of several such organizations. In 1909, Wells-Barnett, Addams, and other reformers created the National Association for the Advancement of Colored People to carry on the fight in the courts. In 1915, the NAACP won a Supreme Court decision outlawing the grandfather clause, which denied the vote to descendants of slaves; but another 40 years passed before it succeeded in overturning *Plessy v. Ferguson*.

# Progressives in State and Local Politics

Progressives were of two minds about the public. Walter Lippmann, a journalist and reformer, could write fondly of "the voiceless multitudes" and contemptuously of the "great dull mass of people who just don't care." Progressives' tactics betrayed this split vision. Their reforms made city government less democratic and more "businesslike." Reforms at the state level, however, expanded voters' power to initiate legislation and remove officeholders. In both cases, the changes enlarged the influence of small-town and urban-middle-class reformers while reducing that of immigrants and the working class.

### Redesigning the City

The machine politicians who ran American cities adapted well to change. To immigrants and factory workers, the local boss was one of the few people looking out for the average person. He rushed to fire scenes to aid homeless victims. He distributed turkeys in poor neighborhoods at Christmas. He could be counted on to post bail or find someone a job. Jane Addams acknowledged that she could not compete with Johnny Powers, the popular local ward boss, this "big manifestation of human friendliness, this stalking survival of village kindness."

Powers and other aldermen sheltered the brothels, saloons, and gambling dens that, in Addams's view, exploited honest workers. Hull House organized to beat Powers in 1895, and in defeat the reformers revealed their frustrations with democracy. The reformers nominated an Irish bricklayer, William Gleeson, whom they thought would appeal to the 19th Ward's working-class voters. But voters said they wanted someone grander to represent them, such as Powers, with his big house and diamond buttons. Gleeson was trounced. Addams was "puzzled, then astounded and indignant" at the outcome.

With officials like Powers in charge, corporations could do what they liked if they padded the right wallets. "If you want to get anything out of the council," the head of the Chicago Chamber of Commerce advised, "the quickest way is to pay for it—not to the city, but to the aldermen." City machines lost their appeal by providing not too few services but too many. As tax burdens grew, wealthier voters clamored for reform. Progressives set out to replace paternalism with efficient, scientific administration.

After the depression of 1893, many groups sprang up to criticize municipal government, which often resembled the federal system in miniature. A mayor, elected by the whole city, presided over a council of representatives from each neighborhood, or ward. This system diluted the influence of the "better classes" and allowed a few powerful wards to rule the city. In 1899, Louisville's Conference for Good City Government proposed a new model, later known as the "strong mayor" system. It gave more power to the mayor and required each council member to represent the whole city. Two years later, after the hurricane and tidal wave destroyed Galveston, Texas, the devastated city tried an even bolder plan (see Chapter 18). The recovery would be run by a commission of five unelected officials, each managing a city department. Des Moines, Iowa, improved on Galveston's design, and by 1911 some 160 cities had commission governments.

The commission resembled a corporate board of directors. Professionalism and accountability, the keys to business success, could make a city run, too. This philosophy led Detroit voters to elect Ford Motor Company's chief efficiency expert, James Couzens, as mayor. Other cities, led by Dayton, Ohio, tried to improve on the city-commission plan by placing local government in the hands of an unelected "city manager."

Middle- and upper-class professionals led this revolution in city government, and they gained the most from it. The new officials could explain where tax money was spent, but there were no turkeys at Christmas. Getting a job from the city meant filling out the proper forms. Reform administrations targeted urban "vice," which included most working-class recreations. Voters also learned that efficiency did not lower taxes. Budgets grew along with the public's demand for services.

## Reform Mayors and City Services

While commissioners rewrote the rules, a new breed of reform mayors cleaned up their cities. Samuel "Golden Rule" Jones, a Welsh immigrant who earned a fortune in the oil fields, won election three times as independent mayor of Toledo. He enacted the eight-hour day for city employees, pushed for public ownership of city utilities, and staged free concerts in the parks. Like Tom Johnson in Cleveland and Hazen Pingree in Detroit, Jones worried less about saloons and more about utilities. Milwaukee, Schenectady, and other cities bought or regulated the private monopolies that supplied lighting, garbage removal, water, and streetcars.

The reform mayors' efforts to humanize the city were supported by architects and engineers who looked to improve urban life through the arrangement of public space. The City Beautiful movement sought to soften the urban landscape with vistas, open spaces, and greenery. The District of Columbia, with its commission government, broad avenues, and parks, furnished a model of city planning, and Congress sought to make it a model of municipal reform as well by introducing a model child-labor law, slum-clearance plan, and school system. The new urban spaces performed social and educational functions as well, especially to Americanize and uplift immigrant city dwellers. New York enacted zoning laws in 1916, and "city planners" joined the ranks of specialists by organizing themselves as a profession.

## Progressives and the States

State reform varied by region. The East mimicked the agenda of urban reform. New York's progressive governor, Charles Evans Hughes, passed laws that prohibited gambling and created a state commission to regulate utilities. In southern states, progressivism often meant refining the techniques of segregation and disfranchisement. Lynching and mob

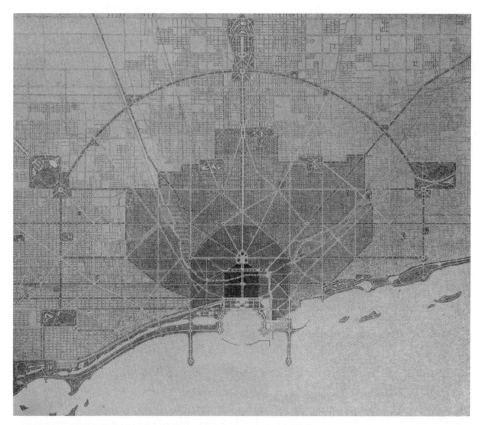

**Daniel Burnham's City Plan for Chicago, 1909** Through comprehensive planning, Burnham sought to save cities from "the chaos incident to rapid growth." He drafted designs for Washington, Cleveland, San Francisco, and Manila.

assaults on African Americans were weekly occurrences in the Progressive Era. White leaders justified segregation and violence in terms used to justify urban reform in the North: the "better classes" had an obligation to rein in the excesses of democracy.

States in the West and Midwest produced the boldest experiments. Oregon introduced the secret ballot, voter registration, and three measures originally proposed by the Populists: the initiative, recall, and referendum. The initiative allowed voters to place legislation on the ballot by petition; the referendum let the legislature put proposals on the ballot; and the recall gave voters the chance to remove officials from office before the end of their terms. Other states soon adopted all or part of the "Oregon system."

The best known of the progressive governors was Robert M. "Fighting Bob" La Follette, whose model of state government came to be known as the "Wisconsin Idea." Elected in 1900, La Follette pushed through a comprehensive program of social legislation. Railways and public utilities were placed under public control. One commission designed a "scientific" distribution of the tax burden, including an income tax, whereas others regulated hours and working conditions and protected the environment. Wisconsin also implemented the direct primary, which allowed party nominees to be chosen directly by voters rather than by party caucuses.

Few machine politicians had as much personal power as the reform governors did. Wisconsin papers would call La Follette a "demagogue," but the reform governors brought policy making out of the "smoke-filled rooms." By shaking up city halls and statehouses, progressives made the public less cynical and government more responsive to reform. They knew, however, that social problems did not respect political boundaries: national corporations and nationwide problems had to be attacked at the federal level, and that meant capturing the White House.

# A Push for "Genuine Democracy" and a "Moral Awakening"

If Theodore Roosevelt stood at the center of the two great movements of his age, imperialism and progressivism, it was because he prepared himself for the part. The Roosevelt family was wealthy and one of the oldest in New York, but Theodore embarked instead on pursuits that were unusual for a man of his class. After graduating from Harvard in 1880, he married, started law school, wrote a history of the War of 1812, bought a cattle ranch in the Dakota Territory, and, most surprisingly, ran for the state legislature.

For Roosevelt's family and friends, government was no place for gentlemen. Roosevelt himself described his colleagues as "a stupid, sodden, vicious lot, most of them being equally deficient in brains and virtue." Avoiding the "rough and tumble," he argued, only conceded high offices to those less fit to lead. Roosevelt's flair for publicity got him noticed, and in 1886 the Republican Party nominated him for mayor of New York. He finished third, behind the Tammany nominee and the Socialist candidate.

A turn as head of New York's board of police commissioners from 1895 to 1897 deepened Roosevelt's commitment to reform. The commission supervised an army of 38,000 policemen. Roosevelt's crackdown on saloons and corruption in the police department earned him a reputation as a man who would not be intimidated, even by his own party's bosses, and when McKinley won the presidency, he named Roosevelt assistant secretary of the navy. The Spanish-American War catapulted him to national fame, and in quick succession he became governor of New York, vice president, and then president of the United States.

Roosevelt believed that to restore democracy—"genuine democracy"—America needed a mission, "a genuine and permanent moral awakening." In the White House, he sought great tasks—duties to be carried out, principles to be upheld, isthmuses to be cut, and lands to be conserved—to inspire a common purpose and test the national will. In the process, he rewrote the president's job description, seizing new powers for the executive branch and turning the presidency into "the administration."

### The Executive Branch Against the Trusts

Roosevelt approached politics the way Jane Addams approached poverty: studying it, living in its midst, and carefully choosing his battles. His fear of radicalism was borne out in September 1901. President William McKinley was shaking hands at the Pan American Exposition in Buffalo, New York, when a man thrust a pistol into his chest and fired twice. The assassin, Leon Czolgosz, came from the Cleveland slums and claimed to seek vengeance for the poor.

At age 42, Roosevelt was the youngest man to attain the presidency. He was the first president to call himself a progressive, and the first, according to Lippmann, "who realized clearly that national stability and social justice had to be sought deliberately and had consciously to be maintained." Unsatisfied merely to lead his party, he set out to remake the executive as the preeminent branch of government, initiating legislation, shaping public opinion, and protecting the national interest at home and abroad. "I believe in power," he explained. Instead of asking Congress for legislation, he drafted bills and lobbied for them personally. He believed government should intervene in the economy to protect citizens or to save business from itself. McKinley had already planned against the trusts, but his plans were not as bold as his successor's.

Challenging the corporations would not be easy. Roosevelt took office less than a decade after J. P. Morgan rescued the federal Treasury. In 1895, the Supreme Court gutted the Sherman Act, one of the few laws allowing federal action against monopolies. The underfunded Interstate Commerce Commission possessed few powers. Roosevelt told Congress "publicity is the only sure remedy which we can now invoke." He used it to the limit, putting Wall Street on notice in his first inaugural when he asserted that trusts "are creatures of the State, and the State not only has the right to control them, but it is duty bound to control them." In 1903, Roosevelt established a Department of Commerce and Labor that required annual reports, making corporate activities transparent.

The Justice Department revitalized the Sherman Act with vigorous prosecutions, and Roosevelt selected cases for maximum publicity value. Attorney General Philander Knox filed suit against J. P. Morgan's holding company, Northern Securities. Morgan expected the matter to be settled in the usual way, and his attorney asked how they might "fix it up." "We don't want to fix it up," Knox replied. "We want to stop it." When the Court handed Roosevelt a victory in 1904, Americans cheered.

With this case, Roosevelt gained an undeserved reputation as a "trust buster." He did oppose serious abuses, but he distinguished between good and bad trusts and believed that government should encourage responsible corporations to grow. He agreed with such progressive writers as Herbert Croly, editor of the *New Republic*, who imagined a central government staffed by nonpartisan experts who would monitor big corporations to assure efficiency and head off destructive actions.

Not all progressives agreed. Louis Brandeis and Woodrow Wilson envisioned a political economy of small, highly competitive firms kept in line by regular use of the Sherman Act. To Roosevelt, there was no future in a small-business economy. Only large combinations could compete on a world scale, and government's obligation was not to break them up but to regulate them. He secured passage of the Hepburn Act (1906), which allowed the commission to set freight rates and banned "sweetheart" deals (of the kind Standard Oil enjoyed) with favored clients. The Elkins Act (1910) regulated telephone, telegraph, and cable communications. The Pure Food and Drug Act (1906) responded to Upton Sinclair's exposé of the meatpacking industry by making it a crime to ship or sell contaminated or fraudulently labeled food and drugs. Under Roosevelt, the federal government gained the tools to counterbalance the power of business. It grew to match its responsibilities. The number of federal employees almost doubled between 1900 and 1916.

## The Square Deal

Roosevelt's exasperation with big business reached a peak during the coal strike of 1902. The United Mine Workers represented 150,000 miners in the coalfields of eastern Pennsylvania. The miners, mostly Polish, Hungarian, and Italian immigrants, earned less than $6 a week, and more than 400 died yearly to supply the coal to run railroads and heat homes. Seventy percent of the mines were owned by six railroads, which in turn were controlled by the usual financiers, including Morgan and Rockefeller. The owners refused to deal with the union, declaring it a band of outlaws. When the miners struck in May, they had the public's sympathy. Editorials, even in Republican newspapers, urged the president to take the mines away from the owners.

The "gross blindness of the operators" infuriated Roosevelt. Coal was the only fuel for heating, and a strike might cause hundreds to freeze. After failing to get the sides to negotiate, he invited union officials and the operators to Washington so that he could personally arbitrate. John Mitchell, head of the mine workers, eagerly accepted the offer, but the owners refused.

For Roosevelt this was the final straw. He prepared the army to move into the coalfields and put the mines under government control. The owners capitulated, agreeing to submit the dispute to a federal commission. The result was a compromise: miners received a 10 percent increase in pay and a nine-hour workday, but owners did not have to recognize the union.

Roosevelt's direct action made the federal government a third force in labor disputes. For the first time a strike was settled by federal arbitration, and for the first time a union had struck a strategic industry without being denounced as a radical conspiracy. The government would no longer automatically side with the corporations. "We demand that big business give the people a square deal," Roosevelt explained. "In return, we must insist that when anyone engaged in big business honestly endeavors to do right, he shall be given a square deal."

## Conserving Water, Land, and Forests

When Roosevelt felt important issues were at stake, he pushed the limits of his office. He enraged Congress by stretching the definitions of presidential power, especially in the area of conservation (see Map 19–1). When Congress sent him a bill to halt the creation of new national forests in the West, Roosevelt first created or enlarged 32 national forests and then signed the bill. To stop private companies from damming rivers, he reserved 2,500 of the best hydropower sites by declaring them "ranger stations." Behind his program was Gifford Pinchot, the chief forester of the United States, who saw conservation as a new frontier. Unsettled, undeveloped lands were growing scarce, and Pinchot convinced the president of the value in managing resources more efficiently. Forests, deserts, and ore ranges were to be used wisely, scientifically, and in the national interest.

One of Roosevelt's first victories was the Newlands Reclamation Act (1902), which gave the Agriculture Department authority to build reservoirs and irrigation systems in the West. In the next four years, 3 million acres were "reclaimed" from the desert and turned into farms. To prevent waste, Roosevelt put tighter controls on prospecting, grazing, and logging. Big lumber and mining companies accepted rationalized resource administration, but small-scale prospectors and ranchers were shut out of federal lands. Naturalists like John Muir also resisted, pointing out that nature was to be appreciated, not used.

By 1909, conservation had become a national issue and created a new constituency of hikers, sightseers, and tourism entrepreneurs. By quadrupling the acreage in federal reserves, professionalizing the Forest Service, and using his "bully pulpit" to build support for conservation, Roosevelt helped create the modern environmental movement.

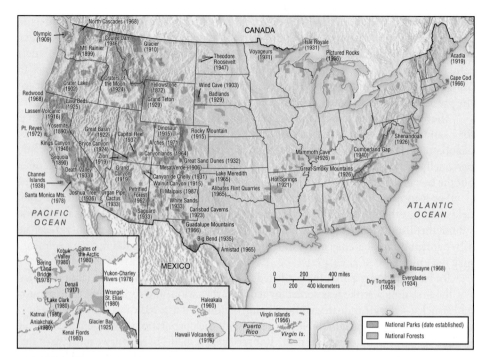

**Map 19-1  Growth of Public Lands** Responding to a national conservation movement, Roosevelt set aside public lands for use as parks and managed-yield forests. The National Park Service was founded in 1916.

## TR and Big Stick Diplomacy

Imperial and commercial expansion put new strains on foreign and military policy after the turn of the century. US investors wanted Washington to protect their overseas factories and railroads against civil wars and hostile governments. Diplomatic and military budgets grew to meet these demands. Diplomats were no longer political cronies but trained professionals, and diplomacy was no longer a matter of weathering "incidents" but of making policy.

Roosevelt's view of world affairs flowed from his understanding of the past and the future. Global trade and communications, he believed, united "civilized" nations. His foreign policy aimed to keep the United States in the mainstream of commerce, imperialism, and military (particularly naval) modernization. He felt a duty to interfere with "barbarian" governments in Asia, Latin America, or Africa that blocked progress. The United States was obliged, he felt, to overthrow governments and even to seize territory when it was acting in the interests of the world as a whole.

Building an interoceanic canal topped Roosevelt's list of foreign policy priorities. A canal would be a hub of world trade and naval power in the Atlantic and Pacific, and Roosevelt aimed to prevent France or Britain from building it. He negotiated a deal to buy out a failed French venture in the Colombian province of Panama.

A civil war in Colombia complicated his plans. In 1902, American diplomats brokered a peace between modernizers led by José Marroquín and traditionalists who fiercely opposed the canal. Marroquín favored it but knew war would erupt again unless the Americans gave Bogotá full control over the canal. For Roosevelt, control was not negotiable.

In the spring of 1903, Panamanian senators, upset by the rejection of the US offer, began planning to secede. Panama had had revolutions before, but the United States had always stepped in to preserve Colombia's sovereignty. Together with Philippe Bunau-Varilla, who represented the French company, the Panamanians lobbied US officials to support their plot. Bunau-Varilla predicted a revolution for November 3, thereby ensuring that the rebels, the Colombian army (which had been bribed into surrendering), and US warships would all be on hand.

The revolution went off without a hitch, and Roosevelt presented the new Panamanian government with a treaty that gave less and took more than the one offered to Colombia. Congress launched an investigation. "I took the canal and let Congress debate," Roosevelt said, "and while the debate goes on the canal does also." The canal, a 50-mile cut built under the direction of George W. Goethals at a cost of $352 million and more than 5,600 lives, opened in 1914.

With construction under way, Roosevelt acted to protect the canal from other powers. Poverty in the region created opportunities for imperial governments to establish bases on Panama's doorstep. In 1902, Germany almost invaded Venezuela over an unpaid loan, but Roosevelt stepped in to mediate. When the Dominican Republic later reneged on its loans, four European nations laid plans for a debt-collecting expedition.

Roosevelt went before Congress in December 1904 and announced a policy later known as the Roosevelt Corollary. It stipulated that when chronic "wrongdoing or impotence" in a Latin American country required "intervention by some civilized nation," the United States would do the intervening. In Roosevelt's view, white "civilized" nations acted; nonwhite "impotent" nations were acted on. The next month, the United States took over the Dominican Republic's customs offices and began repaying creditors. The economic intervention turned military in 1916, when the United States landed marines to protect the customs from Dominican rebels. US troops stayed in the Dominican Republic until the early 1920s.

By enforcing order and efficiency in the Caribbean, Roosevelt extended progressivism beyond the borders of the United States. The movement spread to the Far East, too. In 1906, a US federal court was created in Shanghai, China, to control prostitution in the American community there.

## Taft and Dollar Diplomacy

Enormously popular at the end of his second term, Roosevelt chose his friend William H. Taft to succeed him. Taft gained national attention as a circuit judge whose decisions enlarged federal power to regulate trusts. As governor general of the Philippines, he brought reform to Manila. Taft easily defeated William Jennings Bryan in the 1908 election, and as president he began consolidating Roosevelt's gains. He sent to the states constitutional amendments for the direct election of senators and for the income tax. He increased antitrust enforcement and levied the first tax on corporations. Satisfied that his legacy would continue, Roosevelt left for a tour of Africa.

In the Caribbean, Taft put the Roosevelt Corollary into action (see Map 19–2). The United States bought up the debts of Honduras and Nicaragua. Taft persuaded New York banks to refinance Haiti's debt to prevent German intervention there. Taft intended "dollar diplomacy" to replace force as an instrument of policy, but in most cases, dollars

AMERICAN LANDSCAPE

# The Hetch Hetchy Valley

When landscape painter Albert Bierstadt visited in 1875, he saw a panorama of waterfalls. The canyon walls towered 2,500 feet above a wide, forested meadow populated by herds of elk. Twenty-five years later, San Francisco's mayor James Phelan beheld the cliffs and the pure glacier water pouring into the Tuolumne River and saw his city's answer to the problems of "monopoly and microbes."

The Hetch Hetchy Valley hypnotized naturalists and engineers equally because of its magnificence and its location. It was only 152 miles from San Francisco, close enough both to lure visitors and to channel its waters to the city. A village of less than a thousand in 1848, the City by the Bay was, by 1900, the nation's ninth largest, with 340,000 people. Only water kept it from growing larger.

Hemmed in by ocean on three sides, San Francisco faced a chronic scarcity of fresh water. As the Gold Rush swelled the population, entrepreneurs bought up all available water supplies and formed the Spring Valley Water Company, which monopolized the city's water for 60 years. Water tycoons supported the political machine, led by "Boss" Abe Ruef. The company's water was neither cheap nor safe, causing occasional outbreaks of cholera and typhus.

When voters elected Phelan and a reform ticket in 1897, they expected something to be done about water. The Republican mayor proposed to dam the Hetch Hetchy and build an aqueduct across the Central Valley, breaking the monopoly and making water an abundant, safe public utility.

Many obstacles stood in the way. The city's board of superintendents, controlled by Ruef, sided with Spring Valley and blocked plans for a city reservoir. But it was even harder to get permission from the federal government. Hetch Hetchy was located in Yosemite National Park, one of the first nature preserves, created in 1890 to save its peaks and waterfalls. The parks system was new, and the philosophy of conservation—how to preserve natural resources, and for what purposes—was evolving rapidly. Phelan found an ally in Gifford Pinchot, who filled the newly created office of chief forester.

Pinchot's father had made millions in the lumber trade. Gifford argued that the job of forestry was "to grow trees as a crop." He and Phelan agreed that the two main threats to any resource were inefficient

preceded bullets. For Caribbean nations, American protection meant high import taxes. A revolt usually followed. Marines went into Honduras and Nicaragua in 1912 and stayed until 1933.

Dollar diplomacy also aimed to harness economic power for diplomatic purposes. Taft mobilized a consortium to finance China's Chinchow-Aigun railway. Railroads were instruments of power in North China, and Taft felt he could drive a wedge between the imperial powers—Britain, Russia, and Japan—and compel them to resume open-door trade. Instead, they joined forces against the United States and the Open Door.

use and monopoly control. The few hikers who might enjoy Hetch Hetchy's magnificence were less important than the need "to supply pure water to a great center of population."

Natural and political disasters worked to Phelan's advantage. After the 1906 San Francisco earthquake and fire vividly demonstrated the need for a water supply, Congress allowed the city to apply to use part of Yosemite's land. The following year, a lurid scandal led to a bribery conviction for Ruef and disgrace for his followers. But just as the way seemed clear, a public outcry urged the secretary of the interior to save the Hetch Hetchy.

Behind the campaign were the 1,000-member Sierra Club and its ascetic founder, John Muir. A wilderness explorer and naturalist, Muir was popular for his writings on the transcendent, spiritual aspects of the natural world. "Dam Hetch Hetchy!" he remonstrated. "As well dam for water tanks the people's cathedrals and churches." Historians have characterized the debate between Muir and Pinchot as a contest between rival concepts of environmentalism—conservation for use versus preservation for nature's sake—but the two men also represented opposing interpretations of democracy and the dangers it faced.

"Conservation is the most democratic movement this country has known for generations," Pinchot believed. The Hetch Hetchy project would replace unbridled corporate power with management of natural resources for the public good.

Democratic values were scientific values: efficiency, expertise, and "the greatest good, for the greatest number, for the longest time." For Muir, nature was a refuge where democratic values could survive amid the culture of self-interest and scientific progress. The valley had to be preserved, not just to save the trees but also to "save humans for the wilderness." Only there could people share the nonmaterial values in which democracy took root.

The Sierra Club did not advocate leaving the area pristine. They imagined making Hetch Hetchy a retreat for harried city dwellers, managed by the park service. The public outcry surprised dam advocates, but they managed to cast the "nature lovers" as unwitting tools of the water and power monopolies.

The Roosevelt administration wavered, but in 1913, Phelan got his dam. Muir died a year later. Today the Hetch Hetchy aqueduct delivers 300 million gallons of water a day to San Francisco. But the battle for the valley gave birth to a modern environmental movement. When municipal and mining interests encroached on the Yosemite and Yellowstone preserves in the following decades, they were opposed by a national constituency that saw both activism and wilderness as part of America's heritage.

Despite the setback, Taft still believed that economic power, not military force, was what mattered.

Taft disappointed both conservatives and progressives in his party. He first urged Congress to reduce the tariff, but then he signed the Payne-Aldrich Tariff in 1909, which raised rates on key imports. Taft's secretary of the interior, Richard Ballinger, sided with ranchers and miners who opposed Roosevelt's resource-management policies. When Pinchot, the chief forester, fought back, Taft fired him. When the Ballinger-Pinchot affair revealed the party's divisions, Roosevelt felt his country needed him back.

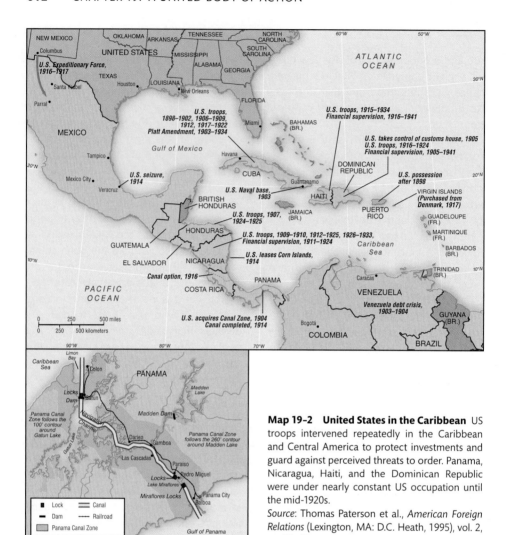

**Map 19-2   United States in the Caribbean** US troops intervened repeatedly in the Caribbean and Central America to protect investments and guard against perceived threats to order. Panama, Nicaragua, Haiti, and the Dominican Republic were under nearly constant US occupation until the mid-1920s.

*Source*: Thomas Paterson et al., *American Foreign Relations* (Lexington, MA: D.C. Heath, 1995), vol. 2, pp. 55, 40.

# Rival Visions of the Industrial Future

After Roosevelt returned from Africa in 1910, Pinchot, La Follette, Croly, and others trooped to his home at Sagamore Hill to complain about Taft. The former president denied any interest in the Republican nomination, but he could not keep his pledge. Roosevelt reentered politics because his views had evolved and because politics was what he knew best. Just 54 years old, his energy undiminished, he took more radical positions on corporations, public welfare, and labor than he had while president. The election of 1912 would define the future of industrial America.

## The New Nationalism

At a sun-baked junction in Osawatomie, Kansas, in August 1910, Roosevelt declared that "the essence of any struggle for liberty . . . is to destroy privilege and give the life of every individual the highest possible value." He laid out a program he called the New Nationalism.

It included the elimination of corporate campaign contributions, the regulation of industrial combinations, an expert commission to set tariffs, a graduated income tax, banking reorganization, and a national workers' compensation program. "This New Nationalism regards the executive power as the steward of the public welfare." The message drew cheers.

Roosevelt had the newspapers, whereas Taft had the delegates. The nomination fight tested the new system of direct primaries. Taft's control of the party machinery helped him in states that chose delegates by convention, but in key states Roosevelt could take his campaign to the voters. At the convention in Chicago in June 1912, Taft's slim but decisive majority allowed him to control the platform and win over undecided delegates. Grumbling that he had been robbed, Roosevelt walked out.

Roosevelt returned to Chicago in August to accept the nomination of the newly formed Progressive Party. The delegates were a mixed group. They included Hiram Johnson, the reform governor of California; muckraking publisher Frank Munsey; imperialist senator Albert Beveridge; and J. P. Morgan's business partner George W. Perkins. The party platform endorsed the New Nationalism, along with popular election of senators, popular review of judicial decisions, and women's suffrage. Women were delegates, and Jane Addams seconded Roosevelt's nomination. The gathering had an evangelical spirit. "Our cause is based on the eternal principles of righteousness," Roosevelt said. "We stand at Armageddon and we battle for the Lord."

## The 1912 Election

In Baltimore the Democrats nominated a former college professor and governor of New Jersey. Like Roosevelt, the young Woodrow Wilson defied his family's expectations by pursuing a political career. He took an unusual route. While studying for a doctorate in government at Johns Hopkins University in 1886, he published his first book, *Congressional Government*, at the age of 28. It advocated enlarging the power of the executive branch. As a professor and later president of Princeton University, he became a well-known lecturer and commentator for new national political magazines such as *Harper's* and the *Atlantic Monthly*. In 1910, he was elected governor of New Jersey and enacted sweeping progressive reforms. For Democrats, smarting from losses under Bryan's leadership, Wilson offered a new image and the ability to unite the South and the East under a progressive program.

With Roosevelt in the race, Wilson had to stake his own claim to the progressive constituency. With the help of Louis Brandeis, Wilson devised a program called the New Freedom. It challenged Roosevelt on his approaches to the economy and politics. Simply regulating the trusts, Wilson argued, would not help consumers, workers, or small entrepreneurs. Instead, it would create a paternalistic bureaucracy. Wilson wanted a lean, strong government and antitrust laws to encourage a return to competition and economic mobility. Both agreed on the importance of a strong executive, but they had different economic formulas. Roosevelt appealed to a collective, national interest, whereas Wilson stressed the needs of individual consumers and investors. The New Nationalism was evangelical, aiming to inspire people to work for the common good. Wilson appealed to reason and self-interest.

On Election Day, the split in the Republican Party gave Wilson a plurality. He won 42 percent of the popular vote, compared with 27 for Roosevelt, 23 for Taft, and 6 for Debs (see Map 19–3). Although his margin was thin, Wilson could interpret Taft's loss and the large combined vote for the progressive candidates as a mandate for change. "What the Democratic Party proposes," he told his followers, is "to do the things the Republican Party has been talking about doing for sixteen years."

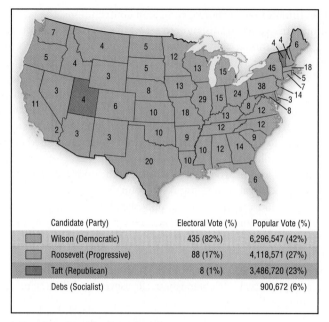

| Candidate (Party) | Electoral Vote (%) | Popular Vote (%) |
|---|---|---|
| Wilson (Democratic) | 435 (82%) | 6,296,547 (42%) |
| Roosevelt (Progressive) | 88 (17%) | 4,118,571 (27%) |
| Taft (Republican) | 8 (1%) | 3,486,720 (23%) |
| Debs (Socialist) | | 900,672 (6%) |

**Map 19-3  The Election of 1912** The election pitted rival visions of progressivism against each other. The decentralized regulation of Wilson's "New Freedom" had more appeal than Roosevelt's far-reaching "New Nationalism."

# Time Line

▼**1889**
Hull House founded

▼**1890**
General Federation of Women's Clubs founded

▼**1893**
Illinois passes eight-hour day for women

▼**1900**
Robert La Follette elected governor of Wisconsin

▼**1901**
Socialist Party of America founded
Galveston introduces commission government

McKinley assassinated; Theodore Roosevelt inaugurated president

▼**1902**
Newlands Reclamation Act funds construction of dams and irrigation systems
*McClure's* publishes first episodes of Ida Tarbell's "History of the Standard Oil Company" and Lincoln Steffens's "The Shame of the Cities"
Roosevelt settles anthracite strike

▼**1903**
Roosevelt establishes Department of Commerce and Labor
Panama declares independence from Colombia

W. E. B. DuBois publishes *The Souls of Black Folk*

▼**1904**
Justice Department sues Standard Oil under the Sherman Anti-Trust Act
US Supreme Court orders Northern Securities Company dissolved as an illegal combination
Roosevelt elected president
The Roosevelt Corollary announced

▼**1905**
United States takes over Dominican customs
Industrial Workers of the World founded

## The New Freedom

Within a year and a half of his inauguration, Wilson produced one of the most coherent and far-reaching legislative programs ever devised by a president. Drawing on his long study of congressional politics, he seized the advantage of his party's majority and exercised an unprecedented degree of personal control through the majority leaders in both houses. The New Freedom advocated lower tariffs, increased competition, and vigorous antitrust enforcement. Three monumental bills passed through Congress in rapid succession.

The first bill was the Underwood-Simmons Tariff (1913), which made the first deep cuts in tariff rates since before the Civil War. The bill overturned a cornerstone of Republican economic policy, the protectionist tariff. It helped farmers and consumers by lowering prices and increasing competition, but Wilson argued that its real beneficiaries would be manufacturers. Lower tariffs would help persuade other countries to reduce taxes on imports from the United States, opening new markets for American-made goods. Wilson created an expert Tariff Commission in 1916 to improve tariff bargaining. The most-favored-nation policies it implemented (and which remain in place) induced European powers to open their empires to American goods. The Singer, Ford, and Camel brand names began appearing in markets from Caracas to Mandalay.

Wilson next targeted the banking system. When Steffens and Lippmann investigated banking for *Everybody's* magazine in 1908, they found that its structure was "strikingly like that of Tammany Hall," with a similar concentration of power, lack of accountability, and extralegal maneuvering. The Federal Reserve Act of 1913 set up a national board to supervise the system and created 12 regional reserve banks throughout the country.

▼**1906**
Hepburn Act passed, allowing the Interstate Commerce Commission to set freight rates
Pure Food and Drug Act requires accurate labeling

▼**1907**
Indiana passes forcible sterilization law

▼**1908**
William H. Taft elected president
Helen Keller joins the American Socialist Party

▼**1909**
Payne-Aldrich Tariff goes into effect
NAACP founded

▼**1910**
Taft fires chief forester Gifford Pinchot
Elkins Act authorizes Interstate Commerce Commission to regulate electronic communications
Roosevelt announces the New Nationalism

▼**1911**
Triangle Shirtwaist Company fire

▼**1912**
US troops occupy Nicaragua
Woodrow Wilson elected president

▼**1913**
Federal Reserve Act reorganizes banking system
Underwood-Simmons Tariff

▼**1914**
Panama Canal completed
Clayton Antitrust Act strengthens antitrust enforcement

▼**1916**
New York City enacts zoning laws
Federal workers' compensation, child-labor, and eight-hour-day laws passed

Banks were now watched to ensure that their reserves matched their deposits. The system's real advantage was the flexibility it gave the currency. The board could put more dollars into circulation when demand was high and retire them when it subsided. Regional banks could adjust the money supply to meet local needs. The system broke Wall Street's stranglehold on credit and opened new opportunities for entrepreneurship and competition.

Finally, Wilson attacked the trusts. He established the Federal Trade Commission (FTC), an independent regulatory commission assigned to enforce free and fair competition. It absorbed the functions of Roosevelt's Bureau of Corporations, but with more authority, including the right to subpoena corporate records and issue cease-and-desist orders. The Clayton Antitrust Act (1914) prohibited price fixing, outlawed interlocking directorates, and made it illegal for a company to own the stock of competitors. To enforce these provisions, citizens were entitled to sue for triple the amount of the actual damages they suffered. In 1916, Wilson produced more reform legislation, including the first national workers' compensation and child-labor laws, the eight-hour day for railroad workers, and the Warehouse Act, which extended credit to cash-strapped farmers.

These programs furthered Wilson's goal of "releasing the energies" of consumers and entrepreneurs, but they also helped business. Businessmen headed many of the regulatory boards, and the FTC and Federal Reserve Board helped stabilize unruly markets. The New Freedom brought reform without the elaborate state machinery of the New Nationalism or European industrial nations. The New Freedom linked liberal reform to individual initiative and free markets.

## Conclusion

By 1900, America's political economy had outgrown the social relationships and laws that served the rural republic for most of the nineteenth century. Squeezed between corporate elites and the large, transient immigrant communities that controlled urban politics, middle-class reformers created a new style of political participation. They experimented with new forms of political decision making and vested the state with responsibility for the quality of life of its citizens. Progressives challenged but never upset the system. Science and the pressure of informed opinion, they believed, could produce managed, orderly change without open conflict.

The progressive presidents took this movement to the national stage. Roosevelt and Wilson touted their programs as attacks on privilege, but both presidents helped position the federal government as a broker among business, consumer, and labor interests. In less than two decades, the federal government overcame its reputation for corruption and impotence and moved to the center of economic and social life. The concept of a "national interest" greater than individual and property rights was now firmly ingrained; so, too, was the need to protect it. The president's leadership now extended beyond the administration to Congress and public opinion. These achievements created a modern central government just as military, diplomatic, and economic victories made the United States a global power. War and its aftermath would curtail the progressive movement, as support for a strong central government would be tested by events unfolding in Europe.

# Who, What, Where

Addams, Jane 596

Chicago 591

City-commission plan 603

Debs, Eugene V. 590

DuBois, W. E. B. 601

Eugenics 600

Hetch Hetchy Valley 610

Hull House 596

Initiative, recall, and referendum 604

Interest groups 593

Panama Canal 608

Roosevelt, Theodore 595

Wilson, Woodrow 606

# Review Questions

1. Why did reformers feel that privately owned utilities caused corruption?

2. What were the Oregon system and the Wisconsin Idea?

3. Choose one level of government—local, state, or federal—and describe three key progressive reforms.

# Critical-Thinking Questions

1. Were the progressives' goals conservative or radical? What about their strategies? Explain your answers.

2. Theodore Roosevelt has been called the first modern president. In what ways did he change the presidency?

3. Did the progressives' emphasis on research and documentation indicate their respect for public opinion or not? Explain your answer.

# Suggested Readings

Bederman, Gail. *Manliness and Civilization: A Cultural History of Gender and Race in the United States, 1880–1917*. Chicago: University of Chicago Press, 1997.

Library of Congress. Progressive Era to New Era. http://www.loc.gov/teachers/classroommaterials/presentationsandactivities/presentations/timeline/progress/

Marten, James, ed. *Children and Youth During the Gilded Age and Progressive Era*. New York: New York University Press, 2014.

McGerr, Michael. *A Fierce Discontent: The Rise and Fall of the Progressive Movement in America, 1870–1920*. New York: Free Press, 2003.

Painter, Nell Irvin. *Standing at Armageddon: The United States, 1877–1919*. New York: W. W. Norton, 1987.

**For further review materials and resource information, please visit www.oup.com/us/oakes-mcgerr**

## 19.1 JANE ADDAMS, EXCERPTS FROM *TWENTY-YEARS AT HULL HOUSE WITH AUTOBIOGRAPHICAL NOTES* (1910)

Jane Addams, inspired by Oxford University graduates who worked in London's poorest neighborhoods, led the settlement house movement in the United States. Addams co-founded Hull House in Chicago, which offered the city's poor a variety of social services and educational opportunities, and advocated on behalf of their rights against corrupt landlords and politicians. Addams celebrated the desire expressed by educated young people of financial means to follow the path of progressive reform and worked to improve life for Americans across social class and status.

This paper is an attempt to analyze the motives which underlie a movement based, not only upon conviction, but upon genuine emotion, wherever educated young people are seeking an outlet for that sentiment of universal brotherhood, which the best spirit of our times is forcing from an emotion into a motive. These young people accomplish little toward the solution of this social problem, and bear the brunt of being cultivated into unnourished, oversensitive lives. They

Jane Addams in 1914, 25 years after she founded Chicago's Hull House.

*Source:* Library of Congress Prints and Photographs Division, Washington, DC.

have been shut off from the common labor by which they live which is a great source of moral and physical health. They feel a fatal want of harmony between their theory and their lives, a lack of coordination between thought and action. I think it is hard for us to realize how seriously many of them are taking to the notion of human brotherhood, how eagerly they long to give tangible expression to the democratic ideal. These young men and women, longing to socialize their democracy, are animated by certain hopes which may be thus loosely formulated; that if in a democratic country nothing can be permanently achieved save through the masses of the people, it will be impossible to establish a higher political life than the people themselves crave; that it is difficult to see how the notion of a higher civic life can be fostered save through common intercourse; that the blessings which we associate with a life of refinement and cultivation can be made universal and must be made universal if they are to be permanent; that the good we secure for ourselves is precarious and uncertain, is floating in mid-air, until it is secured for all of us and incorporated into our common life. It is easier to state these hopes than to formulate the line of motives, which I believe to constitute the trend of the subjective pressure toward the Settlement.

There is something primordial about these motives, but I am perhaps overbold in designating them as a great desire to share the race life. We all bear traces of the starvation struggle which for so long made up the life of the race. Our very organism holds memories and glimpses of that long life of our ancestors which still goes on among so many of our contemporaries. Nothing so deadens the sympathies and shrivels the power of enjoyment, as the persistent keeping away from the great opportunities for helpfulness and a continual ignoring of the starvation struggle which makes up the life of at least half the race. To shut one's self away from that half of the race life is to shut one's self away from the most vital part of it; it is to live out but half the humanity to which we have been born heir and to use but half our faculties. We have all had longings for a fuller life which should include the use of these faculties. . . .

"It is true that there is nothing after disease, indigence and a sense of guilt, so fatal to health and to life itself as the want of a proper outlet for active faculties." I have seen young girls suffer and grow sensibly lowered in vitality in the first years after they leave school. In our attempt then to give a girl pleasure and freedom from care we succeed, for the most part, in making her pitifully miserable. She finds "life" so different from what she expected it to be. She is besotted with innocent little ambitions, and does not understand this apparent waste of herself, this elaborate preparation, if no work is provided for her. There is a heritage of noble obligation which young people accept and long to perpetuate. The desire for action, the wish to right wrong and alleviate suffering haunts them daily. Society smiles at it indulgently instead of making it of value to itself.

We have in America a fast-growing number of cultivated young people who have no recognized outlet for their active faculties. They hear constantly of the great social maladjustment, but no way is provided for them to change it, and their uselessness hangs about them heavily. . . . These young people have had advantages of college, of European travel, and of economic study, but they are sustaining this shock of inaction. They have pet phrases, and they tell you that the things that make us all alike are stronger than the things that make us different. They say that all men are united by needs and sympathies far more permanent and radical than anything that temporarily divides them and sets them in opposition to each other. If they affect art, they say that the decay in artistic expression is due to the decay in ethics, that art when shut away from the human interests and from the great mass of humanity is self-destructive. They tell their elders with all the bitterness of youth that if they expect success from them in business or politics or in whatever lines their ambition for them has run, they must let them consult all of humanity; that they must let them find out what the people want and how they want it. It is only the stronger young people, however, who formulate this. Many of them dissipate their energies in so-called enjoyment. Others not content with that, go on studying and go back to college for their second degrees; not that they are especially fond of study, but because they want something definite to do, and their powers have been trained in the direction of mental accumulation. Many are buried beneath this mental accumulation with lowered vitality and discontent. . . .

Other motives which I believe make toward the Settlement are the result of a certain renaissance going forward in Christianity. The impulse to share the lives of the poor, the desire to make social service, irrespective of propaganda, express the spirit of Christ, is as old as Christianity itself. . . .

I believe that there is a distinct turning among many young men and women toward this simple acceptance of Christ's message. They resent the assumption that Christianity is a set of ideas which belong to the religious consciousness, whatever that may be. They insist that it cannot be proclaimed and instituted apart from the social life of the community and that it must seek a simple and natural expression in the social organism itself. The Settlement movement is only one manifestation of that wider humanitarian movement which throughout Christendom, but preeminently in England, is endeavoring to embody itself, not in a sect, but in society itself.

The Settlement, then, is an experimental effort to aid in the solution of the social and industrial problems which are engendered by the modern conditions of life in a great city. It insists that these problems are not confined to any one portion of a city. It is an attempt to relieve, at the same time, the overaccumulation at one end of society and the destitution at the other; but it assumes that this overaccumulation and destitution is most sorely felt in the things that pertain to social and educational advantages. From its very nature it can stand for no political or social propaganda. It must, in a sense, give the warm welcome of an inn to all such propaganda, if perchance one of them be found an angel. The one thing to be dreaded in the Settlement is that it lose its flexibility, its power of quick adaptation, its readiness to change its methods as its environment may demand. It must be open to conviction and must have a deep and abiding sense of tolerance. It must be hospitable and ready for experiment. It should demand from its residents a scientific patience in the accumulation of facts and the steady holding of their sympathies as one of the best instruments for that accumulation. It must be grounded in a philosophy whose foundation is on the solidarity of the human race, a philosophy which will not waver when the race happens to be represented by a drunken woman or an idiot boy. Its residents must be emptied of all conceit of opinion and all self-assertion, and ready to arouse and interpret the public opinion of their neighborhood. They must be content to live quietly side by side with their neighbors, until they grow into a sense of relationship and mutual interests. Their neighbors are held apart by differences of race and language which the residents can more easily overcome. They are bound to see the needs of their neighborhood as a whole, to furnish data for legislation, and to use their influence to secure it. In short, residents are pledged to devote themselves to the duties of good citizenship and to the arousing of the social energies which too largely lie dormant in every neighborhood given over to industrialism. They are bound to regard the entire life of their city as organic, to make an effort to unify it, and to protest against its overdifferentiation.

It is always easy to make all philosophy point to one particular moral and all history adorn one particular tale; but I may be forgiven the reminder that the best speculative philosophy sets forth the solidarity of the human race; that the highest moralists have taught that without the advance and improvement of the whole, no man can hope for any lasting improvement in his own moral or material individual condition; and that the subjective necessity for Social Settlements is therefore identical with that necessity, which urges us on toward social and individual salvation.

*Source:* Jane Addams, *Twenty-Years at Hull House with Autobiographical Notes* (New York: The Macmillan Company, 1910; twenty-fifth printing, 1968), pp. 200–204.

## 19.2 UPTON SINCLAIR, EXCERPTS FROM *THE JUNGLE* (1906)

Muckraking journalist Upton Sinclair used the power of his pen to expose the corrupt conditions of Packingtown, Chicago's meatpacking district in the early 1900s. In 1906, after spending weeks interviewing and living among workers, Sinclair wrote *The Jungle*, the story of Jurgis Rudkus and his family, which chronicles working-class poverty and the immigrant experience. In the novel, Sinclair detailed the ways packing houses "doctored" the meat sold to the American public. Outrage at the conditions exposed by Sinclair led to nationwide reform.

The people of Chicago saw the government inspectors in Packingtown, and they all took that to mean that they were protected from diseased meat; they did not understand that these hundred and sixty-three inspectors had been appointed at the request of the packers, and that they were paid by the United States government to certify that all the diseased meat was kept in the state.

They had no authority beyond that; for the inspection of meat to be sold in the city and state the whole force in Packingtown consisted of three henchmen of the local political machine!

And shortly afterward one of these, a physician, made the discovery that the carcasses of steers which had been condemned as tubercular by the government inspectors, and which therefore contained ptomaines, which are deadly poisons, were left upon an open platform and carted away to be sold in the city; and so he insisted that these carcasses be treated with an injection of kerosene—and was ordered to resign the same week! So indignant were the packers that they went farther, and compelled the mayor to abolish the whole bureau of inspection; so that since then there has not been even a pretense of any interference with the graft. There was said to be two thousand dollars a week hush money from the tubercular steers alone; and as much again from the hogs which had died of cholera on the trains, and which you might see any day being loaded into boxcars and hauled away to a place called Globe, in Indiana, where they made a fancy grade of lard.

Jurgis heard of these things little by little, in the gossip of those who were obliged to perpetrate them. It seemed as if every time you met a person from a new department, you heard of new swindles and new crimes. There was, for instance, a Lithuanian who was a cattle butcher for the plant where Marija had worked, which killed meat for canning only; and to hear this man describe the animals which came to his place would have been worthwhile for a Dante or a Zola. It seemed that they must have agencies all over the country, to hunt out old and crippled and diseased cattle to be canned. There were cattle which had been fed on "whisky-malt," the refuse of the breweries, and had become what the men called "steerly"—which means covered with boils. It was a nasty job killing these, for when you plunged your knife into them they would burst and splash foul-smelling stuff into your face; and when a man's sleeves were smeared with blood, and his hands steeped in it, how was he ever to wipe his face, or to clear his eyes so that he could see? It was stuff such as this that made the "embalmed beef" that had killed several times as many United States soldiers as all the bullets of the Spaniards; only the army beef, besides, was not fresh canned, it was old stuff that had been lying for years in the cellars.

Then one Sunday evening, Jurgis sat puffing his pipe by the kitchen stove, and talking with an old fellow whom Jonas had introduced, and who worked in the canning rooms at Durham's; and so Jurgis learned a few things about the great and only Durham canned goods, which had become a national institution. They were regular alchemists at Durham's; they advertised a mushroom-catsup, and the men who made it did not know what a mushroom looked like. They advertised "potted chicken,"—and it was like the boardinghouse soup of the comic papers, through which a chicken had walked with rubbers on. Perhaps they had a secret process for making chickens chemically—who knows? said Jurgis' friend; the things that went into the mixture were tripe, and the fat of pork, and beef suet, and hearts of beef, and finally the waste ends of veal, when they had any. They put these up in several grades, and sold them at several prices; but the contents of the cans all came out of the same hopper. And then there was "potted game" and "potted grouse," "potted ham," and "deviled ham"—de-vyled, as the men called it. "De-vyled" ham was made out of the waste ends of smoked beef that were too small to be sliced by the machines; and also tripe, dyed with chemicals so that it would not show white; and trimmings of hams and corned beef; and potatoes, skins and all; and finally the hard cartilaginous gullets of beef, after the tongues had been cut out. All this ingenious mixture was ground up and flavored with spices to make it taste like something. Anybody who could invent a new imitation had been sure of a fortune from old Durham, said Jurgis' informant; but it was hard to think of anything new in a place where so many sharp wits had been at work for so long; where men welcomed tuberculosis in the cattle they were feeding, because it made them fatten more quickly; and where they bought up all the old rancid butter left over in the grocery stores of a continent, and "oxidized" it by a forced-air process, to take away the odor, rechurned it with skim milk, and sold it in bricks in the cities! Up to a year or two ago it had been the custom to kill horses in the yards—ostensibly for fertilizer; but after long agitation the newspapers had been able to make

Upton Sinclair wrote about the hazardous working conditions immigrant and American workers endured as they took up employment in Chicago's meatpacking industry. But while Sinclair hoped to outrage readers about the plight of workers, such as those pictured here, readers generally focused more on the potential health risks they faced as consumers of the meat processed in Chicago's stockyards.

*Source:* Copyright 1909, by Kelley & Chadwick. Library of Congress Prints and Photographs Division Washington, D.C.

the public realize that the horses were being canned. Now it was against the law to kill horses in Packingtown, and the law was really complied with—for the present, at any rate. Any day, however, one might see sharp-horned and shaggy-haired creatures running with the sheep and yet what a job you would have to get the public to believe that a good part of what it buys for lamb and mutton is really goat's flesh!

There was another interesting set of statistics that a person might have gathered in Packingtown—those of the various afflictions of the workers. When Jurgis had first inspected the packing plants with Szedvilas, he had marveled while he listened to the tale of all the things that were made out of the carcasses of animals, and of all the lesser industries that were maintained there; now he found that each one of these lesser industries was a separate little inferno, in its way as horrible as the killing beds, the source and fountain of them all. The workers in each of them had their own peculiar diseases. And the wandering visitor might be skeptical about all the swindles, but he could not be skeptical about these, for the worker bore the evidence of them about on his own person—generally he had only to hold out his hand.

There were the men in the pickle rooms, for instance, where old Antanas had gotten his death; scarce a one of these that had not some spot of horror on his person. Let a man so much as scrape his finger pushing a truck in the pickle rooms, and he might have a sore that would put him out of the world; all the joints in his fingers might be eaten by the acid, one by one. Of the butchers and floorsmen, the beef-boners and trimmers, and all those who used knives, you could scarcely find a person who had the use of his thumb; time and time again the base of it had been slashed, till it was a mere lump of flesh against which the man pressed the knife to hold it. The hands of these men would be criss-crossed with cuts, until you could no longer pretend to count them or to trace them. They would have no nails,—they had worn them off pulling hides; their knuckles were swollen so that their fingers spread out like a fan. There were men who worked in the cooking rooms, in the midst of steam and sickening odors, by artificial light; in these rooms the germs of tuberculosis might live for two years, but the supply was renewed every hour. There were the beef-luggers, who carried two-hundred-pound quarters into the refrigerator-cars; a fearful kind of work, that began at four o'clock in the morning, and that wore out the most powerful men in a few years. There were those who worked in the chilling rooms, and whose special disease was rheumatism; the time limit that a man could work in the chilling rooms was said to be five years. There were the wool-pluckers, whose hands went to pieces even sooner than the hands of the pickle men; for the pelts of the sheep had to be painted with acid to loosen the wool, and then the pluckers had to pull out this wool with their bare hands, till the acid had eaten their fingers off. There were those who made the tins for the canned meat; and their hands, too, were a maze of cuts, and each cut represented a chance for blood poisoning. Some worked at the stamping machines, and it was very seldom that one could work long there at the pace that was set, and not give out and forget himself and have a part of his hand chopped off. There were the "hoisters," as they were called, whose task it was to press the lever which lifted the dead cattle off the floor. They ran along upon a rafter, peering down through the damp and the steam; and as old Durham's architects had not built the killing room for the convenience of the hoisters, at every few feet they would have to stoop under a beam, say four feet above the one they ran on; which got them into the habit of stooping, so that in a few years they would be walking like chimpanzees. Worst of any, however, were the fertilizer men, and those who served in the cooking rooms. These people could not be shown to the visitor,—for the odor of a fertilizer man would scare any ordinary visitor at a hundred yards, and as for the other men, who worked in tank rooms full of steam, and in some of which there were open vats near the level of the floor, their peculiar trouble was that they fell into the vats; and when they were fished out, there was never enough of them left to be worth exhibiting,—sometimes they would be overlooked for days, till all but the bones of them had gone out to the world as Durham's Pure Leaf Lard!

Source:   Upton Sinclair, *The Jungle* (1906; Project Gutenberg EBook, 2006), accessed at http://www.gutenberg.org/files/
140/140-h/140-h.htm#link2HCH0009.

# 19.3 VISUAL DOCUMENTS: LEWIS WICKES HINE, NATIONAL CHILD LABOR COMMITTEE PHOTOGRAPHS (EARLY 1900s)

Lewis Hine worked as an investigative photographer for the National Child Labor Committee, an organization dedicated to child labor reform, between 1908 and 1924. Through his photography, Hine chronicled labor conditions in sites such as coal mines, textile mills, and family farms. Hine's images brought public attention to the conditions under which children labored and effectively underscored the difference between the idealized vision of American childhood and the reality in which many children lived.

Three adults and six children from seven years to twelve years hard at work on a sugar beet farm near Greeley, Colorado. July 1915.

A 14-year-old spinner in a Brazos Valley Cotton Mill in West, Texas. November 1913.

Young drivers and trapper boy, Brown Mine, Brown, West Virginia. September 1908.

*Source:* Lewis Wickes Hine, 1874–1940, photographer. National Child Labor Committee Collection. Library of Congress Prints and Photographs Division, Washington, DC.

## 19.4 HELEN KELLER, EXCERPTS FROM "BLIND LEADERS" (1913)

When she expressed politically and economically radical views, Helen Keller often faced charges that her disabilities made her unfit for social commentary, that her ailments impeded her ability to think rationally. Keller continued to advocate a Socialist position and charged that those who saw the horrors of unfettered industrial capitalism and the inequalities it created, yet allowed the system to continue, were the truly and willfully blind members of American society.

I do not doubt that many persons who read what I am going to write will say to themselves: "She is indeed blind. She is so blind she imagines everybody else to be blind." As a matter of fact, I have been thinking for a long time that most of us are afflicted with spiritual blindness. Certainly, very few people open fresh, fearless eyes upon the world they live in. They do not look at anything straight. They have not learned to use their eyes, except in the most rudimentary ways. They will usually see a lamp-post—if it is a large one—and sometimes they are able to read the danger signal on a railway crossing, but not always. Most of the time they expect some one else to see for them. They often pay fabulous sums to lawyers, doctors, ministers, and other "experts" to do their seeing for them; but, unfortunately, it frequently happens that those hired guides and leaders are also blind. Of course they deny that their sight is imperfect. They claim to have extraordinary powers of vision and many people believe them. Consequently, they are permitted to lead their fellows. But how often do they steer them to their destruction!

When we look about us with seeing eyes, what do we behold? Men and women at our very doors wrung with hard labor, want or the dread of want, needing help and receiving none, toiling for less than a living wage! If we had had penetrating vision, I know that we could not, we would not, have endured what we saw—cruelty, ignorance, poverty, disease—almost all preventable, unnecessary. Our blind leaders whom we have sent away told us that the poverty and misery of mankind were divinely ordained. They taught us that the words, "Ye have the poor always with you," mean that Christ sanctioned poverty as necessary and irremediable. Now we read the Gospel with our own eyes, and we see that Christ meant no such thing.

Much poverty is abominable, unnecessary, a disgrace to our civilization, or rather a denial that we are civilized. Let us try to understand poverty. What is the cause of it? Simply this: that the land, the machinery, the means of life, belong to the few, while the many are born and live with nothing that they can call their own except their hands and their brains. They live by selling their hands and their brains to the few; and all the work they do makes the rich more rich, and gains for the workers a mere livelihood, or less than a livelihood. The ownership of the world by a small class is the main cause of poverty. Strange that we could not see it before, and that when we did see it we accepted it in blind contentment! Our blind guides consoled us by saying that there was much charity, and that the rich were generous and gave to the poor. We now see that what the rich give is only a small part of the money which is made for them by the labor of the poor! They never stop to think that if the workers received an equitable share of their product, there would be no rich, there would be little need of philanthropy. Charity covers a multitude of sins. It does something worse than that. It covers the fact so that they cannot be seen. It covers the fact that the property of the few is made by the labor of the many. The rich are willing to do everything for the poor but to get off their backs. . . .

When we inquire why things are as they are, the answer is: The foundation of society is laid upon a basis of individualism, conquest, and exploitation, with a total disregard of the good of the whole. The structure of society built upon such wrong basic principles is bound to retard the development of all men, even the most successful ones, because it tends to divert man's energies into useless channels and to degrade his character. The result is a false standard of values. Trade and material prosperity are held to the be the main objects of pursuit, and consequently the lowest instincts in human natures—love of gain, cunning, and selfishness—are fostered. The output of a cotton mill or a coal mine is considered of greater importance than the production of healthy, happy-hearted, free human beings.

This unmoral state of society will continue as long as we live under a system of universal competition for the means of existence. The workers cannot lift up their heads so long as a small favored class in each generation is allowed to inherit the accumulated labor of all preceding generations, and many who produce the wealth inherit nothing. (We often forget what wealth is. It is the stored-up labor of men, women, and little children. Money does not create anything. Money is about as productive as a wheel revolving in a void. It has value only in proportion to the toil and sweat of human hands that went into the getting of it.)

During the past century man has gained greater mastery over the forces of nature than he ever had before. Consequently the wealth produced in the world has increased a hundredfold. With the help of the machines he has invented, man can produce enough to provide necessaries, comforts, and even some luxuries for every human being. But in spite of this enormously greater productive power the condition of the workers has not essentially improved. Because the industrial system under which we live denies them the fruits of their labor, they have not received their fair share in the products of civilization.

As a matter of fact, machinery has widened the gulf between those who own and those who toil. It has become a means of perpetuating man's slavery, because it may be run by unskilled laborers who receive low wages, which of course increase the profits of employers and stock holders. So the worker become part of the machine they manipulate; but the machine is expensive, while human life is cheap. When the workers can no longer live, they go on strike, and what happens? The masters evict them from the hovels that they call home; the police and militia break up their protest-meetings, imprison their leaders, and when they can, drive them out of town. This appalling condition of things exists in many different parts of our country at this moment. For even the Constitution does not safeguard the liberties of the workers when their interests are opposed to those of the capitalist. Our administration of justice, which blind leaders used to tell us was a splendid inheritance from our fathers, is grossly unequal and unjust. It is based on a system of money fees. It is so encumbered at every step with technicalities that it is necessary to employ experts at great cost to explain and interpret the law. Then, too, all the petty offenses are punishable by fine or imprisonment. This means the poor will always be punished, while the rich are usually allowed to go free.

We cannot longer shut our eyes to these glaring evils. They divide the world into economic classes antagonistic to each other it is because of all these undeniable evils that I am the determined foe of the capitalist system, which denies the workers the rights of human beings. I consider it fundamentally wrong, radically unjust and cruel. It inflicts purposeless misery upon millions of my fellow men and women. It robs little children of the joy of life, embitters motherhood, breaks the bodies of men and degrades their manhood. It must, therefore, be changed, it must be destroyed, and a better, saner, kinder social order established. Competition must give place to co-operation, and class antagonism to brotherhood. "Each for all" is a far more stimulating and effective doctrine than "each for himself." Private ownership of land and the means of production and distribution of the necessaries of life must be replaced by public ownership and democratic management.

Oh, no, it is not human nature that we have to change. Our task is not so difficult as that. All that is necessary to make this world a comfortable abode for man is to abolish the capitalist system. In the words of Sir Oliver Lodge, "we have entered upon the period of conscious evolution, and have begun the adaptation of environment to organism." In other words, we have learned to curb and utilize the forces of nature. The time of blind struggle is drawing to a close. The forces governing the law of the survival of the fittest will continue to operate; but they will be under the conscious, intelligent control of man.

*Source:* Helen Keller, "Blind Leaders," *Outlook* 105 (September 27, 1913), 231–236.

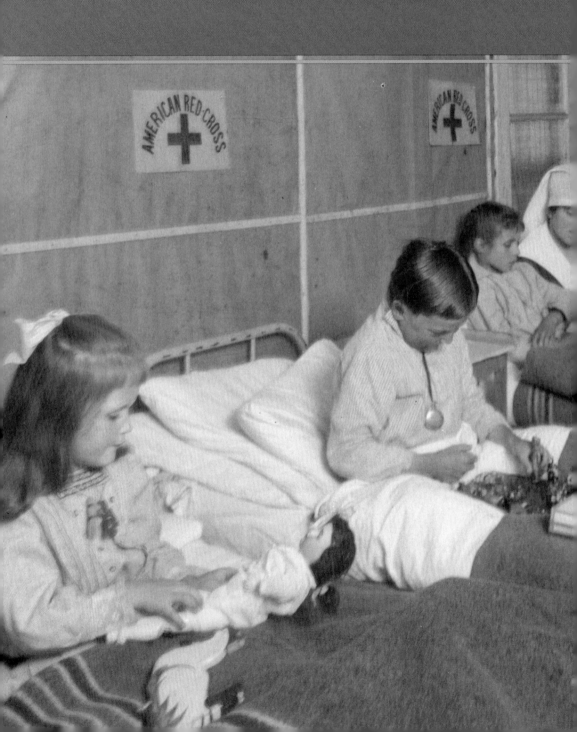

# A Global Power

## 1914–1919

## COMMON THREADS

As a progressive, Wilson was committed to order, efficiency, and gradual reform. How did his policies toward Mexico and Europe reflect this commitment?

Both the Philippine-American War of 1899 and US involvement in World War I in 1917 provoked dissent at home. Why did the government tolerate opposition in the first case but suppress it in the second?

How did the repression of the war years set the stage for the Red Scare?

## OUTLINE

**AMERICAN PORTRAIT: Walter Lippmann**

The Challenge of Revolution
  The Mexican Revolution
  Bringing Order to the Caribbean
  A One-Sided Neutrality
  The *Lusitania*'s Last Voyage

The Drift to War
  The Election of 1916
  The Last Attempts at Peace
  War Aims
  The Fight in Congress

Mobilizing the Nation and the Economy
  Enforcing Patriotism

**STRUGGLES FOR DEMOCRACY: Eugene V. Debs Speaks Out Against the War**

  Regimenting the Economy
  The Great Migration
  Reforms Become "War Measures"

Over There
  Citizens into Soldiers
  The Fourteen Points
  The Final Offensive

Revolutionary Anxieties
  Wilson in Paris
  The Senate Rejects the League
  Red Scare

**AMERICA AND THE WORLD: The American Red Cross and Wartime Civilian Aid**

Conclusion

**< French Children in a Red Cross Hospital**

## AMERICAN PORTRAIT

# Walter Lippmann

**W**alter Lippmann had just landed in Brussels in July 1914 when the trains stopped running. At the station, "crowds of angry, jostling people" were struggling to leave the city. This looked, he confided to his diary, like the beginning of a war. Four weeks earlier, Austria-Hungary's crown prince, Archduke Ferdinand, had been shot in the Serbian city of Sarajevo. Austria threatened to attack unless Serbia punished the terrorists. Russia mobilized to come to Serbia's defense. As stock markets tumbled and banks collapsed, Lippmann found himself caught in a conflict between the world's most powerful states: Austria and Germany on one side, Russia, France, and Britain on the other. As land borders closed, he escaped across the channel to England.

In the twilight of August 4, he stood with an anxious crowd outside the House of Commons, as Parliament passed a war resolution. In Berlin, the Reichstag declared war on France. "We sit and stare at each other and make idiotically cheerful remarks," Lippmann wrote, "and in the meantime, so far as anyone can see, nothing can stop the awful disintegration now."

Twenty-four years old, Lippmann had come of age in the Progressive Era. As a student at Harvard, he came to believe that reason and science would allow his generation to "treat life not as something given but as something to be shaped." After graduation, he set out to become a journalist, studying under the legendary investigator Lincoln Steffens and helping to start a magazine called the *New Republic*. "It was a happy time, those last few years before the First World War," he later remembered; "the air was soft, and it was easy for a young man to believe in the inevitability of progress, in the perfectibility of man and of society, and in the sublimation of evil."

The European war crushed those hopes. Just days after Lippmann left Belgium, German armies slashed through the neutral nation in a great maneuver designed to encircle the French army, but before the ring could be closed, reserve troops from Paris, many of them rushed to the front in taxicabs, stopped the German advance at the Marne River. By November, the western front had stabilized into the bloody stalemate that would last the next four years, taking between 5,000 and 50,000 lives a day. Two inventions first used in the American West, barbed wire and the machine gun, defeated all attempts to break through the enemy's trench lines. Colossal artillery, poison gas, submarine warfare, aerial bombardment, and suicide charges would each be used in desperate bids to break the deadlock, and all would fail.

The carnage horrified Americans. German soldiers terrorized Belgian civilians in retaliation for guerilla attacks, killing over 5,000 hostages and burning the medieval city of Louvain. The gruesome tragedy of modern war made Americans feel both fortunate and guilty to be so uninvolved. "We Americans have been witnessing supreme drama, clenching our fists, talking, yet unable to fasten any reaction to realities," Lippmann told his readers. For three years, Americans watched a civilization they had admired sink into barbarism. They recoiled from the war's violence and the motives behind it, and they debated what, if anything, they could do to stop it.

When the United States entered the fight in 1917, it mobilized its economy and society to send an army of a million to Europe. The war disrupted and culminated the progressive movement. In the name of efficiency, the state stepped in to manage the economy as never before, placing corporations under federal supervision but allowing them profits and some autonomy. The war transformed controversial items on the progressive agenda—women's suffrage, prohibition of alcohol, restrictions on prostitution—into matters of national urgency. The federal government punished political dissenters. On the battlefield, American forces brought swift triumph, but not the permanent peace Wilson sought. Defeated powers collapsed into revolution and anarchy. New ideologies threatened American ideals. The experience of war brought home the dangers of a modern, interdependent world, but it also revealed the United States' power to shape the global future.

# The Challenge of Revolution

Like other progressives, Wilson saw threats to democracy arising from rapid change in industrial society. Revolution, militarism, and imperial rivalries threatened global stability just as surely as labor wars, reckless corporations, and corrupt officials endangered the republic. Wilson opposed radicalism at home and abroad, and he tried to foster orderly change. Stability, like reform, was a process, not a goal, but Wilson believed it had to be forced on those who resisted.

Imposing order, the president believed, was both a duty and an opportunity. An expanding commercial power such as the United States had talent, technology, and capital to share. "Prosperity in one part of the world ministers to prosperity everywhere," he declared, but only in safe markets. Imperialism and revolution endangered the trade necessary for peace in the world and growth at home. It was the government's duty to safeguard goods and investments in order to secure American prosperity and its benefits for the world.

This combination of idealism and self-interest, humanitarianism and force, produced a seemingly contradictory policy. Wilson renounced "dollar diplomacy" only to use Taft's tactics himself in China. He atoned for US imperialism but intervened repeatedly in Central America. Secretary of State William Jennings Bryan negotiated a series of "cooling-off" treaties that required arbitration before resorting to war, but Wilson seldom submitted his own policies to arbitration. He believed the United States had a mission to promote democracy, yet he considered many peoples—including Filipinos—unready to govern themselves.

These contradictions arose from Wilson's view of history. As he saw it, modern commerce and communications were creating a global society with new rules of international conduct. Meanwhile, relics of the past—militarism and revolution—threatened to "throw the world back three or four centuries." Resolving the struggle between the past and the future would require "a new international psychology," new norms and institutions to regulate conflict. Wilson's sympathies lay with Britain and France, but with Europe aflame, the United States, the sole voice of reason, had to remain aloof. "Somebody must keep the great economic processes of the world of business alive," he protested. He was also preoccupied with matters closer at hand. In April 1914, American troops invaded Mexico in an attempt to overthrow its revolutionary government.

## The Mexican Revolution

In May 1911, rebels took control of Mexico City, ending over three decades of enforced order and rapid industrialization under the dictatorship of Porfirio Díaz. Díaz and a clique of intellectuals and planners known as the *científicos* had made Mexico one of the world's leading oil exporters. They confiscated communal lands, forcing Indians to farm as tenants on commercial haciendas. Foreign investment poured in, and by 1911 Americans owned 40 percent of the property in the country. Mexicans grew to resent foreign business and the regime's taxes. When Francisco Madero's revolt broke out, the army folded, Díaz fled to Spain, and power changed hands in a nearly blood-less coup.

The fall of Díaz hardly troubled the United States: Madero held an election to confirm his presidency. But in February 1913, two weeks before Wilson's inauguration, General Victoriano Huerta seized power and had Madero shot. Mexican states raised armies and revolted against Huerta's regime, beginning one of the twentieth century's longest and bloodiest civil wars. In the mountains south of Mexico City, Emiliano Zapata led a guerilla resistance. Meanwhile, along Mexico's northern border, Venustiano Carranza organized a constitutionalist army.

Wilson denounced Huerta, gave arms to Carranza's soldiers, and sent 7,000 marines to occupy Mexico's largest port, Veracruz, in April 1914. The invasion radicalized the rev-olution, unifying all sides against the United States. When Carranza deposed Huerta a few months later, he promised to nationalize US oil fields. Wilson pressured Carranza to resign while providing arms to his enemy, Francisco "Pancho" Villa. Villa briefly seized the capital at the end of 1914, but Carranza drove Villa's army north toward the border. Reluctantly, Wilson recognized the Carranza government and cut ties to Villa. Stung by Wilson's betrayal, Villa crossed the border and attacked the 13th Cavalry outpost at Co-lumbus, New Mexico, killing 17 Americans and stealing horses and guns.

Furious, Wilson sent 10,000 troops under General John J. Pershing into Mexico (see Map 20–1). Pershing never found Villa, but the invasion again unified Mexicans against the United States. Rather than declare war, Wilson ordered Pershing home. After three years of trying to bring democracy and stability to Mexico, Wilson had nothing to show for his efforts. He failed to tame nationalism and revolution in Mexico. The civil war still raged, and American property was more in danger than ever.

## Bringing Order to the Caribbean

In principle, Wilson opposed imperialism, but his desire to bring order to neighbor-ing countries led him to use force again and again. He sent the marines into more countries in Latin America than any other president. Marines quashed a revolution in Haiti in 1915 and then occupied the country. They landed in the Dominican Republic the following year to supervise an election and stayed to fight a guerilla war until 1924. Wilson kept marines in Honduras, Panama, and Nicaragua and briefly sent troops into Cuba.

Progressive senators wondered why Wilson busted trusts and reorganized banks at home but put the marines at their service abroad. Senators Robert La Follette and George

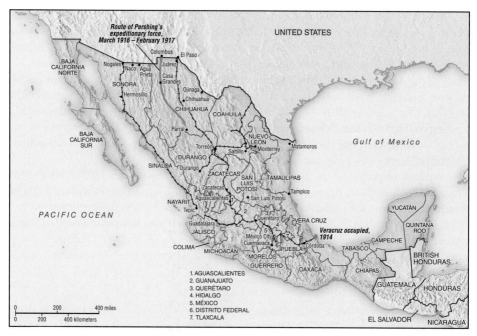

**Map 20-1    The US Invasions of Mexico, 1914, 1917**  General John Pershing led 10,000 troops together with observation aircraft and a convoy of trucks 419 miles into Mexico on a fruitless hunt for Francisco Villa's band. Federal forces loyal to Carranza confronted Pershing near Parral, bringing the US advance to a halt.

Norris argued that revolutions might be necessary in some countries to protect the many against the few. On August 29, 1914, some 1,500 women, dressed in black, marched down Fifth Avenue in New York City to oppose wars in the Caribbean and Europe. Peace advocates, such as Jane Addams, saw signs of a country being drawn toward war.

## A One-Sided Neutrality

As German armies crossed Belgium in August 1914, Wilson declared a policy of strict neutrality. The war took him by surprise, and like Addams he found it "incredible" that civilized nations could display such savagery. His first worry was that America's immigrant communities would take sides. Shortly after the crisis began, 450 steelworkers from Gary, Indiana, enlisted in the Serbian army. Irish Americans, who wanted independence for their homeland, sided with Germany against England. The Allies (Britain, France, Italy, and Russia) and the Central powers (Germany, Austria-Hungary, and Turkey) each used propaganda to manipulate US opinion.

Wilson sent his closest aide, Colonel Edward House, to Europe with offers to broker a peace agreement. Privately the president believed that a German victory would be a catastrophe. Protected by Britain's control of the seas, the United States had expanded its influence during the previous century. In an Allied defeat, he said, "the United States, itself, will have to become a military nation, for Germany will push her conquests into South America." With Europe and possibly Asia controlled by a single power, the United States would be vulnerable and alone.

Modern warfare and commerce made true neutrality difficult. The belligerent powers desperately needed everything the United States had to export. As purchasing agent for France and Britain, J. P. Morgan's firm soon became the world's largest customer, buying more than $3 billion worth of armaments, food, textiles, steel, chemicals, and fuel. US loans to the Allies grew to $2.5 billion by 1917, but the Central powers received only $127 million in credit. Trade with the Central powers meanwhile sank from $170 million to less than $1 million by 1916. An Allied victory would make the United States the world's leading creditor, whereas defeat might mean financial collapse. The United States had not formally taken sides, but the American economy was already in the war on the side of the Allies.

Wilson's response to the British and German naval blockades reinforced the tilt toward the Allies. Both sides violated the "freedom of the seas," Britain with mines and warships, Germany with submarines. Wilson considered Britain's violation justifiable, but not Germany's. Britain's surface fleet was able to capture civilian ships as required by international law, but a German *Unterseeboot*, or U-boat—a small, fragile submarine—could not do that without giving up the stealth and surprise that were its only weapons.

### The *Lusitania's* Last Voyage

Germany used advertisements in American newspapers to warn against travel on ships bound for the war zone. The State Department was divided. Robert Lansing, the department's counselor, condemned submarine attacks as an offense against law and morality, but Bryan wanted to bar Americans from traveling on belligerent ships. Wilson sided with Lansing and declared that Germany would be held to "strict accountability" for American lives or property.

On the afternoon of May 7, 1915, submarine U-20 sighted the luxury liner *Lusitania* off the coast of Ireland and fired a torpedo that detonated against the starboard side. In 18 minutes, the *Lusitania* broke apart and sank. Of almost 2,000 passengers aboard, 1,198 drowned, including 94 children and 124 Americans. The newspapers reacted with rage and horror, but Wilson's advisers again disagreed on how to respond. Bryan wanted to balance a protest with a denunciation of Britain's violation of neutral rights. Wilson ignored him and demanded that submarine warfare stop altogether. He hinted that unless his demands were met, the United States would break relations.

Public opinion was equally divided. Lippmann told a friend in England that "the feeling against war in this country is a great deal deeper than you would imagine by reading editorials." When Germany promised not to attack passenger liners without warning, Wilson accepted this pledge as a diplomatic triumph. It momentarily restored calm, but official and public opinion had turned against Germany. The *Lusitania* crisis, Lippmann predicted, "united Englishmen and Americans in a common grief and a common indignation" and might "unite them in a common war."

# The Drift to War

The *Lusitania* disaster divided progressives on the issue of the war. Peace advocates such as Addams, Bryan, and La Follette urged a stricter neutrality. Others believed war, or preparations for war, were justified. Theodore Roosevelt clamored for it. He endorsed the preparedness campaign mounted by organizations such as the National

Security League and the American Defense Society. Thousands marched down New York's Fifth Avenue under an electric sign declaring "Absolute and Unqualified Loyalty to Our Country."

Preparedness leagues, headed by businessmen and conservative political figures, called attention to the state of the armed forces, equipped only for tropical wars and lacking trucks, planes, and modern arms. The preparedness campaign appropriated patriotic rituals once reserved for elections. Wilson himself led the parade in Washington in 1916, wearing a red tie, white trousers, and a blue blazer. Hundreds of young Americans, positive that a German victory would mean the defeat of civilization, went to Paris to enlist. The French army soon had an American Volunteer Corps and a squadron of American fliers, the Lafayette Escadrille, whose exploits filled American newspapers. Magazines featured the poems of Alan Seeger, a Harvard graduate who joined the foreign legion. While Americans slept "pillowed in silk and scented down," Seeger wrote, "I've a rendezvous with death/At midnight in some flaming town." Wilson felt that to shape the world after the war, Americans would have to meet that rendezvous.

## The Election of 1916

Although Wilson believed the United States would need to enter the fight, he campaigned for reelection under the slogan "He kept us out of war." The preparedness issue reunited Theodore Roosevelt and the Republicans behind Supreme Court Justice Charles Evans Hughes, who attacked Wilson for failing to defend American honor in Mexico and Europe. Woman suffragists campaigned against Wilson and picketed the White House with signs asking, "Mr. President? How long must women wait for liberty?" Although the Republicans remained dominant, Hughes was an inept campaigner. He won New York, Pennsylvania, and Illinois but lost in the South and West. Wilson won narrowly, whereas Republicans controlled the House and the Senate. Still, reelection freed Wilson to pursue a more vigorous foreign policy. As Lippmann realized, "What we're electing is a war president—not the man who kept us out of war."

## The Last Attempts at Peace

After the election, Wilson launched a new peace initiative. Looking for an opening after years of stalemate, he asked each of the belligerent powers to state its war aims. Each insisted on punishing the other and enlarging its own territories. Before Congress in January 1917, the president called for a "peace without victory," based on the self-determination of all nations and the creation of an international organization to enforce peace.

Germany toyed with accepting Wilson's proposals but decided to wait. With the defeat of Russia in 1917, it could shift armies from the eastern front to France. U-boats again torpedoed British passenger liners and American merchant ships. In late February, British intelligence officers showed the US ambassador in London a telegram from the German foreign minister, Arthur Zimmermann, plotting an alliance with Mexico. With the Zimmermann Telegram revealed, if Wilson did not declare war now, Roosevelt declared, he would "skin him alive."

Americans disagreed then, as historians do today, on why the United States went to war. Critics pointed to the corporate interests that stood to gain. Publicly and in private, Wilson stressed two considerations: the attacks on American ships and the peace settlement. The treaty conference would settle scores of issues affecting American interests. Unless it went to war, Wilson told Jane Addams, the United States would have to shout "through a crack in the door."

## War Aims

Rain was falling on the evening of April 2, 1917, as Wilson went to ask Congress for war. Some on Pennsylvania Avenue cheered and waved flags, whereas others stared silently at the president's limousine. The war, Wilson told the assembly, was in its last stages. American armies could bring it to a merciful end. The United States had tried to stand apart, but it had failed. Neutrality had provided no safety for travelers or trade. The only hope for avoiding even more dangerous future wars was for the United States to dictate the peace, to establish a "concert of free peoples." This would be a war to end all wars, to make the world safe for democracy.

In urging the vote for war, the president explicitly rejected the aims of the Allies. "We have no quarrel with the German people," he said, but with the kaiser and all other emperors and autocrats who blocked his road to a new world order. Wilson realized, however, that imperial France and Britain did not stand for democracy or self-determination, either. The United States would fight with Britain and France as an "associated power."

Edward House assembled a secret committee, known as the Inquiry, to draft a peace proposal both generous enough to show "sympathy and friendship" to the German people and harsh enough to punish their leaders. Made up of economists, historians, geographers, and legal experts, with Lippmann as its secretary, the Inquiry produced a set of 14 recommendations that redrew the boundaries of Europe, created a league of nations, and based peace on the principles of freedom of the seas, open-door trade, and ethnic self-determination.

## The Fight in Congress

During the ovation after Wilson's speech to Congress, one senator stood silently, his arms folded. La Follette told his colleagues that if this was a war for democracy, it should be declared democratically. The country had voted for the peace candidate for president, and there were strong reasons to suspect a declaration would fail a national vote. Representatives found that voters opposed American entry, often by two to one. Midwestern farmers, William Allen White reported from Iowa, "don't seem to get the war."

Prowar representatives blocked La Follette's move for a referendum and brought the declaration to a vote on April 6, when it passed 82 to 6 in the Senate and 373 to 50 in the House. Divisions resurfaced over questions of how to pay for the war and who would fight in it. Wilson wanted universal conscription, the first draft since the Civil War. The 1917 draft law deputized 4,000 local boards to induct men between 18 and 45. Both supporters and opponents believed the draft would mold citizens. It would "break down distinctions of race and class," said one representative, turning immigrants into "new Americans." La Follette countered that the new Americans would be like the new Germans, indoctrinated by the army.

Newspapers and politicians denounced the antiwar progressives as traitors. They had too few votes to stop conscription, but they did create an exemption for conscientious objectors and reduced some taxes used to pay for the war. Opposition voices were soon silenced by patriotic calls for unity. "I pray God," Wilson avowed, "that some day historians will remember these momentous years as the years which made a single people of the great body of those who call themselves Americans."

## Mobilizing the Nation and the Economy

News of the war declaration, carried in banner headlines on Easter Sunday, 1917, set the nation abuzz with activity. Wilson recognized that he was asking for an unprecedented effort. Raising an army of over 3 million, supplying it with modern equipment, and transporting it across submarine-infested waters were herculean feats. By midsummer, there were more men at work building barracks than had been in both armies at Gettysburg. Americans would send to Europe 1.8 million tons of meat, 8.8 million tons of grain, and 1.5 million tons of sugar. Factories that produced sewing machines and automobiles would retool to make howitzers and tanks.

The strain war placed on the American people and economy was severe. Wilson and others feared that it could widen political divisions and destroy 15 years of progressive achievements. Others felt that sharing the sacrifices of war would consolidate the gains. "We shall exchange our material thinking for something quite different," the General Federation of Women's Clubs predicted. "We shall all be enfranchised, prohibition will prevail, many wrongs will be righted." Lippmann hoped war would bring a new American revolution.

### Enforcing Patriotism

Authorities dealt severely with dissent. Suspicions about the loyalties of ethnic communities and rumors of German saboteurs fed the hysteria. On July 30, 1916, across the river from New York City, the largest arms storage facility in the country blew up. The explosion destroyed thousands of pounds of shells and guns bound for Russia and tore away parts of the Statue of Liberty. Federal agents responded by rounding up aliens. However, domestic opinion posed a greater danger to the war effort than enemy agents. While initial enthusiasm ran high, the skepticism La Follette expressed was just beneath the surface.

**Wake Up, America!** After a prolonged effort at neutrality, the United States faced the challenge of preparedness upon entering World War I. Propaganda posters encouraged Americans to support the war effort.

## STRUGGLES FOR DEMOCRACY

# Eugene V. Debs Speaks Out Against the War

When the United States declared war on Germany in April 1917, the Socialist Party convened to draft a response to the war. The party committed to an ongoing, active opposition to the war, the draft, and all funding of the war effort. This public stance, combined with steadily increasing membership due to antiwar sentiments from both farm and urban working-class communities, made the Socialist Party a target for those dedicated to promoting "Americanism," unquestioning loyalty, and total support for the war effort. Those who failed to demonstrate their patriotism sufficiently were subject to harassment, violence, or worse. Legislation such as the Sedition Act and Espionage Act made dissent not only unpopular, but illegal.

Eugene V. Debs, a long-time Socialist leader, watched much of this occur from his home in Indiana. After a lifetime of advocating on behalf of the American worker and attempting to spread the party's message, the 63-year-old Debs suffered from poor health and was confined to his bed. But as he saw his friends and associates beaten and jailed, and as he read Socialist views misrepresented in the press, he felt compelled to defend the party to which he had dedicated so much of his life.

Debs traveled to Canton, Ohio, where three local party leaders had been imprisoned under the Espionage Act for publicly opposing the war. After visiting with these men, Debs addressed a crowd of more than 1,000 people in nearby Nimisilla Park. He angrily asserted that his comrades had been persecuted merely for exercising their "constitutional right of free speech." Debs critiqued the American government for failing to live up to its promise as a free republic. He lamented the power of the business elite, who claimed to set the standard for American patriotism even as they made handsome profits from the war effort. These men, Debs proclaimed, "shout their claim from the housetops that they are the only patriots, and who have their magnifying glasses in hand, scanning the country for evidence of disloyalty, eager to apply the brand of treason to the men who dare to even whisper their opposition."

Victories might not come quickly, and if the public should start to turn against the war, consent would have to be manufactured by propaganda or the police.

Congress gave the president sweeping powers to suppress dissent. The Espionage Act (1917) and the Sedition Act (1918) effectively outlawed opposition to the war and used the postal service to catch offenders. Although there was no link between the labor movement and sabotage, unions were the prime target. The Justice Department raided the Chicago offices of the Industrial Workers of the World and sent 96 leaders to prison on charges of sedition. William D. "Big Bill" Haywood was sentenced to 20 years. Eugene V. Debs, leader of the Socialist Party, received 10 years for telling Ohioans they were "fit for something better than slavery and cannon fodder."

The wealthy, he asserted, fervently promoted the war as they happily allowed other men to fight it. To that end, Debs told the crowd, "You are fit for something better than slavery and cannon fodder. You need to know that you were not created to work and produce and impoverish yourself to enrich an idle exploiter. You need to know that you have a mind to improve, a soul to develop, and a manhood to sustain."

In his speech, Debs said nothing he had not said before, but his supporters were not the only ones in the crowd. Also present were stenographers hired by the US Attorney for Northern Ohio, E. S. Wertz. Although the Justice Department in Washington, DC, was not enthusiastic about the possibility of prosecution, Wertz obtained an indictment, charging Debs with 10 violations of the Espionage Act.

When Debs went to trial, he instructed his lawyers not to contest the charges, which had been reduced to two violations. He had given the speech and would stand by it. In his estimation, he had been well within his rights of free speech. As Debs addressed the jury, he invoked great American patriots like George Washington and Thomas Paine, men who had spoken out against injustice, just as he had. Those men were heroes, but contemporaries who followed their examples were subject to persecution. His defense mattered not. The jury found Debs guilty and he was sentenced to 10 years in jail.

Debs's speech and sentencing initially electrified American Socialists, but optimism on the left was short-lived. Debs appealed the decision, but in March 1919, the US Supreme Court upheld his conviction. Ohio Senator Atlee Pomerene feared leniency for Debs would suggest national weakness against the perceived growing threat from radicals and revolutionaries inspired by the Bolshevik Revolution in Russia. Attorney General A. Mitchell Palmer, who would go on to lead raids against political radicals as part of the post–World War I Red Scare, rejected the possibility of clemency altogether.

Debs ultimately served less than three years of his sentence. While in prison, he ran as the Socialist candidate for president of the United States and received nearly a million votes. When he emerged from prison in December 1921, however, he was hobbled by poor health and his party was hampered by an increasingly conservative political climate that would limit radical activism for much of the decade ahead. The rights and freedoms advocated by Debs would be restricted for the foreseeable future.

States also passed laws criminalizing "unpatriotic" activity. Indiana's Council for Defense licensed citizens to raid German homes, prevent church services in German, and make sure German Americans bought war bonds. Towns, schools, and clubs with German-sounding names changed them. East Germantown, Indiana, became Pershing. Hamburgers became "liberty sandwiches." Schools in the Midwest stopped teaching German altogether. Americans who had once proudly displayed their ethnicity now took pains to disguise it.

Pacifist faiths had their own ordeals. Some sects had come to America to avoid conscription in Germany or Russia. Many could not comply with the conscientious objector statute, which required submission to military control. Fifteen hundred Mennonites fled to Canada to avoid being placed in camps. Thirty-four Russian Pentecostals were arrested in Arizona, turned over to the army, court-martialed, and sent to Leavenworth.

The government's propaganda effort was managed by the Committee on Public Information (CPI) under former muckraker George Creel. It made films, staged pageants, and churned out ads, billboards, and press releases. The CPI sold the war by telling Americans they were fighting to save their own homes. One poster showed German bombers over a shattered, headless Statue of Liberty. Like Wilson, propaganda distinguished between Germany and the German people. CPI leaflets in German offered "Friendly Words to the Foreign Born." It cast immigrants as potential patriots and women as symbols of progress and sacrifice. Creel drafted Charles Dana Gibson, whose "Gibson Girl" ads personified glamour, to depict women as mothers, nurses, and patriotic consumers. As advertising mobilized American thought for the war effort, it also advanced progressive agendas.

## Regimenting the Economy

The first prolonged conflict between industrial nations, World War I introduced the term "total war." By 1917, all of the resources, manpower, and productive capacities of the combatants had been mobilized. It soon became clear that the economy of the United States would have to be organized in new ways.

The navy planned a vast shipyard on Hog Island, near Philadelphia, with 250 buildings, 80 miles of railroad track, and 34,000 workers. It would be larger than Britain's seven largest shipyards combined, but in April 1917, Hog Island was 847 acres of swamp. Steelmaker Charles M. Schwab, in charge of the project, signed contracts for machinery, cement, steel, and timber. Materials were loaded on trains headed east. The result was the Great Pile Up, the biggest traffic jam in railroad history. Without enough workers to unload, cars began to back up on sidings in Philadelphia and then all the way back to Pittsburgh and Buffalo, their loads dumped on the outskirts of cities. Schwab begged the railroads to cooperate, to no avail. The voluntary system had failed, and on January 1, 1918, Wilson nationalized the railroads.

The Hog Island fiasco demonstrated the need for supervision of the economy. Wilson created a War Industries Board (WIB) to regulate prices, manufacturing, and transport. The job was enormous, and Wilson found the overseer he needed in Bernard Baruch, a Wall Street financier, who believed in regulation by "socially responsible" businessmen. Baruch recruited corporate executives for top positions and paid them a dollar a year. The president of the Aluminum Company of America became chairman of the WIB's aluminum committee, and a former top executive of John Deere headed the agricultural implements section.

The dollar-a-year men regimented the economy and put business to work for government, but they also guaranteed profits and looked after their own interests. One of their innovations, the "cost-plus" contract, assured contractors the recovery of costs plus a percentage for profit. Under these arrangements, the Black and Decker Company made gun sights, Akron Tire made army cots, and the Evinrude Company stopped making outboard motors and turned out grenades. Each company built up revenues to launch new product lines after the war. Standardization also helped industry. The WIB set standard designs and sizes for everything from shirts to lug nuts. One steel executive observed, "We are all making more money out of this war than the average human being ought to."

**Hog Island Shipyard** Building the massive shipyard at Hog Island was a major feat. The railroad network broke down under the strain, leading Wilson to nationalize the railroads.

Not all businesses submitted willingly to "war socialism." The Ford Motor Company had just set up a national dealer network, and it refused to stop delivering cars. When other automakers followed suit, the board threatened to cut off the industry's supply of coal and steel. After long negotiations, the automakers agreed to cut production by three-fourths. The delay hurt. When American troops went into battle, they had a grand total of two tanks.

The war economy was a culmination of two movements: Wall Street's drive for corporate consolidation and the progressives' push for federal regulation. Businessmen saw that the WIB could rationalize the economy. These "New Capitalists" wanted to end cutthroat competition and make business predictable. They encouraged workers to identify with the company through stock sharing and bonus plans. The WIB's example of government-industry cooperation would serve as a model in national crises to come.

## The Great Migration

The war economy gave Americans new choices and opportunities. As factories geared up, they faced a shortage of labor. The draft took eligible employees from the cities, and the usual source of new workers—Europe—was sealed off by a screen of U-boats. Employers found eager workers in the South. In small towns and rural junctions, labor recruiters arrived offering free rides to the North and well-paid employment on arrival. Manufacturers came to rely on the labor of former sharecroppers. Westinghouse employed 25 African Americans in 1916; by 1918, it employed 1,500. The Pennsylvania Railroad recruited 10,000 workers from Florida and Georgia. Veterans saw no reason to go back to sharecropping after the war. In some northern cities, a thousand migrants were arriving each week. This massive movement from the rural South to the urban North and West came to be called the Great Migration.

Lynchings, intimidation, and a declining southern economy encouraged migration. Almost half a million people came north during the war years—so many that some counties emptied out, creating panic among whites left behind. Mississippi alone lost 75,000 workers. "We must have the Negro in the South," the Macon, Georgia, *Telegraph* pined. "It is the only labor we have. . . . If we lose it, we go bankrupt." Southern states banned recruiters. In some places violence provoked migration. "Every time a lynching takes place in a community down south," one observer noted, "you can depend on it that colored people will arrive in Chicago within two weeks."

African American workers moved into jobs at the bottom of the pay scale: janitors, domestics, and factory hands. Rent, groceries, and other necessities were substantially more expensive in the cities. Still, African American workers could earn wages 70 percent higher than what they were used to at home. Almost no one went back, and the new arrivals adapted to the rhythms of city life. "South State Street was in its glory then, a teeming Negro street with crowded theaters, restaurants, and cabarets," Langston Hughes wrote of Chicago in 1918. Housing was scarce, and African American renters were limited to overcrowded districts wedged between industrial zones and hostile white neighborhoods. W. E. B. DuBois noted that African Americans had lived in many neighborhoods of Philadelphia before the war, but by the end of the war they were concentrated in just one ward. Ghetto neighborhoods were both expensive and decrepit. On Chicago's South Side, rents were 15 to 20 percent higher than in white neighborhoods, and the death rate was comparable to that of Bombay, India. White property owners and real estate agents worked to create the ghettos, enforce their boundaries, and "Make Hyde Park White." A real estate agent said that African American homeowners "hurt our values." When discrimination failed, there was dynamite. From 1917 to 1919, whites bombed 26 African American residences in Chicago. On July 2, 1917, in East St. Louis, an arms manufacturing center in southern Illinois, competition for housing and political offices led a mob of white workers to attack "Black Valley," an African American neighborhood along the Southern Railroad track. Forty-seven people were killed and six thousand left homeless.

After East St. Louis, white mobs found black neighborhoods less easy to attack. When a mob invaded a Washington, DC, ghetto three years later, residents fought back with guns. The novelist Alden Bland wrote that the mood in Chicago's Black Belt, under attack in the hot summer of 1919, was "get them before they get you." An African American newspaper explained drily that "New Negroes are determined to make their dying a costly investment for all concerned." The New Negro, urban, defiant, often a war veteran who demanded rather than asked for rights, became the subject of admiring and apprehensive reports. Police kept files on suspected militants, but the mobility and anonymity of northern cities translated into freedom.

## Reforms Become "War Measures"

On August 3, 1917, thousands of protestors marched in New York under signs demanding "Why not make America safe for democracy?" In the wake of the East St. Louis outrage, the NAACP urged Congress to outlaw lynching as a "war measure." African Americans were not alone in using the president's language to justify reform. Carrie Chapman Catt told Wilson that he could enact women's suffrage as a "war measure." Advocates of progressive change demanded that the United States practice at home the ideals it fought for abroad.

Suffragists hitched their cause to the national struggle. Catt's National American Woman Suffrage Association (NAWSA) abandoned its state-by-state lobbying to identify women with the national cause. Members sold liberty bonds and knitted socks for the Red Cross, making it clear they expected a constitutional amendment in return. Alice Paul's National Woman's Party (NWP) picketed the White House with signs quoting Wilson's demand for all peoples to "have a voice in their own governments." When Wilson announced his support in 1918, he cited women's war service as the reason. The Nineteenth Amendment was finally ratified in 1920, "so soon after the war," according to Jane Addams, "that it must be accounted as the direct result of war psychology."

As it had for African Americans, the labor shortage increased opportunities for women. Although most women workers were already in the labor force, many took jobs previously considered "inappropriate" for their sex. Women replaced men as bank tellers, streetcar operators, mail carriers, and steelworkers. Many of these opportunities vanished when the war ended, but in expanding sectors such as finance, communications, and office work, women made permanent gains. By 1920, more than 25 percent worked in offices or as telephone operators, and 13 percent were in professions such as teaching, nursing, and social work. The new opportunities gave women a source of prestige and enjoyment. Alice Hamilton remarked on the "strange spirit of exaltation among the men and women who thronged to Washington, engaged in all sorts of 'war work' and loving it." Army General Order 13 set standards for women's work, including an eight-hour day, prohibitions on working at night or in dangerous conditions, and provisions for rest periods, lunchrooms, and bathrooms. The government also empowered women consumers, encouraging them to report on shopkeepers who charged above the official price.

Wilson authorized a National War Labor Board to intervene in essential industries. The board set an unofficial minimum wage. For the first time, the federal government recognized workers' rights to organize, bargain collectively, and join unions. Unskilled workers earned higher real wages than ever before. When the Smith and Wesson Company refused to acknowledge its workers' right to bargain collectively, the army seized the factory and recognized the union. There were limits, however, for the administration. When skilled machinists at the Remington Arms plant made demands the board considered excessive, Baruch threatened to have them drafted and sent to France.

Prohibition did not please workers, either, but beer, wine, and spirits were early casualties of war. The Anti-Saloon League and the Woman's Christian Temperance Union had built a powerful antiliquor coalition by 1916. Congress would have passed

Prohibition without war, but temperance became a patriotic crusade. Military regulations prohibited liquor near army camps. Finally, in 1919 the states ratified the Eighteenth Amendment, banning the "manufacture, sale, or transportation of intoxicating liquors." The Anti-Saloon League celebrated the dawn of "an era of clear thinking and clean living." America was "so dry it couldn't spit," according to Billy Sunday. He overstated the case. By some estimates, after the ban illegal speakeasies in New York outnumbered the saloons they replaced. Bootleggers and smugglers slaked American thirsts, but liquor prices rose and consumption declined. Americans never again drank anything like the average two and a half gallons of pure alcohol per person annually imbibed before Prohibition.

The war also lent patriotic zeal to antivice crusaders. During the Progressive Era, muckrakers exposed the police-protection rackets that allowed gambling dens and brothels to thrive. Within days of the declaration of war, reformers identified prostitutes as enemies of the health of American troops. Gonorrhea afflicted a quarter of the Allied forces in France, and middle-class Americans were appalled. Before 1917, reformers targeted commercial vice as a source of political and social corruption, but afterward they directed their efforts at women as carriers of disease.

The army acted against liquor and prostitution to protect the welfare of soldiers, but it did not challenge racial injustice, even when lives were at stake. At camps in the South, it was often unclear who had more authority, uniformed African American soldiers or white local officials. Clashes could easily turn violent. A riot in Houston in August 1917 began when soldiers from nearby Camp Logan rushed to the aid of an African American woman being beaten by police. Twenty policemen and soldiers were killed, and 54 soldiers received life sentences in the largest court-martial in US history.

After the Houston riot, African American units were dispersed across the country, and the army remained segregated. Worse, many southern communities used military discipline to strengthen their own Jim Crow laws. Encouraged by the army's "work or fight" order, which required draft-age men to either enlist or get a job, states and localities passed compulsory work laws that applied to women and older men. The laws were intended to keep laborers in the fields and servants in the kitchens at prewar wages.

In this "war welfare state," the government mediated among labor, industry, and other organized interests. Social activism became a matter of lobbying federal agencies that could either dictate sweeping changes or use wartime powers to maintain the status quo. Success required organization and an ability to tie one's goals to the government's ambitions.

## Over There

When the Senate took up the enormous war budget Wilson submitted in April 1917, the finance committee questioned Major Palmer E. Pierce about what would be done with the money. "Clothing, cots, camps, food, pay," he replied, "and we may have to have an army in France." "Good Lord!" exclaimed Senator Thomas Martin of Virginia. "You're not going to send soldiers over there, are you?" After the horrors of the Somme and Verdun, where men were fed to machine guns by the tens of thousands, it hardly seemed reasonable to send Americans to such a place. "One would think that, after almost four years of war, after the most detailed and realistic accounts of murderous fighting, . . . it would have been all but impossible to get anyone to serve," one veteran later recalled. "But it was not so; we and many thousands of others volunteered."

Americans went to France optimistically believing they could change the war and the peace. Trench warfare was not for them. They planned to fight a war of movement, sweeping in formations across open fields, like those at Antietam and Gettysburg. To a remarkable degree, they got the war they wanted. Europeans watched their civilization destroy itself in the Great War, but Americans saw theirs rising. Soldiers, "doughboys," said so in their letters, echoing the words of their leaders, their newspapers, and the volumes of poetry they carried with them into battle.

## Citizens into Soldiers

Enlisting, training, and transporting soldiers began in a rush. Camps housing 400,000 recruits went up in the first 30 days. Conscription went smoothly, and soon 32 camps were housing 1.3 million men. Commander John J. Pershing arrived in France in June with 40,000 men and the first of some 16,000 women who would serve in the American Expeditionary Force (AEF).

Neither the Wilson administration nor the Allies initially anticipated that soldiers would be the United States' main contribution to the war effort. Britain urgently needed financial support, and Wilson advanced $200 million immediately, the first of an eventual $10 billion in loans to the Allies. Funds, food, and ammunition were needed more urgently than men, but that changed in October 1917, when German and Austrian forces smashed through the Italian lines at Caporetto, capturing 275,000 men and finishing the war on that front. When the Bolshevik Revolution curtailed Russian resistance in the East in November, Britain and France saw that by the next spring Germany would be able to mass its armies on the line from Belgium to Switzerland and break through to Paris. The war became a race to the western front between the United States and Germany.

Getting troops to the war required ships, but the American merchant fleet was smaller in 1917 than it was during the Civil War. For a time the United States had to cut back draft calls because it lacked ships to transport soldiers. The navy, meanwhile, cured the U-boat problem. The American destroyer fleet drove submarines from the sea lanes with depth charges, allowing the Allies to convoy effectively for the first time. By July 18, some 10,000 troops a day boarded the "Atlantic Ferry" for the ride to France.

## The Fourteen Points

In December 1917, the Inquiry sent the president a memorandum titled "The War Aims and the Peace Terms It Suggests." Wilson redrafted it and presented it to Congress on January 8, 1918. The Fourteen Points outlined US objectives, but more fundamentally they offered an entirely new basis for peace. Unlike nineteenth-century wars waged for limited territorial or political objectives, the Great War was a total war, fought for unlimited aims. The principal belligerents—Britain, France, Russia, Germany, and Austria-Hungary—were global empires. Germany hoped both to defeat Britain and to take its empire. France wanted to destroy Germany's future as a great power, economically and militarily. Wilson replaced these imperial visions of total victory with a peace based on limited gains for nations, not empires.

The Fourteen Points addressed four themes: national self-determination; freedom of the seas; enforcement of peace by a league of nations; and open diplomacy. The Inquiry's memorandum included maps marked with new European boundaries based on national, ethnic identities. The new state of Poland, for instance, should govern only territories with "indisputably Polish populations." Point three restated the Open Door, urging international free trade, reflecting Wilson's hope of eliminating what he saw as the two leading causes of war, imperial ambition and commercial rivalry. By calling for an end to secret diplomacy, he appealed directly to the people of Europe. The expectation was that the hope of a just peace would weaken the enemy nations' will and inspire the Allies to fight harder. Creel printed 60 million copies and had them distributed around the world. Planes dropped copies over Germany and Austria.

Wilson hoped the Fourteen Points would dispel both the old dream of empire and the new one of socialist revolution. On November 7, two months before Wilson presented the points to Congress, Russian workers overthrew the Provisional Government of Alexander Kerensky. The one-party regime of the Bolsheviks, led by Vladimir Lenin, summoned workers everywhere to rise against their governments and to make peace without indemnities or annexations. "The crimes of the ruling, exploiting classes in this war have been countless. These crimes cry out for revolutionary revenge." In December, Lenin revealed the contents of the secret treaties, unmasking the imperial ambitions of the Allies. He sued for peace based on the principle of self-determination. The Council of People's Commissars allocated 2 million rubles to encourage revolutions around the world and called "upon the working classes of all countries to revolt."

Two world leaders—Lenin and Wilson—now offered radically different visions of the new world order, and Lenin was putting his into effect. The Bolsheviks' contempt for democracy angered Wilson, but he hoped that Russia would stay in the war. Those hopes ended with the Treaty of Brest-Litovsk, signed by Russia and Germany in March 1918. The treaty showed the fearful price of defeat in modern war. Russia lost the Ukraine, Poland, and Finland, most of its iron, steel, and best farmland, and one-quarter of its population. Those assets went into the German war machine, which began transferring 10 divisions a month to the West, its eastern front now secure.

Wilson was the first, but not the last, American president to be haunted by the specter of a German-Russian alliance, uniting the immense war-making resources of Europe and Asia. In Wilson's strategic vision, the great land powers of Eurasia, not Alfred Thayer Mahan's sea powers, most threatened US security. He refused to recognize the Bolshevik government and sent 7,000 American troops to Russia to support anti-Bolshevik forces on the eastern front. US and Japanese forces invaded Siberia from the east. The Bolshevik government now counted the United States among its enemies. Meanwhile, the battle for the control of Europe was about to begin.

## The Final Offensive

The German high command knew the spring offensive would be the last. Their exhausted economy no longer could supply food or ammunition for a sustained effort. Breadlines, strikes, and industrial breakdowns foreshadowed the chaos that would follow defeat. Risking everything, the German commander Erich Ludendorff launched his offensive on March 21, 1918 (see Map 20–2). Shock troops hurled the British Fifth Army back to Amiens. In May they penetrated French lines as far as Soissons, 37 miles from Paris. As gaps split the lines, French general Ferdinand Foch and General Douglas Haig of Britain appealed urgently to Pershing to put American troops under British and French command. Pershing opposed the idea. He wanted the American army to play its own part in the war.

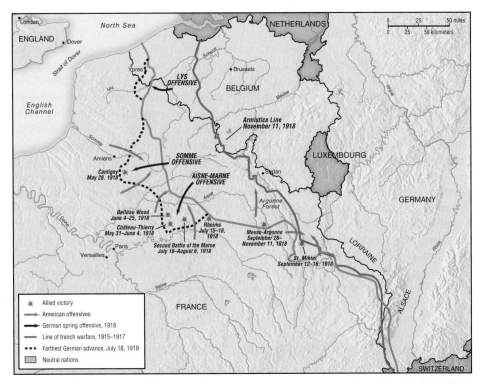

**Map 20-2  Western Front, 1918**  On the western front, the opposing armies fought from trenches forti-fied with earthworks and barbed wire. The parallel trench lines stretched thousands of miles from the North Sea to Switzerland.

Pershing criticized European commanders for remaining on the defensive instead of "driving the enemy out into the open and engaging him in a war of movement." Trained at West Point in Civil War tactics, he imagined himself a General Grant replacing European McClellans and saw trenches as symbols of inertia. Pershing favored massed assaults in which the sheer numbers of American troops would overwhelm the Germans, rifles against machine guns. In seeing Europe's war as a replay of the US Civil War, Pershing revealed a habit of mind that would typify American geopolitical thinking for the next century: the belief that Americans could understand the world through the prism of their own experience. He was not alone in wanting a decisive alternative to trench warfare. Billy Mitchell, head of the army's aviation section, noted that "we could cross the lines of these contending armies in a few minutes in our aeroplanes."

On May 27, German divisions pierced French lines at Château-Thierry and began advancing on Paris at a rate of 10 miles a day. The French government considered whether to abandon the capital or surrender. Bowing to urgent requests, Pershing threw the AEF into the breach. Column upon column of fresh American troops filled the roads from Paris to the front. "We are real soldiers now and not afread [*sic*] of Germans," John F. Dixon, an African American infantryman from New York, wrote home. "Our boys went on the battlefield last night singing." Ahead lay five German divisions, poison gas, minefields, rolling artillery barrages, and machine guns in interlocking fields of fire. The Germans were stopped, but at a fearful cost. The marine brigade that took Belleau Wood suffered 4,600 casualties, half the force. Without artillery or tanks, they assaulted machine gun nests head-on, with rifles.

By mid-July, the initiative passed to the Allies. On September 12, Foch allowed Pershing to try his tactics against the St. Mihiel salient, a bulge in the French lines which, unknown to the Allies, the Germans had already begun to evacuate. The doughboys raced behind the retreating enemy past their planned objectives. Pershing was delighted. St. Mihiel had vindicated his strategy, and he yearned for another chance. It came two weeks later, at the battle of the Meuse-Argonne.

Ten miles northwest of Verdun, the Argonne Forest contained some of the most formidable natural and man-made defenses on the western front. Atop parallel ridges lay three fortified trench lines, *Stellungen*—barriers of concrete pillboxes, barbed wire, artillery, and observation posts. Half a million German troops had defended these fortifications for four years. Against this force, Pershing arrayed the American First Army, 1,031,000 men. The average doughboy at the Meuse-Argonne had a total of four months of training, and some had as little as 10 days. Pershing's battle plan called for overwhelming the German defenses with speed and numbers, reaching the second trench line, 10 miles inside the German front, the first day.

**The Western Front** From 1914 to 1918 the western front was the largest metropolis on earth, in Robert Cowley's phrase, an "unreal city" whose inhabitants—8,000 of whom died each day—worked in an industry of destruction. Here, Australian soldiers tread through the wasteland near Ypres, Belgium, in October 1917.

"Moving slowly forward, never heeding the bursting shells, nor gas, we followed a road forking to the left . . . into no man's land. It was soon noticed that we were in the bracket of a German barrage," a soldier wrote from the battlefield. They broke through the first line of German trenches after a day and a half; then the battle turned into a deadly crawl. In two weeks of fighting, 26,277 Americans died. French soldiers reported seeing the American dead lying in rows, cut down by machine guns as they marched in formation. Finally, on November 10, American troops reached their objective and dynamited the rail line connecting the cities of Metz and Sedan. Meanwhile, Germany announced that it would accept the Fourteen Points as the basis for an armistice and negotiations. At 11:00 a.m. on November 11, 1918, the guns fell silent.

American intervention had been decisive. The American economy, two and a half times the size of Germany's, lent its industrial and agricultural strength to the Allies at a crucial moment. American military power also tipped the balance. Pershing failed to transform strategy—it remained a mechanized war of attrition until the end—but by striking the final blow, Americans had the illusion that their way of war had been triumphant. American losses, 116,516 dead, were smaller than those of the British (908,371), the French (1.4 million), or the Germans (1.8 million), but they still show the colossal destructiveness of industrial war. In just six months, the United States suffered twice as many combat deaths as it would in the Vietnam War and almost a third as many as in World War II.

Americans and Europeans fought two vastly different wars on the same battlefields. The Americans' war was swift and victorious, but the Europeans experienced a catastrophe that consumed an entire generation. For Europeans, their faith in modernity and in the ability of science and democracy to create a better future vanished forever. Confidence in the inevitability of progress became a distinctive feature of US culture in the postwar era. In much of the world, "American" became almost synonymous with "modern," but not everywhere. In the East, another political and economic system shouted its claim to the future.

# Revolutionary Anxieties

Americans celebrated the armistice with bonfires, church bells, automobile horns, and uplifted voices. Wilson told Congress that "everything for which America fought has been accomplished," but he observed that the situation in Russia cast doubt on the durability of peace. Even before the armistice, German revolutionaries took power in Bavaria. Over the next months, revolutions broke out throughout eastern Europe. From the trenches of Flanders to the Sea of Japan, not a single government remained intact, and in Moscow the new Soviet state towered above the ruins of the old regimes.

### Wilson in Paris

For Wilson, the moment he had planned for in 1917 had arrived—the United States could help set the terms of peace—but war had exhausted the president. Confident that the public would view the nation's victory as his victory, he committed mistakes. Had he remained in Washington, some historians argue, he could have taken credit for the peace while keeping a close eye on his critics. Instead, he went to Paris, staking the treaty's success on his own popularity. He passed up a chance to include in the delegation a prominent Republican, such as Henry Cabot Lodge, who could guide the treaty through Congress.

**Wilson in Paris** Woodrow Wilson received a hero's welcome on the Rue Royale when he arrived in France to join the other Allied Powers in crafting the postwar world. His triumph was short-lived, however, as many of his Fourteen Points fell to the wayside during treaty talks at the Palace of Versailles.

In December 1918, Walter Lippmann, now an army captain, watched Wilson's triumphal entry into Paris. Crowds lined the streets, and as the procession crossed the Pont du Concorde, a great cheer echoed off the walls of the Chamber of Deputies. "Never has a king, never has an emperor received such a welcome," *L'Europe Nouvelle* declared. For the next month, Wilson toured France, Italy, and Britain to cries of "Viva Veelson." "They say he thinks of us, the poor people," a workingman remarked, "that he wants us all to have a fair chance; that he is going to do something when he gets here that will make it impossible for our government to send us to war again. If he had only come sooner!"

By the time Wilson arrived for treaty talks at the Palace of Versailles, two of the Fourteen Points had already been compromised. Britain refused to accept the point on freedom of the seas, which would thwart the use of the Royal Navy in a future conflict. Wilson also undercut his own position on point six, respect for Russia's sovereignty, as American troops were occupying Russian Siberia. Wilson was unable to prevent Britain, France, and Japan from dividing Germany's colonies among themselves and imposing harsh peace terms. Germany had to sign a humiliating "war guilt" clause and pay $33 billion in reparations, enough to cripple its economy for decades. Wilson concentrated on the League of Nations, which might make up for the treaty's other weaknesses and provide some safety against the rising tide of revolution. He took the lead in drafting the League Covenant, which committed each member to submit disputes to arbitration and pledged them to take action against "any war or threat of war."

## The Senate Rejects the League

To many observers in the United States the Treaty of Versailles betrayed the goals Americans had fought to attain. "This Is Not Peace," declared the *New Republic*. Congress saw the League of Nations less as a way to prevent wars than as a guarantee that the United States would be involved. Americans were "far more afraid of Lenin than they ever were of the Kaiser," Lippmann wrote. To Republican leaders such as Henry Cabot Lodge, the United States' best bet was to look to its own security, keep its options open, and work out its international relations independently rather than as part of an alliance or league.

In March 1919, before the treaty was concluded, Lodge and 38 other senators—more than enough to defeat the treaty—signed a petition opposing the League of Nations. James A. Reed of Missouri said the covenant would turn American foreign policy over to foreigners. Editorials feared that American troops would be summoned to settle blood feuds in the Balkans. Wilson expected to fight, but he believed that the Senate would not reject the treaty.

In September, Wilson went "over the heads" of Congress and stumped for the treaty on a nationwide tour. He assured listeners in Sioux Falls that "the peace of the world cannot be established without America." He promised the citizens of Salt Lake City that China's independence would be respected. Traveling more than 8,000 miles and speaking before large audiences without loudspeakers took a toll on his health. After a speech in Pueblo, Colorado, he became so ill that he was rushed back to Washington, where he suffered a stroke that left him partially paralyzed and unable to concentrate for more than a few minutes a day. Mrs. Wilson and the president's physician kept his condition a secret and refused to allow anyone to see him.

With Wilson secluded in the White House, the Senate voted against ratification. To the end, Wilson refused to allow Senate Democrats to accept any modifications. Even Lippmann's *New Republic*, a mouthpiece for Wilson throughout the war, called the treaty's demise "desirable and wholesome." Lodge and the Republicans were not ready for isolation, but they preferred diplomatic strategies based on economic strength rather than a relatively weak military. They also saw Latin America as more critical than Europe to US security. Meanwhile, European governments organized the League of Nations without delegations from the United States or the Soviet Union.

Over the next decade, US influence abroad grew enormously. American automobiles, radios, and movies could be seen in far corners of the globe. The United States still practiced cautious diplomacy in Europe and Asia, to avoid being drawn into what the *New York Tribune* called the "vast seething mass of anarchy extending from the Rhine to the Siberian wastes."

## Red Scare

On May 1, 1919, a dozen or more mail bombs were sent to prominent Americans: J. P. Morgan, John D. Rockefeller, senators, cabinet officials, and Supreme Court Justice Oliver Wendell Holmes. None of the packages reached its intended target, but one injured a maid in the home of Senator Thomas Hardwick and another exploded at the residence of Attorney General A. Mitchell Palmer in Washington, nearly injuring Franklin and Eleanor Roosevelt, who lived next door. Investigations later showed that the bombings were the work of lone lunatics, but many people quickly concluded that the United States was under attack. Since the Russian Revolution, newspapers, evangelists, and government officials had fed fears of Bolshevism. Revolution, Palmer alleged, was "licking at the altars of the churches, leaping into the belfry of the school bell, crawling into the sacred corners of American homes."

Revolutions in Europe terrified conservatives in the United States and led them to look for Soviet terrorists, particularly among immigrants and unionized workers. They drew no distinctions among Socialists, anarchists, Communists, and labor unionists; they were all "red." Seattle's mayor called in the army to break a dockworkers' strike. When steelworkers in Gary, Indiana, struck for higher wages and shorter hours in September 1919, Judge Elbert Gary, president of U.S. Steel, denounced them as followers of Russian "anarchy and Bolshevism." During the war they had worked 12 hours a day, 7 days a week, for an average wage of $28 a week. With the help of local loyalty leagues, Gary broke the strike.

AMERICA AND THE WORLD

# The American Red Cross and Wartime Civilian Aid

**B**eyond the financial and material assistance provided by the American government and the military reinforcement provided by the American Expeditionary Force (AEF), Europeans received vital support from the American Red Cross (ARC). Founded in 1881, the ARC was part of the International Red Cross, dedicated to providing neutral wartime aid to soldiers and assisting during natural disasters, famine, and other times of unrest, internationally or at home. During World War I, the ARC moved away from its origins as a neutral organization and engaged in expansive and wide-ranging assistance to soldiers and civilians of Allied nations, supporting the United States' diplomatic efforts to foster global goodwill through the spread of American ideals.

While the ARC had been active in providing assistance to wartime nations since the beginning of World War I, American entry into the conflict marked a turning point for the organization. One-third of the US population became members of the ARC, and donations exceeded $400 million. The vast resources generated by the ARC's popularity allowed the organization to send volunteers to and lead civilian relief efforts in 24 countries, many to which American troops had never been deployed. Influenced by the writings of famed ARC ambulance drivers Earnest

Hemingway and John Dos Passos, popular memory of the ARC often tends toward the organization's military assistance when, in fact, much of its aid targeted the needs of civilian populations.

The model for ARC aid was its operation in France. Homer Folks, a former social worker from New York, became head of the Department of Civil Affairs and worked collaboratively with existing French and American aid efforts. Folks led ARC efforts to establish a vast infrastructure that provided both immediate aid (food, housing, and gainful employment) and set into motion plans for long-term health and welfare programs (an anti-tuberculosis campaign, educational training about public health and nursing for local women, and extensive infant and child health and wellness programs). The ARC justified its focus on education and preventative public health work as war relief, noting that such programs were fundamental to France's long-term stability. In many ways, the strategy and organizational methods of the ARC mirrored the tactics employed by American Progressives of the prewar period, informed as they were by a social scientific method and a commitment to planning, efficiency, and oversight.

The perspectives of the ARC's programs were communicated across numerous forms of media: propaganda

**French Children in a Red Cross Hospital** The ARC assisted civilian populations affected by the tumult of World War I.

posters, films, popular magazines, and its own publication, *Red Cross Magazine*. For progressives and those committed to an effort to establish global health, welfare, and social reform, the ARC's programs provided a model of organization and efficiency, evidence that international reform views were the views of the future, as were international fellowship and global cooperation. Indeed, many ARC volunteers headed overseas were thrilled by the prospect of practicing their ideals, wishing to communicate a global sense of American benevolence and commitment to democracy, contributing to international well-being, and finding professional satisfaction and possible career advancement. Even more, the ARC's efforts to appease civilian suffering provided an answer to those who critiqued the United States' delayed entry into World War I as evidence of its failure to fulfill its responsibility as an ally. Officially, the ARC leadership claimed to assist Allied nations "not in the American way," but in a way "satisfying" to the native populations they assisted. Still, these ways were based on American middle-class values and a faith in expertise, and it was the United States that held the upper hand by providing rather than receiving assistance.

As the war came to a close, the ARC ceded authority to the American Relief Administration and focused on famine relief. The ARC remained committed to a global view of the United States and continued to provide aid to war-torn European nations, but its mission was complicated by the fact that some Europeans objected to a continued American presence and what appeared to be ARC workers' sense of superiority, while volunteers grew frustrated with the limited change they were able to achieve. Many Americans began to yearn for a "return to normalcy" and a decline in international engagement. Yet the ARC remained internationally engaged, assisting when disaster struck across the globe and providing health and hygiene reform in US territories. Even as the US government moved toward a policy of isolation in the 1920s and 1930s, the ARC served an important symbolic function of American international humanitarianism and aid that continues to be among its hallmarks to the present day.

**Wall Street Bombing** On September 16, 1920, Mario Buda detonated a horse-drawn wagon filled with dynamite and scrap metal in front of the J. P. Morgan offices on Wall Street. It was the first use of a new technology of terror, the car bomb. Sending shock waves through an America already anxious about revolutionaries, the blast intensified the hunt for radicals and "reds."

Using the patriotic rhetoric of the war, industry leaders labeled strikers as dangerous aliens. They persuaded allies in the courts to take action, and a series of Supreme Court decisions made union activity virtually illegal. In 1919, the Court allowed antitrust suits to be filed against unions and later outlawed boycotts and picketing. Then, in January 1920, a series of crackdowns known as the Palmer raids rounded up and deported 250 members of the Union of Russian Workers. In one night, 4,000 suspected Communists were arrested in raids across the country.

The most notorious case associated with the "Red Scare" began in May 1920 when Nicola Sacco and Bartolomeo Vanzetti, a shoemaker and a fish peddler, were arrested for robbing a shoe company in South Braintree, Massachusetts. Two men died of gunshot wounds during the robbery, and ballistics experts claimed the bullets came from Sacco's gun.

## Time Line

▼**1911**
Mexican Revolution begins

▼**1914**
US troops occupy Veracruz, Mexico
World War I begins

▼**1915**
US troops occupy Haiti (until 1934)
*Lusitania* sunk

▼**1916**
US forces invade Mexico in search of Pancho Villa
US forces enter the Dominican Republic
Woodrow Wilson reelected

▼**1917**
Russian czar abdicates; parliamentary regime takes power

United States declares war on Germany
East St. Louis riot
Houston riot
October Revolution overthrows Russian government; Lenin takes power

▼**1918**
Wilson announces US war aims: the Fourteen Points
Wilson nationalizes railroads

The trial, however, focused less on the evidence than on the fact that the defendants were Italian and anarchists. The state doctored evidence and witnesses changed testimony, but the judge favored the prosecution. The appeals lasted six years, as protests for their release mounted. With the execution approaching, labor parties organized worldwide boycotts of American products. Riots in Paris took 20 lives. Uruguayan workers called a general strike. Governments called on the president to intervene, but on August 23, 1927, Sacco and Vanzetti died in the electric chair.

Americans who had talked in 1917 about making the world safe for democracy now seemed ready to restrict their own freedoms out of fear. Lippmann found it "incredible that an administration announcing the most spacious ideals in our history should have done more to endanger fundamental American liberties than any group of men for a hundred years." By the end of 1920, the terror subsided, but labor unions and social radicals would have to fight the charge of communism for decades to come.

# Conclusion

Wilson tried to lead America toward what he called a new world order, in which nations and international law would count more than empires and in which the United States could light the way toward progress, stability, and peace. He failed to recognize that for many Americans this future was filled with terrors, as well as promise. The strains of war had introduced new divisions into American society. Progressivism, which had given coherence and direction to social change, was a spent force. The growth of federal administration, the new powers of big business, internal migrations, and new social movements and values added up to what Lippmann called a "revolutionary world." Many of the changes that began during the war had not fully played out, nor were their consequences apparent, but Americans entered the 1920s with a sense of uneasiness. They knew that their nation was now the world's strongest, but they were unsure about what that might mean for their lives.

Sedition Act outlaws criticism of the US government
US troops stop German advance
Wilson sends troops to Siberia
Armistice ends fighting on the western front
Influenza pandemic peaks in September

▼1919
Eighteenth Amendment outlaws manufacture, sale, and transport of alcoholic beverages
Versailles Treaty signed in Paris
Mail bombs target prominent government and business figures
Gary, Indiana, steel strike
US Senate rejects Versailles Treaty

▼1920
Nineteenth Amendment secures the vote for women
Palmer raids arrest thousands of suspected Communists
Sacco and Vanzetti arrested on charges of robbery and murder

## Who, What, Where

Baruch, Bernard  630

Catt, Carrie Chapman  633

Cost-plus contract  630

Creel, George  630

Díaz, Porfirio  622

Hog Island  630

Hughes, Langston  632

Mexico  622

Neutrality  623

Palace of Versailles  640

Pershing, John J.  622

Propaganda  623

Red Scare  641

Suffrage  621

Western front  620

## Review Questions

1. Wilson encouraged Americans to fight a war for democracy, but what other goals did US intervention serve?

2. How did mobilization for war advance the progressive agenda? In what ways did it set progressives back?

3. Where were the main battles in which US troops fought?

## Critical-Thinking Questions

1. Allied commanders wanted to use American troops as a reserve, but Pershing wanted his soldiers to enter the battle as an army. Why was that so important to him?

2. Why did Senate Republicans reject the League of Nations? Did they want the United States to withdraw from the world, or did they want to deal with the world in a different way?

3. Managing the pace of change posed a tricky problem for leaders in the early twentieth century. How did Wilson try to control the dynamic of social and political change? What methods of change was he unwilling to accept?

4. Why were American leaders so much more concerned about sedition and dissent during World War I than they were during the Civil War or World War II?

## Suggested Readings

Capozzola, Christopher. *Uncle Sam Wants You: World War I and the Making of the Modern American Citizen.* New York: Oxford University Press, 2008.

Irwin, Julia F. *Making the World Safe: The American Red Cross and a Nation's Humanitarian Awakening.* New York: Oxford University Press, 2013.

National Archives. World War I Centennial. https://www.archives.gov/topics/wwi#event-/timeline/item/archduke-assassination

Neiberg, Michael S. *The Path to War: How the First World War Created Modern America.* New York: Oxford University Press, 2016.

**For further review materials and resource information, please visit www.oup.com/us/oakes-mcgerr**

# CHAPTER 20: A GLOBAL POWER, 1914–1919
## Primary Sources

## 20.1 WORLD WAR I–ERA MUSIC: "I DIDN'T RAISE MY BOY TO BE A SOLDIER" (1915) AND "OVER THERE" (1917)

Americans viewed their nation's potential involvement in World War I with a healthy dose of skepticism. Many saw no need for the United States to become involved in what they regarded as a European conflict. After the United States joined the war, the Wilson administration recognized right away the need for propaganda efforts to boost support for American war efforts. Music played a fundamental role in reflecting the evolving mood of the population.

### Alfred Bryan and Al Piantadosi, "I Didn't Raise My Boy to Be a Soldier," 1915

Ten million soldiers to the war have gone,
Who may never return again.
Ten million mothers' hearts must break,
For the ones who died in vain.
Head bowed down in sorrow in her lonely years,
I heard a mother murmur thro' her tears:

*Chorus:*
I didn't raise my boy to be a soldier,
I brought him up to be my pride and joy,
Who dares to put a musket on his shoulder,
To shoot some other mother's darling boy?
Let nations arbitrate their future troubles,
It's time to lay the sword and gun away,
There'd be no war today,
If mothers all would say,
I didn't raise my boy to be a soldier.

What victory can cheer a mother's heart,
When she looks at her blighted home?
What victory can bring her back,
All she cared to call her own?
Let each mother answer in the year to be,
Remember that my boy belongs to me!
*(Chorus)*

### George M. Cohan, "Over There," 1917

Johnnie, get your gun
Get your gun, get your gun
Take it on the run
On the run, on the run

Hear them calling, you and me
Every son of liberty
Hurry right away
No delay, go today
Make your daddy glad
To have had such a lad
Tell your sweetheart not to pine
To be proud her boy's in line

*Chorus:*
Over there, over there
Send the word, send the word over there
That the Yanks are coming
The Yanks are coming
The drums rum-tumming
Everywhere
So prepare, say a prayer
Send the word, send the word to beware
We'll be over, we're coming over
And we won't come back till it's over
Over there

Johnnie, get your gun
Get your gun, get your gun
Johnnie show the Hun
Who's a son of a gun
Hoist the flag and let her fly
Yankee Doodle do or die
Pack your little kit
Show your grit, do your bit
Yankee to the ranks
From the towns and the tanks
Make your mother proud of you
And the old Red, White and Blue
(*Chorus*)

*Sources:* Al Piantadosi and Alfred Bryan, "I Didn't Raise My Boy to Be a Soldier," http://historymatters.gmu.edu/d/4942.
George M. Cohan, "Over There," http://www.loc.gov/teachers/classroommaterials/presentationsandactivities/activities/songs/song2.php.

# 20.2 EUGENE V. DEBS, EXCERPTS FROM CANTON, OHIO, SPEECH (1918)

Eugene V. Debs, a leader of the Socialist Party of America, vehemently opposed American involvement in World War I. In June 1918, after visiting several local Socialist leaders who had been jailed for their opposition to the war, Debs spoke in Canton, Ohio. During his speech, he criticized the war as a capitalist undertaking and charged that those who led the patriotic charge did so for purely financial purposes. He called for the working classes to join the Socialist Party and fight for a socialist republic in America. In the aftermath of his speech, Debs was convicted for sedition under the Espionage Act of 1917 and sentenced to 10 years in prison. President Warren Harding commuted his sentence in 1921.

---

I hate, I loathe, I despise junkers and junkerdom. I have no earthly use for the junkers of Germany, and not one particle more use for the junkers in the United States. They tell us that we live in a great free republic; that our institutions are democratic; that we are a free and self-governing people. This is too much, even for a joke. But it is not a subject for levity; it is an exceedingly serious matter.

To whom do the Wall Street junkers in our country marry their daughters? After they have wrung their countless millions from your sweat, your agony and your life's blood, in a time of war as in a time of peace, they invest these untold millions in the purchase of titles of broken-down aristocrats, such as princes, dukes, counts and other parasites and no-accounts. Would they be satisfied to wed their daughters to honest workingmen? To real democrats? Oh, no!

They scour the markets of Europe for vampires who are titled and nothing else. And they swap their millions for the titles, so that matrimony with them becomes literally a matter of money. These are the gentry who are today wrapped up in the American flag, who shout their claim from the housetops that they are the only patriots, and who have their magnifying glasses in hand, scanning the country for evidence of disloyalty, eager to apply the brand of treason to the men who dare to even whisper their opposition to junker rule in the United States. No wonder Sam Johnson declared that "patriotism is the last refuge of the scoundrel." He must have had this Wall Street gentry in mind, or at least their prototypes, for in every age it has been the tyrant, the oppressor and the exploiter who has wrapped himself in the cloak of patriotism, or religion, or both to deceive and overawe the people.

They would have you believe that the Socialist Party consists in the main of disloyalists and traitors. It is true in a sense not at all to their discredit. We frankly admit that we *are* disloyalists and traitors to the real traitors of this nation. . . .

Every solitary one of these aristocratic conspirators and would-be murderers claims to be an arch-patriot; every one of them insists that the war is being waged to make the world safe for democracy. What humbug! What rot! What false pretense! These autocrats, these tyrants, these red-handed robbers and murderers, the "patriots," while the men who have the courage to stand face to face with them, speak the truth, and fight for their exploited victims—they are the disloyalists and traitors. If this be true, I want to take my place side by side with the traitors in this fight. . . .

Socialism is a growing idea; an expanding philosophy. It is spreading over the entire face of the earth: It is as vain to resist it as it would be to arrest the sunrise on the morrow. It is coming, coming, coming all along the line. Can you not see it? . . . It is the mightiest movement in the history of mankind. What a privilege to serve it! . . .

Our hearts are with the Bolsheviki of Russia. Those heroic men and women, those unconquerable comrades have by their incomparable valor and sacrifice added fresh luster to the fame of the international movement. Those Russian comrades of ours have made greater sacrifices, have suffered more, and have shed more heroic blood than any like number of men and women anywhere on earth; they have laid the foundation of the first real democracy that ever drew the breath of life in this world. And the very first act of the triumphant Russian revolution was to proclaim a state of peace with all mankind, coupled with a fervent moral appeal, not to kings, not to emperors, rulers or diplomats but to *the people* of all nations. Here we have the very breath of democracy, the quintessence of the dawning freedom. The Russian revolution proclaimed its glorious triumph in its ringing and inspiring appeal to *the peoples* of all the earth. In a humane and fraternal spirit new Russia, emancipated at last from the curse of the centuries, called upon all nations engaged in the frightful war, the Central Powers as well as the Allies, to send representatives to a conference to lay down terms of peace that should be just and lasting. Here was the supreme opportunity to strike the blow to make the world safe for democracy. Was there any response to that noble appeal that in some day to come will be written in letters of gold in the history of the world? Was there any response whatever to that appeal for universal peace? [*From the crowd, "No!"*] No, not the slightest attention was paid to it by the Christian nations engaged in the terrible slaughter. . . .

Wars throughout history have been waged for conquest and plunder. In the Middle Ages when the feudal lords who inhabited the castles whose towers may still be seen along the Rhine concluded to enlarge their domains, to increase their power, their prestige and their wealth they declared war upon one another. But they themselves did not go to war any more than the modern feudal lords, the barons of Wall Street go to war. The feudal barons of the Middle Ages, the economic predecessors of the capitalists of our day, declared all wars. And their miserable serfs fought all the battles. The poor, ignorant serfs had been taught to revere their masters; to believe that when their masters declared war upon one another, it was their patriotic duty to fall upon one another and to cut one another's throats for the profit and glory of the lords and barons who held them in contempt. And that is war in a nutshell. The master class has always declared the wars; the subject class has always fought the battles. The master class has had all to gain and nothing to lose, while the subject class has had nothing to gain and all to lose—especially their lives.

They have always taught and trained you to believe it to be your patriotic duty to go to war and to have yourselves slaughtered at their command. But in all the history of the world you, the people, have never had a voice in declaring war, and strange as it certainly appears, no war by any nation in any age has ever been declared by the people.

And here let me emphasize the fact—and it cannot be repeated too often—that the working class who fight all the battles, the working class who make the supreme sacrifices, the working class who freely shed their blood and furnish the corpses, have never yet had a voice in either declaring war or making peace. It is the ruling class that invariably does both. They alone declare war and they alone make peace.

What a compliment it is to the Socialist movement to be thus persecuted for the sake of the truth! The truth alone will make the people free. And for this reason the truth must not be permitted to reach the people. The truth has always been dangerous to the rule of the rogue, the exploiter, the robber. So the truth must be ruthlessly suppressed. That is why they are trying to destroy the Socialist movement; and every time they strike a blow they add a thousand new voices to the hosts proclaiming that socialism is the hope of humanity and has come to emancipate the people from their final form of servitude. . . .

[Socialists] are pressing forward, here, there and everywhere, in all the zones that girdle the globe. Everywhere these awakening workers, these class-conscious proletarians, these hardy sons and daughters of honest toil are proclaiming the glad tidings of the coming emancipation; everywhere their hearts are attuned to the most sacred cause that ever challenged men and women to action in all the history of the world. Everywhere they are moving toward democracy and the dawn; marching toward the sunrise, their faces all aglow with the light of the coming day. These are the Socialists, the most zealous and enthusiastic crusaders the world has ever known. They are making history that will light up the horizon of coming generations, for their mission is the emancipation of the human race. They have been reviled; they have been ridiculed, persecuted, imprisoned and have suffered death, but they have been sufficient to themselves and their cause, and their final triumph is but a question of time.

Do you wish to hasten the day of victory? Join the Socialist Party! Don't wait for the morrow. Join now! Enroll your name without fear and take your place where you belong. You cannot do your duty by proxy. You have got to do it yourself and do it squarely and then as you look yourself in the face you will have no occasion to blush. You will know what it is to be a real *man* or *woman*. You will lose nothing; you will gain everything. . . .

*Source:* Jean Y. Tussey, ed., *Eugene V. Debs Speaks* (New York: Pathfinder Press, 1970), pp. 243–279.

# 20.3 GEORGE CREEL, EXCERPTS FROM *HOW WE ADVERTISED AMERICA* (1920)

In April 1917, after the United States entered World War I, President Woodrow Wilson created the Committee on Public Information (CPI) headed by George Creel (1876–1953), a former muckraking journalist, newspaper editor, and politician. The CPI managed the nation's propaganda effort, creating films, staging pageants, and turning out advertisements, billboards, and press releases intended to educate the American public and build support for war efforts such as bond drives and rationing. In this memoir of his years at the CPI, published in 1920, Creel defended the work of the CPI against those who saw the agency as engaging in promotion of the war effort in any way other than an "open" and "positive" manner.

As Secretary Baker points out, the war was not fought in France alone. Back of the firing-line, back of armies and navies, back of the great supply-depots, another struggle waged with the same intensity and with almost equal significance attaching to its victories and defeats. It was the fight for the *minds* of men, for the "conquest of their convictions," and the battle-line ran through every home in every country.

It was in this recognition of Public Opinion as a major force that the Great War differed most essentially from all previous conflicts. The trial of strength was not only between massed bodies of armed men, but between opposed ideals, and moral verdicts took on all the value of military decisions. Other wars went no deeper than the physical aspects, but German *Kultur* raised issues that had to be fought out in the hearts and minds of people as well as on the actual firing-line. The approval of the world meant the steady flow of inspiration into the trenches; it meant the strengthened resolve and the renewed determination of the civilian population that is a nation's second line. The condemnation of the world meant the destruction of morale and the surrender of that conviction of justice which is the very heart of courage. The Committee on Public Information was called into existence to make this fight for the "verdict of mankind," the voice created to plead the justice of America's cause before the jury of Public Opinion. . . .

In no degree was the Committee an agency of censorship, a machinery of concealment or repression. Its emphasis throughout was on the open and the positive. At no point did it seek or exercise authorities under those war laws that limited the freedom of speech and press.

In all things, from first to last, without halt or change, it was a plain publicity proposition, a vast enterprise in salesmanship, the world's greatest adventure in advertising.

Under the pressure of tremendous necessities an organization grew that not only reached deep into every American community, but that carried to every corner of the civilized globe the full message of America's idealism, unselfishness, and indomitable purpose. We fought prejudice, indifference, and disaffection at home and we fought ignorance and falsehood abroad. We strove for the maintenance of our own morale and the Allied morale by every process of stimulation; every possible expedient was employed to break through the barrage of lies that kept the people of the Central Powers in darkness and delusion; we sought the friendship and support of the neutral nations by continuous presentation of facts. We did not call it propaganda, for that word, in German hands, had come to be associated with deceit and corruption. Our effort was educational and informative throughout, for we had such confidence in our case as to feel that no other argument was needed than the simple, straightforward presentation of facts.

There was no part of the great war machinery that we did not touch, no medium of appeal that we did not employ. The printed word, the spoken word, the motion picture, the telegraph, the cable, the wireless, the poster, the sign-board—all these were used in our campaign to make our own people and all other peoples understand the causes that compelled America to take arms. All that was fine and ardent in the civilian population came at our call until more than one hundred and fifty thousand men and women were devoting highly specialized abilities to the work of the Committee, as faithful and devoted in their service as though they wore the khaki. While America's summons was answered without question by the citizenship as a whole, it is to be remembered that during the three and a half years of our neutrality the land had been torn by a thousand divisive prejudices, stunned by the voices of anger and confusion, and muddled by the pull and haul of opposed interests. These were conditions that could not be permitted to endure. What we had to have was no mere surface unity, but a passionate belief in the justice of America's cause that should weld the people of the United States into one white-hot mass instinct with fraternity, devotion, courage, and deathless determination. The *war-will*, the will-to-win, of a democracy depends upon the degree to which each one of all the people of that democracy can concentrate and consecrate body and soul and spirit in the supreme effort of service and sacrifice. What had to be driven home was that all business was the nation's business, and every task a common task for a single purpose. . . .

As swiftly as might be, there were put into pamphlet form America's reasons for entering the war, the meaning of America, the nature of our free institutions, our war aims, likewise analyses of the Prussian system, the purposes of the imperial German government, and full exposure of the enemy's misrepresentations, aggressions, and barbarities. Written by the country's foremost publicists, scholars, and historians, and distinguished for their conciseness, accuracy, and simplicity, these pamphlets blew as a great wind against the clouds of confusion and misrepresentation. Money could not have purchased the volunteer aid that was given freely, the various universities lending their best men and the National Board of Historical Service placing its three thousand members at the complete disposal of the Committee. Some thirty-odd booklets, covering every phase of America's ideals, purposes, and aims, were printed in many languages other than English. Seventy-five million reached the people of America, and other millions went to every corner of the world, carrying our defense and our attack.

The importance of the spoken word was not underestimated. A speaking division toured great groups like the Blue Devils, Pershing's Veterans, and the Belgians, arranged mass-meetings in the communities, conducted forty-five war conferences from coast to coast, coordinated the entire speaking activities of the nation, and assured consideration to the crossroads hamlet as well as to the city.

The Four Minute Men, an organization that will live in history by reason of its originality and effectiveness, commanded the volunteer services of 75,000 speakers, operating in 5,200 communities, and making a total of 755,190 speeches, every one having the carry of shrapnel.

With the aid of a volunteer staff of several hundred translators, the Committee kept in direct touch with the foreign-language press, supplying selected articles designed to combat ignorance and disaffection. It organized and directed twenty-three societies and leagues designed to appeal to certain classes and particular foreign-language groups, each body carrying a specific message of unity and enthusiasm to its section of America's adopted peoples.

It planned war exhibits for the state fairs of the United States, also a great series of interallied war expositions that brought home to our millions the exact nature of the struggle that was being waged in France. In Chicago alone two million people attended in two weeks, and in nineteen cities the receipts aggregated $1,432,261.36. The Committee mobilized the advertising forces of the country—press, periodical, car, and outdoor—for the patriotic campaign that gave millions of dollars' worth of free space to the national service.

It assembled the artists of America on a volunteer basis for the production of posters, window cards, and similar material of pictorial publicity for the use of various government departments and patriotic societies. A total of 1,438 drawings was used. . . .

It organized a bureau of information for all persons who sought direction in volunteer war-work, in acquiring knowledge of any administrative activities, or in approaching business dealings with the government. In the ten months of its existence it gave answers to eighty-six thousand requests for specific information.

It gathered together the leading novelists, essayists, and publicists of the land, and these men and women, without payment, worked faithfully in the production of brilliant, comprehensive articles that went to the press as syndicate features. One division paid particular attention to the rural press and the plate-matter service. Others looked after the specialized needs of the labor press, the religious press, and the periodical press. The Division of Women's War Work prepared and issued the information of peculiar interest to the women of the United States, also aiding in the task of organizing and directing. Through the medium of the motion picture, America's war progress, as well as the meanings and purposes of democracy, were carried to every community in the United States and to every corner of the world. "Pershing's Crusaders," "America's Answer," and "Under Four Flags" were types of feature films by which we drove home America's resources and determinations, while other pictures, showing our social and industrial life, made our free institutions vivid to foreign peoples.

Turning away from the United States to the world beyond our borders, a triple task confronted us. First, there were the peoples of the Allied nations that had to be fired by the magnitude of the American effort and the certainty of speedy and effective aid, in order to relieve the war weariness of the civilian population and also to fan the enthusiasm of the firing-line to new flame. Second, we had to carry the truth to the neutral nations, poisoned by German lies; and third, we had to get the ideals of America, the determination of America, and the invincibility of America into the Central Powers. . . .

Source:  George Creel, *How We Advertised America* (New York: Harper and Brothers, 1920), pp. 3–8.

# 20.4 WOODROW WILSON, "FOURTEEN POINTS" SPEECH (1918)

As Woodrow Wilson addressed Congress on January 8, 1918, he attempted to link American involvement in World War I to a moral cause, much as he had when he asked for a declaration of war in order to "make the world safe for democracy." As he outlined his goals for peace, he attempted to address many of the issues that had led to the outbreak of the war. By eliminating the main causes of the war—imperial desire and commercial competition—and establishing a just peace, he hoped to avoid such conflicts in the future.

It will be our wish and purpose that the processes of peace, when they are begun, shall be absolutely open and that they shall involve and permit henceforth no secret understandings of any kind. The day of conquest and aggrandizement is gone by; so is also the day of secret covenants entered into in the interest of particular governments and likely at some unlooked-for moment to upset the peace of the world. It is this happy fact, now clear to the view of every public man whose thoughts do not still linger in an age that is dead and gone, which makes it possible for every nation whose purposes are consistent with justice and the peace of the world to avow now or at any other time the objects it has in view.

We entered this war because violations of right had occurred which touched us to the quick and made the life of our own people impossible unless they were corrected and the world secured once and for all against their recurrence. What we demand in this war, therefore, is nothing peculiar to ourselves. It is that the world be made fit and safe to live in; and particularly that it be made safe for every peace-loving nation which, like our own, wishes to live its own life, determine its own institutions, be assured of justice and fair dealing by the other peoples of the world as against force and selfish aggression. All the peoples of the world are in effect partners in this interest, and for our own part we see very clearly that unless justice be done to others it will not be done to us. The programme of the world's peace, therefore, is our programme; and that programme, the only possible programme, as we see it, is this:

I. Open covenants of peace, openly arrived at, after which there shall be no private international understandings of any kind but diplomacy shall proceed always frankly and in the public view.

II. Absolute freedom of navigation upon the seas, outside territorial waters, alike in peace and in war, except as the seas may be closed in whole or in part by international action for the enforcement of international covenants.

III. The removal, so far as possible, of all economic barriers and the establishment of an equality of trade conditions among all the nations consenting to the peace and associating themselves for its maintenance.

IV. Adequate guarantees given and taken that national armaments will be reduced to the lowest point consistent with domestic safety.

V. A free, open-minded, and absolutely impartial adjustment of all colonial claims, based upon a strict observance of the principle that in determining all such questions of sovereignty the interests of the populations concerned must have equal weight with the equitable claims of the government whose title is to be determined.

VI. The evacuation of all Russian territory and such a settlement of all questions affecting Russia as will secure the best and freest cooperation of the other nations of the world in obtaining for her an unhampered and unembarrassed opportunity for the independent determination of her own political development and national policy and assure her of a sincere welcome into the society of free nations under institutions of her own choosing; and, more than a welcome, assistance also of every kind that she may need and may herself desire. The treatment accorded Russia by her sister nations in the months to come will be the acid test of their good will, of their comprehension of her needs as distinguished from their own interests, and of their intelligent and unselfish sympathy.

VII. Belgium, the whole world will agree, must be evacuated and restored, without any attempt to limit the sovereignty which she enjoys in common with all other free nations. No other single act will serve as this will serve to restore confidence among the nations in the laws which they have themselves set and determined for the government of their relations with one another. Without this healing act the whole structure and validity of international law is forever impaired.

VIII. All French territory should be freed and the invaded portions restored, and the wrong done to France by Prussia in 1871 in the matter of Alsace-Lorraine, which has unsettled the peace of the world for nearly fifty years, should be righted, in order that peace may once more be made secure in the interest of all.

   IX. A readjustment of the frontiers of Italy should be effected along clearly recognizable lines of nationality.

   X. The peoples of Austria-Hungary, whose place among the nations we wish to see safeguarded and assured, should be accorded the freest opportunity of autonomous development.

   XI. Rumania, Serbia, and Montenegro should be evacuated; occupied territories restored; Serbia accorded free and secure access to the sea; and the relations of the several Balkan states to one another determined by friendly counsel along historically established lines of allegiance and nationality; and international guarantees of the political and economic independence and territorial integrity of the several Balkan states should be entered into.

   XII. The Turkish portions of the present Ottoman Empire should be assured a secure sovereignty, but the other nationalities which are now under Turkish rule should be assured an undoubted security of life and an absolutely unmolested opportunity of autonomous development, and the Dardanelles should be permanently opened as a free passage to the ships and commerce of all nations under international guarantees.

   XIII. An independent Polish state should be erected which should include the territories inhabited by indisputably Polish populations, which should be assured a free and secure access to the sea, and whose political and economic independence and territorial integrity should be guaranteed by international covenant.

   XIV. A general association of nations must be formed under specific covenants for the purpose of affording mutual guarantees of political independence and territorial integrity to great and small states alike.

In regard to these essential rectifications of wrong and assertions of right we feel ourselves to be intimate partners of all the governments and peoples associated together against the Imperialists. We cannot be separated in interest or divided in purpose. We stand together until the end.

For such arrangements and covenants we are willing to fight and to continue to fight until they are achieved; but only because we wish the right to prevail and desire a just and stable peace such as can be secured only by removing the chief provocations to war, which this programme does remove. We have no jealousy of German greatness, and there is nothing in this programme that impairs it. We grudge her no achievement or distinction of learning or of pacific enterprise such as have made her record very bright and very enviable. We do not wish to injure her or to block in any way her legitimate influence or power. We do not wish to fight her either with arms or with hostile arrangements of trade if she is willing to associate herself with us and the other peace-loving nations of the world in covenants of justice and law and fair dealing. We wish her only to accept a place of equality among the peoples of the world,—the new world in which we now live,—instead of a place of mastery.

Neither do we presume to suggest to her any alteration or modification of her institutions. But it is necessary, we must frankly say, and necessary as a preliminary to any intelligent dealings with her on our part, that we should know whom her spokesmen speak for when they speak to us, whether for the Reichstag majority or for the military party and the men whose creed is imperial domination.

We have spoken now, surely, in terms too concrete to admit of any further doubt or question. An evident principle runs through the whole programme I have outlined. It is the principle of justice to all peoples and nationalities, and their right to live on equal terms of liberty and safety with one another, whether they be strong or weak. Unless this principle be made its foundation no part of the structure of international justice can stand. The people of the United States could act upon no other principle; and to the vindication of this principle they are ready to devote their lives, their honor, and everything that they possess. The moral climax of this the culminating and final war for human liberty has come, and they are ready to put their own strength, their own highest purpose, their own integrity and devotion to the test.

*Source:* Woodrow Wilson, Address on the Fourteen Points for Peace, January 8, 1918.

# Photo Credits

**Chapter 1:** Photo by DeAgostini/Getty Images, 2-3; Gianni Dagli Orti/National History Museum, Mexico City/The Art Archive/Art Resource, NY, 4; 100 B.C.-A.D. 200 Mexico, Nayarit Culture Ceramic 30.5 × 25.4 × 17.1 cm. Gift of Joanne P. Pearson, in memory of Andrall E. Pearson, 2015. Metropolitan Museum of Art Accession Number: 2015.306, 7; Cahokia Mounds State Historic Site. Photo by Art Grossman, 9; Bettmann/Getty Images, 15; Photo by DeAgostini/Getty Images, 20; Granger–All rights reserved, 24; Benson Latin American Collection, University of Texas, Austin, 28; Photo by DeAgostini/Getty Images, S1-1; DEA/SIOEN/Getty Images, S1-1.

**Chapter 2:** Indians Fishing (colour litho), White, John (fl. 1570–93) (after)/Private Collection/Bridgeman Images, 32–33, 55; Indian in Body Paint (litho) White, John (fl. 1570–92) (after). Private Collection/Bridgeman Images, 34; Granger–All rights reserved, 42; Governor Peter Stuyvesant (1592–. . .) Couturier, Hendrick (fl. 1648-d.c . . .). Collection of the New York Historical Society, USA/Bridgeman Images, 54; © The Trustees of the British Museum/Art Resource, NY, 56.

**Chapter 3:** Granger–All rights reserved, 60–61; National Portrait Gallery, Washington, D.C. (Photo by VCG Wilson/Corbis via Getty Images), 62; Granger–All rights reserved, 64; Marilyn Angel Wynn/Nativestock.com, 67; Ira Block/Getty Images, 67; Pilgrim Hall Museum, Plymouth, MA, 78.

**Chapter 4:** An American Indian Man and his M . . . Mexican School, (18th century). Museo de America, Madrid, Spain/Bridgeman Images, 88–89, 119; Photo by Briggs Co./George Eastman House/Getty Images, 90; NYC Department of Records & Information Services, 94; Plan et Scituation des Villages Tchikachas Plan and Situation of the Chicksaw Villages, Alexandre de Batz, 1737. French copy of a map made by a visitor to the Chicksaw, 97; Plymouth County Commissioners, Plymouth Court House, Plymouth, MA/Dublin Seminar for New England Folklife, Concord, MA, 105; Courtesy of The Newberry Library, Chicago. Call # Ayer MS map 30, Sheet 77, 115; Kevin Fleming/Corbis/VCG/Getty, 117.

**Chapter 5:** Granger–All rights reserved, 124–125, 149; Courtesy of the Library of Congress, 126; Granger–All rights reserved, 131; Granger–All rights reserved, 138; Mr. Peter Manigault and his Friends, 1854, By Louis Manigault (American, 1828–1899) after George Boone Roupell (1726–1794), Wash and ink on paper, Gift of Mr. Joseph e. Jenkins, 1968.005.0001, Image courtesy of the Gibbes Museum of Art/Carolina Art Association, 140; Courtesy of the Library of Congress, S5–3; GraphicaArtis/Getty Images, S5–7.

**Chapter 6:** Benjamin West, 1738–1820 The Death of General Wolfe, 1770 oil on canvas 152.6 × 214.5 cm National Gallery of Canada Gift of the 2nd Duke of Westminster to the Canadian War Memorials, 1918, Transfer from the Canadian War Memorials, 1921, 156–157, 168; Frontispiece from *A Narrative of the Captivity of Mrs. Johnson* (Bowie, MD: Heritage Books, Inc. 1990), p. v, 181, 158; Granger–All rights reserved, 164; Granger–All rights reserved, 177; Granger–All rights reserved, 180.

**Chapter 7:** Yale University Art Gallery, 188–189, 201; Abigail Smith Adams, c 1766 (pastel on paper), Blyth, Benjamin (c. 1746-c. 1786)/Massachusetts Historical Society, Boston, MA, USA/Bridgeman Images, 190; Granger–All rights reserved, 194; Courtesy of the Library of Congress, 195; Anonymous, 18th century English, after J.F. Renault: The British surrendering their arms to General Washington after their defeat at Yorktown in Virginia, October 1781. Colored engraving, Inv.: CFAc 295. © RMN-Grand Palais/Art Resource, NY, 204; Granger–All rights reserved, 211.

**Chapter 8:** Henry Francis Du Pont Winterthur Museum, 24–225, 233; Courtesy Independence National Historical Park, 226; Henry Francis Du Pont Winterthur Museum, 233; Residence of Washington in High . . . Breton, William L. (fl. 1830). Library Company of Philadelphia, PA, USA/Bridgeman Images, 235; Map located in the Military Journal of Major Ebenezer Denny, an officer in the Revolutionary and Indian Wars (J.B. Lippincott & Co., for the Historical Society of Pennsylvania, 1859), available via the Boston Public Library (E83.79.D4 1859 ×), 244; Granger–All rights reserved, S8-4.

**Chapter 9:** Courtesy of the Library of Congress, 256–257, 267; Anna Claypoole Peale, American, 1791–1878. Andrew Jackson (1767–1845) 1819 Watercolor on ivory 3 1/8 × 2 7/16 in. (7.9 × 6.2 cm) Mabel Brady Garvan Collection 1936.302. Yale University Art Gallery, 258; American

Antiquarian Society copy the gift of Armstrong Hunter, 1991, 265; Kean Collection/Getty Images, 273; Catlin, George (1796–1872) Ten-squát-a-way, The Open Door, Known as The Prophet, Brother of Tecumseh. Shawnee. 1830. Oil on canvas. 29 × 24 in. (73.7 × 60.9 cm) Location: Smithsonian American Art Museum, Washington, DC, U. Photo Credit: Smithsonian American Art Museum, Washington, DC/Art Resource, NY, 280; Image located in Robert Stuart Sanders, Presbyterianism in Paris and Bourbon County, Kentucky, 1786–1961 (First Presbyterian Church, 1961), p. 209, 282.

**Chapter 10:** Granger–All rights reserved, 288–289, 308; McKenney and Hall (19th CE) John Ross, A Cherokee Chief. From History of the Indian Tribes of North America. ca. 1843. Hand-colored lithograph on paper. 19 5/8 × 13 3/8 in. (49.9 × 34 cm). Smithsonian American Art Museum, Washington, DC/Art Resource, NY National Portrait Gallery, Smithsonian Institution, gift of Betty A. and Lloyd G. Schermer, 290; Granger–All rights reserved, 292; Granger–All rights reserved, 299; Page 041, in the Manigault Family Papers #484, Southern Historical Collection, Wilson Library, University of North Carolina at Chapel Hill, 305; Courtesy of the Library of Congress, 320; Gilcrease Museum, Tulsa, OK, 322; Courtesy of the Library of Congress, S10-4.

**Chapter 11:** Geoffrey Clements/Getty Images, 330–331, 345; Courtesy of the Library of Congress, 332; Courtesy of the Library of Congress, 333; Granger–All rights reserved, 335; Photo by: Universal History Archive/UIG via Getty Images, 339; Granger–All rights reserved, 350; Granger–All rights reserved, 354.

**Chapter 12:** Photo by Herbert Orth/The LIFE Images Collection/Getty Images, 360-361, 381; Granger–All rights reserved, 362; Courtesy of the Library of Congress, 365; Apic/RETIRED/Getty Images, 373; George Catlin (1796–1872) [Buffalo Hunt, with Wolf-Skin Mask.], 1844. Toned lithograph with applied watercolor. Amon Carter Museum of American Art, Fort Worth, Texas, 376; Los Angeles Public Library, 386; Thomas Cole, Landscape, 1825 oil on canvas 23 ¾ × 31 ½ in. Minneapolis Institute of Art 15.299 Bequest of Mrs. Kate L. Dunwoody, S12-3; Granger–All rights reserved, S12-4; Louis Rémy Mignot Landscape in Ecuador, 1859 24 × 39 ½ in. (61.0 × 100.3 cm) Oil on canvas. Purchased with funds from gifts by the American Credit Corporation in memory of Guy T. Carswell, and various donors, by exchange 91.2, S12-4.

**Chapter 13:** Granger–All rights reserved, 388–389, 415; Frederick Douglass. ca. 1855.

Daguerreotype, 7.0 × 5.6 cm (2 ¾ × 2 3/16 in.). The Rubel Collection, Partial and Promised Gift of William Rubel, 2001 (2001.756). Image copyright © The Metropolitan Museum of Art. Image source: Art Resource, NY, 390; Outward Bound, The Quay of Dubli . . . Nicol, J (19th century) (after). Collection of the New York Historical Society, USA/Bridgeman Images, 393; Granger–All rights reserved, 399; Granger–All rights reserved, 407; Courtesy of the Library of Congress, 411.

**Chapter 14:** Granger–All rights reserved, 420–421, 446; Penn School Papers, Southern Historical Collection, University of North Carolina at Chapel Hill, 422; Granger–All rights reserved, 431; Granger–All rights reserved, 441; Courtesy of the Library of Congress, 445; David Gilmour Blythe (American, 1815–1865), Lincoln Crushing the Dragon of Rebellion, 1862 oil on canvas 45.72 × 55.88 cm. Museum of Fine Arts Boston 48.413 Bequest of Martha C. Karolik for the M. and M. Karolik Collection of American Paintings, 1815–1865. Photograph © 2018 Museum of Fine Arts, Boston, 451; Culver Pictures/The Art Archive/Art Resource, NY, 453.

**Chapter 15:** Photo by MPI/Getty Images, 458–459, 489; Courtesy of the Library of Congress, 460; Courtesy of the Library of Congress, 468; Courtesy of the Library of Congress, 473; Bettmann/Getty Images, 480; Granger–All rights reserved, 482; Courtesy of the Library of Congress, 486.

**Chapter 16:** The Granger Collection, 496–497, 510; The Granger Collection, 498; The Granger Collection, 505; Curt Teich Postcard Archives Collection (Newberry Library) DPC79785, 507; California History, Vol. 64, No. 3, Summer 1985, page 174 (University of California Press and California Historical Society), 515; The Granger Collection, 522; Courtesy of the Library of Congress, S16-2.

**Chapter 17:** Courtesy of the Ohio History Connection, 524–525, 541; Nebraska State Historical Society, 526; Photo by PhotoQuest/Getty Images, 529; The Granger Collection, 534; Bettmann/Getty Images, 535; Weir, John Ferguson (1841–1926) Forging the Shaft. 1874–77. Oil on canvas, 52 × 73 ¼ in. (132.1 × 186.1 cm). Purchase, Lyman G. Bloomingdale Gift, 1901 (01.7.1). Location: The Metropolitan Museum of Art, New York, NY, USA Photo Credit: Image copyright © The Metropolitan Museum of Art. Image source: Art Resource, NY, 550; Kansas State Historical Society, 553; The Granger Collection, S17-5; Courtesy of the Library of Congress, S17-7; Courtesy of the Library of Congress, S17-7.

**Chapter 18:** Courtesy of the Library of Congress, 556–557, 579; The Granger Collection, 558; Courtesy of the Library of Congress, 563; The Granger Collection, 570; Courtesy of the Library of Congress, 573; North Wind Picture Archives/Alamy Stock Photo, 577; Courtesy of the Library of Congress, S18-7.

**Chapter 19:** Lewis W. Hine/Getty Images, 588–589, 597; Tropical Press Agency/Getty Images, 590; The Kheel Center at Cornell University, 593; Courtesy of the Library of Congress, 599; The University of Chicago Library, Special Collections Research Center, Photographic Archive apf1-08624, 601; Chicago History Museum 139070_6f, 604; Courtesy of the Library of Congress, S19; Courtesy of the Library of Congress, S19-4; Courtesy of the Library of Congress, S19-6; Courtesy of the Library of Congress, S19-7.

**Chapter 20:** Courtesy of the Library of Congress, 618–619, 643; Courtesy of the Library of Congress, 620; Courtesy of the Library of Congress, 627. Courtesy of the Pennsylvania State Archives, 631; The Art Archive/Art Resource, 638; Chronicle/San Francisco Chronicle, 640; Photo by NY Daily News Archive via Getty Images, 644.

**Chapter 21:** Smith Collection/Gado/Getty Images, 648–649, 669; Courtesy of the Library of Congress, 650; Hulton Archive/Getty Images, 652; The Granger Collection, 658; Chicago History Museum/Getty Images, 663; Duke University Libraries Ad Access, BH0714 Ann Elsner in honor of Allan Todd Sagraves, S21-4.

**Chapter 22:** MPI/Stringer/Getty Images, 678–679, 689; Courtesy of the Library of Congress, 680; Three Lions/Getty Images, 685; Bettmann/Getty Images, 686; AP Photo, 697; Getty Images, 703; Courtesy of the Library of Congress, S22-3; Courtesy of the Library of Congress, S22-3; Courtesy of the Library of Congress, S22-3.

**Chapter 23:** Bettmann/Getty Images, 715; Bettmann/Getty Images, 710; Courtesy National Park Service Museum Management Program and Tuskegee Airmen National Historic Site, TUA131, 721; Courtesy of the Library of Congress, 730; Bettmann/Getty Images, 733; Bettmann/Getty Images, 734; Bettmann/Getty Images, 738.

**Chapter 24:** George Tooker, 1920-2011 Government Bureau, 1956. Egg tempera on wood 19 5/8 × 29 5/8 in.: George A. Hearn Fund, 1956. The Met, 742–743, 765; Courtesy Turchinetz family, 744; British Cartoon Archive, University of Kent ILW1059, 748; Photo by Galerie Bilderwelt/Getty Images, 753; Bettmann/Getty Images, 757; AP Photo/File, 761.

**Chapter 25:** Photo by Grey Villet/The LIFE Picture Collection/Getty Images, 772–773, 800; CBS Photo Archive/Getty Images, 774; Guy Gillette/Getty Images, 778; Bettmann/Getty Images, 784; Bettmann, 785; Bettmann/Getty Images, 790; Duke University Libraries Ad Access, T032 Ann Elsner in honor of Allan Todd Sagraves, 795; A 1957 Herblock Cartoon, © The Herb Block Foundation, 801; Duke University J. Walter Thompson Ford Motor Co. Advertisements, 1944–2001: identifier: jwtad150010630, S25-5; Apic/RETIRED/Getty Images, S25-2; The Studebaker National Museum Archives, S25-6; Dmitri Kessel/Getty Images, S25-9.

**Chapter 26:** NASA Image and Video Library, 804–805, 813; GRANGER/GRANGER–All rights reserved, 806; Bob Adelman Archive, 814; British Cartoon Archive, University of Kent ILW3584, 815; © Duke Downey/San Francisco, 827; Hulton Deutsch/Getty Images, 832.

**Chapter 27:** Allan Tannenbaum/Getty Images, 836–837, 843; AP Photo/File, 838; Bettmann/Getty Images, 840; AP Photo, 845; Fred Ward, 847; Bettmann/Getty Images, 865.

**Chapter 28:** AP Photo/Lionel Cironneau, 868–869, 897; Linda Chavez, 870; Authenticated News/Getty Images, 880; Diana Walker/Getty Images, 883; Bettmann/Getty Images, 885; Copyright © 1989 by the New York Times Co. Reprinted by permission, 895; Bettmann/Getty Images, 888; U.S. National Library of Medicine Digital Collections, SP28.

**Chapter 29:** AP Photo/March Neghswanter, 902–903, 915; Ralf-Finn Hestoft/Getty Images, 904; Fritz Hoffman / Redux, 906; AP Photo/Greg Baker, 909; Mark Peterson/Getty Images, 922; Joseph Sohm/Getty Images, 929; Aziz + Cucher Man with Computer, 1992 chromogenic color print mounted on aluminum 85-1/4 × 36-1/4 in. (image/sheet) 88 × 38 × 3 in. (framed/Plexiglass) Indianapolis Museum of Art at Newfields Koch Contemporary Art Purchase Fund 2012.126.1 © Aziz + Cucher, S29-3.

**Chapter 30:** U.S. Navy/Getty Images, 934–935, 943; Craig Mullaney, 936; AP Photo/Laurent Rebours, 940; REUTERS/Jeff Haynes, 944; Glowimages/Getty Images, 954; Economic Policy Institute: http://www.epi.org/publication/charting-wage-stagnation/ (see Figure 2 titled "Workers produced much more, but typical workers' pay lagged far behind"), 955; NurPhoto/Getty Images, 960.

# Index

AAA (*See* Agricultural Adjustment Act)
Abdel-Rahman, Sheikh Omar, 931–32
Abenaki Indians, 158–59
ABM (Anti-Ballistic Missile) treaty, 845
Abolition, 332–33, 339–40, 596, S11–0–1
  African Americans involved in, 236–37, 339–40, 390–91
  colonization solution, 239, 314, 339
  federal government response to, 324–25
  first movements, 211, 235–37
  gradual, state, 442, S8–8–9
  immediatism, 341
  political, 342–43
  Texas annexation and, 370, 378
  violence against, 341–42
Abortion
  clinic bombing, 919
  conservative attack on, 874, 875, 888, 925
  legalization of, 852
  NOW on, 831
  prohibition of, 518
  rates of (1980s), 889(map)
Abu Graib, 940
Acadians, 165
*Account of a Visit to Georgia* (Whitefield, G., 1738), S5–5–6(d)
*Account of a Westward Journey* (Rudd, L. A., 1852), S12–5–7(d)
*Account of Aaron Burr's Farewell Speech to the Senate* (Mitchill, S., 1805), S9–1–2(d)
*Account of Life on the Prairies* (Meidell, F., 1855), S13–1–4(d)
*Account of Reconstruction, An* (Farley, J.), S15–5–6(d)
*Account of the Arrival of the Dutch at Manhattan* (Heckewelder, J.), S2–3–5
*Account of the Murders of Joseph and Hyrum Smith* (Taylor, J., 1844), S11–5–7(d)
Acheson, Dean, S24–6
Achiganaga, 43

Acid rain, 878, 894, 914
Acid rock, 830
Acid test, 830
Ackerman, Gary L., S30–2–3(d)
Acoma Pueblo, 117(photo)
Acquired immune deficiency syndrome (AIDS), 889–90, 909, 925–26
*Acres of Diamonds* (Conwell, R. H., 1860s-1920s), S16–0–1(d)
"Act for the Gradual Abolition of Slavery, An" (1799), S8–8–9(d)
Act of Toleration, 69
Act Respecting Alien Enemies, An (July 6, 1798), S8–5–6(d)
Act to establish an uniform Rule of Naturalization, An (March 26, 1790), S8–5–6(d)
ACT UP (AIDS Coalition to Unleash Power), 889–90
Adams, Abigail, 190, 210, 241
  *Letter from Abigail Adams to John Adams* (1776), S7–3–4(d)
Adams, Brooks, 576, 578
Adams, Charles Francis, 433, 540
Adams, Henry, 558, 586
Adams, John, 175, 181, 190, 210, 241, 260, 261, S7–3–4, S9–0
  American Revolution and, 192
  Declaration of Independence and, 194, 250
  presidency of, 250–51, 254
  vice presidency of, 228, 250
Adams, John Quincy, 295–96, 316
  election of 1828 and, 315, 316
  National Republican philosophy and, 291
  Native Americans and, 291, 318, 319
  as secretary of state, 293, 294, 295
  Texas annexation and, 369, 370, 378
Adams, Samuel, 175, 178, 182, 191, 192
Adams, Samuel Hopkins, 598, 599
Addams, Jane, 601, 605, 623, 626, 633
  Hull House and, 596, 597, S19–0–2

  NAACP and, 602
  Roosevelt's (Theodore) nomination and, 613
  *Twenty-Years at Hull House with Autobiographical Notes* (1910) (excerpts), S19–0–2(d)
  World War I entry opposed by, 625
*Address at Johns Hopkins University, "Peace without Conquest"* (Johnson, L. B., 1965) (excerpts), S26–5–7(d)
*Address Before a Joint Session of Congress on Cessation of Hostilities in the Persian Gulf Conflict* (Bush, G. H. W., 1991) (excerpts), S29–6–7(d)
"Address Before A Joint Session of the Congress on the United States Response to the Terrorist Attacks of September 11" (Bush, G. W. 2001), S2–0–1(d)
*Address to the Nation on Energy and National Goals: "The Malaise Speech"* (Carter, J., 1979), S27–7–9(d)
*Address to the Nation on the Economy* (Reagan, R., 1981) (excerpts), S28–2–4(d)
Administration of Justice Act of 1774, 183, S6–6(d)
Advertising, 656, 670, 779, 801
Affirmative action, 849, 851, 859, 870, 887, 890, 891, 925
Afghanistan, 936, 939–40
  Soviet invasion of, 864, 881, 896, 900, 932
  terrorist presence in, 932
AFL (*See* American Federation of Labor)
AFL-CIO, 776
Africa
  in the age of discovery, 13(map)
  cell phone use in, 905
  cold war and, 746
  origination of humankind in, 5
  Portuguese explorations in, 12, 14, 17
  Reagan Doctrine in, 883–84
  slave trade in, 12, 72, 130

African Americans
  affirmative action and, 849, 851,
    890, 891
  Atlanta Compromise, 571, 601
  Black Power movement, 825–26,
    831, 853
  as Civil War soldiers, 444–46
  Clinton election and, 915
  colleges and universities for, 464
  continued struggle for justice
    (1970s), 849–51
  distribution of population
    (1775), 237(map)
  employment discrimination, 632,
    710–11, 760, 890–92
  Exodusters, 493
  Great Depression and, 684
  Great Migration, 632–33
  labor unions and, 654
  in late 19th century, 567–74
  lynchings of, 448, 570–71, 600,
    603–4, 632, 633, 667, 669,
    700, 720, 760
  in mid-20th century, 783
  in modern era, 668–70
  music of, 657, 786, 891
  New Deal programs and, 697,
    698, 699–700
  New Negro, 632–33, 664, 668–70
  populist, 554
  Port Royal experiment and,
    422–23
  in post-civil rights era, 921–23
  progressivism and, 600–602,
    603–5
  in Reagan era, 890–92
  Reconstruction and, 460–79,
    487–91, 543
    experiments with free labor,
      464–65
    Freedmen's Bureau, 460–61,
      465–67, 478
    land ownership dream, 464–65
    in public office, 472–73, 490
  scientific racism on, 570
  "separate but equal" doctrine,
    570, 798–99
  sharecropping and, 463, 464,
    474–75, 491–93, 632,
    S15-4-5
  Spanish-American War and, 579
  as strikebreakers, 516
  Vietnam War and, 824
  voting rights, 468, 472, 477,
    490, 538, 543, 546, 729,
    759–60, 821
    disfranchisement, 559, 571–74,
      601, 670
    Fifteenth Amendment,
      469(table), 484
    free blacks (during slavery),
      237–38, 300, 313

  grandfather clause, 571–72, 602
  registration drives, 811, 820
  Ten Percent Plan, 462–65
  World War I and, 632–34
  World War II and, 710–11,
    719–21, 727, 729, 759,
    S23-6-7
  See also Civil rights movement;
    Free black population
    (during slavery); Jim Crow
    system; Race riots; Slavery
Afro-American Council, 600
Age of exploration, 11–12
Aging population, 912
Agnew, Spiro, 859, 860
Agrarian Revolt, 551–52
Agricultural Adjustment Act
  (AAA), 692, 696, 701
Agricultural Marketing Act of
  1929, 685
Agriculture (See Farming/
  agriculture)
Agriculture Department, 544, 548,
  607, 692
Aguilar, Jerónimo de, 4
Aguinaldo, Emilio, 581, 582
Aid to Families with Dependent
  Children, 848, 916
AIDS (See Acquired immune
  deficiency syndrome)
AIDS Awareness Poster (1980s),
  S28-0(v)
AIDS Coalition to Unleash Power
  (ACT UP), 889–90
Air Quality Act of 1967, 818
Air traffic controllers' strike, 879
Aircraft
  Lindbergh's flight, 664
  World War II, 722
  Wright brothers' flight, 652
Aircraft carriers, 718–19
Ajax (CIA operation), 790
Akron, Ohio, 655
Akron Tire, 630
Al-Assad, Bashar Hafez, 948
Al Queda, 936–39, S2-0-1
Al Queda in Iraq, 940
Alabama
  Civil War and, 438, 449
  Reconstruction and, 472, 490
  secession of, 424
  settlement of, 231
  slavery in, 376
  statehood, 272
Alamo, Battle of, 369–70
Alaska
  environmental protection
    and, 863
  statehood, 786
Albany, 46, 48, 106, 141, 166
Albany Movement, 811
Albany Plan of Union, 163

Albright, Madeleine, 925
Alcatraz Island, Indian occupation
  of, 856
Alcohol
  Crusade against, 540–41
  Native Americans and, 146
  in New Netherland, 47
  taverns, 141, 232, 241
  taxes on, 246, 262
  See also Prohibition; Temperance
    movement
Alcott, Louisa May, *Transcendental
  Wild Oats* (1873) (excerpts),
  S11-2-4(d)
Alcott, William, 350
*Alexander Hamilton Recommends
  Arming Slaves and George
  Washington Rejects the Idea*
  (1779), S7-1-2(d)
Alexander VI, Pope, 17
Alfonso VI, king of Castile, 10
Alger, Horatio, 514, 518–19
Algeria, 262, 723
Algonquian Indians, 37, 46, 48,
  56(photo), 111–12, 159
  Beaver Wars and, 49
  French and Indian War and, 161,
    165, 170
  French colonizers and, 39,
    41–42, 44, 113
Ali, Muhammad, 824
Alianza Federal de Mercedes, 853
Alien and Sedition Acts, 253, 261,
  265, 324
Allegheny River, 163
Allen, Ethan, 192
Allende, Salvador, 846
Alliance for Progress, 815
Allis-Chalmers, 725
Almshouses, 143, 242
Alonso, 34
Altgeld, Peter, 522
Aluminum Company of
  America, 630
Alvarado, Pedro de, 27–28
Amalgamated Clothing
  Workers, 698
Amazon.com, 910, 954
America First Committee, 713–14
*America First Committee Address*
  (Lindbergh, C. 1941),
  S23-4-5(d)
American Academy of Motion
  Picture Arts and
  Sciences, 676
American Airlines, 794, 795
American Anti-Slavery Society,
  341–43, 357, 390
American Bible Society, 336, 337
American Board of Commissioners
  for Foreign Missions
  (ABCFM), 319, 336, 371

"American Century, The" (Luce), 729
American Civil Liberties Union, 730
American Colonization Society (ACS), 314, 339, 340
American Defense Society, 625
American Expeditionary Force (AEF), 635, 637
American Federation of Labor (AFL), 522, 562, 574–75, 595, 654, 699, 776
American GI Forum, 785
American Indian Movement (AIM), 856
American Medical Association (AMA), 528
*American Mercury,* 665
American Missionary Association, 464
American Party (Know-Nothings), 402, 403
American Professional Football Association, 657
American Protective Association (APA), 536
American Psychiatric Association, 856
American Railway Union (ARU), 562–63, 575
American Recovery and Reinvestment Act of 2009, 944
American Red Cross, 642–43
American Republic, 226–54, 258–87
  borders and boundaries of, 242–43
  conflicting visions of, 238–40
  controlling the borderlands, 243–46
  culture of, 240–42
  economy of, 228–30, 269–78, 280
  extension of territories (1783/1795), 249(map)
  invention and exploration in, 273–76
  politics of transition in, 259–66
  problem of trust in, 284–86
  struggle to form a government, 227–30
  in transition, 230–41
  ways of life in, 278–86
American Revolution, 191–221, 229, 247, 258, 445
  British offensive in, 197–199
  British surrender, 204, 204(photo)
  challenges following, 206–11
  competing strategies in, 196–97
  conflicts leading to, 159, 160, 169, 174–86

first battles of, 191–92
hardships during, 199–201
military ardor during, 193
Native Americans and, 205, 212
Second (Reagan's call for), 894
territory negotiations following, 204–6
American Society for the Promotion of Temperance (ASPT), 351
American System, 292, 296, 364, 377, 379
American Telephone and Telegraph Company (AT&T), 878, 911
American Woman Suffrage Association, 485
*American Women* (report), 830
Ames, Adelbert, 490
Amherst, Lord Jeffrey, 165, 170
Amish, 129
*Amsterdam News,* 710
Anaconda copper mine, 504
Anaconda plan, 432
Anarchists, 522, 641, 666
Anasazi Indians, 9
*Anatomy of a Kiss, The* (film), 659
*And Reform Moves On* (November 18, 1895), S17–1–2(d)
Anderson, John, 875
Anderson, Sherwood, 578, 665, 682
Andros, Edmund, 105, 106, 107
Angelino, Joseph T., 687
Anglican Church, 69, 76, 107, 108, 154, 281
Anglo-Powhatan Wars, 66, 67–68
Angola, 883
*Annexation* (O'Sullivan, J., 1845), S12–7–9(d)
Antebellum era, 390–416
  manifest destiny in culture of, 367–68
  political economy in, 391–97
  politics of slavery in, 397–400
  women's rights in, 354–58
Anti-Ballistic Missile (ABM) treaty, 845
Anti-Imperialist League, 581
Anti-Republicans, 230
Anti-Saloon League, 633–34, 670
Antibiotics, 781
Antietam, Battle of, 439, 440(map), 442, 634
Antifederalists, 219, 220–22, 228
Antimason Party, 301, 364
Antinomianism, 83
A&P grocers, 653
Apache Indians, 117, 119–20, 373, 375, 482
Apartheid, 883
Apollo (moon project), 810
*Apollo Magazine,* 240

Appalachian Mountains, 204, 272–73, 299(photo)
*Appeal to the Christian Women of the South* (Grimké), S11–1
*Appeal to the Colored Citizens of the World, An* (Walker), 340
*Appeal to the People of the United States, An* (American Anti-Slavery Society), 342
*Appeal to the Women of the Nominally Free States, An* (Grimké, A. 1838), S11–1–2(d)
Apple Computing, 871–73
Appleton, Nathan, 276
Appomattox Court House, 454
Apprentice Law, S15–2–3(d)
Arab Spring, 948
Arapaho Indians, 120, 373, 432, 480, 481
Arawak Indians (*See* Taino Indians)
*Arbella* (ship), 79
Arbenz Guzmán, Jacobo, 790
Archaic period, 5, 6
Ardennes Forest, 713, 720, 735
Area Redevelopment Act of 1961, 810
Argentina, 293, 815
Argonauts, 398
*Arizona* (battleship), 716
Arizona, territory acquired by U.S., 382, 383
Arkansas
  Civil War and, 436
  secession of, 426
  slavery in, 376
  statehood, 298
Arkansas River, 106, 371
Arkansas Territory, 295
Arlington National Cemetery, 445
Arminianism, 76, 83, 150
Armour, Philip, 398, 501, 510, 511
Arms reduction
  ABM treaty, 845
  "Atoms for Peace" plan, 791
  INF Treaty, 896
  Limited Test Ban Treaty, 816
  modern era movement, 673
  Reagan administration and, 881, 896
  SALT I, 845
  SALT II, 861, 864, 881
  START, 896
Armstrong, Louis, 657
Armstrong, Neil, 848
Army
  McCarthy hearings, 769
  post-revolution era, 207, 209, 213, 215
Army General Order 13, 633

Army of the Potomac, 438, 439, 443, 450
Arnaz, Desi, 774
Arnold, Benedict, 192, 193, 197
Aroostook Valley, 366
Arthur, Chester A., 543–44
Articles of Confederation, 195–96, 206, 213, 215, 216(table), 221, 238, 242
Asian American Political Alliance (AAPA), 854–55
Asian Americans, activism, 854–55
Asian immigrants, 666, 764, 854–55
Asiatic Squadron, 578
Aspirin, 592
Assemblies of God, 874
Association of Community Chests and Councils, 684
Associationalism, 672, 684
A&T Four, 806, 807
Atchison, David Rice, 405
Atlanta, Sherman's capture of, 452, 453(photo)
Atlanta Compromise, 571, 601, S18-2–4(d)
Atlanta University, 464
Atlantic Charter, 714
Atlantic Monthly, 613, S14-2
Atlantic Wall, 735
Atomic Age, 764
Atomic bomb, 739, 747, 752–53, 756
    American fear of, 764
    development of, 722
    Japan attacked with, 739, 744, 750, 764
    Rosenberg case, 768
    Soviet, 749, 750, 764
Atomic Energy Act of 1954, 787
Atomic Energy Commission (AEC), 752
"Atoms for Peace" plan, 791
AT&T (See American Telephone and Telegraph Company)
Attucks, Crispus, 181, 182
Augusta (cruiser), 714
Auschwitz concentration camp, 731
Austin, Stephen F., 369
Austria
    King George's War and, 160
    Napoleon's victory over, 264
    World War II and, 712, 713
Austria-Hungary, 620, 623, 635, 636
Autarkies, 746
Autobiography of Benjamin Franklin, The (Franklin, B., 1771-1790), S5-0–1(d)
Automobiles
    advertisements, S25-4–6(v)
    consumer safety concerns, 818

decline in industry, 839
Japanese, 841, 886
mass production of, 651–52
in mid-20th century, 775
in mid-m20th century, 778–79
in modern era, 651–52, 653, 655, 656, 662
pollution emission standards for, 818
suburbanization and, 655
World War I impact on industry, 631
youth culture and, 662
See also Chevrolet; Chrysler; Ford Motor Company; General Motors
"axis of evil," 939
Ayllón, Lucas Vázquez de, 23
Aziz, Anthony, S29-3(v)
Azores, 17
Aztec Midwife's Prayer, S1-0(d)
Aztec Priests Respond to the Spanish (1560s), S1-3–4(d)
Aztecs, 4–5, 6–8, 18, 24
    pictographic writings of, 8
    religious practices of, S1-0, S1-3–4
    Spanish conquest of, 19–21, 22–23

B-1 (strategic bomber), 880
B-2 (Stealth bomber), 880
B-17 (Flying Fortress), 715, 722
B-24 (Liberator), 722, 725
B-25 (bomber), 716
B-29 (Superfortress), 722, 725, 736, 739, 750
B-47 (Stratojet), 790(photo)
B-52 (bomber), 846
Babaataa, Afrika, 891
Babbitt (Lewis), 665
Baby boom generation, 782, 842, 874, 912, 916, 956–57
Bacall, Lauren, 767
Backcountry, 202–3, 243, 244, 272–73, 298
Bacon, Francis, 147
Bacon, Nathaniel, 100–101
Bacon's Rebellion, 100–101, 104–5
Baker, Ella, S26-0
Baker, Ray Stannard, 560, 598
Bakker, Jim, 893
Balanced Budget and Emergency Deficit Control Act of 1985, 896
Ball, Lucille, 774
Ballinger, Richard, 611
Baltic Sea, 11
Baltimore, 136, 141
    free black population of, 314
    War of 1812 and, 268–69

Baltimore, Lord (See Calvert, Charles)
Baltimore and Ohio Railroad, 499
Baltimore Sun, 414
Band Aid, 884
Bandits' Roost (Riis, J., 1887), S17-5(v)
Bank holidays, 689–90
Bank of the United States, First, 271 (See also National bank)
Bank of the United States, Second, 278, 291
    Jackson and, 315–18, 364, S10-3–5, S10-9
    panic of 1819 and, 286, 301, 317
    terms of charter, 292
Bank Veto Message (Jackson, A., 1932) (excerpts), S10-3–5(d)
Banking Act of 1935, 690
Banks
    in American Republic, 271, 286
    depression of 1837 and, 318, 365, 366
    Great Depression and, 681–82, 686
    in modern era, 653
    New Deal legislation, 689–90
    panic of 1819 and, 301, 317
    panic of 1873 and, 488
    panic of 1893 and, 499
    Wilson and, 615–16
Banks, Nathaniel, 464–65
Banks Plan, 464–65
Baptists, 112, 153, 236, 281, 283, 336, 463, 595, 874
Barbados, 73, 99
Barbed wire, 504, 620
Baring Brothers, 558
Barnett, Ross, 811
Barrios, 668, 784, 853
Barrow plantation, 476(map)
Barstow family, 788–89
Barton, Bruce, 656, S21-1–4(d)
Baruch, Bernard, 630, 633
Baseball, 657, 761
Bastille, storming of, 247
Bataan Peninsula, 716
Batten, Barton, Durstine, and Osborn, 656
"Battle Hymn of the Republic, The" (Howe, J. W., 1862), S14-2–3(d)
"Battle of Levittown, The" (Greene, G. 1957), S25-0–2(d)
Bavaria, 639
Bay of Pigs incident, 815
Bay of Santiago de Cuba, 578
Bear Stearns, 941
Beat movement, 797
Beatles, 828
Beatniks, 797

Beaver Wars, 49
*Bedford Cut Stone Co. v. Journeymen Stone Cutters' Assn.,* 654
*Bedroom Blunder, A* (film), 659
Beecher, Catharine, 357
Beecher, Henry Ward, 406
Beecher, Lyman, 351
Beekman and Cruger, 239
Belafonte, Harry, 885
Belgium, 620, 623, 635, 685, 713
Bell, John, 415, 416
Bellamy, Edward, 551
Belleau Wood, Battle of, 638
Benevolent Empire, 336–37, 347, 354
Benezet, Anthony, 236
Benin, 12
Benton, Thomas Hart, 365, 382, 402
Beringia land bridge, 5
Berkeley, Lord John, 93, 100–101
Berlin
    airlift, 750
    division of, 747
    Olympics of 1936, 702–3
Berlin Wall
    erection of, 815
    fall of, 896, 898–99, 900
Bernard, Francis, 178, 179
Bernstein, Carl, 859
Berry, Chuck, 786
Bess, Peter, S7–5
Bessemer, Henry, 510
Bessemer process, 510, S16–1–2
*Bessemer Steel Manufacture* (Waud, A. R., 1876), S16–1–2(v)
*Best Years of Our Lives, The* (film), 764
Bethune, Mary McLeod, 700
Beveridge, Albert, 575, 613
Bhopal pesticide plant accident, 894
Biddle, Nicholas, 317
Bierce, Ambrose, 581
Bierstadt, Albert, 610
Big business
    consolidation of, 510–12
    deregulation and, 863
    in modern era, 652–53
    rehabilitation of (1980s), 872–74
    rise of, 508–12
    scandals in (1980s), 893
    *See also* Corporations
Big stick diplomacy, 608–9
Big Three (allies' leaders), 747
Bill Haley and the Comets, 786
Bill of Rights, 213, 218–21, 228
Billion Dollar Congress, 545
Bin Laden, Osama, 932, 937–38, 940, 945

Biotechnology, 910
Bipartisan Campaign Reform Act of 2002, 958
Birkey, Henry, 234
Birmingham
    African American church bombing in, 820
    civil rights activism in, 811, 820
    manufacturing in, 655
Birney, James G., 343, 379
Birth control (*See* Contraception)
Birth control pill, 830
*Birth of a Nation* (film), 601, 667
Birth rates
    in colonial America, 131–32
    of Hispanic Americans, 892
    in mid-20th century, 781
    of Native Americans, 25
Bison, 375, 482
Bizerte, 723
Black, Hugo, 730
Black and Decker Company, 630
Black and Tan constitutions, 472
Black belt, 492
Black Codes, 263, 466, 484, S15–1–4 (*See also* Slave codes)
Black Eagles, 721(photo)
Black Hawk, 321
Black Hawk's War, 321
Black Kettle, 481
Black Lives Matter movement, 951
Black Panthers, 826–27, 830, 856–58
Black Power, 825–26, 831, 853
Black Star Line, 670
Black Tuesday (1929), 681, 896
Blackfoot Indians, 120, 373, 481
Blacklisting, 764
Blackwell, Elizabeth, 447
Blaine, James G., 544, 545
Blair, Ezell, 806, 834
Blair Education Bill, 545
Bland, Alden, 632
Bland-Allison Act of 1878, 543
Bleecker, Harmanus, S9–2–3
Bleeding Kansas, 405–7
"Blind Leaders" (Keller, H. 1913), S19–7–9(d)
Bliss, William Dwight Porter, 595
*Blitzkrieg,* 817
Bloor, Ella Reeve, 599
Blue-collar workers, 656, 781, 910, 911
Blue Eagle banner, 694–95
Blue Lives Matter, 951
Blythe, David, 451(photo)
Board for the Emigration, Preservation, and Improvement of the Aborigines of America, 319

Bob Jones University, 891–92
Boeing, 725
Boesky, Ivan, 872, 874, 893
Bogart, Humphrey, 767
Bohemian Charitable Association, 684
Boland Amendment, 883, 893
Boleyn, Anne, 75
Bolshevik Revolution, 629, 635, 636, 641, 745
Bombs
    neutron, 880
    proximity fuse, 722
    *See also* Atomic bomb; Hydrogen bomb
Bonaparte, Napoleon, 236, 251, 266, 267, 269
    Louisiana Purchase and, 262–64
    trade embargo and, 264–65
Bonds, 172, 229, 434
    junk, 872
    war, 629
Bonus Marchers, 686
Book of Mormon, 286
Booth, John Wilkes, 456
Borden, Gail, 436
Border Ruffians, 407
Border wall, 961
Bosnia-Herzegovina, 929–30, 932
Bosses, political, 536, 548–49, 602
Boston
    American Revolution and, 196, 197
    in colonial era:
        founding of, 78
        growth of, 141
        immigration to, 127
        poverty in, 143
        protest and resistance in, 160, 175–76, 180–82
    free black population of, 314
    port of, 137, 183
    Route 128, 871
    school busing in, 849–51
    slavery in, 143
*Boston Gazette,* 175
Boston Manufacturing Company, 276
Boston Marathon bombing, 949
Boston Massacre, 180–82, 183(table), 191
*Boston News-Letter,* 141–43
Boston Port Act, 183, S6–6(d)
Boston Tea Party, 182–83, 184(table), 191, 850
Botiller, Brigido, 386
*Botiller vs. Dominguez,* 386
Boudinot, Elias, 362–63, 373
Bougainville, 735
*Bowers v. Hardwick,* 889
Boxer movement, 583

Boy Scouts of America, 927
Boycotts
    grape, 853
    Knights of Labor, 574
    Montgomery bus, 799
    outlawing of, 574, 644
Boylston, Thomas, 207
Bozeman Trail, 481
*Braceros,* 727, 784
Braddock, Edward, 164,
    164(photo), 166, S6–0
Bradford, William, 77
Bradstreet, A., *Letter from Anne
    Bradstreet to Her Children*
    (undated), S3–3–5(d)
Bragg, Braxton, 439, 450
Brains Trust, 688, 691
Branch Davidians, 917
Brandeis, Louis, 600, 606, 613
Brandenburg Gate, 898
Brando, Marlon, 796
Brant, Joseph, 212
Brazil, 433
    Dutch claim to, 47
    Portuguese claim to, 17, 22, 29
Brazos River, 369
"Bread-and-butter unionism," 522
Breckinridge, John, 415, 416
Breckinridge, Sophonisba, 594
Breed's Hill, Battle of, 191,
    192(map), 196
Brest-Litovsk, Treaty of, 636
Bretton Woods Conference, 737,
    746, 849
Bridge building, 273
British-American Tobacco
    Company, 577
British East India Company, 173,
    182, 183
Broadsides, 241
Bromley, Dorothy Dunbar, 661
Bronco Busters and Range Riders
    Union, 595
Brooklyn Bridge, 549
Brooklyn Dodgers, 761
Brooklyn Heights, 197
Brooks, David, 252
Brooks, Preston S., 407
Brooks-Baxter war, 476
Brotherhood of Sleeping Car
    Porters, 654, 710, 760
Brown, Charles Brockden, 240
Brown, Helen Gurley, 830
Brown, John, 405, 409, 413–14, 428
Brown, Joseph E., 449
Brown, Linda, 798
Brown, Michael, 951
Brown, Oliver, 798
Brown, Sterling, 669
Brown, Tarleton, 202–3
Brown, William Hill, 240
Brown Berets, 854, 858

Brown Power, 853–54
Brown University, 154
*Brown v. Board of Education,
    Topeka, Kansas,* 798–99,
    807, 921
*Brownlow* (slave ship), 133
Bruce, H. C., 464–65
Brundage, Avery, 702
Bryan, Joseph, 719
Bryan, William Jennings, 566–67,
    609, 613, 621
    "Cross of Gold" speech, 565
    imperialism opposed by, 581
    Scopes trial and, 665–66
    World War I entry opposed by, 624
Bryant, Anita, 889
Bryant, William Cullen, 368
Buchanan, James, 325, 409–10, 416,
    423–24, 436
Buchanan, Patrick, 923
Buchanan's Station, 246
Buchenwald concentration
    camp, 731
Buckeye Rovers, 398
Buckley, William F., 808
Buckner, Simon, 437
Buddhists, 953
Buffalo
    destruction of, 482
    hunted by Native Americans, 10,
        26, 119
    hunted by whites, 375,
        376(photo)
Bulgaria, 900
Bulge, Battle of, 735
Bull Run, Battles of, 427, 429, 439
Bunau-Varilla, Philippe, 609
Bunker Hill, Battle of, 191
Bureau of Alcohol, Tobacco, and
    Firearms (ATF), 917
Bureau of Foreign Commerce, 561
Bureau of Indian Affairs (BIA),
    481, 694, 855, 856
Bureau of Refugees, Freedmen
    and Abandoned Lands (*See*
    Freedmen's Bureau)
Burger, Warren, 858, 887
Burgoyne, John, 199
Burke, Edmund, 91
Burns, Arthur T., 684
Burnside, Ambrose, 443
"Burnwell" (Barnwell), Sherman's
    march through, 452–53
Burr, Aaron, 250, 260, 264, S9–1–2
Burroughs, William, 797
Bush, George H. W., 875, 913–15,
    918, 920, 922–24, 927,
    929, 931
    *Address Before a Joint Session
    of Congress on Cessation of
    Hostilties in the Persian Gulf*
    (1991) (excerpts), S29–6–7(d)

AIDS crisis and, 925–26
Bosnia crisis and, 930
election of 1988 and, 913–14
election of 1992 and, 915, 925
and Guantánamo Bay detention
    center, 942
Persian Gulf War and, 928,
    S29–6–7
Bush, George W., S2–0–1
    "Address Before A Joint Session
    of the Congress on the
    United States Response
    to the Terrorist Attacks of
    September 11," S2–0–1(d)
    and election of 2000, 937
    and election of 2004, 937
    elections of, 920–21, 937
    and financial crisis, 941, 944
    and LGBTQ community, 952
    reelection of, 946
    and September 11 terrorist
        attacks, 938
    and tax cuts, 955
Bush Doctrine, 939
Business (*See* Big business)
Busing, school, 849–51, 858,
    859, 890
Butler, Andrew P., 407
Butler, Benjamin F., 441, 447
Byrd, William, II, 144

Cabeza de Vaca, A. N., *Describing
    North America* (1535),
    S1–4–5(d)
Cable News Network (CNN), 905
Cabot, John, 17, 36
*Caciques,* 16
Cahokia, 9
Cajuns, 165
Cakchiquel Indians, 25
Caldwell, James, 181
Calef, R., *More Wonders of the
    Invisible World* (1700)
    (excerpts), S4–5–7(d)
Calhoun, John C., 295, 301, 316
    National Republican philosophy
        and, 291
    nullification crisis and, 323
    slavery issue and, 378, 379,
        397, 398
    War of 1812 and, 267
California
    acquired by U.S., 382, 383
    gold strikes in, 373, 385, 398,
        481, 504
    Mexican deprived of rights in,
        385–86
    migration to, 785
    Proposition 13, 863
    Proposition 187, 907
    statehood, 398
    Transcontinental Treaty on, 293

Californios, 385
*Call to Action, A* (Weaver, J. 1892),
    S16-6-9(d)
Calley, William, Jr., 846
Calusas, 18
Calvert, Charles (Lord
    Baltimore), 108
Calvert, Sir George, 69
Calvin, John, 75
Calvinism, 76, 91, 92, 147, 150,
    281, 283
Cambodia
    bombing of, 846, 860
    Khmer Rouge in, 861
Camden, Battle of, 199
Cameron, James, 908
Camp David Accords, 864, 884
Camp Logan, 634
Campaign donations, 957–58
Campbell, Archibald, S12-2
Canada
    American Revolution and,
        193, 203
    border dispute with U.S., 366
    French and Indian War and, 169
    French surrender of, 168
    Jay's treaty and, 249
    King George's War and, 160
    King William's War and, 110–11
    NAFTA and, 907–8
    in NATO, 750
    New France, 37, 39–45
    rebellion against Great Britain,
        366–67
    role in French empire, 113
    sovereignty over fisheries and
        seal islands, 547
    War of 1812 and, 268, 269
    Webster-Ashburton Treaty
        and, 377
Canals, 275, 275(map), 391, 394,
    561, 576 (*See also* Erie
    Canal; Love Canal; Panama
    Canal; Suez Canal)
Canary Islands, 13
Cane Ridge revival, 281, 282–83
Cannons, 12
*Canton, Ohio Speech* (Debs, E. V.,
    1918), S20-1-3(d)
Cape Breton Island, 167
Cape Canaveral, 812–13
Cape of Good Hope, 12
Capital gains taxes, 863
Capitalism
    Bellamy's critique of, 551
    in colonial America, 133,
        137, 140
    communism *vs.,* 745
    George's critique of, 549–50
    Puritans and, 80
    Roosevelt (Franklin) and,
        695, 705

Sinclair's critique of, 598
slavery and, 310
welfare, 654
*See also* Industrial capitalism
Caravel, 12
Carey, Mathew, 345
Caribbean, 17, 22, 47, 99, 234,
    270, 271
    British seizure of French
        islands, 168
    French in, 115
    origin of name, 15
    Reagan Doctrine in, 882, 883
    Roosevelt Corollary in, 609
    U.S. presence in, 612(map)
    Wilson administration and,
        622–23
Caribbean Basin Initiative, 883
Caribs, 15
Carmichael, Hoagy, 662
Carmichael, Stokely, 826
Carnegie, Andrew, 508–12, 522,
    558, 562, 571
    imperialism opposed by, 581
    rise of, 508–10
    steel industry dominated by,
        509–10
*Caroline* (ship), 366–67
Carpetbaggers, 472, 487, 490
Carr, Patrick, 181
Carranza, Venustiano, 622
Carson, Rachel, 818
Carswell, G. Harrold, 859
Cartagena, 160
Cartels, 512, 694–95
Carter, Jimmy, 859, 861–66, 870,
    877, 878, 880, 881, 883
    *Address to the Nation on Energy
        and National Goals:* "The
        Malaise Speech" (1979),
        S27-7-9(d)
    background of, 862
    election of 1976 and, 861–62
    election of 1980 and, 874–75
    human rights and, 864, 879,
        881–82, 931
    presidency of, 862–66
Carteret, Lord George, 93
Cartier, Jacques, 37, 40, 58
Casablanca, 736
Casey, William, 894
Casor, John, 74
Cass, Lewis, 379, 397
Cassettari, Rosa, 498, 501, 504, 512,
    513, 522, 532–33
Castle William, 176, 179
Castro, Fidel, 815, 942
Catawba Indians, 783
Catherine of Aragon, 49, 75
Catholicism, 953
    in antebellum era immigrants,
        393, 400–402

anti-Catholicism, 348, 400–402,
    535, 544
Democratic Party and, 673
Dominion of New England and,
    106–7
in England, 49, 75, 91, 92, 108
German Americans and,
    129, 533
in immigrant culture, 531–35
in Maryland colony, 69, 107–9
in mid-20th century, 781
Native Americans and, 41,
    96, 116
nativism *vs.,* 348, 400–402
pastoral letter on nuclear
    weapons, S28-4-6
in the Philippines, 581
Puritan view of, 76
Quebec Act and, 183
Queen Anne's War and, 111
Republican school regulation
    and, 545–46
Roosevelt (Franklin)
    administration and, 699
slaves and, 116, 145
in Texas, 369
in Victorian era, 535
women's suffrage opposed in, 594
Catt, Carrie Chapman, 594, 633
Cattle, 137, 502
Cattlemen, 502–3
Cayuse Indians, 371, 373
CCC (*See* Civilian Conservation
    Corps)
Cellular and mobile
    telephones, 905
Centers for Disease Control, 762,
    889, S28-0(v)
Central America
    Reagan Doctrine in, 881–83
    Wilson administration and, 621
Central Intelligence Agency
    (CIA), 930
    Bay of Pigs incident, 815
    Chilean election and, 846
    cold war activities of, 767, 770,
        790, 791
    contra rebels and, 883
    creation of, 750
    hearings on secret operations
        of, 861
    Nixon's use of, 858
    and September 11 terrorist
        attacks, 938
Central Pacific Railroad, 434, 479
Central Park, 549
Central Treaty Organization
    (CENTO), 794
Chaco Canyon, 9, S1-0-2
*Chaco Culture National Historical
    Park, Pueblo Bonito,*
    S1–0–2(v)

*Challenge of Peace, The: God's Promise and Our Response* (National Conference of Catholic Bishops, 1983) (excerpts), S28-4-6(d)
Chambers, Whittaker, 768
Champlain, Samuel de, 40-42, 58
Chancellorsville, Battle of, 443, 450
Chaney, James, 820
Chaplin, Charlie, 650
Chapultepec, battle of, 381
Charles I, king of England, 69, 78, 91-92
Charles II, king of England, 92, 93, 94, 104
Charleston, 96, 150
    American Revolution and, 197, 199
    Civil War and, 433, 452
    colonial era growth, 141
    free black population of, 314
    French and Indian War and, 166
    port of, 137
    slavery in, 144, 145, 236
Charleston *Mercury,* 323
Charlottesville, 202
Charter colonies, 63, 69, 78, 82
Charter of 1691, 183
Charter of Libertyes and Priviledges, 93
Charters, corporate, 301
Chase, Salmon P., 344
Chase, Samuel, 261
Chattanooga, Battle of, 450
Chávez, César, 854
Chavez, Linda, 870, 886, 892
Cheney, Dick, 938
Chernobyl nuclear accident, 894
Cherokee Indians, 160, 243, 246, 290-91, 373, 432
    attempt to gain legal concessions, S12-0-2
    internal institutions of, 279
    removal policy and, 318-21, 362-63
*Cherokee Nation v. Georgia,* 319
Cherokee National Committee, 290
*Cherokee Phoenix, The,* 362
Cherokee Strip, 560
*Chesapeake* (frigate), 265
Chesapeake Bay, 46, 69, 203
Chesapeake colonies, 63-75, 145
    economy of, 134, 135, 137
    forces shaping, 70
    gender roles and social order in, 72-75
    New England compared with, 78, 85
    origins of slavery in, 70-71
Chesapeake Indians, 57
Cheves, Langdon, 286
Chevrolet, 653, 778

Cheyenne Indians, 120, 373, 432, 480, 481
Chicago
    19th Ward, 597, 602
    African Americans in, 632
    antebellum era growth, 394-95
    Burnham's city plan for, 604(photo)
    business concentration in, 655
    Days of Rage in, 857
    fire of, 506
    industrial era growth in, 506
    in late 19th century, 559-60
Chicago Commons, 498
Chicago Freedom Movement, 826
*Chicago Inter Ocean,* 537
*Chicago Record,* 560
Chicago River, 549
*Chicago Tribune,* 713
Chicano Student Movement of Aztlán (MEChA), 854
Chicanos, 853-54 (*See also* Mexican Americans)
Chickamauga, Battle of, 447, 450
Chickamauga Indians, 246
Chickasaw Indians, 98, 318, 320
Child, Lydia Maria, 350
Child labor, 514, 539, 548, 554, 594, 596, 603, 616, 662-63, 704
Child mortality rates, 132, 534
Children
    in American Republic, 284
    in colonial era, 71, 73, 81
    latchkey, 727
    in mid-m20th century, 781-82
    in slavery, 101-2, 309
    *See also* Youth
Chile, 5, 293
    communism in, 815
    Nixon administration and, 847-48
    Valparaiso riot, 545
China, 939
    Boxer movement in, 583
    Columbus's planned voyage to, 14, 15
    early explorations of, 11-12
    Eisenhower administration and, 791, 792
    globalization and, 906, 906(photo)
    Hollywood's influence in, 909
    imperialism and, 577
    Japanese attack on (WWII), 711, 712, 715
    Japanese war with, 577
    Korean War and, 754
    "loss" of, 752-54
    missionaries in, 577, 582
    Nixon administration and, 845-46
    and nuclear weapons, 948
    oil demand in, 577

Open Door Note, 582-83, 610
    Reagan administration and, 882
    revolution in, 749, 752-54
    Taft administration and, 610
    Taiping Rebellion in, 518
    trade with, 10-12, 234-35, 906, 931
    United Nations and, 736
    U.S. attempts to stablize, 673
    U.S. court in, 609
    Wal-Mart in, 906
    Wilson administration and, 621, 641
China Shock, 954
Chinchow-Aigun railway, 610
Chinese exclusion acts, 521, 535, 543
Chinese immigrants, 480(photo), 518-19, 535, 543, 854-55
Chinook Indians, 373
Chippewa Indians, 42-43, 163
Chisholm, Shirley, 838, 857, 866
Chisholm Trail, 502
Chivington, John, 432
Chocolate, 27
Choctaw Indians, 114, 318, 320
Cholera, 371, 506
Cholonec, Pierre, S2-2-3
*Christian Advocate and Herald,* 371
Christian Broadcast Network, 874
Christian Restoration movement, 283
Christianity, 953
    fundamentalist, 665-66
    Native Americans and, 16, 17, 279, 371
    slavery opposed by, 236, 281
    slaves converted to, 153, 310
    *See also* Evangelical Christianity; Missionaries; individual religions
Chrysler, 863, 944
Chuichi, Nagumo, 719
Chumash Indians, 373
Church, Frederick Edwin, 367
    *Niagara Falls* (1857), S12-4(v)
Church of England, 76, 82, 91
Church of Jesus Christ of Latter-day Saints (*See* Mormons)
Churchill, Winston
    "Iron Curtain" speech, 748, 748(cartoon)
    at Potsdam Conference, 737, 747
    World War II and, 714, 723, 729, 736
    at Yalta Conference, 747
Churubusco, battle of, 381
CIA (*See* Central Intelligence Agency)
Cibola, Seven Cities of, 24
*Científicos,* 622
Cigar Makers' International Union, 574

Cincinnati Redlegs, 770
CIO (*See* Congress of Industrial
    Organizations)
Cities and urbanization
    in American Republic, 231–33
    in colonial America, 141–44
    culture and (*See* Urban culture)
    government of, 548–49, 602–3
    industrial, 506–8
    interstate highway system and, 777
    middle class of, 346–47
    migration to, 348–49
    in modern era, 655
    percentage of population in
        (1890-1920), 592(figure)
    reform and, 344–49
    in the South, 307, 567–68
    turn-of-the-century, 567–68,
        602–3
*Citizens United,* S30–5
*Citizens United v. Federal Election
    Commission,* 958
Citizenship
    African Americans and, 239,
        295, 468
    state, rights affiliated with, 488–89
    women and, 210–11, 594
City Beautiful movement, 603
City busting, 736
Civil Rights Act of 1866, 468
Civil Rights Act of 1875, 488
Civil Rights Act of 1957, 799
Civil Rights Act of 1964, 821, 831
Civil Rights Cases of 1883, 489
Civil rights movement
    COFO, 820
    CORE, 729, 760, 820, 870
    in Eisenhower era, 798–800
    Freedom Riders, 811
    Freedom Summer, 820
    grassroots activism for, 807
    Johnson (Lyndon)
        administration and, 820–21
    Kennedy administration and,
        811–12
    Little Rock school desegregation,
        799–800
    post-oWorld War II, 759–61
    SCLC, 799, 811, 820, 821
    sit-ins, 806, 807
    SNCC, 807, 811, 820, 821, 824,
        826, S26–1
Civil service, 487, 539, 543, 544
Civil Service Commission, 539, 544
Civil War, 422–56, 536–37, 540–42
    antiwar sentiment, 447–49
    beginning of, 425–26
    blockade in, 432–33
    care of casualties, 447
    casualties in, 448(figure), 455
    civilian reactions to, 447–49
    commutation policy, 434, 448

Confederate discontent,
    434–35, 449
Confederate military advantages,
    429–31
end of, 454
final battles in, 450–55
hard war strategy, 436, 450–53
meaning of, 455–56
military scorecard, 429–32
mobilizing for, 428–36
planter's exemption in, 434–35
political economy of, 433–34
popular support for, 426–27
productive capacities of opponents,
    430(figure), 435–36
reasons for fighting in, 427–28
as a social revolution, 436–46
training soldiers for, 428–29
Union naval supremacy, 432–33
Union victories in the West,
    436–38, 437(map)
Civil Works Administration
    (CWA), 690, 699
Civilian Conservation Corps
    (CCC), 691, 692–93, 699
Cixi, dowager empress of China,
    582, 583
Clark, Tom, 765
Clark, William, 263–64
Clay, Henry, 286, 296, 316, 349,
    364, 378, 400
    abolition movement and, 314
    as a Mason, 301
    Missouri Compromise and, 295
    National Republican philosophy
        and, 291, 292
    Native Americans and, 319
    Omnibus Bill, 398–99
    presidential candidacies of, 295,
        296, 377, 378–81
    slavery issue and, 398
    War of 1812 and, 267
Clayton Antitrust Act of 1914, 616
Clean Air Act of 1963, 818
Clean Air Act of 1970, 861
Clean Air Act of 1990, 914
Clean Power Plan, 947
Clean Waters Restoration Act of
    1966, 818
Cleveland, Frances Folsom, 544
Cleveland, Grover, 540, 542,
    544–47, 560, 565
    imperialism opposed by, 574, 581
    Morgan bailout loan and, 558, 564
    Pullman workers' strike and,
        563–64
Cliff dwellings, 9
Climate change, 947
Clinton, Bill, 915–19, 945
    Bosnia crisis and, 930
    compromise with conservatism,
        916–17

"don't ask, don't tell" policy, 926
    elections of, 915, 917, 925
    human rights and, 931
    impeachment of, 920
Clinton, De Witt
    on common school
        movement, 352
    Erie Canal construction and,
        275–76, 368
    War of 1812 and, 268
Clinton, Hillary Rodham, 916, 960,
    S30–5
    criticism of, 960
    and Russian hacking, 962–63
Clothing, colonial era, 139
CNN, 905, 958
Coal mines/mining, 306, 395, 548,
    606–7, 725, 758, 848
Coatzacoalcos region, 4, 19
Coca-Cola, 725
Cocaine, 592
Cody, Buffalo Bill, 529
Coercive Acts (*See* Intolerable
    Acts)
Coffee, 116
COFO (*See* Council of Federated
    Organizations)
Cohan, George M., 728
Coinage Act of 1873, 542
Coit, Stanton, 596
COLAs (cost-of-living
    adjustments), 758
Colbert, Jean-Baptiste, 113
Cold Harbor, Battle of, 450
Cold war, 744–56, 845, 880
    Asian alliances, 793(map)
    Carter administration and,
        863–64
    civil rights movement and, 800
    coining of term, 749
    consumerism and, 774
    in Eisenhower era, 786,
        788–95, 814
    end of, 892, 896, 900,
        911–12, 928
    ethnicity decline and, 781
    gender roles and, 783
    globalization and, 905
    high school and college
        graduates in, S24–1–2
    ideological competition in,
        745–46
    impact on everyday life,
        763–70
    Middle East and, 746, 792–93,
        796(map)
    national security and, 748–56
    origins of, 745–47
    space program and, 802
    and tourism, 794–95
    *See also* Communism; Soviet
        Union

Cole, Thomas, 367–68, S12–3(v)
Coleman, Joseph, 733
*Colgate & Co. Advertisement*
    (1925), S21–4(v)
Collateralized debt obligations
    (CDOs), 941
College of New Jersey, 154
Colleges and universities
    for African Americans, 464
    in colonial America, 81, 150, 154
    flaming youth on campus,
        662–63
    GI Bill and, 756–57
    Johnson (Lyndon)
        administration and, 819
    progressivism and, 600
    protest at, 828–29
    speech codes in, 924
    tuition increases in, 912
    for women, 593
Collier, John, 694
*Collier's* (magazine), 796
Colombia, 22, 160, 608–9
Colonial America
    charter colonies, 63, 69, 78, 82
    children in, 71, 73, 81
    consumerism in, 133–34, 138–40
    east of the Mississippi (1720),
        114(map)
    empires in collision, 113–20
    expansion of settlement
        (1720-1760), 128(map)
    family life in, 134–35
    marriage in, 73, 81, 112,
        131–32, 144
    population explosion in, 127–32
    proprietary colonies, 69, 96, 108
    royal colonies, 67, 69, 85,
        107, 109
    transatlantic economy and,
        133–40
    varieties of experience in, 140–46
    *See also* American Revolution;
        Dutch colonies; English
        colonies; French colonies;
        New World; Spanish
        colonies
Colonizers, 536
Colorado
    gold strikes in, 504
    territory acquired by U.S., 383
Colorado River, 369, 798
Colored Farmers' Alliance, 554
Colored Orphan Asylum, 448
Columbia College, 154
Columbia River, 371
Columbia University, 685, 787, 797
Columbian Exchange, 26–27
Columbian Exposition, 560
Columbus, Christopher, 6, 10,
    14–17, 26, 29, 35, 36, 52,
    147, 240, 560

arrival in Spain, 11
first voyage of, 14–15
theories of, 14
Comanche Indians, 119–20, 159,
    321, 368, 373, 375, 481
Comey, James, 961
Commission on National
    Goals, 802
Commission plan, 603
Committee on Public Information
    (CPI), 630, S20–4–6
Committee to Re-Elect the
    President (CREEP),
    859, 860
Common school movement,
    351–52
*Common Sense* (Paine), 149, 193,
    194(photo), S7–0–1(d)
*Common Sense Book of Baby and
    Child Care* (Spock), 782
Commons, John R., 600
Communications technology, 905
Communism
    capitalism *vs.*, 745
    collapse of, 900
    crusades against, 764–65
    Johnson administration and,
        821–22
    labor unions and, 758, 769
    New Deal programs and, 695
    Nixon administration and,
        845–46
    Reagan administration and, 871,
        880, 881–83, 892
    Red Scares, 629, 641–45, 666,
        764–65, 766–67, 774
    in third world, 751–54, 792–95,
        814, 881–83
    *See also* Cold war; Soviet Union
Communist Party of the United
    States of America (CPUSA),
    695, 765, 768
Communitarians, 333–36
Community Action Programs
    (CAP), 818
Commutation, 434, 448
Company E, 4th United States
    Colored Infantry,
    446(photo)
Compass, 12
Compromise of 1850, 399, 400
Computers, 873–74
    emergence of, 775
    new economy and, 871–72,
        910–11
Comstock, Anthony, 528,
    529(photo)
Comstock Law, 528
Comstock Lode, 505
Concord, Battle of, 191,
    192(map), 196
Conestoga Manor, 170

Confederacy
    capital of, 427, 438, 450–54
    currency of, 434
    discontent in, 434–35, 449
    government of, 424
    military advantages of, 429–31
    motives of soldiers in, 427–28
    slave states refusing to join, 426
    *See also* Secession
Conformity, 780–81, S25–2–4
Confucius Plaza, 854
Congregational Clergy of
    Massachusetts, 348
Congregationalism, 150, 281, 283,
    341, 512
Congress
    in American Republic, 227
    Billion Dollar, 545
    post-revolution problems, 215
    Reconstruction and, 467
    in revolutionary era, 215
    World War I entry debate in, 626
Congress of Industrial
    Organizations (CIO), 699,
    757, 776
Congress of Racial Equality
    (CORE), 729, 760, 820, 870
*Congressional Government*
    (Wilson), 613
*Congressional Pugilists,* S8–4(v)
Congressional Reconstruction,
    470–77, 484
Conkling, Roscoe, 543
Connecticut, 48
    Constitutional ratification
        and, 217
    voting rights in, 300
Connecticut colony, 78, 85, 106
Connecticut Compromise, 217
Connecticut River, 46, 83, 93, 242
Connecticut River valley, 83, 137
Connor, Eugene ("Bull"), 811
Conscientious objectors, 626, 629
Conscription
    Civil War, 434–35, 447–49
    Selective Service Act, 753
    Vietnam War, 824
    World War I, 626, 635
    World War II, 713
Consent, principle of, 174–75, 186
Conservation movement, 607,
    610–11
Conservatism, 870–92
    abortion issue and, 874, 875,
        888, 925
    backlash against 1960s, 831,
        857–59, 886–89
    Clinton's compromise with,
        916–17
    creating a majority, 871–76
    culture wars and, 923–24
    family values issue, 923–24, 926

new, 808, 818
New Deal and, 701–5
in new economic era, 871–72
setbacks for agenda, 894
social values of, 886–93
*See also* Reagan Revolution
Conservative Manifesto, 702–4
*Conservative Mind, The* (Kirk), 808
Conspicuous consumption, 650
*Constellation* (carrier), 719
Constitution, 213, 215–22, 235,
    262, 263, 269, 272, 278, 295,
    312–13, 343, 390
key provisions of, 216(table)
ratification of, 215, 217–22, 238,
    241–43, 324, S7–5–7
strict constructionism, 230
writing, 215–17
Constitution, British, 174
Constitution, Confederate, 424–25
Constitution of the Lowell Factory
    Girls Association (1834),
    S9–3–4(d)
Constitutional Convention,
    215–17, 294, 324
Constitutional Unionist Party,
    415, 416
Constitutionalism, 174–75, 177,
    178, 194
Constructive engagement, 883
Consumer Product Safety
    Commission, 848
Consumer Protection Agency, 863
Consumer revolution, 133–34, 139,
    140, 178
Consumerism
    in colonial America, 133–34,
        138–40
    early 20th century, 598–99
    mid-20th century:
        challenges to, 796–802
        cold war and, 774
    mid-m20th century, 774–79
        the good life and, 775–79
    in modern era, 656, 664
Containment policy, 749–50, 754,
    791, 792
Continental Congress, First,
    185–86, 192
Continental Congress, Second,
    192–93
Continuous flow, 511
Contra rebels, 882–83, 893–94
Contraband camps, 445, 464
Contrabands, 441, 441(photo), 445
Contraception
    birth control pill, 830
    changing attitudes toward, 659
    legalization of access, 819
    restriction of access, 528
    Sanger's activism, 594, 659
Contract labor, 466, 474

Contract law, 277–78
Contract with America, 916
Convention of 1800, 251
Conwell, R. H., *Acres of Diamonds*
    (1860s-1920s), S16–0–1(d)
Coode, John, 108–9
Coode's Rebellion, 69, 108–9
Cooke, Jay, 434
Coolidge, Calvin, 672–76, 682
Cooling-off treaties, 621
Cooper, Anthony Ashley (Earl of
    Shaftesbury), 96, 107
Cooper, Gary, 766
Cooper, James Fenimore, 350, 368
Cooper, Thomas, 253
Cooper, William, 207, 231
Cooper Institute, 415
Cooperationism, 425
Coors brewery, 892
Copper, 37, 505
Copperheads, 448, S15–0–1
*Coquette* (film), 676
Coquille Indians, 783
Coral Sea, Battle of, 716–18
CORE (*See* Congress of Racial
    Equality)
Cornell University, 663
Cornish, Samuel E., 340
Cornwallis, Lord, 200–202, 204
Coronado, Francisco Vásquez de,
    24–25, 116
Corporation for Public
    Broadcasting, 819
Corporations
    chartered, 301
    consolidation of, 564, 910
    downsizing in, 904, 911–12
    economic decline and (1970s),
        839–40
    large-rscale organization, 652–53
    mid-20th century, 775, 801–2
    multinational, 839, 841, 906
    *See also* Big business
Corregidor, 716
"Corrupt bargain" (election of
    1824), 295–96
Corruption
    in early 20th century
        government, 592
    Galveston Plan on, 569
    in Harding administration, 672
    in industrial era government, 547
    in New Deal programs, 697
    in Reconstruction programs,
        486–87
    Roosevelt's (Theodore)
        crackdown on, 605
Cortés, Hernando, 4–5, 19–21, 22,
    27, 28
Cortés, Martin, 52
Corwin, Jonathan, 112
*Cosmopolitan*, 598

Cost-plus contracts, 630, 725
Cottagers, 136
Cotton, 92, 270, 273, 297, 311, 369,
    492, 551
    in antebellum era, 393–94
    Civil War and, 433
    global demand for, 311
    market collapse, 286, 365
    plantations, 303–6
    price decline, 323, 655, 691
    sharecropping and, 464, 474–75
    textile mills and, 271, 276, 311
    transport of, 274
Cotton, John, 82
Cotton gin, 271, 276, 302
Cotton States Exposition, 571,
    S18–2
Cotton Whigs, 398
Coughlin, Charles, 695–96
Council of Economic Advisors, 761
Council of Federated Organizations
    (COFO), 820
Counterculture, 827–28, 923
Country music, 786
Coushatta, 488
Couzens, James, 603
Covenant Chain, 106
Coverture, 210, 240
Covey, Edward, 309
Cowboys, 502–3
Cowpens, Battle of, 200
Cox, Archibald, 859–60
Cox, James M., 671
Coxe, Tench, 241
Coxey, Jacob, 560
Crack, 887
Crandall, Prudence, 342
Crawford, William H., 295, 296
Crazy Horse, 481
Credit, consumer, 272, 298,
    301, 656
Credit cards, 778
Credit Mobiler, 486
Creek Indians, 120, 160, 213, 243,
    246, 268
    Jackson's campaign against,
        258–59, 268
    removal policy and, 318, 320
Creek War, 258–59, 290
Creel, George, 628, 636
    *How We Advertised America*
        (1920) (excerpts),
        S20–4–6(d)
*Creole* (slave ship), 377
Crevecoeur, J. Hector St. John
    De, 238
"Crime Against Kansas"
    (Sumner), 407
Crimea, 948
Crittenden, John J., 425
Crittenden Compromise, 425
*Croatan* (carrier), 719

Croly, Herbert, 606, 612
Cromwell, Oliver, 92
Crop liens, 567
"Cross of Gold" speech, 565, 567
Crow, P., *Letters from Polly Crow to Her Husband during World War II* (1944), S24–7–9(d)
Crow Indians, 373, 480, 481
Crusade, The (against alcohol), 540–41
Crusades, 11
Cuba, 582, 882, 883, 942
   American gunrunners to, 547
   annexation issue, 578
   Bay of Pigs incident, 815
   independence achieved, 580
   missile crisis, 816
   Ostend Manifesto and, 406
   revolution in, 578
   under Spain, 25, 575
   Wilson administration and, 622
Cuban-American Treaty of 1903, 942
Cuban Americans, 892
Cucher, Sammy, S29–3(v)
Cullen, Countee, 669
Cultural feminism, 852
Culture
   of American Republic, 240–42
   of industrial America: immigration and, 531–35
   manifest destiny in, 367–68
   postmodern, 911
   *See also* Modern culture; Urban culture
Culture wars, 921–26
Cumberland River, 274
Cummins, Sarah, 371
Currency
   in American Republic, 229, 271, 286
   in Civil War, 434, 541–42
   in colonial era, 171
   Confederate, 434
   Continental, depreciation of (1770-1781), 208(figure)
   greenbacks, 434, 484, 541–42, 551, 565
   "In God We Trust" added to, 781
   in industrial era, 541–42, 543, 551
   Jackson's policy, 317–18
   in modern economy, 565–67
   panic of 1893 and, 558
   in post-revolution era, 207, 208, 215
   Van Buren's policy, 365
Currency Act of 1764, 171, 182, 183(table)
Cushing, John Perkins, 366
Custer, George Armstrong, 481–82
Cvetic, Matt, 769

CWA (*See* Civil Works Administration)
Czechoslovakia
   communism collapse in, 900
   World War II and, 713
Czolgosz, Leon, 605

D-Day, 734–35
DACA (*see* Deferred Action for Childhood Arrivals program (DACA))
*Daily Record,* 572, 573
Daley, Richard, 826, 827, 833
*Dallas* (television program), 874
Dalrymple, Louis, *School Begins* (1899), S18–6–7(d)
Daly, Marcus, 504
Dams, 277, 691, 694(map), 725, 798, 862
Danbury Hatters case, 574
Dardanelles, 749
Darrow, Clarence, 666
Dartmouth College, 154, 278
*Dartmouth v. Woodward,* 278
Darwin, Charles, 517
Daughters of Bilitis, 783
Davenport, James, 153
Davenport, John, 83
Davidson, Donald, 665
Davis, Benjamin O., 720
Davis, Henry Winter, 462
Davis, Jefferson, 424, 426, 436, 451, 461, 462
   criticism of, 449
   on Emancipation Proclamation, 442
Davis, Jo Ann, S30–2–3(d)
Davis, John W., 672
Dawes, William, 191
Dawes Severalty Act of 1887, 483, 544
Day care, 727
*Day The Earth Stood Still, The* (film), 802
Dayan, Moshe, 719
Days of Rage, 857
Dayton, Jonathan, 252
De Feria, P., *Letter from Fray Pedro de Feria to Phillip II, King of Spain about Paquiquineo* (1563), S2–0–1(d)
De La Warr, Lord, 66
De Salvo, Nicholas, 829
De Soto, Hernando, 23
*Deadly Mantis, The* (film), 802
Dean, James, 796
Dean, John, 859
*Debate in the House of Representatives on a Resolution "That Symbols and Traditions of Christmas Should be Protected"* (2005), S30–3–4(d)

Debs, Eugene V., 563, 575, 628–29
   *Canton, Ohio Speech* (1918), S20–1–3(d)
   imperialism opposed by, 581
   imprisonment of, 628–29, S20–1
   presidential candidacy of, 595, 613, 629
Debtors' prisons, 146, 286, 473
Decade of the Hispanic, 892
*Declaration of a Pueblo Indian Captured by the Spaniards* (1680), S4–4–5(d)
Declaration of Independence, 193–95, 200, 247, 250, 404
*Declaration of Interdependence toward the World--2005* (Ohmae, K., 1990), S29–0–2(d)
Declaration of Rights, 186
Declaration of Rights and Sentiments, 355, 358
Declaration of the Causes and Necessities of Taking Up Arms, 193
Declaration of the Rights of Man and of the Citizen, 247
Declaratory Act of 1766, 177, 183(table)
Deconstruction, 924
Deepwater Port Commission, 568–69
Defense Department, 905
Defense of Marriage Act of 1996, 926, 952, S29–4, S29–4–6(d)
Deferred Action for Childhood Arrivals program (DACA), 952
Deficit spending, 705, 724
Deflation, 543, 551
Deganawidah, 10
Deindustrialization, 842–44, 849, 871, 890
Del Monte Company, 533
Delaware
   in colonial era, 141
   Constitutional ratification and, 218
   emancipation resisted in, 455
   secession resisted by, 426
   slavery in, 211, 238, 455
Delaware Indians, 165, 408–9
Delaware River, 46, 69, 93
   Washington's crossing of, 197–98
Dell Computer, 871
Democracy
   abolitionism and, 324–25
   Adams (John Q.) presidency and, 296–97
   the Barstow family trip and, 788–89
   Boston Massacre and, 180–81
   Bush (George H. W.) and, 927

CCC environmentalism and, 692–93
Chinese exclusion movement and, 518–19
Civil War soldiers and, 428–29
common school movement and, 351–52
Constitution ratification and, 218–19
consumerism and, 598–99
The Crusade (against alcohol) and, 540–41
Debs' anti-war stance and, 628–29
Enlightenment ideas on, 148–50
expert dictatorship vs., 600
flappers, feminists and, 660–61
free blacks and, 74
French-Native American compromise and, 42–43
government shutdowns and, 918–19
the Hollywood Ten and, 766–67
Jacksonian (See Jacksonian Democracy)
Kansas settlement and, 408–9
libraries and, 148–49
limits of dissent and, 252–53
Maryland's demand for new government and, 108–9
participatory, 808
in post-revolution era, 209
Progressivism vs., 596, 600, 602
Puritans and, 80
Reagan at the Berlin Wall, 898–99
Reconstruction and, 488
rise of, 66–67
ROAR and, 850–51
Roosevelt (Theodore) on, 605
Seneca Falls Convention and, 355–56
strain on, 957–64
in Tlaxcalan people, 22–23
Wilmington race riot and, 572–73
women's associations impact on, 594
World War I fought for, 626
Democracy in America (Tocqueville, A., 1840) (excerpts), S11–4–5(d)
Democratic National Committee, 962
Democratic National Convention, 960, S30–2–3
Democratic Party
African Americans and, 700
civil rights movement and, 811
Civil War and, 424, 447, 451
election of 1840 and, 376–77
election of 1844 and, 379

election of 1848 and, 397
election of 1852 and, 400
election of 1856 and, 409
election of 1860 and, 415, 416
election of 1868 and, 483
election of 1872 and, 487
election of 1876 and, 490–91
election of 1880 and, 542, 543
election of 1888 and, 545
election of 1896 and, 567
election of 1912 and, 613
election of 1920 and, 672
election of 1924 and, 672, 673
election of 1928 and, 673
election of 1932 and, 687, 688
election of 1936 and, 699–700
election of 1948 and, 763
election of 1960 and, 809
election of 1964 and, 818
election of 1968 and, 833
election of 1972 and, 858–59
election of 1976 and, 861
election of 1980 and, 874–75
election of 1984 and, 879
election of 1988 and, 913–14
election of 1992 and, 915
election of 2000 and, 920–21
gold standard and, 565
Hispanic vote and, 892
immigrant vote and, 401
in industrial America, 538, 543, 544, 546
Jackson and, 316, 317, 363, 364
Kansas-Nebraska Act and, 402
labor unions and, 698, 699, 757–58
in modern era, 672, 673
New Deal and, 697, 698, 699–700, 704
New Democrats, 915, 916
nullification crisis and, 323
post-World War II troubles of, 761–62
racism in, 572–73, 669
Reagan Democrats, 915
Reconstruction and, 476, 478, 485, 486, 487, 490
sectional split in, 344, 412
slavery issue and, 324–25, 338, 341, 383, 390, 397, 402, 404, 410, 412, 413
on state of the American family, S28–6–9
Thirteenth Amendment and, 455
Van Buren and, 366
Democratic Republicans, 248, 259, 263, 278, 281, 379
Alien and Sedition Acts and, 252, 254
changes in, 291–92
dominance of, 260–62, 264, 266, 278

election of 1796 and, 250
French Revolution and, 252
Jay's Treaty and, 249
trade embargo and, 266
views of, 230
War of 1812 and, 268
Democrats, 958
Denmark, 713
Dennett, John, 460–61
Denver, 506
Dependents' Pension Law, 545
Deposit Act of 1836, 317
Depressions
of 1780s, 231, 233–34
of 1808, 265
of 1829, 345
of 1837, 318, 345, 364, 365, 376
See also Financial crisis of 1890s; Financial crisis of 2008; Great Depression; Panics
Deregulation, 863, 878
Descartes, 45
Describing North America (Cabeza de Vaca, A. N., 1535), S1–4–5(d)
Deslondes, Charles, 263
Détente, 845, 846, 861, 864, 879
Detroit
housing riots in, 727
as "Motor City," 655
race riots in, 729, 825
republic era growth in, 231
War of 1812 and, 268, 279
Detroit, Treaty of, 758
Dewey, George, 578, 580–82
Dewey, Thomas E., 737, 762
DeWitt, John L., 730
Dexter, James Oronoko, 235
Dexter, Sarah, 235
Dexter Avenue Baptist Church, 799
Diaz, José, 732
Díaz, Porfirio, 545, 622
Dickey, Gerald, S27–0–1
Dickinson, John, 195
Diem, Ngo Dinh, 792, 816
Dien Bien Phu, 792
Diggers, 830
Diners Club credit card, 778
Dingley Tariff Act, 567
Dinosaur National Monument, 798
Dinwidde, Robert, S6–0
Dior, Christian, 787
Diphtheria, 781
Disease
AIDS, 889–90, 909, 925–26
in Chesapeake colonies, 70
cholera, 371, 506
in Civil War soldiers, 447
diphtheria, 781
gangrene, 447, 515
gonorrhea, 634
hepatitis, 77

Disease (*continued*)
 influenza, 25, 447
 malaria, 321, 371, 447, 579
 measles, 371, 447
 mill-child's cough, 515
 mumps, 447
 Native Americans and, 19, 21,
  25–26, 77, 120, 165, 321, 371
 plague, 77
 polio, 688, 781
 rickets, 683
 smallpox, 21, 25, 147, 165
 during Spanish-American
  War, 579
 typhoid fever, 64, 371, 781
 typhus, 25
 yellow fever, 506
Disfranchisement, 559, 571–74,
 601, 670
Disney World, 844
Disneyland, 785, 788–89, 844, 926
Diversity, 950–53
 of colonial-iera cities, 143–44
 in Pennsylvania colony, 94–96
 survival of, 785–86
Divorce, 232, 240, 355, 528, 923
Dixon, John F., 637
Dmytryk, Edward, 766, 767
Doby, Larry, 761
Dockworkers' strike, 641, 698
Doctors Without Borders, 906
Dodd-Frank (*see* Wall Street
 Reform and Consumer
 Protection Act)
Doeg Indians, 100
Dole, Robert, 917, 918, 919
Dole, Sanford, 580
Dole, William P., 483
Dollar-a-year men, 630, 724
Dollar diplomacy, 609–11, 621
Dominguez, Dominga, 386
Dominican missionaries, 34
Dominican Republic, 609, 622,
 673, 821
Dominion of New England, 106–7
Domino, Fats, 786
Domino theory, 792, 821–22
Donner Party, 373
Donovan, Raymond, 893
"Don't ask, don't tell" policy, 926
Doolittle, James, 716, 770
"Doom Town," 752
Double V campaign, 729
Doughboys, 634
Dougherty, Esther, 234
Dougherty, John, 234
Douglas, Aaron, 669
Douglas, Stephen A., 395, 403, 404,
 408, 426, S13–6
 Kansas-Nebraska Act and, 402
 Lecompton Constitution
  and, 412

 Lincoln debates with, 412
 Omnibus Bill and, 398–99
 presidential candidacy of, 415
Douglass, Frederick, 303, 306, 309,
 340, 358, 394, 413, 432
 British Isles tour of, 338
 on fugitive slave law, 399–400
 on Harper's Ferry raid, 414
 life and times of, 390–91
 on Lincoln, 417
 on women's suffrage, 355, 485
Dow Jones industrial average,
 912, 941
Downsizing, 904, 911–12
Draft (*See* Conscription)
Draft riots, 448
Drake, Sir Francis, 50, 54, 58
Dreadnought-class warships, 718
Dreamers, 952
Dred Scott decision, 409–12, 467,
 S13–6
Drone warfare, 945
Drug use, 829, 887
Duane, William (newspaper
 editor), 253
Duane, William J. (secretary of
 treasury), 317
Dubinsky, David, 698
DuBois, William Edward
 Burghardt, 600–602,
 632, 669
Dukakis, Michael, 913
Duke, James B., 577
Dulhut, Daniel, 43
Dulles, John Foster, 789, 792
Dumbarton Oaks meeting, 736
Dunmore, Lord, 171, 193
*Duplex Printing Press Co. v.
 Deering*, 654
Dust Bowl, 680, 683, 684(map),
 685(photo), 691
Dutch colonies, 45–49, 83 (*See also*
 New Netherland)
Dutch East India Company, 45
Dutch East Indies, 715
Dutch Reformed Church, 47
Dutch West India Company, 45–47
Dyer, Mary, 104
Dylan, Bob, 829
Dynamic obsolescence, 778
*Dynasty* (television program), 874

Eads Bridge, 510(photo)
Eagleton, Thomas, 859
Early, Jubal, 452
Earth Day, 848
East Louisiana Railway, 570
Eastern Europe
 cold war and, 746, 747, 749
 communism collapse in, 900
Eastern State Mental Hospital, 150
Eastern Woodlands Indians, 9, 243

Eastman Kodak Company, 904
Easton, Treaty of, 167
Eaton, Theophilus, 83
EBay, 910
Echo Park Dam, 798
Eckert, J. Presper, Jr., 775
Economic Opportunity Act of
 1964, 817
Economic recession, 937
Economic Recovery Act of
 1981, 878
Economies of scale, 511
Economy, 953–57
 in 1970s, 839–44
 of American Republic, 228–30,
  269–78, 280
 Carter administration and, 863
 Enlightenment ideas on, 148–50
 global (by 1600), 30(map)
 of industrial America, 540–46
 information, 904, 910–12,
  S29–2–3
 mid-20th century, 775–76
 modern, 565–67
 in modern era, 651–55
 new, 871–72, 910–12
 Nixon administration and, 849
 personal income per capita
  (1840-1880), 379(table)
 post-revolution, 207–9
 post-World War II, 756–57
 Reagan administration and,
  877–79, 894–96, S28–2–4
 of slavery, 393–96
 transatlantic (colonial era),
  133–40
 of Virginia colony, 64–65
 of the West, 502–6
 world (Reagan era), 886
 World War I and, 630–31
 World War II and, 725
 *See also* Political economy
Edict of Nantes, 40
Edison, Thomas Alva, 507, 658
Education
 in American Republic, 242
 bilingual instruction in, 853, 854
 cold war concerns, 802
 in colonial America, 81
 common school movement,
  351–52
 experts' takeover of, 600
 for freed slaves, 422–23, 464, 473
 of immigrant children, 533–35
 under industrial capitalism, 514
 Johnson (Lyndon)
  administration and, 819
 parochial schools, 533, 535, 545
 prayer prohibited in public
  schools, 819
 public, 81, 351–52, 514, 533,
  548, 887

segregated, 798–800, 807, 821, 825–26, 921
vouchers proposed, 887
for women, 210–11, 242, 593
*See also* Colleges and universities
Education Department, 887
Edwards, Jonathan, 150, 154
Egypt
  Camp David Accords and, 864, 884
  cotton from, 433, 551
  Israeli conflicts with, 840, 847–48
  and September 11 terrorist attacks, 937
  Suez Canal crisis, 792–94
Ehrlichman, John, 860
Eight-Hour Leagues, 520
Eighteenth Amendment, 634
Eighth Amendment, 228
Einstein, Albert, 722
Eisenhower, Dwight D.
  background of, 787
  on Buchenwald, 731
  interstate highway system of, 776–77
  as NATO commander, 750, 787
  presidency of, 776, 786–95, 807, 809, 810
    civil rights and, 799–800
    cold war and, 786, 788–95, 814
    farewell address, 802
    Vietnam War and, 792, 816, 821
  and space program, 812
  World War II and, 723, 735
Eisenhower, Mamie, 787, 789
Eisenhower Doctrine, 794
E.J. Korvettes, 778
El Salvador, 881–83
Electoral College (early procedures), 250 (*See also* Presidential elections)
Electricity
  Franklin's experiments with, 147
  industry aided by, 651
  introduction of, 507
  TVA and, 691
Elementary and Secondary School Act of 1965, 818
Elizabeth I, queen of England, 49–51, 56, 63, 72, 75, 91
Elkins Act of 1910, 606
Elkinson, Harry, 313
Ely, Ezra Stiles, 336
Ely, Richard T., 517, 519, 600
Emancipation, 436–37, 440–43, 449, 461
  completion of, 454–55
  military, 441, 454–55
  northern opposition to, 237, 447
  in practice, 444–46
Emancipation Proclamation, 442–43, 445, 710, 812

Embargo Acts, 266
Emergency Banking Act, 689
Emergency Economic Stabiliztion Act of 2008, 941
Emergency Relief Appropriations Bill, 697
Emerson, John, 410
Emerson, Ralph Waldo, 350–51, S11-2–4
Employment, 953–54, 956
Employment Act of 1946, 762
Employment discrimination
  African Americans and, 632, 710–11, 760, 890–92
  women and, 758–59, 783, 831, 852, 887
*Empresarios,* 369
*Encomienda* system, 16, 22, 24, 25, 29, 117, 118
Endangered Species Act of 1973, 862
Energy crises, 840–41, 846, 863, 864
Energy Department, 863
Enfield rifle, 435
England, 939
  African population of, 70
  American Civil War and, 433, 442
  civil war in, 92
  Columbus turned down by, 14
  Dutch conflicts with, 93
  French conflicts with, 105–6, 110–11, 113–14, 159, 248, 249, 264, 270
  Glorious Revolution in, 69, 92, 104, 106–9, 174
  Ireland conquered by, 50
  King George's War, 160
  King William's War, 110–11, 172
  land claims in American Republic, 242, 243
  as Native American allies, 212, 243
  Native Americans in, 52–53
  political hierarchy in, 145
  Puritan movement in, 75, 77, 106
  Queen Anne's War, 99, 110–11, 159, 172
  Samoa claimed by, 545
  slave trade and, 50, 72–73, 93, 101
  slave trade banned in, 236, 344
  slavery abolished in, 236
  Spanish conflicts with, 37–38, 50, 52, 63, 116, 159–60, 248, 264
  tension between American Republic and, 248–50
  textile mills of, 271, 311
  trade with America:
    in colonial era, 176(figure)

  embargo, 264–66
  growth in, 271
  post-revolution policy, 206, 208, 209, 215, 232, 238, 250
  turmoil in 1600s, 91–92
  War of Jenkins's Ear, 159–60
  women's rights discussed in, 240
  *See also* American Revolution; English colonies; English empire; Great Britain; War of 1812
English colonies, 51–57, 62–87, 91–120, 158–85
  impact of global war in, 160–61
  instability in, 91
  new colonies and patterns, 92–99
  New World exploration, 17, 36
  resistance to Crown in, 160, 165–66, 169, 174–86
  unrest and repression in, 106–8
English empire
  attempts at, 49–57
  in crisis, 174–79
  dissent in, 106–8
  enforcing, 169–74
  Native American policy, 105–6
  plan of, 91–92
  victory of, 159–69
ENICAC (Electronic Numerical Integrator and Computer), 775
Enlightenment, 141, 147–54, 194, 201, 210–11
*Enterprise* (carrier), 718, 719
Environmental policy
  Bush (George H. W.) administration and, 914
  Carter administration and, 863
  Civilian Conservation Corps and, 692–93
  conservation movement, 607, 610–11
  Johnson (Lyndon) administration and, 819
  NAFTA and, 910
  Nixon administration and, 848
  Reagan administration and, 878, 894
  rebirth of, 797–98
Environmental Protection Agency (EPA), 848, 878, 893
Episcopalianism, 281, 512, 874
Equal Employment Opportunity Commission (EEOC), 821, 831
Equal Pay Act of 1963, 831
Equal rights amendment (proposed)
  1940s, 759
  1970s, 852, 888
Equal Rights Party, 354

Equiano, O., *The Interesting Narrative and Other Writings* (1789) (excerpts), S4–2–4(d)
Erasmus, 45
Erie Canal, 275–76, 301, 368, 498
Ervin, Sam, 860
Espionage Act of 1917, 628, S20–1
Espy, James Pollard, 350(photo)
*Essay on Slavery and Abolitionism* (Beecher), 357
Establishment democrats, 959
Estate taxes, 878
Esteban the Moor, 24
Estonia, 900
Ethiopia, 712, 884–85
Ethnic cleansing, 929–30
Ethnic Heritage Studies Act of 1972, 858
Ethnicity
    in industrial America, 532–33
    in mid-20th century, 781
    white, 858, 859, S27–6–7
    *See also* Diversity
Eugenics, 600, 601
Euro, 906
Europe
    cold war in, 751(map)
    in pre-Columbian era, 10–14
    World War II in, 724(map), 735
Europe First strategy, 723
European Economic Community, 906
European Union (EU), 906
Evangelical Christianity, 194, 281–84, 888, 889
    growth of, 874
    temperance movement and, 351
Evangelical Protestants, 953
Evans, Hiram Wesley, *The Klan: Defender of Americanism* (1925) (excerpts), S21–0–1(d)
Evarts, Jeremiah, 319
Evers, Medgar, 760
*Everybody's* (magazine), 598, 615
"Evil empire," 881
Evinrude Company, 630
Evolutionary theory, 665–66
*Ex parte Milligan*, 435
Excise taxes, 246
Executive branch, establishment of, 216
Executive Order 8802, 710
Executive Order 9066, 854
Executive Order 9981, 760
Executive power, 947
Exodusters, 493
Expansionism
    commercial, foreign policy and, 545–47
    Native American resistance to, 279

political economy of, 376–84
of settlement (1720-1760), 128(map)
of slavery, 376, 383, 390–91, 396–97, 406
*See also* Land; Manifest Destiny; West
Experts, dictatorship of, 600
Explorer 1 (satellite), 802
Export-Import Bank, 712
Exports
    in 1970s, 841
    in American Republic, 232, 249–50, 270
    in colonial era, 135, 136(map), 137, 176
    Great Depression and, 682
    in industrial era, 545
    in late 19th century, 561
    in post-revolution era, 208, 215
    Reagan administration and, 886, 896
Extract of Remarks at a "Make America Great Again" Rally (Trump, D. 2017), S30–7–9(d)
Exxon Mobil, 564

Facebook, 910, 963
Fair Deal, 763, 787, 808
Fair Employment Board, 760
Fair Employment Practices Committee, 710
Fair Labor Standards Act of 1938, 704
Fairbanks, Douglas, Sr., 650, 664
Fall, Albert B., 672
Fallen Timbers, 246, 249
*Falls of the Kaaterskill* (Cole), 367
Falwell, Jerry, 874, 888, 893
    *Listen, America!* (1980) (excerpts), S28–1–2(d)
Family and Medical Leave Act of 1993, 916
Family Assistance Plan, 848
Family life
    changing American household (1960-2000), 923(table)
    colonial economy of, 134–35
    immigrant culture and, 534–35
    in late 20th century, 923–24
    in mid-m20th century, 781–82
    in modern era, 662–63
    Puritan, 81
    Republican and Democratic party platforms, S28–6–9
    sharecropping and, 474–75
    in slavery, 309
Family values, 917, 923–24, 926
Famine, Ethiopian, 884–85
Farewell Address (Eisenhower, D. W.), 802

Farewell Address (Washington, G.), 250, S8–2–3(d)
Farley, J., *An Account of Reconstruction,* S15–5–6(d)
Farm Security Administration (FSA), 680
*Farm Security Administration Photographs* (Lange, D., 1930s), S22–3(v)
Farmers' Alliance, 526, 551–52
Farming/agriculture, 957
    in Africa, 12
    Agrarian Revolt, 551–52
    in American Republic, 231, 232, 271
    in colonial America, 134, 137
    the Columbian exchange, 26
    decline in (modern era), 654–55
    emergence of, 6
    Great Depression and, 683–84, 686
    in Great Plains region, 503
    in industrial America, 551–52
    in mid-20th century, 781
    Native Americans and, 8
    New Deal measures, 690–94
    Warehouse Act, 616
Farnham, Marynia, 783
Farragut, David, 426, 432, 437, 452
Farrakhan, Louis, 922
Faubus, Orval, 799
Fauset, Jessie, 669
FBI (*See* Federal Bureau of Investigation)
Federal-Aid Highway Act of 1956, 776–77
Federal Alliance of Land Grants, 853
Federal budget
    in 1970s, 840
    in American Republic, 229, 262
    Bush (George H. W.) administration and, 914
    Clinton administration and, 916, 918–19
    Eisenhower administration and, 787
    in modern era, 672
    Nixon administration and, 848
    post-World War II, 756–57
    Reagan administration and, 877, 879, 896
    Roosevelt (Franklin) administration and, 705
Federal Bureau of Investigation (FBI), 730
    Black Panthers infiltrated by, 857, 858
    Branch Davidian siege and, 917
    cold war activities of, 767, 768
    and September 11 terrorist attacks, 938
Federal Communications Commission (FCC), 779

Federal Deposit Insurance
Corporation, 690–91
Federal Election Commission,
957–58
Federal Emergency Relief
Administration (FERA),
690–91
Federal Farm Board, 685
Federal government
abolitionism and, 324–25
Clinton's attempt to limit, 916–17
creation of, 195–96, 213–22,
227–28
Democratic Republicans
and, 291
domestic dissent and (1990s),
917–20
expanding (1955-1970),
819(table)
Great Depression and, 685
in industrial America, 542–46
Jackson's attempt to limit,
297, 366
Jefferson's attempt to limit, 262
Johnson (Lyndon) era growth
of, 819
new conservativism on, 808
new liberalism on, 807–8
Nixon's attempt to limit, 848
Reagan's attempt to limit, 877
Roosevelt (Theodore) era growth
of, 606
shutdowns of, 914, 916, 918–19
Truman era growth of, 761–62
Federal Highway Act of 1921, 672
Federal Meat Inspection Act of
1906, 599
Federal Procession of 1789, 242
Federal Reserve Act of 1913, 616
Federal Reserve Board, 824,
840, 879
Great Depression and, 682
New Deal legislation and,
690–91
Federal Trade Commission (FTC),
616, 672, 861
*Federalist* No. 10,*The,* 222
*Federalist Papers,* 222
Federalists, 230, 259, 291–92
Alien and Sedition Acts and,
252, 254
Bill of Rights and, 228
Constitutional ratification and,
217–22
election of 1796 and, 250
election of 1816 and, 293
French Revolution and, 247, 252
Jefferson presidency and, 260,
262, 263
religious revivalism distrusted
by, 281
states' rights and, 323

trade embargo and, 265
War of 1812 and, 268–69
Feingold, Russ, 958
Felton, Rebecca, 572
Female Moral Reform Society,
336, 354
*Feminine Mystique, The*
(Friedan), 830
Feminism
conservative condemnation
of, 887
cultural, 852
lesbian, 852
in mid-20th century, 783
in modern era, 659–61, 660–61
radical, 852, 857, 858
*See also* Women's rights
Feminization of poverty, 888
Fenno, John, 230
Ferdinand, Archduke, 620
Ferdinand (Fernando), king of
Spain, 11, 15, 35, 49
*Granada Capitulations* (1492),
S1–2(d)
Ferguson, John H., 570
Ferraro, Geraldine, 879
Fertile Crescent, 6, 8, 12
Field, Cyrus, 499
Fifteenth Amendment,
469(table), 484
Fifth Amendment, 228
Filipino immigrants, 854
Fillmore, Millard, 399, 400, 403
Film noir, 764
Financial crisis of 1890s, 499–500,
559–64
Financial crisis of 2008, 940–41,
944–45, 955
and Dow Jones industrial
average, 941
and housing, 941
and loans, 941
and WTO, 941
Finland, 636
Finney, Charles Grandison, 336
Fire department, 507, 549
Fireside chats, 689–90
First Amendment, 228, 764, 939
*First Annual Report to the Congress
on United States Foreign
Policy for the 1970's* (Nixon,
R., 1970), S27–2–4(d)
First Confiscation Act, 441
*First Inaugural Address* (Jefferson,
T., 1801), S9–0–1(d)
*First Inaugural Address* (Roosevelt,
F. D., 1933), S22–0–2(d)
First world, 791
Fish-ins, 855
Fisk, Jim, 486
Fisk University, 464, 601
Fitzgerald, F. Scott, 658, 665

Fitzhugh, George, 412
Five "Civilized" Tribes, 318, 321
Five Nations (of Iroquois), 39, 48
Five Points neighborhood, 345
Flaming youth, 662–63, 665
*Flaming Youth* (Adams), 663
Flappers, 660–61
Flexible response, 815, 821
Flopnik (nickname for first U.S.
satellite), 802
Florida
British claim to, 168
Bush-Gore election and, 921
Civil War and, 426
Jefferson's attempts to obtain,
262–64, 266
migration to, 785, 844
Pinckney's Treaty and, 249
Reconstruction and, 472
secession of, 424
slave revolt in, 145
Spain's ceding of, 259, 293
Spanish in, 18–19, 23, 38, 116,
205, 213
Foch, Ferdinand, 636, 638
Fontana, Marco, 533
Food stamp program, 818
Foot, Samuel A., 325
Football, 657
Foote, Andrew, 432, 437
Force Bill, 327
Ford, Gerald, 860–62
Ford, Henry, 651, 656, 776
Ford Motor Company, 603,
652(photo), 653, 656,
839, 926
World War I and, 631
World War II and, 725
Fordism, 651–52, 656
Fordney-McCumber Tariff of
1922, 672
Foreign policy
Carter's, 863–64
commercial expansion and,
545–47
Ford's, 861
in the global age, 927–32
Monroe's, 293–94
Nixon's, 845–46, S27–2–4
Reagan's, 879–85
Republican (modern era),
673–76
Roosevelt's (Theodore), 608–9
slavery as, 406
Taft's, 609–11
Forests
clearing of, 80
preservation of, 607
*Forging the Shaft: A Welding Heat*
(Weir), 550(photo)
Fort Beauséjour, 164
Fort Biloxi, 106, 114, 115(photo)

Fort Bull, 165
Fort Cahokia, 106
Fort Carillon, 165, 167
Fort Caroline, 38, 39
Fort Detroit, 170
Fort Donelson, 437
Fort Duquesne, 164, 166, 167
Fort Edward, 165
Fort Frontenac, 167
Fort Henry, 437
Fort Kaskaskia, 106
Fort Laramie, 480
Fort Laramie Treaty, 481
Fort Louisbourg, 160, 167
Fort McHenry, 268, 435
Fort Mims, 258
Fort Niagara, 114, 164, 170
Fort Orange, 46, 48
Fort Oswego, 165
Fort Phil Kearny, 481
Fort Pickens, 425
Fort Pitt, 167, 170
Fort Pulaski, 423
Fort St. Frédéric, 114, 164
Fort Sumter, 424, 425
Fort Ticonderoga, 165, 167, 192, 197
Fort Toulouse, 114, 146
Fort Wagner, 446
Fort Walla Walla, 371
Fort William Henry, 165, 166
Fortress Monroe, 438, 441
Fortune, 683, 712
Forty-Niners' gold rush, 504,
    505(photo)
Forty-ninth parallel, 293, 379, 382
Forty-second parallel, 368–69
Fossil fuels, 954
Four Freedoms, 729, 788, S23–0–4
Four Freedoms Speech (Roosevelt, F.
    D., 1941), S23–0–4(d)
Fourteen Points, 635–36, 639, 640,
    S20–6–9
Fourteen Points Speech (Wilson, W.,
    1918), S20–6–9(d)
Fourteenth Amendment, 470,
    484, 485, 488–89, 570, 798,
    799, 851
  origins of, 467–68
  provisions of, 469(table)
Fourth Amendment, 228
Fox, William, 908
Fox News, 958
Fox people, 321
France
  American Revolution and, 199,
    203–6, 247
  arms-reduction accord
    (1920s), 673
  Columbus turned down by, 14
  English conflicts with, 105–6,
    110–11, 113–14, 159, 248,
    249, 264, 270

  imperialism and, 575
  Jay's Treaty and, 250
  King George's War, 160, 161
  King William's War, 110–11
  Non-Intercourse Act and,
    266–67
  Open Door Note and, 583
  Panama Canal and, 608–9
  Quasi-War, 251
  Queen Anne's War, 99,
    110–11, 159
  slavery abolished in, 236
  Spanish colonialism supported
    by, 293
  Spanish conflicts with,
    37–38, 159
  Suez Canal crisis, 792–94
  tension between American
    Republic and, 251
  trade embargo and, 264–66
  United Nations and, 736
  in Vietnam (French Indochina),
    715, 756, 792
  women's rights discussed in, 240
  World War I and, 620, 623–26,
    635–37, 639–40
  World War II and, 711, 713, 719,
    722, 723, 746
  XYZ Affair, 251
  zones of occupation and,
    747, 750
  See also French colonies; French
    empire; French Revolution;
    Louisiana Purchase
Franciscan missionaries, 116, 118,
    S1–3–4
François I, king of France, 37
Franklin, Battle of, 454
Franklin, Benjamin, 147, 148, 150,
    241, 250
  American Revolution and, 199
  The Autobiography of Benjamin
    Franklin (1771-1790),
    S5–0–1(d)
  Declaration of Independence
    and, 194
  French and Indian War and,
    163, 166
  A Narrative of the Late Massacres
    (1764) (excerpts), S6–2–3(d)
  negotiations with France, 203
Franklin, William, 231
Fraternal organizations, 533
Fredericksburg, Battle of, 443
Free black population (during
    slavery), 237–38, 281, 307,
    401–2, 405
  education for, 352
  Fugitive Slave Act of 1850 and,
    399–400
  Missouri Compromise and, 295
  in Philadelphia, 235, 237, 314

  restrictions on, 71, 74, 239, 263,
    300, 313–14, 413
  rights exercised by, 74
  ways of life, 313–14
Free-Soil Party, 344, 390, 391, 397,
    399, 403, 405, 406, 408, 416
Free Speech Movement (FSM), 827
Free State Association, 462, 469
Free State Hotel, 406
Freed, Alan, 786
Freedman's Village, 445
Freedmen's Bureau, 466, 467, 478
  court of, 460–61
  establishment of, 465
Freedmen's Bureau Bill, 468
Freedom Riders, 811
Freedom Schools, 820
Freedom Summer, 820
Freedom Trash Can, 831
Freedom's Journal, 340
Freehold farms, 238
Freeman, Elizabeth (Mum Bett),
    211(photo), S7–4–5
Freeport Doctrine, 412
Freeways (See Highways)
Frémont, John C., 383, 408
French and Indian War, 158–59,
    161–69, 171, 175
  causes of, 161–63
  conclusion of, 169
  from local to imperial, 163–65
  North American colonies before
    and after, 169(map)
  problems with British-iclonial
    cooperation, 165–66
  second phase of, 167(map)
  as Seven Years' War, 163, 172
  start of, 163
French colonies, 113–16
  Beaver Wars and, 49
  in Canada, 37, 39–45
  coffee cultivation in, 116
  exploration and settlement
    (1603-1616), 41(map)
  Louisiana colony, 106,
    114–15, 119
  New World exploration, 36–37
  South Carolina region and, 96
  See also French and Indian War
French empire
  attempts to establish, 113–16
  crumbling of, 161–63
French Revolution, 172, 230, 231,
    240, 247, 252, 269
Freneau, Philip, 230
Frethorne, Richard, 70
  Letter from Richard Frethorne
    to His Parents about Life in
    Virginia (1623), S3–1–2(d)
Frick, Henry Clay, 562
Friedan, Betty, 830
Fries, John, 251

FTC (*See* Federal Trade
    Commission)
Fuchs, Klaus, 768
Fugitive Slave Act of 1793, 226,
    312, 343
Fugitive Slave Act of 1850,
    399–400, 405, 425, 441
Fugitive slave clause of
    Constitution, 217, 312–13
Fulbright, J. William, 824
Fuller, Margaret, 351
Fulton, Robert, 274, 278, 285
Fundamental Constitutions,
    96, 107
Fundamentalist Christianity,
    665–66
*Fundamentals, The* (essays), 665
Funding and assumption, 229
Funelo, Nero, S7–5
Funston, Frederick, 582
Fur trade, 69, 137, 141
    in Dutch colonies, 45–46, 48–49
    French-Indian, 37, 39–42, 44,
        57, 113
    overhunting and, 44, 80, 279
    in South Carolina colony, 97
Furious Five, 843
"Fusion" tickets, 344, 572–73

Gabriel (slave revolt leader),
    259–61, 309
Gadsden, James, 406
Gadsden Purchase, 406
Gag rule, 325, 342
Gage, Thomas, 184, 191, 192
Gallatin, Albert, 262
Galveston, Texas hurricane,
    568–69, 603
Galveston Plan, 569
Galveston Wharf Company, 568
Gandhi, Mohandas, 729, 806
Gang system in slavery, 135, 304–6
Gangrene, 447, 515
Gangsta rap, 891
Ganioda'yo, 279
Garfield, James A., 542, 543
Garner, Eric, 951
Garnet, Henry Highland, 340
Garrison, William Lloyd, 332, 338,
    341, 343, 357, 390, S11–1
    *Liberator* article (1831) (excerpt),
        S11–0–1(d)
Garvey, Marcus, 669
Gary, Elbert, 641
"Gas and water" socialism, 595
Gates, Bill, 871, 874, 910–11
GATT (General Agreement on
    Tariffs and Trade), 906–7
Gay Liberation Front, 856–57
Gays (*See* Homosexuality)
Gaza Strip, 864, 884–86
*Gazette of the United States,* 231

Gellhorn, Martha, 731
Gender roles, 956
    in Chesapeake colonies, 72–75
    in colonial America, 134–35
    in mid-m20th century, 782–83
    in modern era, 659–61
    in Native Americans, 27–29, 120
    slave codes and, 101
    Victorian view of, 527–28
    *See also* Women
General Agreement on Tariffs and
    Trade (GATT), 906–7
General Colored Association of
    Massachusetts, 340
General Electric, 725, 872
General Federation of Women's
    Clubs, 593, 627
*General Jackson Slaying the Many
    Headed Monster* (Robinson,
    H. R., 1836), S10–4(v)
General Motors (GM), 653,
    674–75, 699, 758, 775,
    778–79, 818, 944, S24–3–4
Genêt, Edmond-Charles, 248
Genetics, 910
Geneva Accords, 792
Geneva Convention, 938, 943
*Genízaros,* 119
Gentility, 139, 140(photo), 147
George, Henry, 521, 549–50
    *That We Might All Be Rich* (1883)
        (excerpts), S17–2–4(d)
George III, king of England, 169,
    171, 173, 191, 193, 194,
    195(photo), 200, 278, S6–3
Georgia, 175, 185
    American Revolution and, 199
    Civil War and, 432, 450, 454
    Constitutional ratification
        and, 218
    creation of government in, 196
    founding of, 141, 146
    Native American land in,
        243, 319
    secession of, 424
    slavery in, 146
    Spanish plan to demolish, 160
    territory disputes in, 243
German Coast uprising, 309
German immigrants/Americans
    in American Republic, 251
    in antebellum era, 393, 401
    Catholic Church and, 129, 533
    in colonial era, 123, 129
    during depression of 1837, 366
    in industrial America, 532, 533
    nativism and, 348, 401
    World War I and, 623, 629,
        636–39
Germany
    Berlin airlift, 750
    division of, 747

financial crisis of 1890s and, 561
imperialism and, 575
Manila Bay occupied by, 580–81
nationalism in, 533
Nazi-Soviet pact, 713
Open Door Note and, 583
post-World War I reparations,
    640, 673, 682
post-World War II, 747
Samoa claimed by, 545
Shandong Peninsula occupied
    by, 577
Spanish Civil War and, 713
Taft administration and, 609
Venezuela loan and, 609
World War I and, 620, 623–26,
    629, 635, 640
World War II and, 711–16, 719,
    722, 723, 735, 737, 745, 746
Geronimo, 482(photo)
Gerry, Elbridge, 251
Gestapo, 712
Gettysburg, Battle of, 443–44,
    447, 634
Gettysburg Address, 445
Ghent, Treaty of, 269, 272, 298
Ghettos, 632
Ghost Dance movement, 482
GI Bill, 756–57
Gibbons, Thomas, 278
*Gibbons v. Ogden,* 278
Gibson, Charles Dana, 630
Gibson Girl, 630
*Gideon v. Wainwright,* 819
"Gift for the Grangers" (Power, J.
    1873), S17–7(v)
Gilbert, Sir Humphrey, 51
Gilded Age (*See* Industrial
    America)
Gingrich, Newt, 916, 919, 921
Ginsberg, Allen, 797
Gist, George, 362
Gladden, Washington, 595
*Glasnost,* 896
Glass ceiling, 888
Glass-Steagall Banking Act of
    1933, 690
Gleeson, William, 602
Glenn, John, 810
Glidden, Joseph, 504
Globalization, 905–9, S29–0–2
    cold war and, 905
    communications technologies
        and, 905
    contesting, 907–8
    defined, 905
    foreign policy and, 927–32
    moving people, 907
    multinationals and NGOs, 906
    trade and, 906–9, 931
Glorious Revolution, 69, 92, 104,
    106, 107–9, 174

Gmail, 963
*God and Man at Yale*
    (Buckley), 808
*Godey's Lady's Book,* 350
Goebbels, Joseph, 703, 732
Goethals, George W., 609
Golan Heights, 864
Gold, 317, 486
    in Africa, 12
    in American Republic
        economy, 271
    in Colombia, 22
    in colonial economy, 92, 171
    mercantilism and, 92
    in Mexico, 19, 20
    on Native American land, 318
    in New World, 15, 24, 29, 35
    percentage of world in U.S.
        treasuries, 739
Gold, Harriet, 362, 363
Gold rush(es), 373, 385, 398, 481,
    504–6, 610
Gold standard, 541, 542, 558,
    565–67
    battle of the standards, 565–67
    end of, 849
    in Great Depression, 686
Golden Gate Park, 549, 830
Golden parachutes, 872
Goldwater, Barry, 801, 808, 817,
    831, 875
Gompers, Samuel, 522, 574, 581
Gonorrhea, 634
Good, Sarah, 112
Good Neighbor policy, 712
Goodman, Andrew, 820
Google, 910
Gorbachev, Mikhail, 896–900
Gore, Al, 915(photo), 920–21
Gorgas, Josiah, 435
Gosnold, Bartholomew, 53
Gospel music, 786
"Gospel of prosperity," 475–78
Gould, Jay, 486, 521
Government (*See* Federal
    government; Municipal
    governments; State
    governments)
*Government Bureau* (Tooker),
    765(photo)
Gowrie (plantation), 304–5
Graceland, 797
Gracia Real de Santa Teresa de
    Mose, 116
Grady, Henry, 453
Graham, Billy, 781
Gramm-Rudman Act, 896
Granada, 11, 14
*Granada Capitulations* (King
    Fernando and Queen
    Isabella, 1492), S1–2(d)
Grand Army of the Republic, 538

Grandfather clause, 571–72, 602
Grandmaster Flash, 843, 891
Grange, 551–52
Grant, Ulysses S., 471
    Civil War and, 437, 443–44,
        450–53, 454
    presidency of, 481, 484, 486, 542
Grape boycott, 853
Grateful Dead, 830
Graul, Rita, 850
Gray, Asa, 517
Great Awakening, 133, 146, 150–52
    cultural conflicts and, 152–53
    effects of, 153–54
    origins of, 150
    Second, 281
Great Britain
    arms-reduction accord
        (1920s), 673
    Berlin airlift and, 750
    Canadian border dispute, 366
    Canadian rebellion against,
        366–67
    *Creole* incident, 377
    Fourteen Points and, 640
    Greek civil war and, 749
    imperialism and, 575
    India controlled by, 173, 182
    joint declaration offered by, 294
    limitation of forces on Great
        Lakes/Rockies, 293
    Manila Bay occupied by, 580–81
    national debt of, 173(figure)
    Open Door Note and, 583, 609
    Oregon Territory land claims,
        373, 377, 382
    Panama Canal and, 609
    Potsdam Conference and,
        737, 747
    Suez Canal crisis, 792–94
    Texas annexation issue and, 378
    United Nations and, 736
    World War I and, 620, 623, 624,
        626, 635, 636, 639
    World War II and, 711, 713, 714,
        716, 723, 737, 746
    Yalta Conference and, 747
    zones of occupation and,
        747, 750
    *See also* England
Great Compromise, 217
Great Depression, 680–705,
    711–12, 723–24, 808, 862,
    937, S22–5–7
    causes of, 681–82
    effects of, 682–85
    *See also* New Deal
*Great Gatsby, The* (Fitzgerald), 665
Great Lakes Indians, 243, 249, 318
Great Lakes region, 9, 106, 204,
    242, 244, 293
Great Migration, 632–33

Great Pile Up, 630
Great Recession, 944–45, 946, 954
Great Society, 817–22, 824, 826,
    838, 839, 848, 858, 874, 877,
    890, 895, 923, 924
    coming apart of, 825–33
    major programs of, 818–19
    personal freedom in, 819–20
    white ethnics and, 858
Great Upheaval, 521
Great Western Railroad, 499
Greece, 749
Greeley, Horace, 396, 426, 448,
    462, 487
Green Berets, 815
Green Corn Ceremony, 279
Greenback-Labor Party, 542
Greenbackers, 541–42, S16–6
Greenbacks, 434, 484, 541–42,
    551, 565
Greene, Gael, S25–0–2(d)
Greene, Nathanael, 200
Greenglass, David, 768
Greenland, 17
Greenpeace, 906
Greensboro sit-ins, 806, 807
Greenville, Treaty of, 246, 272
Greenwich Village, 661, 797
*Greer,* USS, 714–15
Gregg, Josiah, 322
Grenada, 883
Grenville, George, 171, 176
Grenville, Sir Richard, 51
Grey, Samuel, 181
Griffith, D. W., 601, 650, 667
Grimké, Angelica, 332–33, 357,
    S11–1–2
    *An Appeal to the Women of
        the Nominally Free States,*
        S11–1–2(d)
Grimké, Sarah, 332–33, 357
Griswold, Roger, S8–4–5
*Griswold v. Connecticut,* 819, 830
Gross national product
    Great Depression, 682
    mid-20th century, 775
Groves, Leslie R., 722
Grundy, F., *Predictions about the
    War of 1812,* S9–2–3(d)
Guadalcanal, 721, 728
Guadalupe Hidalgo, Treaty of, 383,
    385, 386
Guadeloupe, 115
Guam, 575, 580, 716, 736
Guantánamo Bay detention
    center, 938, 942–43,
    943(photo), 948
    and Barack Obama, 943
    torture of prisoners in, 943
Guatemala, 25–26, 28, 791, 815
Guilford Court House, 200
Gullah language, 145

Gunpowder, 12
Gunter, Edward, S12–2
Gutenberg, Johannes, 12
Gypsies, in Nazi Germany, 712

Habeas corpus, 213, 435, 447, 449
Hackensack River, 95
Hacking, 962–63
Haig, Douglas, 636
Haight-Ashbury, 830
Haiti, 250–51
    Clinton administration and, 931
    communism in, 815
    Taft administration and, 609
    Wilson administration and, 622
Hakluyt, Richard, 50
    *The Principal Navigations,*
        *Voyages, Traffiques, and*
        *Discoveries of the English*
        *Nation* (1589-1600)
        (excerpt), S2–1–2(d)
Haldeman, H. R., 859
Haley, Bill, 786
Half-Way Covenant, 104
Hall, Prince, S7–5
*Hall v. DeCuir,* 490
*Halve Maen* (ship), 46
Hamer, Fannie Lou, 821
Hamilton, Alexander, 209, 222,
    231, 242, 250, 260, 262,
    S7–1, S8–7
    *Alexander Hamilton*
        *Recommends Arming Slaves*
        *and George Washington*
        *Rejects the Idea* (1779),
        S7–1–2(d)
    Burr's shooting of, 264, S9–1
    national bank and, 229–30, 291
    *Report on Manufactures* (1791),
        S8–0–1(d)
    as secretary of treasury, 228–30,
        239, 246, 247
    as young man, 126–27
Hamilton, Alice, 593, 596, 633
Hamilton, Andrew, 141
Hamilton, James, 126
Hamilton, Rachel, 126
Hamlin, Hannibal, 415(photo)
Hammon, Jupiter, 236
Hammond, James Henry, 307, 325,
    393–94
    *Speech on the Admission of*
        *Kansas* (1858), S13–4–5(d)
Hampton Institute, 464
Hancock, Cornelia, S14–3–4(d)
Hancock, John, 179, 191, 195,
    209, 219
Hancock, Winfield Scott, 542
Handsome Lake, 279
Hanna, Marcus, 566
*Hard Times* (Terkel, S. 1970),
    S22–5–7(d)

Hard war strategy, 436, 450–53
Harding, Warren G., 672, 673, 682,
    718, S20–1
Hardwick, Thomas, 641
Hariot, Thomas, 54
Harlem, 720, 825
Harlem Renaissance, 668–69
Harmar, Josiah, 246
Harper's Ferry raid, 413–14
*Harper's Magazine,* 613
Harris, Joel Chandler, 529
Harrison, Benjamin, 545–46, 581
Harrison, Shelby, 597
Harrison, William Henry, 378
    death of, 377
    loss to Van Buren, 364
    Native Americans and, 258, 279,
        S9–6–7
Harrison-McKinley Tariff of 1890
    (*See* McKinley Tariff of
    1890)
Hartford Convention, 268–69,
    293, 324
Hartford Wits, 240
Harvard College, 81
Harvard University, 150, 722
Harvey, William ("Coin"), 560
"Haschish, The" (Whittier, J. G.,
    1854), S13–0–1(d)
Hate stikes, 729
Hathorne, John, 112
Havana, 168
Hawaii, 545
    annexation of, 547, 580
    statehood, 786
Hawkins, John, 50, 72
Hawley-Smoot Tariff of 1930,
    686, 712
Hay, John, 566, 575, 583
Hayes, Rutherford B., 490, 542–43
Haymarket riots, 521–22, 549
Hayne, Robert Y., 326
Haynsworth, Clement, 859
Haywood, William D. ("Big Bill"),
    595, 628
Head Start, 818
Headright, 66, 74
Health Care and Educational
    Reconciliation Act of
    2010, 945
Health care crisis, 912 (*See also*
    National health insurance)
Health reform, 350
Health Security Act of 1993, 916
Hearst, William Randolph, 578,
    695, 713
Heckewelder, J., *Account of the*
    *Arrival of the Dutch at*
    *Manhattan,* S2–3–5
Hefner, Hugh, 780
Helsinki Agreement, 861
Hemings, Sally, 265(cartoon)

Hemingway, Ernest, 665
Henry, Patrick, 175, 220
    Caesar-Brutus speech,
        S6–3–4(d)
    Virginia Ratifying Convention,
        speech to, S7–5–7(d)
Henry VII, king of England, 17, 49
Henry VIII, king of England, 49,
    52, 75
Henry of Navarre, 40
Henry the Navigator, Prince, 12
Hepatitis, 77
Hepburn Act of 1906, 606
Heritage USA, 893
Heroin, 592
Herron, George, 595
Hersey, John, 728
Hesse-Cassel, 200
Hessians, 193, 197, 198, 201(photo)
Hetch Hetchy Valley aqueduct,
    610–11
Hewlett-Packard, 873
Hicks, E., S12–2
Hicks, George, S12–2
Hidatsas, 263
*Hidden Persuaders, The*
    (Packard), 801
*High School and College Graduates*
    *in the Cold War* (1948),
    S24–1–2(d)
Higher Education Act of 1965,
    819, 852
Highway Safety Act of 1966, 818
Highways, 776, 779(table)
Hill, Anita, 922, 925
Hill, James J., 508–9
Hill, Lancaster, S7–5
Hill-Burton Act of 1946, 762
Hillman, Sidney, 698, 699
Hillsborough, Lord, 178
Hinckley, John W., 877
Hindus, 953
Hine, Lewis Wickes, *National*
    *Child Labor Committee*
    *Photographs* (early 1900s),
    S19–5–7(v)
Hip-hop, 891
Hippies, 830
Hippisley, Alfred, 583
Hirohito, emperor of Japan, 739
Hiroshima, atomic bombing of,
    739, 744, 764
Hispanics, 950–51
    decade of (1980s), 892
    population decline in mid-19th
        century, 503
    population growth, 907
Hispaniola, 16, 25
Hiss, Alger, 768, S24–6
Historical novels, 321–22
"History of the Standard Oil
    Company" (Tarbell), 597

Hitler, Adolf, 712, 723, 730,
    732–35, 745, 808, 928
  and Olympics of 1936, 702–3
  Roosevelt's cable to, 713
  suicide of, 737
Ho Chi Minh, 719, 792, 816
Hochelaga, 37, 39
Hoffman, Abbie, 857
Hoffman, Frederick I., 517, 519
Hog Island Shipyard, 630, 631
Hohokam Indians, 9
Holding companies, 512
Holland/Netherlands
  American Revolution and, 203
  bonds introduced in, 172
  English conflicts with, 93
  French and Spanish war
    with, 248
  independence secured by, 45
  Puritans in, 76
  World War II and, 713, 716
  See also Dutch colonies
Hollibaugh, Bruce, 829
Hollingsworth v. Perry, 952
Holly, Buddy, 786
Hollywood, 657, 908–9
  sexual harassment in, 956
Hollywood Ten, 764, 766–67
Holmes, John Clellon, 797
Holmes, Oliver Wendell, 641
Holocaust, 731, 764
Homeland Security, 938
Homestead Act, 434, 479
Homestead Steel Works, 562–64
Homesteaders, 503, 560
Homogeneity, 780–87
Homosexuality. See Same-sex
    identity
Homosexuals in the Movement
    (Maxwell, P., 1970),
    S27–4–6(d)
Honda Accord, 886
Honduras, 609
  communism in, 815
  Wilson administration and, 622
Hongs, 233(photo)
Honky-tonks, 530–31
Hood, John Bell, 454
Hooker, Fighting Joe, 443
Hooker, Thomas, 83
Hoover, Herbert, 705, 862
  election of, 673
  Great Depression and, 681,
    685–87, 689, 690, 695, 808
  as secretary of commerce, 672
  World War I charities organized
    by, 685
Hoovervilles, 685, 686(photo)
Hopkins, Harry, 690, 697
Horizontal consolidation, 512
Hornet (carrier), 717, 718, 719
Horses, 10, 21, 26, 119, 120

Horseshoe Bend, Battle of, 258,
    268, 269
Hotline, U.S-Soviet, 816
House, Edward, 623, 626
House I Live In, The (film), 729
House of Commons (Britain), 174
House of Lords (Britain), 174
House of Representatives Testimony
    of Congressman S. Sitgreaves
    (1798), S8–4–5(d)
House of Representatives' Un-
    American Activities
    Committee (HUAC),
    765, 768
Housing
  in American Republic, 234
  in colonial era, 104
  discrimination in, 632, 825
  in modern era, 656, 664
  Powhatan and English,
    67(photo)
  World War II shortage, 727
  See also Mortgages (home);
    Suburbs
Housing and Urban Development
    Department, 818
Housing bubble, 941
Houston, Sam, 370, 425
How the Other Half Lives (Riis),
    506, S17–4–6(d)
How Tim Got the Votes (November
    10, 1892), S17–0–1(d)
How We Advertised America
    (Creel, G., 1920) (excerpts),
    S20–4–6(d)
Howard, Oliver Otis, 465
Howard University, 464
Howe, J. W., "The Battle Hymn
    of the Republic" (1862),
    S14–2–3(d)
Howe, Samuel Gridley, S14–2
Howe, William, 197, 198
"Howl" (Ginsberg), 797
HUAC (See House of
    Representatives' Un-
    American Activities
    Committee)
Hudson, Henry, 45, 58
Hudson River, 45, 46, 93, 273, 278
Hudson River school of painting,
    367–68, S12–3–4
Huerta, Victoriano, 622
Hughes, Charles Evans, 603, 625
Hughes, Langston, 632, 669
Huguenots, 38, 39
Hull, Cordell, 712, 714, 715
Hull-House, 596–97, 602, S19–0–2
Hull-House Maps and Papers
    (survey), 597
Human Be-In, 830
"Human Be-In, The" (Wilcock, J.
    1967), S26–8(d)

Human rights, 107, 864, 879,
    882, 931
Human sacrifice, 8, 19
Humanitarianism, 150
Humphrey, Hubert, 833
Humphrey-Hawkins Bill, 863
Hungary, 791, 900
Hunt, Jane, 355
Hunt-ins, 855
Hunter-gatherers, 5–6, 9, 21, 24
Huntington, Collis P., 510
Huron Indians, 37, 40–42, 44, 49
Hurricane Harvey, 947
Hurricane Irma, 947
Hurricane Katrina, 947
Hurricane Maria, 947
Hurston, Zora Neale, 669
Hussein, Saddam, 928–29, 939–40,
    940(photo), 948
Hutcheson, Francis, 149
Hutchinson, Anne, 82–83
Hutchinson, Thomas, 175, 176,
    182, S6–4–5
  Stamp Act Riots: The Destruction
    of Thomas Hutchinson's
    House, S6–4–5(d)
Hydrogen bomb, 749, 756, 764, 768
Hydropathy, 350

"I Didn't Raise My Boy to be a
    Soldier" (Bryan. A 1915),
    S20–0(d)
I Love Lucy (television program),
    774, 780
I Was a Communist for the FBI
    (film), 765
Iberian Peninsula, 10
IBM, 871, 910
ICC (See Interstate Commerce
    Commission)
Ice Age, 5
Idaho, 504
I'll Take My Stand: The South and
    the Agrarian Tradition
    (essays), 665
"Illegal Immigration" (King, S.
    2007), S30–6–7(d)
Illinois
  pro-slavery advocates in, 323
  settlers in, 298
  statehood, 272
Illinois Board of Trade, 689
Illinois Territory, 115
Illustrados, 581
Immediatism, 341
Immigration
  Alien and Sedition Acts, 254
  in American Republic, 231
  in antebellum era, 393, 400–402
  Asian, 666, 764, 854–55
  in cold war era, 764
  in colonial era, 127–29

culture of immigrants, 534–35
globalization and, 907
illegal, 784, 892, 907
in industrial America, 531–36
labor market and, 498–501
from Mexico, 952
in modern era, 666
nativism *vs.*, 348, 400–402,
    535–36, 666, 666(table)
Proposition 187, 907
World War I and, 623
*See also* Migration, internal
Immigration Act of 1921, 666
Immigration Act of 1924, 666
Immigration Act of 1965, 854
Immigration and Nationality Act of
    1952, 764, 785
Immigration Reform and Control
    Act of 1986, 892
Impeachment
of Clinton, 920
of Johnson (Andrew), 470–71
Imperial Valley Workers
    Union, 668
Imperialism, 575–83
opposition to, 581
sea power and, 575–76
world of, 584–85(map)
Imports
in 1970s, 841
in American Republic, 270
in colonial era, 138
Great Depression and, 682
in post-revolution era, 208
Reagan administration and, 896
*In re Debs,* 575
*Inaugural Address* (Kennedy, J. F.,
    1961), S26–1–2(d)
Incas, 18, 22, 24
*Incidents in the Life of a Slave Girl*
    (Jacobs), 309
Income inequality, 936–37, 956
Income tax, 434, 604, 609, 613,
    696–97, 878, 894
Indentured servants, 64, 66, 71, 74,
    99, 101, 123, 131, 136
in American Republic, 271, 284
in Barbados, 99
importation from Europe to
    America (1580-1775),
    129(figure)
in Pennsylvania colony, 96
profitability of using, 70
Puritans and, 73, 78
treatment of, 70, S3–1–2
India
British control of, 173, 182
Columbus's planned voyage
    to, 15
cotton from, 433, 551
silver minting ceased in, 558
Indian Patrol, 856

Indian Reorganization Act of
    1934, 694
Indian Self-Determination Act of
    1975, 856
Indian Territory, 320, 363, 375 (*See
    also* Reservations (Native
    American))
Indiana
settlement of, 231, 298
statehood, 272
Indiana Plan, 600
Indiana University, 662, 697
Indigo, 92, 134, 135, 270, 272
Individualism, 349, 650
in colonial America, 113
culture of, 663–64
Great Awakening and, 153
politics of, 672
Industrial America
culture of:
    immigration and, 531–35
    urban (*See* Urban culture)
politics of, 526–54
    economic issues, 540–46
    government activism and
        limits, 547–50
    styles, 536–40
rival visions of, 612–16
*See also* Industrial capitalism;
    Industry
Industrial armies, 560
Industrial capitalism, 499–506, 591,
    651, 863
big business rise, 508–12
individualism and, 664
new social order under, 512–16
political economy of global,
    499–508
in the West, 479–83
Industrial Revolution, 311,
    910, 954
Industrial unions, 699
Industrial Workers of the World
    (IWW; Wobblies), 595, 628
Industrious revolution, 133–34,
    140, 154
Industry
deindustrialization, 842–44, 849,
    871, 890
information sector supplanting
    of, 910
major American (ca. 1890),
    511(map)
modern era development of,
    651–52
slavery and, 310–12
Taylorism and, 562, 656
during World War II,
    710–11, 725
*See also* Industrial America;
    Industrial capitalism;
    Manufacturing

INF (Intermediate-Range Nuclear
    Forces) Treaty, 896
Infant mortality rates, 73, 853
Inflation
in 1960s, 824
in 1970s, 839, 840, 848, 849, 861
in 1980s, 879
in 1990s, 912
in American Republic, 271
*Influence of Sea Power upon
    History, The* (Mahan), 575
Influenza, 25, 447
Information economy, 904, 910–12,
    936, S29–2–3
Initiative, recall, and
    referendum, 604
Inoculation (*See* Vaccines/
    inoculation)
Inquiry (secret committee), 626,
    635–36
Installment plan, introduction
    of, 657
Insurance companies, 137,
    271, 311
Intel, 873
Interest groups, 593
Interest rates, 824, 879, 912
*Interesting Narrative and Other
    Writings, The* (Equiano, O.,
    1789) (excerpts), S4–2–4(d)
Intermediate-Range Nuclear Forces
    Treaty (INF), 896
Internal Security Act of 1950,
    769, 784
International Ladies' Garment
    Workers, 698
International Monetary Fund,
    737, 905
International Olympic Committee
    (IOC), 702–3
International Red Cross, 906
Internationalism, 711, 927
Internet, 905, 958
Interstate Commerce Commission
    (ICC), 544, 548, 606, 672
Interstate highway system, 776–77
Intolerable Acts of 1774, 183,
    184(table), 185, 196,
    S6–5–7(d)
*Invasion of the Saucer Men*
    (film), 802
Inventions, 273–76, 395, 651
Iran, 939
American hostages in,
    865(photo), 866, 875,
    877, 893
Carter administration and,
    864–66, 875
cold war era, 747, 789, 794
Iraq war with, 886
and nuclear weapons, 948
Iran-Contra affair, 893–94, 914

Iraq
  economy of, 940
  insurgency, 940
  Iran war with, 886
  Persian Gulf War, 928–29
Iraq War, 939–40, 947–49
  casualties of, 940
  end of, 945
  and U.S. popularity, 940
Ireland, 11, 173
  British conquest of, 50–51
  potato famine in, 348
Irish immigrants/Americans, 500
  in American Republic, 231
  in antebellum era, 393, 401
  Catholic Church and, 348, 533
  Civil War and, 448
  in colonial era, 99, 123
  during depression of 1837, 366
  in industrial America, 533,
    534, 536
  nativism and, 348, 400–402, 536
  World War I and, 623
"Iron Curtain" speech, 748,
    748(cartoon)
Ironclads, "battle" of, 433
Iroquois Indians, 9, 159
  Beaver Wars and, 49
  Covenant Chain joined by, 106
  devastation of during
    revolution, 212
  Dutch colonizers and, 48–49
  French and Indian War and, 163,
    165, 167, 170
  French colonizers and, 37, 39, 44
  region of, in mid-17th century,
    40(map)
Isabel (Isabella), queen of Spain,
    11, 14, 16, 29, 35, 49
  *Granada Capitulations* (1492),
    S1–2(d)
Islamic State in Iraq and Syria
    (ISIS), 948–49
Isolationism
  Bush's (George H. W.)
    repudiation of, 927
  during World War II, 711, 713–14
Israel, 932, 939
  Camp David Accords and,
    864, 884
  Six-Day War, 847–48
  Suez Canal crisis, 792–94
  Yom Kippur War, 719, 840, 847
Isthmus of Panama, 50
*It Came From Beneath the Sea*
    (film), 802
Italian immigrants, 501, 533,
    534, 536
Italy
  arms-reduction accord
    (1920s), 673
  nationalism in, 533

Spanish Civil War and, 713
World War I and, 623, 635
World War II and, 712, 715, 735,
    737, 746
*It's a Wonderful Life* (film), 764
IWW (*See* Industrial Workers of
    the World)

J. Walter Thompson (ad agency),
    656, 674–75
Jackson, Andrew, 290, 297, 300,
    324, 365, 369, 377, 379
  abolition movement and, 314
  background of, 258–59
  Bank of the United States and,
    315–17, 317–18, 364,
    S10–3–5
  *Bank Veto Message* (1932)
    (excerpts), S10–3–5(d)
  censuring of, 364
  "corrupt bargain" accusation,
    295–96
  as a Mason, 301
  Message to Congress "On
    Indian Removal" (1830),
    S10–5–6(d)
  Native Americans and, 258–59,
    268, 286, 293, 318–19, 321,
    362, S10–5–6
  nickname of, 315
  nullification crisis and, 325–27
  Polk compared with, 384
  presidency of, 314–22, 341, 342,
    358, 363
  War of 1812 and, 258, 259,
    268, 269
  western settlement and,
    273, 367
Jackson, Henry, 861
Jackson, Jesse, 826, 891, 924
Jackson, Michael, 885
Jackson, Rachel Donelson Robards,
    258, 314
Jackson, Thomas J. ("Stonewall"),
    439, 443
Jackson State College
    shootings, 846
Jackson-Vanik Amendment, 861
Jacksonian Democracy, 250, 278
  in action, 314–18
  decline of, 363–67
  social and political bases of,
    298–301
Jacobs, Harriet, 309
Jamaica, 25
James, Duke of York, 93
James, Henry, 531
James I, king of England, 57, 63,
    67, 91
James II, king of England, 92,
    106, 108
James River, 64, 67, 69

Jamestown, 34, 53, 57, 62, 64, 66,
    67, 75, 76, 101, 115
  Dutch and, 47
  reason for failure of, 64
  starvation in, 64
Japan
  arms-reduction accord
    (1920s), 673
  atomic bombing of, 739, 744,
    750, 764
  China attacked by (WWII), 711,
    712, 715
  China's war with, 577
  Columbus's planned voyage
    to, 15
  economic rise of, 841
  globalization and, 906
  labor unions in, 757
  Open Door Note and, 583, 610
  Pearl Harbor attack, 711, 715–16,
    718, 730, 737, 745
  post-World War II, 747
  Reagan administration and, 886
  trade with, 545, 886
  World War I and, 636, 640
  World War II and, 711, 712,
    715–19, 723, 730, 735–36,
    739, 745–46, 750, 754
Japanese Americans
  World War II internment of, 711,
    730–31, 854–55
  World War II military service
    by, 720
Japanese immigrants, 854–55
Javits, Jacob, S26–3
Jaworski, Leon, 860
Jay, John, 222, 228, 243, 248–49, S7–1
Jay Cooke & Company, 487
Jay's Treaty, 243, 249, 250
Jazz, 657–58, 786, 891
Jazz Age, 658, 662, 665
*Jazz Singer, The* (film), 657
Jefferson, Thomas, 239, 250, 253,
    274, 281, 298, 315, 347, 368,
    448, 550, 564, S8–1–2, S8–7
  Alien and Sedition Acts and,
    254, 324
  American Revolution and,
    193, 202
  Declaration of Independence
    and, 194
  Enlightenment ideas and, 147
  *First Inaugural Address* (1801),
    S9–0–1(d)
  French Revolution and, 247
  *Letter from Thomas Jefferson to
    William Henry Harrison*
    (1803), S9–6–7(d)
  *Letter to Philip Mazzei* (Jefferson,
    T. 1796), S8–1–2(d)
  Louisiana Purchase and,
    262–64, 266

national bank and, 230, 291
Native Americans and, 279,
    S9-6-7
presidency of, 259-66
as secretary of state, 227,
    229, 248
slaves owned by, 239
vice presidency of, 250, 254
Jefferson Airplane, 830
Jenkins, Robert, 159-60
Jeremiads, 104
Jesuit missionaries, 34, 41
Jewish Charities, 684
Jews
    in American Republic, 242
    in Barbados, 99
    Democratic Party and, 673
    Holocaust and, 731
    immigration of, 501, 534, 536
    in mid-20th century, 781
    in Nazi Germany, 712
    in Netherlands, 45, 47-48
    in Portugal, 10
    Roosevelt (Franklin)
        administration and, 699
    in Russia, 501, 533
    in Soviet Union, 861
    in Spain, 10, 11, 16, 45
Jiang Jieshi, 752
*Jihad*, 932
Jim Crow system, 572, 729, 799
    death of, 820-21
    inventing, 570-71
    World War I and, 634
Jingoes, 547, 575, 577, 578, 581
Job Corps, 818
Jobs, Steve, 871, 873, 874
Jockey Hollow, 199
John Deere tractor company, 630
Johns Hopkins University, 613,
    722, S26-3
Johnson, Andrew, 438, 447
    impeachment and trial of,
        470-71
    Reconstruction and, 461,
        465-66, 470
Johnson, Anthony, 71, 74
Johnson, Hiram, 613
Johnson, Jack, 527
Johnson, James, 158, 167
Johnson, Lyndon B., 849, 858, 895,
    914, 945
    *Address at Johns Hopkins
        University, "Peace without
        Conquest"* (1965) (excerpts),
        S26-5-7(d)
    background of, 817
    Black Power movement and, 826
    civil rights and, 820-21
    election of 1964 and, 817
    election of 1968 and, 832-33
    mandate of, 817

Vietnam War and, 821-24, 826,
    832-33, 846, 860, S26-5-7
    *See also* Great Society
Johnson, Samuel, 543
Johnson, Susannah Willard,
    158-61, 167
Johnson, Sylvanus, 161
Johnson, Tom, 603
Johnson, William, 164
Johnston, Albert Sidney, 438
Johnston, Joseph E., 427, 439,
    450, 454
Joint Chiefs of Staff, 750
Joint-stock companies, 50
Joliet, Louis, 106
Jones, John Beauchamp,
    S14-5-6(d)
Jones, Samuel ("Golden Rule"), 603
Jones, William, 286
Jones Mixer, 511
Jordan, 847
Jordan, Michael, 921
Jorns Family of Dry Valley, Custer
    County, Nebraska (Butcher,
    S. 1886), S17-7(v)
Joseph, Chief, 482
*Journal of Frances Kemble*
    (1838-1839), S10-6-7(d)
JPMorgan Chase, 941
Judge, Andrew, 226
Judge, Ona, 226-27, 236, 237, 254
Judicial branch, establishment
    of, 216
Judiciary Act of 1789, 228, 262
Judiciary Act of 1801, 254, 261
*Jungle, The* (Sinclair), 598-99,
    S19-2-5(d)
Junk bonds, 872
Junto, 148
"Just Say No" campaign, 887
Justice Department, 548, 599, 606,
    628, 811, 917
Juvenile delinquency, 527, 727,
    796, 797

Kaiser Shipyards, 725
Kalakaua, king of Hawaii, 545
Kameny, Frank, 856
Kansas
    admission of, speech, S13-4-5
    bleeding, 405-7
    "crime against" (speech), 407
    Native Americans *vs.* settlers
        in, 409
    sack of Lawrence, 406
    *See also* Kansas-Nebraska Act
        of 1854
Kansas-Nebraska Act of 1854,
    402-6, 408, S13-6
Kasserine Pass, 723
Kearny, Stephen, 382
Keewenaw Peninsula, 42

Keller, Helen, 590-91
    "Blind Leaders" (excerpts),
        S19-7-9(d)
Kelley, Abby, 343
Kelley, Florence, 593-94, 596
Kellie, Luna, 526, 529, 554
Kellogg-Briand Pact, 673
Kemble, Frances, S10-6-7
Kemp-Roth Bill, 878
Kennan, George F., 748, 749
    *The Sources of Soviet Conduct*
        (1947) (excerpt),
        S24-0-1(d)
Kennebec River, 63
Kennedy, Anthony, 887
Kennedy, Edward, 850-51
Kennedy, John F., 809-16, 821, 831,
    833, 834, 848
    assassination of, 816
    Bay of Pigs incident, 815
    civil rights and, 811-12
    Cuban Missile Crisis, 816
    *Inaugural Address* (1961),
        S26-1-2(d)
    Johnson compared with, 817
    and space program, 812
    Vietnam War and, 816, 821
    women's rights and, 831
Kennedy, Robert F., 831, 833, 834
Kent State University
    shootings, 846
Kentucky
    Civil War and, 436
    emancipation resisted in, 455
    Native Americans in, 243
    secession resisted by, 426
    settlement of, 207, 212, 231, 272
    slavery in, 306, 455
    statehood, 300
    voting rights in, 300
Kentucky Resolutions, 254, S8-8(d)
Kenya, U.S. embassy attack in, 932
Kerensky, Alexander, 636
Kerouac, Jack, 797
Kerry, John, 937
Kesey, Ken, 830
Key, Francis Scott, 268, 314
"Key of Liberty" (Manning), 241
Keynes, John Maynard (Keynesian
    economics), 705, 714,
    724, 878
*Keynote Address, Democratic Party
    Convention* (Obama, B.
    2004), S30-2-3(d)
Keystone Bridge Company, 509-10
Khmer Rouge, 861
Khomeini, Ayatollah Ruholla,
    865-66
Khrushchev, Nikita, 816
    Berlin Wall and, 814
    Eisenhower's meeting with, 791
Kickapoo Indians, 318

Kierstede, Hans, 95
Kierstede, Sara Roelofs, 95
Kim Il Sung, 754–55
King, Martin Luther, Jr., 811, 826, 854, 890, 891
    assassination of, 833, 834
    "I have a dream" speech, 812–13
    Montgomery bus boycott, 799
    *Statement to the Press at the Beginning of the Youth Leadership Conference* (1960), S26–0–1(d)
    Vietnam War condemned by, 824
King, Rodney, 922, 951
King, Rufus, 292
    *The Substance of Two Speeches Delivered on the Subject of the Missouri Bill* (1820) (excerpts), S10–1–3(d)
King, Steve A., S30–6–7(d)
King Cotton diplomacy, 433
King George's War, 160, 161
King Philip's War, 99, 104–6
King William's War, 110–11, 172
"Kingdom Coming" (Work, H. C., 1862), S14–6–7(d)
King's fifth, 22
Kings Mountain, Battle of, 200
Kinsey, Alfred C., 780
Kiowa Indians, 373, 375
Kirk, Russell, 808
Kirkpatrick, Jeane J., 882, 888
Kissinger, Henry, 845, 846, 860
Kitty Hawk (airplane), 652
*Kivas,* S1–1
Klamath Indians, 783
*Klan, The: Defender of Americanism* (Evans, H. W., 1925) (excerpts), S21–0–1(d)
Kneel-ins, 807
Knights of Labor, 520–22, 549, 552, 574
Know-Nothings (*See* American Party)
Knox, Henry, 228, 231, 244
Knox, Philander, 606
Koch, Charles, S30–5
Koch, David, S30–5
"Koch Brothers, The" (Reid, H. 2015), S30–5–6(d)
Kodak camera, 789
Kool Herc, 891
Korea
    airliner shot down by Soviets, 881
    Japanese occupation of, 577, 754
    South, 792
    trade with, 545
Korean War, 749, 754–56, 787, 791
Korematsu, Fred, 730
Koresh, David, 917
Kosovo, 930
*Kristallnacht,* 712

Kroc, Ray, 778
Ku-Klux Act, 477
Ku Klux Klan, 477, 488, 601, 673, 811
    emergence of, 477
    rebirth of, 666–67
Kuwait, 928
Kwanzaa, 826

La Follette, Robert M. ("Fighting Bob"), 604–5, 612, 622–23, 625–27, 672
La Salle, René-Robert Cavelier, Sieur de, 105–6, 114
Labor Day, 548
Labor force (*See* Workforce)
Labor unions
    Amalgamated Clothing Workers, 698
    American Federation of Labor, 562, 574–75, 595, 654, 699, 776
    American Railway Union, 562–63, 575
    Bronco Busters and Range Riders Union, 595
    Brotherhood of Sleeping Car Porters, 654, 710, 760
    Cigar Makers' International Union, 574
    communism and, 758, 769
    Congress of Industrial Organizations, 699, 757, 776
    defeat of (modern era), 654
    deindustrialization and, 842
    Imperial Valley Workers Union, 668
    industrial, 699
    in industrial America, 520–22, 548
    Industrial Workers of the World, 595, 628
    International Ladies' Garment Workers, 698
    Knights of Labor, 520–22, 552, 574
    Mechanics' Union of Trade Associations, 299, 345, 353
    mid-20th century, 776
    National Trades' Union, 346
    New Deal legislation and, 695, 698–99
    outlawing of activities, 641
    Pennsylvania Slovak Catholic Union, 533
    post-oWorld War II, 757–59
    Professional Air Traffic Controllers Organization, 879
    Reagan administration and, 877–79
    retreat from politics, 574–75
    Screen Actors Guild, 766, 878

Unión de Trabajadores del Valle Imperial, 668
Union of Russian Workers, 644
United Automobile Workers, 699, 726–27, 758, S24–3–4
United Farm Workers of America, 854
United Mine Workers, 575, 606–7, 698, 758
    women and, 575, 654, 727
    World War I and, 628, 633
    World War II and, 726–27
    *See also* Strikes
*Ladies Magazine,* 350
*Lady Chatterley's Lover* (film), 780
Lafayette Escadrille, 625
Laffer, Arthur, 878
Lake Erie, 268
Lakota Sioux Indians, 481–82
Land
    in American Republic, 231
    in Appalachian region, 272–73
    colonial era supply of, 134, 136–37, 144
    conservation movement, 607
    English encroachments on Indian, 68(map)
    freed slaves' dream of owning, 464–65
    growth of public, 608(map)
    industrial capitalism impact on, 503–4
    Native American use patterns, 80
    obstacles to obtaining, 298
    post-revolution speculation, 207–9, 213
    Puritan distribution and use of, 80–81
    Senate dispute over prices, 325–26
    *See also* Expansionism
Land Act of 1800, 272
Land Act of 1820, 298
Land Act of 1851, 385
Land-grant colleges, 434
*Land of the Dollar, The* (Steevens, G., 1897) (excerpt), S16–2–3(d)
Land Ordinance of 1785, 272
Land pressure, 144
Land riots, 137
Landon, Alf, 700
*Landscape* (Cole), 367, S12–3(v)
*Landscape in Ecuador* (Mignot, L. R., 1859), S12–4(v)
Lane, Ralph, 51–52, 54
Langdon, John, 226, 227
Lange, Dorothea, 680–81
    *Farm Security Administration Photographs* (1930s), S22–3(v)
Lanham Act, 727
Lansing, Robert, 624
Lardner, Ring, Jr., 766

Larkin, Thomas, 382
Lasch, Christopher, 858
*Last of the Mohicans, The*
    (Cooper), 368
Latchkey children, 727
Lathrop, Julia, 596
Latin America
    cold war and, 746
    in colonial era, 113
    Good Neighbor policy and, 712
    Kennedy and, 815
    Rio Pact, 754
    Roosevelt (Theodore) and, 608–9
    Wilson and, 622, 641
Latvia, 900
*Lau v. Nichols,* 855
Laud, William, 91
Lavien, Johann, 126
*Law of Civilization and Decay, The*
    (Adams), 576
Lawrence, D. H., 780
Lawrence, Kansas, 405
*Lawrence v. Texas,* 952
*Laws of the State of New York,* 22nd
    Session (1799), S8–8–9(d)
Lawson, John Howard, 767
Lawyers, 277–78
Lazarus, E., "The New Colossus"
    (1883), S16–4(d)
League of Five Nations, 10
League of Nations, 640–41,
    673, 736
League of United Latin American
    Citizens (LULAC), 668, 784
*Leatherstocking Tales* (Cooper),
    350, 368
Lebanon, 893
    Eisenhower Doctrine, 794
    Israeli invasion of, 884
    and September 11 terrorist
        attacks, 937
Lecompton Constitution, 412
LeConte, Joseph, 517
Lee, Ann, 334
Lee, Charles, 197
Lee, Jason, 371
Lee, Richard Henry, 192, 194, 195
Lee, Robert E., 461
    Arlington estate of, 445
    Civil War and, 439, 443–44,
        449–54
    Harper's Ferry raid and, 414
    surrender of, 454
Left-wing populists, 959
Legal Services Program, 818
Legal Tender Act, 434
Leggett, William, 301
Legislative branch, establishment
    of, 216
Lehman Brothers, 941
Leisler, Jacob, 109
LeMay, Curtis, 736

Lenape Indians, 95
Lend-Lease bill, 714
Lenin, Vladimir, 636, 640, 745
*Leopard* (ship), 265
Lesbian feminism, 852
Lesbian Gay Bisexual Transgender
    and Queer community (*See*
    LGBTQ community)
Lesbians, 925–26
*Letter from Abigail Adams to John*
    *Adams* (1776), S7–3–4(d)
*Letter from Anne Bradstreet to*
    *Her Children* (undated),
    S3–3–5(d)
"Letter from Birmingham Jail"
    (King), 811
*Letter from Fray Pedro de Feria*
    *to Phillip II, King of Spain*
    *about Paquiquineo* (1563),
    S2–0–1(d)
*Letter from George Washington to*
    *Robert Dinwidde, Governor*
    *of New York* (1775), S6–0(d)
*Letter from James G. Thompson to*
    *the Editor of the Pittsburgh*
    *Courier* (1942), S23–6–7(d)
*Letter from Richard Frethorne to*
    *His Parents about Life in*
    *Virginia* (1623), S3–1–2(d)
*Letter from Thomas Jefferson to*
    *William Henry Harrison*
    (1803), S9–6–7(d)
*Letter from William Penn to His*
    *Backers* (1683), S4–1–2(d)
*Letter on the Crisis to the*
    *Philadelphians, A* (Sherman,
    J. 1860), S14–0–2(d)
*Letter to Her Sister* (Hancock, C.
    1863), S14–3–4(d)
*Letter to Philip Mazzei* (Jefferson,
    T. 1796), S8–1–2(d)
*Letters from an American Farmer*
    (Crevecoeur), 238
*Letters from Polly Crow to Her*
    *Husband during World War*
    *II* (1944), S24–7–9(d)
*Letters to Eleanor Roosevelt* (1936),
    S22–4–5(d)
Levitt, William J., 777, S25–0
Levittown, 776, 780
Lewinsky, Monica, 920
Lewis, Ann, 90
Lewis, Diocletian, 540
Lewis, George, 90
Lewis, Jerry Lee, 786
Lewis, John L., 698, 699, 758
Lewis, Mercy, 90–91
Lewis, Meriwether, 263–64
Lewis, Sinclair, 665
*Lexington* (carrier), 716, 718
Lexington, Battle of, 191,
    192(map), 196

LGBTQ (Lesbian Gay Bisexual
    Transgender and Queer)
    community, 925–26, 952–53
    and George W. Bush, 952
    violence against, 949
Libel laws, 141
Liberalism
    in colonial America, 93, 107
    culture wars and, 923–24
    frustrations of, post-WWII,
        761–62
    in industrial America, 539,
        544, 547
    new, 807–8, 817, 819–21, 824,
        825, 858
    Roosevelt (Franklin) and, 704
*Liberator, The,* 332, 341, 390,
    S11–0–1(d), S11–1
Liberia, 314
*Liberty* (sloop), 179
Liberty Baptist College, 874
Liberty Party, 343, 344, 379
Libraries, 150, 241
Library Company of Philadelphia,
    149, 150
Library of Congress, 241
Libya, 885
Lichtenstein, Roy, 830
*Life* (magazine), 729, 749
*Life of Kateri* (Cholonec, P., 1715),
    S2–2–3(d)
Light bulb, invention of
    incandescent, 507
Liliuokalani, queen of Hawaii,
    547, 580
Limbaugh, Rush, 958
Limited Test Ban Treaty, 816
Limited war, 822
Lincoln, Abraham, 350, 423, 454,
    482, 559
    assassination of, 456
    Civil War and, 425–26, 432,
        435, 436, 438–44, 447–51,
        453–54, 456
    Cooper Institute address, 415
    Douglas debates with, 412
    elections of, 414–16, 454
    Gettysburg Address, 445
    Reconstruction and, 461–65
    secession and, 425–26
    *Second Inaugural Address* (1865),
        S14–8–9(d)
    on slavery, 403, 413, 414, 416,
        425, 456, S14–8–9
    *Speech at Springfield, Illinois,*
        S13–6–7(d)
    Thirteenth Amendment
        and, 455
Lincoln Highway, 776
Lindbergh, Charles A., 664, 714
    *America First Committee*
        *Address,* S23–4–5(d)

Linked economic
    development, 137
Lipan Apaches, 368
Lippmann, Walter, 602, 605, 615,
    624, 625, 627, 640, 641, 645
    "cold war" coined by, 749
    League of Nations, 641
    life and times of, 620–21
    as secretary for Inquiry, 626
Lipton, Thomas, 527
Liquor (See Alcohol)
Listen, America! (Falwell, J., 1980)
    (excerpts), S28-1–2(d)
Literacy
    in American Republic, 241
    of freed slaves, 473
    of Mexican Americans, 853
    of Puritans, 75–76
Literacy tests, 484, 536, 593, 821
Literature
    of American Republic, 240
    of antebellum era, 368
    of modern era, 665
    Native Americans depicted in,
        321–22
    self-improvement and, 350
Lithuania, 900
Little Bighorn, Battle of, 482
Little Rock school desegregation,
    799–800
Little Turtle, 245–46
Living Theater, 830
Livingston, Robert, 252, 263,
    274, 278
Lloyd, Henry Demarest, 499
Loans, subprime, 941
Localism, 241, 291, 297
Locke, David Ross (See Nasby,
    P. V.)
Locke, John, 96, 107, 147, 148
Lockheed Aircraft, 840
Lodge, Henry Cabot, 575, 639,
    640, 641
Loewe v. Lawlor, 574
"Log Cabin and Hard Cider
    Campaign," 376–77
Logan, James, 150
Logan, John, 171
Lon Nol, 846
Long, Huey, 696
Long, Lois ("Lipstick"), 660
Longhorn cattle, 502
Look, Job, S7-5
Looking Backward (Bellamy), 551
Looney, John, S12-2
Lord Dunmore's War, 171
Los Alamos nuclear research
    facility, 725, 766
Los Angeles, 732–33
Los Angeles Times, 730
Lost generation, 664–65
Louis XIV, king of France, 106

Louisiana
    Civil War and, 432
    Reconstruction and, 462, 472,
        474, 488, 490
    secession of, 424
    slavery abolished in, 462
    slavery in, 263, 294, 376
    statehood, 272
    voting rights in, 300
Louisiana colony, 106, 114–15,
    119, 165
Louisiana Purchase, 266, 291, 295,
    367, 402
    borders fixed, 293
    details of, 262–64
Louisiana State University, 696
Love Canal, 863
Lovejoy, Elijah, 342
Lowell, Francis Cabot, 276, 311
Lowell, Massachusetts, 276,
    346, 395
Loyalists (American Revolution),
    196, 199, 201, 202, 206,
    210, 231
Loyalty oaths, 769
LSD, 790, 829
Luce, Henry, 729
Lucite, 725
Ludendorff, Erich, 636
Luftwaffe, 713, 720, 725
Lundberg, Ferdinand, 783
Lusitania (ship), 624
Luther, Seth, 346
Lutherans, 129, 533
Lyceum movement, 350,
    350(photo)
Lynch, Joseph M., S12-2
Lynchings, 448, 493, 536, 570–71,
    600, 603–4, 632, 667
    laws against urged, 633, 669,
        700, 760
    during World War II, 720
Lynd, Helen, 664
    Remaking Leisure in Middletown
        (1929) (excerpt),
        S21-5–7(d)
Lynd, Robert, Remaking Leisure
    in Middletown (1929)
    (excerpt), S21-5–7(d)
Lynd, Staughton, 664
Lyon, Matthew, 253, S8-4–5

M1 rifle, 721
Maastricht Treaty, 906
MacArthur, Douglas, 687, 716,
    735, 755
Macdonald, Dwight, 729
Machine gun, 620
Macomb Purchase, 231
Macon, Nathaniel, 252, 295
Maddox (destroyer), 821
Madeira, 13, 17

Madero, Francisco, 622
Madison, James, 209, 222, 229, 248,
    250, 281, 298, 915, S7-5, S8-7
    Alien and Sedition Acts and,
        254, 324
    Bill of Rights and, 228
    Constitutional Convention and,
        215, 217, 220
    French Revolution and, 247
    national bank and, 230, 286,
        291, 292
    War of 1812 and, 266–68
Madison Amendment, 915
Magellan, Ferdinand, 37, 581
Magna Carta, 174
Mahan, Alfred Thayer, 575–78,
    580, 636
Mahattan, arrival of the Dutch at,
    S2-3–5
Mahican Indians, 48
Mahoney, Jeremiah Titus, 702
Maine, 106
    Canadian border issue, 366, 377
    disputes over ownership, 243
    land speculation in, 213
    squatters in, 231
    statehood, 272, 295, 298
Maine (battleship), 578
Mainline Protestants, 953
Mainstream republicanism, 959
Make America Great Again, 957,
    960–64
"Make America Great Again,"
    S30-7–9
Malaria, 321, 371, 447, 579
Malcolm, John, 177(photo)
Malcolm X, 825–26
Mali Empire, 12
Malinche (Malintzin; doña
    Marina), 4–5, 19, 28, 29,
    52, 264
Malone, Dudley Field, 666
Man Nobody Knows, The: A
    Discovery of the Real Jesus
    (Barton), 656, S21-1–4(d)
"Man With Computer" (Aziz
    1992), S29-3(v)
Manchuria, 577, 739
Mandan Indians, 263
Mangum, Willie P., 364
Manhattan
    American Revolution and, 197
    prostitution in, 530(map)
    purchase of, 46
    See also New York City
Manhattan Project, 722, 725,
    726(map), 728, 789
Manifest destiny, 371, 376, 379,
    390, 405, 406, S12-7–9
    in antebellum culture, 367–68
    defined, 367
    in literature, 321–22

Manigault, Charles, 304–5
Manigault, Peter, 140(photo)
Manila Bay, Battle of, 578
Manly, Alexander, 572, 573
Mann, Horace, 352
Manning, William, 239, 241, 298
Manors, 93
Mansfield, Jayne, 782
Manteo, 51, 52, 54, 56, 58
Manufacturing
    in American Republic, 230,
        271, 280
    in antebellum era, 368
    in colonial era, 80, 92
    in late 19th century, 561
    relative share of world
        (1880-1913), 561(figure)
    See also Industry
Manumission, 101, 238
Manzanar Relocation Camp,
    730(photo)
Mao Zedong, 752, 906(photo)
Maps
    Chicksaw, 97(photo)
    early examples of, 12
    first geographically accurate, 17
    King Philip's (Metacom's),
        105(photo)
Marbury, William, 261–62
March Against Death, 846
March on Washington (1894), 560
March on Washington (1932), 687
March on Washington (1962),
    812–13
March on Washington (1969), 846
March on Washington Movement
    (MOWM), 710–11
Marco Polo, 11
Marconi, Guglielmo, 658
Mariam, Mengistu Haile, 884
Marianas, 736
Marijuana, 829
Market revolution, 269, 286, 357
Marquette, Jacques, 106
Marriage
    in colonial America, 73, 81, 112,
        131–32, 144
    freed slaves and, 463, 475
    French-Native American, 44
    in industrial America, 528
    inter-ethnic, 781
    late 20th-century trends,
        923–24
    in modern era, 659
    Mormon, 335
    in Native American culture,
        44, 120
    polygamous/polygynous, 34,
        120, 528
    in post-revolution era, 210
    same-sex, 925–26, S29–4,
        S29–4–6

in slavery, 303, 309
    Spanish-Native American, 27, 28
Marroquín, José, 608–9
Marshall, George C., 714, 715,
    723, 749
Marshall, James, 504
Marshall, John, 251, 262, 264, 278,
    319, S7–5
Marshall, Thurgood, 729, 798,
    799, 922
Marshall Islands, 736
Marshall Plan, 750
Martin, Luther, 218
Martin, Thomas, 634
Martin, Trayvon, 951
Martinique, 115
Mary I, queen of England, 49,
    52, 75
Mary II, queen of England, 92,
    108, 109
Maryland, 207
    Civil War and, 435, 439
    Constitution ratification and, 219
    free blacks barred from, 314
    secession resisted by, 426
    slavery in, 211, 238
    voting rights in, 300
Maryland (battleship), 716
Maryland colony
    establishment of, 69
    Glorious Revolution and, 69,
        107–9
Mason, George, S7–5
Mason, John, 85
Masons, 141, 301
Mass production, 651–52, 653
Massachusetts
    anti-Catholicism in, 348
    in colonial era:
        British war efforts supported
            by, 160
        in Dominion of New England,
            106–7
        Glorious Revolution and,
            107–9
        immigration to, 127
        King Philip's War, 105
        protest and resistance in,
            175–76, 178, 183–85
        as a royal colony, 107
    Constitutional ratification and,
        217–20
    creation of government in, 196
    French and Indian War and,
        166, 175
    slavery issue, 236
    territory disputes in, 243
Massachusetts (ship), 234
Massachusetts Bay colony, 75,
    77–79, 82–85 (See also
    Puritans)
Massachusetts Bay Company, 77

Massachusetts General Court,
    79, 81
Massachusetts Government Act,
    183, S6–6–7(d)
Massachusetts Provincial
    Congress, 185
Massasoit, 77, 105
Massive retaliation doctrine,
    789, 814
Mather, Cotton, 147
Mather, Increase, S4–5
Mattachine Society, 783, 856
Mauchly, John William, 775
Maumee River Indian towns,
    244(photo)
Maverick, Samuel, 181
Maxwell, Jackie, 753
Maxwell, P., Homosexuals in
    the Movement (1970),
    S27–4–6(d)
May Laws, 501
Mayaguez (ship), 861
Mayan Indians, 4, 6–8, 19
Mayflower (ship), 77
Mayflower Compact, 77
Mayors, reform, 603
Mazzei, Philip, S8–1–2
McCain, Franklin, 806
McCain, John, 943–44, 958
McCall's (magazine), 781
McCarthy, Eugene, 831, 833
McCarthy, Joseph, 764,
    769–70, 789
    Wheeling, West Virginia Speech
        (1950) (excerpts), S24–6(d)
McCarthyism, 764, 769–70, 856,
    S24–6
McClellan, George B., 438–39, 447
    Lincoln's firing of, 443
    nominated for president, 451
McCloy, John J., 731
McClure's (magazine), 564, 597, 598
McCormick, Cyrus, 394–95
McCormick reaper, 392, 395
McCulloch, James W., 278
McCulloch v. Maryland, 278, 286
McDonald's, 778, 786, 906
McFarlane, Robert, 894
McGillivray, Alexander, 213, 246
McGirt, Daniel, 202
McGovern, George, 859
MCI, 878
McKay, Claude, 669
McKinley, William, 545, 547, 606
    assassination of, 605
    China policy, 577, 583
    election of, 565–67
    imperialism and, 575
    Philippine-American War
        and, 581
    Spanish-American War and,
        578, 580

McKinley Tariff of 1890, 545, 561, 578, 580
Mclain, Rose, 731
McLane, Louis, 317
McLeod, Alexander, 366–67
McNeill, Joseph, 806
McVeigh, Timothy, 918–19
Me Decade, 857–59
Me Too movement, 956
Meade, George Gordon, 443–44
Measles, 371, 447
Meatpacking industry, 598–99, 606
Mechanics' Institute, 469
Mechanics' Union of Trade Associations, 299, 346, 353
Medicaid, 818, 831, 945
Medicare, 819, 877, 895, 918, 956
Medicine Lodge Treaty, 481
Meese, Edwin, III, 893
Meidell, F., *Account of Life on the Prairies* (1855), S13–1–4(d)
Meigs, Montgomery, 435
Memeskia, 162–63
Memphis race riots, 469
Mencken, H. L., 665
Menéndez, Francisco, 116
Menéndez de Avilés, Pedro, 38–39
Mennonites, 129, 413, 629
Menominee Indians, 43, 318
Mercantilism, 45, 50, 92, 138, 149
Mercenaries, 200–201 (*See also* Hessians)
Merchants, 137–38, 239, 242, 271, 280
Meredith, James, 811
Meredith, William, 718
Mergers, 564, 653, 775
*Merrimac* (ship), 433
Merrimack Manufacturing Corporation, 276
Merrimack River, 275
Merry Pranksters, 830
Mesoamerica, 6–8
Mesquakie Indians, 318
Message to Congress "On Indian Removal" (Jackson, A., 1830), S10–5–6(d)
*Messenger,* 710
*Mestizos,* 28, 119
Metacom (King Philip), 105
Methodist Missionary Society, 371
Methodists, 153, 236, 281, 283, 336, 351, 463, 874
Métis culture, 44
Meuse-Argonne, Battle of, 638–39
Mexica, S1–0
Mexica people, 19–21
Mexican Americans, 892
  activism in (1970s), 853–54
  conservatism and, 870
  derogatory names used for, 784
  in mid-20th century, 784–85
  in modern era, 667–68

music of, 786
World War II and, 720
Mexican immigrants, 667–68, 727, 784–85, 853, 907
Mexican Revolution, 622, 623(map), 667
Mexican War, 344, 380–84, 390, 397, 447
  causes of, 382
  terms of surrender, 383
Mexico, 373, 375, 378, 841
  Aztecs in, 18, 19–21
  cold war era, 791
  commercial expansionism in, 545
  Gadsden Purchase and, 406
  immigration from, 952
  independence from Spain, 293, 322
  lands in trans-Mississippi West, 375
  NAFTA and, 907–8
  pre-Columbian culture of, 6, 8–10
  Reagan administration and, 886
  Spanish conquest and rule, 19–22, 25, 113
  Texas independence, 368–70
  Transcontinental Treaty on, 293
  Wal-Mart in, 906
  Zimmerman Telegram, 625
  *See also* Mexican Revolution; Mexican War
Mial, Alonzo T., S15–4–5
Miami Indians, 161, 162, 245–46
Miami River, 162
Microsoft, 871, 910–11
Middle class, 954–56
  African American, 891, 921
  common school movement and, 351–52
  early 20th century, 592
  immigrant, 534
  in industrial America, 539, 549
  under industrial capitalism, 513
  in mid-20th century, 781
  in new economy, 912
  radicalism in, 549
  self-improvement and, 349
  urban, 346–47
Middle East, 939–40, 947
  cold war and, 746, 792–93, 796(map)
  Nixon administration and, 847–48
  Reagan administration and, 883–86
Middle ground
  abandonment of, 100–101
  creation of, 42–44
  end of, 212–13
Middle passage, 131
*Middletown* (Lynd and Lynd), 664
Middletown, Massachusetts, 179

Midway, Battle of, 717–18
Mignot, Louis Rémy, *Landscape in Ecuador* (1859), S12–4(v)
"Migrant Mother" (Lange), 681
Migrant workers, 655, 853
Migration, internal
  in American Republic, 231–33
  to cities, 348–49
  Great, 632–33
  of pre-Columbian peoples, 5–6
  *See also* Immigration
Military
  gays in, 926, S29–4–6
  racial discrimination in, 634, 760
  Reagan administration and, 880–81
  Truman administration and, 756
  women in, 720, 758, 759, 925
  *See also* Army; Navy
Military-industrial complex, 802
Milk, Harvey, 889
Milken, Michael, 872, 874, 893
Mill-child's cough, 515
Millennialism, 194, 333–36
Millennials, 956–57
Million Man March, 922
Mills, C. Wright, 801–2
Milosevic, Slobodan, 929–30
Mingo Indians, 171
Minimum wage, 633, 704
Mining, 533
  coal (*See* Coal mines/mining)
  copper, 504
  gold, 306
Mining camps, 498, 504
Minnetarees, 263
Minstrel shows, 570
*Miranda v. Arizona,* 819
Miss America pageant, protest against, 831
Missionaries
  in China, 577, 582
  Native Americans and, 41, 116, 118, 279
  in Philippines, 582
  western migration of, 371
Missions, 116
Mississippi
  black codes, S15–1–4
  Civil War and, 443
  French settlement in, 114
  Reconstruction and, 472, 484, 488
  secession of, 424
  settlement of, 231, 298
  slavery in, 376
  statehood, 272
  voter-registration drives in, 811, 820
*Mississippi Black Code* (1865), S15–1–4(d)
Mississippi Freedom Democratic Party (MFDP), 820–21

Mississippi Plan, 490
Mississippi River, 9–10, 24, 170,
    243, 244, 371
  Civil War and, 432, 438, 443
  French explorations of,
    105–6, 114
  great flood of 1927, 685
  Pinckney's Treaty and, 249, 262
  post-revolution negotiations, 203
  steamboats on, 274
  War of 1812 and, 269
  See also Trans-Mississippi West
Mississippi River valley, 159,
    244, 274
Mississippian Indians, 9–10, 24
Missouri
  Civil War and, 436
  secession resisted by, 426
  slavery issue, S10-1–3
  statehood, 272, 295, 298, 342
Missouri Compromise, 337, 397,
    402, 403, 411
  Crittenden Compromise
    and, 425
  tenets of, 294–95
Missouri Crisis, 295
Missouri River, 9, 263
MIT, 722
Mitchell, Billy, 637
Mitchell, John (attorney
    general), 860
Mitchell, John (UMW official), 607
Mitchill, S., Account of Aaron Burr's
    Farewell Speech to the Senate
    (1805), S9-1–2(d)
Mittelberger, Gottlieb, 136
Mobile Bay, Union Capture of, 452
Mobilian Indians, 114
Moctezuma II, 4, 19–21
Model Cities Program, 818
Model T Ford, 651
Modern culture, 655–70, 911
  consumerism in, 656, 664
  family and youth, 662–63
  gender roles in, 659–61
  individualism in, 663–64
  limits of, 664–70
  lost generation in, 665
  recreation in, 657–58
  religion in, 665–66
  sexuality in, 659
  social class and prosperity
    in, 664
Modern era, 650–77
  culture of (See Modern culture)
  economy in, 651–55
  politics and government (New
    Era), 670–76
Modern Republicanism, 786,
    787–88, 809
Modern Woman: The Lost
    Sex (Farnham and
    Lundberg), 783

Modoc Indians, 481
Mogollon Indians, 9
Mohawk Indians, 48, 106, 212
Mojados, 784
Molasses Act of 1733, 171
Molotov, V. M., 747
Mondale, Walter, 879, 891
Monitor (ship), 433
Monongahela River, 274
Monopolies, 278, 606
Monroe, James, S7–5
  New Orleans/Florida purchase
    attempt, 263
  presidency of, 292–94
Monroe, Marilyn, 782
Monroe, Sarah, 346
Monroe Doctrine, 294, 367
Montagnais Indians, 41
Montana, 504
Montcalm, Louis-Joseph de, 165,
    166, 168
Monte Verde site (Chile), 5
Montgomery, Richard, 193
Montgomery, Robert, 766
Montgomery bus boycott, 799
Montréal, 168, 193
Moody, Paul, 276
Moon walk, 848
"Moondog's Rock 'n' Roll Party"
    (radio program), 786
Moore, Amzie, 729
Moors, 10–11
Moral Majority, 875, 893
Moral suasion, 337, 341, 353
Moratorium Day, 846
More Wonders of the Invisible
    World (Calef, R., 1700)
    (excerpts), S4-5–7(d)
Morgan, Edmund, 301
Morgan, J. Pierpont, 508, 510, 607,
    613, 624
  arranges loan to treasury,
    558–59, 564, 606
  consolidation movement led
    by, 564
  gold standard supported by, 565
  Knox's lawsuit against, 606
  mail bomb sent to, 641
Morgan v. Virginia, 760
Mormons, 286, 335–36, 479, 528,
    S11-5–7
Morocco, 262, 723
Morrill Land Grant Act of 1862,
    434, 518–19
Morrill "War Tariff," 433–34
Morris, Gouverneur, 209
Morris, Robert, 209, 234
Morrison, John, 514
Morse, Samuel F. B., 391
Mortality rates
  in Chesapeake colonies, 70
  child, 132, 534
  infant, 73, 853

  in Jamestown, 64
  on slave ships, 131
Mortgages (home), 657, 776
Morton, Jelly Roll, 657
Moses, Robert, 820
Mossadeq, Mohammad, 790
Most-favored-nation policies,
    251, 615
Mother at Home, The (Child), 350
Mott, Lucretia, 355, 358
Mount Vernon, 215
Movement, the, 857–58, 859
Movies
  cold war era, 765, 766–67
  modern era, 650–51, 657–58
Movimiento Estudiantil Chicano
    de Azlán (MEChA), 854
Moynihan, Daniel Patrick, 848
Mozambique, 883
Ms. (magazine), 852
MSNBC, 958
Muckraking, 598–99, 634
Mugwumps, 539
Muir, John, 607, 611
Mujahedeen, 881
Mullaney, Craig, 936–37, 945
Multiculturalism, 924
Multinationals, 839, 841, 906
Mumps, 447
Munich agreement, 713
Municipal governments
  in industrial America, 548–49
  progressivism and, 602–3
Munsey, Frank, 613
Murfreesboro, 447
Murphy Brown (television
    program), 924, 925
Murray, Ellen, 422
Murrow, Edward R., 731
Music
  acid rock, 829
  country, 786
  gangsta rap, 891
  gospel, 786
  hip-hop, 891
  jazz, 657–58, 786, 891
  mid-20th century, 786, 796
  of modern era, 657–58
  popular, 657–58, 786
  rap, 891
  rhythm and blues, 786
  rock and roll, 786, 796, 797,
    828–29, 891
Muslim ban, 961
Muslims, 953
  in Africa, 12, 14
  Nation of Islam, 826, 922
  in Portugal, 10, 11
  reconquista and, 10–11
  in Spain, 10, 11, 16
Mussolini, Benito, 712, 735
Mutual aid societies, 280, 314, 533
Mutual assured destruction, 881

MX Peacekeeper, 880
"My Day" (newspaper column), 700
My Lai massacre, 846

NAACP (*See* National Association for the Advancement of Colored People)
Nader, Ralph, 818
NAFTA (North American Free Trade Agreement), 907–8, 945
Nagasaki, atomic bombing of, 739, 764
Nahuas, S1–0
Namibia, 883
Narragansett Bay, 82
Narragansett Indians, 77, 83–85
*Narrative of the Late Massacres, A.* (Franklin, B., 1764) (excerpts), S6–2–3(d)
*Narrative of the Life of Frederick Douglass, An American Slave* (Douglass), 309, 338, 340
Narváez, Pánfilo de, 23
NASA (*See* National Aeronautics and Space Administration)
Nasby, P. V., *A Platform for Northern Democrats* (1865), S15–0–1(d)
Nashville, Battle of, 438, 454
Nashville sound, 786
Nasser, Gamal Abdel, 792–93
Nast, Thomas, 489(photo)
Natchez Indians, 115
*Nation, The,* 460
Nation of Islam, 826, 922
National Aeronautics and Space Administration (NASA), 810, 812–13, 848
National American Woman Suffrage Association (NAWSA), 539, 594, 633
National Association for the Advancement of Colored People (NAACP), 593, 633, 669–70, 720, 729
  civil rights, 760, 798, 799, 820
  creation of, 602
National Association of Manufacturers, 561, 575
National bank, 229–30, 296, 378, 384, 434 (*See also* Bank of the United States)
National Broadcasting Company (NBC), 658
*National Child Labor Committee Photographs* (Hine, L. W., early 1900s), S19–5–7(v)
National Civil Service Reform League, 539
National Conference of Catholic Bishops, 880

*The Challenge of Peace: God's Promise and Our Response* (1983) (excerpts), S28–4–6(d)
National Consumers League, 593
National Credit Corporation, 686
National Defense Authorization Act of 1994 (1993) (excerpts), S29–4–6(d)
National Defense Education Act, 802
National Defense Mediation Board (NDMB), 726–27
National Endowment for the Arts, 819, 924
National Endowment for the Humanities, 818, 924
National Farmers' Alliance and Industrial Union (*See* Farmers' Alliance)
National Football League, 657
National government (*See* Federal government)
National health insurance
  Clinton's proposal, 916
  Great Society programs and, 818
  Obama's program, 945, 946, 959
  Truman's proposal, 761–62, S24–4–5
National Industrial Recovery Act (NIRA), 694–96, 699, 701
National Institute of Mental Health, 762
National Labor Relations Act (*See* Wagner Act)
National Labor Relations Board (NLRB), 698–99
National Labor Union (NLU), 520
National League, 761
National Liberation Front, 816
National Negro Convention, 340
National Organization for Women (NOW), 831, 852
National Origins Act of 1924, 667
National Refiners' Association, 512
National Republicanism, 291–94, 297, 364
  election of 1824 and, 295
  Jackson and, 316
  Monroe and, 292–94
*National Review,* 808
National Road, 292
National Security Act of 1947, 750
National Security Council (NSC), 750, 756, 899
National Security League, 624
National Semiconductor, 873
National Trades' Union (NTU), 346
National Traffic and Motor Vehicle Safety Act of 1966, 818
National Union for Social Justice, 696

National War Labor Board, 633, 725
National Woman Suffrage Association, 485
National Woman's Party (NWP), 595, 633
National Youth Administration Office of Negro Affairs, 700
Nationalism, 533
  Bellamy's version, 551
  New, 612–13, 616
Nationalist Clubs, 551
Nationalist populism, 959
Nationalists, 209, 213, 215, 217
Native Americans
  activism in (1970s), 855–56
  alcohol consumption in, 146
  in the American Republic, 231, 243–46, 279
  American Revolution and, 205, 212
  attempts to gain legal concessions, S12–0–2
  backcountry land claims, 243
  Bacon's Rebellion and, 100–101, 104–5
  captives taken by, 158–61, S4–2–4
  Cleveland and, 544
  in colonial era:
    Dutch colonies and, 45–46, 48–49
    English colonies and, 53–55, 64, 66–69
    French colonies and, 37, 39–45, 113–15, 119, 159
    New England and, 104–6
    Pilgrims and, 77
    Puritans and, 80, 83–85
    Scotch-Irish and, 127–28
    South Carolina colony and, 96–97
    Spanish colonies and, 16–29, 35, 116–20, 159
    Virginia colony and, 100–101
  Dawes Severalty Act, 483, 544
  destruction of subsistence, 482–83
  diseases affecting, 19, 21, 25–26, 77, 120, 165, 321, 371
  enslavement of, 16, 19, 70, 97, 101, 114, 117, 120
  in European countries, 52–53
  horse impact on culture, 26, 119, 120
  Jackson and, 258–59, 268, 286, 293, 318–19, 321, 362, S10–5–6
  Jefferson and, 279, S9–6–7
  Kansas settlers and, 409
  King Philip's War, 99, 104–5, 106
  King William's War, 110–11

Louisiana Purchase and, 262, 263
major villages and battle sites,
    245(map)
manifest destiny and,
    321–22, 367
in mid-20th century, 783
New Deal legislation and, 694
New World explorations, 16–29
Pontiac's Rebellion, 170–71
precontact world of, 5–10
progressivism and, 601
Queen Anne's War, 99, 110–11
religious practices, 117, 279, 482,
    S1–3–4
removal policy and, 318–22,
    362–63, 375, S10–5–6
Sherman and, 453, 481
treaties signed by, 212, 243, 246,
    258–59, 320, 363, 481
War of 1812 and, 268, 269,
    279, 318
in the West, 212, 371–76, 480–82
    See also French and Indian
        War; Indian Territory;
        Reservations (Native
        American); individual tribes
Nativism, 348, 400–407, 535–36,
    666, 666(table)
NATO, 938, 945 (See North
    Atlantic Treaty
    Organization)
Natural rights, 107
Naturalization Act of 1790, 239
Nauvoo, 335
Navajo Indians, 117, 373, 432,
    481, 720
Navigation Act of 1651, S4–0–1(d)
Navigation Acts, 92, 93, 106
Navy
    in American Republic, 262
    Civil War and, 426, 432–33
    imperialism and, 575–76
    increased strength of, 561
    Korean War and, 756
    War of 1812 and, 268
    warship tonnage of world's,
        576(figure)
    World War I and, 630, 635
    World War II and, 714
NAWSA (See National American
    Woman Suffrage
    Association)
Nazi-Soviet pact, 713
Nazism, 701, 712, 723, 961
NBC, 658
Nebraska (See Kansas-Nebraska
    Act of 1854)
Negro Leagues, 761
Neill, Charles P., 599
Netherlands (See Holland/
    Netherlands)
Neurasthenia, 528

Neutrality Acts, 713, 714
Neutron bomb, 880
Nevada, 504
Nevada Test Site, 752–53
Nevis, 126–27
New Amsterdam, 46, 57, 94–95
"New Colossus, The" (Lazarus, E.,
    1883), S16–4(d)
New conservatism, 808, 818
New Deal, 680–81, 687–705, 725,
    726, 729, 758, 761, 763, 787,
    808, 809, 845, 848, 877, 878
    banking system and, 689–90
    coalition of, 699–700
    crisis of, 700–704
    criticism of, 695–96
    employment programs, 690–91
    farm crisis and, 690–94
    federal relief, 690–91
    first, 687–95
    Great Society compared
        with, 817
    origin of term, 687
    second, 695–700
    Social Security system, 697–98
New Democrats, 915, 916
New Echota, Treaty of, 290, 320
New Economic Policy, 849
New economy, 871–72, 910–12
New England, 75–85
    in 1640s, 84(map)
    American Revolution and,
        196–97, 199, 206
    under assault, 104–6
    captives taken by Native
        Americans, 160–61
    colonial economy of, 134, 137
    Dominion of, 106–7
    early industrial society in,
        276–77
    free black population of, 313
    land pressure in, 144
    tariff of 1816 and, 297
    War of 1812 and, 268
    See also Puritans; individual
        states and colonies
New England Anti-Slavery
    Society, 341
New England Artisan, 346
New England Association of
    Farmers, Mechanics, and
    Other Workingmen, 346
New England Emigrant Aid
    Company, 405
New-England Tale, A
    (Sedgwick), 350
New Era, 664, 670–76
New Federalism, 848, 877
New France, 37, 39–45, 166–68
New Freedom, 613, 615–16
New Frontier, 809–16 (See also
    Kennedy, John F.)

New Guinea, 6, 716
New Hampshire
    Constitution ratification and, 219
    creation of government in, 196
    slavery issue, 236
    territory disputes in, 243
    voting rights in, 300
New Hampshire colony, 78, 106,
    107, 141
New Jersey
    American Revolution and,
        197–199
    Constitutional ratification
        and, 218
    in Dominion of New
        England, 106
    free blacks barred from, 314
    land riots in, 137
    slavery abolished in, 312
    women's suffrage in, 210,
        240, 300
New Jersey Plan, 216
New Left, 808–9, 824, 827, 831,
    852, 857, 858
New liberalism, 807–8, 817, 819,
    820, 821, 824, 825, 858
New Light religious groups, 281
"New Look" strategy, 790,
    790(photo)
New Mexico
    acquired by U.S., 382, 383
    Civil War and, 436
    Spanish conquest and
        reconquest, 116–19
    statehood, 425
New Nationalism, 612–13, 616
New Negro, 632–33, 664, 668–70
New Negro for a New Century, A
    (Washington), 668
New Netherland, 45–49, 92
    becomes New York, 93
    private sector role in, 45–47
New Netherland Company, 46
New Orleans, 146
    Civil War and, 433, 438
    French settlement in, 106, 114
    French surrender to Spain, 168
    jazz in, 657
    Louisiana Purchase and, 262–64
    Pinckney's Treaty and, 249
    port of, 249
    race riots in, 469
    Reconstruction and, 462, 469
    slave market of, 304
    War of 1812 and, 269
New Orleans (steamboat), 274
New Orleans, Battle of, 259
New Republic, 606, 620, 640, 641
New Right, 871
New South, 493
New Spain, 35, 242–43, 244, 368
New Sweden, 47

New Woman, 593–94, 659, 664
New World
  consequences of conquest, 25–29
  division of, 17
  European objectives in, 35–37
  as a geographical barrier, 37
  Spain in, 14–29
New World Order, 927–29
  components of, 927
  retreat from, 929–31
New York
  American Revolution and, 197,
    198(map), 199
  British-Indian alliance
    dominated by, 106
  capital located in, 229
  Constitution ratification and,
    218, 220
  in Dominion of New
    England, 106
  free black population of, 313
  Glorious Revolution and,
    108, 109
  land riots in, 137
  land speculation in, 207, 212
  Native Americans in, 212
  penal reform in, 352–53
  port of, 136, 137
  slavery abolished in, 310, 312, 323
  territory disputes in, 243
  voting rights in, 300
New York, Treaty of, 246
New York Central Railroad, 499
New York City
  American Revolution and, 197
  business concentration in, 655
  colonial era growth in, 141
  colonial era poverty in, 143
  colonial era society of, 94–95
  draft riots in, 448
  free black population of, 237
  industrial era growth in, 506
  library acquired by, 150
  New Netherland becomes, 93
  republic era growth in, 231
  slavery in, 95, 139, 143–44, 236
  South Bronx, 842–43
  See also Manhattan
New York Customs House, 543
New York Herald, 578
New York Journal, 578
New York Post, S25–0
New York Protestant
  Association, 348
New York Radical Women, 831
  Principles (1968), S27–4(d)
New York Stock Exchange, 689
New York Sun, 559, 578
New York Times, 682, 731, 846, 874
New York Times v. Sullivan, 819
New York Tribune, 448, 641
New-York Weekly Journal, 141

New York World, How Tim Got the
  Votes (November 10, 1892),
  S17–0–1(d)
New York Yankees, 657
New Yorker, 660
Newfoundland, 12, 17, 36, 37,
  40, 52
Newlands Reclamation Act of
  1902, 607
Newport, 137, 141, 150, 197
Newport, Christopher, 63
Newspapers, 670, 958
  abolitionist, 342, S11–0–1
  in American Republic, 240,
    252–53
  in colonial America, 141–43, 172
  in industrial America, 537
Newton, Huey P., 826
Newton, Isaac, 147
Nez Percé Indians, 373, 481
NGOs (nongovernmental
  organizations), 906
Niagara Falls (Church, F. E., 1857),
  S12–4(v)
Niagara Movement, 602
Nicaragua, 413, 673
  Reagan administration and,
    881–83, 893
  Taft administration and, 609
  Wilson administration and, 622
Nickelodeons, 657
Nimitz, Chester W., 716–19,
  735, 736
9/11 terrorist attacks (See
  September 11 terrorist
  attacks)
Nineteenth Amendment, 633, 660
Ninth Amendment, 228, 852
NIRA (See National Industrial
  Recovery Act)
Nix v. Williams, 887
Nixon, Pat, 845(photo)
Nixon, Richard, 863, 877, 914
  election of 1960 and, 809
  election of 1968 and, 833
  election of 1972 and, 858
  First Annual Report to the
    Congress on United States
    Foreign Policy for the 1970's
    (1970), S27–2–4(d)
  Ford's pardon of, 861
  Hiss case and, 768
  presidency of, 845–52, 858–61
    affirmative action and,
      849, 852
    foreign policy, 845–46,
      S27–2–4
    southern strategy, 858–59
    Vietnam War and, 833, 846–47
    Watergate scandal, 859–60
    women's rights and, 852
  vice presidency of, 787

Nixon Doctrine, 845, S27–2
No Child Left Behind Act of
  2001, 937
Noble, Harriet, 297
Non-Intercourse Act of 1809,
  266–67
Nongovernmental organizations
  (NGOs), 906
Noriega, Manuel, 927–28
Normandy invasion,
  734(photo), 735
Norris, George, 622–23
Norsemen, 11–12
North
  antiabolition violence in, 341–42
  emancipation opposition in,
    237, 447
  free black population of, 313, 314
  growing estrangement from
    South, 412–13
  political economy in antebellum
    era, 391–93
  Reconstruction impact, 484–85
  slavery in, 236, 310–12
  Union revered in, 423
  West importance to, 396
  See also Civil War; individual
    states and colonies
North, Lord, 179, 191
North, Oliver, 894
North American Free Trade
  Agreement (NAFTA), 907–8
North Atlantic Treaty Organization
  (NATO), 750, 787, 794, 927,
  930, 948
North Carolina
  American Revolution
    and, 199–200
  Civil War and, 427, 432, 449, 454
  Constitution ratification and, 238
  land speculation in, 212
  secession of, 426
  territory disputes in, 242
North Carolina Agricultural and
  Technical College, 806
North Korea, 939, 948
North Pole, 45
North River Steamboat of Clermont,
  274, 275(photo)
Northeast, slavery and
  industrialization in, 310–12
Northern Pacific Railroad, 487
Northern Securities Company, 606
Northwest Ordinance of 1787, 211,
  213, 215, 263, 367
Northwest Passage, 17, 37, 45
Northwest Territory, 222, 246, 273
  Native American claims, 243,
    244–46, 375
  Russian claims, 293
  slavery prohibited in, 211
Norway, 713

*Notes on the State of Virginia* (Jefferson), 238–39
Nova Scotia, 164, 171, 242
NOW (*See* National Organization for Women)
NSC-N68, 756
Nuclear Freeze Rally, 880(photo), 881
Nuclear power, 787, 863
Nuclear weaponry, 948
Nuclear weapons, 961
    advice on surviving an attack with, S25-6-9
    China and, 931
    in cold war era, 752–53, 764, 789, 791
    Kennedy administration and, 814, 816
    "New Look" strategy, 790, 790(photo)
    Nixon administration and, 845, 847
    pastoral letter on, S28-4-6
    Reagan administration and, 880–81
    *See also* Arms reduction; Atomic bomb; Hydrogen bomb
Nueces River, 382
Nullification crisis, 323–27, 364
Nuremberg Laws, 712
Nye, Gerald P., 713

Obama, Barack, 944(photo), 958
    and financial crisis, 944
    and Guantánamo Bay detention center, 943
    and health care, 945
    *Keynote Address, Democratic Party Convention,* S30-2-3(d)
    presidency of, 941–49
    racism against, 951
    reelection of, 946–47
    and Russian hacking, 962–63
    and tax cuts, 955
    unemployment under, 949
    use of executive power, 947
    and war in Afghanistan, 945
    and war in Iraq, 945
Obamacare (*See* National health insurance, Obama's program)
*Obergefell v. Hodges,* 952
*Observations on the Deterioration on the Confederate Home Front* (Jones, J. 1863-1864), S14-5-6(d)
Ocala Platform, 551, 565
Occoneechee Indians, 101
Occum, S., *A Short Narrative of My Life* (1768) (excerpts), S5-1-2(d)

Occupational Safety and Health Administration (OSHA), 848, 878
Occupy Wall Street, 946
O'Connell, Thomas, 850
O'Connor, Sandra Day, 887, 888
Office of Civil and Defense Mobilization, *Survive Nuclear Attack* (1960) (excerpts), S25-6-9(d)
Office of Economic Opportunity (OEO), 817
Office of Price Administration, 726
Office of War Information, 727
Ogden, Aaron, 278
Ogden, William, 394–95
Oglethorpe, James, 146, 147, 160
Ohio
    free blacks barred from, 313
    settlement of, 212, 231, 272
    slavery issue, 323, 343
    statehood, 300
    voting rights in, 300
Ohio Company, 163
Ohio Gang, 672
Ohio River, 9, 213, 274, 395
Ohio River valley, 161–64, 243, 246, 272, 274
Ohio State University, 662
Ohmae, K., *Declaration of Interdependence toward the World--2005* (1990), S29-0-2(d)
Oil
    Carter administration and, 863
    Chinese market for, 577
    embargo, 840–41, 843, 847–49
    exports to Japan ceased (WWII), 715
    in Iran, 790
    Mexican exports, 622
    Persian Gulf War and, 928–20
    price increase, 866
    as principle power source, 757
    Reagan administration and, 878, 883–86
Ojibwa Indians, 318
Okinawa, Battle of, 739
Oklahoma, 362–63, 373
*Oklahoma* (battleship), 715
Oklahoma City bombing, 919
Old Light religious groups, 281
Old Spanish Trail, 371
*Old Time Gospel Hour* (television program), 874
Olive Branch Petition, 193
Olympics of 1936, 702–3
Olympics of 1980, 864
Olympics of 1996 (bombing), 919
Omaha Platform, 552, 565
Omnibus Bill, 398–99
Omnibus Housing Act, 811

Omnibus Trade and Competitiveness Act of 1988, 886
"On Being Brought from Africa to America" (Wheatly), 237
*On the Road* (Kerouac), 797
Oñate, Juan de, 116
Onesimus, 147
Online shopping, 954
Ontario, 212
Oo-watie, 362
OPEC (Organization of the Petroleum Exporting Countries), 840
Opechancanough, 67
Open Door Note, 582–83, 636, 711, 712
Open shop, 654
Open Skies proposal, 791
Operation Annie, 752
Operation Breadbasket, 826
Operation Desert Shield, 929
Operation Desert Storm, 928(map), 929
Operation Iraqi Freedom, 939
Operation Linebacker, 847
Operation Mongoose, 815
Operation PUSH (People United to Save Humanity), 891
Operation Rolling Thunder, 821
Operation Wetback, 784
Oppenheimer, J. Robert, 789
*Opportunity in the New Information Economy* (Trujillo, S. D., 1998), S29-2–3(d)
Oratam, Sachem, 95
Order of Freemasons (*See* Masons)
Ordinance of 1787, 312
Ordinance of Nullification, 327
Oregon system, 604
Oregon Territory, 371–73, 377, 379, 382, 397
Oregon Trail, 371, 372(map)
Organization of American States (OAS), 754, 928
Organization of the Petroleum Exporting Countries (OPEC), 840
Orista Indians, 39
Osborn, Sarah (revival attendee), 152
Osgood, Samuel, 228
OSHA (*See* Occupational Safety and Health Administration)
Ostend Manifesto, 406
O'Sullivan, John, 367
    *Annexation* (1845), S12-7–9(d)
Oswald, Lee Harvey, 816
Otis, James, 175
Ottawa Accords, 714
Ottawa Indians, 43, 163, 409
*Our Country* (Strong), 531

"Over There" (Cohan, G. 1917), S20–0–1(d)
Overland campaign, 450
Overland Trail, 479

P-51 Mustang, 721
Pachucos, 732, 733
Pacific Railroad Act, 434
Pacification, 578
Packard, Vance, 801
Packingtown, 501
Page, Patti, 786
Pahlavi, Shah Mohammad Reza, 790
Paine, Thomas, 147, 149, 193, 197, 222, S7–0–1(d)
Paint-ins, 807
Painters' Row, 512
Painting, 367–68, 830
Pakistan, 945
Pale of Settlement, 501
Paleo-Indians, 5
Palestine Liberation Organization (PLO), 884
Palin, Sarah, 943
Palmer, A. Mitchell, 629
Palmer raids, 641
Palmer v. Mulligan, 277
Pan-American Conference (1889), 545
Pan-American Conference (1933), 712
Panama, 50
  Bush (George H. W.) administration and, 927
  Carter administration and, 864
  revolution in, 608–9
  Wilson administration and, 622
Panama Canal, 545, 791
  Carter's agreement on, 864
  construction of, 608–9
Panics
  of 1819, 286, 297–99, 301, 317, 323, 345
  of 1873, 488, 494, 499
  of 1893, 499, 558–59, 577, 602
  See also Depressions; Financial crisis of 1890s; Financial crisis of 2008
Paquiquineo (See Velasco, don Luis de)
Paris, Treaty of
  American Revolution, 204, 205(map), 242, 243, 244
  French and Indian War, 168
  Spanish-American War, 580, 581
Paris Agreement, 947
Parks, 549, 692–93
Parks, Rosa, 799
Parliament, British, 91–93, 107, 110, 171, 173, 175, 177, 182–83, 186

Parochial schools, 533, 535, 545–46
Parris, Samuel, 90
Participatory democracy, 808
Partisan politics
  decline of, 593
  voluntarism compared with, 538
Patent medicines, 592, 599
Patents, 651
Patient Protection and Affordable Health Care Act of 2010, 945
Patronage system, 539, 543–44, 699
Patrons of Husbandry, 551–52
Patroons, 46
Patton, George S., 687, 723, 731, 734
Patuxet Indians, 77
Paul, Alice, 595
Pawnee Indians, 119, 373
Paxton Boys, 171, S6–2–3
Payne-Aldrich Tariff of 1909, 611
Payola, 801
PBSUCCESS (CIA operation), 790
Pea Ridge, battle of, 436
Peace Corps, 814
Peace Democrats, 448
Peace dividend, 928
Peace movement, 673
Peaceful coexistence policy, 791, 845
Pearl Harbor, 938
  acquisition of, 580
  Japanese attack on, 711, 715–16, 718, 730, 737, 745
Pendleton Civil Service Act, 544
Penicillin, 722
Penis envy, 783
Penn, William, 96
  Letter from William Penn to His Backers (1683), S4–1–2(d)
Penn Central Railroad, 839–40
Penn School, 422
Pennsylvania
  abolitionism in, 236
  Constitutional ratification and, 218
  creation of government in, 196
  German settlers in, 251
  land speculation in, 212
  Native Americans in, 212
  penal reform in, 352–53
  voting rights in, 300
  Whiskey Rebellion in, 246–47
Pennsylvania colony, 92, 136, 162–63
  diversity and prosperity in, 94–96
  founding of, 94–96
  immigration to, 129
  slavery in, 96, 143
Pennsylvania Hospital, 150
Pennsylvania Railroad, 499, 509, 632

Pennsylvania Slovak Catholic Union, 533
Pentagon, September 11 attack on, 938
Pentagon Papers, 846, 860
People v. Zammora, 732
People's Convention, 300–301
People's Party (See Populism)
Pequot Indians, 73, 83–85
Pequot War, 83–85
Perestroika, 896
Perfectionism, 333–37, 341, 343
Perkins, Frances, 697, 700, 701
Perkins, George W., 613
Perot, H. Ross, 915, 917
Perpetual motion machine, 285
Perry, Oliver Hazard, 268
Perryville, battle of, 439
Pershing, John J., 622, 635, 636–39
Persian Gulf War, 928–29, S29–6–7
Personal computer (PC), 871, 872(figure)
Personal income per capita (1840-1880), 379(table)
Personnel management, 562
Peru, 18, 22, 24
Petersburg, siege of, 450, 454
Petition and Memorial of the Delegates and Representatives of the Cherokee Nation, The (Ross, J., 1840), S12–0–2(d)
Petition of Right, 91–92
Phelan, James, 610, 611
Philadelphia, 96
  African Americans in, 632
  American Revolution and, 197, 198
  capital located in, 229, 234, 248
  colonial era growth in, 141
  colonial era poverty in, 143
  commerce and culture in ca. 1760, 142(map)
  free black population of, 235, 237, 314
  French and Indian War and, 166
  industrial era growth in, 506
  library acquired by, 150, 241
  port of, 136, 137
  republic era growth in, 231
Philadelphia and Reading Railroad, 558
Philadelphia Negro, The (DuBois), 601
Philadelphia Plan, 849
Philip II, king of Spain, 34, 38, 52, S2–0–1
Philippine-American War, 581–82
Philippine Sea, Battle of, 719
Philippines, 575, 580–82
  annexation of, 581
  British seizure of, 168

Carter administration and, 864
Eisenhower administration
    and, 792
revolution in, 577, 581
Taft as governor of, 609
U.S. rule phased out, 582
World War II and, 715, 716, 736
Phillips, Wendell, 436
Phips, Sir William, 111
Phonograph, 658
Pickawillany, 162, 163
Pickford, Mary, 650–51, 653, 656,
    659, 664, 676
Pierce, Franklin, 400, 405, 406
Pierce, Palmer E., 634
Pierpont, Jack, S7–5
PIGS (Poles, Italians, Greeks, and
    Slavs), 858
Pilgrims, 75, 76–77
Pina, Marilyn, 921
Pinchot, Gifford, 607, 610–12
Pinckney, Charles C., 251, 266
Pinckney, Thomas, 249, 250
Pinckney's Treaty, 249, 262
Pingree, Hazen, 603
Pinkney, William, S10–2–3(d)
Pinochet, Augusto, 847
Pioneer Hi-Bred Corn
    Company, 691
*Pioneers, The* (Cooper), 368
Piracy, 38 (*See also* Privateering)
Pitt, William, 167, 168, 177
Pittsburgh, 231, 655
*Pittsburgh Courier,* 729
    *Letter from James G. Thompson
    to the Editor of* (1942),
    S23–6–7(d)
Pittsburgh Survey, 597
Plague, 77
Plains Indians, 26, 119–20, 375, 481
Plains of Abraham, 168
*Planned Parenthood v. Casey,* 925
Plantations
    in Barbados, 99
    cotton, 303–6
    culture of, 145
    economic efficiency of, 134
    indentured servants on, 70
    rice, 304–5
    slavery system on, 303–6
    sugar, 99, 464, 474
    tobacco, 135
Planter's exemption from
    conscription, 434–35
*Platform for Northern Democrats,
    A.* (Nasby, P. V., 1865),
    S15–0–1(d)
*Playboy* (magazine), 780
Plessy, Homer, 570
*Plessy v. Ferguson,* 570, 602, 798
Plumbers, White House, 860
Plymouth colony, 75–78, 105, 106

Pocahontas, 53, 62–63, 66
Pogroms, 501
Poindexter, John, 894
Pokanoket Indians, 77
Poland
    communism collapse in, 900
    German invasion of, 711, 713
    Russia's loss of, 636
    Soviet Union and, 746, 747
Police brutality, 951
Police department, 507, 549, 600,
    605, 671
Polio, 688
Polio vaccine, 781
Polish immigrants/Americans, 533,
    534, 786
Political action committees
    (PACs), 958
Political approaches, 959
Political correctness, 924
Political economy
    in antebellum era, 391–97
    of the Civil War, 433–34
    of contract labor, 466
    of expansion, 376–84
    of global capitalism, 499–508
    of mercantilism, 92
    of New France, 44–45
    of New World, 16
    of Puritan society, 80–81
    of sharecropping, 474–75,
        491–92
    of slavery, 70–71
    of South Carolina colony, 96–99
    of trans-Mississippi west, 367–76
    *See also* Economy; Politics
Political machines, 536, 548, 602
Political parties
    in American Republic, 230, 266
    in crisis (Jacksonian era), 363–65
    in industrial America, 536–38
    polarization of, 958
Politics
    of abolition, 342–43
    of American Republic transition,
        259–66
    of individualism, 672
    of industrial America, 526–54
        economic issues, 540–46
        government activism and
            limits, 547–50
        styles, 536–40
    late 19th century retreat from,
        567–75
    machine, 536, 548, 602
    moral reform and, 353–54
    new (early 20th century), 591–95
    New Era in, 670–76
    new national (19th century),
        291–97
    partisan, 538, 593
    popular, 539–40, 571–74

rebellion against (1990s), 914–15
    of slavery, 337–44, 397–400, 404–5
    voluntarism in, 537, 538
    women in, 925
    *See also* Political economy
Polk, James K., 384
    election of, 378–81
    Mexican War and, 382–84
    national bank and, 384
Polygamy/polygyny, 34, 120, 528
Pomerene, Atlee, 629
Pomo Indians, 373
Ponce de León, Juan, 18
Pontiac's Rebellion, 170–71, S6–1
*Pontiac's Speech to the Ottawa,
    Potawatomi, and Hurons*
    (1763), S6–1(d)
*Poor Rich Man and the Rich Poor
    Man, The* (Sedgwick), 350
Pop art, 830
Popé, 118
Pope, John, 439
Popular front strategy, 695
Popular politics
    critics of, 539–40
    decline of, 571–74
Popular sovereignty, 397, 402, 408,
    412, 415
Population
    in American Republic,
        226(table), 231
    black, distribution of (1775),
        237(map)
    of British colonies in America
        (1660 and 1710), 102(table)
    English, of Virginia (1607-1640),
        65(table)
    explosion of 18th century,
        127–32
    of foreign birth by region (1880),
        532(map)
    growth in colonial cities, 141
    Hispanic, decline in, 503
    Hispanic, growth in, 907
    of Mesoamerica, 8–9
    in modern era, 655
    Native American, 25–26, 117,
        855(map)
    of New France, 44
    percentage living in cities
        (1890-1920), 592(figure)
    post-revolution growth, 207
    of pre-Columbian North
        America, 8–9
    proportion living in cities
        (1790-1900), 506(figure)
    slave, 129–32, 236, 302
    world (1650-2000), 27(figure)
Populism, 526, 547, 570
    free silver issue and, 565
    "Fusion" ticket, 572–73
    rise of, 552–54

Port Hudson, 443, 446
Port Huron Statement, 808
Port Moresby, 716
Port Royal experiment, 422–23
Ports, 136, 137, 184, 249, 271
Portugal
    African explorations by, 12,
        14, 17
    Columbus turned down by, 14
    Dutch takeover of Brazil, 47
    Jews of, 10
    Muslims of, 10, 11
    New World colonization, 17,
        22, 29
    slave trade, 12, 72
Postal service, 548, 628
Postmodern culture, 911
Potato famine (Irish), 348
Potatoes, 27
Potawatomi Indians, 394, 409
Potomac River, 69, 215, 443
Potsdam Conference, 737, 747
Pottawatomie Creek slave revolt,
        407, 409
Pound, Roscoe, 600
Poverty
    in African Americans, 891
    in American Republic, 238, 242
    in colonial America, 134, 143
    Johnson (Lyndon)
        administration and, 818, 820
    Kennedy administration
        and, 811
    in Mexican Americans, 853
    in mid-20th century, 776
    in modern era, 664
    Reagan administration and,
        894, 895
    war on, 818, 820, S26-2-5
    women in, 888, 925
    See also Welfare system
Powderly, Terence, 521
Powell, Fenner, S15-4-5
Power
    crisis of misplaced, 801–2,
        806, 807
    new approaches to, 807–16
    restoring American, 880–81
Power Elite, The (Mills), 802
Power of Sympathy, The
        (Brown), 240
Powers, Francis Gary, 791
Powers, Johnny, 602
Powhatan (chief), 62–63, 66, 67
Powhatan Indians, 34, 57, 64,
        69, 74
    destruction of, 67–69
    troubled relations with, 66
Predestination, 75, 76, 82, 91, 111
Predictions about the War of 1812
        (Grundy, F.), S9-2-3(d)
Preparation, doctrine of, 82

Presbyterian Magazine, 665
Presbyterians, 91, 127, 276, 281,
        283, 512, 874
Presidential Commission on the
        Status of Women, 831
Presidential elections
    of 1796, 250
    of 1800, 254, 259–61, 268, 564
    of 1804, 264
    of 1808, 266
    of 1812, 268
    of 1816, 293
    of 1824, 295–96, 363
    of 1828, 314–17
    of 1832, 317
    of 1836, 324, 364–65, 378,
        537(figure)
    of 1840, 363, 367, 376–79,
        537(figure)
    of 1844, 344, 378–81, 537(figure)
    of 1848, 344, 363, 390, 397
    of 1852, 400, 537(figure)
    of 1856, 403, 409, 410(map),
        537(figure)
    of 1860, 414–16, 537(figure)
    of 1864, 450, 454, 537(figure)
    of 1868, 483, 537(figure)
    of 1872, 477, 487,
        537(figure), 542
    of 1876, 490, 491(map),
        537(figure), 542, 543(table)
    of 1880, 537(figure), 542, 543
    of 1884, 537(figure), 543(table)
    of 1888, 537(figure), 543(table),
        545, 545(map), 571
    of 1892, 537(figure), 554
    of 1896, 537(figure), 542,
        565–67, 571, 575, 593,
        594(figure), 670
    of 1900, 537(figure), 594(figure),
        671(figure)
    of 1904, 593, 594(figure),
        671(figure)
    of 1908, 594(figure), 609,
        671(figure)
    of 1912, 594(figure), 595, 612–14,
        614(map), 671(figure)
    of 1916, 594(figure), 625,
        671(figure)
    of 1920, 594(figure), 670, 671–72
    of 1924, 669, 672, 673
    of 1928, 671(figure), 673, 685
    of 1932, 687–88
    of 1936, 699–700, 704
    of 1940, 714
    of 1944, 737
    of 1948, 762, 763(map)
    of 1952, 775, 787
    of 1956, 787
    of 1960, 809, 810(map)
    of 1964, 817, 831
    of 1968, 832–34

    of 1972, 838, 857–59
    of 1976, 861–62
    of 1980, 874–75
    of 1984, 879, 891
    of 1988, 913–14
    of 1992, 915, 925
    of 1996, 917
    of 2000, 920–21, 937
    of 2004, 937
    of 2008, 942–45
    of 2012, 946
    of 2016, 957, 959–60,
        960(photo)
Presidential Reconstruction,
        465–69, 474
Presley, Elvis, 786, 797
Press, freedom of, 143, 228, 819
Preston, Thomas, 181
Price, Looney, S12-2
Princeton, Battle of, 198–99
Princeton University, 154, 613, 663
Principal Navigations, Voyages,
        Traffiques, and Discoveries
        of the English Nation, The
        (Hakluyt, R., 1589-1600)
        (excerpt), S2-1-2(d)
Principles (New York Radical
        Women, 1968), S27-4(d)
Printing press, 12
Prisons/penetentiaries, 352–53
Privateering, 50, 58, 63, 207, 251
Prizefighting (See Boxing)
Proclamation of 1763, 171,
        183(table)
Proclamation of Amnesty and
        Reconstruction, 462
Producers' ideology, 549–50
Professional Air Traffic Controllers
        Organization (PATCO), 878
Progress and Poverty (George), 549,
        551, S17-2
Progressive Party, 613, 672
Progressivism, 591, 596–605, 616,
        653, 659, 661, 664
    experts and, 600
    race issues and, 600–602
    Roosevelt (Theodore) and,
        598–99, 605, 609
    settlement house work, 596–97
    in state and local politics, 602–5
    Wilson and, 613, 621
    World War I and, 621, 624, 631
Prohibition, 554, 621, 633–34,
        662, 672, 687 (See also
        Temperance movement)
Propaganda
    cold war, 791
    World War I, 623, 628
Proposition 13, 863
Proposition 187, 907
Proposition Eight, 952
Proprietary colonies, 69, 96, 108

Prostitution, 232, 336, 529, 621, 634, 659
in China, 609
houses of, 530(map)
Protestantism
in American Republic, 284
Antifederalists and, 221
decline in church membership, 874
in England, 49, 75, 108
in Maryland colony, 108, 109
in mid-20th century, 781
nativism and, 535–36
social class and, 512, 534
Providence Island, 73, 78, 85
Proximity fuse bomb, 722
Prussia, 160
Public Broadcasting Act of 1967, 818
Public education, 81, 351–52, 514, 533, 548, 887
Public Facilities Privacy and Security Act, 953
Public sphere, 141–43
Public Works Administration, 695
Pucinski, Roman, S27-6-7
Pueblo Bonito, 9, S1-0-2
Pueblo Indians, 116–19, S4-4-5
Puerto Ricans, 783, 892
Puerto Rico
under Spain, 25, 575
Spanish-American War and, 580
Pullman workers' strike, 562–65
Pulse nightclub shooting, 949
Pure Food and Drug Act of 1906, 599, 606
Puritans, 73, 75–85, 91, 111–13, 127, 351
beliefs of, 76
dissension in the ranks, 81–85
in England, 75, 77, 106
family life in, 81
political economy of, 80–81
prosperity impact on religion, 104
social organization of, 79–80
*See also* Pilgrims
Putin, Vladimir, 948, 961, 962–63
Pychon, Thomas, 830
Pyle, Ernie, 723

Qaddafi, Muammar, 885–86, 948
Qaeda, Al, 932
Qatar, 941
Qingdao port, 577
Quakers, 109, 112, 351, 596
in England, 94, 104
in Pennsylvania colony, 94, 129
persecution of, 104
slavery opposed by, 236, 341, 413
Quartering of soldiers, 92, 166

Quartering Act of 1765, 172, 178, 182, 183(table), S6-7(d)
Quartering Act of 1774, 183
Third Amendment on, 228
Quasi-War, 251
Quayle, Dan, 923–24
Québec, 41, 113, 183
American Revolution and, 193, 197
French and Indian War and, 168
King George's War and, 160
King William's War and, 111
post established at, 40
Quebec Act of 1774, 183, 184(table), S6-7(d)
Queen Anne's War, 99, 110–11, 159
Quincy, Josiah, 181
Quiz show scandal, 801

Rabaul, 735–36
Race, as concept, 951
Race riots, 811, 820
areas affected (1965-1968), 825(map)
in Detroit, 729, 825
in Harlem, 720, 825
King (Martin Luther) assassination and, 833
King (Rodney) beating and, 922
during Reconstruction, 469
in Watts, 826
in Wilmington, 572–73
during World War II, 720, 727
*Rachel and Reuben* (Rowson), 240
Racial diversity, 950
Racism, 951–52, S17-4-6
in the Democratic Party, 572–73, 669
scientific, 570, 596
slavery justified by, 71, 102
and social Darwinism, 517
Radical feminism, 852, 857, 858
Radical Reconstruction, 472–73, 483
Radical Republicans, 461, 462, 470
Radio
decline of political affiliation, 670
invention of, 658
Radler, D. H., *Teenage Attitudes* (1958) (excerpts), S25-2-4(d)
Railroads
account of construction, S13-1-4
Baltimore and Ohio Railroad, 499
buffalo kills sponsored by, 482
Central Pacific Railroad, 434, 479
Chinchow-Aigun railway (China), 610
Civil War and, 434, 435–36, 455
corruption problem, 486

East Louisiana Railway, 570
expansion of, 382(map), 391, 393–95, 476, 492
first transcontinental, 434, 479
Great Western Railroad, 499
growth of (1850-1890), 508(map)
Interstate Commerce Commission and, 544
labor union for workers, 562–63, 575
New York Central Railroad, 499
Northern Pacific Railroad, 487
panic of 1873 and, 487, 499
panic of 1893 and, 499
Penn Central Railroad, 839–40
Pennsylvania Railroad, 499, 509, 632
Philadelphia and Reading Railroad, 558
Populists demand government control of, 552
racial segregation, 570
Southern Pacific Railroad, 480(photo)
strikes, 499, 543, 562–64, 758
Texas Pacific Railroad, 499
Union Pacific Railroad, 434, 479, 486
the West and, 502, 503
Wisconsin Idea, 604–5
World War I nationalization of, 630
World War II nationalization of, 725
Raleigh, Sir Walter, 35, 51, 52, 54, 55
Randolph, A. Philip, 654, 710–11, 739, 760
Randolph, Edmund, 227
Randolph, John, 259, 266, S9-2
Rankin, Jeannette, 716
Ransom, John Crowe, 665
Rap music, 891
Rape, 16, 24, 119
Rauh, Joseph, 710
Rauschenbusch, Walter, 595
*Raza, La,* 668
Raza Unida, La, 854
RCA, 872
Reagan, Nancy, 877, 887
Reagan, Ronald, 766, 833, 870, 871, 874–89, 893–900, 912–13, 925, 930
*Address to the Nation on the Economy* (1981) (excerpts), S28-2-4(d)
African Americans and, 890–92
AIDS crisis and, 890
assassination attempt on, 877
as California governor, 831
comeback of, 896–900

Reagan, Ronald (*continued*)
  domestic policy, 876–79
  elections of, 874–75, 879
  and Ethiopian famine, 884–85
  foreign policy, 879–85
  Iran-Contra affair, 893–94
  shrinking government, 877
  style of, 876–77
  and tax cuts, 955
Reagan Democrats, 915
Reagan Doctrine, 881–83
Reagan Revolution, 876–86, 894,
    895, 900
  abroad, 879–85
  end of, 913–14
  at home, 876–79
Reaganomics, 877–79, 894, 895
Reapportionment, 872
*Rebel Without a Cause* (film), 796
Recall, 604
Reciprocity, 545
*Reconquista,* 10–11, 58
Reconstruction, 460–87, 543
  account of, S15-5–6
  achievements and failures of,
    472–73
  congressional, 470–77, 483–84
  corruption problem in, 486–87
  end of, 485–91
  the North and, 484–85
  presidential, 465–69, 474
  radical, 472–73, 483
  "redemption" from, 471(map),
    476, 485, 487–90
  resistance to, 467–68
  Ten Percent Plan, 462–65
  terrorism during, 477
  Wade-Davis Bill, 462–63
  wartime, 461–65
Reconstruction Acts, 470, 471, 478,
    483–84
Reconstruction Amendments,
    469(table)
Reconstruction Finance
    Corporation (RFC),
    686, 689
Reconversion, 757–61
Red Cloud, 481
  *Pleads the Plains Indians' Point
    of View at Cooper Union,*
    S15-7–9(d)
*Red Cloud Pleads the Plains Indians'
    Point of View at Cooper
    Union* (1870), S15-7–9(d)
*Red Menace, The* (film), 764
Red River campaign of 1864, 433
Red River parish, 488
Red Scares, 629, 641–45, 666,
    764–67, 774
Red Shirts, 572
Red Stick faction of Creek Indians,
    258–59, 268, 321

Redemption (from
    Reconstruction), 471(map),
    476, 485, 487–90
Redemptioners, 96, 102, 123, 129
Redheffer, Charles, 285
Reed, David A., 701
Reed, James A., 640–41
Reed, Thomas Brackett, 545
Referendum, 604
Reform, 334(map), 344–58
  electoral politics and, 353–54
  health, 350
  penal, 352–53
  progressivism and, 602–5
  religious, 333, 336–37
  the urban classes and, 344–49
  women involved in, 354–58
  during World War I, 633–34
Reform mayors, 603
Reform Party, 917
*Regents of the University of
    California v. Allan
    Bakke,* 850
Rehnquist, William, 887
Reid, Harry M., S30-5–6(d), S30-6
Religion
  African Americans and, 463–64
  in American Republic, 281–84
  in England, 91–92
  Enlightenment ideas and, 150
  freedom of, 213, 221, 228
  mid-20th century resurgence of,
    781, 782(table)
  in modern era, 665–66
  Native American practices, 117,
    279, 482
  "old time," 665–66
  perfectionism and, 333–37,
    341, 343
  prayer prohibited in public
    schools, 819
  scandals in (1980s), 893
  separation of church and
    state, 82
  socialism and, 595
  in U.S., 953
  *See also* Missionaries;
    Revivalism; individual
    religions
Religious Right, 874
Religious tolerance
  Dominion of New England and,
    106–7
  Edict of Nantes, 40
  Enlightenment and, 147
  in Maryland colony, 69, 107–9
  in Netherlands, 45
  in New Netherland, 47–48
  in New York City, 93
  in Pennsylvania colony, 96, 136
  Puritan view of, 82
  in South Carolina colony, 96

*Remaking Leisure in Middletown*
    (Lynd, R. and Lynd, H.,
    1929) (excerpt), S21-5–7(d)
Remington Arms, 625
Remmers, H. H., *Teenage
    Attitudes* (1958) (excerpts),
    S25-2–4(d)
Removal Act of 1830, 319–21,
    362, 367
Removal policy, 318–22, 362–63,
    375, S10-5–6
Reno, Janet, 925
*Report on Manufactures* (Hamilton,
    A., 1791), S8-0–1(d)
*Report on the Uprising of 1622*
    (Waterhouse, E.), S3-0–1(d)
Republic (*See* American Republic)
Republic of Texas, 370(map)
Republic of the Congo, 815
*Republican and Democratic Party
    Platforms on the State of the
    American Family* (1984)
    (excerpts), S28-6–9(d)
Republican Party
  African Americans and, 700
  Civil War and, 425, 434, 436,
    442, 447
  election of 1856 and, 409
  election of 1860 and, 415, 416
  election of 1868 and, 483
  election of 1872 and, 488
  election of 1876 and, 490–91
  election of 1880 and, 542, 543
  election of 1888 and, 545
  election of 1896 and, 567, 575
  election of 1912 and, 613
  election of 1916 and, 625
  election of 1920 and, 671–72
  election of 1924 and, 672
  election of 1928 and, 673
  election of 1932 and, 687, 688
  election of 1936 and, 700
  election of 1940 and, 714
  election of 1948 and, 762
  election of 1960 and, 809
  election of 1972 and, 858–59
  election of 1976 and, 861–62
  election of 1980 and, 874–75
  election of 1984 and, 879
  election of 1988 and, 913–14
  election of 1996 and, 917
  election of 2000 and, 920–21
  emancipation and, 454
  "Fusion" ticket, 572–73
  gold standard and, 565
  Great Depression and, 682
  Hispanic vote and, 892
  in industrial America, 537, 538,
    542–46
  Jackson and, 317, 363–64
  labor unions and, 758
  liberal faction, 487

on "loss" of China, 752–54
Modern, 786–88, 809
in modern era, 670, 672–76
New Deal and, 701, 704
as party of moderation, 483–84
radicals in, 461, 462, 470
Reconstruction and, 461, 462,
    467–70, 472, 474, 483–85,
    487, 490
response to activism of '60s and
    '70s, 858–59
secession issue and, 425
slavery issue and, 344, 391,
    403–5, 412, 425
on state of the American family,
    S28-6-9
Thirteenth Amendment and, 454
Republicanism, 178, 194
Republicans, 958
Republicans (Madison's
    designation), 231
*Requerimiento,* 17
Reservations (Native American),
    375, 482–83, 498, 783, 855–56
New Deal legislation, 694
origins of, 480–82
Restore Our Alienated Rights
    (ROAR), 850–52
Restrictive covenants, 759
Resumptionists, 542
Resurrectionists, 537
Reuther, Walter, S24-3-4
Revenue Act of 1766, 178
Revenue Act of 1935, 696–97
Revere, Paul, 191
Revivalism, 281–84, 334(map) (*See
    also* Great Awakening)
Revolutionary War (*See* American
    Revolution)
Reyes, Manuel, 733
Reynolds, James Bronson, 599
RFC (*See* Reconstruction Finance
    Corporation)
Rhode Island
    American Revolution and, 211
    Constitution ratification and, 238
    voting rights in, 300
Rhode Island colony, 78, 82, 105, 106
Rhythm and blues (R & B), 786
Rice, 99, 134, 135, 232, 270, 272
    plantations, 304–5
    slavery routine, 136
Richardson, Elliot, 859–60
Richie, Lionel, 885
Richmond
    American Revolution and, 202
    as Confederate capital, 427, 438,
        450–54
Richmond, David, 806
Rickets, 683
Ridge, John, 363
Right to Life movement, 888, 925

Riis, Jacob, 506, S17-4-6(d)
Riley, John, 380–81
Rio Grande, 113, 382, 383
Rio Pact, 754
RJR Nabisco, 872
RKO, 657
Road building, 273, 275(map), 292
Roanoke, 51–58, 64
Roanoke Indians, 53–55
ROAR (*See* Restore Our Alienated
    Rights)
Robber barons, 512, 781
Robertson, Pat, 874
Robinson, H. R., *General Jackson
    Slaying the Many Headed
    Monster* (1836), S10-4(v)
Robinson, Jackie, 761
Robinson, Paul, 898–99
Rochefort, Joseph, 716, 717
Rock and roll, 786, 796, 797,
    828–29, 891
"Rock Around the Clock"
    (song), 786
Rockefeller, John D., 508, 510, 512,
    558, 607, 641, 911
Rockefeller, Nelson, 860
Rockhill, William, 583
Rockingham, Marquess of, 176
Rocky Mountains, 264, 373,
    377, 505
*Roe v. Wade,* 852, 888–89, 925
Rolfe, John, 63, 66, 70
Rolling Stones, 828
Romantic movement, 367
Rommel, Erwin, 723
Romney, Mitt, 946–47
Roosevelt, Eleanor, 641, 690–92,
    710, 830
    letters to, S22-4-5
    newspaper column of, 700
Roosevelt, Franklin D., 641,
    687–705, 761, 788, 817, 875,
    915, 945
    African Americans and,
        699–700, 710–11, 720
    background of, 687–88
    as Cox's running mate, 672
    death of, 737–38
    elections of, 687–88, 699–700,
        714, 737
    fireside chats of, 689–90
    *First Inaugural Address* (1933),
        S22-0-2(d)
    *Four Freedoms Speech* (1941),
        S23-0-4(d)
    Holocaust dismissed by, 731
    and Olympic Games, 702–3
    polio of, 688
    World War II and, 711–16, 720,
        722–24, 726, 729, 730, 736
    at Yalta Conference, 747
    *See also* New Deal

Roosevelt, Nicholas, 274
Roosevelt, Theodore, 605–16, 672,
    688, S17-1
    big stick diplomacy, 608–9
    conservation movement, 607
    food and drug regulation,
        598–99
    imperialism and, 575, 577
    on labor strife, 595
    on muckraking, 598
    Philippine-American War
        and, 582
    professional background of, 605
    re-election attempt, 612–13
    Spanish-American War and, 578,
        579, 605
    on sports, 527
    Square Deal, 606–7
    *The Strenuous Life* (1899)
        (excerpts), S18-4-6(d)
    trust busting and, 606
    World War I and, 624, 625
Roosevelt Corollary, 609
Rosecrans, William S., 450
Rosenberg, Ethel, 768, 789
Rosenberg, Julius, 768, 789
Rosie the Riveter, 727
Ross, John, 290–91, 363
    *The Petition and Memorial
        of the Delegates and
        Representatives of the
        Cherokee Nation* (1840),
        S12-0-2(d)
Rough Riders, 579
Route 128, 871
Rowlandson, M., *The Sovereignty
    and Goodness of God* (1682)
    (excerpts), S4-2-4(d)
Rowley, Massachusetts land
    distribution, 79(table)
Rowson, Susanna, 240
Royal Africa Company, 93
Royal colonies, 67, 69, 85, 107, 109
Royal Society of London, 150
Rubin, Jerry, 874
Ruby, Jack, 817
Ruby Ridge siege, 917
Rudd, L. A., *Account of a Westward
    Journey* (1852), S12-5-7(d)
Rudolph, Eric, 919–20, 925
Ruef, Abraham, 592, 610
Ruiz de Burton, María,
    S12-9-11(d)
Rule of law, 174–75, 186, 277–78
Rumania, 900
Rumsfeld, Donald, 942
Rural regions, 957
    in American Republic, 231
    in colonial America, 144
    economic change and, 957
    migration from, 348–49
    in modern era, 655, 957

Russell, Charles, 752–53
Russell, Daniel L., 572
Russell Sage Foundation, 597
Russia, 939, 948
  Bolshevik Revolution in, 629,
    635, 636, 641, 745
  claims in Pacific Northwest, 293
  economic sanctions against, 948
  hacking by, 960, 962–63
  Jews of, 501, 533
  McDonald's in, 906
  nationalism in, 533
  Open Door Note and, 583, 610
  wheat from, 551
  World War I and, 620, 623, 625,
    635, 636, 640
  See also Soviet Union
Russwurm, John, 340
Rustbelt, 843, 871–72, S30-7-9
Rutgers University, 154
Ruth, Babe, 657, 663

Sabin polio vaccine, 781
Sacagawea, 264
Sacco, Nicola, 644–45
Sagamité, 44
Sagebrush Rebellion, 863
St. Augustine, 24, 39, 51, 116, 145,
    146, 160
St. Clair, Arthur, 246
St. Croix River, 242
St. Lawrence River, 37, 39, 40, 41,
    111, 168, 242
St. Louis (refugee ship), 731
Saint-Domingue, 116, 231, 247,
    250, 261, 263
Saipan, 736
Salazar, Rubén, 854
Salem witchcraft trials, 90–91,
    111–13, 143, S4-5-7
Salk polio vaccine, 781
Salons, 241
SALT (See Strategic Arms
    Limitation Treaty)
Salt Lake City, 479
Saltworks, 306
Salvation Army, 593
Same-sex identity, 952
  AIDS crisis and, 889–90,
    925–26
  in cold war era, 764
  conservative criticism of,
    889–90, 925–26
  contesting rights, 925–26,
    S29-4-6
  gay power movement, 856–57
  LGBTQ community, 925–26
  in mid-20th century, 783
  in modern era, 659
  in Nazi Germany, 712
  Victorian view of, 527, 530
same-sex marriage, 952

Samoa, 545
San Bernadino shooting, 949
San Francisco
  beat movement in, 797
  counterculture in, 830
  gold rush in, 398, 506, 610
  "San Francisco" (Wilcock, J. 1967),
    S26-8-9(d)
San Francisco sound, 830
San Jacinto River, 370
San Joaquin Valley, 853
San Juan Hill, Battle of, 580
San Patricios, 380–81
San Salvador, 15
Sand Creek massacre, 481
Sanders, Bernie, 960
Sandinistas, 881–83, 893
Sanger, Margaret, 593–94, 659
Santa Anna, Antonio López de,
    369–70, 382
Santa Fe, 116, 118, 373(map), 382
Santa Fe Trail, 372
Santo Domingo, 72, 116
Saratoga (carrier), 718
Saratoga, Battle of, 199
Satellites, 905
Saturday Night Massacre, 860
Saudi Arabia
  attacks on U.S. soldiers in, 932
  Persian Gulf War and, 928–29
  and September 11 terrorist
    attacks, 937
Sauk Indians, 318, 321
Sault Chippewas, 42–43
Savage, Augusta, 669
Savannah, 146, 150
  American Revolution and, 197
  Civil War and, 454
  colonial era growth, 141
Savannah Indians, 97
Save Our Children, 889
Savio, Mario, 827
Scabs, 516
Scalawags, 472, 476, 490
Scalia, Antonin, 887
Scalpings, 105, 120, 170, 481
Schechter Poultry Corporation v.
    United States, 696
Schine, David, 769
Schlafly, Phyllis, 852
Schlesinger, Arthur M., Jr., 807
School Begins (Dalyrmple, L.,
    1899), S18-7(v)
School District of Abington
    Township v. Schempp, 819
Schools (See Colleges and
    universities; Education)
Schwab, Charles M., 630
Schwarzkopf, Norman, 929
Schwerner, Michael, 186
Scientific management, 559,
    562, 653

Scientific racism, 570, 596
SCLC (See Southern Christian
    Leadership Conference)
Scopes, John (trial of), 665–66
Scotch-Irish, 127–29
Scotland
  emigration from, 123
  religious revolt in, 91–92
Scott, Dred, 409–12
Scott, Tom, 509
Scott, Winfield, 366, 381, 383, 400,
    426, 432
Scottsboro Boys, 695
Screen Actors Guild, 766, 878
SDI (See Strategic Defense
    Initiative)
SDS (See Students for a Democratic
    Society)
Sea Islands, 145, 422–23, 464, 465
Seale, Bobby, 826
Seamstresses, 345
Sears-Roebuck, 778
SEATO (See Southeast Asia Treaty
    Organization)
Seattle, anti-globalization protests
    in, 910
Secession, 423–28, 466
Second Amendment, 228
Second Confiscation Act, 442
Second Inaugural Address (Lincoln,
    A., 1865), S14-8-9(d)
Second world, 792
Secret societies, 301
Securities and Exchange Act of
    1934, 690
Securities and Exchange
    Commission, 690
Sedgwick, Catharine, 350
Sedition Act of 1918, 628
Seeger, Alan, 625
Selective Service Act of 1948, 753
Self-improvement, 141, 349–51
"Self-Reliance" (Emerson), 351
Semiconductors, 871
Seminole Indians, 259, 286, 293,
    318, 321
Seneca Falls Convention, 355–58
Seneca Indians, 279
"Separate but equal" doctrine, 570,
    798–99
Separatists, 76, 77, 82, 333–36
September 11 terrorist attacks,
    936–38, 940, S2-0-1
Serbia, 620
Service sector, 954
Sesame Street (television
    program), 819
Settlement houses, 596–97
Seven Cities of Cibola, 24
Seven Days, Battles of, 439
Seven Years' War, 163, 172 (See also
    French and Indian War)

*700 Club, The* (television
   program), 874
Seventeenth parallel, 792
Seventh Amendment, 228
Seventh Cavalry, 481
Seward, William Henry, 398, 400,
   413, 415, 442, 455, 545
Sewing machine, 395, 514
*Sex and the Single Girl*
   (Brown), 830
*Sexual Behavior in the Human*
   *Female* (Kinsey), 780
*Sexual Behavior in the Human Male*
   (Kinsey), 780
Sexual harassment, 956
Sexuality/sexual relations
   in American Republic, 231–32
   in colonial era, 73, 144
   counterculture, 830
   in mid-20th century, 780, 796
   in modern era, 659
   slave-white, 71, 144, 145, 308
   Spanish-Native American, 27–29
Seymour, Horatio, 483
Shaftesbury, Earl of (*See* Cooper,
   Anthony Ashley)
Shakers, 334
Shakespeare, William, 53
Shandong Peninsula, 577
"Share Our Wealth" program, 696
Sharecropping, 463, 632, 684
   contract for, S15–4–5
   defined, 464
   effect of, 476(map)
   political economy of,
     474–75, 492
   as wage labor, 491–93
*Sharecropping Contract between*
   *Alonzo T. Mial and Fenner*
   *Powell* (1886), S15–4–5(d)
Sharlow, James, 904, 911, 932
Sharon Statement, 808
Shaw, Anna Howard, 594
Shawnee Indians, 246, 268, 279,
   408–9
Shays, Daniel, 209
Shays' Rebellion, 209, 215, 219, 241
Sheen, Fulton J., 781
Sheepherding, 503, 504
Shehaes, S6–2
Shelby family, 349
*Shelley v. Kraemer,* 760
Shenandoah Valley raid, 452
Shepard, Alan, 810
Shepherd, Matthew, 926
Sheridan, Philip, 452
Sherman, John, S14–0–2(d)
Sherman, Roger, 217
Sherman, William Tecumseh, 450,
   454, 465, 481
Sherman Anti-Trust Act of 1890,
   545–46, 548, 574, 606

Shiloh, Battle of, 438, 447
Shipbuilding, 137, 138(photo),
   280, 311
Shipping
   in American Republic, 248–49,
     251, 262, 264–66, 268,
     271, 280
   in colonial era, 92, 134
   in industrial America, 545
Shirley, William, 164
Shoemakers' strike, 280
*Shoho* (carrier), 717, 718
Shopping malls, 778
*Short Narrative of My Life,*
   *A* (Occum, S., 1768)
   (excerpts), S5–1–2(d)
Shoshone Indians, 373
Shriver, Sargent, 859
Siberia, 5, 636, 640
Sicily, 735
Sierra Club, 593, 611, 797–98
Sierra Nevada Mountains, 372,
   398, 505
Silent majority, 859
*Silent Spring* (Carson), 818
Silicon Valley, 872–74
Silver, 317
   in American Republic
     economy, 271
   in colonial economy, 92, 171
   Comstock Lode, 505
   free coinage issue, 551, 560,
     565–67
   India ceases minting, 558
   in industrial era economy, 542,
     543, 545
   mercantilism and, 92
   in Mexico, 22, 25
   in New World, 29, 35
   in Peru, 22
Simon and Garfunkel, 830
Simpson, O. J., 922
Simpson-Mazzoli Act, 892
Sinai Peninsula, 864
Sinatra, Frank, 729, 786
Sinclair, Upton, 591–92, 598–99,
   606, S19–2–5(d)
Sing Sing prison, 353
Singapore, 716
Single-parent families, 888, 891,
   923–24
Single tax, 550
Sioux Indians, 120, 373, 375, 432,
   480, 481–82
Sirhan, Sirhan, 833
Sit-ins, 806, 807
Sitgreaves, S., *House of*
   *Representatives Testimony of*
   *Congressman S. Sitgreaves*
   (1798), S8–4–5(d)
Sitting Bull, 482, 529
Six-Day War, 847

Sixth Amendment, 228
Slater, Samuel, 276
*Slaughterhouse* cases, 488–89
Slave codes, 74, 99, 101, 103(table),
   143, 405, 415 (*See also* Black
   Codes)
*Slave Petition for Freedom to the*
   *Massachusetts Legislature*
   (1777), S7–4–5(d)
Slave power theory, 344, 405,
   406, 412
Slave revolts, 390
   in colonial era, 143–44
   Deslondes', 263
   Gabriel's, 259, 260–61, 309
   German Coast uprising, 309
   Harper's Ferry, 413–14
   Pottawatomie Creek, 407, 409
   in Saint-Domingue, 247,
     261, 263
   Stono Rebellion, 145
   Turner's, 309, 327, 341
   Vesey's, 309
Slave trade, 29, 129–31, 263, 270,
   378, 405, 440–41
   Africa and, 12, 72–73, 130
   banning of, 272, 302, 312
   Constitution and, 233, 272,
     302, 312
   domestic, 302–3
   Dutch and, 47–48, 93
   England and, 50, 72–73, 93, 101
   England's ban on, 236, 344
   number of slaves imported
     (1620-1810), 130(figure)
   slave ship voyage, 131–33
Slavery, 302–10, 393–416, S13–0–1,
   S14–8–9
   in American Republic, 231,
     235–38, 239
   American Revolution and, 193,
     200–201, 206, 211
   birth rate in, 132
   in the Caribbean, 115
   in cities, 143–44
   Civil War and, 427–28, 431,
     434–36, 440–43, 448–49
   common elements in, 101
   Confederate constitution on,
     424–25
   Constitution and, 217, 235,
     312–13, 343, 390
   consumer culture and, 123, 138
   cotton gin and, 272, 302
   Crittenden Compromise, 425
   culture of, 144–45
   Declaration of Independence
     clause (deleted), 194
   economy of, 393–96
   education denied in, 353
   expansion of, 376, 383, 390–91,
     396–97, 406

Slavery (*continued*)
  as foreign policy, 406
  freedom national, slavery local
    position, 343–44, 412
  Freeport Doctrine, 412
  gang system in, 135, 304–6
  in Georgia, 146
  Great Awakening on, 123,
    152–53
  house slaves, 306
  impact on textile mill
    workers, 277
  Jay's Treaty and, 249
  Kansas-Nebraska Act, 402–6, 408
  labor problem and, 404–5
  last-ditch efforts to preserve,
    423–25
  in Louisiana colony, 115
  Louisiana Purchase and, 263
  manumission, 101, 238
  Mexican War and, 383, 385, 390,
    397–98
  middle passage, 131
  Missouri Compromise, 294–95,
    337, 397, 402, 403, 411, 425
  narrative, S5–2–4
  national development and,
    310–14
  Native Americans in, 16, 19, 70,
    97, 102, 114, 117, 120
  Native Americans practicing, 321
  nativism and, 401–2
  in New Netherland, 47–48
  in New York City, 95, 139,
    143–44, 236
  in Pennsylvania colony, 96, 143
  petition for freedom, S7–4–5
  political economy of, 70–71
  politics of, 337–44, 397–400,
    404–5
  population in, 129–32, 236, 302
  in post-revolution era, 206,
    207, 211
  property law on, 302, 397,
    410–12
  punishment practices, 307–8
  Puritans and, 73, 78
  regional tensions caused by, 323
  religious practices in, 281, 310
  in South Carolina colony, 96,
    99, 130
  southern system, 302–10
  Spanish and, 22, 116
  task system in, 135, 145, 305, 309
  in Texas, 369, 370, 376, 378,
    390–91, 398
  Three-Fifths Compromise, 217,
    236, 269, 312, 365, 468
  Tyler on, 377
  Van Buren on, 364, 377, 379
  varieties of, 306–7
  variety of slave reactions, 307–10

  in Virginia colony, 70–71,
    100–103, 145, 236
  *Walker's Appeal,* S10–0–1
  Washington's slaves, 226–27,
    235, 236, 247
  western territory and, 213,
    396–97
  Wilmot Proviso, 397–98
  work routine in, 135–36
  *See also* Abolition;
    Emancipation; Slave revolts;
    Slave trade
Sledge, Eugene B., 720, 736
Sleepy Lagoon Murder, 732
Slenser, Brister, S7–5
Slidell, John, 382
Smallpox, 21, 25, 147, 165
Smallpox inoculation, 147
Smart bombs, 939
Smith, Adam, 149–50
Smith, Al, 673, 699
Smith, Hyrum, S11–5–7
Smith, John, 53, 62, 64, 66, 68, 200
Smith, Joseph, Jr., 285, 335–36,
    S11–5–7
Smith, William, 234
Smith Act, 764
Smith and Wesson Company, 633
*Smith v. Allwright,* 729, 760
SNCC (*See* Student Nonviolent
    Coordinating Committee)
Snowden, Edward, 948
Social class
  in American Republic, 239
  in colonial cities, 141–43
  under industrial capitalism,
    512–16
  of industrial era immigrants,
    534–35
  in mid-20th century, 781
  in modern era, 664
  in new economy, 912
  Puritans and, 80
  in South Carolina colony, 96
  in Spanish colonies, 118–19
  *See also* Middle class; Upper
    class; Wealthy; Working
    class
Social clubs, 593–94
Social Darwinism, 516–17, 536,
    551, 561, 576, 586, 598
Social Gospel, 532, 595
Social media, 958, 963
*Social Problems* (George), S17–2
Social regulation, 349–54
Social Security, 701, 704, 787,
    937, 945
  and baby boomers, 956
  increase in beneficiaries, 912
  introduction of, 697–98
  Reagan and, 877, 895
Social Security Act of 1935, 698

Social Security Reform Act of
    1983, 877
Social workers, 596–600
Socialism, 595, 598, 659, 944–45
Socialist Party, 595, 628
Society for Christian Socialists, 595
Society for Establishing Useful
    Manufactures, 242
Society for Supporting the
    Gospel, 336
Society for the Relief of Free
    Negroes Unlawfully Held in
    Bondage, 235
Society for the Suppression of
    Vice, 528
Sociology, 600
Solomon Islands, 735
Somalia, 932
Somoza, Anastasio, 881–83
Songhay Empire, 12
Sonoma Valley, 382
Sons of Liberty, 175, 179
Sontag, Susan, 830
Soulé, Pierre, 406
*Souls of Black Folk, The*
    (DuBois), 601
*Sources of Soviet Conduct, The*
    (X [Kennan, G. F.], 1947)
    (excerpt), S24–0–1(d)
South
  African American migration
    from, 567
  American Revolution and,
    199–202
  cities of, 307, 567–68
  colonial economy in, 134,
    135–36
  free black population of, 238,
    307, 313–14
  growing estrangement from
    North, 412–13
  growing tension in, 323–27
  Native Americans in, 246, 318
  New Deal and, 699, 704
  party politics in, 537
  populism in, 554, 570
  progressivism and, 596, 601,
    603–5
  racial discrimination in, 570–74,
    596, 760, 799
  railroads in, 393–94, 436, 492
  religious experience in, 281
  secession in, 423–28
  slavery opposition in, 238
  slavery system in, 302–10
  tariff of 1816 opposed in, 297
  World War II industry in,
    725–26
  *See also* Civil War; Confederacy;
    Reconstruction; individual
    states and colonies
South Africa, 754, 883–84

South Bronx, 842–43
South Carolina
    American Revolution and,
        199–203
    backcountry, 202–3
    Civil War and, 427, 452, 454
    Civilian Conservation Corps in,
        692–93
    Constitution ratification and, 219
    creation of government in, 196
    nullification crisis and,
        323–27, 364
    Reconstruction and, 472, 490
    secession of, 423, 424
    slave revolts in, 309
    slavery in, 217, 236, 272, 313, 323
South Carolina colony, 92, 116,
        130, 145, 146
    the Barbados connection, 99
    economic growth in, 134
    political economy of, 96–99
    Spanish and, 96, 160
    *South Carolina Exposition and
        Protest,* 323, 326
South Carolina Forestry
        Commission (SCFC),
        692–93
South Carolina Negro Seamen Act
        of 1822, 313
South Carolina Nullifiers, 364
South Dakota, 481
South Korea, 792
Southdale shopping mall, 778
Southeast
    European colonization of,
        38(map)
    trade routes in, 98(map)
Southeast Asia Treaty Organization
        (SEATO), 792, 794
Southern Baptist Convention,
        665, 874
Southern Christian Leadership
        Conference (SCLC), 799,
        811, 820, 821
Southern Manifesto, 799
Southern Pacific Railroad,
        480(photo)
Southern strategy, 858
*Southern Unionist Judge's Daughter
        Writes the President for
        Help* (Wayne, S. 1874),
        S15–6–7(d)
*Soverereignty and Goodness of God,
        The* (Rowlandson, M., 1682)
        (excerpts), S4–2–4(d)
Soviet Union, 948
    Afghanistan invaded by, 864,
        881, 896, 900, 932
    atomic bomb of, 749, 751, 764
    Berlin airlift, 750
    Carter administration and, 864
    collapse of, 900, 905

    containment and, 749–51, 754,
        791, 792
    détente and, 845, 846, 861,
        864, 879
    Eisenhower adminstration and,
        788–95
    "evil empire" designation, 881
    hotline between U.S. and, 816
    Kennan's article on, S24–0–1
    Kennedy administration and,
        810, 814
    Korean War and, 754–56
    League of Nations organized
        without, 641
    massive retaliation doctrine,
        789, 814
    Nazi-Soviet pact, 713
    Nixon administration and,
        845–46, 879
    official U.S. recognition of, 745
    Open Skies proposal, 791
    peaceful coexistence policy,
        791, 845
    popular front strategy, 695
    post-World War II relations with,
        745–50
    Potsdam Conference and,
        737, 747
    Reagan administration and,
        879–81, 883, 896–900
    space program and, 802, 810, 847
    Spanish Civil War and, 713
    spies for, 767–68
    trade with former republics
        of, 906
    United Nations and, 736, 749
    World War II and, 711, 714, 723,
        734, 737, 746
    Yalta Conference and, 747
    *See also* Cold war; Communism;
        Russia
Space program
    cold war and, 802
    Kennedy administration and, 810
    Nixon administration and, 848
Spaceport USA, 812–13
Spain
    American Revolution and, 204–5
    Canary Islands seized by, 13
    English conflicts with, 37–38, 50,
        52, 63, 116, 159–60, 248, 264
    French and Indian War, 168
    French conflicts with, 37–38, 159
    Jews of, 10, 11, 16, 45
    land claims in American
        Republic, 242–43, 244
    land claims south of 42nd
        parallel, 368–69
    Louisiana acquired from, 262
    Muslims of, 10, 11, 16
    Native Americans and, 16, 51,
        212, 243, 322

    Netherlands independence
        from, 45
    in the Philippines, 581
    Pinckney's Treaty and, 249
    Providence Island destroyed by,
        73, 78
    War of Jenkins's Ear, 159–60
    *See also* Spanish-American War;
        Spanish colonies; Spanish
        empire
Spalding, Eliza Hart, 371
Spalding, Henry, 371
Spanish-American War, 577–81,
        583, 605, 942
Spanish Armada, defeat of, 50
Spanish Civil War, 713
Spanish colonies, 113, 116–20
    exploration routes, 18(map)
    New World exploration, 14–29
    objectives of, 35
    outposts, 37–39, 116
    revolts and independence in, 293
    South Carolina region and, 96
    *See also* Cuba; Florida; Mexico;
        New Mexico
Spanish empire
    establishment of, 21–23
    remnants of, 575
Speakeasies, 634
Special Field Order No. 15, 465
*Special Message to the Congress
        Recommending a
        Comprehensive Health
        Program* (Truman, H. S.,
        1945), S24–4–5(d)
Special Negro Fund, 700
Special privilege, 301
Specie Circular, 317–18, 366
Spector, Ronald, 736
Speech, freedom of, 228, 819, 827
*Speech at Springfield, Illinois*
        (Lincoln, A. 1857),
        S13–6–7(d)
*Speech on the Admission of Kansas*
        (Hammond, J. H. 1858),
        S13–4–5(d)
*Speedwell* (ship), 77
Spheres of influence, 736, 746
*Spirit of St. Louis* (airplane), 664
Spock, Benjamin, 782
Spoils system, 536
Sport utility vehicles (SUVs), 912
Sports
    in modern era, 657
    racial integration of, 761
    women in, 527
Spotsylvania Court House, 450
Spring Valley Water Company, 610
Sprint, 878
Spruance, Raymond, 719
*Sputnik* (satellite), 802
Squanto, 53, 77, 83

Square Deal, 606–7
*Squatter and the Don, The* (Ruiz de Burton, M. 1885), S12–9–11(d)
Squatters, 231, 298
Stagflation, 839, 840, 879
Staines, John, 227
Stalin, Josef, 750
  at Potsdam Conference, 737, 747
  World War II and, 713, 723
  at Yalta Conference, 747
Stamp Act, S6–4–5
Stamp Act of 1765, 171, 175–77, 181, 183(table), S6–3–4
*Stamp Act Riots: The Destruction of Thomas Hutchinson's House* (Hutchinson, T. 1765), S6–4–5(d)
Standard Oil, 486, 512, 548, 577, 597, 606, 911
Stanford University, 873, 924
Stanton, Edwin M., 436, 471
Stanton, Elizabeth Cady, 354(photo), 355, 357, 358, 485
Stanton, Henry, 355
"Star-Spangled Banner, The" (national anthem), 268
*Stark* (destroyer), 886
Starr, Ellen, 596
Starr, Kenneth, 916, 920
START (Strategic Arms Reduction Talks Treaty), 896
State governments
  Bill of Rights and, 228
  Constitutional Convention on, 216
  creation of, 196
  in industrial America, 548
  New Federalism, 848, 877
  progressivism and, 603–5
State University of New York, 757
*Statement to the Press at the Beginning of the Youth Leadership Conference* (King, M. L., 1960), S26–0–1(d)
*Statements by Roman Pucinski Ethnic Heritage Studies Centers* (1970), S27–6–7(d)
*Statements by the United Auto Workers and General Motors* (1945), S24–3–4(d)
Staten Island, 197
States' rights, 291, 323, 413, 434, 449, S8–7–8
Statue of Liberty, S16–4
Steam engine, 273
Steamboat, 274, 391, 394, 500, 711
Steel industry, 500, 508–10, 564, 655, 725, 775, 842, S16–1–2
Steel mills, 491, 508

Steelworkers' strikes, 562–64, 641
Steevens, G., *The Land of the Dollar* (1897) (excerpt), S16–2–3(d)
Steffens, Lincoln, 592, 597, 615
Stein, Gertrude, 665
Steinem, Gloria, 852
Stephens, Alexander, 425, 466
Sterilization, forced, 600
Stevens, Robert T., 769
Stevens, Thaddeus, 462–65, 470–71
Stevenson, Adlai, 787
Stewart, A. T., 393
Stewart, Maria, 340
Stimson, Henry, 714, 725, 727
Stock market
  crash of 1929, 681
  crash of 1987, 896, 912
  in new economy, 912
Stone, Barton W., 276, 283
Stone, I. F., 737
Stone, Lucy, 485
Stonewall Inn riot, 856–57
Stono Rebellion, 145
Stop the Draft Week, 824
Stowe, Harriet Beecher, 400, 405–6
Strategic Arms Limitation Treaty (SALT I), 845
Strategic Arms Limitation Treaty (SALT II), 861, 864, 881
Strategic Arms Reduction Talks (START) Treaty, 896
Strategic Defense Initiative (SDI; "Star Wars"), 881, 930
Strauss, Levi, 398, 504
Streetcar suburbs, 592
*Strenuous Life, The* (Roosevelt, T., 1899) (excerpts), S18–4–6(d)
Stretchout, 653
Strict constructionism, 230
Strikes
  air traffic controllers, 879
  coal miners, 606–7, 758
  criminalization of, 575
  decrease in modern era, 654
  dockworkers, 641, 698
  during Great Depression, 698, 699
  hate, 729
  under industrial capitalism, 515–16
  nationwide, 521–22
  police department, 671
  post–World War II, 758
  Pullman workers, 562–65
  railroad workers, 499, 543, 562–64, 758
  shoemakers, 280
  steelworkers, 562–64, 641
  tailoresses, 346
  tailors, 353–54

textile mill, 277, 346
United Automobile Workers, 726–27, S24–3–4
United Farm Workers of America, 854
Strong, Josiah, 531–32
  *The Superiority of the Anglo-Saxon Race* (1885) (excerpts), S17–4–6(d)
Strong mayor system, 603
Stuart, J. E. B., 414
Student debt, 956
Student Homophile League, 856
*Student Non-Violent Coordinating Committee Statement of Purpose* (1960), S26–1(d)
Student Nonviolent Coordinating Committee (SNCC), 807, 811, 820, 821, 824, 826, S26–1
Student protests, 827, 833, 846
Student Volunteer movement, 577
Students for a Democratic Society (SDS), 808–9, 822, 857
Stuyvesant, Peter, 46–47, 95
Submerged Lands Act of 1953, 787
Subscription schools, 351
*Substance of Two Speeches Delivered on the Subject of the Missouri Bill, The* (Rufus, K., 1820) (excerpts), S10–1–3(d)
Subtreasuries, 552
Suburbs, 513
  in mid-20th century, 776–78, 783
  in modern era, 655
  streetcar, 592
Sudan, 932
Suez Canal, 792–94
Suffolk Resolves, 185
Suffrage (*See* Voting; Women's suffrage)
Sugar, 13, 22, 92, 115
  in Barbados, 99
  Cuban, 577
  in Dutch colonies, 47
  Hawaiian, 545, 547, 580
  increased demand for, 138
  plantations, 304, 464, 474
Sugar Act of 1764, 171, 179, 183(table)
Sullivan, "Big Florry," S17–0
Sullivan, "Boston Tim," S17–0
Sullivan, John, 212
Sullivan, Timothy D. ("Big Tim"), S17–0–1
Sumerians, 12
Summers, Martin, 234
Sumner, Charles, 344, 407, 436, 462–65, 485, 488
Sumner, Newport, S7–5
Sunbelt, 844, 844(map), 858, 871–72

Sunday, Billy, 634
Sunday School movement, 337
Sunday School Union, 281
Super PACs, 958
Super Storm Sandy, 947
Superfund, 863, 894
*Superiority of the Anglo-Saxon Race, The* (Strong, J., 1885) (excerpts), S17–4–6(d)
Supply-side economics, 878, 879
Supreme Court
    on abortion legality, 852, 888, 925
    on affirmative action, 849
    in American Republic, 228
    on antisodomy laws, 889
    on the Bank of the United States, 278, 286, 317
    on bilingual education, 854
    on Bush-Gore election, 920–21
    Civil War impact on influence in, 455
    cold war legislation and, 767
    creation of, 217
    Debs' conviction upheld by, 629
    Democratic Republicans and, 261–62
    on gay rights issues, 925–26
    on Gramm-Rudman Act, 896
    and Guantánamo Bay detention center, 938
    on Japanese American internment, 730–31
    on labor union activities, 641, 654
    on Mexican land claims in California, 386
    "midnight appointees" of, 261–62
    on military trials, 435
    on Native American land rights, 319, 320, 362
    New Deal legislation and, 696, 698, 700, 701–2
    Nixon appointees, 858
    on Nixon tapes, 860
    Pentagon Papers and, 846
    on personal freedom, 819
    on racial discrimination, 488–89, 570, 571, 729, 759, 760, 799, 891
    Reagan appointees, 887
    on school busing, 849–51
    on school segregation, 798–99, 807
    on sexual material, 780
    Sherman Anti-Trust Act and, 545, 548, 606
    on slavery issues, 410–12
    on strikes, 575
    support for market economy, 277–78
    on voting rights, 485, 602, 729, 759

*Survive Nuclear Attack,* Office of Civil and Defense Mobilization (1960) (excerpts), S25–6–9(d)
Susquehanna River, 163
Susquehannock Indians, 49, 69, 101
Sutter, John, 504
Sutter's mill, 504
Swaggart, Jimmy, 893
*Swann v. Charlotte-Mecklenburg Board of Education,* 850
Swansea, 105
Sweatshops, 514–16
Swift, Gustavus, 501, 510, 511
Symes, Lillian, 660
Syngman Rhee, 754
Syria, 840, 847, 948

Taft, Robert, 714, 762
Taft, William H., 609–15, 621, 673
Taft-Hartley Act of 1947, 758, 762
Tailoresses, 346
Tailors, 353–54
Taino Indians, 15, 16
Taiping Rebellion, 518
Taiwan, 754
    Eisenhower and, 792
    Nixon and, 846
Takagi, Takeo, 718
Taliban, 936, 938, 940, 945
Talleyrand, Charles, 251
Tallmadge, James, 294
Tammany Hall, 486, 536, 548, 549, 615, S17–0, S17–1
*Tammany Times, And Reform Moves On* (November 18, 1895), S17–1–2(d)
Tanacharison, 163
Taney, Roger, 317, 410–13
Tanzania, U.S. embassy attack in, 932
Tappan, Arthur, 357
Tappan, Lewis, 357
Tarawa, 736
Tarbell, Ida, 597
Tariff Act of 1789, 229
Tariffs
    of 1816, 297, 323
    of 1824, 297
    of 1832, 326, 327
    of 1833, 327
    of 1846, 384
    of abominations (1828), 323, 327
    in American Republic, 229
    Dingley Tariff Act, 567
    Fordney-McCumber, 672
    globalization and, 906
    Hawley-Smoot, 686, 712
    in industrial America, 544–45
    in late 19th century, 561, 567
    McKinley, 545, 561, 578, 580

Morrill "War Tariff," 433–34
Payne-Aldrich, 611
Reagan administration and, 886
Tariff Act of 1789, 229
Underwood-Simmons, 615
Tarleton, Banastre, 203
TARP (*See* Troubled Asset Relief Program)
Task system in slavery, 135, 145, 305, 309
Tate, Allen, 665
Taverns, 141, 232, 241
Tax Cuts and Jobs Act of 2017, 961
Tax Reform Act of 1986, 894
Taxes, 946
    in American Republic, 246, 251, 262, 264
    Antifederalists on, 221
    and Barack Obama, 955
    Bush (George H. W.) and, 913, 914
    capital gains, 863
    in colonial America, 92, 100, 160, 166–67, 175–77, 182, 185
    estate, 878
    excise, 246
    income, 434, 604, 609, 613, 696–97, 878, 894
    Reagan and, 878, 879, 894
    Roosevelt (Franklin) and, 696–97
    single, 550
    Taft and, 609
Taylor, Frederick Winslow, 562, 653
Taylor, J., *Account of the Murders of Joseph and Hyrum Smith* (1844), S11–5–7(d)
Taylor, Paul, 680
Taylor, Zachary
    death of, 399
    Mexican War and, 380, 382, 383
    presidency of, 397, 398, 400
Taylorism, 562, 656
Tea
    colonial era demand for, 138
    tax on, 182
Tea Act of 1773, 179, 182, 183(table)
Tea Party movement, 946
Teach-ins, 824
Teapot Dome scandal, 672
Technology
    communications, 905
    economic impact of, 871–72
    and employment, 953
    in war, 936
Tecumseh, 246, 258, 268, 279, 377
*Teenage Attitudes* (Remmers, H. H., and Radler, D. H., 1958) (excerpts), S25–2–4(d)
Teenagers (*See* Youth)
Tejanos, 369, 786, 892

Telegraph, 391, 395, 499–500, 552, 711
Telephone, 507
Televangelists, 874
Television
  consumerism and, 779–80
  Johnson-era measures, 819
  religious programs on, 781
Telstar, 810, 905
Temperance movement, 351, 354, 538–41, 594 (See also Prohibition)
Ten Percent Plan, 462–65
Tenements, 514, 534(photo), 592
Tennent, Gilbert, 152
Tennessee
  Civil War and, 438, 443, 449, 454
  Native Americans in, 243
  secession of, 426
  settlement of, 207, 213, 231, 272
  slavery abolished in, 465
  statehood, 300
  voting rights in, 300
Tennessee Valley Authority (TVA), 691, 694(map), 695
Tenochtitlan, 19–20, 21, 22, S1–3
Tenskwatawa (the Prophet), 246, 279, 280(photo)
Tenth Amendment, 228
Tenth Muse Lately Sprung Up in America, The (Bradstreet), S3–3
Tenure of Office Act of 1867, 471
Teotihuacan, 6
Terkel, Studs, S22–5–7(d)
Term limits (proposed), 914
Terrorism, 937–39, 947
  attacks on U.S. embassies, 932
  domestic, 918–20
  and Iraq War, 939
  Reagan administration and, 883–86
  during Reconstruction, 477
  response to, 938, S2–0–1
  World Trade Center bombing (1993), 931–32
  See also September 11 terrorist attacks
Tertium Quids, 266
Testimony of Gerald Dickey, Mergers and Industrial Concentration, S27–0–1(d)
Testimony of Marian Wright, Examination of the War on Poverty (1967), S26–2–5(d)
Tet Offensive, 831
Teton Sioux Indians, 375, S15–7
Tex-Mex cuisine, 892
Texas
  American influx, 368–70
  annexation, 370, 377–81, 390–91, S12–7–9

border settlement, 398
Civil War and, 436
independence issue, 368–70
Reconstruction and, 484
Republic of, 370(map)
secession of, 424
slavery in, 369, 370, 376, 378, 390–91, 398
Slidell's purchase offer, 382
Spanish outpost established in, 159
Transcontinental Treaty on, 293
Texas Pacific Railroad, 499
Textile mills, 276–77, 393, 491, 514
  English, 271, 311
  Lowell mills, 276, 346, 395, S9–3–4
  stretchout in, 653
  Waltham system, 276
Thames, Battle of, 268, 279
That We Might All Be Rich (George, H., 1883) (excerpts), S17–2–4(d)
Third Amendment, 228
Third world
  communism expansion feared, 754, 792–95, 814, 881–83
  Reagan Doctrine in, 881–83
Thirteenth Amendment, 455, 465–66, 469(table)
Thirty-eighth parallel, 754, 755
This Side of Paradise (Fitzgerald), 665
Thomas, Clarence, 922, 925
Thomas, George, 426, 454
Thomas, J. Parnell, 766
Thompson, J. Edgar, 509
Thompson, J. G., Letter from James G. Thompson to the Editor of the Pittsburgh Courier (1942), S23–6–7(d)
Thompson, J. Walter, 674–75
Thoreau, Henry David, 351, 384, S11–2–4
Three-Fifths Compromise, 217, 236, 269, 312, 365, 468
Three Mile Island nuclear accident, 863
3M Corporation, 788, 789
Thurmond, Strom, 762
Tijerina, Reis López ("Tiger"), 854
Tilden, Samuel J., 490, 542
Till, Emmett, 799
Tillotson, John, 150, 152
Timbuktu, 12
Time (magazine), 719, 768
Time Warner, 910
Time's Up movement, 956
Timucua Indians, 24(photo)
Tinian, 736
Tippecanoe, Battle of, 364, 377
Tippecanoe River, 279

Tisquantum (See Squanto)
Titanic (film), 908–9
Title IX, 852
Title VII, 831
Tituba, 90, 112
Tlatoani, 23
Tlaxcalan people, 21–23, 27, 28(photo)
Tlecuiluatzin (doña Luisa), 27–28
To Secure These Rights (report), 760
"To The University of Cambridge, in New England" (Wheatley, P., 1773), S5–6–7(d)
Tobacco, 92, 100, 108, 134, 145, 232, 270, 273, 691
  declining market for, 272
  economic importance of, 64–65, 69, 72
  increased demand for, 138
  labor requirements, 70
  plantations, 135, 305
  sharecropping and, 474–75
Tocqueville, Alexis de, 336, 349, 353, 375
  Democracy in America (1840) (excerpts), S11–4–5(d)
Todd, Silas, 133
Toledo, 10
Tomatoes, 27
Tonkin Gulf Resolution, 821
Toomer, Jean, 669
Tordesillas, Treaty of, 17
Torture, 938
  and Guantánamo Bay detention center, 943
  Native Americans and, 41
  in Philippine-American War, 582
  in Pontiac's Rebellion, 170
  of slave revolt rebels, 143–44
  on slave ships, 132–33
  of slaves, 143–44
Total war, 426–27, 434, 630, 635
Tourgée, Albion, 570
Tourism, 794–95, 910
Toussaint-Louverture, François-Dominique, 247, 250, 261
Town meetings, 80, 107, 175
Towne, Laura M., 422–23
Townsend, Francis, 696
Townshend, Charles, 177–79
Townshend Revenue Act of 1767, 178, 181, 182, 183(table)
Trade
  in American Republic, 232–35, 238, 248–51, 262, 264–66, 269–72
  Bretton Woods Conference on, 737
  in colonial era, 45–49, 92, 93, 176(figure), 182
  GATT, 906–7
  globalization and, 906–9, 931

Great Depression and, 711–12
in industrial era, 545–46
in late 19th century, 561
mercantilism, 45, 50, 92, 138, 149
most-favored-nations, 251, 615
NAFTA, 907–8
in New Netherland, 45–49
North Atlantic routes (end of
   16th century), 36(map)
post-revolution agreements, 206,
   208, 209, 215, 232, 238
in pre-contact Europe, 10, 11
Reagan administration and,
   886, 896
reciprocity, 545
Roosevelt (Franklin)
   administration and, 712
Wilson administration and, 615
world (on the eve of discovery),
   11(map)
World War I and, 624
See also Exports; Fur trade;
   Imports; Slave trade; Tariffs
Trade associations, 280
"Trail of Death," 409
Trail of Tears, 320, S12–0
Tramp laws, 548
Trans-Mississippi West, 367–76
Trans-Pacific Partnership
   (TPP), 948
Transcendental Wild Oats (Alcott,
   L. M., 1873) (excerpts),
   S11–2–4(d)
Transcendentalism, 351, S11–2–4
Transcontinental Treaty of 1819,
   293, 367, 368
Transgender population, 952–53
Transportation
   in early 19th century, 273–76, 292
   racial segregation on, 570,
      759, 799
   See also Automobiles; Bridge
      building; Railroads; Road
      building; Steamboat
Traps for the Young
   (Comstock), 528
Treasure hunters, 285
Tredegar Iron Works, 431
Trent (ship), 433
Trenton, Battle of, 197–99
Triangle Shirtwaist Company fire,
   592, 593(photo)
Tripoli, 262
Tripoli, Treaty of, 262
Trist, Nicholas P., 383
Troll farms, 963
Troubled Asset Relief Program
   (TARP), 941
Troup, George Michael, 318
Trujillo, S. D., Opportunity in the
   New Information Economy
   (1998), S29–2–3(d)

Truman, Harry S., 821, 915, 927,
   945, S24–3
   atomic bombing of Japan
      and, 739
   Chinese revolution and, 751–54
   civil rights and, 760
   cold war and, 744, 748–50, 764,
      765, 768, 769, 788, 791
   comeback of, 762
   Korean War and, 754
   on labor unions, 758
   liberalism and, 761–62
   at Potsdam Conference, 737, 747
   Special Message to the
      Congress Recommending
      a Comprehensive
      Health Program (1945),
      S24–4–5(d)
   women's rights and, 759
Truman Doctrine, 748–49,
   764, 845
Trumbo, Dalton, 766, 767
Trump, Donald, 957, 960–64,
   960(photo)
   criticisms of, 960
   election of, 960
   Extract of Remarks at a "Make
      America Great Again" Rally,
      S30–7–9(d)
   and Russian hacking, 962–63
   use of Twitter by, 961
Trusts
   Clayton Antitrust Act, 616
   motives for forming, 512
   NIRA and, 695
   Roosevelt (Theodore) and, 606
   Sherman Anti-Trust Act, 545–46,
      548, 575, 606
   Taft and, 609
   Wilson and, 613, 615, 616
Truth, Sojourner, 340
Truth in Securities Act of 1933, 690
Tulare Lake, 504
Tunis, 262, 723
Tunisia, 723
Tuolumne River, 610
Turchinetz, John, 744–45
Turkey
   cold war era, 747, 749, 794, 816
   World War I and, 623
Turner, Frederick Jackson,
   560, 561
Turner, Nat, 309, 327, 341
Turner, Ted, 905
Turner Broadcasting, 910
Tuskegee Airmen, 720
Tuskegee Institute, 519, 571, 601
TVA (See Tennessee Valley
   Authority)
Twain, Mark, 581
Tweed, William M., 486
Twelfth Amendment, 261

"Twenty-Negro law," 434–35
Twenty-seventh Amendment,
   228, 915
Twenty-sixth Amendment, 857
Twenty-Years at Hull House
   with Autobiographical
   Notes (Addams, J., 1910)
   (excerpts), S19–0–2(d)
Twitchell, Marshall Harvey, 488
Twitter, 961
Two Treatises of Government
   (Locke), 107
Tyler, John, 321, 377–81
Typhoid fever, 64, 371, 781
Typhus, 25

U-2 spy plane, 791
U-boats, 624, 635, 714–15
UAW (See United Automobile
   Workers)
Ukraine, 636, 948
UMW (See United Mine Workers)
"Uncle Remus" stories
   (Harris), 529
Uncle Tom's Cabin (Stowe), 400
Underwood-Simmons Tariff of
   1913, 615
Unemployment
   in 1970s, 839, 843, 848, 861
   in 1980s, 879
   in African Americans, 921
   and Barack Obama, 949
   depression of 1837 and, 366
   Great Depression and, 682–83
   mid-20th century, 776
   in modern era, 651
   in new economy, 911–12
   panic of 1873 and, 488
   panic of 1893 and, 560
   post-World War II, 756–57
Unified Race, 854
Unión de Trabajadores del Valle
   Imperial, La, 668
Union Iron Company, 509
Union of Russian Workers, 644
Union of Soviet Socialist
   Republics (USSR) (See
   Soviet Union)
Union Pacific Railroad, 434,
   479, 486
Unions (See Labor unions)
Unitarianism, 281
United Arab Emirates, 937
United Artists, 650, 664
United Automobile Workers
   (UAW), 699, 726–27, 758,
   S24–3–4
United Farm Workers of
   America, 854
United Fruit, 776
United Mine Workers (UMW),
   575, 606–7, 698, 758

United Nations (UN), 791, 927, 930
    Korean War and, 754, 756
    Persian Gulf War and, 928–29
    planning, 736, 746
    Soviet Union and, 736, 749
United Nations Declaration on
    Human Rights, 759
United Nations Relief
    and Rehabilitation
    Adminstration
    (UNRRA), 737
United Services Organization
    (USO), 720
United States Information Agency
    (USIA), 791
United States military
    deployments, 949(photo)
United States Military Railroads
    agency, 436
United States Sanitary
    Commission, 447
*United States v. Leon,* 887
*United States v. Windsor,* 952
UNIVAC 1 (Universal Automatic
    Computer), 775
Universal Negro Improvement
    Association (UNIA), 669–70
Universalism, 141, 281
University of Alabama, 812
University of California at Berkeley,
    680, 827, 854
University of California at
    Davis, 849
University of Colorado at
    Boulder, 870
University of Illinois, 662
University of Mississippi, 811
University of Pennsylvania, 775
University of Wisconsin, 560, 600
*Unsafe at Any Speed* (Nader), 818
*Untermenschen,* 712
Upper class, 781 (*See also* Wealthy)
Urban culture, 529–31, 957
Urbanization (*See* Cities and
    urbanization)
Uruguay Round, 906
U.S. Steel, 564, 641
USA for Africa, 885
USA Patriot Act, 938–39
Utah
    nuclear weapons testing and, 753
    territory acquired by U.S., 383

Vaccines/inoculation
    polio, 781
    smallpox, 147
Vagrancy Law, S15–3–4(d)
Vallandigham, Clement L., 435
Van Buren, Martin, 316, 324, 341,
    364–67, 384
    election of 1828 and, 315
    election of 1836 and, 364, 378

election of 1840 and, 363, 376–77
election of 1844 and, 378–79
election of 1848 and, 344,
    363, 397
Native Americans and, 319
presidency of, 365–67
Texas annexation issue, 370
Vance, Zebulon, 449
Vanderbilt, Cornelius, 508
Vanzetti, Bartolomeo, 644–45
Veblen, Thorstein, 600
Velasco, don Luis de
    (Paquiquineo), 34–35, 58,
    S2-0-1
Venezuela, 293
    Columbus's voyage to, 15
    Germany's loan to, 609
Vermont
    land speculation in, 213
    slavery issue, 236
    statehood, 300
    voting rights in, 300
Vermont Green Mountain
    Boys, 192
Verrazano, Giovanni da, 37
Versailles, Treaty of, 640, 711
Vertical integration, 510–11
Vesey, Denmark, 309
Vespucci, Amerigo, 17
Veterans Administration, 762
Vice, crusade against, 634
Vicksburg, siege of, 443
Victoria, Queen of England, 527
Victorian era, 527–29
Viet Minh, 792
Vietnam
    diplomatic recognition of, 931
    division of, 792
    France in (French Indochina),
        715, 756, 792
    trade with, 906, 931
Vietnam syndrome, 880–81, 883
Vietnam War, 639, 821–26, 833,
    859, 864, 880, 927
    anti-war movement, 824–25,
        827, 846, 857, 858
    casualties in, 847
    ending, 846–47
    escalation (1960-1968),
        822(table)
    expenditures for, 840, 849, 895
    Johnson administration and,
        821–24, 826, 832–33, 846,
        860, S26–5–7
    Kennedy administration and,
        816, 821
    limited war, 822
    major battles, 823(map)
    My Lai massacre, 846
    Nixon administration and, 833,
        846–47
    Operation Linebacker, 847

Operation Rolling Thunder, 821
pardons for draft resisters, 862
soldier at jungle camp,
    832(photo)
surrender of South Vietnam, 861
Tet Offensive, 832–33
Tonkin Gulf Resolution, 821
Vietnamization, 846
Villa, Francisco ("Pancho"), 622
*Vincennes* (missile cruiser), 886
Virginia
    American Revolution and, 200
    Civil War and, 426–27, 439,
        442, 443
    Constitution ratification and,
        218–20
    land speculation in, 212
    Reconstruction and, 485
    secession of, 426
    slave revolts in (*See* Slave revolts,
        Gabriel's; Slave revolts,
        Harper's Ferry; Slave revolts,
        Turner's)
    slavery in, 211, 238, 306
    territory disputes in, 243
    voting rights in, 300
*Virginia* (ship), 433
Virginia colony, 63–69, 100–103
    Bacon's Rebellion in (*See* Bacon's
        Rebellion)
    founding of, 63–64
    French and Indian War and,
        162–64, 166
    Massachusetts Bay colony
        compared with, 75
    Pontiac's Rebellion and, 171
    protest and resistance in,
        175, 185
    slavery in, 70–71, 100–103,
        145, 236
    social change in, 100
    tobacco cultivation in, 64–65,
        69, 70, 72
Virginia Company, 53, 63, 64, 66,
    67, 72, 76
Virginia Plan, 216
Virginia Ratifying Convention
    (Henry's speech to),
    S7-5-7(d)
Virginia Resolutions, 254,
    S8–7–8(d)
Virginia Resolves, 175
*Visiting Frenchman's Account of
    Patrick Henry's Caesar-
    Brutus Speech, A* (1765),
    S6-3–4(d)
VISTA (Volunteers in Service to
    America), 817
Voice of America, 791
Voluntarism, political, 537, 538
Voluntary Relocation Program, 783
Voodoo, 310

Voter fraud, 962
Voting
    African Americans and, 468,
        472, 477, 490, 538, 543, 546,
        729, 760, 821
    disfranchisement, 559, 571–74,
        601, 670
    Fifteenth Amendment,
        469(table), 484
    free blacks (during slavery),
        237–38, 300, 313
    grandfather clause,
        571–72, 602
    registration drives, 811, 820
    Ten Percent Plan, 462–65
    in colonial America, 175
    in England (colonial era), 175
    lowering of age for, 857
    Oregon system, 604
    participation (1840-1896),
        537(figure)
    participation (1896-1920),
        594(figure)
    participation (1896-1928),
        671(figure)
    universal white male suffrage,
        299–301, 317, 363
    women and (See Women's
        suffrage)
Voting Rights Act of 1965, 821,
    890, 891

Wabanaki, 90
Wabash River, 274
Waco siege, 917
Waddell, Alfred Moor, 573
Wade, Benjamin F., 462
Wade-Davis Bill, 462–63
Wade-ins, 807
Wage labor
    in American Republic, 271
    in antebellum era, 392, 393
    in colonial America, 137
    discontent in 19th century,
        298–99
    sharecropping as, 491–93
Wagner, Robert, 698–99
Wagner Act (National Labor
    Relations Act), 698–99, 701
Wake, 716
Wal-Mart, 906, 911
Walker, David, 340
    Walker's Appeal (1829)
        (excerpts), S10–0–1(d)
Walker, Quock, S7–4
Walker, Robert, 381
Walker's Appeal (Walker, D., 1829)
    (excerpts), S10–0–1(d)
Wall, Garret, 325
Wall Street bombing, 638(photo)
Wall Street Reform and Consumer
    Protection Act, 944

Wallace, George, 812, 831, 833, 850
Wallace, Henry, 692, 729, 761
Wallace v. Jaffree, 887
Waltham system, 276
Wampanoag Indians, 105
Wampum, 42, 43, 48
Wanamaker's department store,
    507(photo), 508, S16–2–3
Wanchese, 51–53, 58
War. See also specific countries,
        specific wars, etc.
    Afghanistan, war in, 945, 947
    Civil War, 422–56, 536–37,
        540–42
    Cold war, 744–56, 845, 880
    French and Indian War, 158–59,
        161–69, 171, 175
    Iraq War, 939–40, 947–49
    Korean War, 749, 754–56,
        787, 791
    limited war, 822
    Mexican War, 344, 380–84, 390,
        397, 447
    Persian Gulf War, 928–29,
        S29–6–7
    Philippine-American War,
        581–82
    Spanish-American War, 577–81,
        583, 605, 942
    total war, 426–27, 434, 630, 635
    Vietnam War, 639, 821–26, 833,
        859, 864, 880, 927
    World War I, 620–21, 623–40,
        653, 664–65, 682, 685, 686,
        711–13, 723, 724
    World War II, 639, 710–38, 758,
        759, S23–6–9
War bonds, 629
War Brides Act of 1945, 764
War Democrats, 447, 455
War Hawks, 267
War Industries Board (WIB), 630
War of 1812, 266–69, 273, 275, 276,
        279, 291, 297, 298, 301, 311,
        318, 322, 336, 445, 605
    battles and campaigns of,
        270(map)
    Federalist response, 268–69
    Grundy's predictions, S9–2–3
    Jackson and, 258, 259, 268, 269
    Madison and, 266–68
War of Jenkins's Ear, 159–60
"War on Christmas," 953, S30–3–4
War on drugs, 887
War on poverty, 818, 820, S26–2–5
War on Terror, 938–39, 943
War Powers Act of 1973, 860
War Production Board, 732
Warehouse Act, 616
Warhol, Andy, 830
Warmoth, Henry Clay, 486
Warner Brothers, 657

Warner Communications, 910
Warren, Earl, 798, 819, 859
Warren, Robert Penn, 665
Wars of the Roses, 49
Washington, Booker T., 519, 571,
    601, 668, S18–2–4(d)
Washington, D.C.
    capital moved to, 241
    march on (1894), 560
    march on (1932), 687
    march on (1962), 812–13
    march on (1969), 846
    Randolph's march (cancelled),
        710–11
    slavery abolished in, 398,
        425, 439
    War of 1812 and, 268
Washington, George, S7–1
    American Revolution and,
        192, 197–99, 201(photo),
        202, 211
    Constitutional Convention
        and, 215
    French and Indian War and,
        163, 164
    Letter from George Washington
        to Robert Dinwidde,
        Governor of New York
        (1775), S6–0(d)
    Native Americans and, 211, 321
    Philadelphia home of, 234
    Pontiac's Rebellion and, 171
    presidency of, 228, 230, 238, 243,
        244–48
        cabinet, 227–28
        Farewell Address, 250,
            S8–2–3(d)
        proposed title, 227
        Saint-Dominique rebellion
            and, 247
        Whiskey Rebellion, 246–47
    slaves owned by, 226–27, 235,
        236, 247
Washington, Jesse, 570(photo)
Washington, Lewis, 414
Washington, Martha, 226, 227, 235
Washington Naval Conference, 673
Washington Naval Treaty of
    1922, 718
Washington Post, 718, 859
Washita Creek, Battle of, 481
Water conservation, 607
Water cure (torture method), 582
Water Quality Act of 1965, 818, 894
Watergate scandal, 859–60
Waterhouse, Edward, S3–0–1
Watts riots, 826
Waud, Alfred R., Bessemer Steel
    Manufacture (1876),
    S16–1–2(v)
Wayne, Anthony, 246, 249
Wayne, S. A., S15–6–7(d)

WCTU (*See* Women's Christian
    Temperance Union)
Wealth
    in colonial America, 135(table)
    inequality of, 957–58
    percentage of controlled by
        U.S., 739
*Wealth of Nations, The* (Smith), 150
Wealthy
    under industrial capitalism,
        512–13
    in new economy, 911
    *See also* Upper class
Weapons
    in World War II, 721–23
    *See also* Nuclear weapons
Weapons of Mass Destruction
    (WMDs), 939
Weathermen, 857
Weaver, James B., 552, 554
    *Call to Action, A*, S16–6–9(d)
Weaver, Randy, 917
Webster, Daniel, 350, 377, 400
    abolition movement and, 314
    National Republican philosophy
        and, 291
    nullifcation crisis and, 325–26
    presidential candidacy of, 364
    as secretary of state, 378
    slavery issue and, 398
Webster-Ashburton Treaty, 377
Weed, Thurlow, 415
Welch, Joseph, 769
Weld, Theodore Dwight, 332, 341
Welde, Thomas, 81
Welfare capitalism, 654
Welfare system
    Clinton and, 916–17
    conservative view of, 923
    Nixon and, 848
    Reagan and, 877
Wells, William, 366
Wells-Barnett, Ida B., 571, 601,
        601(photo), 602
Welsh immigrants, 123, 129
Wensley, Elizabeth Paddy,
        78(photo)
Wertz, E. S., 629
West
    account of a journey to, S12–5–7
    antigovernment sentiment in,
        862–63
    Civil War and, 436–38, 437(map)
    clearing for capitalism, 479–83
    conflicts over land distribution
        in, 243
    economic transformation of,
        502–6
    Exoduster migration to, 493
    expansion in (1785-1805),
        232(map)
    final land rush in, 560–61

frontier closed in, 479
impact of migration to, 348–49
land cessions, 214(map)
major overland trails, 372(map)
new policy in post-revolution,
    211–13
and Reconstruction, 478
Senate dispute over land prices,
    325–26
settlement of, 213, 272–73
slavery issue, 213, 396–97
trans-Mississippi, 367–76
World War II industry in, 725–26
    *See also* Northwest Territory;
    individual states
West, Dorothy, 669
West Bank, 883–86
West Indies, 93, 113, 116, 134, 136,
    171, 186, 323
    American slaves shipped to, 201
    economic growth in, 137
    trade with, 204, 206, 238,
        248, 249
    *See also* Caribbean;
    Saint-Domingue
*West Rock, New Haven*
    (Church), 367
West Virginia
    secession from Virginia, 426
    slavery abolished in, 462
    slavery in, 306
Westinghouse, 632, 725
Westmoreland, William, 822
Westo War, 97
Weyerhäuser, Friedrich, 509
Wheat, 6, 135, 136, 270, 273, 391,
    395, 455, 479, 503, 551, 566,
    655, 691
Wheatley, Phillis, 237
    "To The University of
    Cambridge, in New
    England" (1773), S5–6–7(d)
Wheeler, Burton, 714
*Wheeling, West Virginia Speech*
    (McCarthy, J., 1950)
    (excerpts), S24–6(d)
Wheelwright, John, 83
Whig Party, 344, 363, 366, 384,
    390, 415
    decline of, 400, 401(figure)
    election of 1836 and, 364
    election of 1840 and, 367, 376–77
    election of 1844 and, 378–81
    election of 1848 and, 397
    election of 1852 and, 400
    election of 1856 and, 403, 409
    formation of, 364
    political philosophy of, 364
    slavery issue and, 342, 390,
        397, 402
    Tyler and, 378
Whiskey Rebellion, 246–47

Whiskey Ring, 486
White, E. B., 767
White, Hugh Lawson, 364
White, John, 54, 55(photo)
White, William Allen, 626
White Citizens' Councils, 799
White-collar workers, 513, 514,
    653, 655, 656, 910–11, 925
White ethnics, 858, 859, S27–6–7
White Leagues, 488, 490
White Lives Matter, 951
White supremacy, 490, 572–73,
    581, 601, 858, 918–20,
    951, 961
Whitefield, George, 141, 150–52
    *Account of a Visit to Georgia*
    (1738), S5–5–6(d)
Whitman, Marcus, 371
Whitman, Narcissa Prentiss, 371
Whitman, Walt, 530
Whitney, Eli, 271, 276, 302
Whittier, J. G., "The Haschish"
    (1854), S13–0–1(d)
*Why Not the Best?* (Carter), 862
Wichita Indians, 119
Widows, 73–75, 141, 143
*Wieland* (Brown), 240
Wilberforce, William, 323
*Wild One, The* (film), 796
Wilderness Act of 1964, 818
Wilderness campaign, 450
Wilderness Road, 207
Wilderness Society, 797–98
Wilkie, Wendell L., 714
Willamette Valley, 371
Willard, Frances, 538, 540
William of Orange, 92, 108
Williams, Roger, 82, 83
Wilmington, 136, 572–73
Wilmot, David, 397
Wilmot Proviso, 397–98
Wilock, John, S26–7–9(d)
Wilson, Charles, 775
Wilson, James, 218, 219, 645
Wilson, Woodrow, 606, 613–16,
    621–30, 671, 673,
    687–88, 927
    Fourteen Points, 635–36, 640,
        S20–6–9
    *Fourteen Points Speech* (1918),
        S20–6–9(d)
    League of Nations, 640–41
    Mexican Revolution and, 622
    New Freedom, 613, 615–16
    Paris peace negotiations, 639–40
    stroke suffered by, 641
    women's suffrage supported
        by, 633
    World War I and, 621, 623–30,
        633–36
WIN (Whip Inflation Now)
    program, 861

*Winesburg, Ohio* (Anderson), 665
Wingfield, Edward Maria, 64
Wingina, 54
Winnebago Indians, 318
Winthrop, John, 79, 82, 83, S3-3
Wirt, William, 301
Wisconsin Idea, 604–5
Wise, John, 150
Witchcraft trials, 90–91, 111–13, 143, S4-5-7
Witte, Edwin, 725
Wolfe, James, 166, 168
Wolfe, Tom, 858
Woman's National Loyal League, 485
Women
  in the abolition movement, 343, 357
  African, 71
  African American, 340, 463, 474, 492, 514, 891
  in American Republic, 233, 240
  in Benevolent Empire, 337
  Civil War and, 447
  in colonial America, 69, 72–75, 134–35, 179
    Puritan, 81, 82
    witchcraft accusations and, 90–91, 111–12
  as delegates in 1912 election, 613
  education of, 210–11, 242, 593
  in industrial America, 538
  labor unions and, 575, 654, 727–28
  middle-class (19th century), 347
  Native American, 10, 27–29, 117, 120
  New Woman, 593–94, 659, 664
  political voluntarism and, 538
  in post-revolution era, 207, 210–11
  in post-World War II era, 758–59
  in postfeminist era, 925
  property rights denied to, 210, 240, 354–57
  Roosevelt (Franklin) administration and, 700
  self-improvement and, 350
  in Shakerism, 335
  single mothers, 888, 891, 923–24
  social clubs, 593–95
  in textile mills, 276–77
  in the workforce, 240, 393, 514, 548, 561–62, 633, 653–55, 727–28, 758–59, 783, 831, 842, 852, 887–89, 925
  World War I and, 630, 633, 635
  World War II and, 720, 727–28, 758
  *See also* Feminism; Gender roles; Women's rights; Women's suffrage

Women Accepted for Volunteer Emergency Service (WAVES), 720–21
Women's Army Corps (WACs), 720, 759
Women's Christian Temperance Union (WCTU), 538–40, 633–34
Women's Health Protective Committee (WHPC), 569
Women's liberation movement, 831, 852–53
Women's rights
  Adams (Abigail) on, 210, S7-3-4
  in American Republic, 240
  in antebellum era, 354–58
  conservatives on, 887–89
  post-World War II, 759
  rebirth of movement, 830–31
  women's liberation movement, 831, 852–53
  *See also* Feminism
Women's Strike for Equality, 852
Women's suffrage, 354–58, 485, 537–39, 554, 591, 594–95, 613, 621, 625
  African American suffrage and, 485
  in New Jersey, 210, 240, 300
  Nineteenth Amendment, 633, 661
Woodstock music festival, 857
Woodward, Bob, 859
Woolman, John, 211
Woolsey, James, 932
Woolsey, Lynn C., S30-2-3(d)
Woolworth stores, 653, 806, 807
*Worcester v. Georgia,* 319
Work, H. C., "Kingdom Coming" (1862), S14-6-7(d)
Workers' compensation, 515–16, 613, 616, 697
Workers productivity, 955(figure)
Workforce
  African Americans in, 632, 710, 760, 890–92, 921
  in American Republic, 280, 284
  blue-collar workers in, 656, 781, 910, 911
  in colonial era, 70, 138
  contract, political economy of, 466
  deindustrialization and, 842–44
  downsizing in, 904, 911–12
  experiments with free labor, 464–65
  global migration of, 500(map), 501
  in industrial America, 548
  makeup of (1938-1947), 728(figure)
  mid-20th century, 776

minimum wage and, 633, 704
modern era transformation of, 653–54
New Deal programs, 690
in new economy, 910–12
political mobilization in, 353–54
scientific management and, 559, 562, 653
Taylorism and, 562, 656
wage dependency and protest, 344–46
white-collar workers in, 513, 514, 653, 655, 656, 910–11, 925
Wilson administration and, 616
women in, 240, 393, 514, 548, 561–62, 633, 653–55, 727–28, 758–59, 783, 831, 842, 852, 887–89, 925, 956
World War I, 633
World War II, 726–27
*See also* Employment discrimination; Labor unions; Unemployment; Wage labor; Working class
Workhouses, 143
Working class
  African American, 891
  common school movement and, 351–52
  under industrial capitalism, 514–16
  middle class distinguished from, 346, 348
  *See also* Workforce
Working Men's Association of New York, 351
Working Men's Party, 353
Workmen's compensation (*See* Workers' compensation)
Works Progress Administration (WPA), 697, 699, 700
World Bank, 737, 905
World Economic Forum, 906
World Trade Center bombing (1993), 931
World Trade Organization (WTO), 907, 909, 913, 941, 954
World War I, 620–21, 623–40, 653, 664–65, 682, 685, 686, 711–13, 723, 724
  aims in, 626
  American Red Cross in, 642–43
  armistice in, 639
  casualties in, 639
  Congress urged to vote for entry, 626
  conscientious objectors, 626, 629
  dissent suppressed, 627–30
  economic regimentation during, 630–31
  election campaign of 1916 on, 625

World War I (*continued*)
final offensive in, 636–39
last attempts at peace, 625–26
*Lusitania* incident, 624
music of, S20–0–1
neutrality during, 623–24
Paris peace negotiations, 639–40
preparedness campaign, 624–25
reforms during, 633–34
training of soldiers, 635
U.S. entry, 621, 626
Western front, 637(map),
638(photo)
World War II, 639, 710–38, 758,
759, S23–6–9
atomic bomb deployed, 739,
750–51
Axis powers in, 712
casualties in, 739
D-Day, 734
declaration of, 711, 713
in Europe, 724(map), 735
Europe First strategy, 723
Holocaust and, 731, 764
idealism and fear during, 728–31
industry during, 710–11, 725
isolationism during, 711, 713–14
Nazi-Soviet pact, 713
negotiations following, 746–47
Normandy invasion,
734(photo), 735
in the Pacific, 717(map), 735–36
recruitment and training of
troops, 719–21
second front in, 723, 735
surrender of Germany, 737
surrender of Japan, 739
turning the tide in, 716–23
U.S. entry, 716
weapons technology in, 721–23

World Wide Web, 905
Wounded Knee
Native American demonstration
at, 856
Native Americans massacred at,
482, 564
Wozniak, Steve, 873
WPA (*See* Works Progress
Administration)
Wright, Frances, 298–99
Wright, Marian, S26–2–5
Wright, Orville, 652
Wright, Wilbur, 652
Wrigley gum, 725
WTO (*See* World Trade
Organization)
Wyandot Indians, 371
Wyman, David, 731
Wyoming
statehood, 537
territory acquired by U.S., 383
Wythe, George, S7–5

Xicallanco, 7–8
Xicotencatl, 22–23, 27
XYZ Affair, 251

Yakima Indians, 373
Yale University, 150
Yalta Conference, 747
Yamamoto, Isoroku, 716, 717
Yamasee War, 98
Yamato race, 712
Yellow-dog contracts, 654
Yellow fever, 506
Yeltsin, Boris, 900
Yippies (Youth Independent
Party), 874
Yom Kippur War, 719, 840, 847
York, John, 232

York River, 69
*Yorktown* (carrier), 716–19
Yorktown surrender, 204
Yoruba people, 12
Yosemite National Park, 610, 611
Young, Brigham, 336
Young Americans for
Freedom, 808
Young Ladies' Academy of
Philadelphia, 242
*Young Mother, The* (Alcott), 350
Young Women's Christian
Association (YWCA), 594
Youngstown Sheet & Tube,
S27–0–1
Youth
conformity in, S25–2–4
counterculture, 827–28, 923
in mid-20th century, 796–98
in modern culture, 662–63
YouTube, 963
Yucatan Peninsula, 6, 19
Yugoslavia, 929
Yuma Indians, 373
Yuppies, 874
YWCA (Young Women's Christian
Association), 594

Zapata, Emiliano, 622
Zenger, John Peter, 141–43
Zimmerman, George, 951
Zimmermann, Arthur, 625
Zimmermann Telegram, 625
Zones of occupation, post-WWII,
747, 753
Zoot suit riots, 732–33
Zoot suits, 720, 732, 733
Zuni Pueblo, 24
Zyklon-B gas, 731